The Labour Movement in Europe

WALTER KENDALL

ALLEN LANE

My interest in the international labour movement dates back to 1944 when at the age of eighteen I first joined the ranks of organized labour. My first direct participation in activity alongside comrades from overseas I owe to Eric Heffer, now MP for Walton, Liverpool. My introduction to the labour movement in Europe I owe more than any other person to Giulio Seniga of Turin. It is to Giulio Seniga, who typifies all that is best in the Italian socialist movement, that I wish to dedicate this book.

Contents

List of Maps and Diagrams

Acknowledgements

I can hardly hope to express my thanks and appreciation to every one of those individuals and organizations who over a period of some six years have contributed in one way or another to the appearance of the present volume. However, within the limitations of that proviso I should like in particular to mention the following: the Centre for Contemporary European Studies, University of Sussex, which financed the larger part of the work; Nuffield College, Oxford, which generously allowed me to use part of the time originally allocated for another project to prepare this study for publication.

I have also to express appreciation for assistance rendered by the following organizations and institutions: the Institut Émile Vandervelde, the Parti Socialiste Belge (PSB), the Fédération Générale du Travail de Belgique (FGTB), the Confédération des Syndicats Chrétiens (CSC) in Belgium; the Trades Union Congress (TUC) and the Labour Party in Britain; the Confédération Française Démocratique du Travail (CFDT), the Confédération Générale du Travail – Force Ouvrière (CGT–FO), the Confédération Générale du Travail (CGT), in France; the Deutsche Gewerkschaftsbund (DGB), the Sozialdemokratische Partei Deutschlands (SPD), the Industriegewerkschaft Metall (IG Metall), the Friedrich Ebert Stiftung in Germany; the Confederazione Generale Italiana del Lavoro (CGIL), the Confederazione Italiana dei Sindacati Lavoratori (CISL), the Unione Italiana del Lavoro (UIL), the Partito Socialista Italiano (PSI), also the Istituto per la Ricostruzione Industriale (IRI) in Italy; the Nederlands Verbond van Vakverenigingen (NVV), the Christelijk Nationaal Vakverbond (CNV), the Partij van der Arbeid (PvdA), the joint NVV–NKV–CNV Coordinating Committee, the Dr Wiardi Beckman Stichting, and the International Institute for Social History in the Netherlands; the United Automobile, Aerospace and Agricultural Implement Workers of America (UAW) in the USA.

Also my thanks to the following individuals whose personal knowledge, assistance and advice has materially contributed to the text:
Wolfgang Abendroth, Valerio Agostinone, Giuliano Angelini, Enzo Bartocci, Émile Le Bellet, Irving Bluestone, Piero Boni, Walter Braun, Tom Barry-Braunthal, Edward Brown, Roland Van Buven, Tony Carew, Jack and Laura Carper, Sanford Cohl, Giuseppe Faravelli, Charles Ford, Walter Freitag, Albert Fried, Dan Gallin, Charles Gladstone, Ken Grieve, Eric Heffer, Bob Holton, Julius Jacobson, James Keeney, Otto Kersten, J. Kulakowski, Gerhardt Lauschke, Charles Levinson, Heinz Markmann, Eli Marx, Th. Offermans, Linda Van Olffen, Fritz Opel, Berndt Otto, Oskar Paskal, Renata

Peltzer, Enzo Pontarello, Bruno Rizzi, W. J. J. Rotermundt, Robert de Rovi, Walter Schutz, Anja Schweiker, Giulio Seniga, Wilebaldo Solano, Bruno Trentin, Jan Vanek, Nat Weinberg, Stan Weir, Bill and Lil Whitney, B. J. Widick.

Limited aspects of the material covered in the text have been discussed in seminars at the University of Sussex, the University of Oxford, the University of Warwick and the Business School of the University of Columbia in New York. I express my thanks to all those who participated in those rare events.

The typescript has been re-written from end to end several times. I cannot express appreciation individually to everyone who shared in this monumental labour but at the University of Sussex I would like to thank in particular Rita Waddingham and Eleanor McLeod, each of whom repeatedly produced fresh drafts without complaint and did much to lighten my days into the bargain; also Yvette Stone and Shirley Rooth, whose personal qualities and secretarial ability also did a great deal to make life easier.

I also have to express thanks for assistance received from the offices of the International Confederation of Free Trade Unions (ICFTU), and what is now the European Confederation of Trade Unions (ECTU), the offices of the World Confederation of Labour (WCL) and its European organization, the CGT–CGIL Standing Committee, all in Brussels, the office of the Socialist International in London, also the offices of the International Federation of Chemical and General Workers' Unions (ICF), the International Union of Food and Drink Workers (IUF), the International Metalworkers' Federation (IMF), and the International Labour Office (ILO) in Geneva; also the staff of the Press and Information Service of the European Economic Community in Brussels and in London. I have also to thank the staff of the British Museum, the Bodleian Library, and the libraries of Nuffield College and the University of Sussex, without whose aid this work would have proved impossible.

I have to thank in particular the following persons who read drafts at various stages and as a result of whose advice and criticism the manuscript benefited beyond measure. David Goldey of Lincoln College, Oxford and Duncan Gallie of Nuffield College and the University of Essex, Philip Williams of Nuffield College, Oxford, for the French chapter; Gustave Dermine of the FGTB for the Belgian chapter; Bill Conboy of the University of Oxford, Extra-Mural Department, for the British chapter; Alberto Aquarone of the University of Pisa, Gino Bianco of *Avanti!*, Guido Franzinetti of the University of Turin, for the Italian chapter; Daniel Benedict of the IMF for the chapter on European auto industry, R. Bruce Aubry, Archivist of the Independent Labour Party for the introductory chapters.

The text is my responsibility alone. No one but myself is responsible for factual errors which may have escaped repeated revisions, nor for views, whether orthodox or heterodox, to be found in the text.

Introduction

Internationalism has been a watchword of labour for more than one hundred years. Yet information regarding the international labour movement remains astonishingly hard to find. This work in its own limited and pioneering fashion sets out to remedy that omission.

The integration of each nation state into a world economy, as endless indoctrination regarding the 'balance of payments' makes us all aware, is now a cardinal feature of economic life. Capital, as the spread of empire shows, has long possessed a high degree of global mobility. The same is not true of labour. Human beings in the main move long distances only under the pressure of the strongest local compulsion or the attraction of quite exceptional opportunities.

This relative immobility has meant that in the past, despite labour's ideology of internationalism, the larger part of labour's practical activity has not extended beyond the boundaries of separate national states. Only now, with the rise of the giant international corporation, the emergence of trans-national bodies such as the European Economic Community, have the practical questions of international labour organization and behaviour begun to come seriously to the fore.

This work lays claim to originality less in the detail of the information which it places before the reader than in the manner of its presentation. What it seeks to do is to present the labour movements of six European countries in such a fashion as to make their manifold differences comprehensible, to show them as the product of socio-economic factors at variance with those usually taken for granted in the Anglo-Saxon world.

Too often it has been assumed that the mode of operation of labour movements in Britain and the USA conforms to some objective norm from which the labour movements in other countries diverge, for unexplained, but by implication irrational, reasons. The burden of this author's conclusions is that on the contrary the British–United States experience has many of the marks of an atypical, special case.

The labour movement stands at a nodal point in human society. The nature, the pattern of activities of each national labour movement, are conditioned by the multi-faceted socio-economic features of its specific national environment. The labour movements of continental Europe differ from those of Britain and the USA simply because in different circumstances even equivalent goals have to be fought for by different means.

Yet when all such qualifications have been made the common factors continue, as a rule, to overshadow all the others. The job problems of auto workers in Dagenham, Boulogne-Billancourt, Genk, Cologne, Turin or Detroit vary surprisingly little. Increasingly the workers of FIAT, British Leyland, Volkswagen, Renault, Ford, Chrysler or General Motors are constrained to take common action in order to achieve their aims.

This book will I hope be read not only by students and those involved in higher education, not only by management, but above all by those involved in the practical day-to-day activity of the labour movement, for whom in particular it is intended. Up till now the cultural–linguistic barriers separating national labour movements and indeed whole nations from one another have been, for most people, almost insurmountable. These barriers are increasingly outdated and ought to be broken down.

This volume seeks to introduce, across national frontiers, the workers and intellectuals of each nation to the other. If as a result it helps to eliminate past misunderstandings and contribute towards the creation of a common consciousness and sense of purpose, towards a rise in practical working-class and human solidarity, then it will have fulfilled its purpose.

Abbreviations

INTERNATIONAL ORGANIZATIONS

CI	Communist International
CISC	Confédération Internationale des Syndicats Chrétiens – International Federation of Christian Trade Unions
Comintern	Communist International
ECCI	Executive Committee of the Communist International
ECSC	European Coal and Steel Community
ECTU	European Confederation of Trade Unions
EEC	European Economic Community
ICFTU	International Confederation of Free Trade Unions
IFCTU	International Federation of Christian Trade Unions
IFTU	International Federation of Trade Unions
ILO	International Labour Office
ITS	International Trade Secretariat
IWMA	International Working Men's Association (the 'First International')
OECD	Organization for Economic Cooperation and Development
RILU	Red International of Labour Unions
WCL	World Confederation of Labour
WFTU	World Federation of Trade Unions

ITS – International Trade Secretariats

IFBW	International Federation of Building and Woodworkers
IFCCTE	International Federation of Commercial Clerical and Technical Employees
IFFTU	International Federation of Free Teachers' Unions
IFPAAW	International Federation of Plantation, Agricultural and Allied Workers
IMF	International Metal-workers' Federation
ISETU	International Secretariat of Entertainment Trade Unions
ITGLWF	International Textile Garment and Leather Workers' Federation
ITF	International Transport Workers' Federation
IUF	International Union of Food and Allied Workers' Association

MIF   Miners' International Federation
PSI   Public Services International
PTTI   Postal Telegraph and Telephone International
UAD   Universal Alliance of Diamond Workers

OTHER ORGANIZATIONS

AFL   American Federation of Labor
AFL – CIO   American Federation of Labor – Congress of Industrial
             Organizations
CIO   Congress of Industrial Organizations
UAW   United Automobile, Aerospace and Agricultural Imple-
             ment Workers of America

FRANCE

BC   Bureau Confédéral
CA   Commission Administrative
CC   Congrès Confédéral
CCN   Comité Confédéral National
CD   Comité Directeur
CFDT   Confédération Française Démocratique du Travail –
             French Democratic Confederation of Labour
CFT   Confédération Française du Travail – French Con-
             federation of Labour
CFTC   Confédération Française des Travailleurs Chrétiens
             – French Confederation of Christian Workers
CFTC (Maintenu) – The section of the CFTC which seceded when the
             CFTC transformed itself into the CFDT
CGC   Confédération Générale des Cadres – General Con-
             federation of Supervisory Workers
CGPF   Confédération Générale de la Production Française
             – General Confederation of French Industry
CGPF (after 1936) Confédération Générale du Patronat Français –
             General Confederation of French Employers
CGT   Confédération Générale du Travail – General Con-
             federation of Labour
CGT – FO   Confédération Générale du Travail, Force Ouvrière
             – General Confederation of Labour, Force Ouvrière
CGTU   Confédération Générale du Travail Unitaire – General
             Confederation of Labour, Unity Wing
CNPF   Confédération Nationale du Patronat Français –
             National Confederation of French Employers
EGF   l'Electricité et le Gaz de France – French Electricity
             and Gas Board
FDL   Fédération du Livre – Printers' Union
FEN   Fédération de l'Éducation Nationale – Teachers' Union
FO   Force Ouvrière: abbreviation for CGT–FO

FTSF	Fédération des Travailleurs Socialistes de France – Socialist Workers' Federation of France
MRP	Mouvement Républicain Populaire – Popular Republican Movement
PCF	Parti Communiste Français – Communist Party of France
POF	Parti Ouvrier Français – French Workers' Party
POSR	Parti Ouvrier Socialiste Révolutionnaire – Revolutionary Socialist Workers' Party
PTSF	Parti des Travailleurs Socialistes de France – Socialist Workers' Party of France
RATP	– Paris Transport Authority
SFIO	Parti Socialiste, Section Française de l'Internationalé Socialiste – Socialist Party, French Section of the Socialist International
SMAG	Salaire Minimum Agriculture Garanti – Guaranteed minimum wage, agriculture
SMIG	Salaire Minimum Interprofessional Garanti – Guaranteed Minimum Wage, urban area employment
SNCF	Société Nationale des Chemins de Fer Français – French National Railways
UD	Union Départementale – Regional trade union organization
UIMM	Union des Industries Métallurgiques et Minières – Engineering Employers' Association

GERMANY

ADA	Allgemeiner Deutscher Arbeiterverein – General German Workers' Association
ADB	Allgemeiner Deutscher Beamtenbund – General German Federation of Civil Servants
ADGB	Allgemeiner Deutscher Gewerkschaftsbund – General German Trade Union Federation
BDA	Bundesvereinigung der Deutschen Arbeitgeberverbände – German Confederation of Employers' Associations
CDU	Christlicher Demokratische Union – Christian Democratic Union
CGB	Christlicher Gewerkschaftsbund Deutschland – German Christian Workers' Union Confederation
DAF	Deutsche Arbeitsfront – German Labour Front
DAG	Deutsche Angestellten Gewerkschaft – German Salaried Employees' Association
DBB	Deutsche Beamtenbund – German Civil Servants' Union
DGB	Deutsche Gewerkschaftsbund – German Trade Union Federation

DKP	Deutscher Kommunistische Partei – German Communist Party (after 1971)
FDGB	Freier Deutscher Gewerkschaftsbund – Free German Trade Union Federation (after 1945 state-controlled labour organization in Eastern zone)
IG	Industriegewerkschaft – Industrial Union
IG Metall	Industriegewerkschaft Metall – Metal-workers' Industrial Union
KAPD	Kommunistische Arbeiterpartei Deutschland – Communist Workers' Party of Germany
KPD	Kommunistische Partei Deutschlands – Communist Party of Germany (1919–1971)
OTV	Gewerkschaft Offentlichedienste Transport und Verkehr – Public Service, Transport and Communication Workers Union
SAD	Sozialistiche Arbeiterpartei Deutschlands – Socialist Workers' Party of Germany
SAP	Sozialdemokratische Arbeiterpartei – Social Democratic Workers' Party (1869)
SAP	Sozialistischer Arbeiterpartei – Socialist Workers' Party (1931)
SED	Sozialistische Einheitspartei Deutschlands – Socialist Unity Party of Germany
SPD	Sozialdemokratische Partei Deutschlands – Social Democratic Party of Germany
USPD	Unabhängige Sozialdemokratische Partei Deutschlands – Independent Social Democratic Party
VDA	Verband der Deutschen Arbeiterverein – Union of German Workers' Societies (see p. 92)
VDA	Vereinigung der Deutschen Arbeitgeberverbände – Federation of German Employers' Associations (see p. 97)
WWI	Wirtschaftswissenschaftliches Institut – Institute for Economic Research

ITALY

ACLI	Associazione Cristiani dei Lavoratori Italiani – Christian Association of Italian Workers
CGIL	Confederazione Generale Italiana del Lavoro – Italian General Confederation of Labour
CGL	Confederazione Generale del Lavoro – General Confederation of Labour
CISL	Confederazione Italiana dei Sindacati Lavoratori – Italian Confederation of Workers' Unions
CLN	Comitato di Liberazione Nazionale – Committee of National Liberation
CLNAI	Comitato di Liberazione Nazionale dell' Alta Italia – Committee of National Liberation, Northern Italy

Confagricoltura	Confederazione Generale dell' Agricoltura Italiana – Italian General Confederation of Agriculture
Confindustria	Confederazione Generale della Industria Italiana – Italian General Confederation of Industry
DC	Democrazia Cristiana – Christian Democracy
ENEL	Ente Nazionale Energia Elettrica – National Electricity Board
ENI	Ente Nazionale Idrocarburi – National Petrochemical Board
FIM	Federazione Italiana Metallmeccanici – Federation of Italian Metal Workers (CISL)
FIOM	Federazione Impiegati Operai Metallurgici – Federation of Metal Workers and Employees (CGIL)
Intersind	Associazione Sindacale Intersind – State and para-state employers' association
IRI	Istituto per la Ricostruzione Industriale – Institute for Industrial Reconstruction
PCI	Partito Comunista Italiano – Communist Party of Italy
PSDI	Partito Socialista Democratico Italiano – Social Democratic Party of Italy
PSI	Partito Socialista Italiano – Socialist Party of Italy
PSIUP	Partito Socialista Italiano del Unità Proletaria – Italian Socialist Party of Proletarian Unity
UIL	Unione Italiana del Lavoro – Italian Union of Labour
UILM	Unione Italiana Lavoratori Metalmeccanici – Metal Workers' Federation of the Italian Union of Labour (UIL)

BRITAIN

AEU	Amalgamated Engineering Union
ASE	Amalgamated Society of Engineers
AUEW	Amalgamated Union of Engineering Workers
CBI	Confederation of British Industry
EETU–PTU	Electrical, Electronic, Telecommunications Union–Plumbing Trade Union
ETU	Electrical Trades Union
GMWU	General and Municipal Workers' Union
ILP	Independent Labour Party
LRC	Labour Representation Committee
NALGO	National and Local Government Officers' Association
NATSOPA	National Society of Operative Printers and Assistants
NUBPW	National Union of Book Binding and Paper Workers
NUM	National Union of Mineworkers
NUPE	National Union of Public Employees
NUR	National Union of Railwaymen
PTU	Plumbing Trade Union
SDF	Social Democratic Federation

SOGAT — Society of Graphical and Allied Trades
SPGB — Socialist Party of Great Britain
TASS — Technical and Supervisory Section of the Amalgamated Union of Engineering Workers (AUEW)
TGWU — Transport and General Workers' Union
TUC — Trades Union Congress
USDAW — Union of Shop Distributive and Allied Workers

BELGIUM
CGTB — Confédération Générale du Travail de Belgique – Belgian General Confederation of Labour
CLS — Comités de Lutte Syndicale – Trade Union Struggle Committees
CSC — Confédération des Syndicats Chrétiens – Confederation of Christian Trade Unions
FGTB — Fédération Générale du Travail de Belgique – Belgian General Federation of Labour
FIB — Fédération d'Industrie Belge – Federation of Belgian Industry
MMU — Mouvement Métallurgiste Unifié – United Metalworkers' Movement
MSU — Mouvement Syndicale Unifié – United Trade Union Movement
PCB — Parti Communiste Belge – Communist Party of Belgium
POB — Parti Ouvrier Belge – Belgian Workers' Party
PSB — Parti Socialiste Belge – Belgian Socialist Party
PSC — Parti Sociale Chrétien – Christian Social Party

NETHERLANDS
ANMB — Algemene Nederlandse Bedrijfsbond voor de Metallnijverheid en de Elektrotechnische Industrie – General Union for the Metalworking and Electro-technical Industry
CNV — Christelijk Nationaal Vakverbond – Protestant National Trade Union Federation
CSWV — Centraal Sociaal Werkgevers Verbond – Central Social Federation of Employers (1945–1967)
EVC — Eenheids Vakcentraal – Trade Union Unity Centre
FCWV — Federatie van de Katholieke en Protestants–Christelijke Werkgeversbonden – Federation of Catholic and Protestant Employers' Associations
KAB — Katholiek Arbeidersbeweging – Catholic Workers' Movement (1946–64)
NAF — Nederlands Arbeidsfront – Netherlands Labour Front (1942–45)
NAS — Nationaal Arbeids Secretariaat – National Labour Secretariat

NKV	Nederlandse Katholiek Vakverbond – Netherlands Catholic Trade Union Federation
NKWV	Nederlands Katholiek Werkgevers Verbond – Netherlands Catholic Employers' Federation
NVV	Nederlands Verbond van Vakverenigingen – Netherland Federation of Trade Unions
PvdA	Partij van den Arbeid – Labour Party
SDAP	Sociaal Democratische Arbeiders Partij – Social Democratic Workers' Party
SDB	Sociaal Democratische Bond – Social Democratic League
SDP	Sociaal Democratische Partij – Social Democratic Party
VPCW	Verbond van Protestants Christelijke Werkgevers in Nederland – Federation of Protestant Employers in the Netherlands

1. The Industrial Revolution in Europe

The European Economic Community established in 1958 is only a small part of continental Europe. Great Britain and the Irish Republic stand outside its original boundaries. The Scandinavian countries – Norway, Sweden, Denmark and Finland – are similarly excluded from its original domain. Austria, Switzerland, the Balkan states, whether 'East' or 'West', all the Russian bloc countries, indeed the Russian Federal Soviet Republic itself, all properly speaking part of Europe, stand outside the EEC.[1]

Until the conclusion of the First World War, Europe dominated the whole globe, as it had done from the rise of sail, gunpowder and cannon, in the sixteenth and seventeenth centuries. In the last decades of the nineteenth century and the first decades of the twentieth, the United States first caught up, then surpassed, the industrial might of its European competitors. The First World War shook Europe's hold on its colonies. Russia, reorganized on the basis of a state-owned economy controlled by a self-appointed Communist elite, split off from Europe and set out on an autarchic course all of its own. The United States emerged for the first time as a power of world rank, a role in which it was confirmed by the Second World War. After 1945 Russia, now buttressed by a whole chain of satellite states along its eastern borders, emerged as a fresh power of global status in its own right.

In each of the two world wars it was the working populations of the combatant powers, victor and vanquished alike, who were truly the losers. Devastation, slaughter and economic blockade reduced whole nations to beggary, so loosening the ties that bound colonial to metropolitan territories as eventually to set them free. In the years immediately following 1945 the nations of western Europe were dependent on American aid for survival, confronted with social dislocation which, in the eyes of many observers, involved a real physical danger of revolution.

1. Geographers are accustomed to divide the earth into 'eastern' and 'western' hemispheres along the lines of the meridians 20° west and 160° east. On that basis, part of Iceland, and all of Britain, to say nothing of the rest of 'western' Europe, are properly speaking in the east. This is a case in which political propaganda has quite eclipsed reason and common sense.

Neither a shattered and fragmented German state, nor a weakened and chronically disunited France, could any longer claim great power status. The British Empire was heading rapidly towards dissolution.

The Second World War led to an irretrievable decline in the global power of European capitalism. The European labour movement, by contrast, emerged from the turmoil and suffering of hostilities stronger and more powerful than ever. The trade unions and the socialist and communist parties, once outcast and scorned, now came forward to the very centre of the political scene.

The world labour movement, the product of the industrial revolution, began in Britain and in continental Europe. Trade unions arose in direct defence against the exploitation to which the largely defenceless individual wage worker is subject in an industrial society. The Socialist Party began as a means to bring capitalist exploitation to an end. These organizations have since become implanted across the world wherever the process of industrialization has taken place. Yet the labour movement of Europe, its organization, its models of behaviour, its origins, its hopes and aspirations, remain surprisingly unknown.

In the United States the trade union movement organizes across a whole continent extending some 2800 miles from Atlantic to Pacific, 1600 miles from Canada to the Mexican frontier. Yet, 'independents' such as the mine-workers, teamsters and auto workers apart, the whole movement is united in a single union confederation, the American Federation of Labor and Congress of Industrial Organizations, the AFL–CIO. The unions, while pursuing pressure-group aims of their own, do not set out either directly or indirectly, to enter the lists as representatives of the 'class interests' of labour. The unions accept the social system. Their objective, succinctly expressed by Samuel Gompers, a former President of the AFL, is 'More . . . Now!'

In the United Kingdom the unions, organizing a higher proportion of the workforce than in the United States, are, like their US counterparts, linked in a single national union centre, the Trades Union Congress (TUC). British politics revolve around a two-party, Labour–Conservative axis. Union affiliations provide the majority of the members, the bulk of Labour Party finances. The unions have an important, although not decisive, voice in Labour Party councils. These political differences apart, British and United States unions have a great deal in common. Both are primarily wage-bargaining institutions. Both are solidly financed by membership subscriptions. Both have elaborate procedural devices which enable them to encompass widely different views within their ranks. That either the TUC or the AFL–CIO might split over political or religious issues seems inconceivable.

Brought up in this school the British or American observer finds the labour movement in Europe simply incomprehensible. In France, socialist and communist and formerly Catholic union organizations compete with one another in a confusing pattern of continually changing conflicts and alliances. The membership of any two major British or United States unions outnumber by far that of whole national union confederations in France.

In Italy, where in recent years strike figures have been the highest in Europe, the unions have no strike funds. Stoppages are momentary and episodic, rarely long-drawn-out affairs. Italian unions can muster large demonstrations on the streets. Union bargaining power at the point of production remains very low indeed. Christians, communists, socialists (of three different doctrinal varieties) and republicans rally to three main union confederations, within which they are mixed in an astonishing confusion of attitudes and organizational combinations. Are Italian unions, in the past largely dependent on financial subventions from external sources, properly to be understood as industrial organizations at all? Can they be better comprehended as extended arms of one or other political party?

In the Netherlands, by contrast, strikes are rare. The unions, divided between Catholic, Protestant and socialist confederations, nevertheless maintain a remarkably tight common front. In post war years all three confederations have pursued a restrictive incomes policy. The individual wage-earner's freedom to capitalize on the opportunities of the labour market has been restricted to an extent unknown outside totalitarian regimes. How could that be?

Belgian unions divide approximately equally between Catholic and socialist confederations. The socialists are moderate rather than revolutionary in character. Yet Belgian socialist unions have launched two political general strikes in the years since 1945, six at least since their foundation. One can drive across Belgium in any direction, in a long afternoon. Yet hostility between French and Dutch speaking Belgians has grown so sharp as to pose the union confederations regional–linguistic problems which it requires the greatest skill and tact to overcome.

'A country in which industrial development is more advanced than in others simply presents those others with a picture of their own future,' wrote Marx in his 1867 preface to volume 1 of *Capital*. The history of Europe shows that no view could be more misleading. The continental powers were less well situated to make the industrial transition than Britain. They had the misfortune to face the problem of the industrial revolution with a technical–productive leader *already* in the field. Continental powers faced a challenge to 'catch up and surpass' foreign competition not unlike that imposed on Russia by Stalinism a century or so later. The industrial revolution in Europe differed from that of either Britain or the USA. Since labour movements arise as a human response to external social and economic conditions the labour movements of Europe in their turn come to assume forms significantly different from those of either Britain or the USA.

The United Kingdom has existed as a single unit of sovereignty for over 200 years, England alone for more than eight centuries. The United States, the brief years of the Civil War apart, has been one unified state throughout its existence. Europe through most of history has represented more a patchwork quilt of petty kingdoms, duchies, bishoprics, free cities, often with separate courts, coinage and customs barriers, than the system of nation states we see today.

Britain and to an important degree also the United States are homogenous societies by comparison. Each occupies a territory united over centuries, within a common market area. No such homogeneity exists in continental Europe. Linguistic barriers between French, German, Dutch, Belgians, Italians and Scandinavians are difficult to surmount. Regional conflicts, as between Flemings and Walloons in Belgium, or north and south in Italy, can be questions of major national significance. Regional dialects are widespread and important. Local traditions remain powerful. Folk memory may go back over centuries. The traditions of whole regions, the location and character of cities, are to be explained by events which antedate not only the industrial revolution but indeed modern society altogether. By modern standards distances in Europe are not great. In terms of psychic perception they can be immense. Each factor exercises its influence on the behaviour of labour movement organizations in Europe.

Inside the United States the work of colonizing a continent has made a high degree of labour mobility commonplace. Europeans too, in tens of millions, left their homelands to migrate to the USA. Yet that enormous migration, amongst the greatest in history, ought not to blind us to the fact that over centuries the degree of labour mobility within Europe has remained low. Feudal obligations fixed millions of peasants to the soil until the French Revolution brought their release. Peasant proprietorship continued to tie many millions just as firmly thereafter.[1] Limited communications and tiny market areas have restricted the consciousness of the labourer, over many past generations, to a petty rural or urban world in his immediate vicinity. After the 1707 Act of Union there was no customs barrier between London and Edinburgh. Over the similar distance between Strasbourg and Rotterdam there were several hundred.[2]

1. 'As late as 1861 more than nine out of ten in seventy of the ninety French departments lived in the department of their birth', Hobsbawm, *The Age of Revolution*, p. 10.

2. Despicht, 'Esquisse historique de la politique britannique des transports intérieures', *Transports*, Nov. 1967, p. 590; see also Despitcht, *Policies for Transport in the Common Market*, p. 179.

When feudal ties were ended, national frontiers erected during the nineteenth century took their place. Europe has never known the steady forward movement of millions towards an open frontier on the American model. Widespread regional, national, religious and linguistic differences all bear witness to that fact.

The capitalist–industrialist ethic was generated in Britain. In the United States it was implanted in a hitherto virgin soil. In Britain the entrepreneurial class was clearly established as part of the ruling elite, the political monopoly of the monarchy and the landed interest broken, before the eighteenth century began. The United States was a lay republic from the moment of its birth. In most continental European countries the power of monarchical semi-absolutism was not broken until the revolutions which followed the First World War.

The ideology of free trade and *laissez-faire*, the ideas of Adam Smith, Cobden and Bright, were born in Britain and here they gained the widest acceptance. Nascent American society knew no other ethical and cultural guidelines than those of Weber's 'protestant ethic'. 'Go West, young man,' advised Horace Greeley. 'Go West' to get rich. In a lecture at Oakland, R. W. Emerson affirmed that 'if you can build a better mousetrap, although you live in the deepest forest, yet the world will beat a path to your door'. Such an optimistic belief in the universality of a competitive ethic, unrestricted by inhibitions from an earlier age, unalloyed with belief in any other source of power and prestige but that of hard cash, was unique to the USA. It found no counterpart in continental Europe.

The philosophy of capitalist society is one of open entry. The devil takes the hindmost. The winner collects the prize. Yet in Europe, open entry was always the exception rather than the rule. 'Far more than in Britain', one commentator has written, 'continental business enterprise was a class activity, recruiting practitioners from a group limited by custom and law.'[1] In the United States by contrast the citizen inherited a seemingly limitless frontier on which he was able to forage almost unopposed. Those who were tough, able, ruthless and enterprising enough did indeed possess exceptional opportunitites to succeed, even if their initial capital was not great. In Europe 'take-off' to entrepreneurial success did not come from any egalitarian plain but from a series of stepped class plateaux. Ease of entry to entrepreneurial activity bore direct relation to previous social status and economic circumstances. Widespread awareness of this fact may indeed be one explanation of the greater receptivity of workers in Europe to socialist ideas.

In Europe the relationship between state and industry was often quite different also. Many of the more important manufactories in Europe were of state or semi-state origin, producing in some cases luxuries, in

1. Landes, *The Unbound Prometheus*, p. 129.

other cases arms, and catering to the needs of aristocratic, clerical or commercial ruling elites. The mass of subsistence consumers bought elsewhere in a series of markets served by local craftsmen, dominated by tradition rather than more modern innovatory techniques. For reasons of state the governments of France, Prussia and Austria had set out to encourage industrial development as early as the seventeenth and eighteenth centuries. In this they were aided by the ready availability of standing bureaucracy, always of greater importance in the government of European states than in Britain or the USA. British competition after the industrial revolution thus only gave added impetus to a movement already under way.

The European enterprise, too, was far more likely to be a family undertaking. This meant that the family income, the family status, the whole family way of life, were inextricably linked with the fortunes of only one particular firm. Close family involvement discouraged the use of outside capital, minimized incentives for growth beyond a size optimal for family needs and encouraged high profit margins on small production runs, rather than the reverse. Such entrepreneurs were inclined to see the market as fixed and limited, rather than as dynamic and expanding. The accumulation of riches at the expense of the ruin of one's neighbours, seemed contemptible, rather than praiseworthy. The 'laws of competition' failed to take proper effect. Enterprises survived which in Britain or America would rapidly have gone to the wall.

Again, British and United States entrepreneurs, certain public utterances notwithstanding, took the maintenance of social order and stability for granted. British industrialists remembered Chartism and recalled that it had been defeated. The European entrepreneur, by contrast, took note of the French Revolution and remembered the Terror, the tumbrils and the guillotine.

For the British [or American] employer the best remedy for insubordination was technological unemployment. It hardly occurred to him to allow social considerations to modify the rational organisation of his enterprise. . . His French counterpart – and to a lesser extent, the German or Belgian manufacturer – was never sure when labour unrest or unemployment would turn into political revolution.[1]

That such fears were by no means unfounded was shown by the revolutions which swept across the breadth of Europe in 1848, the Paris Commune of 1871, the two revolutions in Russia during 1917, the revolutions in Germany, Bavaria and Hungary at the end of the First World War.

Paternalism was in part a defensive reflex to putative social revolt, in part an attempt to stabilize a workforce with skills in short supply. The

1. Landes, pp. 190–1. The reader might care to ponder the psychological connotations of the term 'labour unrest'. On this also, Chevalier, *Classes laborieuses et classes dangereuses en France.*

entrepreneur's view of his workforce itself reflected earlier feudal and manorial traditions. The entrepreneur came to see himself not as an 'employer' on the Anglo-American model, but as the *patron*, a 'master' standing in a particular, paternalistic relation to his 'man'. Yet it would be wrong to deny paternalism genuine altruistic motivation altogether. It was this very sincerity which brought harmful social consequences in its train. British and United States employers fought union organizations, but once unions were firmly in the field they were prepared to deal with them, to discuss what were, after all, essentially economic issues. 'For the continental employer, however, a union was a conspiracy against public order and morals; a strike an act of ingratitude; the effort of labour to raise wages the indiscipline of an impatient son. All of this was evil. And there is no negotiating with evil.'[1]

British industrialization got under way with funds derived from the exploitation of the whole world. Industrialization in the United States, which came later, was eased by relatively unrestricted access to scarce investment funds which could be acquired from abroad without any serious threat to national sovereignty. The Atlantic and Pacific Oceans effectively insulated the vast territories of the United States from unwanted foreign interference.

In Europe by contrast, investment funds were harder to come by, sovereignty more permanently at risk. Britain, an island, protected by her navy, never maintained more than a small professional army, mainly for overseas duties. In the United States the army, before 1850, stood at below 10,000 men, between 1871 and 1897 it never exceeded 30,000, and even in 1916 on the eve of the United States entry into the First World War barely exceeded 100,000 men. In Europe, the powers retained great armies of conscripted citizens, numbered collectively in millions, permanently in the field. British and American workers never knew conscription. Workers in continental Europe came to accept it as a customary rule.

Shortage of available capital underlies a further factor distinguishing the industrialization process in continental Europe from that in Britain and the USA; the role of the banks. Banking in Britain began primarily as a *commercial* operation and remains so to this day. In Europe, where capital and entrepreneurial skills were more scarce, where the pressures of industrialization were greater, the bank became the crucial intermediary between collective investment and individual savings. Nowhere in Europe does the stock market play a role comparable to that of 'the City' in Britain or Wall Street in the USA.

Between the English bank essentially designed to serve as a source of short-term capital and a bank designed to finance the long-run investment needs of

1. Landes, p. 192.

the economy there was a complete gulf . . . A German bank . . . accompanied an industrial enterprise from the cradle to the grave, from establishment to liquidation through all the vicissitudes of its existence . . . the banks acquired a formidable degree of ascendancy over industrial enterprises, which extended far beyond the sphere of financial control into that of entrepreneurial and managerial decisions.[1]

Lenin, who like most Marxists of his day had been brought up to see British capitalism as the classical model, found in this phenomenon 'the turning-point from the old capitalism to the new, from the domination of capital in general to the domination of finance capital'.[2] In fact this was not the case. The conclusions Lenin drew, which continue to motivate the world communist movement to this day, were erroneous. Continental investment banking is properly to be understood as a specific instrument of industrialization in a backward country. This 'proto-socialist' mode of behaviour, far from representing 'the highest stage of capitalism' foretold by Lenin, was rather the forerunner of the industrialization methods used by the Bolsheviks themselves after the Russian Revolution.

The nature of the economy, we have sought to argue, is both formed by and itself forms the nature, methods and behaviour of the entrepreneurial class in a process of continually repeated mutual interaction. This process is conditioned by the particular strategic needs of specific states. The behaviour of the economy, the entrepreneurial class and the state establish the environmental conditions in which the modern urban working class is formed, the social pressures in response to which its own forms of consciousness, its own modes of organization arise. It is here that we hold the key to the specific characteristics of the various sections of the European working class and the working class in general. It was not, after all, formal rules and procedures which created the modern labour movement. Rather these rules and procedures were the outcome of ideas and attitudes already present in the minds of the working class.

All coal-mines have common features, but some are deep and others are shallow, in some the seams are thin, in others they are thick, in some the coal is soft, in others it is hard, some may be operated through horizontal shafts into the hillside, others may go down a thousand feet into the ground and extend a mile or more under the sea. Each variation has a direct impact on the nature and outlook of the work force. The more complex a productive operation, the more the possible variants in a production process, the greater the scope for pre-existing markets, habits, techniques, locational siting factors, to exert an influence. As production processes and other factors change so the work force organization and outlook alters as a direct response.

1. Gerschenkron, *Economic Backwardness in Historical Perspective*, pp. 13–14.
2. Lenin, *Imperialism, the Highest Stage of Capitalism*, p. 57.

The degree of development of the economy, the balance of the factors of production, the extent of enterprise size, the degree of industrial concentration, all these both quantitatively and qualitatively affect the character and outlook of labour. The number of British coal-miners increased from 314,000 in 1871 to 517,000 in 1891 and some 830,000 in 1911. There were 120,000 German coal- and lignite-miners in 1865; this number rose to 247,000 in the next twenty years; 300,000 more workers entered the pits over the next two decades. The mining population was highly concentrated. The average coal-mining concern employed over 800 men (lignite pits were much smaller). That being so, the factors tending to the growth of unionism and social democracy were far more powerful than if the rate of growth had been lower, the degree of geographical and industrial concentration less. Similar factors, working for example in an area of predominantly female employment like textiles, might have been expected to produce a profoundly different result.

If some factors speed up the pace of labour movement development others may work in the opposite direction. Peasant society with its emphasis on subsistence economy limits the market for the circulation of commodities, and places limits on recruitment for large-scale industry. That is not all. Peasant economy also constantly produces and reproduces modes of behaviour appropriate to an earlier age, not only in its own ranks and to some extent those of the bourgeoisie, but also in the ranks of the urban working class many of whose members retain a close and familiar connection with the peasant economy of the rural village.

The nature of the labour movement in each territory also finds roots in particular national conditions. Centralized unions in post war Germany are a reaction, at least in part, one suspects, to a highly cartelized industry, and to the threat posed by the stalinist state across the border. The difficulties of working class organization in Italy are partly due to the pronounced regionalism of a country long divided into local fiefdoms, which for generations lacked an adequate national transport system. The cautious conservatism of Netherlands labour finds much of its origins in social traditions of oligarchic rule derived from a far earlier age.

The worker's view of himself and his patterns of socio-political and organizational behaviour cannot be arbitrarily separated from the history of the society or state, and of the classes, of which, independently of his will, he is an integral part. The very question whether a particular industrial or political response to a given social situation will be effective or ineffective will depend on attention to the social context established by these facts.

The worker is not a worker in the abstract, he is a specific worker, in a specific situation, at a specific moment in time, at a particular place, in a particular conjunction of circumstances and social forces which are to a large extent determined by history. The British worker cannot but be aware of Britain's imperial and maritime tradition, its relatively secure situation, and its former high status in the world. The German worker, before 1939, could not have been unaware of the exposed situation of Germany in central Europe, with the vast plains of Poland, Prussia and Russia on its eastern borders. The Italian worker could not fail to be influenced by the localized traditions of an aristocratic bourgeoisie, the long standing clerical domination of a large part of the Italian mainland. The Dutch, inhabitants of a small maritime nation with large land powers on its borders to the south and east, had to behave circumspectly and to learn to accept with tolerably good grace matters which, albeit by no means to their natural taste, could not be changed by the forces at their command. The great French Revolution and the tradition of Napoleonic military glory which emerged as a result are, as de Gaulle and the colonels have shown, by no means invalidated up to the present time. Yet a Napoleonic tradition is one with quite different social consequences to the British cult of Nelson 'turning a blind eye' at the Battle of Trafalgar. Naval imperialism protects national security while not in the least threatening to undermine the political power structure at home. No military imperialism could have the same consequences at all.

The labour movement in short is not a thing in itself but a social organism responding to particular social circumstances. These circumstances differ a great deal between one place and another. It is only to be expected that where social circumstances differ, labour movements should differ too.

2. The Rise of the Labour Movement

The precondition for the emergence of a modern labour movement in Europe was the existence of a fully developed society based on capitalist commodity circulation, the separation of millions of individuals from ownership of means of production, whether as peasants or as artisans, their entry into the newly formed 'labour market' as wage labourers. Society had to change from a static, essentially rural construct, based in most areas on production for use or limited local exchange, to one of vastly larger market size.

The bedrock of Europe's modern industrial society was laid in the years between 1850 and 1870. In Germany in these years rail mileage jumped from 3600 to 14,800, in France from 1900 to 11,500, in Belgium from 500 to 2300. Ruhr coal output, 1,600,000 tons in 1850, rose to 11,800,000 by 1869; production in the French Pas-de-Calais field rose from 4700 tons to 2,200,000 tons between 1851 and 1871; production in Germany as a whole rose from 4,200,000 to 23,800,000 tons; in France from 4,400,000 to 13,300,000 tons. Consumption of raw cotton, an index of the growth of the textile industry, rose from 17,000 to 118,000 tons in Germany; from 10,000 to 18,000 tons in Belgium, over the years 1850–73.[1]

These production figures need to be translated into human terms to be properly understood. The creation of a railway network abolished distance at a stroke. Cheap, fast rail transport served to unify the market, to eliminate enclaves previously immune to outside competition. The railway was by the standards of the time an enormous organization, the largest standing body outside the conscript army. Hierarchically organized, the railwaymen with their manifold occupations, many of an unprecedented nature, some highly skilled, represented an entirely new element in the labour force. Employed in some cases by private companies, more often by state or para-state organizations, drilled into a common sentiment by the requirements of their employment, they were bound in time to think and to organize in terms of collective action.

Miners had been extracting coal from the surface of the earth as far back as the Middle Ages and earlier. Their numbers and work situation

1. Landes, *The Unbound Prometheus*, pp. 194, 203.

were now miraculously transformed. The railway, like the motor car today, was distinguished by the range and extent of its forward and backward linkages. It not only called into existence a new body of men to handle day-to-day operations, it also called up increased output from the metal-producing and machine-building industries. These industries in turn made demands on the mines. Cheaper transport widened and diversified the market for coal, which the railways themselves consumed in vast quantities simply for their own needs. The rise of large-scale production, dependent on cheap, easy transport for market realization, demanded further huge amounts of mechanical power, steam fed out of boilers fuelled by coal. Between 1871 and 1900 coal output in Germany, France and Belgium, the main continental producers, rose from 56 million to 206 million tons, by 1913 it had climbed to 256 million. Lignite output increased these figures by 19 million tons in 1871, by 87 million in 1913. British output, roughly comparable in 1913, required the labour of over 800,000 men. Total employment in France, Belgium and Germany in these years is not likely to have been significantly less.

These changes in the economy transformed the whole physiognomy of human society. In Germany, population increased by 24 million between 1871 and 1910. At the beginning of this period, 64 per cent of the population was rural, 36 per cent lived in towns; at the end, the ratio was almost exactly reversed. The rate of industrial transformation in Germany was rapid. 'Some trades even passed in a single generation through the three stages – independent handicraft, outwork, and the factory system – an evolution which . . . had taken several centuries in earlier ages.'[1] In chemicals and electrical engineering Germany became a world leader by the turn of the century. These industries were not only new, they were highly concentrated. By 1961 three firms dominated the electrical engineering industry. One, AEG, employed 31,000 out of a total industry work force of 107,000.

The tumultuous onrush of industrial growth at first produced no visible counterpart in the field of labour organization. A kind of psychic delay factor intervened, a time of adjustment to the mood of anomie and helplessness induced in those plunged into the urban maelstrom of industrial employment. The individual worker, pitchforked into a strange, rapidly changing urban environment, badly informed, if informed at all, about the labour market situation, was confronted, not with a multitude of individual employers, but with a relatively small number of larger undertakings. Such employers could readily dispense with any single element in their labour force. The labourer stood in the position of a forced seller, whose commodity, the power to work, on the sale of which he depended for very existence, was irretrievably lost when not used. It was to remedy this inequality of bargaining power

1. Clapham, *The Economic Development of France and Germany*, p. 301.

that labour set out to organize.[1] Factory discipline required a new breed of worker, a man broken to the inexorable demands of the clock. In time the wage worker came to realize that this same discipline, once learned, could be used for his own social and political emancipation.

The repeal of the Combination Acts in 1824 largely cleared the decks for union organization in Britain. The obstacles faced by labour in Europe were of a more serious order. The general level of social conditions and economic deprivation was a great deal worse. Political rights were more limited. The unions in particular were the victims of severe legal discrimination.

The French Revolution of 1789 abolished the guilds and established that henceforth every citizen was 'free to do such business, exercise such profession, art, or trade, as he may choose'. Alongside this went an express legal recognition of the rights of assembly and free association. One result was an upsurge of militancy amongst the building trade workers of Paris. The 'masters' petitioned the municipal authorities for action. The municipality in its turn appealed to the National Assembly. The outcome was the Chapelier Law of June 1791.

The Chapelier Law, whilst clothed in all the individualist rhetoric of the Revolution, was an explicitly anti labour measure. The guilds and all other organizations of particular estates having been abolished, it was made illegal to re-establish them in any form whatever. Thus 'gatherings composed of . . . working men . . . or instigated by them and directed against the free exercise of industry and work' were deemed 'riotous, to be dispersed by force . . . and . . . punished with all the severity which the law permits'. It was clear to the legislators that the general terms of this law caught employers associations equally with workmen's combinations. Accordingly the Chamber added a specific rider to the effect that: 'The National Assembly, considering that the law which it has just passed does not concern the Chambers of Commerce, passes to the order of the day.' The French Assembly, by a law of 1803, also made 'workbooks' compulsory. Without such a book and a satisfactory entry in it from his former employer, no worker could be re-hired. In such case he was liable to arrest for vagrancy.[2]

In France laws against strikes were enforced with some severity; over 13,000 persons were prosecuted in the four decades before their repeal in 1863. Even after this date the right to organize still remained much more formal than real: not until 1884 was labour conceded anything

1. For this summary of the situation I am indebted to Nathan Reich, *Industrial Relations in the Weimar Republic*, pp. 10–11.

2. Levine, *The Labor Movement in France*, pp. 15–19. The workbook was re-introduced by Hitler in Nazi Germany (Nathan, *The Nazi Economic System*, p. 194) and has been for decades a feature of the worker's life in Soviet Russia. A similar document, the 'passbook', is obligatory for the native population of South Africa.

approaching full freedom of industrial organization. The workbook requirement was not abolished until 1890.[1]

The Chapelier Law and other French legislation applied, as a matter of course, to the whole territory of France, which at this time included both present day Belgium and the Netherlands.[2] When the Netherlands was reconstituted as a separate kingdom in 1815 much of this legislation was retained on the statute book. When the Revolution of 1830 gained Belgium her independence from the Netherlands, the same procedure was followed here too. In the Netherlands legislation banning both strikes and union organization was not repealed until 1872.[3] In Belgium the right to strike was not conceded before 1886 and only explicitly recognized in 1921, after the First World War; the workbook survived until 1890.[4]

If the worker's freedom to organize was limited, his right to a say in the government of his country was no less severely circumscribed. In Italy the number entitled to vote was no more than 630,000 as late as 1880. The electorate was raised to 3 million soon after but did not acquire anything approaching a popular character until raised to 8 million in 1913 on the eve of the First World War.[5] In Germany, not only was the suffrage limited, but representation was grossly and dishonestly weighted in favour of the middle and upper classes. Electoral rights apart, the Reichstag itself possessed only the most limited powers. In Belgium the mass of the working class was not enfranchized until 1893. Universal suffrage once achieved, a gerrymandered electoral system, based on multiple voting rights for members of the middle and upper classes, continued to deny workers the electoral majority to which they were entitled.

The Constitution of the United States made the USA a lay state from the beginning. In Britain the power of the Catholic Church was broken in the sixteenth century. The Church of England, the 'Tory Party at prayers', like its counterpart the Greek Orthodox Church in Tsarist Russia, was never more than a shabby and unrespected defender of the *status quo*. Anti clericalism was never a major force in nineteenth or twentieth century British or United States politics simply because the special privileges of the Church in social and political life had been disposed of long ago. In Europe the power, privilege and income of the Church, still intact, were threatened by the rise of rationalism which accompanied the bourgeois revolution, land reform and the division of

1. Landauer; *European Socialism*, vol. i, p. 288; Levine, *The Labor Movement in France*, pp. 17–22.

2. For the shocked reactions of a United States labour leader to this situation see Gompers, *Labour in Europe and America*, p. 217.

3. Windmuller, *Labor Relations in the Netherlands*, p. 8.

4. Chlepner, *Cent ans d'histoire sociale en Belgique*, pp. 22–4.

5. The population of Italy was 36 million in 1911.

large estates which it brought in its train. The Catholic hierarchy saw the state as a secular arm, established to protect the true faith, indoctrinate the population and repress heresy wherever it might arise. Thus in France political Catholics, royalist rather than republican through most of the nineteenth century, were not regarded as loyal citizens of the Republic. In Italy the Church excommunicated the king and went so far as to forbid the faithful to vote or stand for election to the Chamber.

Education had hitherto been largely the preserve of the ecclesiastical authorities. The provision of popular lay education, coming at a time when urbanization was threatening the faith of a hitherto predominantly rural population, was seen as a direct blow at the Church. Clerical obscurantism brought the hierarchy into headlong conflict with both the liberal bourgeoisie and the rising socialist movement. The socialists, understandably, saw the Church as a bastion of the most reactionary elements in society. The Church in return condemned the doctrines of socialism out of hand. The socialists became strongly anti clerical and, to the extent that they were Marxists, atheistic as well. Anti clericalism in Europe, it is important to note, was not socialist in origin but was rather a respectable bourgeois phenomenon.[1]

Europe in the nineteenth century remained a predominantly rural society. The rural population, dominated by the parish priest, constituted a most important voting bloc at the disposal of the hierarchy and through it the Vatican. Confessional issues were at times a cardinal factor in the political life of France, Germany, Belgium, Italy and the Netherlands during the nineteenth century. Multi-class Catholic parties remain an integral part of the political life of these countries up to the present time. No equivalent problem faced the labour movement in either Britain or the United States.

This situation was made more difficult by the fact that to the hierarchy in these years, even the ideology of simple trade unionism was unacceptable. The Church denied the existence of any fundamental conflict of interest between 'master' and 'man' and sought to organize both together in associations based on an essentially corporative model. Hostility to unionism became a further factor driving a wedge between the Church and the rising working class movement.

If we take into account the social situation of the European worker living surrounded by poverty, hardship and insecurity, denied the right to vote, often cheated of the vote's proper weighting even when he did possess the suffrage, liable to criminal sanctions if he sought to better his wages and conditions and threatened with eternal damnation if he dared to stand up for his rights, it is perhaps not surprising that the socialist movement in Europe initially advanced at a faster rate than in Britain

1. See the perceptive article, 'Roman Catholicism and socialism', in Connolly, *The Workers' Republic*, pp. 56–62.

and the USA. Major political reforms were self evidently required to clear the way for any thoroughgoing social change.

Utopian socialist doctrines of one kind or another had a long history in European thought. Socialism as a mass phenomenon waited on the emergence of an industrial working class and the establishment of wage labour as the predominant mode of employment. Thus although the First International, set up in London in 1864, inspired terror in the hearts of many governments, its physical support was never more than very limited. Riven by internal disputes, the First International ended its effective existence in 1873.

In the next decade, as the pace of industrialization increased, Marxist parties grew rapidly in a number of European countries. In Germany, the Socialist Labour Party, later the Social Democratic Workers' Party (*Sozialdemokratische Partei Deutschlands*: SPD), could muster a vote exceeding 1·4 million already in 1890.

In France, the socialists fully recovered from the repression that followed the Paris Commune within ten years. Unfortunately the French seemed to divide as easily as the Germans combined. The French Socialist Workers' Party (*Parti des Travailleurs Socialistes de France* : PTSF) founded by Jules Guesde in 1880, with a programme in the drafting of which both Marx and Engels had collaborated, split within three years. In 1882, one wing, the 'Possibilistes' led by Paul Brousse, whose reform aspirations were too moderate for Guesde, set up the Federation of French Socialist Workers (*Fédération des Travaileurs Socialistes de France*: FTSF). The Guesdists meanwhile reformed themselves as the French Workers' Party (*Parti Ouvrier Français*: POF). In 1890, Jean Allemane, too revolutionary for his own party, not dogmatic enough for Guesde, split off from Brousse to found a fresh, Revolutionary Socialist Workers' Party (*Parti Ouvrier Socialiste Révolutionnaire* : POSR). Deputies elected by these organizations apart, the French Chamber also housed a number of socialist 'Indépendants'. Two, Jean Jaurès, a university professor and Alexandre Millerand, a lawyer, were each in their very different ways very representative figures of French socialism. Significantly, of the forty-eight socialist deputies returned in the election of 1893, no less than thirty were 'Indépendants'.

In Italy, where the anarchists had dominated the First International, where industry was more retarded, socialism was a little slower to enter the field. An Italian Socialist Party (*Partito Socialista Italiano* : PSI) was not founded until 1892. The PSI elected twelve deputies in the election of 1895, fifteen in that of 1897, and thirty-three in the election of 1900, when the party polled 13 per cent of the vote.[1] The Belgian Workers' Party (*Parti Ouvrier Belge* : POB), established in 1885, mustered 300,000

1. The PSI vote was 76,000 in 1895, 135,000 in 1897, 175,000 in 1900.

THE RISE OF THE LABOUR MOVEMENT 17

votes and elected twenty-eight deputies by 1894. In the Netherlands, a Social Democratic League (*Sociaal Democratische Bond:* SDB) had been established, under the inspiration of Domela Niuwenhuis, a former Lutheran pastor, as early as 1881. At a conference held in Paris in 1889, the 100th anniversary of the French Revolution, a new International, linking these and many other socialist organizations around the world, was set up.

The advances in the field of union organization, although less startling, were equally significant. In Belgium, the country in which industrialization had got under way the earliest, a number of locally based union organizations had affiliated to the First International. Twenty local unions were amongst the fifty-nine organizations, which combined to set up the POB in 1885. These socialist unions, reconstituted in 1898 as the *Commission Syndicale*, became the forerunner of the present Belgian socialist union confederation, the *Fédération Générale du Travail de Belgique* (FGTB). In these early years membership of Belgian unions is not likely to have exceeded 20,000.

In Germany the first unions were established by the socialists 'primarily as recruiting agents for the political labour movement'.[1] Membership of the German General Workers' Association (*Allgemeiner Deutscher Gewerkschaftsbund:* ADGB), 200,000 in 1890, reached the million mark by 1904, making the German unions by far the strongest and best-organized in continental Europe.

In the Netherlands local unions of skilled diamond workers and printers had been set up as early as the 1860s. The first national trade union centre was set up in 1871. In 1903 a split between socialists and syndicalists led to the foundation of a new confederation, led by moderate socialists. This organization, the Netherlands Federation of Trade Unions (*Nederlands Verbond van Vakverenigingen:* NVV) established in 1905, soon came to dominate the field.

In France, although socialist ideas early came to dominate the organized labour movement, the bulk of organized unionists, after an initial hesitation, adopted a critical, even anti political stance. The General Confederation of Labour (*Confédération Générale du Travail:* CGT) disillusioned with French parliamentary socialism, influenced by anarchist ideas, developed a syndicalist ideology all of its own. In the eyes of the CGT leaders, the workers, schooled by militancy, made irresistible by the all-powerful weapon of the general strike, would take over society themselves, without need of a political party. The French unions, some 300,000 strong by 1906, perhaps twice as powerful by 1914, thus stood separate and apart from, sometimes even hostile to, the Socialist Party.

Italian industry, concentrated around Milan, Genoa and Turin, the

1. Schorske, *German Social Democracy,* p. 9.

'iron triangle' of the north, lagged behind its rivals; so, as a consequence, did Italian union organization. The first national trade union centre, the General Confederation of Labour (*Confederazione Generale del Lavoro*: CGL), was not established before 1906. Italian society remained extremely backward, with advanced industry in the north, near-feudal conditions for land workers in the centre and the south. The CGL was unusual in that it comprised an important contingent of workers from the land as well as industrial workers. The Italian Socialist Party, under Turati, pursued a moderate course. Elements in the CGL were much more radical. The outcome was marked tensions, both within the CGL, and, at times, between the CGL and the PSI. In pre war years the CGL enrolled between 300,000 and 500,000 members.

By 1900 it was plain that a radical change had come upon the political scene. Previously politics had been the preserve of propertied elites. Hitherto the 'patron', aided at moments of crisis by the police, the army and the law, had been unchallenged 'master' of those in his employ. The rise of the mass Socialist Party and the mass trade union began to change all this, and by 1910 the advance had gone so far as to be virtually irreversible.

The mass Socialist Party as it first appeared in Germany was an unprecedented phenomenon. The success of the German SPD made it a model for socialists all around the world, including the Bolsheviks in Russia. The SPD was the first political party to base itself on permanent, firmly organized mass support. Hitherto parties had been shifting alliances of individuals centred round the legislative chamber, cliques which from time to time appealed to the arbitrament of a limited number of voters at infrequent elections. SPD individual membership, 300,000 by 1906, exceeded 1 million by the eve of the First World War. The party's vote reached 3 million in 1903, passed 4 million by 1912. The SPD's objective was nothing less than the organization of the whole proletariat, its indoctrination with socialist ideas in preparation for the social revolution. A host of full-time functionaries, a network of local and national newspapers, bound the Socialist Party into a single unit. The party press had reached a circulation of 1·5 million by 1912.

The SPD was the steam-engine of the socialist new moral world. In every country of Europe the socialists set out to imitate the SPD and did so with considerable success, forcing even opponents to adopt its organizational–agitational scheme as the price of survival.

Congresses of the International at Brussels in 1891, Zürich in 1893, London in 1896, Paris in 1900, Amsterdam in 1904, Stuttgart in 1907, Copenhagen in 1910 and Basle in 1912 testified to the astonishing growth of socialist forces over little more than two decades. The Amsterdam Congress of 1904 took place at the height of the Russo-Japanese War. The sight of Katayama of Japan and Plekhanov of Russia on the same platform, shaking hands in the midst of hostilities between the armed forces of their two nations, indicated that a new ideal of international solidarity was indeed at work in the world. Growth and organizational consolidation was not restricted to the socialist parties alone. The unions also were on the move.

Trade unionists attended international congresses alongside the socialists. The general discussion which took place on these occasions proved inadequate to meet the specific industrial needs of groups of organized workers. As early as 1896 British unionists, headed by Tom Mann, James Sexton and Havelock Wilson, had established an International Federation of Ship, Dock and River Workers. One aim of this federation was to prevent the workforce in one port being used to undermine working conditions achieved in another. Organizers from Britain visited harbours as far apart as those of France, Germany, Belgium, the Netherlands, Spain and Scandinavia with this end in view. A branch of the British Dock, Wharf, Riverside and General Labourers' Union, was established at Rotterdam, in 1889.[1]

The transport workers' initiative was notable more because those involved were organizing *unskilled* workers than for any other reason. International organization amongst skilled workers had begun some years earlier. Cigar-makers, hat-makers and shoe-makers had set up their own international links in 1889. The miners, numerically much more powerful, followed in 1890. Glass-workers and print-workers established their separate liaison offices in 1892, the tailors and the engineers (metal-workers) in 1893, the textile-workers in 1894. Much the strongest numerically were the textile-workers, the miners and the engineers. Twenty eight trade based internationals (or International Trade Secretariats: ITS, as they later came to be known) were in operation by 1914.

International co-operation at a more general level followed rather than preceded that between unions with common craft or industrial interests. Not until 1901, on the initiative of the Danish trade union president Jensen, did the unions of Germany, France, Britain, Belgium and the five Scandinavian countries meet in Copenhagen to set up the International Federation of Trade Unions (IFTU). Congresses of the IFTU were held at Dublin in 1903, Amsterdam in 1905, Oslo in 1907, Paris in 1909, Budapest in 1911 and Zürich in 1913. At the time of the Zürich Conference, affiliated membership had risen to some 8 million. The largest contingents came from Germany (2·5 million), the United States (2 million) and Britain (1 million). That same year the first International Congress of the ITS was held.[2]

1. See Mann, *Tom Mann's Memoirs*, pp. 135–49, and Windmuller, p. 13.
2. On these events, see in particular Schevenels, *Forty-five Years of the IFTU*, pp. 20–23, 26–46, 54–6.

The trade union and socialist movements arose as a response to the inhuman conditions to which tens of millions of human beings were subject during the industrial transformation of Europe in the latter part of the nineteenth century and the first decades of the twentieth. By 1910 however it was becoming apparent that the socialists faced real problems as a result of their own success, problems which the ideology bequeathed by their founders was no longer adequate to resolve.

A socialist party, outcast, persecuted and in perpetual opposition, was driven by the very nature of its situation to maintain doctrinal purity substantially intact. The party programme, as a rule modelled on that of the German SPD adopted at Erfurt in 1891, provided both minimum and maximum objectives. The minimum programme proposed reforms to be sought within the framework of capitalist society. The maximum programme outlined the course of historic development and proposed the ultimate goal of the achievement of a socialist order. The implicit, but not always explicitly revealed assumption, was one of a substantially linear increase of socialist consciousness and socialist organization, accompanied by a deepening crisis of the capitalist economic and social system. At some imminent, foreseeable, but not precisely to be foretold future date, the ascending and descending graphs of socialist and capitalist power would cross in a 'breakdown of the capitalist system'.[1] At that point, social democracy, now an overwhelming majority of the nation, would acquire political power and refurbish society on a socialist model.

There are several points to be made if subsequent developments are properly to be understood. In the first place, although the 'crisis of capitalism' was undoubtedly growing deeper, as shown both by the growth of working class socialist forces and by the cataclysm of the First World War, the capitalist system was also growing stronger, more powerful, and more all embracing. The hidden assumption that the growth of socialist forces was taking place within a static and not a dynamic expanding system was entirely erroneous. The rise of socialist consciousness was at least as much a consequence of the *extensive* growth of the system as it was of the system's own internal 'contradictions' and 'decline'. If the rate of growth of the system as a whole should slow down it seemed likely that the rate of recruitment of the socialist banner would in turn decline. This is in fact remarkably close to the pattern subsequently assumed by events.

In the second place, the socialists had a reform programme for

1. Thus William Morris, one of the founders of Britain's first Marxist–Socialist Party, the Social Democratic Federation (SDF), in his utopian romance *News from Nowhere* (1891) set the date for the revolution as 1952 (pp. 61, 110). For the text of the Erfurt Programme see Lidtke, *The Outlawed Party: Social Democracy in Germany, 1878–1890*, pp. 353–8.

capitalism and a revolution programme for socialism, but there was no adequate bridge between the two. If the two lines on the graph had continued to converge, this might not have been an insuperable obstacle. In such circumstances the inherent rationale of the system, like a kind of inbuilt autopilot, might have carried the socialist parties through to victory. In some sense this seems to have been the hidden theoretical assumption which guided the major parties of the second International in the classic years before the First World War. But the line of linear progression broke up some time before 1914. The relationship of forces between capitalist and working classes at times assumed more a model of free floating comparability than that prescribed by the inexorable determinism of classical theory. Neither by training, nor by temperament, nor by theoretical understanding, were the socialist parties prepared to handle such a situation. As a result they failed to turn to advantage the opportunities offered by the general breakdown of the system which followed the end of the First World War.

Thirdly, because the socialists proved unable to turn to advantage their peaks of opportunity during a period of disjointed development, and because in the interwar years the system failed to grow, the projected 'crossing of the graphs' failed to materialize. In country after country the socialist vote stuck fast and failed to surpass the '$33\frac{1}{3}$ per cent barrier' as it came to be called. The inability to gain more than one third of the votes meant that they could not win through to capture an overall majority.

Fourthly, in such a situation the socialist parties and the union organizations came to develop conservative bureaucratic interests of their own, quite apart from those which they were orginally founded to serve.[1] Instead of acting as agents for social revolutionary change they tended instead to become modes of accommodation of working people to their existence within the system.

The turning point proved to be the First World War. In a perverse, dialectical fashion, it simultaneously destroyed and renewed the socialist movement. The whole international socialist and trade union movement was committed to oppose any war between capitalist powers. The issue had been discussed at length, notably at the Stuttgart Congress of the International in 1907. Prescriptions had been adopted by which all were bound. In the event formal prescriptions proved useless. The socialist parties found themselves confronted with mobilization and the threat of martial law, without having any properly prepared plans of action to deal with hostilities should they break out. Their leaders were torn by an unresolved dilemma over the extent to which the socialists ought to

1. For a revealing account of some of the factors at work, and in particular the fashion in which the *apparat* began to assume disproportionate influence in party affairs, see Landauer, *European Socialism*, vol. i., pp. 482–9.

assume responsibility for national defence. Once confronted with the armed might of the state, the socialist parties, essentially legalistic machines geared to parliamentary manoeuvre, felt themselves powerless. The socialist leaders, with scarcely an exception, failed to offer any resistance to the war at all.[1] The masses in many cases responded enthusiastically to the martial calls of their national governments. In Germany workers rallied to the flag to defend western European culture from the onrush of Tsarist Despotism advancing headlong through East Prussia. In Britain their counterparts volunteered to resist aggression, to defend the sovereignty of 'poor little Belgium'. In France worker conscripts marched off to defend the democratic French Republic from the onslaught of Prussian Militarism.

The consequences for the European labour movement were manifold. The revolution in industrial technique was now applied to the mass production of death. The output indices surpassed all levels hitherto known in history. In the end much of Europe's social structure broke down under the strain of human agony and despair. Revolution intervened in Russia, Germany and Hungary. Elsewhere society was severely at risk. During the war years limitless demands for more production and the pressing need for internal social stability brought socialist and trade union leaders within the inner circles of power and influence for the first time. The enhanced bargaining position of the unions, the semi-official tolerance they received during the war years, enabled them to grow enormously. Despite subsequent heavy losses in membership, a part of the gains became permanent. War badly discredited the old ruling classes. In the post war wave of radicalization the socialists were driven forward to fill a great part of the void.

The Russian Revolution now came to provide an alternative focus of allegiance for all those who came to regard socialist support for the war as an act of betrayal. On Russian initiative, paid for to a large extent with Russian money, there now appeared new 'communist' parties, which in these early years were dedicated to the launching of revolution on an imminent, almost day-to-day basis. The two halves of the Erfurt Programme, reform and revolution, it seemed at first, had split asunder.

The two lines on the graph of social revolution moved together convulsively at the end of the First World War, ran parallel, and then instead of coming together once again diverged. The forces which led

1. The Bolshevik view of the world, still widely accepted by non-communists, seeks to make this fact carry a greater load than the facts will bear. 'In not a single one of the eight Great Powers, in July, 1914, was a Socialist Government in power, nor were any of the eight governments dependent on their Parliamentary existence upon the Socialist vote. Hence the Socialists were powerless to prevent the war.' The outbreak of hostilities in 1914 abruptly revealed a pre-existing weakness, hitherto largely unobserved; it did not in itself bring this weakness about. Rosenberg, *A History of Bolshevism*, pp. 64–5.

to the steady growth of socialist support, the hidden postulate of classical Marxism, no longer operated as in the years before 1914. In Italy the revolutionary impetus given to social democracy by the war seemed for a while to threaten the whole existing order. Then the mass organizations, built at the cost of so much sacrifice, went down to destruction before the onslaught of fascist gangs aided and supported by the official regime. In Germany the Weimar Republic, established after the Revolution of 1918, survived, torn by severe internal dissensions, only until destroyed by the Nazis in 1933. In Belgium the Workers' Party, unable to muster the strength to form a government on its own account, abandoned non-participation and served in three coalition cabinets between 1918 and 1939. In the Netherlands the Social Democratic Workers' Party maintained a stance of pure opposition. Then, in 1939, it too entered the Cabinet under the threat of German invasion. In France the gains made by the unions in the war and immediate post war years were quickly lost. The already existing divisions in the working class movement were increased by the communist–socialist split. The brief experience of a socialist led coalition government in 1936, which was backed by a massive upsurge of militant union action, led to a number of very important gains. Yet the movement rapidly fell into dissension once more. In France the greater part of the gains of 1936 had been lost before world war broke out again in 1939.

The labour movement had emerged from the First World War greatly strengthened and with high hopes for the future. Tested in the furnace of events during the two decades 1919–39, those high hopes had not been fulfilled. Not the approach of final victory, but a struggle for mere survival, was now on the order of the day.

3. The Modern Labour Movement

The generalized social crisis which followed the end of the First World War had a far-reaching effect on the European labour movement. The breakdown of the old monarchist semi-absolutist institutions under the stresses produced by the war projected the mass organizations of the working class into hitherto unthought-of positions of power and responsibility. The war itself created an unprecedented dislocation of human society. The break up of the Austro-Hungarian Empire, the border changes imposed by the Versailles Treaty throughout central and southern Europe, the breakdown of Russian society which accompanied the Revolution, the Revolution itself which went far towards removing Russian economy from the sphere of European circulation, were all contributory factors. For a while it seemed that the 'breakdown' of capitalist society, so long foretold by the socialists, was at hand. Such indeed was the fundamental and now forgotten creed of the world communist movement at its foundation. Yet once revolution failed to mature at the end of the war, stabilization, even if at heavy human cost, was bound to follow not long after.

The German socialist party, the SPD, polled 11·5 million votes in 1919, approaching three times the highest figure recorded in pre war years.[1] The Weimar Constitution made Germany for the first time a republic organized on modern lines. Germany's underlying social structure, however, changed very little. The heavy burdens imposed on Germany by the peace treaty, the problems of post war readjustment, violent internal dissensions, all reached a kind of insane fulfilment with the Nazi conquest of power in 1933. The whole regime had lasted less than fifteen years.

In Italy, where the socialist successes were more limited, the capitalist reaction was more prompt, if in the end not so far-reaching. The Italian socialist party had opposed the war and was greatly strengthened by the wave of radicalization which followed the Armistice. The socialists preached revolution; the workers, in 1920, occupied the factories:

1. The Independent Socialist Party of Germany (USPD) which had split from the SPD polled a further 2,700,000. The SPD polled 3,259,000 in 1907, 4,250,000 in 1912. Pinson, *Modern Germany*, pp. 572–5.

neither made any serious plans for insurrection. The ruling elite took fright. The outcome was a fascist reaction which destroyed the labour movement, the whole apparatus of Italian political democracy, for over two decades.

In France too the mass labour movement was greatly strengthened by the war, but proved incapable of transforming society in a socialist direction. Membership of the CGT, France's leading trade union confederation, doubled, rising to 2 million in 1920. An unsuccessful general strike and an employer counter-offensive cut membership to pre war levels by 1921. Under the impact of the communist bid for the control of the labour movement both socialist party and trade union confederation split in two.

In the Netherlands, Troelstra, the socialist party's most respected leader, under the influence of events in Germany across the border, experienced a brief conversion to revolutionism. The Netherlands government reacted vigorously. Social Democracy flinched and withdrew. The Netherlands had not been a combatant power. In the absence of a fully fledged wartime boom the unions, though strengthened, did not benefit to the same extent as in other countries. The Netherlands communist party did not prove a serious contender for power in either the socialist or the trade union movement.

The situation in Belgium was more complicated. The German advance in 1914 rapidly overran the country's main industrial complex around Liège and the Borinage. Throughout the war the larger part of Belgium was under German occupation. The occupying power exploited the genuine social and political grievances of the Flemish Catholic population to encourage pre-existing separatist tendencies. Linguistic, confessional, regional differences now superimposed themselves on existing class tensions to influence deeply the pattern of political life in Belgium.

The conflicts between socialists who supported and socialists who opposed the First World War made a temporary split in the International inevitable. Bolshevism institutionalized this split, ensured that it took a specifically Russian form. The parties of the Communist International were all conceived and organized on the Russian model. All were dependent on the prestige of the Russian Revolution and on large scale material aid from the Russian government for such limited successes as they achieved. All the communist parties were riven, during the 1920s, by fierce factional struggles. In these, hidden behind impressive smokescreens of ideology, there was concealed one basic issue. Could the interests of the Russian state and the world revolution conflict? In such a case should the interest of the revolutionary movement or the Russian state prevail?

Such internal conflicts were not confined to the ranks of the Communist

International. There were many social democrats who rejected the reformist policies of their own leaders. The communist–socialist split indeed soon no longer represented a division between revolution and reform at all. Rather it represented the organizational divide between those who did and those who did not unconditionally and at all times support the policies advocated and pursued by the rulers of the Russian state. The dividing line between reform and revolution, by the mid-twenties at the very latest, now ran through socialist and communist organizations alike. In the years before 1914 the socialist movement had undoubtedly harboured a limited measure of apocalyptic ideology. Under the impact of the socialist–communist split the degree of mystification now began to increase enormously and with extremely harmful effects.

The communists failed to win a majority of the labour movement in any major European country.[1] There ensued not a successful revolution but a disastrous and long lasting split in labour's ranks. Conservative opponents equated socialists with communists. Communists in their turn denied that the socialist leaders were socialists at all. Highly centralized bureaucratic organizations, the communist parties served to accentuate bureaucratic tendencies already existing in the labour movement. As a result the socialist movement was driven to the right.

European economy had recovered from the aftermath of the war by the mid-1920s, stabilizing itself at a level somewhat higher than that of 1913. The collapse of the Credit Anstalt in May 1931, a bank which controlled some two thirds of Austrian industry, precipitated an economic crisis in country after country in Europe. Unemployment had never fallen to the pre-war figure even in the years of recovery; now it soared to unprecedented levels.

In France and Italy the shock of the crisis was cushioned to some extent by the survival of large reservoirs of peasant economy, able to absorb workers displaced from the towns. France in particular was able to improve employment prospects for French citizens by shifting the burden towards foreign workers who represented an important constituent of the French labour force.

The Italian economy was hit hard. Three leading banks, the Banca Commerciale, Banca di Roma and the Credito Italiano, followed the Credit Anstalt into ruin, dragged down by the bankruptcy of hard-pressed industrial concerns in which they were involved. Italy's Fascist government moved in hurriedly to guarantee the bankrupt institutions. The result was the nationalization of large sections of the Italian economy, notably in banking, ship-building and engineering. The Istituto per la Ricostruzione Industriale (IRI), formed, to administer these bankrupt

1. Bulgaria, Yugoslavia and Czechoslovakia are possible exceptions; they are hardly relevant to our argument here.

holdings, subsequently became one of the most important employers in Italy.[1]

The real test for the 'breakdown' theory came in Germany, the industrial heartland of European economy. Here unemployment reached 7 million by 1932. In some cases trade unions found over half their members out of a job. Instead of unifying labour's ranks this terrifying social crisis split them still further. It proved impossible to form a united front against the Nazi onslaught. Instead, German communists denounced the socialists as 'fascists', going so far as to vote with the Nazis against the social democratic government of Prussia, the largest German province, in the infamous Red Referendum of 1931. The communists' naïve belief, that 'after Hitler it will be our turn', proved unfounded. Early in 1933 the most powerful labour movement the world had ever known went down to defeat before the Nazis. Not until the military conquest of Germany by Allied arms in 1945 would it be able to raise its head again.[2]

The Nazi conquest of power in Germany altered the whole relationship of social forces in Europe, putting at risk all the gains achieved by the labour movement since its foundation.

In neither Belgium nor the Netherlands did social democracy face a strong challenge from a communist 'left' wing. Perhaps for that reason native fascist movements were unable to present a threat that could not be contained. In both countries the division of the labour movement between socialist and confessional wings made difficult the election of a socialist majority. In each the parliamentary system placed strong pressure on the socialists to participate in coalition cabinets.

In Belgium the Workers' Party, under the influence of its leader Henri de Man, adopted a neo-Keynsian programme of reform, designed to counter the worst effects of the slump. In pursuance of this policy the Workers Party entered the Cabinet in 1935. The Netherlands Social Democratic Labour Party (*Sociaal Democratische Arbeiders Partij*: SDAP) cautious and conservative, also found De Man's proposals attractive. Majority opinion however remained opposed to participation in any governmental coalition.

The labour movement in France found itself in a much more serious situation. The victory of fascism in Italy and Germany, both countries bordering France, the social strains of the depression, seemed to put the fate of the republic, never properly secure, once more into the balance. In part as a response to communist pressure designed to

1. See, for example, Posner and Woolf, *Italian Public Enterprise*, pp. 23–6. There were 350,000 IRI employees in 1970. IRI, *Annual Report, 1970*, Rome, 1971, p. 49.
2. For an accessible account of these events, see Borkenau, *World Communism*, pp. 339–80.

safeguard the Russian state by means of a Franco–Soviet military alliance, both the French socialist party and the CGT moved farther to the right, growing closer together in the process. Earlier both lost blue-collar support to their communist rivals. The communists made import-ant gains. Already, in 1928, the communist trade union confederation (CGTU) could claim one half the membership of the CGT. More surprisingly, the Communist Party (PCF) could muster a vote almost two thirds that of the SFIO. In the six years of the 'socialists are fas-cists' policy imposed on the Communist International by its dominant Russian section which followed, the communists lost ground. Then, a new turn in Russian diplomatic policy towards a united front of 'demo-cratic' powers against Hitler enabled the PCF to emerge from isolation. In 1934, the communist PCF signed a 'Unity of Action' pact with the socialist SFIO. In 1936 the CGTU dissolved. The communists rejoined the CGT.

The general election of 1936 made the socialist leader Léon Blum prime minister in a Popular Front Government. The SFIO became the largest single party in the French Assembly. Much in the manner of May 1968, an enormous spontaneous sit-down strike paralysed a large part of French industry. The unions, with some difficulty, persuaded the strikers to return to work, with major gains. CGT membership trebled in a matter of months, shifting the internal balance of power strongly in favour of the PCF. By the end of 1938 internal disputes and a counter-offensive by the employers had brought CGT membership down again to the pre 1936 level. When the French communists sup-ported the Nazi–Communist Pact in August 1939, the socialist leaders made this the pretext to expel all communists from the CGT.

By late summer or early autumn of 1939 the mass labour movements of Germany and Italy had long been destroyed. In France the Popular Front Government had collapsed, the communists were expelled from the CGT, the PCF was now an illegal organization. In Belgium under the threat of imminent invasion the Workers' Party was about to enter a coalition once again. In the Netherlands the Social Democratic Labour Party, abandoned its past opposition and did the same. The develop-ments in Belgium and the Netherlands were of some importance. Socialist ministers continued to serve in governments in exile through-out the war years and were thus encouraged to join post war coalition governments when hostilities were over.

Thus on the eve of the Second World War the apocalyptic hopes of the early socialists had in no sense been realized. In Germany and Italy the socialist movements had been obliterated. In France, Belgium and the Netherlands socialist and union growth had slowed up or stopped. Nowhere had the socialists been able to muster sufficient strength to govern on their own account, let alone overthrow the capitalist system.

If the hopes of the socialists had not been realized those of the communists had proved even more displaced. The German party, the largest in the world outside Russia, had gone down before the Nazi regime, firmly convinced that this was a mere temporary setback, preceding final victory. The Italian communist party, whilst contributing to the disarray of the labour movement before Mussolini, had neither prevented nor delayed the fascist conquest of power. In Belgium the communists, while drawing some support from industrial workers, never at any time posed a serious challenge to the Workers' Party. In the Netherlands the communists failed to do much more than take over political territory already occupied by syndicalists and left-wing socialists before the First World War. The communists had neither conquered the labour movement, nor had they made a revolution. On the contrary they had played an important part in producing the causes of the present defeats.

The Second World War did not scar the labour movement like that of 1914–18. There was widespread recognition that Hitler's Nazism was something qualitatively different from the old-fashioned authoritarianism of the Hohenzollern regime. Participation in government was no longer an innovation. Socialist parties and unions were already committed to some degree of co-operation with the existing regimes. The Spanish Civil War, the communist campaigns for a Popular Front of workers and employers, had prepared the road for a further accommodation with the *status quo*. Paradoxically, the abandonment by the communists of their own Popular Front Policy, following the Nazi–Communist Pact of 1939, made it easier for others to take it over when hostilities broke out at a later date.

Hitler's military successes in the west and the struggles which preceded the eventual liberation radically changed political alignments in the occupied territories. In Belgium and the Netherlands old alignments broke and then, following a period of post war fluidity, reasserted themselves. Germany, defeated and in ruins, was cut up into Russian and western zones of influence. In France and Italy the war created conditions which enabled the communists to become, for the first time, the dominant force in the labour movement. In Germany by contrast, the communists who made an initial comeback in 1945–7 lost ground rapidly thereafter. Social Democracy became the unchallenged spokesman of working-class interests to an extent never achieved during the Weimar Republic.

The First World War split the socialist movement into hostile communist and socialist wings. The Second World War produced no new organizational alignments of a similar order. Although post war Europe manifested many of the features of a revolutionary situation, neither socialist nor communist parties showed any will to power. Quite the reverse: the First World War domesticated the socialists of France, Belgium and Germany, brought them to play a part in government for the first time; the Second World War domesticated the communists in their turn. Defeatists in 1940, the communists of France and Belgium, became patriotic participants in bourgeois governments when once the war was over. So indeed did their allies, the communists in Italy.[1]

The key to this remarkable transformation lies in Russia's reluctant involvement in the war and its consequences for the communist parties of Western Europe. Following the Nazi–Communist Pact of 1939 the communists dismissed the war as an imperialist conflict of no interest to the working class. Communist propaganda laid emphasis on the malevolent intentions of aggressive Anglo-French imperialism and issued a call for a negotiated peace with Hitler. The communist parties set out to sabotage and undermine the war effort in France, to hinder preparation for national defence in Belgium and the Netherlands. Until the German invasion of Russia in 1941 Nazi aggression and German occupation did nothing to alter this stand.

The communist record was shameful. Nor was the socialist record without blemish. In France a section of the socialist party and the CGT, profoundly affected by the massacres of French workers in the First World War, opposed the war on principle. One leader of this tendency within the CGT, René Bélin, subsequently became Minister of Production and Labour in the Vichy Government. In Belgium the Workers' Party leader, Henri de Man, changed his coat, collaborated with the Nazis and helped set up a Belgian version of the Nazi Labour Front. A limited number of union leaders, some Flemish Catholics, others socialists, initially supported this venture. In the Netherlands the socialist trade union confederation – NVV – continued to function even after Dutch Nazis had been placed in command. NVV top officials did not abandon their posts until the Germans proposed the establishment of a Netherlands Labour Front in 1942.

The socialist parties had been primarily electoral organizations. The 'functionaries', as Carl Landauer has written, 'had been chosen for qualities other than readiness to sacrifice their own lives and those of their family members'.[2] The Communist Party activists in western Europe as elsewhere, saw themselves as expatriate citizens of the USSR. After Hitler's attack on Russia in July 1941, the communists became a most important force in the Resistance in every one of the occupied territories. The Resistance itself everywhere experienced a marked surge in influence, once conscription for forced labour in Germany began to get under way in 1943.

1. For a contemporary comment on this situation see Dwight Macdonald, *Memoirs of a Revolutionist*, pp. 153–4.
2. Landauer, *European Socialism*, vol. 2, p. 1528.

The situation varied greatly from one country to another. In France business was collaborationist, favouring not the Resistance but the Vichy regime. In Belgium and the Netherlands by contrast, business favoured the Resistance and the governments in exile, rather than the occupying authority. In these two countries Nazi behaviour tended to solidify the whole body of the nation against the occupying regime. Workers and employers, socialists, communists and conservatives stood together in the Resistance, laying the basis for a continuing coalition in the immediate post war years. Italy was something of a special case. The Italian ruling class had solidly backed fascism. Nevertheless, when once Mussolini had been deposed in 1943 a fresh government, formed in the liberated zone, rapidly acquired the status of a co-belligerent. After 1943 a major partisan movement in the centre and the north did much to clear the way for an important communist presence in Italy when once hostilities were over.

The communists made bigger inroads into the labour movement in France and Italy, where business was collaborationist, than they did elsewhere. Allowed to re-enter the underground CGT as a minority in 1943, PCF members were accorded parity on the CGT executive in 1945 by which time they had gone far towards acquiring majority support amongst the rank and file. In Italy the role of the communists in the resistance enabled the PCI to make large gains by the time that hostilities came to an end.

In both Belgium and the Netherlands the communists made ground. Yet in each country there also arose a new left-wing socialist opposition, if anything more critical than the communists of the pre war behaviour of the labour movement. In Belgium two fresh rank-and-file union organizations, one socialist, the other communist, bid hard to replace the socialist trade union centre only to fuse, on a parity basis, into a fresh *Fédération Générale du Travail de Belgique* (FGTB) in 1945. In the Netherlands in 1945 a new left-wing Trade Union Unity Movement (*Eenheids Vakcentraal*: EVC) claimed 176,000 members against the 240,000 of the socialist NVV. This in turn collapsed as a result of internal conflicts and external hostility in the years that followed.

The extent of devastation in Europe in 1944-5 is too easily forgotten. The cities of Germany lay in ruins. The former Reich, now without any central administration, was divided into four sealed zones, governed by mutually suspicious and antagonistic military commanders. Italy had been fought over from one end to another between 1943 and 1945. Whole regions of France, Belgium and the Netherlands were in ruins. Allied and German bombing aircraft had caused immense devastation in areas far behind the fighting lines. Poverty, chronic undernourishment, starvation, had become part of the common currency of human experience. In the Netherlands, during the last year of the war 'endless trains of people walked with a handcart, or a bicycle without tyres, to the north or east of the country, trying to obtain food . . . in exchange for everything the farmers might be willing to accept'.[1] The situation was not markedly different elsewhere.

The objective prospects for Revolution at the end of the Second World War were far more favourable than at the end of the First. In Germany, in Italy, to a large extent in France as well, the old ruling class, discredited by its association with fascism was in disarray, the old state structure in ruins. The whole framework of European society had been disrupted by war and occupation. New bodies of disciplined men, armed by the Resistance, were everywhere in existence. Pre war organizations were either disbanded or discredited, the masses radicalized by terrifying experiences of hardships, suffering and brutal oppression. The last prop of social stability, the Allied armies, almost to a man, were clamouring angrily to go home.

Revolutions, however, do not take place simply because for millions social conditions are almost unbearable. If that were so they would happen all the time. Social revolutionary change requires long preparation in the minds of the population, organizations to embody this consciousness and carry it through to fulfilment. In the eyes of the radicalized European masses, the communist parties which had sprung from the Russian Revolution of 1917 were the fore-ordained agents of revolutionary change. In fact, as far as western Europe was concerned, no conception could have been farther from the truth. Potsdam and Yalta had allocated spheres of influence both to Russia and to the western Powers. Russia acquired a whole string of buffer states along her immensely long western border. The price, gladly paid by Stalin, was the social passivity of the communist parties in the west.

Thus the communist parties of Western Europe, in the words of the former Foreign Editor of the New York (Communist) *Daily Worker* saw Europe

essentially as a peninsula of the Eurasian continent which the Soviet armies had been unable to reach in time. . . The communists conceived of their task as holding fast to post-war positions (they were almost everywhere members of the government) until the Soviet Union's recovery could stalemate Anglo–American military power. . . This required avoiding the seizure of power in any country where . . . it threatened to involve the weakened Soviet Union.[2]

In the stabilization of Europe after the Second World War, the communist parties thus played the role classically attributed to the social democrats after the First. The years which followed the end of the First

1. Verkade, *Democratic Parties in the Low Countries and Germany*, pp. 206–7.
2. Starobin, 'Communism in Western Europe', in J. Calmann, ed., *Western Europe*, pp. 300–303.

World War had seen widespread social unrest, particularly in Germany, Italy and France. After 1945 the social surface was a millpond by comparison. The great waves of political strikes which remain in popular memory as the communist contribution to the post war world did not come at the end of the war, in 1945. They were launched only after the Cold War got under way in 1947. They were intended not to precipitate revolution but to lever the communist parties back into coalition Cabinets from which they had been expelled in the early months of that year.

Western Europe, devastated by the war, had been heavily dependent on short-term US aid for survival. Yet even with this aid, one prominent economist has written that 'two full years after hostilities had ceased Europe found itself on the verge of a financial bankruptcy whose economic consequences threatened to topple over a political and social structure already weakened by ten years of depression followed by the most destructive war in history'.[1] The onset of the Cold War made a permanent stabilization of western Europe, a thorough revitalization of European economy, essential. Marshal Aid alone, on whatever scale, was clearly insufficient. The restoration of German economy was also required. This in turn involved the formation of a West German state, the danger that a rearmed Germany might once more come to dominate the continent of Europe. It was to insure against this possibility that proposals for western European integration were first brought onto the field. The formation of the European Coal and Steel Community (ECSC) in 1952, the signing of the Rome Treaty in 1957, Britain's application to enter the Common Market and its approval in 1971–2, all spring from this same situation.

One cannot say, in retrospect, that the pioneers of the labour movement were at fault in anticipating apocalyptic events. The twentieth century, as shown by the First and Second World Wars and the Great Depression of the 1930s, has proved to be replete with them. The error lay rather in the failure to foresee accurately the nature of such events and the assumption that they would lead to a socialist society.

If the labour movement had continued to grow at the same rate after 1914 as before, then the expectations of the early socialists might well have been fulfilled. In fact it has been war, rather than social crisis, which has added most to the strength of the labour movements since 1914.

Classical Marxist socialism, it is clear, gravely overestimated the role of objective forces in the social process. The Leninist emendation, with its strictly 'idealist' view of the party as a voluntaristic organization able to overcome all obstacles, reversed the balance in the opposite direction. Neither theory possessed any clear understanding of the

1. Triffin, *Europe and the Money Muddle*, p. 31.

causes of the bureaucratization of the labour movement. Neither grasped the extent to which this might lead not only trade union organizations, but also socialist and communist parties, to subvert the aims for which they had been established in the first place.

The generation now assuming the field is one which has never known the great issues which dominated the lives of their forebears: the Russian Revolution, the British General Strike, the Nazi conquest of power, the French sit-downs in 1936, the Spanish Civil War, the Moscow trials, the Second World War, the Occupation, the Resistance, the bitter internecine conflicts of the Cold War and after. To this generation the Soviet Union appears as one mighty military power, much like any other, not as the 'Fatherland of the Toilers of All the World'. The sclerotic hold of the communist parties over some of the best elements of the working population is in serious decline. The events of May 1968 in France, Italy's 'hot autumn' of 1969, widespread unofficial strikes in Germany, Sweden and the Netherlands in 1969–72, the rise in industrial militancy in Britain, all suggest that a new spirit is afoot in the world. The nearest parallel would seem to be the international upsurge of militancy which spread across Europe in the years before the First World War. Only the future will show the final outcome.

4. France

France in the eighteenth and nineteenth centuries was a unified state, the largest in Europe, at a time when Germany remained a shapeless mass of petty dukedoms and principalities, at a moment when the state of Italy did not exist at all. Power in this, for its time, enormous state, was highly centralized, a tradition carried through into the twentieth century by a post-revolutionary society based on the norms of Napoleonic administration. Although France is around double the area of either Italy or the Federal Republic of Germany, her population remains less than that of either her largest co-founders of the EEC.[1] In the event, the relative decline of France over the last two centuries, *vis-à-vis* the rest of European society, is probably the most decisive factor in the cultural experience of the French people as a whole.[2]

While the rise of the commercial class in Britain was signalled by the triumph of the English revolution in the seventeenth century, the emergence of the new commercial order in France waited upon the Revolution of 1789. The French Revolution of 1789, the Revolutions of 1838 and 1848, the Paris Commune of 1871, all made with the flesh and blood of the French people, represent a very different tradition from the gradualism of which the English and the Americans are, by repute, so proud: 1789 has given the idea of revolution in France a respectable and patriotic air quite lacking in Britain. The Paris Commune of 1871 opened a breach between the social classes for which neither Britain nor the USA has any parallel. Some 20,000 *communards* were either killed by government troops or executed by summary courts martial; some 4000 persons were transported to the 'Devils' Islands' of France's New Caledonia penal colonies. Sixty years after the event, the moderate founder of the French Catholic trade union movement could still write

1. France 212,919 sq. miles – 48,992,000 population
   Germany 95,959 sq. miles – 56,839,000 population
   Italy 116,290 sq. miles – 51,576,000 population
2. For this important insight I am indebted to Nigel Despicht.

with bitterness of the '110,000 victims dead, wounded, deported; women, children, or old people left without support'.[1]

The Revolution of 1789, despite its vast impact on Europe as a whole, failed to clear the ground for sharp and rapid industrialization in France itself. The very success of the Revolution, on the contrary, fixed the peasantry so firmly to their land as materially to delay the process of industrialization altogether.[2] France experienced no industrial revolution on the British model. A leading authority has written: 'The slow transformation accomplished in a century was in many ways less complete than that which Germany experienced in the forty years after 1871'. 'In the course of the nineteenth century most French industries were remodelled, but it might be said that France never went through an industrial revolution.'[3]

The French employer, the *patron*, and the attitudes of his class organizations, reflect this path of development. As late as 1906, workshops employing fewer than ten workers still hired one third of the industrial labour force; 59 per cent of all industrial workers worked in establishments of fewer than one hundred employees. 'A large part of France's industrial life centred on luxury articles, "articles of Paris", which lent themselves to the little workshop.'[4]

Small business continues to play a disproportionate role in French economy and to influence the political and social outlook of the French employer class, big business included. 'The business is not an end in itself, nor is its purpose to be found in any such independent ideal or service. It exists by and for the family, and the honour, the reputation, the wealth of the one are the honour, wealth and reputation of the other.'[5] As a result the employer frequently views the trade union not merely as a threat to his profits but also as a direct threat to inviolable family property, a threat which he will resist to the utmost. The employer in France is the *patron*, his national association is the *patronat*, and in these words is embodied an almost feudal flavour which contrasts strangely with our modern age. '*C'est moi, le patron ici*' (I'm the boss here) continues to represent the spirit of the age.[6]

1. Zirnheld, *Cinquante années de syndicalisme chrétien*, quoted in Lorwin, *The French Labor Movement*, p. 14.

2. The rural population amounted to 76 per cent of the total in 1876, some 56 per cent in 1911 and was only surpassed by that of the urban areas in the inter war years. In 1968 the agricultural workforce still represented some 15 per cent of the employed population.

3. Clapham, *The Economic Development of France and Germany 1815–1914*, p. 53.

4. Lorwin, *The French Labor Movement*, p. 15.

5. Landes, 'French Business and the Businessman', in E. M. Earle, ed., *Modern France*, p. 336; see also Ehrmann, *Organized Business in France*, pp. 420–24.

6. For the views of one French management theorist, see Cuthbert, 'Fayol and

The French economy stagnated in the inter war years. In 1939 the active population was 1,500,000 fewer than in 1929, industrial production was 14 per cent down on what it had been before the slump, energy utilization per capita was down by 13 per cent. Caution and conservatism, writes one commentator, 'drained away the sources and energy of enterprise and energy in the bourgeoisie and made even Paul Reynaud declare at one stage, "It seems to be contemplating its own funeral." '[1]

RISE OF LABOUR MOVEMENT

The French worker has been moulded by his environment no less than the French employer. The slow rate of industrial growth during the formative period of French unionism, the extent to which the movement was consequently one of relatively skilled workers in comparatively small plants, gave it an elitist philosophy which saw in a minority of highly conscious workers the conscience and leadership of a less conscious and largely unorganized mass. France's major trade union federation, the CGT (*Confédération Générale du Travail*), organized no more than 400,000 of the 6 million French industrial workers in 1914. There were more trade unionists outside the CGT, it seems clear, than inside.[2] *Élan révolutionnaire*, originally seen as a substitute for solidly organized dues-paying membership on the British model, became rationalized into a virtue in itself, conferring status and prestige upon an ideologically privileged, self-appointed elite, within the working-class movement.[3] Here is one reason at least for the failure of French unions to achieve a mass base comparable to those of Germany, Britain, Belgium, Scandinavia and the USA. Also perhaps one explanation for the ability of the French Communist Party (*Parti Communiste Français*: PCF) to 'take over' an earlier revolutionary syndicalist tradition.[4]

1. On this, Kemp, *The French Economy, 1913–1939*, especially pp. 162–76.
2. The miners for example did not join the CGT before 1908. Of the 860,000 persons recorded as union members in 1906 the CGT *claimed* only 300,000 and even this figure is likely to have been an overestimate. The same holds for the 1914 figure too. On this; Georges, Tintant and Renauld, *Léon Jouhaux, cinquante ans de syndicalisme*, pp. 11–12; Lefranc, *Le Mouvement syndical sous la troisième République*, pp. 409–11.
3. For a valuable elaboration of this point and a parallel with the theory of the offensive which dominated the French General Staff during the First World War, see Bowditch, 'The Concept of Elan Vital, a Rationalization of Weakness', in Earle, ed., *Modern France*, pp. 32–4.
4. See for example the quotation from the syndicalist Émile Buget, who one authority considers 'sounds almost like Lenin in his call to this elite'. Kassalow, *Trade Unions and Industrial Relations*, p. 111.

the Principles of Organisation', in Tillett *et al*, eds., *Management Thinkers*, pp. 108–9.

The theory of this revolutionary syndicalist minority held that economic struggle alone was sufficient to achieve the workers' emancipation. Political parties, parliamentarianism were a fraud and a delusion. Direct action, the strike, and ultimately the general strike, would enable the working class to expropriate capital and build the new collectivist society. In place of the shattered capitalist state, the 1906 constitution of the CGT proposed that 'the trade union, which is today a fighting organization, will in the future be an organization for production and distribution and the basis of social reorganization'.[1] The Charter of Amiens, the 1906 basic text of French unionism, separated the organized working class from any direct links with the newly unified Socialist Party and rendered impossible the foundation of any Labour Party on the British model.[2] Nevertheless there are good grounds for the belief that unions in present day France are at least as much means of political action as of wage bargaining. In the past the worker's decision to join a union has represented at least as much a reflex of class consciousness as any intent to organize in a practical fashion for better conditions and improved job control. In France there was no scope for narrow business unionism precisely because there did not exist any solely cash-oriented bourgeoisie as in the United States.

The French socialist movement goes back far beyond Marx through Proudhon, Fourier and Blanqui to Babeuf and the French Revolution of 1789. This rich tradition is expressed, at least in part, in doctrinal divergence. In the years from 1880 on, socialism in France comprised at least five different tendencies (Guesde, Brousse, Allemane Vaillant, and the 'Independants'), of which only one, that of Jules Guesde, could properly be termed Marxist. There were thirty-seven socialist deputies of one kind or another as early as 1893. The entry of the socialist deputy, Millerand, into the Cabinet of Waldeck Rousseau in 1899, alongside General Gallifet, an executioner of the Commune, became the cause of bitter controversy in France and a socialist international *cause célèbre*. After fierce and long-drawn-out polemics from all sides, the International Socialist Congress, meeting at Amsterdam in August 1904, condemned Millerand's action and issued what came close to a mandatory directive, albeit in judicious terms, for the unification of the competing groups in France. In response to this initiative there arose a united *Parti Socialiste – Section Française de l'Internationale Socialiste* (Socialist Party – French Section of the Socialist International, usually abbreviated as SFIO). The party vote, 878,000 in 1905, passed 1 million

1. *L'Action syndicaliste*, 1908, quoted in Lorwin, *The French Labor Movement*, p. 30.
2. The text of the Charter of Amiens will be found in Lefranc, *Le Mouvement Syndicale sous la Troisième République*, p. 406; English translation in Lorwin, *The French Labor Movement*, pp. 312–313.

by 1910 and reached 1·4 million in 1914. On the eve of the First World War the SFIO was 90,000 strong, with over 100 members elected in its name to the French Chamber of Deputies.[1]

In the pre war years the anti-militarism of sections of the SFIO and CGT had caused the authorities great concern. Attempts to co-ordinate French and German socialist activity against the war were under way right up to the outbreak of hostilities. The assassination of Jaurès, the party's most popular leader, did much to disarm French socialism at the hour of its greatest need. A wave of patriotism, a deep seated willingness to defend the Republic against external aggression, swept through the ranks and carried almost the whole of the CGT and SFIO before it.[2] The Socialist Party, placing on one side the Millerand debate, sent three of its leaders, Maurice Sembat, the old Marxist Jules Guesde, and later Albert Thomas, into the oddly named wartime Cabinet of 'sacred unity' (union sacrée). The CGT too traversed a watershed in its history. Its Secretary, Léon Jouhaux, became a 'commissioner of the nation', lining up the CGT behind the war effort, doing favours to friends and supporters which were to stand him in good stead at a later date.[3]

THE FIRST WORLD WAR

The First World War mobilized 8 million Frenchmen, one-sixth of the population of France. In the four years of war 4·5 million were wounded and over 1·3 million killed. Widespread army mutinies in May–June 1917 threatened the whole front with collapse. In September of that year the socialists under rising pressure from below withdrew from the Cabinet. In July 1918 the previous 'minority' assumed control of the Socialist Party on the platform of a negotiated peace. The catastrophic blood-letting of the years 1914–18 dealt the French nation a blow from which it has still to recover.

The war, its horrors, hardships and slaughter apart, materially changed the composition of the working class. At the close of hostilities a great mass of new members flooded into the ranks of the CGT. A minority within the CGT had consistently opposed the war. This

1. Lefranc, *Le Mouvement socialiste*, pp. 187, 435; Saposs, *The Labor Movement in Post-war France*, p. 428.

2. 'On the 14th July, we were voting Vaillant's resolution "Rather insurrection than war". On the 31st July, we were picking up our rifles and rushing to the frontier shouting "*Vive la France*"': Frossard, *De Jaurès à Lénine*, quoted Lefranc, *Le Mouvement socialiste*, p. 196.

3. Lefranc, *Le Mouvement socialiste*, pp. 198, 205; Lorwin, *The French Labor Movement*, p. 49; Monatte, *Trois scissions syndicales*, pp. 142–5. For a fascinating account of all this see Rosmer, *Le Mouvement ouvrier pendant la guerre*.

minority now received a marked accession of strength from the Russian Revolution and the dangerously high social tensions which the war had generated. The foundation of the Communist International in March 1919, and the establishment of its subsidiary, the Red International of Labour Unions (RILU), in summer of 1920, helped to bring tension between the Jouhaux majority and the CGT revolutionary wing towards breaking point. A non-communist revolutionary syndicalist tendency came close to winning control of the CGT in 1921. The Jouhaux leadership, feeling their power rocking in the balance, made refusal to disband this tendency organization the excuse for wholesale expulsions. The outcome was the foundation of a new *Confédération Générale de Travail Unitaire* (CGTU) in opposition to the CGT.

Inside the CGTU, the communists, backed by the propagandist and practical support of the Russian Revolution,[1] after bitter battles, succeeded in gaining control. The hitherto united union movement was now divided into majority, reformist, and minority, communist-controlled, wings. One authority, who credits the CGTU with over 550,000 members at the time of its foundation, claims that under its communist leadership two thirds of the membership was subsequently lost.[2] Be that as it may, the breach in the union ranks has proved to be permanent,[3] and a serious blow to the progress of the French Labour Movement as a whole.

The behaviour of French unionism in the inter war years did not entirely match the tone of its leaders' fiery proclamations. The CGT lost much of its industrial working class base. In practice it became as much involved with political lobbying and the defence of social security as with the direct action of which its leaders had once been prone to speak. By 1927 three quarters of CGT membership was concentrated in government service or public utilities. Altogether the record of the French union movement was one of no marked success. Overall, a nett decline in the strength of the unions in regard to management may even have taken place.

The post war split in the labour movement also extended to the

---

1. The interested reader should consult J. Humbert-Droz, *L'Oeil de Moscou à Paris*. Humbert-Droz was the official representative of the Executive Committee of the Communist International to the French Communist Party. The full text of his instructions from Moscow and his replies will be found in Humbert-Droz, *Origines et débuts des partis communistes des pays latins, 1919–1923*.

2. Raoul Lenoir, quoted in Lorwin, *The French Labor Movement*, p. 71. Saposs, pp. 136–7, credits the CGT with 750,000, CGTU, 400,000, CFTC, 100,000 in 1931.

3. The communists were re-admitted to the CGT in 1936, expelled again in 1939, readmitted in 1943. Jouhaux and the former majority split off in their turn in 1947, leaving the communists in control.

Socialist Party. At the Congress of Tours in December 1920 the pro-Russian wing gained control, changed the party's name to *Parti Communiste Française* and affiliated to the Communist International. Most of the deputies and best known party leaders now split off and re-established the SFIO under its old name. At Tours the pro-Russian majority has been credited with the support of 150,000 of the SFIO's 200,000 members. By 1933, PCF membership had fallen to 28,000. In terms of votes, however, the PCF was more successful. The PCF polled 875,000 votes in 1924, 1,063,000 in 1928, 796,000 in 1932. The SFIO vote was 1,690,000, 1,720,000, 1,975,000 on these same occasions.

INTER WAR YEARS

The course of subsequent events in the French Labour Movement was deeply influenced by a series of confusing shifts in the policy of the French Communist Party which need some explanation to be properly understood. In 1928-9 the Russian leaders, with the Comintern and all its affiliated parties following meticulously at their tail, decided that the 'final crisis' of capitalism, and with it imminent social revolution, were now on the order of the day. In this six-year-long ultra-left 'Third Period', which lasted until 1934-5, the communists treated socialists and social democrats, rather than conservatives and reactionaries, as the main enemy of the working class. Socialists and fascists were the same; in Stalin's famous phrase they were 'not antipodes but twins'. If anything the socialists (social fascists) were the worst of the two. A Nazi victory in Germany, it was devoutly believed, would rapidly be followed by a successful communist revolution.[1] Following Hitler's triumph and the total destruction of the German working-class movement, socialist, trade union, co-operative and communist alike, the Russian leaders sought to insure themselves by a military alliance with the 'democratic' capitalist powers. When this move failed, a sudden about-turn led to the conclusion, in 1939, of the Nazi-Communist, Russian-German Pact. Less than two years later Hitler invaded his communist ally, throwing Churchill, Stalin and later Roosevelt into one another's arms for the duration of the war. Each shift in this policy merry-go-round of the Russian state produced an equivalent gyration in the Communist Party of France.

At the end of 1933 and the beginning of 1934, the government of Daladier was severely shaken by a financial scandal which led to the

1. On this see in particular the excellent article by Theodore Draper, 'The Ghost of social fascism'; Borkenau, *The Communist International*, pp. 338-56.

mysterious 'suicide' of a banker named Stavisky and appeared to involve in its complications a number of well-known politicians.[1] On 6 February 1934, the communists and right-wing near-fascist leagues rioted together against the government outside the Chamber. By the time the day was over, sixteen demonstrators were dead, 660 injured. Next morning the government resigned. A right-wing *coup d'état* seemed the order of the day. The CGT, as an emergency measure, called a twenty-four hour demonstration strike in defence 'of the fundamental liberties without which life is not worth living', for the following Monday, 12 February. As socialists and unionists combined in a massive campaign of agitation and propaganda, the communists and their union confederation the CGTU found themselves increasingly isolated. At the last moment the Russian government now became deeply concerned that the French Republic might go the way of Weimar. On the eve of the strike, the PCF received fresh instructions, switched its line and marshalled all its forces into support of the stoppage called by the CGT.[2] The strike proved a massive success. The immediate fascist danger to the Republic was driven to one side. Yet the internal and external threat remained very real and gave great impetus to demands for working-class unity. Moscow's rising concern about the international situation enabled the PCF to move sufficiently far from the doctrine of social fascism to enable the conclusion of a socialist–communist 'Unity of Action pact' in July 1934.[3] Negotiations for a reunification of the CGT and the CGTU followed.

The communist shift to the right was confirmed by a growing *rapprochement* between the French and Soviet governments. On 2 May 1935, in Paris, Foreign Minister Pierre Laval signed a Pact of Mutual Assistance with the Soviet Union. On 15 May, in Moscow, he obtained a declaration that 'Stalin understands and fully approves the policy of national defence adopted by the French Government in order to maintain its armed forces at the level necessary for security'.[4] The Moscow declaration involved a complete about-turn for the PCF and CGTU, which had hitherto maintained an adamant refusal to vote credits for national defence. Communist leaders had gone so far as to denounce as

1. Lefranc, *Histoire du Front Populaire*, pp. 12–14. The suggestion has been made that Stavisky's 'suicide' was arranged by the police to prevent revelations damaging to those in high places.

2. ibid., pp. 18–28; Ehrmann, *French Labor*, pp. 27–30. For another view see Trotsky, *Whither France?*

3. The very notion of working class/socialist parties signing 'pacts' indicates how deeply Russian ideology had influenced socialist and communist behaviour by this time.

4. '*Stalin comprend et approuve pleinement la politique de défense nationale faite par la France pour maintenir sa force armée au niveau de sa sécurité*', Lefranc, *Histoire du Front Populaire*, pp. 72–3, 435–6.

'monstrous treason' the very idea of national solidarity as a counterpart to a treaty with the USSR.[1] The communists, moving rapidly across the socialist front from left to right, now sought to include even capitalist parties in an oddly named 'Popular Front', as part of a global effort to build national multi-class alliances aimed at tying the western capitalist powers to the USSR in a firm military pact.

POPULAR FRONT

Now that the PCF no longer regarded the Socialist Party (SFIO) as a fascist organization, one fundamental cause of working-class disunity faded away. At Toulouse in March 1936 the CGT and CGTU were re-unified, largely on the basis of the CGT programme. On the new executive the CGT had a six-to-two majority over the old CGTU. At the May 1936 elections a Popular Front of socialists, communists and radical socialists gained a major victory. The combined socialist–communist vote at over 3·4 million was without precedent. The communists doubled their vote, but increased their representation from twelve deputies to seventy-two.[2] The SFIO, with 146 deputies, became the largest party in the Chamber. On 5 June the socialist leader, Léon Blum, now prime minister, was at the head of a socialist–radical Popular Front government.

The victory of the Popular Front at the poll brought entirely un-planned events in its train. In a spontaneous upsurge, upwards of one million workers downed their tools and struck work, demanding union recognition, wage increases and improved working conditions. Beginning five days after the election this tumultuous manifestation rose to a crescendo at the end of May and beginning of June. Three quarters of the strikes involved 'sit-ins' where the workers refused to leave the plant, ate, slept and played in good humour on the premises, refusing either to work or to leave until their demands were met. The newly unified CGT, the socialists, the communists, still more the employers and the government were completely taken by surprise.

When union–management negotiations failed to bring a resumption of work, Blum moved onto the scene, summoning both the CGT and the employers' association, the CGPF (*Confédération Générale de la Production Française*), to meet him at the Hotel Matignon, his official quarters.

The employers and union leaders met at Matignon at 3.00 p.m. on

1. ibid., pp. 72–4; also Lefranc, *Le Mouvement socialiste*, p. 319; Ehrmann, *French Labor*, p. 30.
2. Lefranc, *Le Mouvement socialiste*, p. 324. The interested reader can find a not unsympathetic view of the communist role in these and later events in Jacques Fauvet, *Histoire de parti communiste français*.

Sunday 7 June 1936. In a set of incredibly rapid negotiations the whole matter was settled by 1.00 a.m. the next Monday morning. Wages were increased by an average of 12 per cent, and the right to organize and protection of union members against victimization were promised. The employers agreed in principle to the 'immediate conclusion' of collective bargaining agreements. This last undertaking, however, by failing to enforce a necessity to 'bargain in good faith', left a loophole of which the employers were very prompt to avail themselves. The CGT thereupon ordered a return to work. A situation of some confusion followed.

Important elements in the rank and file considered the Matignon agreement[1] inadequate, others saw the factory occupation as no more than the first springboard of a socialist revolution in France. The PCF, concerned not to compromise the possibility of Franco-Soviet *rapprochement* on the basis of the *status quo*, threw all its weight into the scales for a resumption of work. The slogan of the left was 'all is possible'. Maurice Thorez, the Communist Party secretary, counterposed 'to this dangerous formula' the communist slogan, 'all is not possible'; the party's main line of action remains 'All for the Popular Front: all by means of the Popular Front'.[2] Eventually the return to work began.[3]

In line with undertakings given at the Hotel Matignon, Blum rushed laws through the Chamber which established the forty-hour week and guaranteed paid holidays for the first time in French history. The new labour legislation specified in detail matters to be covered by collective agreements, made provision for their geographical and temporal extension by legal enactment and also specified arrangements for employee representation at the place of work. All in all, the social legislation of the Popular Front represented a major milestone in French history, only to be compared with that of the British Labour Government in 1945–51 or the Roosevelt New Deal in the USA.[4]

The immediate outcome of the Popular Front legislation, the nation-wide sit-downs, the veritable employers' surrender embodied in the Matignon Agreement, was a tidal wave of recruitment into the unions, notably the CGT. Over a million workers joined the CGT in May and June. By the end of the year the original membership had multiplied several times over and stood at over 5 million. This mass influx shifted

1. For an English version of the text see Lorwin, *The French Labor Movement*, pp. 313–15.
2. Lefranc, *Histoire du Front Populaire*, pp. 163–6. The interested reader may find the PCF view of this and other events in the official history, Bruhat and Piolot, *Esquisse d'une histoire de la CGT*.
3. Thus on 7 July, *one month* after the Matignon signature, 1171 plants were still occupied by 120,381 workers; on 14 July there were still 73,700 strikers occupying 613 plants. Lefranc, *Histoire du Front Populaire*, p. 175.
4. The Bank of France and the railways were nationalized, for example.

the balance of power in the direction of the communists whose *apparat* of rigidly disciplined ex-CGTU militants rapidly acquired great influence as leaders of the radicalized but inexperienced new recruits inside the CGT.[1] According to one account, by 1939 the communists had 'gained control of twelve of the CGT's thirty national unions, amongst them the key federations in engineering, chemicals, electrical power and construction industries'.[2] A furious faction fight now developed in which international political issues soon came to overshadow those native to the CGT.

The Matignon Agreement was considered by most French employers as an abject surrender. The outcome was important changes in the national employers organization the CGPF, a hardening of attitudes towards the unions and a determination to shift the balance of power back in the opposite direction. An attempt to reconvene the Matignon conference in November 1936 brought an abrupt refusal from the employers.

Inside the plants every effort was made to undermine union organization and re-establish management prerogative. Outside the plants a strengthened, renamed and reinvigorated employers' organization mustered powerful and effective resistance against union endeavours to set up a national network of collective bargaining agreements.[3] By the end of 1938 the wage boost which followed Matignon had been completely wiped out by rising prices.

The Popular Front government, rent with internal dissensions, confronted with a hostile ruling elite and seemingly insurmountable problems of foreign policy, went out of office in June 1937. Successive governments moved steadily further to the right. France failed to endorse collective resistance to the Nazi encroachments on Czechoslovakia at the time of the Munich crisis in autumn 1938. Instead, the French government moved away from a Russian alliance towards a policy of appeasement. The issues of war and peace produced no heart-searchings for the PCF faction inside the CGT, which was content to defend the Soviet interest, as presented by the Russian leaders from day to day. The situation of the old-time leaders of the CGT was more difficult.

1. If, as Prost suggests, the CGT membership in 1934 was 490,000 as against 260,000 of the CGTU, then the original 3:1 CGT: ex-CGTU ratio in the leadership of the reunited CGT was an exaggerated one: Prost, *La CGT à l'Epoque du Front Populaire*, pp. 177–94; Ehrmann, *French Labor*, p. 73, Lefranc, *Le mouvement syndical sous la Troisième République*, p. 377.

2. Ehrmann, *French Labor*, p. 123; also textiles and agriculture, see Lefranc, *Le mouvement syndical sous la Troisième République*, p. 374.

3. The Confédération Générale de la Production Française was reorganized as the Confédération Générale du *Patronat* Français in 1936 and re-established as the Conseil National du Patronat Français (CNPF) in 1945.

The ex-CGTU faction had maintained their journal *Vie Ouvrière* inside the CGT, with a circulation of 100,000, even after the merger. A section of the old CGT leadership, led by René Bélin, determined to resist PCF penetration and gathered around the new journal *Syndicats*, founded in October 1936.[1] Another group centred around the syndicalist publication *Révolution Prolétarienne*. Léon Jouhaux and his associates, the CGT majority, occupied a centre position with the official press of the CGT at their disposal. *Syndicats*, *Révolution Prolétarienne* and Jouhaux, though united in opposition to the PCF, proved badly divided in their attitudes to the threat of a new world war.

SECOND WORLD WAR

At this time the communist PCF was firmly in favour of French resistance to Hitler even if this meant war. *Révolution Prolétarienne* stood for revolutionary opposition to any Second World War. Bélin and the *Syndicats* tendency, associated with Paul Fauré in the SFIO, conscious of the terrible losses sustained by the French working class in 1914–18, sought almost at any cost to avoid the outbreak of a new world war. Jouhaux and the CGT majority leaned more towards the communists on the issues of war and peace than to the '*ex-confédérés*', their natural allies on other matters. This confusion aided the communist advance within the CGT.[2]

The Nantes CGT Congress of November 1938, the first since the unification at Toulouse, was held in the shadow of Munich, in the face of an imminent government offensive against the remnants of the gains of 1936, including the hard-won forty-hour week.[3] Ribbentrop, the Nazi foreign minister, visited Paris that same month and talk of a Franco–German Pact was in the air. The communists backed the Jouhaux foreign policy resolution, winning a two-to-one majority over the Bélin conciliationist position. The Congress unanimously declared its forthright opposition to the government's proposed withdrawal of the forty hour week. In this decision the PCF saw an opportunity to strike a blow against the government and its foreign policy. Jouhaux and his allies allowed themselves to be stampeded into an ill-managed twenty four

1. Circulation 60,000. The editor's chair was originally reserved for Jouhaux but he failed to assume that post. Lefranc, *Le Mouvement syndical sous la Troisième République*, pp. 374, 375.

2. For a clear account of this very confusing situation see Lefranc, *Le Mouvement syndical sous la Troisième République*, pp. 373–80.

3. Ehrmann, *French Labor*, pp. 93–4; Lefranc, *Le Mouvement syndical sous la Troisième République*, pp. 380–82. The Congress was held at Nantes, opening 14 November. The Munich agreement of 29–30 September, from which Russia was excluded, represented a major step away from the policy of Franco-Russian collective resistance to Hitler.

hour general strike on 30 November. The government took forceful
counter measures. The strike was a disastrous failure. The spirit of
the CGT declined, the differences amongst its leaders grew even
wider.

It was in the aftermath of this situation that on 23 August 1939 the
signature of the Russo-German, Communist–Nazi Pact was announced
to a shocked and astonished world. The next day the communist faction
of the CGT leadership, which forty eight hours previously had been all
out for the fight against Hitler fascism, moved a resolution welcoming
the Russian initiative. Hitler's invasion of Poland on 1 September, and
the Soviet Union's own invasion of Polish territory which followed on
17 September, dealt the CGT's already precarious unity a further blow.
France declared war on Germany on 3 September. The CGT seems to
have been forewarned of government countermeasures against the
PCF, whose pro German attitude consequent on the Nazi–Communist
Pact was considered a threat to national security. On the day following
Russia's invasion of Poland, the CGT executive condemned both the
Communist–Nazi Pact and the invasions of Polish territory, declaring
'collaboration no longer possible with those . . . who do not wish to condemn an act that amounts to the negation of the very principles of
human solidarity on which the honour of the labour movement is
based'.[1]

There followed a wholesale purge. In flat defiance of the Charter of
Amiens and all the professed principles of the CGT, a political test for
membership was imposed. Pro communist CGT leaders, individual
members and union locals were asked whether or not they approved of
the Communist–Nazi Pact. An affirmative reply, as indeed no reply at
all, was followed by expulsion.[2] The well known French unionist Pierre
Monatte, with some justification, has described the whole sorry business
as no more than a combat between two factions, one pledged to French,
the other to Russian, patriotism, and there is much to commend this
view.[3] Yet it should be realized that PCF control had advanced sufficiently to threaten the position of the existing CGT leadership. The
Nazi–Communist Pact, the Russian invasion of Poland, France's ally,
constituted a most useful pretext for large scale expulsions which
enabled the Old Guard to retain control of the CGT. One week after
the communists were expelled from the CGT the French government

1. Quoted in Ehrmann, *French Labor*, pp. 144–5; Lefranc, *Le Mouvement
syndical sous la Troisième République*, pp. 386–7.
2. Ehrmann, *French Labor*, pp. 144–7; Lefranc, *Le Mouvement syndical sous
la Troisième République*, pp. 386–7. The PCF and all its affiliated organizations
were dissolved by government decree on 26 September 1939, only a week after
the CGT's action. Ehrmann, *French Labor*, p. 148, Lefranc, *Le Mouvement
syndical sous la Troisième République*, pp. 378, 386–7.
3. Monatte, *Trois Scissions*, p. 41.

decreed the dissolution of the PCF and all its affiliated organizations. The view that the expulsion of the communists from the CGT was intended at least in part to protect the organization from government countermeasures would thus seem to be well founded.

Although France entered the war in September 1939, no large-scale hostilities took place in the West until the German offensive in May 1940. This 'phoney' war saw widespread infringement of civil liberties. Thousands of suspects were detained in concentration camps without trial. Heavy prison sentences were imposed on some union leaders. The draconian measures taken by the government against its political opponents, by no means all of whom were communists, the serf like regulations with which it surrounded workers in the war production industries, did much to undermine the will to resist. Long before the Vichy regime assumed power, fascism was being prepared in the guise of resistance to Hitler.

At the same time government repression served to give an aura of martyrdom to the PCF. Through most of the first two years of the war, the French communists decried national defence, damned what they termed Allied aggression against Hitler, sabotaged war production where possible and generally carried out a policy calculated to aid a Nazi victory. This policy did not change even after the French defeat and the Nazi German occupation. One of the PCF's first acts following the Nazi conquest of Paris was to open negotiations with the German authorities for the publication of the party daily *L'Humanité* which had been banned by the French government in 1939. In November 1940 a condemnation of Resistance attacks on German troops, signed by the veteran communist leader Marcel Cachin, was widely posted through Paris by the occupying power. Only after 22 June 1941, when Hitler's attack on Russia broke the Nazi–Communist Pact, did the PCF belatedly espouse the cause of Resistance to the Nazi invaders. Conducted in secrecy, a large part of this communist activity in the years 1939–41 never saw the full light of day. To this day the majority of French people are unaware even of its existence.[1]

As for the CGT, membership had fallen by 1939 to around a quarter of the 5 million claimed for 1936. By 1940 the CGT itself claimed only 800,000 members. The blame for this catastrophic decline lay more with its leaders, of whatever political persuasion, than in any other cause.

The Franco-Prussian War and the Paris Commune laid the basis on which French socialism and French syndicalism arose in the years before

1. On this see Rossi, *A Communist Party in Action*, pp. 17–20, 82–105. This edited English-language edition of Rossi's *Physiologie du parti communiste français* does not do justice to the original which is superior in every way. On this see also Rossi, *Les Communistes français pendant la drôle de guerre. Sunday Times*, London, 6 Sept. 1970.

1914. The First World War and the Russian revolutions split the working-class movement into reformist, revolutionary, and later also Stalinist wings. Hitler's attack on Russia in June 1941, which allowed the PCF to base itself on the seemingly coincident interests of French and Soviet Russian patriotism, cleared the way for its subsequent conquest of the organized mass labour movement.

The CGT and the CFTC were formally liquidated by the Vichy government in November 1940. The Vichy regime enrolled a number of individuals formerly prominent in the pacifist wing of the CGT whom resistance to communist demagogy had driven into a neo-corporatist position. Bélin, a former leader of the *Syndicats* tendency, became Minister of Labour responsible for the Charter of Labour enacted in October 1941, intended as a major step in the transformation of French society into a corporate state on the Nazi model.

French employers on the whole were collaborationist, not above taking steps to rid their plants of active labour organizers by facilitating their deportation to forced labour in Germany. 'In general the *"haute bourgeoisie"* and the nobility gave their wholehearted support to the régime which had resulted from the defeat. In doing so they renounced the role of societal leadership for which they believed themselves to be pre-ordained.'[1] As a result, promptly following the involuntary switch of alliances which swept Russia pell mell from the side of Germany to that of Britain and the USA, the PCF was able to take up the standards of French patriotism discarded by the bourgeoisie and launch a belated cry for resistance to the *boche* and the Nazi invader.[2] Once wartime hardship cut down living standards, once Vichy subservience to the Nazis began to outrage national sentiment, once large scale conscription for forced labour in Germany got under way in 1943, the preconditions for a movement of resistance, with its main basis amongst the working class, were created.

The PCF with its centralist leadership, pre-existing Russian links and conspiratorial mode of organization, already underground in 1940, was supremely well fitted to take advantage of this situation. Not only did the French communists play a leading role in the Resistance; at the same time they were able to recruit and train cadres which were to give them an inestimable advantage over their rivals in the post war years.[3]

1. Ehrmann, *Organized Business in France*, pp. 58, 94–100, 104.
2. Full details will be found in Rossi, *Les Communistes*. The PCF had denounced de Gaulle as a hireling of the City of London for his 18 June 1940 appeal to continue the struggle.
3. By 1944 the PCF front, the 'Committees of Peasants' Defence and Action', had already 2500 sections in 33 departments. Earle, ed., *Modern France*, p. 225. The post war failure of the communist parties of Belgium and the Netherlands certainly owes much to the more patriotic stand of the Belgian and Dutch bourgeoisie during the Occupation.

Union opposition to Nazism had rallied long before the communist about-turn. As early as November 1940 leaders of the CGT and Christian *Confédération Français des Travailleurs Chrétiens* (CFTC) met to demand the lifting of the bans on their organizations and to call for the re-establishment of free and independent trade unions. An underground CGT was re-established. In May 1943, some two years after Hitler's attack on the Soviet Union, the communists were re-admitted to the CGT with three out of the eight seats on the central executive board. The unified CGT now became a key element in the Resistance. As the Allied armies converged on Paris, CGT and CFTC combined to launch a general strike for liberation, linked to a Resistance rising in that city. Since Eisenhower, unlike Marshal Rokossovsky before Warsaw, did not halt his troops whilst the Nazis slaughtered the partisans, the unions and the Resistance entered the last months of the war with an aura of a self-won victory around their heads.

FRENCH LABOUR AFTER 1945

The decisions taken at the Great Power Conferences at Yalta and Potsdam in February and July–August 1945 placed France firmly within the western bloc.[1] When the French government was re-established in France under General de Gaulle communist leaders, amongst them Maurice Thorez, the party secretary, accepted Cabinet posts. In the years between August 1944 and their ejection from the coalition in May 1947, the number of communist ministers in successive cabinets varied between two and seven. Thorez, the communist party secretary was Vice-Premier from November 1945 to May 1947.[2] In the post war euphoria the PCF thus figured in a strangely contradictory role. As a party of government and Resistance it represented patriotic and even chauvinistic forces in the nation. As a party of communism it was believed to bear the red flag of revolution. As an ally of the Communist Party of the Soviet Union it shared the prestige conferred by Russian military victories which created millions of 'Red Army Communists' throughout the Western world. As a party of revolution and a party of order, as the prime claimant to the French patriotic legitimacy abandoned by a collaborationist bourgeoisie, it subsumed, Bonapartist fashion, the most wildly conflicting hopes and aspirations within its ranks.

Perhaps for this very reason, the Communist Party enrolled between 800,000 and one million members in the immediate post war years,

1. And equally the nations of Poland, Hungary, Roumania and Bulgaria in that of the 'East', hence the post war division of Europe.
2. For details see Williams, *Crisis and Compromise*, pp. 16–20, 368, 378–9, 436–7.

sufficient to give it a dominating influence over wide areas of national life. A whole generation of French workers and intellectuals thus came to be trained in the Stalin school, identifying the socialist future with the model of soviet totalitarianism; the time serving morals of the cynical party *apparatchik*, with those of a new liberated Soviet man. Although in subsequent years party membership has fallen, the PCF's hold on the working-class vote has remained substantially intact. The direct result has been a major sclerotic degeneration of the French working class.[1]

The SFIO lacked the conspiratorial, centralist tradition of the PCF. The socialists possessed no close knit party organization with a unified theory and programme of action during the Resistance. Nor, unlike the communists, were they supported by the prestige and backed by the material aid of one of the major combatant powers. In 1940 thirty-six of the eighty votes cast against conferring full powers on Marshal Pétain were cast by the socialists. Yet the fact remained that three quarters of the socialist deputies voted on the other side.[2] Léon Blum, the party's leader, did not return from German imprisonment until May 1945. A drastic purge of those who had supported Pétain weakened the party's old-line leadership considerably.[3] The anti political traditions of French unionism pre-empted the party's working class base, leaving it with an ageing and predominantly middle class leadership.[4]

'Socialism is the master of the hour,' Blum declared on his return from captivity.[5] Hopes that the socialists would play a leading role in post war France nevertheless proved illusory. In the election of 1945 the socialists polled only 4·5 million votes against the 5 million of the PCF.[6] Locked into a government coalition between the communists and the Catholic *Mouvement Républicain Populaire* (MRP), the SFIO found itself being ground to powder between the millstones on either side.

1. See, for example, the style and content of the official history of the CGT, Bruhat and Piolot, *Esquisse d'une histoire de la CGT*.
2. Williams, p. 89; Graham, pp. 15–16.
3. The PCF deputies had been unseated in 1939. As a result the question of their voting for Pétain did not arise.
4. Thus in 1951 none of the members of the *comité directeur* of the SFIO came from a working class family. The PCF on the other hand had carefully cultivated the existing *ouvriériste* mystique, especially in regard to the composition of its leadership; see Earle, ed., p. 186. Herriot's cynical aphorism regarding the SFIO; '*Restaurant ouvrière, cuisine bourgeoise*', seems very apt on this; see Williams, p. 95.
5. Graham, p. 2.
6. It would be a mistake to assume that the whole of the working-class vote goes to either the SFIO or the PCF. In fact between 1946 and 1956, around one third went to the parties of the orthodox right and centre. In later years the proportion seems to have been even higher. On this see Adam *et al.*, *L'Ouvrier français en 1970*, p. 124.

Concerned to prevent the conquest of power by either the communists or the orthodox right, it gave the impression of a party dedicated to ineffectual parliamentary manoeuvre, a stance which did little to extend the base of popular support; 340,000 strong in 1945, the party shrank to 156,000 by 1949 and 100,000 by 1962. The bulk of the members were teachers, professional and white-collar workers, lower-grade civil servants and municipal officials.

The decline in the SFIO has not brought any accession of strength to the PCF. Party membership a claimed one million in 1946 had fallen to around 200,000 by 1968.[1] The PCF vote in 1962 was more than one million below the 5 million peak of 1945.

The PCF remains able to exercise disproportionate power and influence, not least due to the power and size of its bureaucratic apparatus. 'Taxation' of party deputies provides more income than membership fees. The party owns numerous business enterprises, among them twelve printing firms, a fleet of taxis and a record company. In 1972 the party treasurer, George Gosnat, put the party's income at a figure in excess of £3 million a year.[2]

Increasingly apathetic and disillusioned with politics and parties, the French working man has tended to drop out of political life altogether. The decline of French socialism is thus a problem not of the working class alone, but of French democracy as a whole.

Mass post war recruitment enabled the PCF to consolidate the positions they had gained after 1943 and to make still further gains. Communist cadres used the Liberation to wipe out old scores, not least against former party members and rivals on the left, by methods which went beyond character assassination to those of simple murder.[3] In March 1945, whilst Léon Jouhaux, the best-known figure in the CGT, was still a prisoner in Germany, the PCF, at the first meeting of the CGT Confederal Committee since the Liberation, gained parity with the non-communists on the crucial Bureau Confédéral.[4] In September 1945, Benoît Frachon, a prominent communist leader, was elevated to a freshly created post of General Secretary alongside the now returned and ageing veteran Léon Jouhaux. Jouhaux, specially concerned with

1. A. Kriegel, *Les communistes Françaises*, Paris 1968, pp. 297–8 calculates the claimed membership for 1968 at 275,000–300,000. This however makes no allowance for bombast and exaggeration. A true figure would probably be up to one third lower.

2. On this, *France Nouvelle*, Paris, 9 Dec., 1970; *Le Nouvel Observateur*, Paris, 4 Oct. 1971; *Observer*, London, 11 June 1972. The Conservative Party in Britain reported an income of £1,800,000 in 1970–71, *Guardian*, 7 Oct. 1972.

3. Rossi, *Physiologie*, quoted in Williams, p. 74; also Rieber, pp. 178–82.

4. Lebrun and Saillant, two '*ex-confédérés*', increasingly supported the communists, giving them effective control: V. R. Lorwin, p. 108. Louis Saillant, as a non-communist, was later appointed General Secretary of the World Federation

international affairs, was largely isolated within the national committee in which a number of ex-CGT leaders were moving towards the communists. Frachon's appointment thus gave to the communists decisive power at the centre of the CGT. At the April 1946 Congress the communists emerged with a four-to-one majority over their opponents.[1] The maintenance of nominal parity on the Secretariat enabled the new communist majority to utilize the prestige of its main opponents whilst being able to restrain and contain them at the same time. By 1947 the CGT, at almost every level, was firmly in the hands of the PCF.[2]

The communist victory was due as much to the weakness of their opponents as to any other reason. Some of the former CGT leaders seem to have taken the PCF's post war endorsement of bourgeois democracy at its face value. 'The Communists have understood at last and come over to our platform; from now on we can work together in open agreement', Raymond Bouyer, a close associate of Jouhaux, is reported as saying.[3] The PCF had indeed shifted to a position so thoroughly reformist that it stood to the right of the old CGT leaders on a number of issues.[4] These were understandably bewildered as a consequence.

The former CGT chiefs in the main were older men than their communist rivals. Some found the semi-insurrectionary atmosphere of the Liberation a little frightening. Others lacked faith in both themselves and in the working class. Among their old friends were some who had gone over to Vichy. The PCF, despite its own despicable role in 1939–41, did not hesitate to use moral terrorism against them on this account. The '*ex-confédérés*' were men from an earlier era. The bulk of the CGT membership were now new recruits easily won over by PCF propaganda which cast a discreet screen over aspects of the communists'

1. V. R. Lorwin, p. 109. For a most illuminating account of the atmosphere at this Congress see Monatte, *Trois scissions*, p. 20. The vote on the communist constitutional amendments was 6 to 5 in the Bureau, 20 to 15 in the Administrative Committee. A little latitude in the question of who was and who was not communist at this time should be allowed, as the issue is open to dispute.

2. For an account of methods used in the Postal Workers' Federation see Rioux, *Le Syndicalisme*, p. 76.

3. Monatte, p. 12; Rioux, p. 75.

4. 'The national committee ... considers the promoters of disorder [i.e. strikes] ... as saboteurs and provocateurs ... the comrades who fought under the occupation ... will not allow the post office workers to serve as a springboard ... in the service of a reborn fascism.' The sinister and threatening overtones of this post-Liberation CGT ultimatum to militants in the post office workers union speak for themselves: Rioux, p. 78.

---

of Trade Unions (WFTU). Saillant subsequently sided openly with the communists. After the ICFTU–WFTU split he remained WFTU General Secretary for more than twenty years.

own past while relentlessly exposing weak spots in that of their opponents. The PCF's opponents were in disarray. Some at least seem to have considered final Russian victory inevitable and thought that all one could hope to do was to retard it,[1] a view, one might add, a great deal more comprehensible in 1945 than it appears today.[2]

A lack of faith in the prospects for the future, an inability to resist effectively the rough house tactics by which the CGT on occasion sought to gain control, resulted in a fall of morale. The fact that the communists were willing to leave the 'ex-confédérés' in office for the time being undermined their will to resist. Léon Jouhaux had been closely involved with the politics of power ever since he had put antiwar sentiment aside and joined the union sacrée as pro war commissioner in 1914. His closest associates, deferentially attached to the authority of power, saw no reason to split with the PCF. After all the communists appeared to share their own reformist opinions. Additionally all the signs showed they were urgently required to shed a mantle of respectability on a now thoroughly communist controlled CGT.

At the end of hostilities hopes ran high that the French nation, reinvigorated, would set out on a new, radically different course. Vichy had thoroughly discredited the old right. The employers 'record during the most difficult hours of the country had been at best undistinguished, in many cases despicable'.[3] Several thousand firms were either shut down or run by workers' committees which took over what they regarded as collaborationist property. Renault and other large plants were summarily transferred to state ownership. In 1944 sovereignty over a large part of liberated France was shared between Gaullist authorities and communist dominated Committees of National Liberation, guns in hand. The true location of political legitimacy was swinging in the balance. In fact, once an initial wave of settling of accounts with the more obvious and vulnerable collaborators was over,[4] the old forces of French society, initially in retreat and disarray, rapidly emerged to reassume their ascendant position in society.

The French peasantry had done well out of the war, the business classes little less. The main burden had been borne by the urban working classes. The sufferings and hardships of wartime France lasted until long after the Liberation. Inflation remained rampant, the black market, social injustice and inequality were rife. In August 1947, two

1. For an example: Monatte, Trois scissions p. 13.
2. For an excellent evocation, see Koestler, The Age of Longing.
3. Ehrmann, Organized Business, p. 103.
4. As a result of an agreement between de Gaulle and the communists no industrialists were tried for collaboration. See Galtier-Boissière, Histoire de la guerre, 1939–45, vol. 5, quoted in Ehrmann, Organized Business, p. 104.

years after the end of the war, 'the average town worker was spending almost three quarters of his wages on food'.[1] Real earnings remained far below pre war levels.[2]

The French Communist Party, now the decisive force in the organized working class movement, joined the government under General de Gaulle in October 1945. Within the underground the PCF had acted as a moderate wing and lagged behind its allies in proposing specific socialist measures for a post Liberation transformation. As a party of government, the PCF put all its power and prestige behind forceful appeals for increased production and a standstill on wage increases for the sake of national recovery.

In 1945, Maurice Thorez, Communist Party General Secretary, now returned from Russia where he had gone to avoid conscription into the French army at the outbreak of war, informed the miners that to dig coal 'was the highest form of their duty as Frenchmen'. In accord with this directive the communist controlled miners' union announced that the pitmen would abandon their holidays. The same year Gaston Monmousseau, a former syndicalist, now a PCF–CGT functionary, denounced the strike as 'a weapon of the trusts and enemies of the working class'.[3] The PCF–CGT control of the working class movement, its assaults on strikers as scabs, fascists and traitors, its great hold on working-class loyalty negated hopes of any effective mass movement to redress the manifest social injustices from which the workers suffered. Statistics show that in 1946, the first year for which strike figures are available, man-days lost amounted to only 312,000, a figure so close to zero as to be ignored.

Two PCF ministers possessed special responsibility for industrial relations: Ambrose Croizat, Minister of Labour, and Marcel Paul, responsible for Industrial Production. Croizat continued to hold his post as secretary of the CGT Metal-workers' Union, a dual responsibility which did not prevent him denouncing a Paris print workers' strike on the radio.

The astonishing policy of the French communists, who at this time were some way to the right of the Labour government in Britain, is only to be explained by their conscious subordination to the needs of Soviet foreign policy. Allied unity after 1945 carried with it an obligation for the Russian satellite parties in the west to maintain an alliance between the classes which matched the Big

1. Williams, p. 26.
2. Skilled workers at 59 per cent of the 1938 level, unskilled workers at 69 per cent of the 1938 level. These figures are for a married man with two children living in Paris; they include family allowances. V. R. Lorwin, p. 113.
3. *L'Humanité*, 19 Sept. 1945. Monatte, *Trois scissions*, pp. 10, 27; Rioux, p. 68.

Three unity at international level. PCF participation in the government offered the opportunity to influence the post war settlement in the Russian direction, an opportunity in no circumstances to be disregarded.

By mid-1947, however, the PCF was in grave danger of losing control of its base. Not even the denunciation of strikers as 'fascists' and 'agents of the trusts' could any longer conceal the total failure of wages to keep pace with the cost of living.[1] If the PCF–CGT wage standstill had continued much longer it is probable that the newly won communist control over the CGT would have been shattered altogether.

Yet at this moment the international constellation of forces on which CGT policy depended was being called into question. Repeated Big Power conferences had failed to agree a post war settlement in Europe. The eventual division of Germany into 'Eastern' and 'Western' sectors was already getting under way. Britain's inability any longer to maintain its hold on Greece had led to her replacement by the United States. In March 1947 came the Truman Doctrine in favour of containment of communism everywhere. In April 1947 an unofficial strike closed the nationalized Renault motor plant at Boulogne-Billancourt in Paris, hitherto regarded as a fortress of PCF support in the labour movement. The CGT denounced the stoppage. When denunciation failed to get the men back to work, the CGT privately urged the management to fire the organizers. Finally, unable to smash the strike, the PCF–CGT wheeled about and took it over.[2] A short while later, the PCF voted against the government wage policy in the Chamber. On 5 May 1947, in an atmosphere of general surprise, the five communist ministers were dismissed from the government. (The socialists and communists were eased out of the Cabinet in Italy during this same month.)

The dismissal of the five communist ministers was followed by a wave of strikes in June which cost the economy twenty times the number of man-days lost in the whole previous year (6·416 million as against 312,000). Yet the communist reaction remained measured. There is every reason to believe that the PCF considered it would be able to force readmission to the Cabinet on its own terms. These hopes went unfulfilled. The announcement of the Marshall Plan in June, Molotov's walk out at the Marshall Plan talks at Paris in July, the foundation of the

1. A detailed account of how the CGT sought to refuse wage increases offered by Renault management to its workers during 1945–7 will be found in Tiano, Lesire-Ogrel and Rochard, see esp. pp. 69–71.
2. Lefranc, *Les Expériences syndicales en France*, pp. 177, 178; Rioux, pp. 68–9; V. R. Lorwin, pp. 116–17. A detailed account of conditions in Renault will be found in Tiano, Lesire-Ogrel and Rochard.

Cominform as a riposte in September set the scene for a direct confrontation.

At Paris, Molotov warned Bevin and Bidault that if they went ahead with the European Recovery Programme, they would face serious disturbances at home.[1] In response to Cominform reprimands, the PCF now denounced the Marshall Plan, and set a course towards a series of wildly adventurist political strikes.[2] In a matter of months the post war unity of the CGT was irretrievably destroyed.

In November, against the opposition of Jouhaux and his allies, the CGT national committee voted to 'consult' all workers in the plants, whether CGT members or not, on the advisability of a general strike for increased wages. The stoppage was already under way before the recalled national committee could meet to consider the outcome. A special committee, packed with communist national and regional leaders, but without constitutional authority, was set up to lead the strike. The Jouhaux minority on the national committee was excluded from its deliberations. By 22 November large scale stoppages were under way in Paris, Marseille and the north. By December pits and ports were shut down completely. Building and engineering in Paris and a number of other cities was largely halted. Gas, chemicals, textiles, post, telephones and railways were all seriously affected. The CGT claimed 3 million participants, 2·5 million at the peak and 1·5 million still out at the conclusion on 9 December.

CGT SPLITS AGAIN

In December 1945 the Jouhaux grouping had established a journal, *Force Ouvrière*, round which it sought to organize resistance to the communist colonization of the CGT. Force Ouvrière (FO) strongly opposed the course events had taken in November–December 1947. During the strike itself, Force Ouvrière and the PCF-sponsored strike committee issued rival strike communiqués day by day. By the time the strike was over, the rift was wide and deep. Jouhaux himself was reluctant to leave the CGT. The communists however had assaulted Force Ouvrière members in northern coalfields. A majority of the Force Ouvrière faction, at a meeting held in Paris the week following the conclusion of the stoppage, declared themselves unwilling to remain in the CGT.[3]

1. *Hansard*, vol. 446, 1947–8, pp. 387–94. *The Times*, 22 Jan, 1948.
2. The Soviet Union and Eastern Europe sent large sums as subsidies for strikes in 1948. See V. R. Lorwin, p. 241. Report of Debate in National Assembly, *Débats*, 16 Nov. 1948, pp. 7005 ff.; 7129 ff. That similar subsidies were forthcoming in 1947 also seems highly likely.
3. The Jouhaux leadership had met on 8 Dec. and made plans to continue inside the CGT. The meeting on the 18th, called at the request of the rank and

The FO meeting was held on 18 December. In the afternoon of the following day Jouhaux and four other members (Botherau, Bouzouquet, Delamère and Neumeyer) resigned from the executive of the CGT. This was the third split in little more than twenty years. On each of the other occasions, Jouhaux and his friends had emerged as the majority. Now this was no longer the case. The bulk of the CGT membership, its offices, buildings, press and equipment remained under the control of the communists. The rival, CGT–Force Ouvrière, launched in April 1948, was forced to start almost from scratch. Ex-functionaries of the CGT claimed most of the posts within the CGT–FO. The insurgents of 18 December were largely excluded from power.

At the end of the war, when the Jouhaux group might indeed have been able to outflank and outvote the communists, they had foregone the opportunity because of their genuine belief in a reformist programme. When now the CGT abandoned that policy and enlisted the mass dissatisfaction accumulated by their earlier line as the thrusting force behind wildly adventurist strikes, the FO leaders continued to hold to their original and now largely discredited position. The stalinists stole the verbal radicalism of the old CGT and made it a smokescreen for Soviet foreign policy. Jouhaux and his allies, accustomed to dressing up a policy of cautious reformism in high-sounding phrases, found themselves at a dead end, quite unable to cope effectively with the problems by which they were faced. A whole era of the French Labour Movement had come to an end.

Force Ouvrière, handicapped by shortage of funds, personnel, physical resources,[1] and above all by the circumstances of the split itself, failed to prove a serious challenge to the CGT and remained primarily based in white collar and government service.[2]

The blame for the 1945 split, unlike those of 1921 and 1945, fairly or unfairly, was placed squarely on Jouhaux and the Force Ouvrière. Many non-communists, in the print unions for example, stayed with the CGT as a result. The large teachers' union, the *Fédération de l'Education Nationale* (FEN), seceded from the CGT but refused to join FO

1. Daniel Meyer, Socialist Minister of Labour, handed the FO 30 million francs of ex-Vichy 'union funds' soon after the split. Money also came from the AFL–CIO and also later from the CIA via Irving Brown. On this, see Thomas W. Braden, *Saturday Evening Post*, 20 May 1967; *Voice of the Unions*, May 1967. The communists had of course for decades been using Russian money in a similar way; e.g. Godfrey, pp. 55–6. On this see also Dallin, *Soviet Espionage*, p. 2570. The CGT and CFTC also received shares of the Vichy money.

2. For a recent account of Force Ouvrière's view of itself, see Pierre Galoni, *Free Trade Union News*, Dec. 1971.

file, voted a resolution calling on Jouhaux and his allies to resign from the CGT leadership. Godfrey, *The Fate of the French Non-Communist Left*, pp. 52–3.

for fear of producing a split in its ranks. The CGT continued to hold a clear majority of the *organized* industrial workers.[1] FO became a minority organization with its main base in white collar, government and municipal service. Once the split had taken place the FO was forced to maintain a total ban on common action with the CGT. This decision, coupled with an initial reluctance to embarrass the fragile government coalition by pressing wage demands, enabled Force Ouvrière to be easily outbid by the CGT.

The CGT, undeterred by the failure of its semi-insurrectional stoppage at the end of 1947, returned to the fray with a violent eight-week coal strike, in the autumn of 1948. Pierre Monatte, a revolutionary syndicalist of an earlier generation, relates of the years 1947–50 how he had beforehand criticized communist passivity and now received the reply, 'You ought to be satisfied. You wanted strikes. Now you have them.'

Yes, [Monatte replied,] strikes against the dismissal of Thorez from the Government. Strikes to upset Ramadier. Strikes to please Moscow. Strikes to upset Washington... Strikes against acceptance of the Marshall Plan. Strikes to make the Americans change their mind about the Plan. Strikes on orders from Warsaw. Strikes to outbid the movement launched by the opposition. Strikes to make the opposition look like scabs. Strikes to bring discredit on the strike weapon. Strikes to make trade unionists fed up... All this is truly too complicated for an old hand like me, used only to strikes for working class objectives.[2]

In 1946 the unified CGT could claim a membership of over 5 million. six years later this had fallen by more than half and was destined to fall a great deal lower. French labour, demoralized, weak and divided, riven by political schisms, out-manoeuvred by management, was chronically unable to exert its full weight on either the industrial or political scene.

UNION MEMBERSHIP

To study the strength of French trade unionism is to take a roller-coaster ride through history. Surges into the heights are followed by plummets into the depths. A sense of dizziness impedes perception. One finds it difficult to describe the position accurately from one moment to another.

The membership of the CGT in 1914 could be counted as between 300,000 and 400,000 members.[3] In 1920, according to some accounts, it

1. But given the French situation a small minority of the workforce overall.
2. Monatte, *Trois scissions*, pp. 176–7.
3. Lefranc, *Le Mouvement syndical sous la Troisième République*; according to Jouhaux a maximum of 350,000 (p. 410).

had risen as high as 2 million.[1] An ill-prepared, ill-managed general strike in April–May 1920 resulted in a catastrophic reversal of fortune. Membership fell to one million or below by the beginning of 1921.[2] By 1931–2 a measure of recovery had taken place. The membership claims of CGT and CGTU combined amounted to some 1·2 million.[3]

The CGT and CGTU merged in 1936, with a membership that had fallen during the depression to less than one million.[4] In May to June of that year came the Popular Front victory at the poll and an unprecedented wave of sit-down strikes. By the beginning of 1937 membership stood at over 4·5 million and was later claimed to have run as high as 5·3 million. In some sectors membership rose fortyfold in twelve months.[5] Bitter internal faction fights, employer pressure, a disastrous general strike call in 1938, combined to send membership plunging downwards. Within two years 3 million of the new recruits walked out of the CGT. By the outbreak of war in 1939 membership certainly did not exceed two million. That year the mass expulsion of communists and their supporters which followed the Nazi–Communist Pact reduced membership still further.[6] In 1940 the CGT was dissolved altogether by the collaborationist government at Vichy.

Reconstituted illegally during the war, the CGT grew enormously at the time of the Liberation. In 1947 the CGT issued 6,440,000 union membership cards. Of these, 849,000 were returned unpaid giving a nominal membership of around 5,600,000.[7] Jouhaux and his adherents split off to form the CGT–FO in 1947. Force Ouvrière at its foundation Congress in 1948 claimed 2 million members. The CGT that same year claimed 4,080,000. Thus we are asked to believe that the elephantine convulsions undergone by the French labour movement in the year 1947–8 resulted in a nett gain of around 500,000 members. The official figures plainly partook more of myth than reality. CGT membership fell dramatically over the next decade. By the leadership's own count,

1. The CGT claimed 2,400,000 in January 1920. Governmental statistics registered 1,580,000. A critical examination by Annie Kriegel has suggested 1,050,000. Lefranc, *Le Mouvement syndical en France*, p. 220.

2. V. R. Lorwin, pp. 54–5; Lefranc, *Le Mouvement syndical sous la Troisième République*, p. 315.

3. Lefranc, *Le Mouvement syndical sous la Troisième République*, pp. 410–11. For a breakdown, see V. R. Lorwin, pp. 324–5.

4. V. R. Lorwin, pp. 70–71; see also Lefranc, *Le Mouvement syndical en France*, p. 315, which suggests 755,000.

5. See breakdown of membership in Montreuil, *Histoire du mouvement ouvrier*, p. 488; V. R. Lorwin, pp. 74–5, 324–5; Lefranc, *Les Expériences syndicales en France*, p. 336, and *Le Mouvement syndical sous la troisième République*, pp. 348–9.

6. V. R. Lorwin, pp. 82–4.

7. Lefranc, *Le Syndicalisme en France*, p. 107. The claimed distribution figure for 1945 was 5,600,000; for 1946 6,369,000. See Lefranc, *Les Expériences syndicales en France*, p. 367.

membership stood at slightly more than 2 million in 1957, at 1·7 million in 1961.

The true membership of the French unions at the present time must in the nature of things be to some extent a matter for conjecture. In 1968, the *claims* of the three main confederations were: CGT 2,300,000, CFDT 700,000, FO 700,000. In addition the FEN claimed 450,000, the CGC[1] (white-collar) 250,000, the CFTC (Maintenu) 145,000. The 1968 census showed an active labour force of some 20·5 million.[2] Out of this total on the basis of official *claims* some 4,545,000 were organized. However, the official membership figures are undoubtedly a gross exaggeration.[3] Eugène Deschamps, CFDT General Secretary, in another connection, has made estimates which would suggest a membership amounting to only 2·7 to 3 million overall in 1968.[4] This last figure is certainly a great deal closer to the truth than the official claims.

If we accept the official figures of the FEN and CGC at around their face value, which is not intrinsically unreasonable, this leaves us with a figure of 2 to 2·3 million for the CGT, CFDT, FO and CFTC (Maintenu) combined. Since May 1968 there has been an additional enrolment into the unions, which has been put at some 400,000 to 450,000. This would give us a membership allocation in the region of 1·3 million for the CGT, 700,000 for the CFDT and 500,000 for Force Ouvrière. French unions therefore still remain amongst the weakest in Europe. None of the three major confederations musters as many members as the single German union IG Metall. The membership of the two largest British unions, the transport workers (TGWU) and the engineers (AUEW) together equals or outnumbers that of all the three major French union confederations combined.[5]

1. The CGC – Confédération Générale des Cadres – is a specifically white-collar organization, the CFTC (Maintenu) a breakaway from the CFDT.

2. Of which 2·5 million are registered as '*agriculteurs exploitants*', 1,960,000 as '*patrons de l'industrie et du commerce*' and 990,000 as '*professions libérales et cadres supérieurs*'. These categories undoubtedly reduce the total organizable labour force. Yet in Italy both CGIL and CISL organize peasants. In Britain quite high-level civil servants and managers are looking towards protection via union organization. Precisely what adjustment one ought to make is not clear.

3. The CGT constitution (article 9), defines a member in compliance as one who pays only ten (not twelve) dues stamps per year. Even on this somewhat unusual basis of calculation, the dues payments recorded in the report to the CGT Congress of 1969 represent a membership of only 1·2 million or approximately one half of the figure officially claimed by the confederation at that time. On this and other matters see Adam *et al., L'Ouvrier Français en 1970*, pp. 15–16. It appears that no proper figures are available even within the CGT; see Barjonet, *La CGT*, pp. 64–5; also Lefranc, *Le Syndicalisme en France*, pp. 105–21.

4. Deschamps in Spitaels, ed., *La Crise des relations industrielles en Europe*, p. 102.

5. André Barjonet, CGT research director until May 1968, gives a valuable insight into the comparative strength of the three confederations, their influence

In the past the results of enterprise elections to boards which administer social security funds, elections fought on competitive union lists, has provided an index if not of union membership, at least of relative popularity. In the election of 1962, the CGT obtained 44 per cent of the votes cast, the CFTC 21 per cent, the FO 15 per cent. The white-collar CGC outvoted FO in Paris (8 per cent against 7 per cent) and overall polled 4·6 per cent although it did not contest all elections. Some 15 per cent of votes were cast for non-union lists. Significantly, 30 per cent of the potential electorate of 11·6 million did not find it worth their while to vote at all.[1]

A more up to date if less all inclusive popularity index is provided by the results of *comité d'entreprise* elections. In 1970 the CGT polled 46 per cent of votes cast, the CFDT 19·6, FO 7·3, CFTC 2·7 leaving the balance divided between other unions and the unorganized. In the years 1966–70 inclusive the CGT vote varied between 50·8 per cent (1966) and 40·9 per cent (1969), the CFDT vote varied between 17·7 per cent (1967) and 19·6 per cent (1970), that of the FO between 7 and 8 per cent of CFTC between 2 and 3 per cent. Significantly in all these elections the votes for non-union candidates exceed those for all other groups except the CGT and CFDT. In the 1970 elections the votes of the unorganized claimed 30 per cent of the seats as against 35 per cent for the CGT.[2]

By these tests the CGT emerged as the strongest force in French unionism, in most, but not all areas, receiving an absolute majority of the votes cast. Yet this is not the whole picture. The distinctive feature of French unionism remains less the shifting relations between competing minorities than the chronic incapacity of all the factions together to organize more than a small minority of the labour force. The existence of up to 2 million foreign workers, some notoriously difficult to organize, is certainly a mitigating circumstance of which one ought to take account.[3]

1. These elections are no longer held. For tables of results, 1947–1962, with geographical allocation, see Reynaud, *Les Syndicats en France*, pp. 129–31, 136–7; on this see also Adam, *Atlas des élections sociales en France*.

2. G. Adam *et al.*, *La Négociation collective en France*, Paris, 1972, pp. 120–3. The analysis is based on an electorate of 1,420,000 in the private sector.

3. In 1965, the Ministry of the Interior reported figures for foreign *residents* as follows: Italians 680,000, Spaniards 585,000, Algerians 500,000, Portuguese 157,000, Poles 145,000, Belgians 80,000, Germans 50,000, Moroccans 77,000, Yugoslavs 21,000, Tunisians 46,000, Africans 30,000 – a total of some 2,300,000. In addition there are some one million former aliens who have acquired French nationality. An official *estimate* of foreign *workers* in 1968 put the number at

in industrial sectors and regions of France, in *La CGT*, pp. 64–70. The membership of I. G. Metall is 2,300,000, that of the TGWU 1,500,000, of the AUEW 1,200,000.

Yet this cannot counterbalance the distressing impression of overall weakness which any examination of the French trade union movement conveys. Competitive bidding is one source of confusion regarding French union strength. Lack of proper statistical information is another. French unions (some federations of the CFDT constitute an exception) pay neither strike nor welfare benefits, so that some incentives to proper accounting are lacking. The theory of elite unionism, which originated with the old CGT, remains a powerful force. The CGT goes so far as to 'consult' unorganized workers and even to set up joint committees of organized and unorganized workers to lead specific actions at the base.

COMITÉS D'ENTREPRISES

ALLOCATION OF VOTES IN ELECTIONS 1966–70, BY PERCENTAGES

	1966	1967	1968	1969	1970
CGT	50·8	45·0	47·9	40·9	46·0
CFDT	19·1	17·7	19·3	18·2	19·6
CGT–FO	8·0	7·5	7·7	7·0	7·3
CFTC	2·4	2·1	2·9	2·7	2·7
CGC	(4·2)	(3·9)	(5·1)	(4·9)	(5·5)
Other unions	3·5	3·9	5·4	5·9	7·0
Unorganized	12·0	19·9	11·7	20·4	11·9
Total	100·0	100·0	100·0	100·0	100·0

ALLOCATION OF VOTES AND SEATS 1970, BY ABSOLUTE NUMBERS AND PERCENTAGES

	Votes	%	Seats	%
CGT	652,441	46·0	12,253	35·0
CFDT	278,279	19·6	5,214	14·9
CGT–FO	104,160	7·3	2,363	6·8
CFTC	38,856	2·7	772	2·2
CGC	77,929	(5·5)	1,932	(5·5)
Other unions	99,342	7·0	1,894	5·4
Unorganized	168,720	11·9	10,561	30·2
Total	1,419,727	100.0	34,989	100·0

SOURCE: Minister of Labour. Ex tables Adam *et al.*, *La négociation collective en France*, pp. 120–21.

around half this figure, but the accuracy of the estimate is open to dispute: *Note d'information*, French Embassy, London, Oct. 1968, pp. 1–2. *The Times*, 15 May 1972 puts the number of foreigners in France at 3·2 million of whom 1·5 million are wage-earners.

Thus at the margin the boundary between a member and a sympathizer becomes blurred.[1] There can be no doubt that the PCF prefers the CGT to remain a cadre organization tightly under party control. A more widely based union confederation would require to be more responsive to the needs and desires of its members and less to those of the party leadership.

The problems of the unions are accentuated by the artificially low level of subscriptions which directly undermine both autonomy and effectiveness. The CGT, in words at least, has set as a target the payment of dues equivalent to one hour's pay per month. This target is far from being reached. Dues, which vary both within and between confederations, are, as a rule, far below this level. Even these low dues are paid at irregular intervals.

In Britain or the USA, a member who is in arrears beyond a fixed period is automatically struck off the books. No such provision exists in France. The member buys a card at the beginning of each year, thus renewing his membership annually. Properly speaking he should then buy a dues stamp for each of the succeeding twelve months, thus presenting, at the end of each year, a fully paid up card. Outside the virtual closed shop of the CGT's printing federation and the ranks of certain white-collar organizations, the fully paid up member does not exist, and indeed never did exist, in France.[2]

In the years before 1914 the average dues payment has been put at eight months out of twelve. During the inter war years dues payment seems to have remained around the same level.[3] In the years 1947–57, published CGT figures (which certainly exaggerate) show an average of seven to eight months' payment per member, not least because after October collectors hesitate to press too hard for fear members will not buy a new card the following year.[4] Yet in the year 1959 (allegedly a bad one), even the CGT vanguard, the metal-workers' federation, received

1. For the origin of this procedure in a Red International of Labour Unions (RILU) directive see E. Frow and M. Katanka, *Strikes*, London, 1971, p. 197. For a belated recognition of its harmful effects, by Georges Séguy, General Secretary of the CGT, see *World Trade Union Movement*, Prague, May–June 1971, p. 14.

2. See Barjonet, *La CGT*, pp. 64–5; Lefranc, *Les Expériences syndicales en France*, p. 368. The closed shop itself is illegal in France and the unions manifest no desire to see a change in the law.

3. Lefranc, *Le Mouvement syndical sous la Troisième République*, p. 407; also *Les Expériences*, p. 368. For FO dues 1947–59, see Adam, 'Situation de force ouvrière', *Revue Française de la Science Politique*, 1964, p. 108.

4. Lefranc, *Le Syndicalisme en France*, p. 108. The published figures take account of a virtual 100 per cent in the print unions, so that the level of payments in the rest of the confederation must be lower than indicated. Lefranc, *Les Expériences*, p. 368. See also Tiano, *et al.*, p. 44.

only an average of 6·7 months' dues from each of the members enrolled on its books.

Trade union membership in France is plainly an elusive concept composed at least as much of bluff and bluster as of solidly organized support. On the more rigorous criteria applied by unions in Britain, the United States, Germany, the Netherlands, Scandinavia or elsewhere, it must be concluded that anything up to 50 per cent of those claimed as 'organized' in France are not properly speaking trade union members at all.

THE CFDT

In addition to the CGT–FO tradition, there exists another in France, so different in its internal history as to require separate treatment, that of the CFDT (*Confédération Française Démocratique du Travail*). The conflicts between Church and state in the nineteenth century, the royalist and anti republican attitudes of French Catholics[1] and the anti-clerical commitment of a socialist movement which arose in this context, ensured the violent hostility of the hierarchy to the aspirations of the rising working class movement. In the last decades of the nineteenth century more far seeing elements in the hierarchy sought to re-establish contact with the increasingly laicized urban working class and to combat the growth of socialist ideas within its ranks. Some socially-minded Catholics, among them paternalistic employers, concerned at frightful social conditions and the growing gulf between the classes, also sought to find means to ameliorate the situation. These two strands mingled inextricably together. Attempts were made to organize Catholic workers and Catholic employers in a common, essentially corporate organization on the basis of an idealized version of the old medieval guilds. Clerically oriented, anti socialist, 'yellow',[2] company unions, such as those founded at Schneider-Le Creusot in 1899, were also set up; in one case at least the founders did not hesitate to announce the aid of money from 'good Frenchmen and big industrialists'. The Fédération des Jaunes de France claimed 375,000 members in 1907.

The rise of social catholicism during the first decades of the twentieth century, the undeniable evidence that labour unions had come to stay, both exercised an influence on this heritage. Environmental pressures combined to produce a decline in the ethos of corporative ideas and

1. For a brief account of these matters which, though not unbiased, is essentially fair minded and correct, see *Histoire du mouvement ouvrier et des Centrales Syndicales en France*, published by CFDT (hereafter cited as *CFDT*).

2. 'Yellow' because when strikers broke the windows of the company union office it was with yellow paper that they were covered to keep out the draught and the rain: *CFDT*, p. 55.

'yellow' unionism. In its place came the idea of a Catholic labour union for Catholic workers, and more especially those in Catholic districts working for Catholic employers. Catholic unionism thus tended to be restricted to the more devout communities, areas concentrated in an ambience dominated by Catholic employers. The first Catholic union was one of white-collar workers, although other organizations followed not far behind.

The First World War, the radicalization of the masses that followed, the split of the Second International into discrete social-democratic and communist wings, was accompanied by a significant rise of the ideas of social Catholicism over a large part of Europe. In France this trend led to the establishment in 1919 of the CFTC (*Confédération Française des Travailleurs Chrétiens*), with a membership of around 100,000.[1] Internecine warfare between the CGT and CGTU in the 1920s and 1930s gave the CFTC opportunity to consolidate its position as a separate organization, independent of both its rivals. Notably less authoritarian than its counterparts in other European countries, the CFTC from the beginning elected its leadership at an annual congress.

The mass unionization which followed the sit-downs of 1936 benefited the CFTC as well as the CGT. At the end of that year membership had risen to 500,000. Exempt from the bitter quarrels which rent the CGT, the CFTC suffered fewer losses than its rival in the pre-Vichy years that followed. CFTC militants fought alongside those of other organizations in the underground, separating themselves clearly from the Catholic corporatist elements associated with Vichy. At the Liberation the CFTC again emerged as a separate force, unwilling to merge with the CGT. As a result, the CGT–FO split in 1947–8 had no direct effect on the CFTC, which thus became the only major union organization in France with an unbroken continuity reaching back to the end of the First World War.

The tragic disarray caused by the CGT–FO disputes, the communist manipulation of the CGT in the interest of Russian state policy, both added to the status of the CFTC as an independent force. Differences of doctrinal emphasis inherent in the CFTC since its foundation, which had grown in significance since the mass recruitment of 1936, now began to assume major importance. Was the CFTC a confederation of Catholics foremost, or of workers? If the first, then confessional denominational criteria must be decisive. If the second, the class interests of the members as workers must predominate. In the first case, there were predetermined limits, defined by confessional allegiance, to the extent

1. For an allocation, see Lefranc, *Le Mouvement syndical sous la Troisième République*, p. 240. Employees 43,000, railwaymen 35,000, textile workers 14,800, miners 10,000, constituted the largest blocks of membership.

of CFTC organization. In the second, to the extent to which Christian social attitudes might be acceptable by others, in no sense theologically devout, the boundaries of recruitment were limitless. The internal history of the CFTC is the account of a gradual switch from the first position to the second.

At its first post war Congress in June 1946 the CFTC, taking note of the situation in the CGT, where communist ministers retained their posts as union functionaries, voted a resolution declaring the incompatibility of trade union and political office, by a three-to-one majority.[1]

At the next Congress, in 1947, the CFTC deleted the constitutional provision which based its activity on the social doctrine defined in the papal encyclical *Rerum Novarum*. A fresh text which declared that 'limiting its action strictly to the defence of the general interests of labour the CFTC determines its conduct on its own responsibility, and with full independence of all external political and religious groups' took its place.[2] A new force, rejecting equally the instrumentalization of CGT, FO and the Catholic Church, was entering the French union scene.

The CFTC reformers were based in: engineering, building, gas and electrical industries; the chemical and teaching federations. In the course of a long, hard struggle, which included their withdrawal from the leadership between 1953 and 1957, the CFTC began to move towards a non-confessional, democratic socialist, position. The reformers sought a reorganization of structure, a redefinition of outlook and leadership, which would enable the CFTC to challenge the CGT for the place of major union federation in the country. The issue came to a head at a specially convened Congress in November 1964. The delegates, by a five-to-one vote, ratified the change of title from CFTC to CFDT. Changes in statutes followed, calculated to assist the CFDT to play a new role. An important minority, comprising the bulk of the miners' and several white-collar federations, now walked out of the Congress. Some time later these established a fresh organization, preserving the old name, now known as the CFTC (Maintenu). Meantime, at its March 1970 Congress which registered a further shift to the left, a strengthening of anti-capitalist attitudes and a swing towards ideas of *auto-gestion* the CFDT has undergone a further phase in its evolution.

The changes in the CFTC–CFDT illustrate the failure of the CGT–FO to constitute itself an alternative pole of attraction to the CGT. CFDT recruitment, unlike that of its rivals, has been biased

1. This same principle was to become an important issue in Italy and Belgium in the 1960s.

2. '*Bornant strictement son action a la défense des interêts généraux du travail la détermine cette action en pleine responsabilité et en toute indépendance a l'égard de tous les groupements extérieurs politiques et religieux*', *CFDT*, p. 77.

towards the 'hard' territory of private capitalism, rather than the 'soft' territory of state and public employment.[1] Even before the split, the white-collar federations had lost out in terms of membership to the blue-collar engineers, who, in 1961, comprised some 15 per cent of the confederation enrolment. CFDT members are younger and less marked by the faction wars of an earlier generation than those of other confederations. Already, with 700,000 members, the CFDT has displaced FO as the major alternative to the CGT. Thus, in the 1970 *comité d'entreprise* elections the CGT polled 46 per cent of the electorate, the CFDT 19·6 per cent, the FO 7·3 per cent.[2] Whether with its foundation of soundly based, militant, dues-paying, non-instrumental unions it can displace the CGT as the major organization of the French working class remains to be seen.

UNION STRUCTURE

In reality, as we have seen, '*leur grande et puissante CGT*', as militants are somewhat romantically prone to describe it, is neither great nor powerful. In this dissonance between words and reality there lies something essential to the understanding of the French Labour Movement.[3] That an outside observer can describe CGT regional secretaries as '*préfets d'un gouvernement peu centralisé*'[4] is a further indication of a discrepancy between the theory and practice of France's nominally ultra democratic modes of union organization.

French unions are organized, in the main, on industrial union lines. Thus the CGT comprises only some forty national federations, the CFDT a few more, FO a few less. Some federations, like the metalworkers, organizing such diverse elements as steel, ship-building, auto, aircraft, and electrical engineering, are in reality general unions. Others, such as the railwaymen and the miners, are defined by boundaries a great deal more precise. The benefits of rational division of labour are limited however by the inter confederation competition which exists in all sectors of industry. The fact that each centre has only one federation

1. One indication of this trend; in 1968 the CFDT metal-workers' union broke its ties with the confessional metal-workers' international and joined the International Metal-workers' Federation, IMF, to which the major British, German and US organizations in the field are affiliated.

2. Based on 750,000 workers in 690 plants. Source: CFDT, quoted in Kassalow, *Trade Unions and Industrial Relations*, p. 123.

3. Thus all three confederations, the CGT included, conduct part of their member-training programmes 'under the aegis of the universities' and with the aid of state funds. On this see Marcel, 'Universities and workers' education in France', *International Labour Review*, Geneva, Feb. 1970; for critical appraisal, Barjonet, pp. 74–5.

4. Reynaud, p. 120. The role of a *préfet* is somewhat akin to that of a governor.

for engineering does not prevent there being three, four or more competing organizations in the field.

The nature of the federations has been determined in part by the general absence of in-plant bargaining, in part by the political role undertaken by the unions in the past.

Union locals have found it difficult to establish a firmly implanted membership at the base. Low membership, linked with low dues, infrequently paid, have made it difficult to build a solid and effective union organization. Multiple unionism has weakened the fragile structure still further. Nominally independent, national unions (*fédérations*), are frequently dependent on confederal aid for their continued existence. Union locals are customarily locally rather than plant based. Branches may vary in size from a few dozen up to several thousand. In a limited number of cases, such as, for example, Renault at Boulogne-Billancourt, *de facto* plant-based unionism has overridden the original union structure. The Law of December 1968, enacted in the wake of the May–June events, which confers recognition on the plant based, *section syndicale*, as the fundamental unit of union organization, may prove to have great significance for the future. It is as yet too early to express a definitive judgement. There is clearly a great mass of social inertia and resistance to be overcome. Local union branches are linked to the confederation in two ways. Firstly by their integral membership of an industrial '*fédération*'; secondly by their membership of the provincial organization of the confederation itself.[1] The *unions départmentales* (UD) tend to assume a greater importance in the less well organized areas of the country, where membership is more limited and widely dispersed. In such cases the UD secretary is called upon to perform tasks which in different circumstances might have been performed by the members, the locals, or even the federations themselves. The UD frequently represent the national union (*fédération*) in negotiations with the employers. Similarly it is an important factor in rallying members, adherents and sympathizers to the *mots d'ordre* (literally 'word of command', i.e. slogans) issued by the confederation leadership from time to time[2] and is thus important as an organ of *political* mobilization. At the annual provincial conference, the local unions affiliated to the UD possess, in theory, at least, the possibility of arranging their own regional affairs.

1. *Unions départementales* or *unions régionales*, the difference in title signifying that the association does, or does not, coincide with the administrative divisions of the French state.

2. On this one can report changes in attitude. Thus, commenting on the events of May 1968, Eugéne Deschamps, General Secretary of the CFDT, 'In the past one gave slogans as the call to action. Now we say to the workers, Pursue your own demands! We will give our support. The union will give you support': Spitaels, *La Crise*, p. 891.

In areas such as Paris, where the engineering industry is highly concentrated and relatively well organized, union branches may federate into such bodies as the CGT Metal-workers' Council and thus perform both coordinating and bargaining functions on their own behalf. In certain locations there may also exist the equivalent of a British 'trades council' or an AFL–CIO City Council in the form of a town-based union local. Affiliation to the UD is mandatory; to the union local, optional.

The power exercised by the national federation in confederation affairs varies in accordance with its membership, strength and organization, bargaining potential, sense of independence and financial autonomy. Some, such as the printers' *Fédération du Livre*, with a non communist leadership, manage to go much their own way, even within the PCF-controlled CGT. Others should more properly be seen as dependencies of the national centre. Federation conferences are held, normally, every two years. In between conferences a *Bureau Fédéral*, comprised of several full-time secretaries, each with specific responsibilities, runs affairs under the general supervision of a national committee chosen by the conference. One of the members of the *Bureau Fédéral* will be nominated general secretary with overall responsibility. Since the relatively large national committee meets only infrequently, detailed control of policy is entrusted to a small body, meeting more regularly, chosen by the conference. The extent to which the federation, nationally and locally, is staffed by full-time officials is dependent on resources available and differs greatly between one organization and another.

The competitive, politically oriented nature of French unionism, the undeveloped character of collective bargaining, endows the national confederations with more power than they might otherwise possess. The highly federated structure of French unions provides for a great deal of autonomy at the base. In fact the operation of political factionalism makes this autonomy less than appears on the surface, and has enabled the PCF almost totally to dominate the CGT.

The day-to-day management of the main confederations is vested in a four-tier structure of organization. A Congress, held normally every two years, is constitutionally sovereign. A smaller but widely representative body, meeting around twice a year, a kind of congress in miniature, decides policy issues between conferences. This body in turn appoints a smaller committee, meeting at approximately monthly intervals, charged with supervision and control of the executive, the *Bureau Confédéral*, itself composed of a number of full-time secretaries, and a single overriding General Secretary.

In the case of the CGT, this resolves itself into:

1. *Bureau Confédéral* (BC), comprising twelve to fourteen full-time *secrétaires confédéraux* and one *secrétaire général*.

2. *Commission Administrative* (CA), comprising thirty-five members, meeting once a month, entrusted by the constitution with the task of controlling the affairs of the CGT jointly with the BC.
3. *Comité Confédéral National* (CCN), comprising the general secretary, plus the general secretaries of each national federation and the secretaries of each *union départementale*.[1] Required by the constitution to meet at least twice a year. The only organ constitutionally empowered to call a general strike.
4. *Congrès Confédéral* (CC), comprised of delegates elected by union locals. Entrusted with the formulation and control of Confederation policy, but, it will be noted, without power to elect either CCN, CA, or BC, the decisive levels of power in the confederal hierarchy.

A number of comments are called for. In the first place, it will be observed that, while the Congress is entrusted with the formulation of policy, it has no means of deciding the composition of the *Bureau Confédéral* and thus ensuring its execution. The two-year intervals between meetings in any case make the enunciation of effective policy decisions difficult and tends to pass authority elsewhere. In fact, in the years since 1947, the Congress has become a stage for a theatrical performance produced by the ruling caucus. Federation and UD secretaries, constitutionally present only as guests, monopolize the sessions with lengthy speeches on behalf of the platform, robbing rank-and-file delegates of any effective voice in the proceedings. The Congress has become an occasional mass demonstration and is no longer a serious policy-making body.[2]

CCN meetings have little more significance than those of the Congress, being devoted to 'one or two speeches of a magisterial quality, delivered by the top leaders, received in a religious silence and followed in the midst of general indifference by inevitably laudatory contributions of the federation and department chiefs'. Key decisions have already been taken elsewhere and those present are well aware of the fact.[3]

It is the *Bureau Confédéral* which governs the CGT. Through its proceedings, members such as Séguy and Frachon, who hold interlocking directorates with the Political Bureau and Central Committee of the Communist Party, carry the PCF's directives, via the 'transmission belt' of the CGT, down to the masses.

The constitutional structure of the FO, taken over from that of *la vieille maison*, is essentially that of the CGT, although in this case the

1. Since the UD secretaryships are frequently a fief of the BC, this body is in large measure self-perpetuating.
2. Barjonet, *La CGT*, pp. 58–9, describes the proceedings as a High Mass (*Grande Messe*). The religious, mystical connotation is apposite.
3. Barjonet, *La CGT*, pp. 59–61. Barjonet gives specific examples of disregard of constitutional statute by the leaders.

BC numbers only five, not all of whom are professionals. The FO, however, is in no sense a monolithic organization. Important differences of opinion exist and these are reflected in the leadership of both the confederations and the various federations. As a result, the congress is a more lively affair. Policy is decided not solely by a hidden hand but also by an open struggle of opinion and tendencies.

The confederal structure of the CFTD has undergone important changes as that organization has moved farther away from the original confessional statutes of the CFTC. In place of the CCN, the CFDT elects a *Conseil Confédéral* (CC). The CC meets every two months. One half of the forty-four members are elected direct by the *Congrès Confédéral*, one half nominated by the twenty-two largest unions and regional federations.

The composition of the CGT confederal leadership has remained remarkably stable. Léon Jouhaux, secretary of the CGT in 1909, remained in office until the split in 1947, when he moved over to fill the same function in the CGT–FO. Benoît Frachon, a functionary in the PCF-controlled CGTU, joined the CGT *Bureau Confédéral* in 1936, was appointed General Secretary alongside Jouhaux in 1946 and remained at the top of the CGT until promoted to glory as President. Frachon was then replaced by Georges Séguy. In the CFDT the key post of President has been occupied since 1945 by Gaston Tessier, Maurice Bouladoux, Georges Levard, and André Jeannson. In 1973 the holder was Laurent Lucas. The present FO General Secretary is André Bergéron. The secretary of the CFDT until recently Eugène Deschamps[1] is now Edmond Maire, formerly a leader of the Chemical workers' federation. The breakaway CFTC (Maintenu), is headed by Joseph Sauty.

Although firmly under PCF control the CGT nevertheless tolerates a 'loyal opposition'. As a means of disarming external criticism the non-Communists receive approximate parity of representation on the formal policy-making boards. The 80–100 strong central apparatus of the Confederation and all the CGT publications remain firmly in the hands of the PCF.

INDUSTRIAL RELATIONS

'In most of French private industry, genuine collective [bargaining] relations have scarcely been tried.'[2] One might dismiss such a view of French industrial relations, written by an outsider in 1954, were it not confirmed by native and contemporary observers of the French labour scene. Thus Yves Delamotte considers

1. For a valuable autobiography, Deschamps, *Militer en toute liberté*.
2. V. R. Lorwin, p. 190.

'collective bargaining has never bulked as large in France as it has in other countries . . . nor has it any past or tradition behind it since, leaving out of account brief bursts of activity (1919–20 and the Popular Front in 1936), it did not really take root until the passing of the Act of 11 February 1950 (still in force), which established its legal framework.'[1]

'Collective bargaining is a new practice in France', writes another authority. 'Neither the laws brought forth by 1919 and 1946, nor the exceptional moments like those of 1936 and 1945 have been propitious for the establishment of permanent structures of collective bargaining'.[2]

The disproportion of power between management and unions is so great that labour has only most rarely been able to 'take on' capital at the bargaining table. The employers' associations are highly representative, well staffed, well equipped, disciplined and above all unified. The unions are outmatched in each respect. The industrial weakness of the French unions has led them, despite their professed concern for political independence to depend to a great extent upon political manoeuvre, state intervention and governmental legislation to achieve their demands. This has applied to all confederations without exception. Even the outcome of the mass sitdowns in 1936 was less a marked increase in the number of freely negotiated collective contracts than an upsurge of state incursion into the field of industrial relations. The outcome of this intervention has not always been favourable to the growth of union organization.

Unlike the United States Wagner Act of 1935, which constituted the firm bedrock on which took place the organization of mass production industry and the CIO, the Matignon legislation of 1936 did not specify *a sole bargaining agent* in respect of workers within a given plant. Instead, it provided for union agreements to be signed by 'most representative organizations'. 'Most representative', however, did not mean 'majority'. Unions could receive legal entitlement to bargain, even if they constituted a clear minority of the work force involved.[3] Thus the Ministry of Labour reports as 'representative' 61 trades union organizations which, collectively, in *comité d'entreprise* elections, mustered less than 10 per cent of the total vote.

Since unions received bargaining entitlement without any parallel obligation to achieve majority status, one fundamental incentive to large-scale organization was removed. The Matignon decision to allocate bargaining rights to *minority* unions goes some way towards explaining the chronic weakness of French trade unionism, which it has done much to

1. Yves Delamotte, 'Recent Collective Bargaining Trends in France', p. 351. Yves Delamotte is Director of the Institut des sciences sociales du travail, Paris, (Sceaux).
2. Adam *et al.*, *La négociation collective*, p. 12.
3. Adam *et al.*, *La négociation collective*, p. 81.

institutionalize.[1] The CFDT has proposed that representation should be restricted to those organizations commanding 10 per cent of employees' votes or failing that the three trade union organizations which top the poll. This suggestion has not received support from elsewhere.

The Matignon legislation also buttressed minority unionism in another way. Negotiation of all the 1936 agreements was in the nature of things put in hand around the same time. Once the *patronat* had recovered its breath, the government faced the possibility of widespread, interconnected conflicts in the event of a 'failure to agree'. The CGT, in which the communists were already an important component, like the Popular Front government, feared that widespread strikes would alienate public opinion. Accordingly, at the CGT's request, one of the last acts of the Popular Front was to enact, in December 1936, a law providing for compulsory arbitration of disputes.

Solidly organized unionism and effective bargaining procedures take time and harsh experience to mature. Compulsory arbitration removed from the French unions the necessity to prove their claims by going to the final test of direct action. Instead unions were enabled to shrug off their responsibilities onto the shoulders of third parties nominated by the state.[2] The terms of collective contracts were repeatedly extended on expiry by the intervention of the final arbitrator. Over the passage of time they became reduced to no more than a catalogue of legally obligatory clauses. The significance of the union in the eyes of the worker diminished in favour of the state. This tended to undermine his weak union loyalty still further.

The abnormal economic conditions in France at the end of the war, the initial timidity of the labour movement before the problems it faced, did not aid a reorganization of industrial relations on more rational lines. Although the French employers were largely absent from the social scene in 1944–6, management, more conscious, better led, more united, re-established all its old superiority within a decade. As a result, the character of French collective bargaining, the nature of industrial relations, is backward almost beyond belief. The social outlook of French employers, their unwillingness to recognize unions and bargain collectively, is certainly the first cause. The failure of the unions, notably the CGT, to muster the forces or the will to force the employers to heel is certainly the second.[3]

French labour's initial complaisance during the post war re-establish-

1. Adam *et al.*, *La négociation collective*, p. 81.

2. Of 2471 awards between March 1938 and February 1939, no less than 96 per cent were allocated by the 'super arbitrator' appointed by the state. Ehrmann, *French Labor*, p. 48.

3. For an unconvincing official explanation of this failure, by Georges Séguy, General Secretary of the CGT, see *World Trade Union Movement*, 1971, pp. 12–13.

ment of the old regime under de Gaulle, the subsequent wild adventurism of the Russian inspired mass strikes against the Marshall Plan, destroyed the organized power of the greatest union movement France had ever known, without bringing any benefit in return. Adventurist political strikes demoralized workers, strengthened employer resistance and gained this resistance public support at the same time. The attitudes of the *patronat* and the PCF are self-reinforcing and may even be perceived by the conflicting parties as such. The employers need the empty demagogy of the PCF–CGT in order to justify their intransigent stand. The PCF–CGT equally need reactionary employers to justify their sterile and unproductive denunciations of French society.[1] Apocalyptic immobilism becomes the order of the day. The unions deny the possibility of any effective reform this side of revolution.[2] By denouncing reform as 'integration' and 'betrayal', unions and political parties make it impossible. Thus the sterile prophecy becomes self-fulfilling. The mass organizations remain immobile awaiting the apocalypse, modern Micawbers, waiting against all the odds, 'for something to turn up'.

It is probably only in the CGT that serious discussion could have taken place around a communist thesis of 'absolute pauperization' which held that the French workers were *worse off*, in material terms, than in 1939. There are obviously certain limits to the credibility of trade unionism which argues that wages *must* go down, whatever struggles the masses may undertake to improve their conditions. This is the more so when the workers' own experience of increased consumption, in items as diverse as holidays, radio and television sets, motor cars and refrigerators, proves the reverse.[3]

The failure of French unions to organize private industry as effectively as state or para-state employment is a further factor retarding the development of modern industrial relations. The existing imbalance of membership between private and public sectors encourages union leaders to seek to achieve industrial aims by means of political pressure.

1. Thus one authority has written, 'Collective bargaining is not the main process for determining conditions of employment in France. The unions exist more for reasons of political protest and political pressure than for economic bargaining': Lorwin, *The French Labor Movement*, p. 212. The situation has changed since, but not fundamentally.

2. Not only the CGT. For the influence of this pernicious theory on the CFDT and indeed to some extent on the FO see Adam *et al., La négociation collective,* pp. 12, 77–9. The British equivalent would seem to be the socialism of the Socialist Party of Great Britain (SPGB) which however has never mustered as many as 1000 members.

3. For this theological disputation see, for example, Belleville, *Une Nouvelle classe ouvrière* (pp. 8–9); 'According to the leaders and theoreticians of the PCF and the CGT. . . . the situation is getting worse, the working class is subject to absolute pauperization.' See also: Lebrun, *Questions actuelles du syndicalisme,* pp. 9–19; Barjonet, *La CGT,* pp. 132–3.

The very reliance on such measures weakens the unions' ability to force changes in the private sector where they are most urgently required.[1]

The archaic French bargaining situation is also to be explained by the confrontation between united disciplined employers and divided unions. In the past labour organizations have frequently been more concerned with internecine warfare amongst themselves than with advancing the day-to-day interests of their members. The CGT, the strongest of the confederations, as one might expect, has always been loudest in its calls for unity of action, seeking either to swallow its rivals or to detach the rank and file from their leaders.[2] The CFTC–CFDT, doctrinally independent, has shown itself willing to cooperate with either CGT or FO, or, on occasions, both. FO has objected on principle to a united front with the CGT, although, on rare occasions, this aversion has been overcome. If one takes into account not only the political orientation of the union centres, but also the varying industrial problems of specific individual federations, then the possibilities of shifting alliances between CGT, CFDT, FO, CFTC, CGC and FEN become kaleidoscopic. The prospects of disagreement in negotiations when the 'workers' side' at negotiations exceeds 100 in number is self-evident. If one can form any conclusion at all from these events it is that the CFDT, by far the most serious and militant of the three main federations, is forging ahead and growing proportionately stronger than its rivals.

Collective bargaining in post war France remained under firm government control until 1950. A new 1950 law, like that of 1936, provided for both full collective agreements (*conventions collectives*) eligible for legal extension[3] and simple wage agreements (*accords salaires*). A legal minimum wage – SMIG (*salaire minimum interprofessionel garanti*) and a lower counterpart for agriculture – SMAG (subsequently raised to the SMIG level) were also established. SMIG increases rapidly became reflected in the general wage-level. In turn, the calculation of SMIG's level began to be conducted with less than magisterial impartiality, thus undermining the intended purposes of the SMIG legislation altogether. At present directly affecting only 4 per cent of wage-earners, SMIG no longer exercises the influence it formerly enjoyed.

1. It is interesting in this connection that Gabriel Ventejol, a national secretary of FO, should write of the 'old CGT, whose work is now continued by Force Ouvrière . . . its activity was decisive along two lines, *the first was the struggle for protective legislation*, the second the creation of a collective strength to put the workers on an equal footing with the exployers in negotiations': 'The Trade Unions' Role in Society', *Free Labour World*, February 1972 (italics added).

2. For example Lecoeur, quoted in Lorwin, *The French Labor Movement*, p. 201. For an estimate of the success of this tactic see Barjonet, *La CGT*, pp. 105–23.

3. For full text of obligatory clauses see Reynaud, p. 201.

The wave of union demands which followed the end of restrictions in 1950 were rebuffed by the employers in a fashion which made clear how far the balance of power had shifted since 1945. The strikers, in general, failed to move management from their original terms. The *patron* showed himself a virtually unchallenged master of the wages he paid and of the general conditions of labour. *Accords salaires*, simple wage agreements, rather than the *conventions collectives* eligible for extension, were the order of the day. Major issues – holidays with pay, plant committees, employee 'in-plant' representation – continued to be decided by law and not by union negotiation.[1] The general level of wages and conditions was, and continues to be, decided more by autonomous managerial decisions made in the light of prevailing market conditions than by serious negotiations between employers and employed.

French industrial relations have been complicated by the fact that until quite recently the same mode of wage determination has not applied to both public and to private sectors. The government employs, overall, around one quarter of the non-agricultural workforce in France. Some public undertakings, notably the nationalized Renault concern, have possessed the same wage autonomy as any other commercial enterprise. Most other fields of public employment, the nationalized railways (SNCF), the nationalized gas and electricity industry (EGF), the nationalized coal mines, the civil service itself, have been in a different case.[2] As far as these categories are concerned the final decision regarding wages and conditions has rested with the government and thus partaken of the nature of a political act. Once a wage and conditions leader, the public sector had begun during the early sixties to lag, in important respects, behind the advanced sectors of private industry.

The fact that although unions could exercise pressure on the management of public industry and the government as a civil service employer, they have been unable until recently to conclude agreements, has caused much dissatisfaction. Certainly it has helped to maintain the backward nature of industrial relations in private industry. Limited changes in this system (the so-called 'Toutée' procedure) were introduced in 1965. In

1. On this it has been written: 'The negotiation of wage agreements in France is far from holding the same place as collective bargaining in Britain and the USA. It is neither the principal pre-occupation, nor the most absorbing task of the partners. It has much more limited effects, other modes of solution are often equally effective, the mass of wage earners do not attach to it the same importance. The similarity in nomenclature ought not to lead us to confuse a British agreement or a United States contract with a French "convention". The differences exist not only in the law but also in the historical experience and special circumstances of each country': Reynaud, pp. 160–61. This statement is certainly true but the present author suspects that there is an element of apologetics in its presentation.

2. For a list see Lorwin, *The French Labor Movement*, pp. 320–21.

the aftermath of May–June 1968, the authorities decided to advance the process further. Far-reaching innovations followed initiatives undertaken by the Chabon-Delmas administration in 1969. In a statement to the National Assembly Chabon-Delmas announced the government's intention to institute, for the first time, a system of union–employee negotiation to settle wages in the nationalized industries. A series of negotiations followed resulting in agreements for the nationalized electricity and gas industry (EGF) in December 1969, the nationalized railways (SNCF) in February 1970, the nationalized coal mines (Charbonnages de France) in March 1970 and the Paris transport authority (RATP) in October 1970. The content of these agreements was not particularly remarkable. Far more important was the fact that the government had voluntarily decided to negotiate them, rather than as hitherto, making a unilateral decision, or as under the 'Toutée' procedure of 1965 allowing the unions some very limited rights of consultation. Whether any subsequent administration can revert to the old system of unilateral or virtually unilateral decision making is doubtful although the prospect ought not to be excluded altogether. Given the important weight of nationalized industry in the French economy the precedent of government–employee negotiation in this sector, if maintained, must surely exercise an important influence towards the development of more meaningful industrial relations in private industry as a whole. That this at least in part, has been the intention of the administration does indeed seem likely. It is, however, too early yet to point to any very remarkable shifts in private sector behaviour as a result of the Chaban-Delmas initiative of 1969.[1]

In private industry, management has until now largely succeeded in excluding union representation from the plant. Negotiations are handled normally through the agency of the appropriate section of the French national employers association (*Confédération Nationale du Patronat Française*: CNPF) thus enabling the individual employer to avoid meeting union representatives face to face. Bargaining has as a rule been held to the level of the *département* structure of the CNPF.[2] Thus the engineering employers (*Union des Industries Métallurgiques et Minières*: UIMM) negotiate an agreement covering some 600,000 workers in the Paris region, one third of the industry work force, whilst at the same time resisting nationwide bargaining, which it is felt would redound to the benefit of unions rather than management.[3]

1. On this see Delamotte, pp. 356–61, 366–70; Adam *et al.*, *La négociation collective*, pp. 38–44.
2. The chemical industry employers, presumably because of the special circumstances of that industry, have however recently agreed to national negotiations.
3. The Paris agreement itself dates only from 1954.

The employers' ability to fix the level of negotiations to their own advantage, the technical and material superiority of the CNPF over the unions, has not been without effect. In general, negotiated wage levels are minima fixed in relation to the economic viability of the marginal enterprise, which leave the more efficient undertakings ample leeway to conduct an autonomous wage policy on their own account. The result has been a form of institutionalized wage drift. Average real wages in the Paris area in 1960 were between 18 and 40 per cent above the negotiated rates.[1] The direct impact of negotiated agreements on real wages is thus very limited. Organized pressure on individual management after a negotiated settlement will frequently provide an increase designed to maintain the existing differential. Usually this will be unilaterally conceded and not subject to local negotiation. The result is that union negotiations and union rates continue to mean little to most workers. The *patron* remains master in his own house. For many ordinary workers valid motivations for union membership must remain slight indeed.[2]

The CFDT has sought, as a matter of policy, to break down the engineering industry into sector agreements, but its ability to do so must plainly be dependent on a far higher level of organization than that which exists at the moment.[3] One pointer to the general situation is given by Renault, at Boulougne-Billancourt (Paris). Here only some 20 per cent of the workforce are organized[4] and this despite the plant's reputation as a union stronghold. On this basis the estimate of 20 to 25 per cent organization amongst the 2 million workers in the engineering industry would seem to be something of an exaggeration to say the least.[5] In the building industry it has been estimated that only some 75,000 of the 1.4 million workers are organized. Minimum wage rates between workers of the same category are reported as varying between 3.83 francs in the Lot Department and 5.48 francs in the Paris region.[6] Wages are fixed by agreement in seventy-five of the ninety French *départements*, by unilateral employer decision in fifteen. Here too the gap between negotiated and real wages is wide. The level of organization in French *private*

1. See Reynaud, pp. 171–5; Lesire-Ogrel, *Le Syndicat dans l'enterprise*, pp. 79–88.
2. See particularly Reynaud, pp. 172–5; Adam *et al.*, *La négociation collective*, p. 85.
3. For one CFDT view, see Soulat, 'No there are no industrial relations in France', in *UNIAPAC International*, no. 5, Brussels, 1972.
4. These are 1970 figures. This is an improvement on 1959 when it was reported that of 35,000 workers, the CGT organized 3000, the CFTC 400 and FO 200: Galenson, *Trade Union Democracy in Western Europe*, p. 9.
5. This estimate is given by Reynaud, p. 128.
6. Adam *et al.*, *La négociation collective*, p. 34.

industry as a whole has been put by one reputable authority at between 15 and 20 per cent overall.[1]

WORKERS' PARTICIPATION

Recognition of the chasm which separates capital and labour in France and a desire to construct a bridge seem to have been major motives behind the Gaullist measure of 17 August 1967 designed to give workers a greater share of the fruits of expansions of the enterprise in which they are employed. The law provides that workers may benefit from growth to the extent of a maximum of 6 per cent of their annual income, the sum to be calculated in proportion to salary received. In the event that there is neither profit nor growth the worker receives no added return. The capital sum concerned cannot be realized by the employee until five years have elapsed thus contributing to a process of enterprise self-financing and enforced individual saving. Much the most important part of the new legislation is perhaps the provision that the management of the scheme must be subject to joint agreement, a provision which has led to an upsurge of interest in the *comités d'entreprises*, proposed by Article 10 of the legislation as one of three possible channels of administration.[2]

The Gaullist 'participation' legislation has not been welcomed by any of the three main union confederations. CGT, CFDT and FO have rather been inclined to condemn the measure as an endeavour to 'integrate' the French worker within the system. Some 5800 agreements covering 2,500,000 workers in enterprises had been concluded by December 1970. The nett benefit accruing to the worker by that date (but still largely 'frozen') has been put at some 354 francs per head or some 2·75 per cent of the wage bill. The cost, as one union leader has icily pointed out, is being 'borne entirely by the Treasury through tax relief'.[3]

PLANT NEGOTIATIONS

The archaic character of French labour relations correlates with the general backwardness of much of French society. A series of violent clashes at Nantes and Saint-Nazaire in June 1955, with plant offices invaded, workers wounded and killed, brought their participants a wage increase of 22 per cent. In the summer holiday that followed other employers took advantage of the vacation to concede increases of 10

1. Reynaud, pp. 175–6; Lesire-Ogrel, p. 9.
2. A summary of the provisions of the law and a text of the law itself will be found in *Notes et études documentaires*, No. 3460, Paris, 5 February 1968.
3. R. Lovet, 'Financial Participation: Change or illusion for the ordinary man?' *Free Labour World*, Brussels, June 1971, p. 9.

to 15 per cent so as to avoid similar troubles of their own.[1] It was in the aftermath of this situation that the nationalized Renault corporation unilaterally offered major concessions to its workers as part of a plan to enter into more realistic relations with its workforce. Renault's wages and conditions were already materially above negotiated Paris rates. Renault now promised a guaranteed 4 per cent increase in *real* wages in each of three successive years, an extra week's holiday and other concessions as part of a proposal for an *agreement with the unions* designed to limit unofficial strikes and establish better labour–management relations. The 'negotiations' took only one day to complete. The contract has since been renewed.[2]

The Renault initiative was followed during the next year by over fifty similar agreements, all involving major concessions in large-scale, modern, frequently highly capitalized enterprises, covering auto, aircraft, ship-building, steel and chemicals. The objective of the employers seems to have been to improve industrial relations, stabilize workforce turnover and domesticate both workforce and unions. Also involved perhaps was an ambitious project to bring wage drift in larger enterprises under control. Certainly to the extent that the concessions impinged immediately on the workers' living standards there can be no doubt that they represented a genuine attempt to make the contract a real force and increase the workers sense of involvement in the plant and its future.[3]

The 'Renault initiative' led to protests from other French employers, who complained that the higher wage-rates paid by more modern firms jeopardized the future of smaller and less efficient enterprises. The unions too seem to have had their doubts, 'prompt to fear' suggests one commentator 'that their weakness at plant level might lead to their integration, more or less, into the system'.[4] By the mid-sixties the impetus of the original initiative had exhausted itself without bringing in its train any fundamental change in the French system of industrial relations. Nevertheless, this innovation points to the existence of some more far sighted groups among the employing class whose attitudes, given appropriate social and economic conditions, might contribute to a more rational and effective organization of industrial relations in France. The existence of such groups is further confirmed by the election and subsequent confirmation in office of M. Seyrac as president of the national employers' association CNPF in October 1972–January 1973.

The Matignon Agreements of 1936 led to legal provision for *délégués*

1. For a brief summary see *Histoire du mouvement ouvrier et des Centrales Syndicales en France*, published by CFDT (hereafter cited as *CFDT*), p. 88.

2. Reynaud, pp. 180–84. The conflict between the Renault initiative and the 'pauperization' theory made the CGT hesitate to sign: see *CFDT*, p. 88.

3. For a detailed view on this, see 'Renault-type agreements', in *International Labour Review*, March 1960, pp. 205–32.

4. Adam *et al.*, *La négociation collective*, p. 12.

du personnel (employees' representatives) elected by *all* those employed in the plant, not by union members alone. In form at least election is compulsory in all undertakings with more than ten employees.[1] The post war upsurge of militancy led, as we have seen, to plant takeovers by workers and technicians. In an endeavour to head off this semi-insurrectionary venture, the coalition government, by an ordinance of February 1945 and a law of May 1946, established *comités d'entreprise* (works committees) in all plants with over fifty employees.[2] In these elections all workers, organized or unorganized, have the right to vote. The poll takes place on the basis of union lists. The function of the *délégués du personnel* is prescribed as that of presenting individual or collective grievances 'related to the *application* of wage rates and other occupational classifications, of the Labour Code and of the other laws and regulations for the protection of workers' health, safety and social insurance'.[3] Management is required to meet the *délégués du personnel* at least once a month and to allow up to fifteen hours per month for this activity. *Comités d'entreprise* are allocated authority over company welfare schemes; the employer is also required to consult them on a whole range of matters concerning the economic policy of the enterprise.[4]

In fact both laws have been more honoured in the breach than in the observance. According to the estimate of Maurice Montuclard, a distinguished French authority, there ought, if the legal statutes were properly enforced, to be some 25,000 *comités d'entreprise* in France. Until recently the total was nearer 9,000, of which only a very few function as was intended by the original legislation.[5] A large number are 'ghost committees' whose functions are more nominal than real. The rest, perhaps the largest number, are essentially welfare-sports-social-canteen type committees without serious influence on the enterprise or its conduct.[6] The gap between legal requirement and actual performance

1. At Matignon, Bélin had proposed union representation in place of the *délégués du personnel* proposed by the *employers* but this proposal was not accepted by Jouhaux.

2. For further details, see Lorwin, *The French Labor Movement*, pp. 262–3; Lesire-Ogrel, pp. 25–7; Reynaud, p. 212.

3. Quoted Lorwin, *The French Labor Movement*, p. 259.

4. For a summary of the *comité d'entreprise* situation see Sturmthal, *Workers' Councils*, pp. 32–45.

5. There is evidence which suggests that the powers conferred on *comités d'entreprise* by the Gaullist profit sharing legislation of 17 August 1967 has led to an increase in the activity rate of up to 50 per cent.

6. V. R. Lorwin, pp. 262–7; Reynaud, pp. 212–14. M. Montuclard, 'La participation ouvrière dans l'institution française des comités d'entreprise', paper presented at International Seminar on Workers' Participation in Management, Experiences, Institutions and Perspectives, University of Bologna, Dec. 1969. One Minister of Labour is reported to have estimated that only 1500 *comités d'entreprises* were functioning as the law originally envisaged; on this see Lesire-Ogrel, p. 57.

springs from employer reluctance to carry out the terms of the law and the absence of any effective enforcement authority. The situation is but little different in the case of *délégués du personnel*. The CNPF has expressed the opinion that 'the workers have the right to be unionized, but there are not truly any union rights as such; that is a different thing'. The worker has the right to join the union as an individual, but the union as such has no right in the plant. Thus, although a union militant may benefit in theory from protection as *délégué du personnel* or member of a *comité d'entreprise*, in practice the employer may dismiss him at any time in exchange for by no means excessive compensation. Given the low level of organization and union militancy, the prospect of a strike forcing re-engagement is rarely a real one.

French business operates with a mixture of paternalism and repression more appropriate to the nineteenth century than to the twentieth. Workers at Clermont-Ferrand, it has been said, belonged, until recently, to the Michelin company from cradle to grave. Born in a Michelin hospital, they were educated in a Michelin school, lodged in Michelin houses. When they died, the company, with pious wisdom, paid for a mass to be said for the good of their souls. The same company, it has been alleged, pursues an aggressive anti-union policy. Citroën and Simca have been accused of employing veritable anti-union 'commandos' on the lines of Harry Bennett's 'militia' at the Ford plant in Detroit in the 1930s, a force specifically hired to forestall and break up incipient union organization. Citroën and Simca are also accused by union critics of backing the *Confédération Française du Travail* (CFT) a 'yellow' union, with its main base in auto. Distribution of leaflets in the vicinity of factories in France has, on occasion, been declared illegal. Facilities for posting union notices in the enterprise are denied. Workers are fired for distributing union literature in the plant. Possession of union literature is frowned upon. Union propaganda by word of mouth is banned. Workers may find their lockers opened and searched for 'incriminating' material.[1]

The law of December 1968 conferring legal recognition on the plant based *section syndicale* has set out to remedy the worst elements of this situation. The measure of its success should become apparent in the course of the next few years. One presumes that its importance will be found greater in large plants where a measure of organization already exists than in smaller ones where the *patron* still reigns quite supreme.

Legal provisions up until now have clearly not solved the problem of adequate worker representation in the plant. In the absence of effective

1. On all this, Lesire-Ogrel, pp. 25–30, 40–88; Lorwin, *The French Labor Movement*, p. 261; de Gramont, *New York Times Magazine*, 16 June 1968, p. 11.

union organization there are indeed good grounds for doubt whether it can be achieved. There is indeed substance in the argument which maintains that legal provision, on the French model, militates against effective union organization. If the vote in an occasional election gains the worker collective representational rights with management, why should he trouble to join a union at all?

STRIKES

The 1946 French Constitution, with magnificent ambiguity, guarantees the right to strike 'within the framework of the laws which regulate it'.[1] Nevertheless unless five days' notice was given, a requirement which largely neutralized their efficacy, 'surprise' and 'irritation' strikes were banned in 1963. More important, the 1938 National Service Law, voted by both socialist and communist deputies, empowers the state to requisition workers to maintain production in establishments 'indispensable to meet the needs of the nation'. These powers of requisition, which subject the individual to heavy penalties in case of a breach, played a major role in breaking the 1938 general strike. On the other hand, the use of this same weapon on striking railwaymen in 1951 and striking miners in 1963 resulted in failure. In each case, mass refusal to obey requisition orders made the law powerless. The effective use of these enormous and dictatorial powers clearly depends on the circumstances of the hour.

The general absence of industrial procedure agreements and the consequent absence of precise contractual obligation mean that although spontaneous strikes are becoming much more frequent, 'unofficial' or 'wildcat' strikes (grèves sauvages) are hardly a problem in the Anglo-Saxon sense. The French strike is frequently accompanied by impassioned class-war oratory. It may, as at the Liberation in 1944, or as at the time of the Algerian crises of 1958 and 1961, have specific and legitimate national political objectives. On the other hand, it is likely soon to be over. French unions have no strike funds. Strikes are essentially short-term affairs. It is precisely because French unions are weak that the incidence of 'pin-prick' stoppages is so high. Only by calling a stoppage can unions convince employers that union demands command genuine support.[2] Strike stoppages, even when called, are rarely fully obeyed. Average support in 'struck' plants is sometimes less than 50 per cent.[3] In 1954 32 per cent was indicated; in 1957 49 per cent.

1. Lorwin, The French Labor Movement, p. 244.
2. 'It is striking to note that quite often in France one launches a strike in order to get negotiations to begin. In other countries one only has recourse to a strike when negotiations, already begun, come to a deadlock': Eugène Deschamps, in Spitaels, ed., La Crise des relations industrielles en Europe, p. 100.
3. Reynaud, p. 147.

The French term for strike, *la grève*, refers to a stoppage for a fixed period, limited in advance, and thus has a qualitatively different significance from its Anglo-Saxon counterpart, which denotes a combat which by definition continues until one party or the other bends or breaks under the strain. A strike on the Anglo-American model merits the special title of *grève illimitée*, a strike of unlimited duration. The 'go-slow' and 'work to rule', which in Britain and the USA would not be regarded as a strike at all, in France are accorded the title of *grève perlée* and *grève du zèle*.

The absence of strike funds, which fatally undermines the credibility of much of French unionism, is in part at least the result of a deliberate political doctrine. The PCF views the CGT as an arm for political pressure and demonstration rather than an organ of serious social struggle on its own account. The collection of funds for strikers on a national scale, although monumentally inefficient, provides occasion for the manufacture of propaganda and demagogic nostalgia. A strike fund based on a solidly organized dues system would enhance CGT independence and threaten PCF control. In recent years the CFDT miners, postmen, engineers and railwaymen have however sought to establish strike funds and gained material advances in consequences. The CFDT slogan, *'Cotisations fortes = syndicats forts'* ('tough dues make a tough union') represents an innovation in French union practice.[1]

The need for 'tough unions' to deal with tough *patrons* ought to be plain enough. Out of fifty-three workers fired for striking at the Bouyer plant in Montauban for example, eighteen were out of work for six months or more. Fourteen had to leave home to seek employment elsewhere. Significantly, amongst those forced to leave the district were three of the four *délégués du personnel* and three out of the five members of the *comité d'entreprise*.[2] Elsewhere the custom of offering a substantial 'anti-strike bonus', forfeited in the event of stoppage, has become widespread. On other occasions, employers such as the Rouen tramway company have paid what amounts to a strike-breaking bonus to workers who failed to honour a union strike call.

MAY 1968 AND AFTER

The volcanic social upheaval which threatened to shatter the obsolescent fabric of French society in May–June 1968 should not strain the comprehension of the reader of these pages.[3] French capital and French labour

1. 'Check off', the deduction of union dues from wages is still illegal in France. Act No. 56–416, *Journal Officiel*, 28 April 1956. In view of its importance for unions in Italy after 1962–3, this is a question to which the CFDT and other organizations might well give attention.

2. Lesire-Ogrel, pp. 20–21.

3. The opinions expressed in this section are my own. For factual material I

have shown the ability to produce conflict without manifesting either the talent or the will to achieve an effective resolution. Equally, in French society as a whole, conflicting group interests have generated problems which the political parties and government machinery have proved chronically unable to resolve. Lacking the means of expression, the suppressed conflicts in 1968, as in 1936, found their outlet in an explosion. A vast university expansion generated tensions in the educational sector, which spread outside and detonated long standing discontent with the centralized authoritarianism of French society as a whole.[1] In terms of social movement and participation the sequence of events far outran those of 1936. At its peak, the 1968 uprising saw no less than ten million workers, some half the labour force, five times the union membership, out in a spontaneous rash of sit-down strikes.[2] In the experience of a new generation in the plant, May–June 1968 is the most significant event in a lifetime up to now. Its effects in the medium–long term may well rival those of 1936.[3]

The first swing of the working class into the struggle alongside the students came on 8 May in the western regions of Brittany and the Loire, where at this time CFTD influence was predominant.[4] The CFDT throughout remained the most militant of the three key confederations. Whilst the CGT looked askance at the whole student movement, the CFDT sought consistently to maintain links between students and the working class. Whilst the CFDT sought to use the mass movement to force the employers to gain concessions ensuring for the first time a guaranteed and continuing union presence in the factory, to sign agreements benefiting especially the lower-paid workers, the CGT, like

1. A style brilliantly epitomized by Crozier in *The Bureaucratic Phenomenon*, as one which encourages autocracy at the top and anarchy at the bottom at one and the same time.

2. The strikes were of course *subsequently* legitimized by the confederation leaderships. The point is that the confederations did not start them and were all, as in 1936, taken unawares by the onrush of events.

3. For one view of these events and their significance, see Deschamps, 'La France, pratique syndicale, action directe et mouvements spontanées' in Spitaels, ed., *La Crise des Relations industrielles en Europe*, for another Shaw, 'The French General Strike of 1968', in Kamin, ed. *Western European Labor and the American Corporation*, pp. 119–38.

4. On this, 'Positions et action de la CFDT au cours des évenements de mai-juin, 1968', *CFDT*, p. 180.

am indebted especially to my friend David Goldey and in particular to his excellent and well informed article 'The events of May and the French general election of June 1968', published in *Parliamentary Affairs*. For the CFDT position I have also drawn on the November 1969 special issue of *Syndicalisme: Position et action de la CFDT au cours des évènements de mai-juin 1968*. The views of a PCF dissident will be found in Barjonet, *La CGT*.

the PCF, was clearly embarrassed by the whole affair and concerned to wind it up as soon as possible.

The attitude of the PCF and CGT is not difficult to explain. General de Gaulle's antagonism to NATO, his opposition to US policy in Asia and elsewhere, his flirtations from time to time with Moscow, made his government, in the eyes of the PCF, infinitely preferable to any other that seemed likely to arise out of the crisis. The great proletarian mass movement had begun quite independently of the party and union of the proletariat. The movement's development leftward threatened to leave the proletariat's doctrinally prescribed representatives stranded high and dry. The confused excitement of May–June offered an unprecedented opportunity for revolutionary students to break through the wall which insulated the CGT's doctrinally insulated base from outside influence. This threatened organizational and political disaster for the PCF in France. Thus, in a potentially revolutionary situation, the PCF, in 1968 as in 1936, acted as a party of order. The CGT limited its aims to the industrial field and here, essentially, only to questions of wages and hours, leaving the far more significant question of union recognition discreetly to one side.[1]

The Grenelle negotiations for a settlement to the strike were called for 3 p.m. on Saturday 25 May and ran, with scarcely a break, until 7.15 a.m. on Monday morning, 27th. According to André Barjonet, at that time research chief of the CGT, the Grenelle talks were preceded by private assurances to Huvelin, the CNPF President, that the CGT had no more than limited economic demands to make. The atmosphere of haste around the Grenelle discussions, the apparent endeavour of CGT and CNPF to resolve matters amongst themselves during the proceedings, support Barjonet's testimony. It seems probable that without the presence of rival organizations on the CGT's flank, the Grenelle agreement would not have been referred to the strikers for approval at all.[2]

In the event, presented to the workers for approval, the over-hastily concluded Grenelle agreement was turned down. A shift in the political situation made government and employers unwilling to reconvene. In place of the resounding victory of an overall global settlement the strikers were forced to settle for piecemeal agreements the value of

1. Barjonet, *La CGT*. For an interesting light on the 'false consciousness' exhibited by PCF–CGT leaders see Barjonet, 'CGT 1968: Subjectivism to the rescue of the status quo' in Posner, ed., *Reflections on the Revolution in France, May 1968*, pp. 154–62.

2. There was no reference to the strikers in 1936. Thus although the CGT limited its terms of negotiation at Grenelle to purely economic questions, it never considered it necessary to have a brief prepared setting out its aims, objectives and rationale for the discussion, and this as late as 23 May, ten days after the outbreak: Barjonet, *La CGT*, pp. 156–7.

which varied greatly from place to place and sector to sector. Nevertheless, May 1968, as the shift in Government attitude towards wage negotiations in the nationalized sector shows, has given an impetus to the development of collective bargaining which signs suggest is already beginning to reach over into the field of private capitalist industry as well.

The immediate outcome, negotiated gains apart, of the May–June strikes proved to be a considerable but short term increase in union membership. This, however, was by no means on the scale of 1936. One authority has estimated the total number of recruits for all three confederations at no more than 400,000–450,000. Most of these have, however, subsequently been lost. What lessons will French workers draw from the events of 1968? What morals from the differing conduct of the various confederations?[1] The situation is as yet too little advanced for a definite conclusion to be drawn. A tentative assessment may nevertheless be made. The events of 1936, the war, Vichy, the Liberation, constitute the life experience of a generation which has been decisive in the French labour movement in the last two decades. The signs suggest that May 1968 constitutes the first part in a new cycle likely to prove vastly more productive, and markedly less tragic, than the old.

1. For a CFDT union leader's view of the 1968 events, see Jeansson, 'The CFDT and the May–June crisis', in Posner, ed., *Reflections*, pp. 143–52.

5. Germany

German labour became a national force at a later date than labour in England. Once in existence it grew a great deal more rapidly than labour in France. The explanation of both factors is to be found in the pattern of industrial development which took place in Germany. Large-scale industrialization waited on the unification of Germany and did not finally get under way until after the defeat of France in the Franco–Prussian conflict of 1871. Once started, industrial development went ahead at a tumultuous pace that soon enabled the new German state to outdistance all its rivals on the European mainland. German steel production, roughly equivalent to that of France in 1880, exceeded its closest rival by almost four to one by 1910. German coal output increased seven times over between 1870 and 1913, a period in which British coal production increased less than two and a half times. Germany's coal output barely exceeded that of France and Belgium combined in 1871. Forty years later the growth of the German industry had so outpaced that of its competitors as to exceed their combined output by a margin of three to one. German industry was able to take advantage of the latest techniques, building plant and equipment exempt from the inbuilt obsolescence which threatened to overtake earlier rivals in the field. Not only this, the growth of German industry coincided with important technical and scientific breakthroughs. In the industrial uses of electricity and chemicals Germany soon began to set the pace for the world. The commercial application of the telephone, the dynamo, of electrical traction, provided the basis for a large scale industry. In 1882 the weight of the electrical industries in the economy was too small to merit a category of its own in the census. By 1907 the industry, already employing 107,000 workers, was dominated by two giant firms, AEG and Siemens Halske. The AEG payroll alone numbered 31,000. German industry, a latecomer in the field, not only benefited from earlier technical innovation, not only grew rapidly in the years after 1870, it also proved singularly uninhibited by the free trade ideology which proved so powerful a factor in deciding the social attitudes of both capital and labour in Great Britain. The ideology of German industry was exemplified by semi political doctrines of national economic interest, by Freiderich List rather than by the ideas of Cobdenite *laissez-faire* and free trade. Late development, heavy concentration, tariff protection, encouraged the growth of a cartel system unparalleled elsewhere in Europe. German industrial interests thus possessed a force of organization of a very high order.

The growth of German industry, and with it the social influence of its owners, went alongside a massive increase in population. Forty-one million in 1871, Germany's population rose to 65 million forty years later. Perhaps more important, the balance between urban and rural areas changed decisively. In 1871 two thirds of the German population lived in the countryside; by 1910 almost two thirds lived in the towns.

These vast changes in the social structure of German life and industry were reflected in the consciousness of the German population. The German labour movement scarcely existed at the time this headlong industrial revolution began. By its conclusion Labour had emerged as one of the greatest single powers within the modern German state.

The French labour movement came to birth in a bourgeois republic in which the aims of the new middle class had been largely achieved.

The British Labour Movement, after the period of Chartism, never had to fight for political democracy; it grew up with it . . . When British Labour began to stake its political claim, political democracy had long since become an unquestioned *national inheritance*. When German Labour entered the political arena, the fight for democracy meant fighting against an existing Constitution and, what is more, against the accepted way of life of the rest of the nation.[1]

In the Revolution of 1848, the working class, small though it was, made its debut on the political stage simultaneously with the revolutionary bourgeoisie. Although little organized, the workers in certain industrial areas already manifested a sense of class interest separate from that of the middle class . . . The middle-class leaders of the Revolution of 1848 recoiled from the revolution they had conjured up, and, leaving political power in the hands of the aristocracy, placed their hope for the achievement of a constitutional order in legal methods.[2]

The unification of modern Germany was accomplished by the forces of Bismarck's 'blood and iron'. Two thirds of the population of the new state resided in Prussia. The King of Prussia was the Emperor of Germany. The Chancellor of the Reich was the prime minister of Prussia. The dominant position of the *Junker*, military landed aristocracy, found a rationale in the exposed situation of the new state,

1. Anderson, *Hammer or Anvil*, p. 9.
2. Schorske, *German Social Democracy 1905–1917*, p. 1. See also Schlesinger, *Central European Democracy and its Background*, p. 4.

flanked in the east by the North German plain and on the west by the Netherlands and France.

Germany industrialized, adopted parliamentary forms of government, yet without producing either a classic individualistic bourgeoisie or undergoing a full bourgeois democratic revolution. There thus came about a combination of modern economic patterns and an authoritarian political order, an 'industrial society with an authoritarian welfare state'.[1] In this fusion between past and present, rather than a clear break between one and the other, the mode of social development in Germany is closer to that of Japan than to the customary classic capitalist, Anglo-American model. In line with this German tradition, paternalistic social welfare schemes, endowed both by employers and the state, have sought to immobilize individuals in the place of their birth, to domesticate them within their place of employment. A labour force conditioned by such policies values security highly, tends to restrict its own vision of potential horizons of opportunity. One outcome is diminished motivation to explore alternative labour market options, a tendency to perpetuate a feudal domestic, rather than a market rational outlook, on individual and social affairs. Thus Alfred Krupp in a speech to the firm's employees:

Enjoy what is granted to you . . . remain in the circle of your family . . . think upon household matters and education . . . as for the high politics of the country, do not waste your breath. Higher politics requires more time and greater insight into conditions than are given to the workers . . . you will do nothing but damage if you try to interfere with the helm of the legal order.[2]

The German middle class, instead of leading a struggle for the democratic state against the Emperor, the *Junker* landed aristocracy and its offspring the Prussian army, became their ally in the defence of the *status quo*. The integration of the middle class in an order in which middle class aims were as yet unachieved forced the working class into the forefront of the struggle for democratic rights and liberties against an aristocratic and capitalistic state. The sanctions to which it was exposed gave to its ideas and actions a revolutionary tone, not entirely in line with the immediate tasks which history had placed on the agenda. The labour movement thus came to organize, under the phraseology of socialist theory, the achievement of essentially liberal democratic

1. Dahrendorf, *Society and Democracy in Germany*, pp. 31–7, 39, 42, 60.
2. In 1877, quoted in Grebing, *The History of the German Labour Movement*, p. 53. In 1972 Krupp continued to provide no less than 52,000 apartments for its employees. Krupp also built two hospitals, still used primarily for its own employees. Until the end of the Second World War Krupp also ran 120 company stores, access to which was restricted to Krupp employees only. See 'Krupp's slide into the shadows', Norman Crossland, *Guardian*, London, 13 January 1972.

objectives. On the one hand it grew stronger from its ability to rally to its banner elements which might otherwise have been excluded. On the other hand the contrast between its aims and ideology laid the basis of dangerous weakness for the future.

The slow pace of industrial development in Germany before the last decades of the nineteenth century meant that guild organization survived as a powerful force until the 1850s and even beyond. The master craftsman and the apprentice, with the tiny scale of enterprise which this involved, survived until an astonishingly late stage: 'Before 1840 large enterprises of the factory type were extraordinarily rare.'[1] As a result, change when it came, was all the more sharp and brutal in its effects. 'Some trades even passed in a single generation through the three stages – independent handicraft, outwork, and the factory system – an evolution which, as has been said, had taken several centuries in earlier ages.'[2]

RISE OF THE LABOUR MOVEMENT

The labour organizations which had appeared on the scene at the time of the Revolution of 1848 were driven underground and destroyed in the years that followed. Not until the upturn in German industry did working class organizations again begin to emerge as a factor of importance upon the social scene. In 1863 at Leipzig a group of workers' educational societies, under the leadership of Ferdinand Lassalle, founded the General German Workers' Association (*Allgemeiner Deutscher Arbeiterverein*: ADA). Lassalle stood for a programme of socialism to be achieved via workers' co-operatives, subsidized by a state in which the working class, by the exercise of universal male suffrage, would exercise a powerful influence.

Another group of workers' organizations, the Union of German Workers' Societies (*Verband der Deutschen Arbeiterverein*: VDA) was set up in 1864, under the chairmanship of August Bebel. In 1868, under the influence of both Bebel and Wilhelm Liebknecht, a close associate of Marx, the VDA voted to join the First International.

In 1869 at Eisenach Bebel's Union of German Workers' Societies fused with dissident members of the Lassallean ADA to form the Social Democratic Workers' Party (*Sozialdemokratische Arbeiterpartei*: SAP), the forerunner of modern German Social Democracy. The theoretical programme adopted at Eisenach reflected the Marxism of the International; the immediate demands scarcely differed from those of the ADA. By 1875 the SAP had enrolled 9100 members against the 16,500 of the ADA. In the Reichstag election of that year the Lassalleans

1. Clapham, *The Economic Development of France and Germany*, p. 385.
2. ibid., p. 301.

polled 180,000 votes and returned three deputies, the Eisenachers 171,000 and five deputies. That same year both organizations merged at Gotha to form the Socialist Workers' Party of Germany (*Sozialistische Arbeiterpartei Deutschland*: SAD), later renamed the Social Democratic Party of Germany (*Sozialdemokratische Partei Deutschlands*: SPD). The unification of Gotha, like its predecessor at Eisenach, represented a compromise between the tendencies of Marx and Lassalle which gave birth to Marx's *Critique of the Gotha Programme*. After only three years of life the newly founded party was dissolved by Bismarck's Anti-Socialist Law of 1878. All meetings attacking the state or private property were forbidden. The publication and distribution of socialist literature was banned. 'Professional agitators' were threatened with deportation. Social Democratic candidates nevertheless retained the right to stand for election. Parliamentary immunity allowed them to speak and vote freely in the Reichstag if elected.

The rigours of the Anti-Socialist Law, although grave and brutal for their time, scarcely compare with restrictions on civil liberty which have become commonplace in both East and West in recent times.[1] The 1900 deportations, the 1500 sentences totalling 1600 years in jail, the 1300 publications prohibited, failed to arrest the growth of social democracy. The party's vote, which stood at 493,000 (9 per cent of the total) in 1877, rose steadily to reach 1,427,000 by 1890, when the legislation was finally allowed to lapse.

Fritsche, a supporter of Lassalle, organized the first German trade union, that of the cigar-makers, in 1865. The printers' union followed in 1866, the tailors' and the woodworkers' in 1868. On 26 September 1868 a Congress attended by 206 delegates, representing some 142,000 workers in 110 different localities, set up a national union organization, the General German Trade Union Federation (*Allgemeiner Deutscher Gewerkschaftsbund*: ADGB). The Anti-Socialist Law severely circumscribed union growth and activity. Once it expired the way was clear for a fresh development. A census taken in 1890 reported a total of fifty-three national unions with 228,000 members, plus an additional 73,000 organized only at local level. In November of that year a General Commission of German Trade Unions, headed by Karl Legien, was set up to lead the movement. The unions remained organizationally independent of the party although the General Commission itself was

1. For example, in Czechoslovakia, after 1948, according to the London *Observer* (28 July 1968), 'there were probably 100,000 persons imprisoned for long sentences ... perhaps 2000 died in prison from fever and other diseases. About 30,000 people served 15 years.' Czechoslovakia is a far less populous country than Germany. The record of the Nazis and the Greek colonels is too well known to need repetition here. The text of the Anti-Socialist Law will be found in Lidtke, pp. 339–45.

staffed almost entirely by Social Democrats. The ADGB had originally
been seen primarily as a recruiting agency for the political labour movement. The strengthened trade union movement which emerged after the
Bismarck repression soon began to make it clear that such a subordinate
status could not continue.

Trade union membership doubled between 1891 and 1899, increased
by half a million between 1899 and 1904. One million strong in 1904, the
unions added a further million to their ranks in the six years that
followed. In 1898 it was still possible for Karl Legien to state that 'the
members of the German trade unions are for the most part members of
the Social Democratic Party'. By 1913, union membership exceeded
that of the party by approximately two and a half to one. The ratio of
party votes to union members, eight to one in 1893, fell to less than
two to one by 1912. The increasing strength of the unions led to an
increasing affirmation of autonomy from the party. At the same time,
within the unions, centralizing forces gained at the expense of local
autonomy. The primitive radicalism which originally opposed the
negotiation of labour contracts as reactionary was forced to give ground
under the pressure of events. The control of strike funds gradually
passed from the localities towards the national union centres. At the
same time the General Commission strengthened its position in regard to
the individual unions. A view gradually, almost imperceptibly, gained
ground that unions and political party were 'two pillars' of the working
class movement, the unions 'to discharge the economic functions . . .
the party, the political ones'.[1] The unions, although still led almost to a
man by Social Democrats, were shaking off the paternity of the party,
asserting their right to deal with the party as a separate, equal and
autonomous group, with duties and responsibilities which might
override the demands of party discipline.

The Anti-Socialist Law served to radicalize the SPD. The 1883
Congress, held in Copenhagen due to the Anti-Socialist Law, 'declared
the party to be revolutionary, with "no illusions" concerning the
realization of its goal by parliamentary methods'.[2] The Erfurt Congress
of 1891 adopted the party's first thoroughly Marxist programme. This
later came to serve as a model for socialist parties throughout the world.
The Erfurt Programme, the principle author of which was the party's
leading theoretician Karl Kautsky, comprised two parts. The first laid
down the theoretical basis of the party's Marxist programme. This
foretold mounting crises, an 'ever more bitter' class struggle, the final
acquisition of political power by the proletariat, and the transformation
of capitalist private property into social ownership. The second comprised the immediate aims to be pursued within capitalist society:

1. Schorske, pp. 15–16.
2. ibid., p. 3.

universal suffrage, democratization of the German state, the eight hour day, extension of social insurance, guarantees of the right to organize, and similar measures of this nature. The immediate demands comprised the platform around which the party might rally the working class. The struggle for these immediate demands, it was held, the very development of capitalism itself, could be relied on to create both working class awareness of the need for socialism and the desire and will to realize it. The Erfurt Programme provided a synthesis acceptable to both revolutionary and reform wings of the party, yet one which carried within itself the danger of a split should ever the two elements find themselves in confrontation.

The growth of the Social Democratic Party of Germany was phenomenal. The party's vote, 763,000 in 1887, rose to 3,011,000 by 1903 and 4,250,000 by 1912, by which time it represented over one-third of the total poll. The party itself, the first true political mass organization in history, set a pattern or organization since followed all over the world. Year by year membership of the SPD grew with an inexorable quality which seemed to bear out all Marx's prophecies of the approaching doom of the capitalist system. By 1906 membership exceeded 384,000. In the years up to 1912 the annual rate of increase varied between 10 and 30 per cent. On the eve of the First World War the SPD, despite all the barriers the Kaiser's Reich placed in its path, enrolled rather more than one million individual members. In power, in size, in theoretical influence, the German Social Democratic Party overshadowed every other socialist organization in the world.

The growth of the party was marked by recurrent conflicts between revolutionary and reformist wings. In these disputes the trade union leaders, at first silent observers, later played a decisive role. As early as 1898, only seven years after the adoption of the Erfurt Programme, a leading German Social Democrat, Eduard Bernstein, in his *Die Voraussetzungen des Sozialismus und die Aufgaben der Sozialdemokratie*,[1] challenged the apocalyptic perspective on which the Erfurt synthesis was based. In contrast to Marx, to Engels and to Kautsky, Bernstein perceived a world in which capitalist contradictions were growing more muted rather than more acute, one in which the historical inevitability of socialism disappeared altogether. In Bernstein's eyes the socialist programme ceased to be the objective expression of the revolutionary class interests of the rising proletariat. It became instead the reformist classless expression of a general humanitarian ideal. Bernstein's 'revisionist' thesis, sarcastically termed by Kautsky 'the first sensational piece of writing in the literature of German Social Democracy', was rejected in

1. *The Presuppositions of Socialism and the Tasks of Social Democracy*, published in English as *Evolutionary Socialism*, London, 1909.

a series of prolonged debates which engaged the SDP between 1898 and 1903. In the event the defeat proved more formal than real.

Belgian and Swedish workers' organizations had both launched general strikes in 1902 as part of their struggle for universal suffrage. Dutch labour adopted the same measure to prevent the passage of a strike-breaking law in 1903. The revolutionary strikes which swept across Russia during the Revolution of 1905 now found their echo in Germany.[1] Greatly impressed by the Russian experience, Rosa Luxemburg who, as a Pole, had participated in the Russian Revolution of 1905, now began to advocate the political mass strike, as an additional weapon in the armoury of German social democracy.

At this time, in Germany as a whole the suffrage extended to only some 20 per cent of the population. Women were denied the suffrage altogether. The varying size of constituencies, which ranged from an electorate of 9500 (Schaumburg-Lippe) to 247,000 (Berlin-Teltow), rigged the scales against Social Democracy. Thus in the 1902 general election the Conservatives received one seat for every 18,000 votes, the Social Democrats one seat for every 76,000. Prussia, the largest and most important state in the Reich, represented a road block of cardinal importance to the progress of Social Democracy. A discriminatory three class franchise delivered one third of the seats to 3 per cent of the electorate. A further one third of the seats were allotted to 12 per cent of the electorate. By this legal jerrymander a mere 15 per cent of the population were guaranteed a two-to-one majority in the Chamber before the election even began. In the 1903 *Land* elections in Prussia, the SPD and the Conservatives each polled 19 per cent of the vote. The Conservatives were allotted 143 seats, the Social Democrats none.[2]

The German government was not responsible to the Reichstag. The state voting procedures were highly discriminatory and undemocratic. The strength of the Prussian government within the Federal Council of the Reich gave it the opportunity to veto any reform of which it did not approve. The prospect of an anti-SPD revision of the electoral system, the need to break through the 'suffrage barrier' if the party was to win a parliamentary majority, made Luxemburg's proposal highly relevant. The 'mass strike' as conceived by Luxemburg was indeed more than a simple political tactic. In her eyes it was the spontaneous elemental expression of the revolutionary will of the masses, 'the form of movement of the proletarian mass, the form of the proletarian struggle in the revolution itself'.[3]

1. It must be remembered that at this time present day Poland did not exist, being divided between Russia, Austria–Hungary and Germany. Russia and Germany thus shared a common frontier.

2. Grebing, *History of the German Labour Movement*, p. 73.

3. Schorske. p. 55.

The radicals' endorsement of the mass strike, coupled with marked unrest of their own members, caused the union leaders great concern. Criticizing 'our literati' who had 'no notion of the practical labour movement for propagating general strike discussion from their summer resorts', the union leaders disassociated themselves from the idea of any mass strike and placed all responsibility for finance and leadership squarely on the shoulders of the party. The SPD was forced to recognize that 'in actions which affect equally the interest of trade unions and party the central leadership of both organizations should seek a mutual understanding in order to achieve a unified procedure'.[1] The union leaders were thus removed from the direct discipline of Social Democracy and recognized as an independent force, equal in their sphere to the party leadership. 'Since the executive could undertake no action which the trade unions would not approve, it came almost imperceptibly to be responsible more to the general commission than to the party itself.' In the opinion of one authority the decision 'accorded institutional recognition to the primacy of the material interest of German Labour in the existing order, represented by the trade unions, over the "ideal" interest of the working class, heretofore represented by the party, in the overthrow of capitalism'.[2]

The mass strike debate was followed by a whole series of struggles during the years before 1914, not least over SPD attitudes to antimilitarism, to its youth organization, and to its willingness to form alliances with bourgeois parties. These served to polarize conflicting forces within the part. The war, when it came, finally split the SPD asunder.

The unions, which grew so rapidly in the pre war years, were confronted by a unitary Federation of German Employers' Associations (*Vereinigung der Deutschen Arbeitgeberverbände*: VDA) which remained 'aggressively opposed to the unions and used their entire arsenal of weapons to defeat the claims of organized labour'.[3] Whilst making ground against the employers' resistance, the German unions proved refreshingly immune from the jurisdictional disputes which plagued labour in both Britain and the United States. Despite an eightfold increase in membership between 1890 and 1913 the number of national unions fell from 62 to 49. On the eve of the First World War, five large unions, the metal-workers (529,000), the building-workers (327,000), the transport-workers (201,000), the woodworkers (189,000) and the general factory-workers (184,000) between them comprised more than half the socialist trade union strength. Most unions possessed strike funds. Most also provided social services, sickness and unemployment benefits

1. ibid., pp. 39, 44, 49.
2. ibid., pp. 52–3.
3. Galenson, *Comparative Labor Movements*, p. 269.

to their members. Yet despite gains and successes registered in the negotiation of agreements at regional and national level the progress made at the work place, which remained a stronghold of employers' autocracy, remained very small indeed. Well before the First World War the unions, like the SPD, had accumulated large assets and employed a professional staff in considerable numbers, acquiring thus a deep stake in the existing order. This stake the union leaders were increasingly unwilling to hazard by serious gestures against an unremittingly hostile government.

FIRST WORLD WAR

After the outbreak of war in 1914 almost every major socialist party abandoned its prewar internationalism to line up behind the nation state and its own national government in the interests of 'national defence'. The German Labour Movement was internationally renowned, the SPD seen as 'the Marxist model organization, the revolutionary workers' party *par excellence*'. The German socialists' vote for war credits on 4 August 1914 dealt the International a blow from which it has never recovered.[1]

The support of the SPD and the unions for the war, their abandonment of the class struggle for the duration, marked a crucial stage in the evolution of the labour movement. Acceptance and involvement with government policy 'drew the leaders psychologically closer to the ruling groups – it raised the importance of the leaders within the labour movement by confining political and economic action essentially to the negotiating level – it compelled Social Democracy to adhere fully, in word as in deed, to a strictly reformist course'.[2]

During the war years of full employment and limitless demand for output and in the aftermath of the revolution of 1918, union membership more than doubled, rising from 2,076,000 in 1914 to 5,479,000 in 1919. The war rallied labour *leaders* to the government and incorporated them into the system. At the same time the savagery and suffering brought about by the war alienated the *rank and file* from the system and opened a wide breach between leaders and 'led'. The labour *movement* was enormously strengthened in an exceedingly short space of time. The mixture was to prove highly explosive.

The Social Democratic Party of pre war Germany had adopted a tactic

1. The SPD at the last minute had sought assurances that common action would be joined by the SFIO, but failed to receive them. The SPD saw Germany menaced by the Tsarist invasion of East Prussia. In view of Marx's strictures on Russian barbarism, their decision for national defence could claim a certain Marxist rationale. See for example, Anderson, pp. 17–22.

2. Schorske, pp. 293–4.

of 'pure opposition' which found symbolic expression in the refusal to vote for a national budget, or to participate in the '*Hoch!*' to the Kaiser. The Social Democrats used parliament more as a platform of agitation than as a legislative organ. One, perhaps unduly harsh, critic has written:

Pre-war Social Democracy . . . combined activity for the workers' welfare with a passive and theoretical radicalism in other spheres of public life. In general the Social Democratic Party official had no real interest in problems of foreign policy and the army, education, the administration of justice, the civil administration, and even economic problems as a whole . . . he never realized that the day might come when the Social Democrat would be called upon to decide all these matters . . . German socialists as a whole up to 1914 unconsciously regarded social policy and the suffrage as the most important things in the world, and let all other questions sink into the background.[1]

This history could not be without its effect on the party's behaviour, when the revolutionary upsurge of 1918–19 catapulted the SPD into office as the major political party in the post-Kaiser state. The Weimar Constitution was something of a model of its kind. For the first time the forms and content of a thoroughgoing parliamentary democracy were introduced into German political life. In this it expressed very well the attention which the pre war party had devoted to the field. Yet what Social Democracy proposed to do, and in this it reflected once again the formal socialism which characterized it in pre war years, was to superimpose a parliamentary constitution on a post war Germany in which the balance of social forces which maintained the old order had remained unchanged.[2]

The power of the military caste, on which in moments of crisis the government came to depend, remained almost unchallenged.[3] The vast estates which provided the social basis of the *Junker* aristocracy and the subordination of the peasantry upon their soil were left intact and undivided.[4] 'Genuinely desirous of suppressing private capitalism . . . in the hopeless economic conditions which prevailed in Germany . . . [the Social Democrats] . . . were unwilling to make any economic experiments . . . that might still further interfere with essential production.' Hypnotized

1. Rosenberg, *A History of the German Republic*, pp. 13–14.
2. See for example the section on the army quoted in Rosenberg, *A History of the German Republic*, pp. 105–6.
3. On this see Carsten, *Revolution in Central Europe, 1918–1919*, pp. 55–77. This dependence was in no sense obligatory as the account given by Carsten of the Austrian *Volkeswehr* (pp. 78–126) makes plain.
4. This was a question to which German socialism, preoccupied with a classical Marxist vision of an urban confrontation between bourgeoisie and proletariat, had paid little previous attention. Gerschenkron, *Bread and Democracy in Germany*, pp. 24–7, 92–5.

by a Fabian gradualism clothed in Marxist phrases, the SPD hesitated to take over industry not 'ripe' for nationalization and so failed to change the structure of private ownership at all. Since the ruling social classes of the old order never truly accepted the new, the Weimar Republic was threatened by hostile forces from its inception. The middle classes too, their savings virtually expropriated by the inflation of 1921–3, were impoverished and degraded, with little reason for faith and loyalty to the new regime.

The downfall of the old regime was brought about by widespread mutinies of Germany's soldiers and sailors. Two hundred thousand Berlin metal-workers had struck already in 1917. These same workers now become a leading force in the Berlin general strike of 9 November 1918, which forced the abdication of the Kaiser. The first Republican government of Germany was elected on 10 November by the Workers' and Soldiers' Council of Berlin. For a while regimes of parliamentary democracy and elected Workers' and Soldiers' Councils existed side by side.

At Easter 1917 those socialists opposed to the continuation of the war, many already outside the SPD, had met to found a new Independent Social Democratic Party (*Unabhängige Sozialdemokratische Partei Deutschlands*: USPD). The membership was wide ranging. Kautsky and Bernstein favoured a 'peace of understanding' but opposed revolution. Luxemburg and Liebknecht felt that without revolution no satisfactory peace would be forthcoming. By 1919 members of the former left and right wings of the SPD were facing one another on opposite sides of the barricades.

In December 1918, before the Communist International had been founded in Russia, Luxemburg and Liebknecht split off from the USPD to set up a new explicitly revolutionary Communist Party of Germany (KPD). The KPD declared for a workers' and soldiers' republic based on the existing Workers' and Soldiers' Councils rather than a 'bourgeois regime' based on parliamentary democracy.

The newly founded KPD blundered into a muddled and confused revolutionary venture in January 1919. The Social Democratic government called out the mercenary armed bands of the 'Free Corps', the only military units still remaining loyal to the officers of the old regime. Luxemburg and Liebknecht were murdered in the ensuing repression. Thousands were killed in the punitive expeditions which followed, not least in Bavaria, where a short lived Soviet Republic had been established. In its efforts to maintain the existing order against attack feared from the left, the government thus became the prisoner of its own most inveterate enemies on the right.

The KPD, which was independent enough to dispatch a delegate to Moscow early in 1919 opposing the foundation of the Communist

International, rapidly fell under Russian domination after Luxemburg's death. When the USPD decided to affiliate to the Comintern in October 1920 KPD membership grew from 80,000 to 380,000 in a single stride.

THE WEIMAR REPUBLIC

The weight of the Versailles Treaty on the Weimar Republic, the burden of reparations, the dislocation caused by the war, the runaway inflation which pauperized the middle classes, the sharp class tensions which characterized German society, the final economic collapse in the Great Depression which raised unemployment to over 7 million in 1932, constituted problems which it would have strained the wits of any working-class movement to overcome.[1] In Germany these immense problems were complicated by a fratricidal conflict within the working class itself.

The bloodshed in the post war stabilization, the foundation of the Comintern, the Russian domination of the KPD, drove a wedge between the different elements of the working class which were to prove fatal for the hopes of German Socialism.

The SPD mustered its greatest vote in the first post war election of 1919 when it polled 11,509,000 votes, 37·9 per cent of the total. This represented a peak never regained although the party continued to poll over 7 million votes (18·3 per cent), even after the Nazi accession to power in 1933. The combined votes of the working class parties reached a peak of 13,826,000 (45·5 per cent) in 1919. This vote remained fundamentally stable although latterly that of the KPD grew considerably at the Social Democrats' expense. In November 1932 the combined poll exceeded 13 million (37·3 per cent). This vote remained at over 12 million (30·5 per cent) even after Hitler came to power. The solidarity of this bloc despite all adversity is remarkable. Yet it also testifies to the inability of the labour movement to make electoral gains amongst the population during the life of the Weimar regime.

Almost 9 million strong in 1921, the socialist and christian unions lost ground in the years that followed. Union membership barely exceeded 5 million on the eve of the Nazi rise to power. Nevertheless the labour organizations of the Weimar Republic were considerably stronger than those of the pre war years. At their 1921 peak the unions enrolled treble the pre war maximum. Even in the midst of the mass unemployment of 1932 the enrolment still exceeded that of 1914 by some 2 million members. The unions nevertheless were weakened by divisions within their own ranks. In 1931, the Social Democratic trade unions enrolled some 4·4 million members. Yet there also existed two rival national

1. Woytinsky, *The Social Consequences of the Economic Depression*, p. 333. Anderson, p. 135, puts the unemployment figure as high as 8 to 9 million.

confederations, plus a number of independent organizations mainly in white-collar and public service. The Christian trade unions, linked with the important Catholic Centre Party, mustered some 700,000 members. A 'Liberal' Hirsch-Duncker union confederation numbered 180,000 more. Although not comparable in size to the social democratic ADGB these organizations had a history almost as long. There can be no doubt that the resulting political and confessional differences, the pointless jurisdictional disputes, weakened the German labour movement a great deal.

SPD individual membership, despite losses to the USPD and KPD, surpassed the million mark in 1919. Recovering from heavy losses in the mid-1920's, membership reached the million mark once again in 1929. The German worker had a sense of loyalty, devotion and above all discipline to these great organizations which made them a formidable force indeed.

The numerical strength of the German labour movement was only one side of the coin. Inside these organizations the domination of bureaucracy and conservative routine was beginning to become the rule.

The Social Democratic Party, oriented almost totally towards the parliamentary–gradualist aspect of the Erfurt Programme, proved quite unable to cope with the disjointed development of the post war era. Bossification, ossification, bourgeoisification (*Verbonzung, Verkalkung, Verburgerlichung*) wrote Sigmund Neumann, and it was not so far from the truth.[1] Paralysed by a kind of arterial sclerosis, its vast organisations suffocated the movement below by their own dead weight.[2]

A tendency for the existing leadership and the 'apparatus' to emerge as a self-perpetuating oligarchy was already apparent before the war. The overburdening strains which post war disorder, inflation, unemployment and ruthless employer offensives put upon the unions and their leadership accentuated these trends.[3] Precise figures for the number of persons employed by the SPD are difficult to establish. Party commercial enterprises it is known employed some 7,400 persons. An official SPD authority has given the number of party employees at 10,000. Party critics have proposed the seemingly astronomical total of 70,000–80,000. The figure has been put even higher. A median figure of 20,000–30,000 functionaries has been suggested by one authority.[4] That the large body

1. Quoted in Hunt, *German Social Democracy*, p. 240.
2. Thus in 1912, by one account, the German unions spent 42 per cent of their income on their apparatus, the British 18 per cent. Landauer, *European Socialism*, vol. i, p. 134.
3. Schorske, pp. 116–45; Schlesinger, pp. 69–84. The classic study is Michels, *Democracy and Political Parties*.
4. On this, Hunt, *German Social Democracy*, pp. 56–7; Grebing, p. 73. Oliveira, in *A People's History of Germany*, p. 174, proposes the astonishing figure of ' 300,000 salaried workers on the staff, of whom 52,650 were concerned with management, 162,325 were officials and secretaries, the rest printers,

of functionaries and full-time employees dependent on the party for jobs and careers developed a life and activity in its own right there can be no doubt. That party functionaries possessed a disproportionate control of party policy seems quite plain.[1] The staff of the unions, with their social service, and other benefits to administer, would, one imagines, be at least as large as that of the SPD.

The KPD threat to the existing union and party leadership forced the apparatus of each group to consolidate its own strength. At the same time party and union organizations moved farther to the right to consolidate their defence against onslaughts from the 'left'. The KPD, after its initial years an externally financed annexe to the Russian-dominated Comintern, was organized on far more bureaucratic lines than either unions or the SPD. Communist Party membership proved highly volatile and unstable. In 1930 70 per cent of the German Communist Party had only one year's membership to their credit. That year 143,000 members joined the KPD; 95,000 left. Around its cadre of Russian financed professionals the Communist Party became in the end largely an organization of the unemployed.[2] SPD membership, by contrast, proved more stable. Losses of younger people to the communists increased the age level of the membership and further consolidated the power of the party's existing regime.

The events of 1930 onwards the great depression, which hit Germany particularly hard, made socialists and communists alike the victims of their own propaganda. One participant has written:

In the summer of 1931 the German banking system came literally to a standstill under the intolerable pressure of the crisis. The banks suddenly found themselves unable to make further payments. The 'collapse of capitalism', to which reference had so often been made in Socialist and Communist literature as to a vague future possibility, suddenly became a fact. The temper of the people was such that any Social Revolutionary movement that had made a determined effort could have achieved power. Neither the SPD nor the KPD, however, seized the opportunity . . . Since the Marxist parties took no advantage of the situation, the mass of the dissatisfied populace went over to National Socialism.[3]

More detached observers may question this judgement. Yet the possibility of success is not arbitrarily to be excluded. Certainly it would not

1. On this, Petroff and Petroff, *The Secret of Hitler's Victory*, pp. 48–51. Landauer, vol. pp. 483–6; Schorske, pp. 116–45; Hunt, pp. 63–83, 90.
2. On this Borkenau, *The Communist International*, p. 365; Rosenberg, *A History of the German Republic*, p. 289.
3. Rosenberg, *A History of the German Republic*, pp. 308–9.

transport workers, typists, clerks, etc.' Unfortunately Oliveira does not indicate the source of his figures. The whole question is one which would well repay further study.

be reasonable to suggest that a labour movement which had bid for power and failed would have suffered a worse fate than that which subsequently ensued under the Nazi regime.

The truth was that the SPD at this moment, as at the time of the formulation of the Erfurt Programme, remained without any realistic model for the transition to socialism, without any practical bridge between its immediate and its ultimate programme. In the midst of the economic crisis Fritz Tarnow, President of the ADGB, the principal speaker at the party's 1931 Leipzig Congress, made this plain.

> Standing at the sickbed of capitalism is our position . . . that of a physician who wishes to heal the patient? Or of the joyful heir who can hardly wait to see the end and who would really love to accelerate it with a little poison? . . . The patient's agony means starvation for the masses . . . Right at this moment we cannot remember so vividly that we are the heirs and that we are looking forward to the end of the patient's life.[1]

The SPD was unsure of its role. The KPD by contrast was absolutely certain. Only it seems in retrospect that the communists had totally parted company with their senses. At the Russian's behest the KPD, after 1928, had adopted an ultra-left policy. In the eyes of the KPD the Social Democratic Party was fascist, the trade unions were fascist, the government was fascist too. In that case why on earth should the working class be afraid of Hitler? In August 1931 communists and Nazis united in a plebiscite designed to overthrow the Social Democratic government of Prussia, the largest and most important state in the German Reich. The communists' main enemy became the Social Democrats. Once the Nazis 'are in power, the united front of the proletariat will emerge and make a clean sweep of everything . . . we are not afraid of the fascists. They will shoot their bolt sooner than any other Government',[2] one leader of the KPD declared.

The communist prophecy proved totally in error. On 30 January 1933, Hindenburg appointed Hitler Chancellor. On 27 February 1933 the Reichstag was set on fire. The general election which followed on 5 March was held under the shadow of a rising wave of Nazi terror. Later that month, on Hitler's initiative, the Reichstag, against the vote of the SPD passed an Enabling Law which legally enthroned the Nazis in office with virtually unlimited powers. Before the year was out Germany

1. Quoted in Landauer, vol. 2, pp. 1393–4. Recognition of this dilemma is essential to the understanding of the history of Social Democracy, both in Germany and elsewhere. For a partisan account of some of the differences of opinion in the SPD and ADGB which lay behind this formulation of Tarnow, see Woytinsky, *Stormy Passage*, pp. 457–72; for further details see Baade in Woytinsky, ed., *So Much Alive*, pp. 61–6.
2. Remmelle, quoted in Anderson p. 144.

was in the grip of a totalitarian dictatorship from which it would not emerge until after the military defeat of Hitler in 1945.

THE GERMAN LABOUR FRONT

The Nazi Party in its struggle against the Weimar Republic had formed its own cells in factories and unions. Nevertheless, even after the Nazi accession to power some union leaders seem to have continued to believe that their organizations might survive under the new regime.[1] Negotiations actually took place between union leaders and the Nazi 'workers organizations . . . [for] . . . a merger of all trade unions in which the trade unions would sever their connection with the Social Democratic Party . . . receiving in return the promise of being maintained in existence'.[2] In trying to save the existence of the unions, the trade union leaders went so far as to state that the social tasks of the unions must be fulfilled irrespective of 'the prevailing forms of government'. The ADGB chairman, Leipart, handed Hitler a declaration to this effect on 21 March 1933. On 19 April 1933 the ADGB officially called for union participation in the forthcoming Nazi-sponsored May Day celebrations. Some union leaders even marched in the Nazi demonstrations. In an endeavour to save itself the ADGB also broke off its links with the International Federation of Trade Unions. These concessions proved unavailing. On the day following the 1 May celebrations, union headquarters were invaded by Nazi storm-troopers. All union assets were confiscated. Union leaders were beaten up and arrested. Within the year, the unions themselves were wound up.

In place of the unions, the Nazis set up a new unitary German Labour Front, which embraced both workers, salaried employees and employers. Organized on the military 'leadership principle' the Labour Front by 1939 included the whole workforce of the state, a total of some 30 million people.[3] Membership of the Labour Front was compulsory; national leadership rested with the Nazi Party, to which all full-time officials belonged. Dues amounting to 1·5 per cent of wages or salary, compulsorily deducted, receipts from confiscated union property and investments, direct grants from the Nazi state, made the Labour Front

1. There seem to have been private discussions with Strasser for example. Gottfurcht, *Trade Unions in Germany*, p. 21.

2. Neumann, 'The labor movement in Germany', in Morgenthau, ed., *Germany and the Future of Europe*, p. 103.

3. Twenty million individual members plus 10 million more through collective affiliation; agriculture through the National Food Estate, lawyers through the National Socialist Lawyers Association, intellectuals through the Chamber of Culture, etc. For a valuable account of the operation of the Labour Front, see Hamburger, 'The German Labor Front', *Monthly Labor Review*, Washington, D.C., Nov. 1944, pp. 932–44.

a very wealthy and powerful organization; in 1939 it employed 36,000 paid officials, their activities supplemented by those of no less than 2 million unpaid, non-professional workers.[1]

The structure of the Labour Front reached right down to the floor of the plant, where a whole apparatus of cells, cell leaders and, in large factories, professional leaders, was installed. Wage determination was entrusted to a series of regional labour trustees, appointed by the Minister of Labour.[2] Free collective bargaining was replaced by dictatorial control of every aspect of the individual working life. The Labour Front became the most powerful single propaganda arm of the Nazi regime, an endeavour to establish the Nazi Party's own 'transmission belt' to the masses.

The Labour Front took over the social security functions of the former unions. The Labour Front nominated the lay assessors both to the Labour Courts of the Weimar Republic, which continued to exist, and to the new Courts of Social Honour established by the Nazi regime. The Labour Front acted as representative of worker and employer to either court where required. Labour Front advisory offices, which became an obligatory stage of consultation before recourse to the courts, set themselves the tasks of resolving as many issues as possible without a contest. Since the Labour Front was the advocate of the 'social peace' insisted upon by the Nazi state, its 'advice' was a factor of some importance.

In place of the class struggle in the enterprise the Nazis introduced the 'enterprise community' (*Betriebsgemeinschaft*) in which the entrepreneur acted as 'leader', the wage-earners as 'followers'. The worker now became a 'soldier of labour' participating in 'factory roll-calls' 'serving the Führer and the nation' in 'work battles' and 'labour action'. The propaganda style, its militarist rhetoric apart, had much in common with that in force around the same time, in the Russia of the Five-Year Plan.

The leisure and travel organizations of the pre-Nazi labour movement were fused into the Labour Front subsidiary Strength Through Joy.[3] Seeking to monopolize workers' leisure time by using sport and travel for political propaganda, the Strength Through Joy, with its swimming, boating and hiking activities, its own hotels and health resorts, even its

---

1. Hamburger, pp. 934–5. Another source estimates the number of Labour Front functionaries as 44,500 in 1939: see Mason, 'Labour in the Third Reich, 1933–1939', *Past and Present*, April 1966, p. 120. The size and scope of the Labour Front was clearly enormous.

2. Twelve of the original thirteen appointees were former legal advisers to employers' associations: Gottfurcht, p. 23.

3. A full account of the Labour Front will be found in Mason, 'National Socialist policies towards the German working classes', D.Phil. thesis, Oxford, 1971, pp. 214–328.

own ships and mass foreign travel schemes, achieved important propaganda successes for the Nazi regime.[1] Paid for with the deposits of 300,000 Labour Front members, the world-renowned Volkswagen (People's Car), originated as a product of a specially built factory, owned by the Labour Front, at Fallersleben near Hanover.

The Nazis achieved remarkable successes in getting the German economy under way. By 1939 unemployment was down to less than half a million. If we take into account this added employment, the stabilization rather than massive decline of wages, which followed the Nazi regime, the real living standards of the German working class must have been higher in 1939 than at the time of the Nazi conquest of power. Despite all this, amongst the working class itself, the Labour Front, whilst in the end winning acquiescence, never gained full and active support.

RE-ESTABLISHMENT OF THE GERMAN STATE

There are moments when the hard, steel like surface of society melts and becomes plastic; usually, in our age, times of war and the social discontents and upsurges which follow. These moments past, society congeals once more, but in a fresh and novel mould. This is particularly true of the origins of the present Federal German Republic and the regime on its eastern border. The foundation of each is to be traced directly to the unforeseen consequences of decisions taken by the leaders of the Great Powers in the concluding stages of the war against Hitler's Germany.

Insistence on unconditional surrender forced the Allied powers to envisage the administration of the conquered territory by the direct agency of the occupying powers.[2] The final lines of demarcation were settled in part by the strategic disposition of the British, United States and Russian armies in the final assault upon Hitler's 'fortress Germany'; in part by political decisions taken beforehand.[3]

1. Mussolini's 'Opera Nazionale Dopolavoro' was the forerunner of Hitler's 'Strength Through Joy'; see Sarti, *Fascism and the Industrial Leadership in Italy, 1919–1940*, p. 93.

2. There was originally no plans for a French zone of occupation although one was subsequently carved out of territory held by the British and Americans. French intransigence subsequently held up plans for zonal unification. This may not have been entirely unwelcome in the West. Balfour and Mair, *Four-Power Control in Germany and Austria 1945–1946*, pp. 36–7.

3. Thus, for example, Allied troops held back, allowing the Russians alone to occupy Berlin. The entry of British, United States and French troops and subsequent Four-Power administration did not take place until July although Berlin had been occupied by the Russians in May 1945: Balfour and Mair, pp. 74, 75.

The decisions taken at Teheran in 1943, at Yalta and Potsdam in 1945 all rested on the explicit assumption that Great Power unity would survive the end of the war.[1] In fact, even the wartime alliance had been full of stresses, strains and ill-concealed differences. Once the war was over the practical business of administering defeated Germany rapidly brought these differences into the open. It very soon became apparent that hopes of a united Four-Power administration of conquered German territory were illusory. Instead each segment of a formerly united German state was run as an independent economic entity, hermetically sealed, economically unviable.

The Allies had at one time seriously considered shutting down the bulk of German industry and reducing Germany to a largely agrarian state. The British zone, predominantly industrial, was burdened with a massive influx of refugees from the east, as was that of the United States. Each zone required costly external subsidies and the import of food which was in extremely short supply, to maintain even the deplorably low level of human existence at which the population subsisted in the immediate post war years. Eventually it was realized that Germany was deeply integrated into European economy, that the pauperization of the occupied territories would involve the pauperization of a large part of Europe as well.

In July 1946 the first steps towards the economic unification of the British and United States zones were put in train. In September, the United States Secretary of State, Byrnes, in a speech at Stuttgart, set a course towards restoring German economy to a state of reasonable prosperity.

Relations between the Great Powers had already suffered a marked deterioration as the nations lurched towards the Cold War. Proposals for Western zone unification, which moved towards a formalization of the divided *status quo* in Germany and tended to cut off the Russians from an effective say in the reconstruction of the Ruhr, marked a further stage in this process. The Moscow Conference to discuss a German peace treaty, called in March 1947, ended without practical result. The launching of the Marshall Plan which followed in June 1947 constituted a decisive turn towards the reconstruction of European economy and led to an open breach in the former Great Power alliance. The Russians retaliated with the foundation of the Communist Information Bureau (Cominform) in September 1947. Widespread strikes in France and Italy that year were followed by the communist *coup d'état* in Czecho-

---

1. It was these conferences that decided post war policy towards Germany, also the revisions of Germany's eastern frontiers and the mass population expulsions which followed. The Teheran Conference was held from 28 Sept. to 1 Oct. 1943, the Yalta Conference from 4 to 11 Feb. 1945, the Potsdam Conference from 17 July to 2 Sept. 1945.

slovakia during February 1948. A stable and secure West German state now became the keystone of plans for the stabilization of Western Europe in face of what was deemed a Russian threat.

In June 1948 a unilateral currency reform in the three Western zones, which bore most heavily on the employed population, cleared the way for industrial recovery. The currency reform formalized the breach between Eastern and Western zones. The Russians responded with the Berlin Blockade, which lasted from June 1948 all through the following winter until abandoned in May 1949. The blockade failed to force the Western powers to relinquish their position in Berlin. The way was left clear for the establishment of the Federal German Republic, which, following elections held in August 1949, united the territory of what had formerly been the three Western zones.

The present Federal German Republic occupies approximately half the land area of the Weimar Republic. Around one-quarter of the former German territory was involuntarily ceded to Poland at the end of hostilities.[1] The balance represents the territory of the East German regime. In the absence of any peace treaty the issue of the status and demarcation of the German–Polish frontier has been the source of continuing tension in Central Europe. However, treaties concluded between the Federal Republic, Poland and Russia in 1971–2, as part of Chancellor Brandt's *Ostpolitik*, now accept the permanence of the existing boundaries and have done much to take the tension out of this matter. The Federal Republic is more than double the size of its East German neighbour (96,000 against 42,000 square miles), its population (62 million) is more than treble that of its rival in the east (17 million). West Germany, despite territorial losses, remains by far the most powerful state in continental Europe.

GERMAN LABOUR AFTER 1945

At the conclusion of hostilities,

in Cologne 66 per cent of the houses were totally destroyed; in Düsseldorf 93 per cent were uninhabitable: 80,000 out of 180,000 houses in Frankfurt were wrecked. In Berlin, it was calculated that, at the rate of ten trains a day of fifty wagons each, removing the rubble would take fifteen years. Of five and one half million houses in the British zone, three and one half million were

---

1. The land area of the Reich in 1937 was 182,000 sq. miles. The lost territories amount to some 44,000 sq. miles. The Russians had availed themselves of a large slice of the territory of the former Polish state. By allowing the Poles to reimburse themselves at German expense they sought to ensure that Poland would stay close to the USSR in order to safeguard itself against any German attempt at restoration.

either destroyed or seriously damaged. Of 16 million houses in 'Potsdam' Germany, 2,340,000 were destroyed and 4 million more damaged at least 25 per cent.[1]

At the close of hostilities 12,000 of the 13,000 kilometres of rail track in the British zone was out of action, almost half the rolling stock was unusable and most of the rest had severe defects. Over 3 million Germans were killed in the Wehrmacht, 500,000 civilians killed as a result of air attacks and a further 100,000 in the course of fighting. Increased mortality due to the war has been estimated at 400,000. 'A pre war surplus of 1,463,000 women had increased to one of 7,279,400.'[2] The German government itself, in a reign of terror on a scale hitherto unparalleled in human history, had murdered the larger part of the 600,000 German Jews formerly resident in the territories of the Reich.

At Potsdam in 1945, the Russians, British and Americans agreed that all Germans at that time living in Poland, Czechoslovakia and Hungary should be expelled from their homes. As a result several million people were uprooted and driven across the face of Europe into the desperate sanctuary of the shrunken and now near-starving Reich. The total number of refugees has been put as high as 9 million.[3] In 1950 the refugee population in Württemberg, Baden and Greater Hesse exceeded 20 per cent of the total. In Lower Saxony it exceeded 30 per cent and in Schleswig-Holstein the proportion rose as high as 38 per cent.[4] In the years up to the building of the Berlin Wall in 1961 a further 3 million German citizens voluntarily left the 'socialist' regime in the east in order to start life anew in the Federal German Republic. There can be no doubt that the experiences of these 12 or 13 million refugees, the circumstances of their flight or expulsion, have brought great benefit to the cause of Christian Democracy in the post war years. The cause of German socialism has suffered in equivalent measure.

'At the end of 1946, sixteen months after the war was over, there were in Hamburg 10,000 sufferers from oedemas due to undernourishment.' In Cologne only 12 per cent of the children were of normal weight. According to United Nations experts, the daily requirements of calories for health and normal work was 2650 calories. The official ration in

1. Balfour and Mair, pp. 7–8.

2. Balfour and Mair, pp. 9–10. According to one account only 130,000 of the 750,000 German prisoners-of-war deported to Russia at the end of hostilities were still alive in 1955; see Prittie, *Konrad Adenauer, 1876–1967*, pp. 248–9.

3. For estimates, see Lowie, *Towards Understanding Germany*, pp. 169–70. Proudfoot, *European Refugees*, pp. 369–77. The Federal German Republic puts the figure at 10 million; 'The Federal Republic at a Glance', p. 8.

4. Dahrendorf, *Society and Democracy in Germany*, p. 107.

Germany was 1500 calories. The ration actually received often fell below 1000.[1] It was against this sombre background that the reconstruction of German society and political life began.

If one considers the total character of the Hitler tyranny, the overwhelming volume of Nazi propaganda to which the defenceless population had been exposed, the poverty, starvation and destruction in post war Germany, the revival of the German labour movement acquires an almost miraculous character. In an important degree this was due to the extent to which active and passive resistance to the government continued, even under the Nazi regime. Many socialists and trade unionists, amongst them Otto Brenner, later President of Germany's largest union, I G Metall (Metal-workers' Union), went to jail. Others, like Walter Hesselbach, subsequently director of the German Workers' Bank (*Bank für Gemeinwirtschaft*), were conscripted into penal battalions in the German army during the war. Still others, like Willy Brandt and Ludwig Rosenberg, later President of the D G B (*Deutsche Gewerkschaftsbund*), Germany's T U C, went into emigration in order to continue the struggle. Already in 1946, the membership of the S P D in the Western zones alone, a far smaller area than that of the whole Weimar Republic, exceeded 700,000. The following year membership rose to 875,000, and by mid-1948 reached a peak of 896,000, a figure which must by far have exceeded the membership in this same area before the Nazi's rise to power.

The German Communist Party (KPD), too, showed an astonishing capacity for revival. This was true not only in the Russian zone where the party was rapidly elevated to the role of a puppet government by the occupying authority. In the Allied zones too, notably in the Ruhr, the KPD made a significant comeback. In the event, however, the reparations policy of the Russians, the conduct of affairs in the Eastern zone, the forced fusion of the Social Democratic S P D in the East into a communist-run, oddly titled, Socialist Unity Party (*Sozialistische Einheitspartei Deutschlands*: S E D) did much to discredit the Communist Party in the West. Well before the mid-1950s what had once been the most powerful communist party in the world outside Russia was no longer an important force to be reckoned with at all.

THE RECONSTRUCTION OF THE UNIONS

As the Allied troops rolled into defeated Germany in 1945, they entered not only a territory in ruins, but also one in which democratic institutions

1. Balfour and Mair, pp. 14, 73–6, 131–2, 149–52. For eyewitness accounts from two very different viewpoints see Fenner Brockway, *German Diary*; Richard Brett-Smith, *Berlin '45: the Grey City*. For the general level of German production at this time, Landes, *The Unbound Prometheus*, pp. 487–9.

had been totally suppressed for twelve to thirteen years, in which every citizen had been subjected to wholesale indoctrination on what was, for Western Europe, an unprecedented scale. To those who have not experienced totalitarian rule the significance of these statements can never be entirely plain. By 1939 about one million Germans had served sentences in concentration camps on political charges. In that year the number of political prisoners held by the authorities exceeded 200,000. In the six years before, 225,000 men and women had been sentenced to approximately 500,000 years in jail on political charges. The bomb plot against Hitler in 1944 cost the German people 7000 arrests and 4980 executions by the Nazi authorities. All the more astonishing therefore that almost immediately the Allied armies arrived, the organs of the German labour movement began to reappear. By 1949 the trade unions in the Western zone alone already equalled the strength achieved in the whole land area of Germany under the Weimar Republic. Union membership soon came to exceed that of the Weimar Republic by a very wide margin. This success is the more remarkable when one takes account of the freeze on wages and hours maintained by the Allied Control Council from the inception of the Occupation, which placed close limits on the scope for trade union action.

The division of occupied Germany into four military zones (British, American, Russian and later also French), at first rigidly demarcated one from another, did nothing to make the reconstruction of the unions easier. In the Western zones where zonal authorities provided little or no direct material aid, where interzonal union links were at first prohibited, unions developed on a local basis and then spread upwards and outwards. The process was slow and cumbersome, not least through the provisions for Occupation supervision and control.

The situation was very different in the Soviet zone. As early as 10 June 1945 an eight-man provisional committee, appointed by the Soviet military government, announced itself as the Federation of Free Trade Unions (*Freier Deutscher Gewerkschaftsbund*: FDGB). This rump committee then set about the establishment of an organization to justify its claim. In the months that followed, sections of a highly centralized FDGB, controlled and initiated by this self-appointed clique at the top, were set up throughout the Soviet zone. The FDGB was from the beginning firmly under the control of the Communist Party and its Russian advisers.[1]

The trade union leaders who emerged in the Western zone, in the main veterans of the Weimar era, were uniformly 'determined to avoid any splintering of the new trade union movement into ideological factions. They were in favour of a single organization grouping all

1. On this, Matthew A. Kelley, 'The reconstitution of the German trade union movement', *Political Science Quarterly*, March 1949, pp. 26–7, 36.

workers regardless of ideology, religion or party affiliation.'[1] A decision
in favour of reconstruction of the unions along industrial union lines
had already been taken by a conference of German trade unionists held
at Stockholm, where there had long been a concentration of political
emigrants, in February 1944.

Nevertheless important differences of opinion developed regarding
the proper structure for the reconstituted trade union organizations.
The British zone included the Ruhr and with it the larger part of German heavy industry. It was here that the issues were fought out. One
tendency, with its spokesman Hans Böckler and support in the Ruhr,
favoured a single centralized union centre with a number of integral
industrial departments, rather than a series of autonomous unions linked
on the federal model of the pre-Hitler ADGB, the TUC or the American AFL–CIO. In Hamburg, however, already in November 1945, there
existed a federation of thirteen autonomous unions with an organized
membership of 120,000.[2] The issue was not one of trade union concern
alone. The communist controlled FDGB, which operated in the Soviet
zone, was already organized on a unitary model. Böckler was no
communist (he later became President of the DGB) but the fact remained that the KPD exercised considerable influence in the Ruhr,
where in 1946 some 38 per cent of works councillors in the pits were
elected on a KPD ticket, as against 33 per cent for the SPD and 14 per
cent for the Christian Democratic Union (CDU). As late as 1947 the
KPD could still muster 31 per cent against 46 per cent and 14 per cent
for its rivals.[3] A centralized West German trade union federation would
be more easily fused with the FDGB should the occasion ever arise.[4]
Equally, if the KPD could ever capture control of such an apparatus, it
would prove difficult to dislodge it from such a position of centralized
command. The issue of post war trade union structure thus became a
matter of some importance to the occupation authorities in the British
zone.

In September 1945 the TUC was invited by the War Office to send a
delegation to Germany. The delegation, during its trip, which lasted

1. Lepinski, 'The German Trade Union Movement', *International Labour
Review*, 1959, vol. 79, p. 65.

2. The first unions in Hamburg had been dissolved by the British in June
1945, 'because they were alleged to be too strongly political in character':
Friedmann, *The Allied Military Government of Germany*, p. 158.

3. In 1947, the number of pit workers councils controlled by the KPD fell
from 25 to 14 whilst those controlled by the SPD rose from 28 to 44. Sixty
failed to elect a clear majority. In 1948–9 the KPD share of the poll fell from
15 to 13 per cent: Kelley, 'Communists in German labor organizations',
Journal of Political Economy, June 1949, pp. 216–17.

4. At the end of 1946 the (artificially inflated) membership of unions in the
Soviet zone was 4,000,000, in the (artificially retarded) British and U.S. zones
2,700,000, a matter of importance in this regard. Friedmann, p. 156.

from 22–29 November, was induced to take a stand on the serious problem of German trade union structure, then under debate. The delegation, which included Jack Tanner of the engineers and Will Lawther of the miners, delivered its verdict in a letter to the Ruhr organization, dated 27 November 1945:

We are disturbed about your desire to have one trade union for the North Rhine (i.e. Ruhr) Province, even if you have separate sections for each industry. Even if this desire comes from the workers we feel it will mean in practice all effective power will ultimately reside in a small group of men at the top. Although arrived at by a different path, this will be the same position as when the Nazis took power . . . Our experience as representing the oldest trade union movement in the world is that . . . the strength of trade union-ism depends largely upon . . . members' . . . active participation in all deci-sions . . . If the workers are too far away from the centre . . . they will lose interest and merely obey orders. We therefore, as representatives of a great trade union movement, which sincerely desires to see a real democracy in Germany, ask you to modify your plan so that a small number of unions shall have complete autonomy over the industrial affairs of their members.[1]

The TUC's advice, which was backed by the refusal of both British and American occupation authorities to permit the formation of cen-tralized unions on a zonal basis, tipped the scales against the Böeckler proposals. In April 1947 the unions of the British zone, now with Occupation authorization, approved the constitution for a zonal federa-tion, the German Trade Union Federation, the DGB. Böckler was elected President.

In November of that same year, a joint trade union council linking organizations in the British and American zones was established. Later the unions in the French zone were also allowed to join.[2] In 1949 the three Western zones were fused into one. In August elections to the Bonn Parliament of the newly established Federal Republic took place. At its Munich Congress, the following October, the DGB with its sixteen autonomous unions was consolidated into a national union confederation for the whole of the Republic. Headquarters were established at Düsseldorf in what had formerly been the British zone. Böckler was re-elected as President. With a membership of 4,800,000 in 1949, the DGB soon enrolled more than 6 million workers, the most powerful trade union federation in continental Europe.

As will be seen the reconstruction of the German unions took place in conditions of extreme difficulty, complicated by the local implications of the conflicts between the Great Powers of the wartime alliance. What was at stake in Germany was not merely the aspirations of millions of workers, but also a struggle between two power blocs for domination of

1. Quoted in Trades Union Congress, *Trades unionism in Central Europe*.
2. Grebing, *History of the German Labour Movement*, p. 173.

the central European heartland. The original restrictions on trade union organization in the West were due to a pro-employer bias and an exaggerated concern for *some* of the niceties of democratization. Their removal was linked to the hardening of lines of struggle in the Cold War. In the East the rapid creation of the FDGB from the top down, the ruthless elimination of socialist influence from the unions and the forcibly fused SED, were a function of the Russian desire to ensure hegemony in the Eastern zone. Between 1945 and 1949 union leaders took part in no less than nine meetings in an endeavour to form a single all-inclusive union federation covering both East and West. The last meeting, in August 1948, adjourned on failure even to agree an agenda. Each meeting foundered on issues which, whatever form they nominally assumed, were essentially a function of the growing rift between East and West. The existence of free trade unions on the DGB model was incompatible with the Russian-supported, centralized, stalinist, Ulbricht regime. The existence of centralized, party controlled, state-servile, 'labour front', unions, was unacceptable equally to the workers of the Federal Republic and to the Western powers.

UNIONS IN GERMANY

The sixteen industrial unions affiliated to the DGB are each independent organizations, freely affiliated to the central confederation. The largest, IG Metall, enrols over 2·3 million members. DGB membership overall exceeds 6·5 million. The policy of the individual unions is decided at congresses held every two or three years. Delegates to these General Assemblies (*Gewerkschaftstag*) are elected by secret ballot from local and district units of the unions. The General Assembly itself elects a full-time management committee (*Hauptvorstand*) which conducts the day-to-day business of the union, also a larger executive council comprising both full-time management committee members and unpaid representatives of the rank and file. The work of management committee and executive council is, between conferences, supervised by an elected general committee. 'Attached to the Executive Council is an advisory body in which the various districts are represented according to size. In this body the district representatives sit together with members of the Council.'[1] The base of each union is the local, and above this, district association. Internally each union is organized into vertical trade groups. Strike, victimization, pension and sickness benefits are provided for members, as is free legal aid where required. In line with the fresh start made by the DGB after 1945 all sixteen industrial unions are organized on similar lines.

1. Lepinski, 'The German trade union movement', *International Labour Review*, 1959, vol. 79, p. 66.

The rank order, in terms of enrolment, of the German union movement, in 1971 showed I G Metall at the head with 2,300,000 members,
almost one third of the D G B's affiliated membership. Next came the
Public Service, Transport and Communication Workers (*Gewerkschaft
Offentlichedienste Transport und Verkehr*: O T V) with 990,000. There
followed the chemical workers with 600,000 members, the builders with
over 500,000, the miners and the railwaymen, each around 400,000; the
textile, postal, food and restaurant workers, each in the vicinity of
300,000. The remaining seven unions rolled up only some 700,000
members between them.

One natural consequence of industrial union organization seems to be
that some categories benefit from a 'catch all' jurisdiction, whilst others
do not. Thus in the Federal Republic, the metal-workers and the public
service unions have grown very large. Other jurisdictions, smaller in
scope and more closely defined, such as banking, education and the
media have remained a great deal smaller. One result is that the larger
unions like I G Metall, Public Service, Chemicals and Building can
afford to steer a course fairly independent of the D G B should they so
decide. The smaller unions, like those for teaching and science
(120,000), leather-workers (59,000), agriculture and forestry (43,000),
art (34,000), are more in need of aid, counsel and in the end, support,
from the D G B.

German labour law carries an inherent bias against the conflictual
solution of disputes. This bias has been stringently interpreted by
jurists and the courts. As a result the right to strike has become circumscribed by severe constraints. In part as a reflex to these judicial provisions, the rule books of German unions customarily require that the
strike is to be utilized only as a measure of last resort. The constitution
will normally lay down that an official stoppage requires a prior vote
giving 75 per cent majority of all those likely to be involved. Even after
this authorization a strike does not become obligatory. The final decision
whether to launch a stoppage or not still remains with the union executive. In the event of a major stoppage the D G B must be notified beforehand and given the opportunity to express an opinion.

Most post war German union leaders gained their formative experience
in the middle ranks of the labour movement during the Weimar regime.
Many were victims of the Nazi era. The German unions operate within
the context of a divided Germany, whose eventual fate has been, and
remains, one of the central issues in the Cold War. In these circumstances it is not surprising that the German unions, which are powerful
organizations, have been cautiously led by moderate men.

Constitutionally without political involvement the unions are led in
the main by Social Democrats. Most unions also contain a liberal sprink-
ling of Christian Democrats in their leadership. Ever since the trans-

formation of the SPD from socialist to a 'Peoples' Party at the Bad
Godesberg Congress in 1959, the DGB unions have shown an increasing
tendency to adopt specific social and political perspectives of their own.
The DGB itself stands somewhat to the left of the SPD.[1] Within the
confederation IG Metall has been a customary spokesman of the left and
finds allies amongst the unions organizing chemicals and print.

GERMAN TRADE UNION CONFEDERATION – THE DGB

The DGB is governed by a Federal Congress (*Bundeskongress*) which
meets every three years. Congress delegates are elected directly from
locals of the sixteen affiliated unions. The President of the DGB, the
two Vice-Presidents, who each head one of the eight departments
handling DGB affairs, and the six other department heads, are all
elected at this *Bundeskongress*. Each holds office subject to re-election
at three-year intervals. The President is the chief spokesman of the
DGB with status analogous to the Secretary of the TUC.

Main policy issues, the general line of conduct of DGB affairs,
between meetings of the *Bundeskongress*, are decided by the DGB
Federal Executive Council (*Bundesausschuss*). The Federal Executive
Council comprises the President and two Vice-Presidents of the DGB,
the six remaining department heads, members of the executive boards of
all sixteen affiliated unions, plus the members of each of the nine *Land*
executives (*Landesbezirkevorstand*) of the DGB. The Federal Executive
Council meets at three-monthly intervals. Amongst other powers it
has the right to pass on elections to the Land executives. These are not
valid without Federal Executive Council endorsement.

A disputes committee (*Revisionskommission*) comprised of one representative of each of the sixteen affiliated unions works alongside the Federal
Executive Council. This body, among other tasks, acts as a conciliator
in jurisdictional disputes. In the event of a failure to agree the matter is
referred to an arbitration tribunal whose decision is final.

The Federal Executive Council is clearly a somewhat unwieldy body.
In between the meetings of the Federal Executive Council, the general
execution of policy laid down by the Congress and Council is in the
hands of the Federal Executive Board (*Bundesvorstand*). The *Bundesvorstand* comprises the President, the eight DGB department heads
(which includes the two Vice-Presidents), plus the Presidents of the
sixteen industrial unions. Day-to-day conduct of DGB business is
handled by a nine-man committee of the *Bundesvorstand* (*Geschafts-
fuhrender-Bundesvorstand*) comprising the President plus the eight
department heads.

1. For an indication of the DGB outlook see *The Basic Programme of the
German Trade Unions Federation.*

In addition to its national organization based at Hans Böckler House in Düsseldorf, the DGB also maintains regional offices, each with a jurisdiction approximately corresponding to one of the nine *Länder* of the Federal Republic.[1] Each regional office is governed by a *Land* executive, election to which needs to be approved by the *Bundesausschuss*.

Each DGB *Land* executive region is divided into DGB districts (*Kreise*) of which there are 270 in all. Of these the great bulk are in the four most strongly organized *Länder* of the Federal Republic, Bavaria (67), Nordrhein-Westfalen (59), Baden-Württemberg (44), Niedersachsen (36). Where membership warrants there may also be city and regional council below DGB *Kreise* level. On all these bodies DGB affiliates are represented in accordance with their strength in the locality. DGB activities are financed from fees paid by affiliated organizations. Each pays a standard 12 per cent of its own dues income to maintain the organization and activity of the federation. In case of special need the full executive board may propose a special levy on the funds of affiliated unions, but such a proposal requires Congress's approval before it becomes effective.[2]

The DGB has never concluded nationwide confederal contracts with the employers on the lines of those formerly negotiated between the CGIL and Confindustria in Italy. Nor has the DGB ever been the master of its affiliated unions in the same way as some confederations in France and Italy. Yet if this be true, the fact remains that now, as during the Weimar Republic, the hierarchy of union officials does exercise disproportionate powers, both within the DGB and its affiliated organizations.[3] Collective bargaining remains the jealously guarded prerogative of the affiliated unions. Nevertheless, as will be appreciated, one of the main functions of the DGB is to seek to produce a common union front in face of the employers and the state.

German union dues, by the standards of France and and Italy, are high and consistently well paid, despite the fact that the 'check off' (deduction of trade union subscriptions from wages) is the exception rather than the rule. Dues are related to wage income with an objective of a scale equivalent of from one to one and a half hour's pay per week. Dues in IG Metall range from a monthly minimum of DM 5·20 to a monthly maximum of DM 32. One result is that by comparative European standards German unions are soundly based and very rich. An important part of these large union funds have been invested in enterprises under

1. Baden-Württemberg, Bavaria, Berlin, Hessen, Niedersachsen, Nordmarck, Nordrhein-Westfalen, Rheinland-Pfalz, Saar.
2. Galenson, p. 305.
3. For a stringent criticism of the working of bureaucratic control in German unions see Mincus, in Dietz *et al.*, *Le Syndicalisme allemand contemporain*, pp. 75–90.

direct or indirect union control. The union sponsored *Büchergilde Gutenberg*, founded in 1924, was one of the world's first book clubs. Between 1945 and 1967 union funds financed the building of some 500,000 housing units, many of these through the union-owned *Neue Heimat* housing and property development group. Germany's fourth largest bank, the *Bank für Gemeinwirtschaft*, is owned by the unions. Germany's second largest insurance company, the *Volksfürsorge*, with 5·5 million policy-holders and 10 per cent of the total life assurance business, is also under union control. The DGB also owns a travel savings bank, the BSV, with 700,000 accounts, and jointly with IG Metall a travel company, GUT, which sold 200,000 package tours in 1972. The *Neue Heimat* building society has built over 250,000 dwellings and has an output of some 25,000 housing units a year.[1]

The unions are also involved in the administration of the social security system. At the present time tens of thousands of union officers are associated with the administration of sickness, employment, injury and pensions insurances schemes, on the basis of the equal representation of the assured and the employers.

The industrial unions affiliated to the DGB seek to organize all workers, whether blue- or white-collar, within their ranks. Considerable success has been achieved. The DGB Public Service union includes amongst its 960,000 members soldiers and officers serving in the *Bundeswehr* on behalf of whom it is an officially recognized bargaining agent. Reports indicate that 77 per cent of DGB members were paid by the hour in 1968. The remaining 23 per cent were either salaried employees in private industry (14 per cent) or government officials.

Nevertheless the DGB has met very real problems in its endeavours to step up the level of white-collar organization. German white-collar workers, more than most, have a highly developed sense of status. Many are reluctant to marshall themselves in the ranks alongside workers from the shop floor. One result has been the emergence of a separate union federation, organizing white-collar workers alone, the German Salaried Employees' Association (*Deutsche Angestellten Gewerkschaft*: DAG), which now organizes some 500,000 members. Some 700,000 of the Federal Republic's civil servants are also organized outside the DGB in their autonomous *Deutsche Beamtenbund* (DBB). An autonomous policeman's union enrols a further 140,000 members. The DGB, the DAG, and the public service unions listed above are Germany's main union organizations. The German Christian Workers' Union Confederation (*Christlicher Gewerkschaftsbund Deutschlands*: CGB) which arose from an unsuccessful attempt to split the DGB on religious–confessional lines in the 1950s is not a factor of significance at the present time.

Although separate white-collar organizations exist outside and separate

1. Hesselbach, *Co-operative Enterprises in West Germany*, pp. 16–53.

from the DGB, these indicate more a sense of craft differential than major conflicts in social and political outlook. Whereas before Hitler's rise to power German unions were divided on confessional and political lines, now they are substantially united. The police union has for some time past sought admission to the DGB. The constitutional barrier to its admission was lifted at the DGB's Extraordinary Federal Congress, held in 1971. In the event that the police union should be accepted into affiliation, similar moves by other salaried employees' organizations might follow. Not the least success of the DGB has been its ability to unite both socialist and Christian workers within its ranks. When one takes account of the power of Christian Democracy in Germany and looks at the unions divided on confessional lines in some other countries of the Nine this unity emerges as a considerable achievement.

One ought also to draw attention to the extent to which German unions have ensured that an unprecedented influx of voluntary migrant labour into the German economy has neither undermined union wages and conditions, nor resulted in uniformly deplorable conditions for the migrants themselves. In June 1971 official statistics recorded the number of foreign workers as 2,170,000 or some 10 per cent of the labour force. Significantly these were not from the neighbouring EEC territories of France, Belgium, Luxembourg and the Netherlands. The bulk of the foreign workers came from four countries, Yugoslavia (470,000), Turkey (430,000), Italy (410,000) and Greece (260,000) none either culturally or linguistically close to Germany.[1] Reports suggest that around one half of the labour force in the Ford plants at Cologne are of Turkish origin. In this case, the large scale of the plant and the presence of union organization ensure a measure of protection and job advancement. Immigrant workers employed by small undertakings are by no means so well placed. The fact that these vast numbers of foreign workers have been received with so little social friction is a major achievement. On the other hand there can be no doubt that the immigrant worker as a rule suffers badly from social isolation, that his opportunities for job advancement are unduly limited, and that in respect of housing in particular his situation leaves a very great deal to be desired.

German union strength stands at around 8 million out of a total

1. It should not be thought that migrant labour is a new phenomenon in Germany. Much of the harvest labour force for the East Prussian estates always came from abroad. The Ruhr labour force was recruited from as far away as Poland and Hungary. The Catholic faith of these immigrants served to divide them from the local, predominantly Protestant, population. As long ago as 1907, there were over 1 million foreign workers in Germany. In the last years of the Second World War the number of non-German nationals employed on forced labour in Germany exceeded 5 million. On this, Bohning, *Foreign Workers in Post-War Germany*; Weckelmann, 'Immigrant workers and trade unions in the Federal Republic', *Free Labour World*, Brussels, Dec. 1970.

working population of some 23 million. Given that the unions are disproportionately strong in the key sectors of the economy, the figures somewhat understate the real level of union power. German labour, whilst it retains a great deal of scope to grow still further, nevertheless remains amongst the best organized in the world.

INDUSTRIAL RELATIONS

The nature of much of German labour relations is difficult for the outsider to grasp, largely one feels because it partakes of social and cultural conceptions less firmly established elsewhere. Thus the prevailing concept of the state does not spring from any perception of an aggregated series of individualized Hobbesian men. Rather, in line with preceding German thought, it springs from a philosophy that puts the state in the centre of social life. Thus it has been written that 'the two basic principles underlying the economic provisions of the Weimar Constitution were the supremacy of the group over the individual and the ultimate supremacy of the state over the interests of its constituent groups'.[1] Certain attitudes of strongly inculcated upward deference seem deep-rooted in German society, not least the high value placed on security by the average worker and his unusually marked respect of received authority.[2] For this the universities, which until very recent years have survived largely unchanged in structure and outlook from the imperial regime, bear heavy responsibility.[3] An organic view of society seems to have led to endeavours to seek legalist solutions to problems of social conflict. The study of law occupies a high place in German universities which are themselves 'almost exclusively public, government controlled', with the faculty involved in 'prescribed career patterns and formalized status systems which are borrowed from the administrative bureaucracy'.[4] More than half of the German higher civil servants have legal training. Law students, it has been suggested, are drawn from the more conformist elements of a quite unrepresentative, class-selected, university elite, with a pronounced authoritarian bias. The tendency for the intellectual to see himself as a member of a service class, rather than a member of a liberal profession or an entrepreneur in the field of ideas,

1. Reich, *Labor Relations in Republican Germany*, p. 14.
2. M. Edelman and R. Fleming, *The Politics of Wage-Price Decisions*, pp. 85, 120–21.
3. The universities, it was written in 1947, contain 'too large a proportion of ex-conservatives and nationalist professors who have just managed to avoid denazification, but whose outlook cannot possibly provide the inspiration for a new educational approach'. Friedmann, p. 182. The Allied Occupation authorities who talked a great deal about democratization but did nothing in this crucial field share the blame.
4. Dahrendorf, pp. 276–9.

would seem to explain a great deal of the conformism which continues to characterize German society. There can certainly be no doubt that the class, authoritarian bias of the legal profession[1] has shown marked impact on the nature and interpretation of labour law in regard to union conduct, strikes and industrial relations in general.

The specific nature of Germany's transition to an industrial society has also exercised its own direct effect on the character of the wage relationship which has emerged within German society. The concept of the Federal Republic as a 'social state' means that the freedom of the employment contract is limited 'not only by laws and government regulations but also by concepts of social rights and obligation based on custom, practice and social justice'.[2] It is this conception of the wage relationship as something other than the one which has 'pitilessly torn asunder the motley feudal ties that bound man to his "natural superiors", and has left no other nexus between man and man than naked self interest, than callous "cash payment"',[3] which underlie much of the complex legalism of German industrial relations. As a result the German law concerns itself with the employment contract in a whole series of matters which elsewhere would be outside the sphere of legal enactment altogether. Thus the 'law of socially unjustified dismissals' insists that the employer shall be able to give 'socially justifiable' reasons in cases of dismissal. In such matters his decision can be contested in the Labour Courts as a whole body of legal doctrine bears witness. One consequence, among many, of this 'social' view of the wage relationship has been to ensure that the temporary 'lay-off' as an employer reaction to falling consumer demand is practically unknown in German industry.

LABOUR RELATIONS AND THE WEIMAR REPUBLIC

The present pattern of labour relations in the Federal Republic of Germany owes its origins and most of its institutions to the Weimar Republic. The need of the Kaiser's government to win labour collaboration in the First World War led to the first moves by state and business to come to terms with organized labour. In November 1918, under the pressure of the revolutionary upsurge which established a government of People's Commissars in Berlin, the German employers' federation conceded a whole series of longstanding union demands. These included the eight hour day and recognition of the unions as proper representatives of the workers. Provision was made for the establishment in every enterprise employing more than fifty persons of works councils

1. A tendency already clearly apparent under the Weimar Republic; see for example, Neumann, *Behemoth*, pp. 27–9, 361–4.

2. Seyfarth *et al.*, *Labor Relations and the Law in West Germany and the United States*, p. 119.

3. Marx and Engels, *Communist Manifesto*, Centenary edn, 1948, p. 16.

charged with various social functions, including overseeing the terms of collective agreements. In the two years that followed over 2 million new members joined the union ranks. These sudden gains largely reconciled the union leaders to the existing order. The unions became a particularly staunch bastion of the Weimar regime.

The gains made by the organized workers of this time were real and should not in any sense be underrated. Thus Article 159 of the Weimar Constitution for the first time specifically guaranteed the right of combination. Article 165 similarly endorsed the right of wage-earners to participate collectively in the determination of their working conditions. The change from the pre war situation, sardonically described by the economist Brentano as one in which 'the German workers enjoy the right of combination but if they make use of it are punished',[1] amounted to a minor revolution. At the outbreak of the war only 2 million workers had been covered by union agreements. In the post war years, union agreements, which in one form or another covered between 12 and 14 million workers, became the decisive method of wage determination.

THE FEDERAL REPUBLIC

When, in the aftermath of the war and the first years of the Federal Republic, the pattern of labour relations began to be laid down, the structures created under the Nazi regime were put almost entirely on one side. Both the individual German unions, and the DGB were reformed anew, with a total breach in continuity. On the employers' side, there emerged the German Confederation of Employers' Associations (*Bundesvereinigung der Deutschen Arbeitgeberverbände*: BDA). German private employers are accustomed to bargain through the intermediary of the BDA and its thirty-seven industrial and fourteen regional associations, rather than on their own behalf. The BDA is a strongly disciplined body which not only bargains for its members but also provides strike insurance, conducts propaganda and lobbies in their interest. The coal, iron and steel employers, where full co-determination is practised, are not members of the BDA.[2] Subject to these exceptions and that of Volkswagen, which is accustomed to bargain separately, the great bulk of private German employers are members of the BDA.

1. Quoted in Reich, p. 37. The Constitution provided that 'the right of combination for the protection and promotion of labour and economic conditions is guaranteed to everybody and to all professions. All agreements and measures which attempt to limit or restrain this liberty are unlawful.'
2. For one account of the activities of the BDA see Braunthal, *The Federation of German Industry in Politics*.

COLLECTIVE BARGAINING

There can be little doubt that with collective contracts covering 17 million workers the unions are a decisive force in German economic life. German collective bargaining procedures are governed by the Collective Agreement Statute (*Tarifvertragsgesetz*) as enacted in 1949 and subsequently amended in 1952. In essence the modes and procedures follow those already established under the Weimar regime.[1]

Although national bargaining between employer association and individual union may take place, negotiations are usually conducted at *Land* or regional level. Union–employer bargaining at plant level is unknown. The closed shop is illegal. Confederal bargaining between the DGB and the BDA, on the lines at one time customary between the CGIL and Confindustria in Italy, is unknown.

In respect of each industry, and covering a specified region, a general frame contract agreement (*Manteltarifvertrag*) establishes obligatory general principles and remains valid for three years or even longer. The *Manteltarifvertrag* lays down working hours, overtime rates, holiday pay and holiday entitlement, shift-work regulations and procedures for settlement of disputes. Within the framework established by the *Manteltarifvertrag* and perhaps covering a smaller area there may be one or more wage-contract (*Lohntarifvertrag*) regulating actual wage levels. Duration of the *Lohntarifvertrag* will normally be shorter than that of the frame agreement, probably one to two years.

Separate agreements may also be concluded regulating such matters as holiday entitlement and apprenticeship procedures. Thus by no means all contract provisions need arrive on the bargaining table at the same time. The Federal and *Lande* ministers of labour have powers, on application, to declare that union–employer association agreements represent obligatory minimum standards. Owing to tight labour market conditions these provisions seem to have been a declining importance in recent years.[2]

Conclusion of an agreement commits the signatories to an obligation to keep its terms. Failure of either employers' associations or individual unions to hold their members in line can result in reference to the Labour Court or to the termination of the contract. In cases of dispute, comprehensive conciliation services are provided by the *Land* govern-

1. For an account of recent events, see Reichel, 'Recent trends in collective bargaining in the Federal Republic', *International Labour Review*, Dec. 1971.
2. Between 1949 and 1960, 41,882 collective agreements were registered by the Federal Minister of Labour. Of these 165 were declared universally applicable at Federal level, 1296 at *Land* level, overall less than 3 per cent. Whether the numbers covered were proportional to the contracts involved is not clear.

ments. The DGB and the BDA have also adopted their own model conciliation agreement, recourse to which, in case of need, each has recommended to its constituents. Where a conflict of terms occurs between the union agreement, the individual terms of employment, or other provisions governing the worker's wages and conditions, the employee is entitled to avail himself of the most favourable option. Differences of interpretation are a proper matter for reference to the Labour Court.

Once an agreement is concluded the labour law of the Federal Republic, following that of Weimar, considers that both parties have assumed an implicit duty to maintain industrial peace. Jurists and the courts have interpreted this intention stringently in the post war years. Thus only unions may call strikes. Unofficial strikers are liable to prosecution. Thus 238 unofficial strikers were fined a total of £75,000 in 1956.[1] A strike in which the 'losses caused by the dispute do not stand in a reasonable relationship to any advantage which may accrue from it', for example a stoppage in transport, hospitals or public services may similarly be the subject of prosecution. While the right to strike of manual workers in the public sector is recognized, the situation of salaried public employees is by no means so clear. Established civil servants are denied the right to strike. The right of non-established public servants to strike is disputed on the grounds that it is not the employer but the *Bundestag* that determine salaries. Therefore it is alleged that a strike would possess a political connotation. Strikes for other than purely economic objectives may be deemed political and declared illegal. Certainly any stoppage designed to exercise pressure on either Federal or *Land* governments would be so construed at the present time. Strikes during the term of an agreement are banned, irrespective of whether specific provisions are included in the agreement or not. Unions are forbidden to bring economic sanctions to bear on an employer, in respect of renewal or renegotiation, before the terms of the agreement have legally expired. Even then a strike may be held illegal if the court deems all avenues leading towards a peaceful settlement have not been explored. Thus in 1958 the employers took IG Metall to court for an alleged breach of this 'peace obligation' and collected judgement for damages of DM 10 million.[2] There is no limit to the damages which may be awarded by the Labour Court.

One might add that whilst the union's right to strike is severely restricted, the employer's liberty to lock out has been subject to no such demanding constraint. In 1963, when selected plants with a labour force of 100,000 were struck by IG Metall, the BDA was able to lock out

1. Their unions paid the fines.
2. In the end the damages remained unpaid. The unions and employers settled for a conciliation agreement instead.

350,000 workers, 250,000 of whom had not been engaged in the stoppages at all.

WORKS COUNCIL

The structure of German industrial bargaining, with its emphasis on regional agreements, has meant that formal union structures have possessed only limited relevance to union activity at the level of the enterprise. Nevertheless there exists a longstanding view that the workers are entitled by a kind of 'natural right' to a say in fixing terms of employment through direct relations with the employer. The concept may be traced back at least as far back in German history as the Revolution of 1848 and the Frankfurt Assembly of 1849. The German Revolution of 1918 brought this issue to the fore again. A law of 1920 provided for the establishment of the works council as a permanent statutory agency charged with representing the workers in relation to the employers. In these years conflicts between works council and employers were frequent, hard-fought and bitter. Employers did not hesitate to exercise sanctions against militant employees and troublesome works councils. Thus, in 1929, a government inspector reported that in one locality 40 per cent of large undertakings were without a works council altogether.

The works councils sprang into activity again almost immediately Nazi rule was over; in the Ruhr especially, they played an important part in economic reconstruction. The works council became an obligatory part of the machinery of industrial relations in the Federal Republic with the passage of the Works Constitution Act (*Betriebverfassungsgesetz*) enacted in October 1952. At present some 300,000 works councils are reported in existence.

The German works council (*Betriebsrat*) is a body analagous to the French *comité d'entreprise* and the Italian *commissione interne*. Endowed with powers greater than either its French or its Italian counterparts, the works council has become a pivotal point in the whole structure of German industrial relations.[1]

Although elected by the workforce, the powers of the works council are so defined as to make it an intermediary between capital and labour rather than in the full sense a workers' representative organization. Thus section 49 of the Works Constitution Act lays it down that in pursuit of the tasks allocated to them 'the employer and the Works Council shall work together in a spirit of mutual trust . . . for the good of the undertaking and its employees, having regard to the interests of the community'. The works council does in fact perform functions which elsewhere would be performed by collective bargaining, but it does so

1. For an easily accessible account, see Sturmthal, *Workers' Councils*, pp. 53–85.

in a specifically German way, and in a fashion which broadly differentiates its own tasks from those of the unions. In British terms the works council performs some of the functions of a joint production committee and some of the functions of a shop stewards' committee, without being exactly equivalent to either.[1]

The works council is entrusted with responsibility for the enforcement of the terms of the collective agreement, for supervising the application of existing factory legislation, promulgating plant regulations and works rules, handling employee grievances, administering social welfare services attached to the undertaking and exercising limited rights over the use of the employers right to hire and fire. The works council also possesses the right to negotiate works agreements with management regarding aspects of working conditions not covered by collective agreement, notably piecework rates and incentive payment systems.

In recent years some unions have expressed discontent with the extent to which the works council rather than the union has become the means for determining the real wage level. Regional agreements in the nature of things leave some margin between the wages which the least efficient and most efficient employers can afford to pay. In engineering and textiles a wage drift of up to 50 per cent in excess of negotiated union rates has been reported. Both the chemical and metal workers' unions are now seeking to achieve an 'opening clause' which would entitle them to undertake plant and company bargaining within the framework of the existing regional agreement. At present, although an employer may unilaterally allocate special increases to his workers, or do so via a 'works agreement' with the works council, the union is legally forbidden to negotiate direct. The employer obviously prefers dealing with the negotiators of the works council, who are less experienced and legally barred from launching a stoppage in the event of a dispute, to dealing with the union. The employer too, can, if he chooses, absorb locally negotiated special increases into subsequently negotiated union increases. A similar divergence from a negotiated union rate would be open to appeal as a breach of agreement. There can be no doubt that the rigidity of regional agreements and the resulting gap between negotiated rates and real earnings was a prime cause of the flush of unofficial stoppages which brought some 150,000 workers out on strike in September 1969.[2]

The terms of the Works Constitution Law expressly forbid the works

1. The union 'confidence men' in the plant are not empowered to bargain on the union's behalf. There are moves, notably by I G Metall, to increase the status and powers of 'confidence men' in the plant. A union 'confidence man' may of course be elected to the works council, but in that case he exercises power only by reference to the second function, not the first.

2. See Markmann, 'Les grèves spontanées de l'automne 1969', in Spitaels, ed., *La Crise de relations industrielles en Europe*, pp. 167–70.

council to exercise economic sanctions against the employer and enforces an obligation to exhaust all internal modes of conciliation before reference of the matter in dispute to an outside body.[1] The works council is expressly excluded, by statute, from organizing its own independent sources of revenue and is dependent on the employer for the finance and facilities essential to its effective operation. Works council meetings are private and not open to attendance by members of the workforce at large. Works councillors are bound by strict regulations regarding the protection of 'company secrets' which limit their freedom to report freely to other members of the work force. A works councillor reporting confidential business to his union, even involuntarily, may serve up to one year in jail. 'The Works Council,' one commentator has written, 'is situated between the economic interests of the employer and those of the employees, although it is of course nearer to the employer interests.'[2]

The works council is chosen from the whole body of the employees at a properly constituted election. Chairman and vice-chairman are drawn respectively from the ranks of wage and salary earners. Election is for a three year term. The works council varies from one to thirty-five members, according to the size of the enterprise. Special provision is made to ensure the protection of white collar interests by the council. Elections are conducted on the basis of competing lists of candidates, rather than individual candidatures. Each list cover must cover twice as many candidates as there are council members. Seats are allocated by a system of proportional representation which delivers places in relation to votes polled and the location on the respective list. Elections are conducted at the employer's expense, during working hours. Disputes regarding the outcome of elections may be referred to the Labour Court for settlement. Although unions play no formal part in election proceedings, in fact, most candidates on election lists are union members. Ninety per cent of works councillors are union members.

The works council, unlike the French *comité d'entreprise*, meets separately, on its own account, without the employer present. Meetings with the employer, to discuss outstanding issues, take place not less than once a month. Works council meetings take place during working hours with the expenses, including lost time, paid by the firm. In plants with over 100 employees, works councillors may claim the right to deal with complaints and inquiries, during company time, at the employer's expense. In large plants the chairman of the works council and one or

1. The Works Constitution Law, approved by the Federal Parliament at the end of 1971, has enlarged the powers of the works council, in particular in regard to matters of personnel policy and redundancy. The unions' right to enter the enterprise has also received added legal sanction: see *DGB Report*, Düsseldorf, April 1972.

2. Seyfarth *et al.*, *Labour Relations and the Law in West Germany and the United States*, p. 98.

more of the other members are likely to be engaged full time on works council business.[1]

In cases where the works council exceeds ten in number (i.e. in plants with over 1000 employees) the law makes provision for the council to elect a smaller executive to handle day-to-day business. Sub committees may also be established to deal with special aspects of works council business. Where there are several works in a single company, a central works council, comprised of representatives from each plant, may be set up to deal with common problems.

The works council is required to report to a works assembly (*Betriebsversammlung*) not less than once every three months. At these meetings, which are held during working time, the employer has the right to attend and to speak. Expenses are for the charge of the company. The works assembly may comment on works council activity or make proposals for future action. Such proposals are advisory only and not binding. Union representatives may attend and participate in both works council and works assembly meetings, provided a request to this effect is made by one quarter of the members.

In sharp contrast to the experience of earlier years, relations between works councils and employers have been smooth under the Federal Republic. In part this has been due to changed social circumstances, in part to the nature and composition of the works council itself. It seems clear that employers, once forced to concede the presence of union organizations, have been sophisticated enough to prefer dealing with works problems through the works council, rather than by direct union–employer negotiations. German workers change their jobs infrequently. Works councillors tend to be long-service employees who are frequently re-elected time and time again. One result is the build-up of strong company loyalties. Shrewd management, too, is able to present problems to the works council in a fashion which leads directly to the solution which management considers best. Lacking knowledge, professionial advice and full access to company books, the works council finds it difficult to make alternative proposals. Management is able to direct works council attention into fringe areas and away from issues which are considered central to company policy. Finally, although the works council has power to refer disputes to arbitration, it lacks any effective sanctions of its own. Without such sanctions, and especially the willingness to have recourse to them, it is difficult to see how a much greater level of independence could be maintained.

1. There were some 14,000 works councillors elected for approximately 25,000 enterprises in 1961. DGB, *The Educational Activities within the German Federation of Trade Unions*, p. 7.

STRIKES

During the last two decades the general level of recorded industrial disputes in Germany has been so low that one might fairly say that for practical purposes they did not exist at all.[1] Between 1958 and 1962, man-days lost in the Federal Republic were proportionally only 2 per cent of those in the USA. In 1968 the Federal Republic lost 25,000 man-days through recorded strikes. That year Britain lost 4 million.

The widespread view that this phenomenon is in some sense a function of deferential qualities inherent in the German labour force is a little difficult to sustain in the light of the historical record. In the years before the First World War the German working class was the most politically advanced in Europe. In any one year between 1920 and 1924 the man-days lost through strikes exceeded those lost in the whole decade 1950–60. Clearly some more sophisticated explanation must be sought.

The causes of the post war quiescence of the German labour force would seem to fall under several heads. In the immediate post war years the prostration of the economy forced standards of the workers and their families down so close to subsistence level that it is arguable that the labour force did not in fact have the capacity to conduct large-scale struggles at all. In the years that followed, the fruits of recovery, although limited, were so disproportionately significant, the starting point having been so low, as to undermine any will for hard-fought disputes. This must have been particularly true of the millions of hard pressed refugees from the East who had to commence their lives again from the beginning in the Federal Republic.

Thirdly, the Cold War, the presence of the stalinist regime across the border, cautioned the bourgeoisie against precipitating any major struggles, thus making possible a loyalist approach by union leaders which in turn was backed by the members. Fourthly, continual legal encroachment on the right to strike has inhibited, if only for the time being, the incidence of industrial disputes.

It is arguable also that a unitary industrial union structure makes it possible for unions and employers to impose a greater degree of discipline on the workforce than would be possible where confederations or

1. Whether all disputes are recorded is another matter. A strike, as legally defined, may take place only between a legally recognized union and a legally recognized employers' association. What in Britain would be termed an 'unofficial stoppage' or in the USA a 'wildcat strike' is termed in Germany an 'Arbeitsniederlegung' or 'work pause'. Between January and March 1970, there were at least forty in German engineering alone. Whether these appear in the official statistics seems questionable: *Labour*, London, Oct 1970, p. 15.

craft unions are in competition for membership one with another. The substitution of the works council for union 'in-plant' bargaining probably also has some effect. This may well have lowered the level of stoppages although at the price of reducing the employee's degree of job control and his ability to exercise individual autonomy at the point of production.

One also needs to take express account of the fact that within living memory the German working population has twice been the victim of terrifying inflation. The older generation not only saw its savings wiped out in 1923, it also lived to see the experience repeated by the 'currency reform' of 1948 which reduced the value of the mark by 90 per cent at one stroke.[1] In such circumstances arguments, however ill founded, that union wage claims cause inflation are bound to carry especial weight with union members and the population at large. This has certainly conduced to moderation, even excessive moderation, in union demands and thus limited the very probability of union–employer conflicts and disputes. 'Inflation' to the German worker represents a trauma comparable to, but of greater significance than, that which 'unemployment' represents for his counterpart in Britain.

One ought to add that strikes in Germany, in the nature of things, are likely to be more serious affairs than the momentary stoppages customary in France and Italy. The German employers' association, BDA, commands massive mutual assistance funds. These funds are available to finance and maintain employers engaged in strikes or lock outs. A German trade unionist who pays a monthly contribution of DM.15 on a monthly income of DM. 1000 will receive between DM. 660 and DM. 880 in strike pay monthly. In such circumstances a stoppage, once entered into, is likely to be a long drawn out struggle, rather than a brief skirmish.[2] Employers, aware of the facts, are more likely to settle without a strike than they would be if unions were weak, disorganized and financially insecure. The heavy weight of the potential combatants means that part at least of the absence of strikes in the Federal Republic may be put down to a balance of mutual terror.

LABOUR COURTS

The Labour Courts, like other organs of the industrial relations system of the Federal German Republic, trace their origins to antecedent bodies established under the Weimar regime. The vast crop of labour laws and

1. The German currency moved from 39,750 marks to 72,006 million marks o the dollar between January and October 1923: Rosenberg, *The German Experiences with Inflation*, pp. 6, 13.

2. Thus an official strike launched by IG Metall in Schleswig-Holstein in October 1956 was not concluded before February 1958.

administrative regulations inspired by the Weimar Republic were deemed unsuited for the interpretation by the protracted, formal and expensive procedure of the normal courts. The outcome was the passage in December 1926 of an act establishing a system of labour law courts in the German Reich. This statute, substantially amended in 1953, remains the basis of the Labour Court system today.

In line with the prevailing preference for legalistic rather than conflictual solutions to problems of industrial relations, the Labour Courts are bodies of major importance in the Federal Republic at the present time. These courts exist at three separate levels.

The local Labour Court (*Arbeitsgerichte*) is a court of first resort and the place at which most cases are heard. Appeals from local Labour Court judgements may be made to the *Land* Labour Court (*Landesarbeitsgerichte*). A Federal Labour Court (*Bundesarbeitsgerichte*) handles both appeals from *Land* Labour Court decisions and also cases of major legal importance in their own right. A prime function of the Federal Labour Court is to ensure a unified interpretation of legislation which might otherwise be treated very differently in the different *Länder* of the Republic.

Local and *Land* court judges are appointments of the *Land* government. The composition of the Labour Court at local and *Land* level depends on whether it is hearing cases which arise from the individual employment contract or matters which arise from the collective bargaining relationship. The composition of the court will always include one professional judge specializing in labour law. Where individual employment cases are concerned the professional judge is supplemented by two lay assessors chosen by the *Land* government from panels of qualified persons drawn up by unions and employers' associations. In matters relative to collective bargaining, the number of lay assessors chosen from the respective panels rises to four, two being chosen from each panel. In individual cases the court thus numbers three, in collective bargaining cases five.[1]

The jurisdiction of the Labour Court is wide and comprehensive. Included are disputes between employers and employees arising out of the individual employment relationship, disputes arising out of the interpretation of collective agreements; liability for damages in respect of strikes or lock outs which may be held in breach of agreements; decisions regarding certain matters related to the functioning of the works councils not expressly provided for elsewhere.

Much of the legal interpretation of Federal labour law under the Weimar Republic was markedly hostile to the intentions of its initiators. One commentator has gone so far as to see in the rulings of the Reich

1. There were some 5000 lay judges in 1962; D G B, *The Educational Activities*, p. 6.

Labour Court (equivalent of Federal Labour Court today) a 'definite tendency towards the reshaping of labour laws in the spirit of the fascist corporate state'.[1] The German legal profession remains profoundly unrepresentative of the nation at large. Post war decisions have tended to follow the tradition of an earlier era although in a less forthright and pronounced fashion. In their tendency to restrict the right to strike in particular, post war judgements and legal opinions seem, to this author at least, to err grossly on the wrong side of equity between the conflicting parties.

CO-DETERMINATION

At its founding congress in 1949 the DGB set itself important social objectives, notably labour participation (co-determination) in the management of the economy, and 'collective ownership of the key industries, particularly mining, steel, chemicals, power and the principal centres of communications and credit'.[2]

In respect of co-determination (*Mitbestimmung*) the union demands went a great deal further than the somewhat illusory rights embodied in the Works Councils Act of 1920. The unions were asking in essence for the institutionalization of arrangements that had existed in the then de-cartelized steel industry since 1947. The post war collapse had seen what proved to be a temporary eclipse of German business management which had been totally identified, at all echelons, with the Nazi regime.

At the conclusion of hostilities the property of the big industrial monopolies in Germany was confiscated under SHAEF Law No. 52. I G Farben, with 169 factories in the Western zones, was taken over in autumn 1945, Krupp on 16 November, all pits in the British zone on 22 December. Ownership of the steel industry was transferred to the Military governments as trustees on 20 August 1948. In the case of the Ruhr pits, the British authorities declared themselves to be acting 'as trustees for the German people' and added that 'those industries will never be returned to their former owners'. The sequestrated assets remained in a kind of limbo until the Cold War and the restoration of German sovereignty brought a return of these properties to private capitalist ownership.[3]

The unions themselves had at one stage advanced radical socialization proposals.[4] The task of re-starting production among the ruins had been

1. Otto Kahn-Freund, quoted in Reich, op. cit., p. 265.
2. *Report* of the Constituent Congress of the DGB, Cologne, 1949, p. 318.
3. Grosser, *Western Germany*, p. 96.
4. See for example, Friedmann, *The Allied Military Government of Germany*, p. 160.

assumed by works councils, re-constituted from Weimar days. The DGB justifiably considered that the maintenance and extension of these rights was essential if Germany was to be safeguarded from a relapse into another business-financed Nazi regime. When, in 1950, it became obvious that the newly formed federal government was unwilling to concede the DGB demands for a voice in key management decisions, a crisis arose. Under official DGB leadership, 90 per cent of the workers in the coal, iron and steel industries voted for a political stoppage. In the face of this strike threat the government thought again. In May 1951 an act conceding many of the DGB demands for co-determination in the coal, iron and steel industries passed into law.

German company law rests on a three tier structure, the share-holders, a supervisory board appointed by the shareholders (*Aufrichtsrat*), and a board of management (*Vorstand*) appointed by the supervisory board. Under the provisions of the law of 1951, the workers and their unions acquire 50 per cent representation on the supervisory board and the right, in effect, to appoint one of the three working directors. These provisions apply to all coal, iron and steel enterprises with more than 1000 employees.

The supervisory board comprises eleven members, among them four appointed by the owners, four by the employees. Each party also nominates a fifth member not connected with the firm in any way.[1] The eleventh 'neutral' member is a joint nomination with provision for arbitration in case of inability to agree.[2] Two of the four labour representatives come from staff employed in the enterprise, one worker and one employee. The remaining two are union appointees, one nominated by the union organizing the plant, the other by the DGB.

The three man board of management comprises a business manager, a production manager and a labour manager. The labour manager is by common consent the nominee of the worker–trade union side and cannot be dismissed without their approval. The supervisory board normally meets three to four times a year in sittings of three to five hours' duration.

The DGB was dissatisfied with the restriction of the *Mitbestimmung* provisions to basic industry and continued to agitate for its extension to the rest of the economy. The outcome was the Works Constitution Law of July 1952 which extended a much more limited form of co-determina-

1. In the case of the workers' representation the fifth member is a nominee of the DGB.
2. In the case of the larger firms the size of the board may rise to 15 to 21 members. The same principles of proportionality apply. In 1962, there were 560 board members who were union–workforce nominees and 90 labour directors. The number today one presumes is larger: DGB, *The Educational Activities*, p. 45.

tion to the larger firms in the rest of German industry.[1] The 1952 law provides for only one-third worker representation on the supervisory board and none whatever for appointment of a labour director.[2] Union representation is precluded and the DGB has strongly criticized these arbitrarily limited provisions from the beginning. In the absence of parity representation, with the consequent worker veto which this involves, hopes that the law would make any significant inroads in management prerogative and behaviour have proved largely illusory.

Whilst it would be absurd to suggest that *Mitbestimmung* has revolutionized labour management relations in Germany, there does seem evidence that it has made inroads into the traditional highly conservative and paternalistic pattern of labour relations in heavy industry. *Mitbestimmung* has materially eased and humanized the post war run down of the coal industry in particular. Nevertheless the gulf between workplace and supervisory board remains very wide.

In the seventy or so coal, iron and steel enterprises there are over 500 posts as workers' representatives to be filled. These positions are highly rewarded. They represent a source of patronage for the union hierarchy and contribute to some extent at least to the formation of a privileged stratum within the Labour Movement.[3]

Overall, the German labour movement is firmly convinced that co-determination in heavy industry has proved a marked success. The demand for the extension of *Mitbestimmung* to the rest of the economy is a major plank in the programme of the DGB. The unions want co-determination extended, by law, to all enterprises which fulfil at least two of the following three criteria: more than 2000 employees, more than DM 7·25 million capital, more than DM 15 million annual turnover. Adoption of these criteria would bring the 500 largest German private companies within the scope of the co-determination proposals.

Support for the union view has been provided, unexpectedly, by the report of a special commission, headed by Professor Biedenkopf, set up in 1968 to look into the whole question of co-determination. To the dismay of some of its advocates the 180-page Biedenkopf Report, published in 1970, gave a clear endorsement to the success of co-determination in coal, iron and steel. Instead of proposing to limit existing co-determination provisions, Biedenkopf recommends extension. The report proposes to strengthen limited co-determination in

1. For a full account see DGB, *Co-determination*, pp. 5–12. (This work provides a succinct account of the background, principles and practice of co-determination.)

2. There were some 7000 appointments in force under this Act in 1962: DGB, *The Educational Activities . . .*, p. 6.

3. The DGB ask that all union nominated board members contribute part of their salary to the work of the union Co-determination Foundation at Düsseldorf. Many do so. The income of the Foundation exceeded DM 12 million in 1962.

those private companies where it already exists. Thus if the Biedenkopf recommendations are passed into law, the composition of a twelve-man supervisory board (*Aufsrichtsrat*) would be altered to consist of six members nominated by the shareholders, four workers' representatives (two chosen by the unions) plus two members jointly nominated by both groups. The shareholders' representatives would thus lose their absolute majority on the supervisory board. In the event that workers and jointly appointed nominees voted together a veto on the wishes of the shareholders would result.

GERMAN SOCIALISM AFTER THE WAR

In October 1945 the British Occupation authorities took over the Ruhr coal industry, later announcing that 'these industries would never be returned to their former owners'. The British Foreign Secretary, in a speech to the House of Commons in October 1946, denounced the magnates of the Ruhr industries as being 'closely allied to the German military machine, who financed Hitler'. The Foreign Secretary continued:

We have no desire to see those gentlemen or their like return to a position which they have abused with such tragic results ... Our intention is that those industries should be owned and controlled in the future by the public ... The case for the public ownership of those heavy industries was never stronger than it is in Germany today.[1]

In 1946–7 a former high-ranking British Control Commission official could write, that

a majority of organized political opinion in Germany today, but in particular the entire organized working class in Germany, believes that the socialization of basic industries is the only logical and constructive answer ... to the evils of uncontrolled capitalism ... the association of the industrial class with the Nazi regime and the subsequent dispossession ... by the Allies. To ignore this faith means ... taking the side of the industrial and business class against the organized working class and a large proportion of the independent voters.[2]

Feeling on this question was so strong that the 1947 Ahlen Programme of the Catholic Christian Democratic Union (CDU) went so far as to state: 'The capitalist economic system has not satisfied the vital state and social interests of the German people. After the frightful economic, political, and social collapse, the consequences of a criminal policy of

1. Ernest Bevin, Hansard, *House of Commons Debates*, vol. 427, col. 1515/15, 22 Oct. 1946, see also Bevin's declaration of 4 Aug. 1947 referred to by Friedmann, p. 143.
2. Friedmann, pp. 165–6.

power, only a new order that starts again from the foundations is possible.'[1]

The Ruhr, the industrial heartland of Germany, was part of the British zone. If a policy of nationalization had been determinedly carried out in the initial months of the Occupation there is no doubt that it could have been enforced without difficulty. The will proved lacking. Once the winds of the Cold War began to blow, a reconstructed Germany was seen as an essential bulwark against the threat of Russian state power in the East. When the Rhineland–Westphalia Diet voted for nationalization of industry in the Ruhr this decision was vetoed by British Military government. Similarly, when the *Land* of Hesse decided on the transfer of the chemical giant I G Farben to state ownership the US Occupation authority enforced a veto, and this after a plebiscite carried out on their own instructions had expressly confirmed popular support for the original decision.[2]

In these post war years the Social Democratic Party (SPD) was by far the largest political party in the Western zones. Given a free run it would probably have emerged as the major party in the East as well. Led by the concentration camp veteran Kurt Schumacher, re-established on essentially pre-Hitler lines, the SPD by 1946, enrolled over 700,000 members and 875,000 by 1947. The German business class responsible for Hitler's rise to power had fallen with him and was now discredited. The SPD considered that the German bourgeoisie would never be able to recover their former position. 'Socialism is no longer a distant goal, it is the task of the day,' declared the 1946 Congress of the SPD.

The SPD was the only really democratic, anti-Nazi force in Germany. If the nation had been free to elect a government in these first post war years it seems certain that the SPD would have been returned to power. Authority during these years rested not with the German people but with the Occupation authorities. By the time the German state was re-established in 1949 the Cold War had begun, and the capitalist system, aided by the Occupation forces, had drawn second breath. The 1949 elections, in a fashion quite inconceivable in the first years after the war, returned not the SPD but a Christian Democratic Union coalition, to govern the Federal Republic.[3]

The German Communist Party (KPD), the largest outside Russia in pre-Hitler days, made a rapid recovery after 1945. Membership in the

1. Quoted in Abendroth, *Wirtschaft, Gesellschaft, und Demokratie in der Bundesrepublik*, p. 126 ff; see also Balfour and Mair, *Four-Power Controls in Germany and Austria*, p. 205.

2. Friedmann, pp. 144, 146.

3. It has to be remembered that the pre-Hitler SPD also drew strong support from what was now the Russian zone so that it by no means follows that in a united Germany the outcome would have been any different.

Western zone has been put as high as 300,000.[1] KPD agitation in support of enormous Russian reparation claims, which amongst other demands required the dismantling of whole factories and their shipment to Russia, a social policy which placed it a long way to the right of the SPD, did nothing to add to this support. Nevertheless, even as late as 1949, when the tide had turned firmly against it, the KPD could still muster 1,360,000 votes, 6 per cent of the total, and return fifteen members to the Bonn Parliament.[2]

What finally discredited the KPD was the course of events in the Russian zone. In the first months of 1946, under Russian pressure, the socialist party (SPD) in the Eastern zone was shut down and forcibly fused into a communist-controlled, ironically titled Socialist Unity Party (SED). Berlin, in the midst of Russian zone, remained under four-power control. Here the SPD continued to exist. In 1932 the communist vote in Berlin had exceeded that of the SPD. In the October 1946 elections the SED vote failed to reach that attained by the KPD alone in 1932. Overall the SPD vote exceeded that of the SED by a majority of two and a half to one.

The KPD vote at the Federal election of 1953 was down to 600,000, some 2 per cent of the total vote. The behaviour of the Ulbricht regime in the East reduced the KPD to a largely ineffectual sect in the years that followed. Banned by the federal government as an unconstitutional party in 1956, the KPD continued to maintain a skeletal organization underground in the Federal Republic. A change in federal policy allowed the party to be reformed as the *Deutsche Kommunistische Partei* (DKP) in 1969-70.[3] There is nothing to suggest that the DKP will be more successful in the future than the KPD in the post war years already past.

The Cold War, the seemingly permanent division of Germany, the unexpected boom and economic recovery, the CDU's successive victories at the polls in 1949 and 1953, led to a marked shift in SPD policy. Under Schumacher's leadership the SPD had fought vigorously against Western proposals for German rearmament. Schumacher's death in 1952 and the passage of the rearmament proposals into law cleared the way for a re-examination of SPD policy and attitudes. The defeat of the SPD in the September 1953 election, following the Russian repression of the East German Rising the previous June, proved a turning point.

Schumacher had represented the Marxist tradition in which the

1. Vincent, *The Socialist Register, 1964*, p. 70. The KPD won ministerial posts in some *Land* governments. Grebing, p. 163.
2. Grebing, p. 163-4; Vincent, pp. 71-3. Strangely enough 'No annexations, No reparations' had been a key Communist demand in 1917. Now the French communists went so far as to vote in the Chamber for separation of the Ruhr and Rhineland from Germany: Hill, *The Struggle for Germany*, p. 17.
3. The SPD remains illegal in the East.

SPD had been born. A new group of leaders, the *Burgermeister-Faktion*, with a power base amongst SPD-controlled administrations in Bremen, Hamburg and Berlin, now began a move for the transformation of the SPD into a classless 'People's Party' of liberal reform. At the Bad Godesberg Congress, held in November 1959, their campaign was crowned with success. Marxism was written out of the party constitution. The SPD began to cultivate a new 'People's Party' image designed to attract middle class and confessional groups hitherto outside its clientele. The aim, finally realized in 1969, was to replace the CDU with a SPD-led government on a platform of moderate social reform.

The present SPD, although it retains the original title and continues to attract the preponderant part of the German working class vote, has little in common with the organization which first bore that name. The shift in outlook between the SPD which saw socialism around the corner in 1947 and the SPD whose leaders regard socialism as utopia in 1974, seems at first sight to be astonishing. Yet it is difficult to resist the thought that to a marked degree German socialism has been the victim of forces beyond its own control. The monopoly of power held by the military occupation in the crucial post war years, the expulsion of millions of Germans from the East, the flight of 3 million more from the dictatorial statized regime in East Germany, the Berlin Wall and the anti-socialist feeling these events engendered confronted the SPD with obstacles which even the most correct principles, the most consummate tactics and leadership, might well have proved unable to surmount.

Whether, as a new generation replaces the old, these factors will continue to carry the same weight as hitherto seems open to doubt. The experience of the post-1950 generation has very little in common with that which went before.[1] The long term stability of the regime in the East remains questionable. Student revolt and the unofficial stoppages in the Ruhr in autumn 1969[2] indicate the nature of the forces that might be released in the West as the relationship of factors changes in the years to come. Classical Marxism, in retrospect, seems to have been in many ways a strangely simplistic doctrine. Whether the experience of the twentieth century will lead to a revival of socialist ideas in a more relevant and sophisticated form remains to be seen. If this is to be so, Germany may well be the place.

1. The age gap due to war losses and the Hitler regime implies an abrupt separation between the present and succeeding generation of working class leaders and activists. Changes when they come, might be sweeping.
2. On this see Markman, 'Les grèves spontanées de l'automne 1969 dans la République Fédérale d'Allemagne', in Spitaels, ed., *La Crise des relations industrielles en Europe*, pp. 160–74.

6. Italy

The peculiar and specific characteristics of the Italian labour movement have been conditioned by a social experience unique amongst its associates in the territory of the European Economic Community. Until the last twenty years Italy has been an almost Balkan peninsula, studded with cities famous in a bygone age, with modern industry closely confined and limited to the northern 'iron triangle' of Milan, Genoa and Turin.

In a nation with about the population of Britain, a labour movement split into three politically divided union confederations organizes at most one half, probably nearer one quarter, the number of workers organized in Britain's TUC.

Italy has existed as a unified state only since 1861. Unification, despite Garibaldi's original heroic initiative, was carried out from above rather than below. In this mountainous peninsula with poor communications, where local loyalties have been a traditional base of allegiance, political unification did little to bring them to an end. Italian allegiance continued to be awarded to a heterogeneous cluster of local, regional and even family loyalties, rather than to any all pervading national idea. Generations of foreign occupation have formed a mentality which views government and the state as alien and hostile phenomena. An essentially Napoleonic constitution under which prefects, rigidly controlled from Rome, are charged with overseeing every detail of local administration serves to perpetuate this outlook amongst the population. The unique position occupied by the Vatican as the long standing administrative centre of an immensely rich cult of global proportions, the power exercised by the hierarchy within Italian society itself, are further factors reinforcing qualities of upward deference among the people as a whole.

Italian industry, concentrated almost wholly in the North, grew up as an island in a sea of largely unchanged social and economic relationships. At the time of unification the Central Italy railway line ended at Bologna. Italy's total rail mileage only amounted to some 2800 km. That same year British mileage was seven times this figure, French five times, German six. The rail routes broken through the Alps in the closing years of the century served to link the North with France, Germany and central Europe, rather than with its own national hinterland in the Centre and the South. There thus developed a form of dual development with highly capitalized modern industrial plant existing alongside semi-stagnant peasant and artisan economy. This pattern, to a marked degree, has survived up to the present day.

Italian industry emerged in a period of rapid growth between 1880 and the outbreak of the First World War. Lacking iron ore, possessing only the smallest supplies of low-grade soft coal, heavy industry was dependent from the first on tariff protection and the import of costly raw materials. As much of industry depended 'on the state for its prosperity it was from the first a corrupting influence, and it financed newspapers, deputies and high-ranking officials in order to persuade the government that such a costly, artificial industry was necessary for the country's greatness and should be protected to the limit'.[1] Thus Italy never saw the development of the *laissez-faire* 'night-watchman' state. Entrepreneurial activity and governmental decision were interlocked to a surprising degree from the very beginning.

Agriculture continued to account for 56 per cent of the Italian labour force as late as 1921, when industry in all its spheres still embraced only some 24 per cent of the population.[2] As late as 1969 the agricultural labour force continued to total slightly more than 4 million or some 21 per cent of total employment.[3] The proportion of the labour force in Britain engaged in agriculture had fallen to 9 per cent by 1900. Even in France, by comparison a case of retarded development, the figure in 1901 stood at 33 per cent, a far lower level than in Italy.[4] Official statistics of illiteracy, hardly likely to underrate the problem, show a 75 per cent illiteracy rate in 1861, 48 per cent illiteracy in 1901, 27 per cent illiteracy in 1921, and a continuing substratum of 13 per cent overall as late as the 1950s. In the South, Basilicata and Calabria, where the problem was greatest, illiteracy continued to run as high as 30 per cent.[5]

Italy, with a population larger than that of France, occupies little more than half of the area and of this some 40 per cent is mountain and a

1. Mack-Smith, *Italy*, p. 155.
2. Neufeld, *Italy*, pp. 298–9. In Great Britain during 1841 industry already absorbed 46 per cent, agriculture only 23 per cent.
3. Istituto Nazionale di Economia Agraria (INEA), *Annuario dell' Agricoltura Nazionale*, vol. 23, 1969, p. 135.
4. Neufeld, p. 298. 'In the Community as a whole the agricultural sector accounts for 14 per cent of the working population; in France it is 14 per cent, in Italy 22 per cent and in Germany 9 per cent. In certain regions of the Community it may be 50 per cent or more'; Michael Berendt, 'An end to farm surpluses?', *European Community*, London, Sept. 1971, p. 9.
5. For an excellent insight into the weaknesses of the Italian education system see The School of Barbiana, *Letter to a Teacher*.

further 40 per cent hilly terrain. Population, 26 million in 1861 at the time of unification, rose to 36 million in 1911, and some 54 million at the present time. In the years 1900 to 1920 emigration rarely fell below 500,000 a year, and reached a peak of 870,000 in 1913. Between 1900 and 1914 the enormous number of 8·5 million Italians emigrated. Despite this massive human outflow, population growth in Italy has consistently outmatched employment opportunity. Italy remains today by far the largest source of migrant labour in the European Economic Community, with some 1·5 million workers employed abroad in France, Germany, Switzerland and the UK.

Overpopulation, open and concealed rural unemployment, has been accentuated by the system of land tenure. As late as 1957 large properties of over 250 acres, 0·3 per cent of the total, occupied 38 per cent of the productive land. At that time 5,400,000 (54 per cent) of Italian holdings were less than 1·25 acres in extent. Too many, even after bitterly hard labour, failed to provide adequate subsistence. Such unfortunate peasants were driven to supplement their income by joining the over-crowded ranks of *braccianti*, day labourers, working on larger farms. The *braccianti*, then one quarter of the rural labour force, were fortunate if they received the legal minimum wage and doubly so if they could find work for more than 100 days a year.[1]

In addition to the regular labour hired on annual contracts (*salariati*) of the more modern farms of the Po valley in the North and the *braccianti* of the large estates in the Centre and the South, there exists an alternative form of rural employment, the *mezzadria*, or sharecrop tenancy.[2] Prevalent in Tuscany, Umbria, the Marches and the hill country of Emilia, the central region of Italy, sharecrop tenancies involved some 1,750,000 people, 23 per cent of the agricultural work force, in 1950 and around half that figure even today. It is no coincidence that the areas where this anachronistic social relationship has prevailed have been amongst the greatest strongholds of the communist and socialist parties in Italy.

Modern Italian society from the very beginning has thus been characterized by a process of dual development in which modern industry has been grafted onto a substantially unchanged and outdated social base. Endowed after unification with the institutions of parliamentary democracy, Italy has lacked, even up to the present day, the support of social forces sufficient to ensure that they function effectively.

The parliamentary reforms instituted in 1861 cloaked a system in which the suffrage was restricted to a small and unrepresentative oli-

1. Carlyle, *Modern Italy*, p. 124–6.
2. Under a sharecrop tenancy the landlord receives a proportion of the crop in lieu of rent providing certain limited (and sometimes valuable) services in exchange.

garchy. Some 300,000 in 1861, the electorate did not exceed 3,000,000 until the election of 1913 when it was raised to 8·5 million. Participation at the polls fluctuated between 50 per cent and 60 per cent in the years before 1914. In the South especially, the survival of pre capitalist relations of near feudal obligation and reward (*clientela*) led to a system of pocket boroughs at the disposal of the dominant elite. One participant, the former prime minister Bonomi, 'estimated that three quarters of the electoral districts in Italy were feudal enclaves or private perquisites where there was never a serious contest. The moral significance of an election,' Bonomi concluded, 'would emerge just from that hundred or so seats where there was a genuine fight.'[1]

In these circumstances there developed a system of jobbing and corruption in political affairs which typified the British Parliament of the eighteenth rather than the twentieth century. This system of *trasformismo*, based on the absence of clear cut party divisions, the ability of judiciously administered patronage to 'transform' the opponents of yesterday into the government ministers of today, became the standard method by which parliamentary majorities were composed. Although the balance shifted between outright military and police repression to liberal and almost enlightened reform, the system of rule, rooted as it was in backward, rural economy, remained always essentially the same. It was under such a system, against such a system, that the Italian labour movement was born.

RISE OF THE LABOUR MOVEMENT

The Italian Socialist Party (*Partito Socialista Italiana*: PSI), established at Genoa in 1892, was heavily influenced by the thought and organization of the German SPD. The PSI, with its local, regional and national organization, mass individual membership, its national press, the formally constituted authority of its elected party organs to which its parliamentary deputies were responsible, established a pattern which in the end all its rivals were forced to follow. Within twelve months the PSI was able to claim an affiliated membership of 107,000 members in some 300 organizations. The socialist vote, 26,000 in 1892, rose to 135,000 in 1897, and 1·8 million in 1919. The PSI elected 33 deputies in 1900 and 156 in the election of 1919.

There were a number of factors behind this phenomenal growth. The unification of Italy, conducted essentially from above, which left the social aspirations of the masses and sections of the intelligentsia unfulfilled, did not set in motion sufficiently deep seated processes of struggle to produce a feeling of involvement with the new regime. The Church hierarchy was alienated from the secular state, not least by the

1. Mack-Smith, p. 221.

annexation of the Papal States and the occupation of Rome in 1870. One result was that local priests were by no means averse to encouraging popular agitations against the new regime and even the formation of primitive 'white' Catholic agricultural labour unions. The hierarchy's unwillingness to permit Catholic participation in the electoral and parliamentary processes of the lay Italian state weakened one major source of electoral competition the PSI might otherwise have had to face.

The Italian section of the First International had claimed a membership of 26,000 in 1864. Although the majority undoubtedly adhered to Bakunin rather than to Marx, a part at least of this tradition came over to the PSI at its foundation. The PSI also attracted support from intellectuals of national standing. The university professor Antonio Labriola announced his adherence to Marxism in 1889. *Critica Sociale*, founded at Milan in 1891 by Filippo Turati and Claudio Treves, has remained an influential voice of socialism up to the present. The party's growth coincided with the emergence of large scale industrialism, the growth of large combines such as FIAT, Ansaldo, Pirelli, Breda and Montecatini in the North. Thus to some extent the emergence of political socialism and industrial capitalism took place side by side. Italian agriculture had undergone a radical transformation in the 1870s and 1880s. The large numbers of day labourers and sharecroppers created in the process provided a ready audience for the socialist message.

The electoral and organizational strength of the PSI was buttressed by major expansion in labour unionism which took place under socialist inspiration after the turn of the century. Agricultural labourers set up their own national organization, *Federterra*, in 1901. A confederation of existing national unions (*Confederazione Generale del Lavoro*: CGL), claiming 250,000 members, was set up in 1906. Local Chambers of Labour, uniting all the unions in a given locality, had begun even earlier. By 1901 the number had risen to fifty-five. A rival Catholic union movement, the *Confederazione Italiana dei Lavoratori* (CIL), grew rapidly after 1906, establishing its first main base in agriculture, its second in textiles. Growth did not take place easily. One authority has estimated that forty workers were killed and 202 wounded in the course of labour disputes between 1900 and 1904.[1]

The high proportion of agricultural unionists, who constituted around half the CGL membership and the important role played by the Chambers of Labour combined to give an especially radical tinge to the unions in these years. Rural unionism operated in an isolated and extremely hostile environment. Labour disputes tended to be unusually violent and to demand tactics of mass demonstrations and widespread all-inclusive local strikes, if they were to be brought to a successful conclusion.

1. Rinaldo Rigola, quoted in Horowitz, p. 67.

Viewed in retrospect, the parliamentary wing of Italian socialism does not seem to have been so soundly based. Filippo Turati, the theoretical spokesman and parliamentary leader of Italian socialism, and with him the party majority, seem to have exaggerated the stability of bourgeois democracy in Italy, and to have been markedly over-optimistic about the ease with which a peaceful transition to socialism might be made.[1] Giovanni Giolitti, Prime Minister almost without interruption from 1903 to 1914, early concluded that the uprising of the working classes was an 'unconquerable movement'.[2] Accordingly this unusually able politician sought by a process of conciliation and reform to incorporate the socialist and working class movement within the ambit of the existing regime. As a result, Turati's policy of seeking gradual reform, while the working class movement accumulated strength and became better able to transform Italian society on socialist lines, assumed considerable credibility. Italian socialism from the beginning thus subsumed within the framework of Marxist terminology both reformist and revolutionary attitudes. Each equally possessed legitimate bases in the uneven development of Italian society.

The level of violence used against the working class movement nevertheless remained high enough to spark off a general strike in 1904. The Giolitti regime's decision in 1911 to launch an aggressive war for the conquest of Libya, then Turkish territory, was met with the call for a general strike by the CGL. The Libyan war drew marked hostility from the PSI. Three right wing leaders who supported the government were expelled from the party. The Reggio Emilia conference in 1912 enthroned the party left wing as the acknowledged leadership. Lazzari was appointed General Secretary, Mussolini became editor of the party daily *Avanti!*

Under Mussolini's editorship *Avanti!* adopted a near insurrectionary tone. Circulation trebled. PSI membership doubled in the next two years. In the 'Red Week' of June 1914 events in many parts of Italy assumed the character of an insurrection. The Marches and the Romagna declared themselves independent republics. Soldiers were disarmed, arsenals occupied. In one case at least a despairing general surrendered his troops to the insurgents.[3]

FIRST WORLD WAR AND AFTER

The Italian government, after secret and disreputable bickering for terms and the use of secret service funds to whip up a spurious inter-

1. See Arfé, *Storia del Socialismo Italiano*, pp. 97–103, 247–8, 257–8.
2. Quoted in Horowitz, pp. 48–9.
3. Horowitz, pp. 56–7; Neufeld, pp. 243–4, 349; Borghi, *La revoluzione mancata*, pp. 36–42; Sprigge, *The Development of Modern Italy*, pp. 108–10.

ventionist agitation to silence an initially hostile parliamentary majority, finally brought Italy into the war on the side of the Allies on 23 May 1915. The war was never popular. The PSI, unique among the socialist parties of Western Europe, inoculated against war hysteria by the Libyan episode of 1911, refused support outright. Under the slogan 'Né aderire – Né sabotare' – neither support nor sabotage the war it disowned all responsibility for the proceedings and sought a negotiated peace. The war itself raised the social tension already apparent in 1914 to an even higher level. Forty one deaths were recorded in Turin alone when police fired on bread rioters in the summer of 1917. The discontent of a peasantry forcibly conscripted into the trenches of a grossly mismanaged war in which they felt no interest was at least one major cause of the rout at Caporetto in the autumn of the same year. At the end of hostilities in November 1918, official records listed 150,000 deserters; one million cases of indiscipline were awaiting trial by court martial.[1]

The end of hostilities saw the ruling elite largely fail to achieve the territorial and other gains for which they had begun the war. The population as a whole, the rank and file of the army in particular, were enormously radicalized by their experiences. Not only socialists, but also demobilized soldiers, peasants and industrial workers saw the transformation of Italian society by a revolution on the Russian model as an immediate prospect.

The Socialist Party, now led by its left (*Maximalist*) wing, while preaching the imminence of revolution had no practical programme to bring it about. Labour union membership rose rapidly. The CGL claimed over 2 million members in 1920, the CIL over 1 million. The unions made major gains all along the line, achieving the eight-hour day in 1919, surpassing pre war real income levels by 1920. Yet when in August 1920 the metal-workers in Milan, responding to a lock-out, occupied the factories in a move which rapidly acquired general and semi-insurrectionary proportions, neither the CGL nor PSI had any clear idea what course to pursue. The return to work in September 1920, in exchange for purely economic gains, marked the end of the post 1918 high tide of revolutionary fervour.

In the countryside the tumultuous growth of unionism and socialist militancy had called the dominance of the rural landowners into question. In a movement initiated in the Po Valley, the landowners, with the connivance and at times outright assistance of the police and military, hired bands of mercenaries largely recruited from demobilized ex-servicemen, to shatter and destroy the socialist organizations and peasant leagues which had emerged in post war years. In the words of a fascist apologist,

1. See, for example, Forcella and Monticone, *Plotone di Esecuzione*; Sprigge, p. 161.

thus 'opened the great fascist era – the law of brutal retaliation, atavistic and savage, reigned in the peninsula'.[1] Important elements of the revolutionary and syndicalist wings of the Italian labour movement had gone over to support the war in 1915, Mussolini amongst them. Their conversion to nationalist enthusiasm proved to be in almost direct proportion to their previous revolutionary fervour and belief in violent direct action. Mussolini now took the anti labour commando of the rural landowners, in a stroke of innovatory genius gave it an ideology, and implanted it in the city with the greatest success. By November 1921 the Fascist Party numbered 320,000 members. Armed to the teeth its 90,000 militants inflicted on the working class movement the violence which socialist leaders had threatened but failed to use. All over Italy labour organizations were terrorized into impotence, their members beaten and killed, their buildings and printing plants burnt, shattered and destroyed.

The inherent legalism of the PSI leadership prevented any adequate militant defence against the fascist onslaught. A shift in the attitude of the hierarchy, generated by fear of revolution, had allowed the formation of a Catholic 'People's Party'. This *Partito Popolari* elected 100 deputies and polled 1·2 million votes in its first campaign in November 1919. The emergence of this party completely disrupted the essentially lay basis of the earlier *transformismo* regime. Yet the People's Party interposed itself between socialism and the masses, preventing the emergence of a socialist majority, only at the price of itself disrupting the solidity of the conservative bloc. Mussolini, backed by landowners and big industry, tacitly aided by the forces of police, military and state bureaucracy, and not least the hierarchy, was thus able to mount a dynamic offensive against no more than limited resistance.

Prospects of united resistance by the working-class movement were themselves shattered by the actions of the Communist International. By 1922 the formerly united Socialist Party had split into three hostile organizations, a majority PSI, a reformist PSU (*Partito Socialista Unitario*) and a communist PCI (*Partito Comunista Italiano*). Mussolini, carefully combining parliamentary manoeuvre with extra parliamentary pressure in a model which Hitler was later to follow, was invited to form a Cabinet in October–November 1922. Parliament now legally voted Mussolini authority to govern with special powers. Once in office, his offensive facilitated by the hesitations and divisions in the ranks of the opposition, Mussolini proceeded by legal and extra-legal means to 'slice off' sections of the opposition one by one.[2] In December

1. Quoted in Guérin, *Fascism and Big Business*, p. 97.
2. This same technique of 'revolution from above' was applied in post-Second World War Hungary. The Hungarian Communist dictator, Rakosi, termed it 'salami socialism'.

1923 *Confindustria*, Italy's main employer organization, conferred formal recognition on the fascist unions. In October 1925 this was extended to a monopoly of representation. Within two more years, all opposition was legally banned, the press under censorship, the right to strike prohibited, the unions destroyed. Italy's bourgeois democracy had come to an end.

RISE AND FALL OF FASCISM

Although Mussolini gave to Hitler the Roman salute, the title *Führer*, which is no more than the Germanization of *Duce*, the model of the terrorist political party and the technique of the legalist *coup d'état* Italian society was never remodelled with the same harsh seriousness as that of Germany. In the field of industry the state did no more than continue the old policy of subsidizing private industry, although on a bigger scale and with the aid of an exaggeratedly large state, party and corporatist bureaucracy. A major economic legacy of Mussolini was the nationalization of Italy's key banks and dominant sectors of the engineering and ship-building industry which followed from the financial collapse of the Banca Commerciale Italiana and the Credito Italiano in the world depression of 1931. The Institute for Industrial Reconstruction (*Istituto per la Ricostruzione Industriale*: I RI), formed to take over and administer these assets, was to become in the post fascist era one of the most important entrepreneurial undertakings on the Italian scene, with over 300,000 employees.[1]

The regime's most important political legacy was the Concordat with the Vatican, negotiated in 1929. The Concordat abolished the hitherto lay character of the Italian state and ended the rift between Church and state which had lasted through the sixty years since its foundation. The privileges which the Concordat accorded to the Church give it a special position within the state, unique amongst the major powers of contemporary Europe. Catholic Action became the only social organization allowed to continue independently of the fascist regime. The continuity of operation, the training in leadership which this provided was of major importance in enabling the Catholic Church to exercise far greater political power and influence after Mussolini's fall than it had done before his rise to power.

By the early 1930s the fascist secret police had for practical purposes wiped out effective organized opposition in Italy. In real terms, socialist and communist activity existed only in exile. Italian socialists reunited into a single organization, the *Partito Socialista Italiano* (PSI) at a Congress held in Paris during 1930. The communists, despite losses at

1. 321,000 in 1969, *Annual Report*, p. 65. For further details see Holland, ed., *The State as Entrepreneur*.

the hands of both Stalin's and Mussolini's secret police, also kept a narrow framework of organization intact. The survivors of the repeated purges of the PCI provided a schooled, disciplined, totally Russian-oriented apparatus of considerable talent and capacity. Participation in the International Brigade during the Spanish Civil War placed at the communists' disposal activists whose military experience was to prove of major importance in the months which followed the downfall of the Mussolini regime. With the advent of the Popular Front the PCI, which had hitherto fought the socialists as if they were fascists, now changed its line and sought them as allies. In 1934 the PSI and PCI signed a Pact of Unity. Here, for the first time the PSI accorded the PCI recognition as an equal and provided for future co-operation between the two organizations. In 1936 both parties 'announced agreement upon the principle of trade union unity' thus broadening still further the scope for common action when once the downfall of fascism was complete. These events were to have great significance for the course of events when once the fascist regime fell and the liberation of Italy got under way.

Allied forces landed in Sicily on 10 July 1943, precisely one month to the day from the date on which the Russians as part of a *quid pro quo* had dissolved the Communist International.[1] The fascist Grand Council, seeing the invasion of the mainland in the offing, deposed Mussolini on the night of 24–25 July. After a period of vacillation, a new government under General Badoglio, in fact 'a monarchical autocracy based on the army, the royal household administration, the ex-fascist civil service and the police', concluded an armistice on 8 September.[2] In the meantime Germany had reinforced her hitherto scanty manpower on the Italian peninsula. Rome did not fall until June 1944. The liberation of northern Italy was delayed until April 1945.

In these two years, as the Allied armies slowly fought their way up the length of the Italian mainland, the framework of the pre-Mussolini society was gradually reconstructed, piece by piece. Badoglio's government declared war on Germany on 13 October 1943 and thereafter was accorded the status of a co-belligerent. There existed however a rival source of authority, the six party (Socialist, Action, Communist, Christian Democrat, Liberal and Democratic Labour) Committee of National Liberation (CLN), set up illegally in Rome during the first days of the Badoglio regime.

An independent Committee of Liberation of Northern Italy (*Comitato di Liberazione Nazionale dell'Alta Italiano*: CLNAI) was soon directing powerful partisan forces which had gone into action against the Germans in the Centre and the North. The CLN–CLNAI, thus

1. See Sobolev *et al.*, *Outline History of the Communist International*, p. 514; Neufeld, p. 444.
2. Mack-Smith, p. 487.

represented an alternative claimant to sovereignty in the areas under both German and Allied occupation. The King of Italy, who had welcomed Mussolini, refused to accept political party nominees in the Badoglio Cabinet. The CLN congress at Bari in January 1944 accordingly demanded responsible party government and the abdication of the King. Neither was forthcoming.

The German defeat at Stalingrad in February 1943 marked a turning-point in the general strategy of the war which immensely increased Russian, and thereby Italian communist, prestige.[1] In the two years of the Italian campaign, under the leadership of the CLNAI, the partisans of the Centre and the North, whose casualties in these years exceeded those of the combatant units of the regular Italian army, assumed real importance. On 1 March 1944 over a million workers responded to a strike call issued by the CLNAI. Early in 1945 Mussolini's Salo Republic in the North, on the verge of collapse, offered to cede its sovereignty to the CLNAI. The offer was refused, under communist influence, as an infringement of the terms of unconditional surrender. In April widespread strikes in the North culminated in open insurrection. Milan, Genoa, Turin, Cremona and Mantua were liberated by partisans. The CLNAI was thus in effective control of the North even before the Allied armies arrived. The CLNAI, at the head of a semi-insurrectionary regime, remained in control all through May 1945. Not until after the Allied Military Government assumed control in June did the popular power of the CLNAI evaporate in favour of the infinitely less representative royal cabinet in Rome.[2]

The predominant role of the communists in the partisan movement now assured the PCI of a crucial role in the development of Italian society. The main line of communist world strategy at this time was determined by an assessment of the military needs of Russia's war against Germany. As a gesture of reassurance to their capitalist allies, designed to hasten the establishment of a fullscale second front in Europe, the Russians dissolved the Comintern in June 1943. On 13 March 1944, in response to an Italian approach, the Russian government accorded recognition to the Badoglio regime. On 27 March Palmiro Togliatti, leader of the Italian Communist Party, was flown back to Italy from the Soviet Union. The programmes both of the

1. On the fashion in which the wartime prestige of Stalin benefited the PCI see Paolo Spriano, 'I Comunisti nella Resistenza', in *Rinascità*, Rome, 30 July 1971, p. 34.
2. There is no fully satisfactory account of the confusing interplay of political and industrial conflict, diplomatic intrigue and factional warfare which attended the reconstruction of the Italian labour movement and the Italian state. Mack-Smith, Horowitz, Neufeld and Galli are each illuminating in their own way; Valiani, *L'Avento di De Gasperi*, provides valuable insights from an unorthodox viewpoint.

party and of the now defunct Communist International forbade communist participation in bourgeois cabinets. Nevertheless Togliatti unilaterally announced that the PCI was willing to enter the government, and this without making any prior condition about the abdication of King Victor Emmanuel as head of state. The remaining five parties to the now disrupted popular alliance, instead of leaving the PCI in ridiculous isolation, reluctantly decided to follow suit. Following the occupation of Rome in June, a new Cabinet under Ivanoe Bonomi, former President of the Rome CLN, was formed, with all six parties of the CLN represented. The democratic and socialist forces in Italy, following the communist lead, thus surrendered their own claims to legitimacy, embodied in the CLN–CLNAI, to a government of the old order, in direct line of continuity and administration from that of Mussolini. The old state, particularly in the North, had gone to pieces under the shocks of liberation. The participation of the parties of the left in the government enabled Italy's severely threatened ruling elite to ensure that the traditional apparatus of ministries, prefectures, Carabinieri and magistrates, would be reconstructed and preserved. In the end, only the monarchy, badly compromised by its links with fascism, was sacrificed to the storm of popular resentment.

RE-ESTABLISHMENT OF ITALIAN STATE

The events of the second half of 1943 and the first months of 1944 were crucial for the destiny of the labour movement and Italian society. Badoglio, anxious to keep spontaneous agitation under control in the weeks after the fall of the Mussolini regime, offered to appoint representatives of the anti-fascist parties to posts of command in the fascist 'unions'. Socialists, communists, and Christian Democrats, the three parties with proven interests in the field, instead of demanding a dissolution of the fascist labour organizations, accepted Badoglio's proposition.[1] Thus two most important precedents were established. First, by taking over and restaffing fascist organizations, the new authorities implicitly accepted both their legitimacy and their existing obligations. Second, and more important, the principle was established that in the new regime labour organizations were to be seen as fiefs of political parties, rather than as the expression of the interests of their members. From this it clearly followed the allocation of officerships must be decided by political cliques rather than subjected to the uncertain vagaries of a system of elected choice.

The backward, illiterate, hitherto unorganized areas of the South were the first to be liberated. The acknowledged strong points of socialism and labour unions were in the Centre and the North. These remained under

1. Horowitz, pp. 185–6; Galli, *La Sinistra italiana nel Dopoguerra*, pp. 227–8.

German occupation for almost two years after the fall of Mussolini. The labour unions were thus reconstituted, by agreement of the political factions, in areas where the mass organizations had but little strength or tradition of struggle. The leadership and forms of organization thus arbitrarily established were later imposed on the areas most highly developed politically and organizationally. The instrumentalization of the Italian unions by political factions which has characterized the post-war Italian labour movement is thus a product of the circumstances of their initial reconstruction in 1944–5.

In June 1944, under German occupation, socialist, communist and Christian Democrat trade union 'leaders' hammered out a unification deal, significantly later known, like a diplomatic agreement, as the Pact of Rome. This agreement provided for the establishment of a single trade union centre, the Italian General Confederation of Labour (*Confederazione Generale Italiana del Lavoro*: CGIL) nominally independent of all political parties. The CGIL was to be without bias in respect to the political and religious opinions of its members. In flat contradiction to the terms of this agreement the Pact nevertheless provided that each of the three factions would have equal representation on the executive bodies of the CGIL. The first full congress of the CGIL was held at Naples between 28 January and 1 February 1945. The 322 delegates represented an authenticated, dues-paying membership of only 275,000, although the total membership *claimed* in liberated Italy already amounted to 1·3 million.[1] The main base of activity continued to rest with the regional Chambers of Labour rather than national unions. There can be little doubt that one of the main purposes of this congress was to legitimize the CGIL as an institution in being, to strengthen the hold of the existing officers against any challenge that might later be forthcoming from insurgent North. Indeed when later the liberation of the North more than *tripled* the membership of the CGIL, no fresh congress was held. Instead, in June 1945, at a meeting between Chambers of Labour in the North and what was by comparison a rump of national officials of the CGIL, the *status quo* was legitimized. Provision was now made to fill the executive places left vacant by the unrepresentative Naples congress earlier that year. Nominally in the possession of its members, the CGIL was thus in fact the creation of a trio of tightly knit, allied, but at the same time essentially competitive, party oligarchies. While that alliance remained unity was assured. When once it ended the whole organization split asunder.

The decision of the Socialist, Communist and Action Parties to enter the king's cabinet voluntarily surrendered all the powerful authority of the embryo new order incarnated in themselves, the CLN and CLNAI, as genuinely popular forces of resistance, and admitted the legitimacy

1. Horowitz, pp. 186–7, 196–7; Neufeld, pp. 454–6.

and continuity of the old state. This act provided the foundation upon which the subsequent restoration of pre-Mussolini Italian society took place. The position of the socialist and communist parties within the government was downgraded in direct proportion to the extent to which social stability was restored. In November 1945 the Christian Democrats precipitated a parliamentary crisis. The outcome was the fall from office of Ferruccio Parri, former partisan Joint Commander-in-Chief, who the previous June, following the liberation of the North, had replaced Bonomi as Prime Minister. In December 1945 Alcide de Gasperi, a former Foreign Minister, political secretary of the Catholic Popular Party in the pre-Mussolini regime, the first militant Catholic ever to be Prime Minister in the Italian state, took Parri's place. De Gasperi's emergence as Prime Minister dealt the socialist–communist alliance a blow from which it never recovered.

ITALIAN LABOUR AFTER 1945

In the first post war elections of June 1946, the Christian Democrats mustered 8,100,000 votes against 4,760,000 of the socialists and 4,360,000 of the PCI, and emerged for the first time as the largest single party in the Italian state. Under De Gasperi's premiership, with the socialist leader Pietro Nenni and the communist leader Togliatti (until July 1946) and their parties represented in the Cabinet, the reconstruction of Italian society proceeded along lines considerably to the right of that of the Weimar Republic after 1914–18. Thus, to quote one example, in 1947 the Italian communists cast the decisive votes (the socialist PSI abstained) for the incorporation of the fascist Concordat with the Vatican in the terms of the new constitution. The pronounced confessional bias in the education system which was one result has delivered a virtually guaranteed Christian Democratic majority amongst the new voters who have gone subsequently on the register. The privileges accorded the Catholic Church by the Italian constitution continue to this day to be more appropriate to the eighteenth century than the twentieth.

Rising international tensions, the failure to reach an agreement over a German Peace Treaty, put strains on the Great Power alliance which finally brought it to breaking-point. Not even the communist vote for the Concordat was sufficient to keep the PCI a continuing place in the coalition. Early in 1947 De Gasperi left for an official visit to the United States. Here it seems discussions took place regarding the plans for Marshall Aid and the desirability of levering the communists and their socialist allies out of the Italian cabinet as a necessary preliminary. In a new government formed on 31 May 1947, after his return from the USA, De Gasperi found places for neither socialist nor communist ministers. The transition from near-revolution to reconstruction was now complete. Out of the turmoil which followed the collapse of Italian fascism, with which the Vatican had been allied, the Christian Democrats now emerged as the major party in the Italian state. Alone or in coalition, Christian Democrats continued to rule Italy for the next quarter of a century. Thus in the twentieth century Catholicism won a position of political primacy and privilege in the Italian state which it had proved unable to conquer in the nineteenth. In part this represents a tribute to the considerable strategic and tactical ability shown by Christian Democracy and the hierarchy which stands at its side. Even more it is a measure of the extent to which incompetence and concern for the short term foreign policy interests of the Russian state caused socialist and communist parties to squander the opportunities for social change inherited at the end of the war.

ITALIAN LABOUR DIVIDES

The exclusion of socialist and communists from the government threatened the three-party alliance which controlled the CGIL, which by 1947 was able to *claim* some 5·7 million members. The communists operated a strict factional discipline within the CGIL, to which the socialists, with greater or less degree of unanimity, tended to conform. The Catholic faction was mobilized in a similar fashion by the Christian Association of Italian Workers (*Associazione Cristiani dei Lavoratori Italiani*: ACLI). ACLI had been established by Catholic Action at the time of the original Christian Democrat decision to join the CGIL in 1944. At the Florence Congress of the CGIL in June 1947, the month following the exclusion of socialists and communists from the government, the PCI proposed to scuttle the previous parity agreement and replace it with one of representation in accordance to factional strength. A communist, Di Vittorio, was installed as General Secretary under whom were placed three co-equal secretaries, one from each of the three parties involved.

The exclusion of communist and socialist ministers from the government in May 1947 had brought no violent reaction from the PCI. This situation did not last. At the founding session of the Cominform in September 1947 the PCI was severely reprimanded for its quiescence. Thereafter it launched, through the medium of the CGIL, a series of widespread industrial stoppages accompanied by large and frequently violent demonstrations. In the general election of April 1948 the PCI–PSI alliance was defeated. The Christian Democrats, with 12·7 million votes, achieved an overall single party majority in the Chamber for the first time. This development did nothing to ease the now rapidly deepening divisions inside the CGIL. An assassination attempt which seriously injured the communist leader Togliatti on 14 July 1948, sparking off a spontaneous nationwide strike wave of near-insurrectionary proportions, now brought the CGIL, in its turn, to a split. The PCI, taken by surprise, quickly sought to bring the strike under control and to restrain its ranks, some of whom were already preparing onslaughts on barracks and power stations, as part of the insurrection they believed to be the order of the day. The Christian Democrats threatened a walk-out unless the CGIL called off the stoppage. On 22 July the ACLI National Council met, declared the general strike had 'destroyed the Pact of Rome' and called for the establishment of a new, noncommunist dominated, trade union confederation. This proposal was endorsed by a specially convened ACLI National Congress held between 15 and 18 September 1948.[1]

There now ensued two years of almost indescribable turmoil and confusion in the labour movement. Christian Democrats, communists, republicans, socialists of both left and right wing, communist and noncommunist orientation, fought one another both for control of the CGIL and for the establishment of a fresh union confederation outside its ranks. When by 1950 the smoke surrounding this mutual organizational slaughter had cleared, three main trade union organizations held the field. The CGIL had lost about half its membership. Still the largest, still the strongest among the organized section of the manual working class, the CGIL was dominated by communists with, as increasingly critical allies, adherents of the major socialist party, the PSI. The Italian Confederation of Workers Unions' (*Confederazione Italiana dei Sindacati Lavoratori*: CISL), an expressly non-confessional organization, dominated by Christian Democrats but with very limited Social Democrat participation as well, challenged the CGIL as a major contender, but with a heavier white collar base. Far smaller than either CGIL or CISL, but with important representation in certain sections of Italian industry, the Italian Union of Labour (*Unione Italiana del Lavoro*: UIL) was led by social democrats and republicans who could stomach neither the communist control of the CGIL nor the Christian Democrats' domination of the CISL. The CGIL retained affiliation to the indisputably Russian-dominated World Federation of Trade Unions (WFTU). CISL and, in due course UIL also, became affiliates of the Western-oriented International Confederation of Free Trade Unions (ICFTU).[2] Any cold examination of the facts would lead us to believe that the consequence of two years of organizational disruption and Cold War hostility, combined with a universal failure adequately to protect

1. For one account, Horowitz, pp. 215–18.
2. However, the Christian Association of Italian Workers (ACLI), the Catholic faction inside CISL, is an 'Extraordinary Member' of the European Organization of the predominantly Christian, World Confederation of Labour (WCL) formerly the International Federation of Christian Trade Unions).

living standards, would have seen a massive loss in union membership. In fact, competitive bidding raised the total claimed by the
three confederations in 1950 to 6·9 million. This was no less than
1·2 million above the figure claimed by the CGIL alone in 1948.
One reliable authority has put the actual membership in 1948 at
only some 4·5 million. The real membership figure in 1950, on the
most optimistic estimate, is likely to have been a great deal lower than
that.

The first and most important political factor affecting the post war
Italian labour scene has been the emergence of a state with a pronounced
religious bias governed by a ruling Christian Democratic Party, backed
in its turn by a major Christian Democrat-oriented labour union confederation. The second factor has undoubtedly been the success of the
communist PCI in displacing the socialists as the major party resting on
working class support. In the pre-Mussolini era, the PCI possessed most
of the characteristics of a schismatic sect and occupied a clear minority
position in both political and trade union life. The underground party
probably numbered no more than a few hundred militants and party
functionaries. As late as 1943, two years after Russia's involuntary entry
into the war, PCI membership, according to an official communist
historian, did not amount to more than 5000.[1] In the first years of the
CGIL it seems probable that socialist support outweighed that of the
communists. At the election of 1946, despite the unity pact, the socialist
poll still exceeded that of the PCI by some 400,000 votes. Yet by 1948
the socialists had lost the primacy they originally possessed and become
very much the junior partner in the PCI–PSI alliance. The PCI, with
2·3 million members, was now the largest party in the Italian state.[2]
The PCI, of course, both from its foundation and up to the present
time, has received financial and organizational backing from Moscow.
At the time of the Liberation the communists seized valuable and
important assets which they have never relinquished. Nor did the PCI
hesitate to murder a number of its opponents and critics on the left
at the time of the liberation.[3] These facts are important. They are
not sufficient to explain the gains made by the PCI in the post war
years.

1. Spriano, 'I Communisti nella Resistenza', *Rinascità*, p. 33.
2. Communist Party membership at the present time is around 1·5 million.
One estimate puts the number of employees on the party payroll as 12,000, and
the annual income at some 12 to 30 *billion* lire. The same source reports the
party's official total of employees as 6000. The best comparison known to this
author is the apparatus of classical German Social Democracy: see Giovanni
Sartori in Lapalombara and Weiner, eds., *Political Parties and Political Development*, pp. 144–8.
3. See, for example, Zaccaria, *200 Communisti Italiani tra le Vittime dello
Stalinismo*, pp. 99–113.

The leaders of the socialist PSI, Nenni especially, seem to have seen in the disunity of the Italian working class a prime cause of the triumph of fascism. After the mid-1930s socialist–communist collaboration became a basic axiom of PSI policy. This was despite the fact that the communists themselves were primarily responsible for the disunity in the socialist ranks in front of Mussolini. The socialists, too, at this time, shared the PCI's professed belief in the mythical 'Socialist Soviet Union – Fatherland of all the Toilers'. Thus many PSI members came to feel themselves only 'second grade' socialists. Before the PCI, on which the Russian mantle of socialist legitimacy rested direct, they felt a sense of inferiority. The PSI leaders, not daring to act independently for fear of being charged with breaking the working class front, became for practical purposes a fifth wheel of the PCI. In the early post war years independent action by the PSI would have isolated the PCI and discredited its conservative and reactionary policies. Instead the PSI legitimized the policies of the communists. As a result the socialists took more than their share of the electoral and organizational consequences. PSI collaboration with the PCI and insecurity about its role precipitated splits within its own ranks. A section of the PSI critical of the socialist–communist alliance split off to form the Italian Social Democratic Party (*Partito Socialista Democratico Italiano*: PSDI). This split and others like it, further weakened the socialist position. Not until after Stalin's death did the PSI begin to move gradually away from the PCI. The Poznan and Berlin Risings of 1953 and the Twentieth Congress denunciations of Stalin in 1956 speeded up the process. Russia's armed suppression of the Hungarian revolution that same year helped bring a decisive separation. Since 1963 the breach at national level has been complete.[1] The socialists thereafter have comprised an essential element of the governmental coalition.

Since the end of the war the combined socialist–communist vote has remained substantially static. The PCI's much vaunted electoral gains, the trumpeting of which puts the vulgar parliamentarianism of German social democracy before the First World War to shame, represent only marginal shifts within the working class bloc. No major realignment in the boundaries of the electoral territory, which this bloc divides with its opponents, has yet taken place. The split in the Italian working class created by the foundation of the Communist Party thus emerges as one major cause of the paralysis which characterizes Italian political society today. A united socialist party would, on all the evidence, have constituted a valid alternative to the Christian Democrats at the polls, in most of the post war years. But for these internal divisions, it seems clear that

1. Entry into the Centre–Left Coalition led to a further split when a wing of the PSI hostile to this decision broke away to form the Italian Socialist Party of Proletarian Unity (*Partito Socialista Italiano del' Unità Proletaria*: PSIUP).

for a number of years at least, Italy would have been ruled by a Socialist, rather than a Christian Democrat, government.[1]

A conservative, anti-revolutionary force in the transitional post war years, the PCI has proved unable to attain an electoral majority in the decades that have followed. Nor have its endeavours to gain acceptance as a suitable member of an extended centre–left coalition proved any more successful. Whether viewed as a party of revolution or a party of reform, it stands condemned as a failure.[2]

Locked in a seemingly permanent stalemate, Italian political life is characterized at national and local level by the wheeling and dealing of a select, self-appointed and largely self-reproducing few. The manoeuvres within this oligarchic elite are transmitted into the mass by manipulative party, and to some extent union, organizations, which have a life and reason for existence all of their own, quite separate and apart from the needs of the masses they purport to represent.

Giustino Fortunato declared in the 1920s that while the Italian Parliament was 'definitely mediocre, extremely mediocre, it was better than the country'. There is no doubt that even today Italian society suffers from a profound lack of developed civic consciousness, of which narrow particularism and the triumph of sectional and corporate over community interests, are clear and obvious symptoms.

We are confronted in the second half of the twentieth century with a new form of *trasformismo* one which substitutes a party political, oligarchic bureaucratic procedure, for the individualist negotiations which existed beforehand.

INDUSTRIAL RELATIONS

The generally retarded character of Italian political life has not been without its impact on modes of labour movement behaviour. All Italian political parties were reconstructed bureaucratically from the top down in the post war years, new oligarchies in an already oligarchic society. Behind Christian Democracy stood the organized power of the Vatican, without which its successes could never have been achieved. Behind the Italian Communist Party stood the direct organized power, political and financial support, of the Russian state. The strength of the PCI, the strategic position of Italy on NATO's exposed Mediterranean flank, made the policies of the PCI a crucial bargaining counter in the Cold War. In the years which followed the union splits of 1947–8 the labour

1. Thus calculations appear to show that 25 per cent of Italian workers vote for the PSI, 28 per cent for the PCI and 38 per cent for the DC: Doggan in Lipset and Rokkan, eds., *Political Party Systems and Voter Alignments*, p. 140.

2. For a perceptive account, Gino Bianco, 'To use the Communist Party – or be used?', *Socialist Affairs*, March 1972, pp. 55–6.

movement became a battleground in which the Great Powers fought by proxy. CIA funding for CISL and UIL in the early years seems quite clearly established. The dependence of the CGIL and the PCI on Russian sources of financial aid is equally plain.[1]

Italian industry had from the beginning established the closest political ties with government. Italian labour too, perhaps in part as a response, had long manifested political allegiances of its own, as least as explicit as those of the employers. The political and union organizations of the working class now became an arena for Cold War combat. Battles were fought out by hostile elites, each with self-interested backers hidden in the shadows at its rear. In a society where it is common knowledge that the main organs of public opinion are in the pockets of one or another group of vested interests, this perhaps is not surprising.[2] At any rate, without a recognition of these facts it is impossible to make head or tail of the course of labour movement affairs in Italy during the post war years.

The post war decade was characterized by chronic unemployment, certainly never less than 1·5 million and perhaps rising as high as twice this figure. The unions' weak bargaining position was accentuated by internecine divisions and the markedly hostile stance of Italian employers. Confindustria, Italy's archaic, centralized and reactionary employers' organization, seems to look back with nostalgia to the 'peace and order' which reigned under Mussolini. In Italian business the objective rational values of a developed capitalist society are far from the accepted norm. It has been said that Italian industrial owners and managers 'manifest the same attitudes towards labour that are characteristic of the Southern landlord . . . Both are referred to as *padrone*, and the social distance of the rural, semi-feudal South can quickly and readily be transferred to the industrial plant. In many instances management's attitude towards labour is at best condescending; the factory is viewed as personal, inviolable property; trade unionists are considered social upstarts and dangerous revolutionaries.'[3]

1. The CIA annual budget for unions in France and Italy in the late 1940s has been quoted as $12 million. The amount of Russian money going into the Western European labour movement at this time was certainly at least as large. On this: Thomas W. Braden, *Saturday Evening Post*, June 1967; *Voice of the Unions*, July 1967; Galenson, *Comparative Labor Movements*, p. 478; Edelman and Fleming, *The Politics of Wage-Price Decisions*, pp. 12–13; Raffaele, *Labor Leadership in Italy and Denmark*, pp. 291–3.

2. The two most important dailies are *La Stampa* (circulation 470,000) and the *Corriera della Sera* (circulation 570,000). *La Stampa* is owned by FIAT. *Corriere della Sera* is owned by the Crespi family, and with *Il Sole* and *24 Ore* is widely regarded as an organ of Confindustria. On this and related matters, del Boca, *Giornali in Crisi*; Adams and Barile, *The Government of Republican Italy*, pp. 190–92.

3. Lapalombara, *Interest Groups in Italian Politics*, p. 40.

Article 2094 of the Civil Code requires employees to be 'diligent' and 'follow the orders given by the entrepreneur . . . [and others] . . . who are hierarchically superior to him'. Article 30 of the metal-workers' agreement, even as late as 1966, still contained a discipline clause requiring the worker not only 'to maintain proper relations with his fellow workers' but also to 'maintain relations of subordination towards his superiors'.[1]

Even where, as in the case of FIAT, Olivetti and Montecatini, management makes use of modern technology and mass production, it is likely to rely on quite outdated nineteenth century paternalism to tame and domesticate its labour force. Thus workers will be cocooned in company housing, welfare and leisure schemes designed to strangle incipient labour union activity at the first moment of birth. FIAT, Italy's largest private employer, with 100,000 on its payroll in Turin, has distributed its favours amongst the CGIL, the CISL and what is generally regarded as a company union in turn. At one time FIAT is reported as transferring all known members of the CGIL to a single plant, preparatory to closing that same plant and laying the unwanted activists off its staff.[2] Turin it would seem manifests many of the characteristics of a company town.[3] Economists generally recognize a dual economy in Italy, an advanced market for capital and labour and a retarded sector of semi-artisan economy, each existing side by side, with only the most limited interaction. One must also take into account pronounced regional differences between the North and South of the country. Thus in 1950 only 25 per cent of industrial plants in the North employed fewer than ten workers. In the South the proportion was 60 per cent. In 1950 per capita income in the South was estimated at 45 per cent of that in the North. In 1969, per capita income in the South amounted to only £336 as against £595 in the North.[4] The social chasms which separate human experience within this single society are undoubtedly one cause of the archaic social attitudes which continue to exist inside modern Italian industrial plants.

Given the character of the Italian labour movement and the im-

1. Seyfarth *et al.*, *Labor Relations and the Law in Italy and the United States*, pp. 299–300. '*Art. 30 – Discipline azienalde . . . . Egli deve conservare rapporti di educazione verso i compagni del lavoro e di subordinazione verso i superiori . . .*': FIM–FIOM–UILM, *Contratto Nazionale del Lavoro, 15 Dicembre 1966*, Rome, 1967, p. 57.

2. Edelman and Fleming, pp. 39–42, 53.

3. For allegations of 'undue influence' exercised by FIAT in municipal affairs, see the Press Conference of 22 Sept. 1971 held by *La Lotta Continua* in Turin. For one account *Soccorso Rosso*, 8 Oct., 1971, pp. 15–16. For a subsequent British report which refers to 'FIAT'S secret files on more than 200,000 people', *Sunday Times*, 4 June 1972.

4. Vera Lutz, quoted in Edelman and Fleming, p. 9. *Guardian*, 16 Sept. 1970.

portance of Italy as an arena of confrontation in the Cold War, it is understandable that the changes which have taken place since the middle 1950s have been linked with developments on a more global scale. A whole series of events culminating in the Russian invasion and counter-revolution in Hungary in 1956 provoked marked strains in the PSI–PCI alliance. The socialist–communist front had in any case failed to deliver the electoral successes originally anticipated. In these same years, elements of the Christian Democratic left began to look towards an alliance with the PSI, as the basis of a centre–left, Christian Democrat–Socialist coalition, which might break the impasse in Italian politics. After some hesitation, Nenni, the PSI leader, broke with the PCI alliance and gave his support to this new orientation.

By the mid-1950s, despite all attempts of the CGIL to drive them out of the plants, CISL and UIL had finally established themselves as valid union organizations in their own right. CISL and UIL together probably commanded 50 per cent of the organized labour force at this time, a proportion which they have continued to hold up to the present. CGIL membership is more blue-collar, CISL more white. By the end of the 1950s it became plain that the demarcation lines between the unions were now firmly drawn. CISL and UIL proved well able to exert a competitive influence on the CGIL at all levels of activity.

Inside the CGIL the Nenni socialist minority was beginning to make its presence felt over a whole number of points of difference with the PCI.[1] Union weakness and disunity had ensured that productivity and profit increases markedly outran wage rises all through the 1940s and 1950s. Not until 1949 did real wages regain the level of 1921. As new men came to the fore and old bitterness waned, so pressures for greater union unity began to make themselves felt.[2]

The PSI decisions first to support, and later in 1962 to *enter* the coalition, provided the hinge about which subsequent developments in the labour movement have begun to turn. The presence of the PSI in the government alongside the Christian Democrats and the Social Democrats (PSDI) could not be without its effect on relations between the labour unions associated with these organizations. The PSDI command a small minority tendency within the CISL and with the PSI and Republicans represent the ruling group within the UIL. The PSI constitutes a minority within the CGIL, but one which, for historical reasons, is over represented in its ruling circles. The PSI presence within the government thus provided a bridge between communists and

---

1. For one view of the power relationship between PCI and PSI see Neufeld, *Italy*, p. 555.
2. An excellent symposium showing these developments through the eyes of leaders of some of the main tendencies involved will be found in *New Politics*, vol. 1, no. 4, pp. 124–72.

non-communists within the trade union movement. At the same time it gave assurance that a co-ordinated union strategy, backed by political manoeuvres aimed at gaining concessions from employers, had some prospect of success.

In the 1950s and 1960s the economic climate in Italy changed considerably too. A self-started 'second industrial revolution' got under way. An unprecedented mass immigration caused a population shift of some 1·9 million northwards from the overpopulated, underprivileged South in the years 1951–61.[1] The boom elsewhere in Europe has drawn some 1·5 million Italian workers to employment in Switzerland and the nations of the EEC. The economic boom and the virtual elimination of mass unemployment markedly altered the balance of social forces in favour of the working class. The economic success of the EEC, the employment generated for Italian workers within its boundaries, rendered untenable the CGIL's initial Russian-inspired total opposition to the European Economic Community. The CGIL, and in turn the PCI, gradually shifted towards a position of critical support of the EEC, thus eliminating one major cause of internal differences within the labour movement. The leftward shift of the hierarchy which began under Pope John also helped to reduce internal tensions within the labour movement. The general move towards a *détente* in the Cold War had the same effect. Under these pressures the Communist Party monolith showed signs of beginning to shiver. It became clear that a section of the leadership under Amendola was in favour of integrating the PCI into the coalition should the opportunity offer. Thus the decade that begins in the mid-1950s represents a watershed in Italian labour politics. The modes of behaviour which have followed it are markedly different from those that went before.

A further factor of great importance to an understanding of the contemporary Italian labour scene is the unique significance of the public sector in Italian socio-economic and political affairs. The post war years have seen the rise of the *Ente Nazionale Idrocarburi* (ENI), a major Italian state trust operating in oil and natural gas, which, under the daring if somewhat piratical genius of Enrico Mattei, challenged the might of the great oil companies all around the world. The giant IRI complex which inherited the assets taken over by Mussolini in the great depression employs in all some 300,000 workers. Out of this total, 180,000 are in manufacturing. IRI plants comprise the largest single section of the engineering industry. IRI also employs some 90,000 in motorways, telecommunications, radio, television, shipping and airlines.

1. Between 1951 and 1961 there was a net loss of 1,866,000 from Southern Italy, a net gain of 1,029,000 in the North. Between 1954 and 1962, the labour force in agriculture decreased by 1,100,000 (17 per cent). Employment in industry rose by 2,600,000 (47 per cent); Edelman and Fleming, pp. 8, 27.

The I R I–E N I complexes constitute virtual empires in their own right. These giants exercise political influence on their own behalf and enjoy a very large measure of scope for independent action. Italian society fails to conform to the norm of a highly disaggregated, decentralized open market economy. In the advanced sectors, oligopolies like F I A T, Montecatini, Olivetti, E N I and I R I predominate, with all the political and social consequences that this involves.

UNIONS AND COLLECTIVE BARGAINING

The industrial bargaining structure in Italy is directly descended from that of the fascist regime. During its brief interregnum the Badoglio government appointed socialist, communist and Christian Democrat trade unionists to the vacated posts of command in the existing fascist labour organizations. In the words of one Italian authority, the fascist regime had set up a 'bureaucratic bargaining system in which industrial disputes, attenuated by the doctrine of inter-class collaboration, were settled by the intermediary of the all powerful bureaucratic machinery of the legally recognized workers' and employers' organizations'. Face-to-face negotiations between union officials and individual employers rarely if ever took place.[1] In the post war years fresh national agreements between the union confederations C I S L and U I L, the national industrial employers' association (*Confindustria*) and the national agricultural employers' association (*Confagricoltura*) simply replaced those formerly existing between the fascist syndicates and the employers.

The unions, centrally controlled, closely subordinated to the political parties, in the case of the CGIL at least, committed to a schematic theory of 'class unionism', and with it conceptions of overall across-the-board increases, found this inheritance a desirable one. The employers' association, composed of a majority of small employers, concerned to protect marginal enterprise and above all to keep the union presence outside the plant, saw no reason to propose any innovation. As a result a rigid bargaining structure appeared, one functionally hostile to democratic participation, ill suited to maximizing either workers' welfare or industrial productivity, but eminently fitted to maintain indefinitely the arbitrary rule of the union hierarchy over the union base. National all-industry wage agreements (interconfederal agreements) set wage rates for four basic skill classifications and established sliding-scale cost-of-living allowance which with zonal differentials covered the whole country. These agreements were made, it should be emphasized, not by the individual unions (federations) but by the national union centres

1. Giugni, 'Articulated bargaining in Italy', in Flanders, ed., *Collective Bargaining*, p. 269.

(confederations: CGIL, CISL, UIL). Demands were formulated, agreements concluded, without either prior consultation, or the submission of contract texts for ratification by the membership. Right up to 1954 these interconfederal agreements, in a super-centralized wage bargain, continued to set wage rates right across the country.

Interconfederal agreements decided wage policy and laid down terms governing holidays, redundancy, grievance procedure, etc. In the years after 1954, a shift towards national sectoral agreements has taken place, although not without strong resistance from the employers and some initial hesitation amongst unions. In all cases employers, while reserving to themselves the right unilaterally to pay over the rate, explicitly refused to bargain with the unions below the confederal or national federation level. With one or two notable exceptions employers continued to handle negotiations through Confindustria rather than accept 'in plant' management relations of a type customary in Britain and the United States. The pattern of the original post war agreements represented first, the dominance of the employers over the unions; second, the dominance of a self-reproducing union bureaucracy with political manipulative interests of its own to serve, over and above and those of the workers themselves.

The first steps towards a breach with the centralized confederal agreement came from the UIL and the CISL. After 1953 both began to move towards industry-wide and later plant-level agreements with a specific union presence in the plant.[1] This initiative at first came under heavy fire from the CGIL 'as an effort to fragment the working class, to develop a new corporativism and basically to serve the interests of the employers'. By 1956 however, the CGIL, under pressure from its own members and successes gained by CISL and UIL had adopted a similar position.

The *conglobamento* agreement signed by CISL and UIL in 1954, first denounced, then tacitly accepted by the CGIL, which consolidated a number of war and post war allowances into the basic pay, was the first major step forward in collective bargaining in the post war years.[2] The weakness of the Italian unions is shown by the fact in the eight years following the *conglobamento* agreement of 1954 there were only three confederal agreements negotiated. None of these registered a major wage advance. Confederal agreements, fixing wage rates, as they did, on a national scale, at rates which marginal employers could afford to pay,

1. In proposing that the unions organize their own sections in the plants CISL and UIL also had in mind to neutralize the power of CGIL which at this time exercised a predominant influence within many *commissione interne*.

2. For details, Edelman and Fleming, pp. 34–6; see also Giugni, 'Recent developments in collective bargaining in Italy', *International Labour Review*, April 1965 pp. 273–91.

left the larger companies ample scope to cream off labour and undermine unionism by paying over the rate.

The changed economic situation, the shift in the balance of the governmental coalition, the growing conviction in all three unions that workers were failing to gain an adequate share of growing prosperity, led to major shifts away from confederal bargaining during the 1960s. The law of 22 December 1956 cleared the way by requiring state-owned companies to set up their own independent employers' association separate from that of *Confindustria*. The attitudes of central management in the IRI, ENI, ENEL (*Ente Nazionale del Energia Elettrica*) nationalized sectors are more forward-looking than those of Confindustria. *Intersind*, the new state employers' association, formed as a result of the 1956 law, at first presented a common front alongside Confindustria. Later it began to adopt a more enlightened attitude of its own.

A series of strikes in the electrical manufacturing industry in 1960–61 led, following ministerial intervention, to a separate agreement in the state electrical engineering sector, the first breach in the system of central agreements. The IRI complex employs some 180,000 of the 1·3 million workers in the metal-working (engineering) sector, which represents the key bargain for the Italian economy. The unions now sought to break down the central confederal contract for the metal-working industry, due to expire in October 1962, into a series of sectoral agreements. When negotiations with Confindustria broke down Intersind continued to bargain separately. The outcome was a system of 'articulated' bargaining. The settlement conceded by Intersind without a stoppage in November 1962 was substantially conceded, after widespread strikes, by Confindustria in February 1963.

The 'articulated' agreement negotiated by the metal-workers made provision for bargaining at three levels. In addition to general provisions appropriate to the whole metal-working industry the new 'articulated' contract also made provision for negotiations at the level of six newly established sectors of the metal-working industry itself. These covered iron and steel, ship-building, electrical and electronic engineering, automobile and aircraft manufacture, foundries and non-ferrous metals and general engineering. Within the framework of the national contract provision was made for negotiations of job categories, hours and minimum wages at the sector rather than the national level.[1] A very limited number of matters, not precisely elaborated at the higher stages, were also open for bargaining at plant level by full-time officials of the *provincial* unions. The agreement stood, however, as a whole. Commence-

1. Alan Ross has reported that over a quarter of Italy's larger factories have job-evaluation systems, most imposed by unilateral management initiative; on this see Seyfarth *et al.*, *Labor Relations and the Law in Italy and the United States*, pp. 162–3.

ment and expiry of the contracts for each sector took place on the same dates. On their part the unions conceded a no-strike pledge in respect of all matters specifically settled by the three year confederal contract. As other major confederal agreements have fallen due for renewal they have tended to move towards the 'articulated' model although frequently a sector breakdown has not been required.

In retrospect, probably the most important single clause in the 1962 agreement was one which provided for the 'check-off' (deduction of union dues from wages) in the metal-working industry. Italian workers have proved chronically unwilling to pay union dues. The institution of the check-off with the regular subscriptions that this involved may have increased the income of some metal-working unions by as much as 50 per cent. The ensuing shift from financial dependence on the con-federation or other more dubious sources to one of virtual financial self-sufficiency, has been of crucial importance to subsequent develop-ments in the metal industry. There are signs that in the seventies even the confederations themselves are at last moving towards greater self-sufficiency. Thus the CISL journal *Conquista del Lavoro* writes that recent developments have enabled the organization to achieve financial autonomy and thus to guarantee an ever more rigid autonomy of the entire organization.[1] In this connection the public recognition of past dependence is surely of comparable importance as the aspiration to future freedom. If the check-off spreads to other sectors to a sufficient extent to make most unions financially autonomous it must alter the whole landscape of Italian labour relations in the years to come.

COMMISSIONE INTERNE

The absence of 'in-plant' unionism in Italy has many causes. It is to be explained in part by simplistic class conceptions of the socialist movement, in part by attitudes carried over from the fascist era, in part by the instrumental uses to which unionism has been put, first by the communists and later by others, after the Second World War. Yet there exists also another cause of primary magnitude. In the *commissione interne* (best translated as works councils although there is in fact no *exact* equivalent), which first became important on a large scale following the metal-workers' agreements of 1919 and 1920, there has existed an alter-native and more widely acceptable mode of representation to the union in the plant. Elected by all workers, organized and unorganized, in the plant, the *commissione interne*, suppressed by Mussolini, were re-established by agreement between Confindustria and the nascent unions in September 1943. This represented one of the first acts which followed the establishment of the ephemeral Badoglio regime. The German re-

1. *Conquista del Lavoro*, Rome, July 1973, pp. 23–5.

occupation, the failure of the Allied offensives, delayed reconstruction of the unions until after the liberation was complete in 1945. Thus for two crucial formative years the *commissione interne* became the only legal and recognized form of labour representation over large areas of Italy. In the absence of strong union representation, the *commissione interne*, originally intended to 'police' the union collective agreement, handle grievances, and concentrate on social welfare and advisory functions,[1] came to be seen as a substitute for the union in the plant. Even now the *commissione interne* continue to be the first stage in the processing of individual grievances. As such it continues to rival the union for the loyalty of the individual worker in the plant. The tendency of the *commissione interne* to substitute themselves for the union was particularly strong in the post war era of mass unemployment since they possessed important consultation rights over individual dismissals and general reductions in the workforce. The employers had no wish to deal with the unions. 'Negotiations' with the *commissione interne* enabled the employers to short-circuit the unions whilst still maintaining contact with 'representatives' of their workforce. Since the *commissione interne* could exercise no effective sanctions in the event of a failure to agree, since their members possessed no serious protection against victimization, the employer, understandably, found them an excellent partner at the bargaining table.

The fact that the *commissione interne* lacked bargaining power meant that, properly speaking, they were not very powerful institutions at all. Nevertheless, *commissione interne* elections, held at annual intervals, contested by the slates of the three rival unions, came to be regarded as vital indices to shifts in the political allegiance of the working class. The elections frequently took place in an atmosphere of outrageous interference by plant managements. Contested with an expense of time and money more appropriate to a political party in a general election, the *commissione interne* elections came to represent a monumental diversion from proper union activity. Thus it has been said that in the 1950s the *commissione interne* elections in large companies overshadowed in importance not only the congresses of the respective confederations but also the periodical contract negotiations themselves.[2] With the parliamentarian bias which is its distinctive characteristic the Italian Communist Party, like its rivals, treated the outcome of elections to these largely powerless bodies as a matter of vital importance. In fact never at any time did votes polled in *commissione interne* elections indicate actual

1. The best brief discussion of the role of the *commissione interne*, easily available to the reader, will be found in Seyfarth *et al.*, *Labor Relations and the Law in Italy and the United States*, pp. 38–44.
2. Baglioni, 'L'istituto della Commissione Interne e la questione della rappresentanza dei lavoratori nei luoghi di lavoro', *Studi de Sociologia*, June 1970, p. 188. On this see also, Neufeld, *Labor Unions and National Politics in Italian Industrial Plants*, in particular, pp. 85–92.

union strength. A 1970 investigation conducted in one medium-size plant showed that whilst 400 employees supported CISL in the *commissione interne* elections only forty were union members. In the same elections only ten of the fifty workers who supported CGIL and ten of the fifty who supported UIL were members. Thus in a plant where 500 employees voted for union candidates only slightly over one in every ten thought it worth his while to join the union to which he gave his vote.[1]

As all three union confederations are now beginning to recognize, representative bodies inside productive undertakings which are not backed by strong union organization are worth very little more than the value of the paper their constitutions are written upon. Furthermore, once union organization exists their presence as an alternative mode of representation is a liability rather than an asset. Even according to the contractual provisions which governed their establishment (frequently not fulfilled) the *commissione interne* never covered more than an atypical minority of the workforce, some 1 million employees in the 3000 largest enterprises. At all times the bulk of those voting have never belonged to the confederation to which they gave their ballot. The *commissione interne* have provided a means whereby the employer might 'treat with his workforce' without dealing with the union. As such they have materially assisted the efforts of Italy's employers to maintain a quite outdated atmosphere of neo-feudal paternalism in their plants. Recent years have seen union attention swing away from the *commissione interne* towards the problem of a proper union presence in the plant. The 1966 confederal agreement expressly excluded the *commissione interne* from participation in wage-bargaining procedures. The move towards the substitution of the union for the *commissione interne* as the authentic representative of the workforce in the plant has been carried still further by the confederal agreements concluded in 1969 and 1972–3.

UNION STRENGTH AND STRUCTURE

The structure and nature of Italian unionism is closely linked with the circumstances of its origin. Italian unions grew up under political tutelage, in a backward country without a long standing tradition of craft unionism, encompassing within their ranks major organizations based on the agricultural work force.[2] Understandably its first major points of strength were the regional and city Chambers of Labour (on the lines of the French *Bourse de Travail*) rather than 'trade' unions on the British

---

1. Seyfarth *et al.*, *Labor Relations and the Law in Italy and the United States*, p. 22.

2. In the mid-1960s CISL continued to claim a membership of 525,000 in agriculture (175,000 sharecroppers and 350,000 day labourers). CGIL agricultural membership would be of the same order. ibid., p. 3.

and United States models. Chambers of Labour were able to rally a series of relatively weak union sections into a social force of some significance. Chambers of Labour were better fitted to rally masses of workers behind demands of a political party than a series of sectional unions. The fact that Italian unionists lacked basic political rights and needed political reforms as a precondition for effective union action was also a factor of importance adding credence to the predominant role of Chambers of Labour. The Chamber of Labour, it is clear, was a response to a specific series of socio-political and organizational problems. Equally the Italian emphasis on 'class' rather than 'trade' unionism is as much a specific response to practical problems as an indication of an ideological preference in itself.

The basic structure of all three rival union confederations, CGIL, CISL and UIL, is essentially similar. Each comprises a series of industrial federations, combined into a single national confederation. Given the unwillingness of the Italian worker to pay regular union dues, the limited membership, itself divided between three rival organizations, the framework of many federations remains skeletal to say the least. Lack of financial resources makes many federations heavily dependent on the confederation for staffing, personnel and guidance, thus limiting autonomy and reinforcing instrumentalism.[1] In Italy it is the central confederation which dominates the national unions and not the affiliated unions which grudgingly concede powers and finance to a central body as in the cases of the TUC, the AFL–CIO and the unions of Belgium and Germany. The low density of membership in most areas of Italy emphasizes the importance of the local Chamber of Labour. The Chamber, by combining the resources of the various federations in a given area, is able to provide services, leadership and representation, which none of the federations would be able to provide for themselves individually.

Traditionally the Chamber of Labour is the organization closest to the worker and the one to which he is most likely to turn for aid and assistance. The absence of union 'in-plant' bargaining means that in most cases the federations are a series of local associations of workers in similar trades and occupations linked horizontally through the Chamber of Labour and vertically through the national offices of their federation. Thus in agriculture the federation combines sections for sharecroppers (*mezzadri*), agricultural day labourers (*braccianti*) and small peasant farmers (*coltivatori diretti*). In most cases these do not maintain separate headquarters at local level but operate instead either through common

1. Suggested as exceptions to this rule are the metal-workers', textile, chemical and agricultural-workers' federations of CGIL; metal, textile, chemical-workers' federations in CISL, the chemical-workers' federation of UIL: Edelman and Fleming, p. 12.

services provided by the Chamber of Labour or through the national or provincial structure of the federation. Only the strongest federations, such as the metal-workers, and even here not in all cases, are able to maintain offices and organization at local level, with a fully developed city, regional, provincial structure up to national level. Thus in 1961 the CISL Food Industry Federation could claim only 20,000 members out of a workforce of 250,000 eligible for membership. The equivalent CGIL federation claimed 30,000 members. The headquarters of the CISL federation numbered only two full-time officers and a typist. The CGIL headquarters is not likely to have been much better staffed.[1]

The Chamber of Labour, properly speaking, should be seen as a co-ordinating arm of the confederation on which it will usually be dependent. The Chamber of Labour aims to provide at city or provincial level the range of services provided by the confederation itself nationally. Thus the chief officials of the Chamber of Labour will frequently be the best-known and most experienced union 'leaders' in the locality. A secretary general, assisted by as many other secretaries as its own income and the Chamber's importance to the confederation can support, will seek to elaborate and apply confederation policy to its area. The Chamber will rally popular support to political campaigns inaugurated by the confederation at national level, and seek to provide negotiating and technical assistance to category federations whenever this is required. The Chambers of Labour are, it will be seen, extremely important bodies. Nevertheless, the Milan Chamber, the most important in the CGIL, was 9 million lire in the red at the end of 1955. The debts of the Milan provincial federation, if included, would have raised this figure still higher. The same year the Turin Chamber of Labour, the CGIL's second largest, closed its books owing 7 million lire in unpaid rent and a further 8 million lire in unpaid social insurance contributions for its employees.[2] The Turin Chamber, in 1961, in a city where FIAT alone employs 100,000 workers, housed a staff of fifty. Twenty were on the Chamber's own payroll, the rest on the staff of the various national federations, with, one imagines, the metal-workers predominating.[3]

Given the lack of developed bargaining structures, the congresses of the confederations and of the national federations have been in the past

1. Galenson, *Trade Union Democracy in Western Europe*, p. 10. The CISL claim for 1972 had increased to 45,000. *Conquiste del Lavoro*, Rome, July 1973, p. 24.

2. Neufeld, *Italy*, p. 508. In Turin during 1959 one investigation reported only 20 CGIL and 40 CISL locals functioning, none of them with 'real power or contact with employers'. In Bologna, a communist stronghold, a city of 400,000 inhabitants with a PCI dominated municipal council, 'not a single local union was functioning': Galenson, *Trade Union Democracy in Western Europe*, p. 9.

3. Galenson, p. 10.

occasions of political rather than industrial importance. Confederation congresses are held in most cases at three-year intervals. The conduct of proceedings ensures the domination of the platform over the rank and file. The number of delegates normally gives proceedings more the character of a rally than a serious congress. According to repute, one CGIL general secretary opened proceedings with a speech which continued, with a break for lunch, for seven hours, through the whole course of a day's proceedings. Since the mid-1960s however the control of the platform over the floor has loosened. Congresses have come to be a much more genuine forum for debate and decision.

Between congresses power is delegated to a large National Council on the continental model comprising both persons chosen by the congress and representatives of the national federations. The Council is called only two or three times a year. Since it is too unwieldy to conduct detailed business, powers are delegated to an executive chosen from its ranks. The executive meets monthly and supervises the work of a full-time professional secretariat. The secretariat handles the day-to-day business and controls the life and activity of the organization. A general secretary heads the secretariat. Under his jurisdiction are a number of secretaries each with a specific field of authority. The UIL secretariat numbers ten, the CGIL twelve, the CISL eight.

The political associations of Italian unions, the excessive parliamentarian bias of Italian society, has meant that key union posts traditionally have been fiefs at the disposal of political parties. Union secretaries have been political figures and parliamentary deputies as well. Political office has supplemented the income of union leaders and opened the way to a more lucrative career.[1] Political and union career structures have become so interconnected that in many cases it is impossible to separate one from another. An important number of union officials have seen their posts only as a stepping-stone to higher political office. Trade union work and activity have suffered greatly as a result.

While for a union with an empty treasury a deputy's salary may temporarily provide sustenance difficult to find elsewhere, the practice of dual office-holding is plainly harmful to the effective conduct of union business. In recent years experience has led to this view becoming much more widely held among the rank and file of all three confederations. Agonizing debates around the principle of *incompatibilità* have now spread to all three confederations. Certain union leaders have been forced to choose between one career structure and the other. Some have resigned their union posts as a result. Others have abandoned their positions as parliamentary deputies. Pressures are mounting to declare

1. An Italian MP is paid around £7000 a year. RAI, the Italian TV network, employs some 21,000 'outside collaborators', many of them sinecures awarded as a result of political affiliation. *Guardian*, 13 May 1971, 9 Feb. 1972.

incompatibilità also applicable to the holding of dual office as union leader and member of the formal leadership of any political party. The intent is to reduce the high degree of instrumentalism which has characterized Italian unionism in the past.[1]

The real spokesmen for most Italian union organizations are to be found in the secretariats of the various confederations. Here the key decisions are taken, here the key battles are customarily fought. Until recently the main role of the rest of the union structure has been to carry out decisions already made above, in the secretariat of the confederation. As a rule it has been the confederation which subsidizes the national unions, not, as elsewhere, the national unions which from their own dues income maintain the apparatus of the confederation.

One root cause of the weakness of Italian unionism is the unwillingness of the Italian worker to pay even the low level of existing union dues. This unwillingness is attributed by some to the Mediterranean climate and a happy-go-lucky Latin temperament. A more likely explanation lies in worker recognition of the political instrumental character of Italian unionism, and the inability of too many unions to deliver serious wage gains or offer perceptible 'on the job' protection or services.[2] Thus although US official statistics are more detailed, precise and comprehensive, Italy reports one million industrial accidents a year against two million in the USA which has a workforce three and a half times as large. Italian unions have neither sought nor been accorded closed-shop provisions which might have heightened their bargaining power at the point of production. The fear that closed-shop provisions might strengthen the CGIL is one reason for the legal contention that compulsory union membership would be outside the terms of the constitution.

A further factor conducive to union weakness in Italy *may* be an unusually high ratio between social wage and cash wage. Figures have been published which indicate that although average hourly rates in the USA are approximately four times those of Italy, fringe benefits in Italy exceed those of the USA by a perceptible margin. If, as these figures suggest, the Italian social wage approaches the cash wage then

1. CISL and UIL are proposing that positions of leadership in any merged union confederation should be incompatible with office at any level in a political party. As far as the CGIL is concerned this would involve a choice between the Communist Party and CGIL for some 50,000 persons. At present some eighteen top CGIL leaders, including Lama, the General Secretary, are reportedly members of the Central Committee of the Italian Communist Party (PCI). For one view of this see Montana, 'The plight of Italian democracy', *Free Trade Union News*, March 1972.

2. 'Until the early 1960s both wage rates and earnings in Italy were held well under the rise in productivity, though they exceeded the increases in consumer prices': Edelman and Fleming, p. 29.

this would certainly militate against union membership.[1] In the past party organizations, confederation officials, individual militants, have seen the unions more as agents for mobilizing the masses than as self-acting organizations designed to deliver social and economic benefits.[2] Some years ago a CISL official in Turin, an industrial city, reported that only less than half his 'members' paid dues regularly. There is no reason to believe the past experience of CISL in this regard to be any different from that of CGIL and UIL. The average level of dues payment in the CGIL metal-workers' union, one of the best-organized in Italy, before the institution of the check-off, has been put at between six and seven out of the twelve months in the year. An increase to ten months out of twelve followed the institution of check-off. Yet even this 50 per cent increase of dues income would still leave a very large part of the membership out of compliance by British and United States standards.

Even if all Italian union members paid union dues regularly, and this clearly is in no sense the case, Italian unions would still be short of funds since the dues level itself is low. The dues requirement of CISL membership has been put, over the years 1968–72, at between 6500 and 12,000 lire a year in industry and between 3000 and 6000 in agriculture. In 1970 CISL minimum dues were reported as 4000 lire a year.[3] Of this sum, 800 lire represented the fee for the membership card issued by the confederation, on the sales of which membership claims are based.[4] The balance of 3200 lire represents the total of twelve months' dues. In fact, as is well known, workers frequently buy cards at the beginning of the year and then fail to pay any dues at all. In most cases dues will certainly be paid only for part, not for all of the year. Unless there exists a check-off, the payments actually made to the federation are not likely to exceed one half or at most two thirds of the amount nominally due. No fund, no services; no services, no membership strength. This is the vicious circle from which the Italian unions have yet to break out.

To understand the behaviour of sections of the Italian labour force, the contradictory phenomena of upward deference in unions and labour force coupled with near-anarchist outbreaks of strikes, demonstrations

1. Seyfarth *et al.*, *Labor Relations and the Law in Italy and the United States*, pp. 141–2. This issue merits further investigation. One problem is that whereas 'fringe benefits' may be defined in the same way, the weight of the specific components may vary a great deal between one country and another. Such shifts in balance can have great significance for union organization.

2. Thus one authority reports that in 1965 Confindustria found CGIL easier to bargain with than CISL, no doubt because CGIL, under competition for membership, wished to gain tacit management support so as to maintain its position: Edelman and Fleming, p. 46.

3. Seyfarth *et al.*, *Labor Relations and the Law in Italy and the United States*, pp. 8–9. *Conquiste del Lovaro*, July 1973, p. 25.

4. For a detailed breakdown of union dues in all three confederations as of 1957–8, see Neufeld, *Italy*, App. B, p. 554.

and even violence, one must take account of the rural origin of much of the modern working class. Mass immigration from South to North has meant that the predominant life experience of a large part of the labour force (including for example workers on the FIAT assembly line) has been that of the underprivileged agrarian South. To such a first-genera-tion proletariat, the ideas of union organization and union negotiation are alien. The union organizer who is confronted with the question 'We have something to eat, what more do we want?' clearly faces problems which vanished from the labour movements in most industrial countries a long time ago.

On balance it is doubtful if any of the three union confederations and more than a few of the category federations are financially self-support-ing. All three union confederations have negotiated state subsidies which are used for 'vocational training'. The government also 'grants money for social welfare services operated by the trade unions'. All unions similarly participate in the social service programme and receive cash from the state for the service they provide in this regard. The CGIL in the past has been dependent on subventions from the Com-munist Party and indirectly the Russian government. CISL has cer-tainly received aid from the Church hierarchy. At the time of the split and for some years after both CISL and UIL received substantial aid from the United States. FIAT and Montecatini are alleged to have given financial aid to both CISL and UIL in the past.[1] Equally there have been allegations of an exchange of favours between FIAT and the PCI and CGIL following the allocation to FIAT of a contract for a motor plant employing 20,000 workers at Togliattigrad in Russia.

Given the political importance of the Italian unions, the essentially competitive relations of the confederations one to another, the absence of any concept of a 'a fully-paid-up member', the membership figures claimed have usually owed more to romantic imagination than statistical accuracy. Thus when in 1973 CISL for the first time made available precise *claims* for both federation and confederation membership, this was described as giving the example of a major trade union organization which 'opens its secret books'. This decision was publicized as a breach with past Italian tradition in which 'for reasons of organizational patrio-tism there had taken place a certain artificial inflation of membership figures'. In the case of CISL this had led to *claims* of a membership of more than a million and a half, even reaching almost two million at a time in which as now revealed the true *claim* was 1,620,000. There is no reason to suppose that the past practice of CISL has differed from that of CGIL and UIL in this regard. Comparable figures for both organiza-tions are still lacking. Even in the case of the CISL figures published in

1. Edelman and Fleming, p. 13; ILO, *The Protection of Trade Union Funds and Property*, p. 26.

1973 the extent to which these represent fully paid up membership cards, as against cards merely issued, is not clear.

It seems reasonable to conclude that all figures quoted in Italy are inflated. Regularly included are whole contingents of old-age pensioners[1] whose connection with the field of productive labour is tenuous to say the least. The author's estimate would put the CGIL ahead in blue-collar, CISL ahead in white.[2] UIL is based mainly in metal-working, chemicals and the ENI complex generally. In 1968 the membership officially claimed by each confederation was CGIL – 3·3 million, CISL – 2 million, UIL – 1·5 million. A more realistic estimate would put CGIL at a maximum of 1·7 million, CISL at no more than 1·2 million, UIL at around 300,000. In a labour force of some 19 million this is no large proportion. Attested by the rigid accounting procedures of Britain, Germany and the USA the figures might fall even lower.

The metal-working trades are far and away the best-organized sector of the Italian economy. Yet even here membership can be highly volatile. According to one authority CGIL organized 40,000 employees at FIAT in 1950. Ten years later, out of 100,000 FIAT employees in Turin the CGIL could claim no more than 1000.[3] In 1969–70, after the institution of the check-off, and according to official union claims, less than 600,000 of the 1·3 million workers in the metal-working industry were organized. Out of these FIOM–CGIL claimed 300,000, FIM–CISL 180,000 and UILM–UIL 80,000.[4] The balance of these figures is probably unduly favourable to the CGIL. If figures derived from check-off records examined by the author are representative, then CISL and UIL combined probably narrowly outweigh the CGIL all along the line. In the FIAT plant at Turin, at most 30 to 40 per cent of workers are organized and this despite the high strategic importance accorded to FIAT by both the unions and political parties.[5] If the level

1. 300,000 in the case of CISL in the mid-1960s, 160,000 in 1972; the number in CGIL is presumably greater.
2. A table showing distribution of union loyalties in a single plant, which indicates a clear bias in favour of CGIL amongst blue-collar and in favour of CISL–UIL in white collar, will be found in Seyfarth *et al.*, *Labor Relations and the Law in Italy and the United States*, p. 22.
3. Sergio Garavini, 'Gli anni cinquanta alla FIAT: un esperienza storica', p. 44. One view of FIAT in the immediate post war years will be found in Lanzardo, *Classe operaia e Partito Communista alla FIAT*.
4. *Unity and Victory*, published by FIM/FIOM/UILM, Rome, 1969, p. 5. FIOM (*Federazione Impiegati Operai Metallurgici*) is the metal-workers' federation of CGIL, FIM (*Federazione Italiana Metalmeccanici*) and UILM (*Unione Italiana Lavoratori Metalmeccanici*) the metal-workers' federations affiliated to CISL and UIL respectively.
5. For two views and some factual background see Garavini, pp. 44–55, and Castellina, 'Rapporto sulla FIAT', *Il Manifesto*, July–Aug. 1970, pp. 12–24; see also Lanzardo.

of organization at FIAT is any indication the figures claimed for the metal-working industry as a whole are considerably exaggerated.[1]

One indication of Italian union membership is given by recently published *claims* of CISL. These show a total of 1,160,000 members who are either pensioners, agricultural or white-collar workers: the farm bloc comprises 350,000 farmhands and 175,000 sharecroppers, 300,000 pensioners constitute the next largest category, 100,000 municipal employees and 85,000 civil servants come next in line. CISL claimed 260,000 metal-workers in 1970 after the conclusion of the highly successful 1969 contract negotiations. The most important of the thirty-five federations in the CGIL are, according to official *claims* metal-workers – 450,000; agricultural workers – 360,000; building-workers – 300,000; and chemical-workers – 200,000. The character of any confederation must be influenced by the relative weight of its constituents. The fact that CISL until recently organize double the number of workers in agriculture than in engineering, the fact that its enrolled pensioners outweighed its municipal employees and civil servants combined, cannot be without influence on the conduct of its affairs. The CGIL also organizes large numbers of agricultural-workers and old-age pensioners, though it generally has a heavier blue-collar weighting than the CISL.

The air of mystery with which most of the essential credibility data regarding the strength of Italian unions has been deliberately shrouded in the past, an air which remains, if less impenetrably up to the present day, makes it difficult to assess the present situation. In retrospect, however, the metal-workers 'check-off' agreement of 1962–3 consolidated and extended to some other federations in 1966, 1969 and 1972 does seem to have assumed an importance quite disproportionate to that which its apparent 'technical' nature would initially lead the observer to assume. The 'check off' does seem in practice, and quite apart from membership claims, to have increased real membership and to have strengthened the financial autonomy of federations and even confederations. If the 'check off' agreements are maintained and extended this process is likely to continue with important consequences for the future. The Italian unions, although still weak by comparison with Germany, Britain and Belgium are certainly stronger now in real terms, than at any time since 1950.

Clearly, neither from the viewpoint of finance nor that of membership are the Italian unions in a strong position as against the business class. Additionally, due partly to ideology and partly to financial weakness, none of the three confederations nor their federations possesses a strike

---

1. *Sull 'Organizzazione*, no. 3, 1971, an official publication of the CISL–FIM metal-workers' union, shows a membership of 80,000 in 1951 rising in a most uneven fashion to 260,000 in 1970: see tables pp. 68–75.

fund. The dominant view that strike funds inevitably lead to reformism and bureaucracy is hardly to be taken seriously. All Italian unions, not least those of the CGIL, are reformist and bureaucratic at the present time. The absence of strike funds enhances union dependence on external party political support. In strikes the political parties may mobilize popular goodwill, raise funds through public subscription and provide open and concealed subsidies via municipalities under party control. Strikes are seen less as a means of winning specific socio-economic demands than as an exercise in mass mobilization and propaganda. Strikes are accordingly short and normally not particularly well supported, a stoppage for a day here, a day there, an hour in one part of the factory, an hour in another. Such measures, while causing losses and inconvenience, do not bring determined management quickly to the bargaining table. Italian business knows this. So, one suspects, despite their wordy bluffing, do Italian union leaders. It is not without significance that although Italian labour is a great deal stronger now than before the First World War the average duration of strikes is a great deal shorter. The longer a strike continues the greater the danger the workers will develop a consciousness of their own, with objectives separate from those of party and union bureaucrats.

Italian union constitutions, unlike those of many other countries, do not contain well-thought-out provisions indicating by what method, whether by membership poll, conference decision, or executive vote strikes may be launched and settled. Effective decisions consequently rest with their leading elites. Lack of membership involvement means membership loyalty to strike decisions is limited. Willingness to accept the suffering and hardship which long stoppages involve is lacking. Instrumental unionism[1] develops a vested interest in bureaucracy and union weakness. The whole Italian labour scene bears eloquent witness to the fact.

FUTURE TRENDS

The growing distance between the present generation and the events that followed 1947-8, the changed economic and political situation, has led in the 1960s to a marked trend towards union reunification. These developments have gone farthest in the metal-working industry where the unions are strongest and most financially independent. In the negotiations of 1962-3 and again, more confidently, in 1966, 1969 and 1972, the three metal-workers' federations, FIOM, FIM and UILM (CGIL, CISL and UIL respectively), presented a common platform of demands to the employers. In the past union demands had been decided arbitrarily by union leaders without much regard to the

1. I use this term in the sense that the unions are used by outside forces for the achievements of ends external to the wishes and desires of the members themselves.

wishes and needs of individual members. To some extent in the negotiations of 1962–3 and 1966, to a much larger extent in the negotiations of
1969 and 1972, preliminary consultation on a fairly wide scale took
place. The union contract renewal campaign which took place during
the so-called 'hot autumn' of 1969 produced a range of popular
response which caused wide sections of the overseas press to anticipate a repetition of the Paris events of May 1968. The unions proved
able to muster more rank and file support than at any time in the
last twenty years. The outcome was the most successful contract negotiations since the Second World War. These gains have however to be
understood within the context of the Intersind Leverage Strategy of 1962
already outlined. The union campaign involved mass demonstrations,
coupled with a series of rolling, local, regional or enterprise stoppages,
varying according to location from a matter of hours to at most two or
three days. Confindustria broke off negotiations early in September.
Union pressure now built up on Intersind. Intervention by the Christian
Democrat Minister of Labour, Donat Cattin, a former union official,
caused Intersind, already markedly more conciliatory than Confindustria
to give further ground. On 2 November, on the eve of a 100,000 strong
union demonstration in Rome, Cattin, at a meeting with the state sector
employers, made fresh proposals for a settlement. These proposals led to
an agreement early in December. Confindustria, bowing to union and
government pressure, settled on substantially the same terms some two
weeks later. Much the most important innovation of the 1969 contract
was the recognition for the first time of a union presence in the plant.
Limited rights to rank and file representation within the enterprise have
been conceded. Union full-time officials may now hold meetings on
plant property. Union members attending such meetings may receive up
to ten hours' pay, per year, paid for by the company at basic rate.[1]
One further outcome has been the passage into law during 1970 of the
Statuto dei Lavoratori, a law governing union rights at the place of
work which has done a great deal to strengthen union credibility and
union organization in general.

There can be no doubt that both union militancy and the willingness of
mployers to make concessions sprang from exceptional elemental militancy from the base. The willingness of the unions to consult their members
and the workforce at large was conditioned by the growing emergence
of independent 'rank-and-file' committees (comitati di base) which
threatened the unions' claim to be valid representatives of the working
class. Thus at Pirelli, already in 1968, an unofficial movement organized
by the comitati di base forced the overthrow of an agreement negotiated

---

1. The best easily accessible account of the strikes and their outcome will be
found in the *Bulletin of the International Metal Workers' Federation*, Geneva,
Dec. 1969, pp. 22–3, 43.

by the unions and its replacement by an improved agreement closer to the aspirations of the workforce. The employers too seem to have sensed that their previous hostility to 'in-plant unionism' had allowed a dangerous vacuum to appear under their feet. The May 1968 events in France showed conclusively that the failure of unions to express the needs of rank and file workers and to orchestrate them into bargaining demands can result in a spontaneous explosion of discontent on a near-cataclysmic scale. The autumn 1969 negotiations showed that the key elements of that situation were to be found in Italy as well.

Almost a decade of growing unity of action has brought all three confederations closer together. Unity is in the air, detailed negotiations have taken place yet somehow never quite achieve fulfilment. Con-federal unity, at one time proposed for 1972, is still not a fact. Instead the bureaucratic alternative of a Federation of Confederations, the 'Federa-tion CGIL, CISL and UIL', in which each retains freedom and autonomy of action, has taken its place. Unification of the three metal-workers' federations seems more likely. Yet here too the fusion promised for 1973 has failed to take place.[1] The emergence of a single, united metal-workers' non-party, federation, independent of CGIL, CISL and UIL, would indeed totally disrupt the existing confederal power structure and set in train forces of dissolution which would prove difficult to restrain. Given the political, personal and bureaucratic vested interests in the present confederal power structures it is difficult to believe that even the unification of the metal-workers will be accom-plished in the immediate future.

Italian society in the years since 1948 has undergone a social and economic transformation without precedent in the present century. Yet despite these massive socio-economic changes the sterile irrelevance of Italian political life, its manifest inability to relate effectively to the problems facing the Italian people, has continued almost unchanged. In the years since 1965 the three union centres, on a basis of common action, have sought, as an independent power and pressure group, to force upon the government reforms in housing, schools, health and pensions which are long overdue, but which the secret intricacies of Roman coalition politics have brought to nought up to now. If the unions should prove able to break free of the sterile, largely spurious confrontations of Italian politics, organize the waiting millions, who in the past have with some justification stayed outside their ranks, it is possible that they may become the new motor of reform and social change for which the archaic structure of Italian society has already waited far too long.

1. For a revealing light on these negotiations, the AFL–CIO view and the prospect of a new split in the event that a merger goes through, see Montana, 'Projected "Merger" of Italian Unions follows Communist Blueprint' and 'The Plight of Italian Democracy', *Free Trade Union News*, January and March 1972.

7. Britain

The British labour movement is the oldest in the world, the product of the first industrial revolution in history, of the unique political and economic circumstances under which this revolution took place.

The past pre-eminence of British industry, the global extent of British trade and bygone imperial interest, has given the British population a worldwide, rather than predominantly European horizon. British cultural experience too, has specific characteristics of its own. A unified state free of foreign occupation since the twelfth century, English society is one in which the issues of Church versus State were settled in the reign of Henry VIII, over four hundred years ago. The fact that Britain has been for centuries a predominantly maritime power, without either a large standing army or a powerful state bureaucracy, has left its mark on the outlook and attitudes of the British people. Britain too is the nation in which the ideas of *laissez-faire* and parliamentary democracy first took firm root. The power of the monarchy was broken in the seventeenth century. Conflicts between the classes, although sometimes severe, have normally been resolved without recourse to revolution as a court of last resort. Peasants have long vanished from the social scene. Wage labour and capitalist farming, which have been the predominant mode of rural employment for the best part of two centuries, provide occupation for only a minor part of the population. In this surprisingly tolerant society, the British labour movement grew up under a set of constraints very different from those imposed upon its continental neighbours. It is for this reason that it assumes in many ways a markedly different form.

In outlook, organization and behaviour the labour movement in Britain is closer to the labour movements of Australia and New Zealand half the globe away, than it is to its nearest neighbours in France, Belgium and the Netherlands, across the narrow width of the 'English' Channel. The 'Empire', the opening-up of North America, gave Britain, like the USA, a vast 'open frontier', a fact too often unobserved since the new territories were not geographically contiguous to the United Kingdom. This frontier is not yet closed. Three-quarters of the white population of Rhodesia have been resident less than twenty years, a crucial factor underlying the equivocation by successive British governments in their dealings with the Smith regime. Through most of the nineteenth century, in terms of travel time and opportunity cost, Liverpool was a great deal closer to New York than New York itself to San Francisco or the West.

During the nineteenth and early twentieth century over 21 million British citizens emigrated, most to the United States, the British colonies and the dominions overseas.[1] In the British Empire and to a lesser extent in the USA, they imposed their pre-existing attitudes and modes of behaviour on the new social environment. Branches of British craft unions, like the Amalgamated Society of Engineers (ASE), were founded in places as far apart as Australia, New Zealand, South Africa and the USA.

The number of British emigrants in the nineteenth and twentieth centuries is to be counted in millions. Yet it is doubtful whether the number that left for any European country could be counted even in tens of thousands during this period. The British working population had wide horizons, horizons which encompassed the earth. Yet, whilst their sympathy for popular and revolutionary movement in nineteenth-century Europe was real, as their support for the causes of Polish liberty, Italian unification, the Paris Commune, the victims of Russian terror and the Balkan atrocities of the nineteenth century all showed, for British workers these events remained happenings in strange and alien countries, far away. The English-speaking world shared a common language and culture, was peopled with relatives and friends from one's own land. Although more distant, these territories seemed far closer than any nation across the Channel.[2] The Trades Union Congress (TUC) decided to exchange fraternal delegates with the Congress of the American Federation of Labor (AFL) in 1894. It has continued to do so each year ever since. The TUC has yet to establish a regular exchange of delegates with any national trade union centre across the Channel.

The British labour movement is different because the cultural experience of the British people has been different too. The Industrial Revolution in Britain took place in an unique conjunction of social and political circumstances. All have left their mark on the British labour

1. Between 1815 and 1912 the largest single contingent went to the United States. For annual figures see Carrothers, *Emigration from the British Isles*, pp. 305–6.

2. The population of England and Wales was 7·5 million in 1780, 23,000,000 in 1871, that of the United Kingdom, 21 million in 1821, 45 million in 1911. The number of emigrants between 1815 and 1912 was equal to the whole UK population in 1821, slightly less than half that of 1912. Carrothers, pp. 305–6.

movement, and separated it from others whose social experience has been different from its own.

The British industrial revolution took place in a society where the political–religious issues of Church versus State had been settled by Henry VIII in the sixteenth century. Much of the wealth, a large part of the lands confiscated from the Catholic hierarchy, were disposed of by the Crown in the endeavour to balance its own hard pressed finances. The English aristocracy never recovered from the Wars of the Roses which brought Henry VII, father of Henry VIII, to the throne.[1] These factors, each in their own way, helped to bring about in British society a spread of economic, and by implication political, power. In Britain, after the sixteenth century, the 'Church of England' was a state Church, servile and at the behest of the ruling elite. Thus in Britain, unlike in Continental Europe, the introduction of widespread popular education during the last quarter of the nineteenth century produced no great conflicts between Church and state. Popular education remained predominantly secular in content. Such controversy as arose was primarily concerned with the rights of dissenting groups, notably the low church nonconformists, as against the high church episcopalian establishment.[2] The Established Church was predominantly Tory in composition, its local appointments largely at the disposal of Tory landowners, its bishops sitting in the House of Lords. Non-conformisn was to a large extent Liberal in outlook, as were important sections of the urban and industrial working class. In Britain therefore conflicts over the religious content of education served to strengthen Liberalism rather than any other political force.

England was unusual, too, in that it had been a unified state within substantially unchanged boundaries for some seven centuries. Wales was forcibly enjoined in the fourteenth century and formally united with England in 1536. Scotland was added to England when the Crown passed to the Scots King James in 1688. France apart, Britain is the oldest unitary state in Europe. 'Occupation' and 'Resistance' are terms which the British can grasp only by an act of imagination, for these are happenings of which the British people have no personal or folk experience whatever. Armed hostilities have not taken place on British soil since the

1. 'From the reign of Henry VII down to the last days of James I by far the better part of English landed estates changed owners and in most cases went from the old nobility by birth and the clergy into the hands of those who possessed money in the period of the Tudors, i.e. principally the merchants and the industrialists or the newly created nobility and gentry who, to a great extent, were allied to the former class of people in England': Liljegren, *Fall of the Monasteries and Social Changes in England Leading up to the Great Revolution*, pp. 130–31.

2. In Britain the Catholics, like the Jews, were part of an underprivileged minority.

end of the Civil War in the seventeenth century.[1] True, the Irish remained a subject people in a situation in some ways like that of the Poles under the Tsar.[2] Yet, in the end, independence left Britain with only the intractable problem of Northern Ireland which it continues to face up to the present time. The British people thus possessed a quite marked sense of national identity at a time in which many other modern nations were only about to begin to acquire their own.

The close proximity of the territory of what is today Belgium, the Netherlands and northern France to her own south coast gave England a permanent strategic interest in maintaining friendly governments in these domains. The descendants of William the Conqueror indeed for several centuries laid claim to the throne of France. Only the discovery of America turned English attention away from continental involvement towards a wider and more global role. Britain became a maritime, a naval, and in the end, an imperial power.

The British Parliament viewed the maintenance of a large standing army with pronounced disfavour and consistently refused to vote funds to keep one in being. All through the nineteenth century, when the conscript armies of the continental powers were numbered in millions, the British army consisted exclusively of volunteers. Military conscription was never enforced in Britain before the twentieth century.[3] Until 1916 even the First World War was fought entirely by volunteers. At least one prominent historian implies that the war could have been fought through to a successful conclusion without recourse to conscription at all.[4]

The British Parliament had gained its supremacy over the Crown only by a bloody civil war. Parliament remained profoundly suspicious of any institution likely to limit or undermine its powers. A large standing army was anathema. A powerful navy, away from home, ever ready to protect trade, was quite another thing. In the ideology of the British political system it was the citizen who came before the state, rather than the other way about. The British state never acquired a great standing bureaucracy, nor any centralized administration on the Napoleonic model.

The ideology of modern 'bourgeois democracy' originated in Britain. Economists like Adam Smith, politicians like Cobden and Bright, originated and propagated the ideas of *laissez-faire*. The British believed in a 'night watchman' state, the role of which was to be minimal. In line

1. The Scots rebellions of 1715 and 1745 involved some combat on English soil but only of a very limited order. Ireland, of course, was another matter.
2. The Poles however were more cultured than the Russians.
3. Although the 'press gang' continued to take citizens for enforced service in the navy until the Peace of 1815.
4. This appears to be the view of A. J. P. Taylor; see quotation from Auckland Geddes, in Taylor, *English History, 1914–1945*, pp. 84–5.

with this view the ruling class resorted to violence less easily than elsewhere, being more inclined to retreat from untenable positions than to
seek to hold them by violent and possibly self-defeating means. The
British parliamentary system, although through most of the nineteenth
century it excluded the bulk of the population from the franchise,
nevertheless for most people remained a system to be improved and
amplified rather than overthrown. The Reform Act of 1832 enfranchised
the rising entrepreneurial class, thus pre-empting any subversive alliance
between the middle and working classes. Then, too, Britain's social
structure never knew an intelligentsia on the European, still less the
Russian model. The British socialist intellectual was usually 'Fabian'
and reformist, when elsewhere he was Marxist and, at least in form,
revolutionary as well. Russia produced Lenin and Trotsky, Britain
produced Sidney and Beatrice Webb. In the late nineteenth century and
to a marked degree in the twentieth, the Indian Civil Service and the
Colonial Administration, offered an acceptable middle-class career,
governing 'native' peoples overseas. This was a bureaucratic career
structure. Yet it did not engender a large self-sufficient bureaucracy at
home in Britain.

The Industrial Revolution in Britain was eased by the wealth already
accumulated before the take off point was reached. The exploitation of
India, the three cornered trade in slaves and sugar, the piratical exploits
of English freebooters, provided funds which made investment easier
than elsewhere. Entrepreneurial skills were in relatively abundant
supply. At home by the eighteenth century enclosures had turned farming into a capitalist, predominantly market-oriented activity. Agricultural wage labourers employed by capitalist farmers, rather than
independent peasants, sharecroppers, or landless peasants working on
large estates, came to be the natural representatives of the rural workforce. During the nineteenth century free trade, later the railway, the
steamship and refrigeration, combined to reduce the importance of the
agricultural sector in the economy. Agriculture absorbed one quarter of
the adult male labour force in 1851. By 1911 agricultural wage labour
was down to one twentieth of the employed population, the agricultural
workforce overall down to 8 per cent of the whole.[1] Britain was a
predominantly urban society already in 1860, a situation not achieved in
Germany until the last years of the nineteenth century, in France until
the years between the two world wars.

Laissez-faire, in comparison with what had gone before, was a
liberating ideology. The first generation of labour leaders were deeply
influenced by it. Yet by the use of only a modicum of expertise they were

1. On this Court, *A Concise Economic History of Britain*, pp. 200–207. Rural
depopulation was relative, not absolute. The rural population of England and
Wales in 1911 was larger than in 1841; see Court, p. 232.

able to use the dominant ideology to provide a rationale for their own activity. If labour was bound to provide a 'fair day's work', it was self-evidently entitled to a 'fair day's pay' in exchange. The individual wage worker, unsupported by collective organization, was at a manifest disadvantage when it came to bargaining with his employer. Thus union organization was a logically admissible innovation, even within the limits of the system. The union was a protection without which the worker would be forced to accept a lower wage than that to which he was properly entitled. Liberal union leaders could thus assert the right to organize and defend the short term interests of labour without in any way challenging the legitimacy of the system as a whole.[1] To the miners, concentrated in one industry communities, with a great need for legislation in respect of safety provisions and hours, often with Tory landowners taking royalties or owning the mines, political action seemed an urgent necessity, the Liberal alliance almost a matter of course. The modern labour movement thus rose alongside and even in alliance with liberalism, rather than direct contradiction to it, as in most countries of continental Europe.

RISE OF THE LABOUR MOVEMENT

The British working class was formed in the first industrialized country in the world in an era in which the ideas of *laissez-faire* were dominant within the state. The relatively open character of society, one which had recognized the supremacy of parliamentary institutions since the seventeenth century, could not be without influence on the nature of both the class and its organizations. Thus while the authorities made widespread use of informers and even provocateurs, the British state possessed no secret political police until the Special Branch was set up to counter Irish revolutionism in 1883. Britain to this day does not possess any national police force, nor any special armed force with public order responsibilities like the Gendarmerie in France and Belgium, the Marechaussee of the Netherlands, or the Carabinieri in Italy. Nor does Britain possess any special para military riot police, such as the French CRS or the Italian Pubblica Sicurezza. Although the authorities at one time had recourse to a newspaper tax[2] designed to price radical publications out of the working-class market, Britain never knew a direct censorship of the press at any time between 1815 and the outbreak of the First World War. The rights of free speech and assembly, although not invariably

1. See for example, Howell, *Labour Legislation, Labour Movements and Labour Leaders*, pp. 338–9, 451, 489, 493, and esp. 495–8.
2. In 1819. The tax was widely evaded by radical publicists hundreds of whom went to jail for their pains. Prosecutions were commonplace until 1834. The tax was not abolished until 1855.

honoured, extended far beyond the narrowly circumscribed ranks of the propertied electorate.

Workmens' combinations were penalized by such measures as the Combination Act (1799) and the Act against Unlawful Oaths (1797) which made offenders liable to seven years transportation. The Combination Act was repealed in 1824. When in 1834 six Dorset farm labourers were sentenced to transportation to Australia for administering illegal oaths in a trade union ceremony, trade union feeling was outraged. Within a month 'an enormous procession of trades unionists' estimated at between 30,000 and 100,000 strong demonstrated, peacefully, in London. In response to a public campaign which gathered over a quarter of a million signatures, a free pardon was granted in 1836. After two years' delay the victims were brought home and re-established in relative comfort with funds raised by public subscription.[1] British trade unionists, during the nineteenth century, were far from possessing untrammelled freedom to organize before the law. Hostile legislation and a prejudiced judiciary continued to hamper the growth of British trade unionism until the turn of the century and even beyond. Yet, as this example illustrates, the social context of British society was very different from that of continental Europe. The legal sanctions which British labour movement pioneers had to face were a great deal less than those which confronted their brothers across the North Sea and 'English' Channel. The 'free born Englishman' may have looked much less free from the USA, yet in regard to continental Europe, he was free indeed. The list of political exiles who took refuge in Britain during the nineteenth century, which includes Marx, Engels, Garibaldi, Mazzini, Kropotkin and Zola, makes this plain.

The disenfranchised working population, under its own leaders, and with its own programme, 'the Charter', organized to demand the vote as early as 1838. The Chartist agitation lasted for some ten years before going down to defeat. Reform Acts in 1867 and 1884 subsequently widened the electorate to include the bulk of the adult male population. Universal male suffrage had to wait until 1918. Elder women received the vote for the first time this same year, all women over the age of twenty-one, ten years later in 1928. The suffrage issue never assumed the same importance in the formative period of the British labour movement as it did elsewhere, notably in Belgium, Germany and Italy during this same period.[2]

The extension of the franchise in 1867 was followed by the establishment of popular education in 1870. In the absence of a strongly

1. Webb and Webb, *History of Trade Unionism*, pp. 129–33; Pelling, pp. 39–42.

2. There was, of course, an intense militant campaign for *women's* suffrage in the years before the First World War, but this was not the same thing.

entrenched Catholic Church there were no confessional issues to precipitate wide divisions between sections of the working class. Nor was
there any cause for socialists and Liberals to present a common front
against clerical reaction. The way was left clear for some British socialists
to rationalize their attitudes in religious terms. 'Christian Socialism',
unknown in most of Europe, became a force of some importance, influencing leaders of the stature of Keir Hardie and Philip Snowden in the
early days.

The British labour movement was influenced too by the fact that the
composition of the working class was more chemically pure than in most
countries elsewhere. Britain was a predominantly urban society already
in the second half of the nineteenth century. The agricultural sector, no
longer primary, was of rapidly decreasing importance. The town
worker was fully urbanized, maintaining none of those personal links
with the countryside which have remained of importance in Italy,
France and Belgium almost to the present day.

TRADE UNIONS

The skilled worker, especially the craftsman whose abilities were
indispensable for the building of machines, occupied a strategic bargaining position of great importance during the industrial revolution. The
origins of the trade societies to which many such men belonged often
ante dated the industrial revolution. 'Combinations' of English working
men can be traced as far back as the fourteenth century. More permanent
and continuing forms or organizations were firmly established during the
eighteenth century. Organizations like the Amalgamated Union of
Engineering Workers (AUEW; formerly the Amalgamated Society of
Engineers: ASE) can trace their origins back to 1851 or even before.
Such a line of unbroken continuity surpasses that of states like Germany
and Italy in continental Europe.

Originally such craftsmen did not seek to 'bargain' with their employer
at all. Rather, through their 'trade societies', they fixed the minimum
rates of wages, the hours and conditions of labour, on which alone they
were prepared to provide their services to employers. Union benefit
funds were available for the support of members out of employment
whether due to depression in the trade or to a refusal to 'work below the
rate'. Union dues were high, but they entitled the member to a whole
series of friendly benefits, thus giving him a vested interest in maintaining continuous union membership.

British trade societies were cautious bodies. Nevertheless they
possessed real fighting power in case of need. Coal-miners in Durham
were able to organize a ten-week stoppage as early as 1851. Over
£100,000 was raised to support Preston operatives in a six-month

stoppage during 1853-4. In London, during 1859-60 the building unions stayed out for six months in order to defeat the employers' imposition of a no-unionization clause on their employees.[1]

British trade union activity based itself on a presence at the point of production from the very beginning, establishing itself on a local basis, only later extending organization to a district and national level. The first trade unionists organized round their craft and places of employment, producing forms of organization as manifold and varied as the work situation itself. The class-consciousness expressed by British trade unionism sprang from the practical experience of wage workers, rather than out of a socialist critique of a class society, as in some other countries in Europe. In Britain the unions came first, the emergence of a socialist party only a great deal later. If British workers to this day retain a pragmatic approach to problems, something of an innate suspicion towards intellectual schemas, it is in part the outcome of a soundly based awareness of their ability to do things for themselves, without outside intervention, however well meaning.

British unionism remained based on skilled workers until around the turn of the century, when advances in the organization of the unskilled began to be made. The Trades Union Congress, the first national all-union body in Britain, was founded in 1868 and has met annually ever since. At its foundation in 1868 the TUC affiliates enrolled some 120,000 members, by 1900 the number had climbed to 1·2 million, by 1910 to 1·7 million, by 1914, on the eve of the First World War, to 2·7 million, by 1919 to the impressive total of some 6·5 million.[2]

The British socialist movement, by contrast, was a very late developer. Britain's first socialist organization, the Marxist, Social Democratic Federation (SDF), was founded in 1884. The SDF, whilst influential, was never numerous and failed to elect a member to Parliament on its own account. The Independent Labour Party (ILP), founded in 1893, less orthodox but numerically more important, provided the nucleus of Labour's later socialist representation in Parliament. In 1900 a number of unions affiliated to the TUC; the SDF, the ILP and the Fabian Society, combined to establish the Labour Representation Committee (LRC). This was a coalition of organizations, not an institution in its own right. Not until the Labour Party opened its doors to individual membership in 1919 did Britain see the establishment of a mass socialist party on anything approaching the continental model.

1. For these examples, Pelling pp. 44-8, 52-3; for contemporary documents bearing on twenty stoppages before 1860, see Frow and Katanka, *Strikes: A Documentary History*, pp. 1-88.

2. These figures, if anything, understate the position since there were also a number of unions outside the TUC. Thus the all-union figure for 1900 is 2 million, 1910 – 2·6 million, 1914 – 4·1 million, 1919 – 7·9 million: Pelling, tables, pp. 261-2; TUC, *Annual Report*, 1971, pp. 668-9.

LABOUR PARTY

The British labour movement was characterized by the early growth of union organizations, led in the main by skilled craftsmen, which originated locally and only subsequently extended to national level. These trade societies were founded and firmly established long before anything approximating a modern socialist movement came into being. The union leaders who sat alongside Marx in the General Council of the First International were in no sense socialists. The British labour movement had acquired its own leaders, sprung from its own ranks, with their own traditions of organization, long before the socialist movement came upon the scene. The socialists who formed first the Social Democratic Federation (SDF), later the Independent Labour Party (ILP) were confronted with a labour movement fixed not plastic, one with its own leadership, predominantly Liberal in composition, already formed.

Two miners' leaders, Alexander MacDonald and Thomas Burt, were elected to Parliament on a Liberal ticket as early as 1874. By 1895 the number of Liberal–Labour (Lib–Lab) MPs had risen to eleven, six of them miners. This was at a time when the socialists had proved unable to gain any parliamentary representation at all. The precondition for a big move forward proved to be a clear breach with Liberalism, the conversion of the unions to the socialist cause. This process was largely completed between 1898 and 1918. Once this was accomplished the Labour Party moved forward rapidly, replacing the Liberals as the official opposition in 1918, forming notably unsuccessful minority governments in 1924, and again in 1929–31. The Labour Party participated in the wartime coalition from 1940 to 1945, and has since formed one-party governments, which have lasted from 1945 to 1951, and 1964 to 1970.

The relation between unions, TUC and Labour Party are complex. First, not every union is affiliated to the TUC.[1] At times in the past the discrepancy between overall union membership and TUC affiliation has been quite large. At present, only a few unions, mainly white-collar, stand outside the TUC. The TUC is the only British national trade union centre and there has never been another. Between the TUC and the Labour Party there is no organic link. Each stands as an independent body in its own right.

1. The best short account of the principles and practice of the TUC will be found in its own publication, *Trade Unionism*, 1966. This comprises the evidence submitted by the Trades Union Congress to the Royal Commission on Trade Unions and Employers' Associations. In 1970 the returns of the Registrar of Friendly Societies listed 9,277,000 union members as against 8,875,000 for the TUC.

Just as not all unions are affiliated to the TUC, so not all members of individual unions are affiliated to the Labour Party. Every union, irrespective of whether it affiliates to the Labour Party, maintains a separate political fund, financed from a special subscription, held in a separate account. (This is a legal requirement.) Most British unions do in fact affiliate to the Labour Party. Yet a decision to affiliate does not automatically commit every union member. Any member, if he so desires, may contract out of that part of the union subscription, which is devoted to political purposes. The picture which emerges is an interesting one. In Britain there are some 10 million union members affiliated to the TUC. Only some 5·5 million are also affiliated to the Labour Party. The British unions organize throughout the United Kingdom. Some also organize in the Irish Republic although most of the unions in Ireland have only southern Irish jurisdiction.

The British Labour Party is an unusual coalition of forces, something on the lines of the original Belgian Workers' Party (POB). Membership falls into two distinct categories, individual and affiliated. Individual membership, first constituted in 1919, stood at 200,000 when the first count was made in 1928 and reached a peak in excess of 1 million in 1952. Since that time membership has fallen sharply. The present claim of 700,000 is certainly exaggerated. The real figure is probably at least one third less.[1] Affiliated membership falls under two heads, trade unions and affiliated societies. The affiliated societies are few in number and small in membership. Although they command one seat on the party executive they are not otherwise of great importance. The 5·5 million affiliated trade unionists provide the bulk of the party finances and a large majority of votes at the annual party conference. Each trade union casts its vote as a single block so that where several large unions are in agreement, they exercise a disproportionate influence on conference proceedings. In the past this system has assured the parliamentary party (i.e. the deputies) of a solid block of right-of-centre support. In recent years shifts to the left in some major unions have upset the previous balance. The consequences for the party power structure and policies are not yet clear.

The British unions have for many years made it a general rule that service as a Member of Parliament should be incompatible with full-time union office. Thus when Frank Cousins, General Secretary of the 1·6 million strong, Transport and General Workers' Union (TGWU), was asked to serve in the Labour Government of 1964–70 he was required temporarily to relinquish union office in order to do so.

1. Basically because each of the 635 constituencies needs to register a minimum of 1000 members in order to achieve representation at the party conference. It is well known that many have a far lower enrolment. For membership figures, see *Annual Report*, 1972, p. 47.

Exceptions to this rule are rare. In a similar fashion top union leaders have to choose between service on the TUC General Council and membership of the National Executive of the Labour Party. A rule, unwritten but firmly enforced, makes dual membership quite unthinkable. Unions do however send a number of their members to Parliament as trade-union-sponsored Labour MPs. At the present time the 'trade union group' of members sponsored to protect union interests in this way numbers some 116 Labour MPs.

The broad character of the Labour Party as a coalition of trade union and socialist interests is reinforced by the working of the British electoral system. Based on simple majorities in single-member constituencies, the electoral system works to the advantage of the two major parties and discounts minority representation.[1] Experience shows that dissidents who seek to express views outside the broad range of permissible Labour opinion are likely to be summarily obliterated at the polls.

The British Communist Party, founded in 1920, never split the mass labour movement with the same success as its counterparts in France, Germany and Italy. Party membership, never large, is now around 29,000. Communist influence within the unions is greater than numbers might suggest, but overall not of great significance. In recent years communists have controlled only one major union, the Electrical Trades Union (ETU). This control was lost when inquiry established that their majorities was achieved by unscrupulous rigging of the ballots for officers and executive. There are no communist MPs in the House of Commons. There is however one communist, Lord Milford, who sits in the House of Lords.

UNION SIZE AND STRUCTURE

Labour relations in Britain, until the most recent days, have been distinguished by a pronounced bias against either legal or state intervention. Perhaps because, in a situation the converse of that in most continental European countries, British workers possessed real industrial bargaining power before they acquired substantial political influence, the British unions have always preferred to settle matters direct with employers. Recourse to the law has been envisaged only as a last resort. In the words written some years ago, of one leading authority, 'there is, perhaps, no major country in the world in which the law has played a less significant role in the shaping of industrial relations than in Great Britain and in which today the legal profession have less to do with industrial relations'.[2]

1. No one party, Labour, Tory or Liberal, has achieved an overall majority of the votes in the years since 1945. Nevertheless Britain has known only one-party governments through all these years.
2. Otto Kahn Freund, in Flanders and Clegg, p. 44.

The Industrial Relations Act of 1971 set out to change all this, met
with no marked success and was repealed in 1974.

Much of the character of British industrial relations springs from the
specific features of the British unions and the British social situation,
already outlined. In all there are some 142 unions affiliated to the
TUC.[1] The three largest British unions, the Transport and General
Workers' Union (TGWU, 1·6 million), the Amalgamated Union of
Engineering Workers (AUEW, 1·3 million) and the General and

MEMBERSHIP OF THE LARGEST TUC AFFILIATES, 1960 TO 1966

Membership in thousands	1960 TUC (Dec. 1959 membership)	1966 TUC (Dec. 1965 membership)	Change as%
Membership growing			
TGWU	1,240·8	1,443·7	+16
AEU	907·7	1,049·0	+16
NALGO*	273·6	348·5	+27
ETU	233·6	292·7	+25
NUPE†	(200)	248·0	+24
SOGAT‡	193·1	225·0	+17
Total 'rounded'	3,050	3,607	+18
Membership static			
GMWU	769·0	795·8	+3½
USDAW	351·5	349·2	−1
Total 'rounded'	1,120	1,145	+2
Membership falling			
NUM	639·0	446·5	−30
NUR	333·8	254·7	−24
Total 'rounded'	970	700	−28

NOTES
* Affiliated 1965.
† Affiliation to TUC in 1960 was given in a rounded number.
‡ The Society of Graphical and Allied Trades. This union was formed late in
1965 by the amalgamation of the NUBPW and NATSOPA. In the table the
1960 affiliation figures for the two constituent unions have been combined.
SOURCE: John Hughes, *Trade Union Structure and Government*, 1968.

1. There are also certain problems about the count. Thus the Draughtsmen's
and Allied Technicians' Association (DATA) has merged into the AUEW of
which it is now the Technical and Supervisory Section (TASS). However in
many ways both bodies continue to function as independent unions. For statistics
of TUC membership, TUC, *Annual Report*, 1971, pp. 636–82.

Municipal Workers' Union (GMWU, 850,000), together represent some 37 per cent of the TUC's affiliated membership. The TGWU and the GMWU are 'general' unions, each with specific areas of regional and industrial strength. The AUEW, a craft union expanded to include both semi-skilled and unskilled workers, now also has something of a 'general' character. The AUEW occupies what is in continental terms a 'metal-working' jurisdiction.

The ten largest unions comprise some 62 per cent of the TUC affiliated membership. Four are unions with a general recruitment within a single economic sector; of these two, the AUEW and the Electrical, Electronic, Telecommunications Union – Plumbing Trade Union (EETU–PTU) are sector-general unions with a craft union base, whilst two more, the Union of Shop, Distributive and Allied Workers (USDAW) and the National Union of Public Employees (NUPE) are simple sector-general unions. Two organizations, the National Union of Mineworkers (NUM) and the National Union of Railwaymen (NUR) are industrial unions. One, the National and Local Government Officers' Association (NALGO), is a white-collar, public service sector union. One, the Society of Graphical and Allied Trades (SOGAT), is a sector-general–industrial union hybrid. Evidence submitted to the Royal Commission on Trade Unions and Employers' Associations provides interesting details regarding the fortunes of the ten leaders. Over the years 1960–66 the membership of the two industrial unions, NUM and NUR, fell sharply alongside the contraction of coal-mining and railway employment, a drop overall of 270,000 members or 28 per cent. The membership of two unions, the GMWU, a general union, and USDAW, a sector-general organization, remained static. The six remaining organizations, TGWU, AUEW, NALGO, EETU–PTU, NUPE and SOGAT, recorded an increase of some 550,000 members or 18 per cent over their enrolment at the beginning of the period. NALGO and NUPE with interests in public employment and the EETU–PTU with a sector-general jurisdiction were proportionately ahead with membership increases of between 24 per cent and 27 per cent although, due to their larger size, the increases registered by TGWU and AUEW were numerically the larger.[1]

Trade union bargaining in Britain it should be emphasized, remains the preserve of the individual national unions, and not the TUC. The TUC possesses only such powers as are freely delegated to it by the constituent unions. Since the leading committees of the TUC are manned by the more important officers of the national unions there are clear constitutional safeguards to ensure that this situation remains unchanged. The TUC General Council, which meets monthly, comprises thirty-nine members, fixed numbers being allocated to each of the

1. On this see Hughes, *Trade Union Structure and Government*, pp. 2–12.

nineteen trade groups, thus ensuring representation of all major industrial sectors in the day-to-day deliberations of the TUC.[1] Consultation between TUC and government on matters of importance to the trade union movement takes place as a matter of course.

Union congresses meet annually as a rule although in some cases only at two-yearly intervals. A fair measure of conflict between platform and floor is customary. The normal practice of preparing the agenda around several hundred resolutions submitted from the base adds an element of uncertainty to the outcome of the proceedings. As a result the 'feeling' of the labour movement emerges from the series of union conferences lasting from March to early June. The process achieves its consummation at the conferences of the TUC and the Labour Party which take place in the first weeks of September and October each year.[2]

The union conference determines and if necessary amends the union constitution and decides union policy. The union conference is normally composed of delegates 'working at their trade' elected direct to the conference by union 'branches' which may vary in size from less than 100 to 1000 members or more. In the case of the TUC however union national officers play a predominant role.

In a minority of cases, such as the engineering section of the AUEW, elections may be indirect. In this case the district committees, which are chosen by branches and shop stewards, appoint delegates to divisional committees which in turn select delegates to the National Committee which fulfils the functions of a conference. In the GMWU delegates to the national conference are chosen at regional level. Once at the conference they sit and vote as a block, much in the manner of individual union delegations at the TUC and the Labour Party Conferences. The business of the union conference comprises as a rule two sections; consideration of the report submitted by the executive on its activity since the last conference and discussion of policy resolutions. The latter normally occupies by far the larger portion of the time. The major part

1. The nineteen trade groups, with their membership, as reported to the 1971 Congress, are; Mining and Quarrying 300,000, Railways 300,000, Transport (other than Railways) 1,760,000, Shipbuilding 127,000, Engineering, Founding and Vehicle Building 1,540,000, Technical Engineering and Scientific 360,800, Electricity 420,000, Iron and Steel and minor Metal Trades 160,000, Building, Woodworking and Furnishing 375,000, Printing and Paper 400,000, Textiles 150,000, Clothing, Leather and Boot and Shoe 270,000, Glass, Ceramics, Chemicals, Food, Drink, Tobacco, Brushmaking and Distribution 475,000, Agriculture 100,000, Public Employees 135,000, Civil Servants 600,000, Professional, Clerical and Entertainment 350,000, General Workers 860,000. The breakdown and nomenclature of the trade groups itself gives an insight into origins of the TUC.

TUC, *Annual Report*, 1971, pp. 644–82.

2. In the British labour movement the terms 'conference' and 'congress' are used indifferently, each signifying the same thing.

of the conference will be occupied with resolutions and amendments to resolutions submitted by the branches or local organizations (the floor), although the executive (the platform) can and does also submit major policy resolutions on its own account. The largest conferences like those of the TGWU, USDAW and the TUC, which may comprise as many as 1000 delegates, last normally three to four days.[1] The smaller conferences such as that of the AUEW National Committee and the NUR may last several weeks. As may be appreciated the style and content of the proceedings at large and small conferences varies a great deal.

Conduct of union business between conferences is customarily in the hands of an executive elected by the membership, normally on the basis of geographically defined divisions, or in some cases, as with the TGWU, a mixture of geographical and trade divisions. The chief officer is normally the general secretary, although he may, in some cases, be the president. In a majority of cases the general secretary is elected by the membership as a whole. Once in office he will usually retain the post until retirement. The locus of sovereignty rests in president, general secretary and executive combined. There are variations in emphasis depending on circumstance, constitution, tradition and personality. There is no constitutional provision for presidential leadership on the US union model, nor for the kind of pre-eminence of one leading official above all others frequently found in both Catholic and communist organizations. There is for example, no automatic 'changing of the guard' in the central office whenever the incumbent president or general secretary is replaced by another with different opinions. Nevertheless institutional factors do tend to make the general secretary the most important single figure within the union. In the case of the TGWU in particular, the policy and attitudes of the union have been closely linked with the outlook and attitudes of the union's successive general secretaries.

Full-time union officials are in most cases appointed by the executive. Officials of the railwaymen (NUR), the engineers (AUEW), and some other unions are elected by the members.[2] Responsible downwards to their electorate, upwards to their executive, elected union officials sometimes find life difficult. The appearance of a 'militancy cycle' which reaches a peak as the ballot for re-election looms ahead is not unknown. There have been many criticisms of the system of electing full-time

1. It is interesting to note that over the years it has become customary to hold union conferences at seaside resorts. One presumes the practice began in part because delegates had to forego their holiday entitlement in order to attend, in part as a perquisite for delegates and their families. Nowadays Blackpool is the only resort with halls big enough to handle the proceedings of the larger conferences and sufficient accommodation to house the influx of delegates and visitors.

2. For a valuable elaboration on these topics see Hughes, Part 2, pp. 41-8.

union officials, not all from inside the labour movement. Nevertheless, those trade unionists who do elect their officials seem well satisfied with the result. Proposals to change the procedure rally but little support.

INDUSTRIAL RELATIONS

British employers' associations arose, in part at least, as a reaction to the rising pressures of trade union organization. In their early years employers' associations often fought bitterly to deny union recognition and enforce the 'open shop'. Nowadays the principle of union recognition is more generally conceded. The main national employers' association is the Confederation of British Industries (CBI). The CBI does not bargain on its own account. The bargaining role rests with the hundred or so national employers' associations who are members of the CBI. Probably the most important single association is the Engineering Employers' Association, which covers some 4600 establishments employing several million workers. Evidence to the Royal Commission estimates that 14 million of 16 million manual workers in employment, and 4 million of the 7 million non-manual workers, were covered by national negotiating machinery.

The structure of collective bargaining in Britain is too complex to permit of any simple description. Voluntary negotiating bodies, either in the form of Joint Industrial Councils or comparable *ad hoc* institutions, covered all major sections of British industry by the end of the Second World War. The demarcation of an industry for bargaining purposes depends far more on the practical exigencies of employers' interests and union jurisdictional boundaries than on any intellectually precise definition. Multiple union organizations do not usually constitute any obstacle to joint union representation in industrial bargaining. The Confederation of Shipbuilding and Engineering Unions (CSEU), encompasses some thirty affiliates and some 1,900,000 members. Nevertheless it usually manages to present a common front to the employers without experiencing undue strain. Not all employers are members of their respective employers association. Ford and Vauxhall in engineering, ICI in chemicals, bargain on their own account, direct with the unions. Agreements with such *non-federated* firms may be company-wide or concluded on a plant-by-plant basis. Industry-wide or company agreements do not normally preclude bargaining at enterprise level, by local union representatives. Evidence submitted to the Royal Commission on Trade Unions and Employers' Associations of 1965–68 suggests that workplace negotiations take place in as many as 80 per cent of the cases in which union organization exists.

SHOP STEWARDS

Plant negotiations in Britain are largely the responsibility of local shop steward organization. To catch the essence of shop steward activity in a form communicable to a foreign audience is not an easy task. The shop steward is more than the French *délégué du personnel*, he bears comparison with the German *vertrauensmänner* and the German Works Councillor, the Italian *uomo di confianza* or a member of the *commissione interne* but he is not the same as any of these. The shop steward is by definition an employee[1] of the enterprise. Inside the workplace he functions not as a representative of the workforce as a whole but only of those employees who hold union membership. As such the steward must hold credentials from the union of which he is a member. Yet he is not normally *appointed* by the union. Rather he is the *elected* representative of a section of the workforce, who happen to be union members, and are perhaps divided amongst more than one union organization. In most places of work, there is likely to be more than one shop steward. If the plant is large enough, a 'chief shop steward', 'senior steward', 'convenor' or 'chairman of the shop steward committee', will be elected by the stewards themselves. The convenor will co-ordinate activity and in case of need head any delegation to management. According to circumstances a proportion of the time spent by the shop steward on union business, during working hours, will be paid by the company.

Rank and file workplace negotiation is a crucial part of the structure of British union activity, an essential part of the mechanism of British industrial relations. The high level of rank and file activity is one explanation of the otherwise low level of union dues and professional staffing which characterizes much of British trade union life. A large part of the responsibilities which in other countries would be assumed by union full-time officers in Britain fall upon rank and file members. Accurate estimates of the number of full-time union officials in Britain are hard to come by. One estimate has put the figure at 2600.[2] Included were a number of officials at union headquarters not directly involved in the bargaining process. According to the TUC the number of shop stewards continually involved in day-to-day activity in British industry during 1960 was in the region of 200,000. More recent research suggests that the true figure may be far higher.[3] One survey suggests that union officials

1. i.e. on the payroll. In Britain in the term 'employee' carries no exclusively white-collar connotation.
2. Clegg, Killick and Adams, *Trade Union Officers*, pp. 38–9, 90–91.
3. This is a question which would repay further examination. For the figure of 200,000, TUC, *Annual Report*, 1960, p. 128. For a much lower figure of 90,000, 'no better than a guess', Clegg, Killick and Adams, p. 153. For the view of McCarthy, that 'the truth is probably somewhere between the two figures', *The Role of Shop Stewards in British Industrial Relations*, p. 5. McCarthy and

work on average fifty-seven hours a week.[1] Evidence to the Royal Commission indicates that stewards spend on average six hours a week on union business.[2] If we make the legitimate assumption that the work of both officials and stewards is necessary to the effective conduct of union business we can make an assessment of the relative loads they bear. On the basis of a nominal forty hour week shop steward activity gives us a manning equivalent of 30,000 full-time union employees. The 2600 union officials, spend on average fifty-seven hours a week on union business. On the basis of a nominal forty hour week this gives us the equivalent of 3700 union full-time employees. In short, of necessary union activity, as defined above, 90 per cent is conducted by shop stewards and only 10 per cent by union officials.[3]

The shop steward movement provides a continually bubbling reservoir of militant rank and file activity within the official union movement. At times, notably, during the war of 1914–18, it emerged as a force in its own right, with leaders and an ideology of its own.[4] In a number of industries there can be no doubt that the steward organization exercises a powerful influence on the pattern of national union behaviour. There have been proposals, utopian but recurrent, that a nationwide shop steward movement could itself replace the 'bureaucracy' of the official union movement.[5] Hugh Scanlon, the President of the AUEW, is a former shop steward and there can be no doubt that this experience has deeply coloured his outlook and actions. The desire to curb the growing power of the shop steward movement, to bring it under greater disciplinary control from the official union machinery, was certainly one of the moving forces behind the Industrial Relations Act of 1971.[6]

Union–employer agreements fall into two categories, substantive

1. Clegg, Killick and Adams, p. 63.
2. McCarthy and Parker, p. 17.
3. For this novel presentation I am indebted to my colleague W. Conboy of Oxford.
4. On this Kendall, *The Revolutionary Movement in Britain, 1900–1921*, pp. 105–69; Pribicevic, *The Shop Stewards' Movement and Workers' Control*; for the ideology, Murphy, *The Workers' Committee*.
5. For one such proposal see Murphy, above. Utopian because a nationally organized shop steward movement would rapidly begin to reproduce the very 'bureaucratic' features it was set up to oppose; misplaced, because, as we have shown, the stewards already exercise great power within the unions and could exercise more if they really so desired.
6. McCarthy and Parker give detailed information regarding the range and scope of shop steward activity. A table of issues covered by shop steward bargaining will be found on pp. 83–4.

Parker, *Shop Stewards and Workshop Relations*, p. 16, provides figures ranging between 168,000 and 222,000, and finally opts for 175,000. The Commission of Industrial Relations study, '*Industrial Relations at Establishment Level*', London, HMSO, 1973, pp. 3, 4, 72/4 puts the the figure of union stewards at 285,000.

agreements which regulate wages and conditions, procedural agreements which establish a recognized method of reaching substantive agreements and resolving disputes which may arise during their terms. Procedural agreements usually allow for local differences to be processed through several main stages. First, reference to local supervision, the steward, through to the convenor and up to the plant top management. Second a 'works conference' at which 'full-time' union officials are called in to meet the employers with a view to resolving the difference. Thereafter there may be a reference to a local or regional body comprising employers' and union representatives (formerly known in engineering as a 'local conference'). In some cases a reference to a similarly composed national, industry-wide body (formerly known in engineering as the 'central conference') may follow. The exact method varies from industry to industry but in all cases two characteristics emerge. Settlement is arrived at as near to the source of grievance as possible. The parties themselves almost always attempt to settle without outside help, whether legal or otherwise. At each stage settlement depends on agreement between the parties, arbitration normally is not involved. The union aim has always been to settle as many issues as possible in the plant rather than at the higher level of the machinery. The evidence shows that most disputes are, in fact, settled within the plant. Nevertheless the excessive delays which such lengthy procedures may involve, are one factor leading to unofficial strikes. In engineering the delays in procedure are such that many stewards consider limited local stoppages a far more efficient method of settling disputes.[1] During 1972 differences between the AUEW and the Engineering Employers' Federation grew so sharp that the national procedure agreement ceased to be recognized by the unions. Whether national negotiating machinery will be re-established, and if so on what basis, remains at this moment uncertain.

MEMBERSHIP

The effectiveness of workers' representation in British industry which rests on a conflictual rather than a legal representative base, is largely a function of the level of membership and extent of activity of rank and file trade union organization. Important to the working of this system is the fact that in most cases employers have now, however reluctantly, come to concede that once a fair measure of blue collar union organization has been achieved in their enterprise, then they should be prepared both to meet and negotiate with union full-time officials.[2]

1. For an account of industrial relations in this sector: Marsh, *Industrial Relations in the Engineering Industry*.
2. For an elaboration of this question, as far as white-collar organization is concerned see Bain *Trade Union Growth and Recognition*, pp. 31–97.

One important factor in this regard is the 'closed shop'. In this by means of a variety of different procedures and union enforced job employment constraints, trade unionists refuse to work alongside non-union members, thus 'closing the workshop' to all but *bona fide* trade union members.[1] This process, is of course, not original. It is only the extension to the manual and white-collar working classes of a practice already of long standing among doctors and other professional men. Bodies such as the British Medical Association (BMA) and other 'trade associations' of the professional classes have long enforced job employment constraints of a similar and indeed far more wide-ranging order. The leading authority on the closed shop in Britain, W. E. J. McCarthy, has calculated that roughly 3·8 million workers, some 39 per cent of the unionized labour force, or some 16 per cent of the labour force overall, are employed in closed shops. The closed shop is likely to appear wherever the nature of the job situation makes it appear desirable and the work force possesses the bargaining power to enforce it on the employer. The largest single groups covered by the *fully* closed shop are the miners, process and skilled workers in iron and steel, workers in the printing industry, co-operative employees, shipyard workers, seamen, port workers, and bus crews and maintenance staff on London Transport. The closed shop is also enforced widely, although not universally, in the engineering industry.[2]

Widely criticized, the closed shop has been declared illegal in more than one country in continental Europe. In Britain, where the population is noted for its longstanding concern for the cause of civil liberty,[3] the closed shop does not provoke any widespread concern as a threat to the freedom of the individual. If anything, it is becoming more rather than less important, as the years go by. The short lived Industrial Relations Act of 1971 (apart from certain minor exceptions) declared the open-entry closed shop void. Nevertheless it continued to function, for practical purposes, as before.

The density of union membership in Britain can be measured fairly accurately. A research paper submitted to the Royal Commission reported, on the basis of 1964 figures, a labour force of 23·6 million, a union membership of 10·1 million overall and a density of organization of 42·6 per cent. Global figures however do not give the full picture. A

1. For the nature and operation of the closed shop see McCarthy, *The Closed Shop in Britain*, pp. 16–26.

2. The co-operative movement is one case in which the closed shop is enforced rather more from above than from below, for example, McCarthy, pp. 58–60.

3. British citizens have, for example, steadfastly resisted proposals to require individuals to carry a national identity document. Such a document was briefly accepted during the Second World War but once hostilities were over public opinion rapidly forced a reluctant government to abandon the measure.

proportion of the total labour force are workers in part-time employment, notoriously difficult to organize. Three million persons are engaged in the distributive trades where the multitude of small undertakings with only a handful of employees pose great organizational problems. If the level of organization in these areas is lower than average, so, in others, it is a great deal higher. Evidence submitted to the Royal Commission during 1965–68 reported densities of organization which varied from 12 per cent in distribution to 95 per cent in coal-mining. Shown with a density of over 50 per cent were engineering 55 per cent; paper, print and publishing 59 per cent; footwear 63 per cent, railways 73 per cent; transport excluding railways 76 per cent; gas, electricity and water 81 per cent; local government 82 per cent; national government 87 per cent; coal-mining 95 per cent.[1]

The high density of organization in national and local government is worthy of note. Government employees gained recognition of the principle that they should be entitled to join a union and to negotiate their terms of employment collectively, as a result of the Whitley Report, in the years following the First World War. Local government employees subsequently sought and gained the same rights. Since the number of persons in national and local government service totals some 5,250,000, these rights, plus the obligation implicit on public undertakings to be a 'good employer', have exercised a marked influence on the level of union membership. On the other hand, the fact that in these sectors recognition was, as a result of external factors, conceded from above, often before a thoroughgoing membership at the base had been built up, does seem to have effected the situation. There is some evidence to suggest that the extent of local bargaining is less, the concentration of power at the top of the system rather more, than in most areas of private industry.

Another factor of importance has been the obligation imposed by statute on nationalized industry to draw up with the unions joint machinery 'for the settlement by negotiation of terms and conditions of employment'.[2] This provision has served to enhance the already high level of unionization amongst manual workers in these industries and to clear the way to a marked increase in organization amongst white-collar employees where the level hitherto had been low.

Nevertheless there remain important areas of the economy which up to now the unions have proved unable to organize effectively. In these sectors Wages Councils settle the wages of some 3·5 million workers. The Wages Council consists of equal numbers of union and employers'

1. Statistics for the year 1964, *Selected Written Evidence to the Royal Commission*, p. 23.
2. Clegg, p. 388. The quotation is from the wording of the Coal Industry Nationalization Act.

representatives, plus up to three 'independent' members appointed by the state. One of the independent members acts as chairman. Proposals agreed by the parties, or carried by the casting votes of the independents, are then referred to the Minister who will normally embody them in an order. This minimum is then the subject of statutory enforcement. It is characteristic of the British labour movement that the unions should up to now have preferred this somewhat involved method of negotiation to the enactment of a legal minimum wage. In recent years Wages Councils have come under criticism. Their activity has failed to raise the chronically low level of organization in the sectors which they cover. The effectiveness with which their statutory minima are enforced leaves much to be desired.[1]

The complexity of British wage bargaining is enhanced by a further factor which has come to the fore in the years of full employment since the Second World War. In private industry at least, there is likely to be a marked difference between nationally negotiated rates and actual weekly earnings. National negotiations produce what have come to constitute base rates only. Over the years local negotiations have aggregated special increases of one kind or another which in some cases bring 'earnings' up to 100 per cent or more over nationally negotiated figures. Bargaining thus takes place at two related but largely independent levels. 'It means . . . that from time to time an industry agreement adds to the levels of pay, themselves largely or partly determined in the plants.'[2] In the past none of these agreements have been deemed legally binding, nor has it been the prevailing wish of either unions or employers to make them so. It is significant that the outcome of negotiations between unions and employers is in Britain termed an 'agreement' whereas in many other countries it is known as a 'contract'. The Industrial Relations Act of 1971 sought and failed to enforce changes in this situation. The Act has now been repealed.

Working hours in Britain have fallen by between one third and one half since the turn of the century. The reduction, however, is less than a first reading of union agreements might suggest. A normal working week was down to 47-8 hours by 1920. Although mines, building and printing did better than this, the general level held until 1939. Hours fell to 44 in the aftermath of the war. A further reduction to 40 hours had become general by 1967. In fact however the work week of male employees continued to average 46 hours, even in 1969.[3] Management

1. On this evidence of the Ministry of Labour to the Royal Commission, p. 119.
2. Clegg, pp. 138-40.
3. Perhaps an understatement since the official figures subsume short-time working and lost time in the overall count. On the other hand employers may use payment for somewhat notional overtime to bid up the going rate.

and men have both used overtime as a means to make up what were tacitly conceded to be unduly low earnings. Part of this overtime is real. Part should be regarded as 'manufactured'. Among women, who at the margin would appear to value leisure time more highly than money, average working hours, at 38, are a great deal lower than for men.

Rather less than one half of British workers were entitled to holidays with pay in 1938. By the end of the Second World War one week's holiday had become customary. The general level has since risen to two weeks and is now approaching three. Although Wages Councils fix holidays as well as wages and hours, holiday provisions remain a subject for trade union bargaining rather than governmental legislation. Annual holidays with pay apart, the number of public holidays in Britain stands at a lower level than in most continental European countries.[1] The same holds true of annual holiday provisions.

STRIKES

In Britain strike statistics, like the football results, receive a great deal of publicity, although in their case the emphasis is on grim despair, rather than joy and jubilation. The true significance of these statistics seems to this author much overrated. Production and wages lost one day are likely to be made up the next. Cargo intended for British industry, shut out of the Port of London, can hardly be offloaded at Antwerp and delivered by road from there. A strike which removes causes of tension in the workplace may increase, rather than decrease, output and productivity. In the international league strike tables, Britain normally appears way above Scandinavia, the Netherlands and Germany, where in most recent years the man hours recorded as lost by strikes have been for practical purposes negligible. On the other hand, British strike figures have been consistently lower than those of Italy, and in particular those of the USA. Major official stoppages in Britain, in post war years, have been rare. The miners' strike of 1972, the Industrial Relations Act of 1971, both suggest that this pattern may be about to change.

A study conducted for the Royal Commission showed that in the years 1964–6 unconstitutional stoppages accounted for 95 per cent of strikes and 70 per cent of working days lost through industrial disputes. Most of these stoppages were brief and localized, affecting only one plant or part of a plant, lasting a few days at the most. There is a great deal of evidence about the causes of unofficial strikes, much of it

1. Five to six public holidays in Britain, as against ten in Belgium, nine in France, ten to thirteen in Germany, seventeen in Italy, six to seven in the Netherlands: see *The Common Market and Common Man*, p. 17, London, EEC Information Office, 1969.

inconclusive. Evidence submitted to the Royal Commission suggests that insecurity of employment and sharp variations in earnings due to causes beyond the workers' control are important contributory causes.[1]

A taste for history is required to put this much-exaggerated issue into proper perspective. Between 1891 and 1926, a yearly average of 17 million working days were lost through strikes. The annual average in the years 1956–68 was rather less than one quarter of this figure. In 1971 man-days lost through strikes amounted to 13·5 million. In this same year man-days lost through unemployment amounted to 164 million, those lost by illness to 314 million and by industrial injuries to 20 million.[2]

The provisions made by union constitutions for calling official strikes vary. In some cases the power to call a strike may be vested in the union executive. In others, as in the case of the miners, where in this century official stoppages have been industry-wide, the rules may demand an affirmative vote of the whole membership. In most cases however a simple majority of the competent union body and the subsequent endorsement of the union executive is all that is required. There are no complicated and restrictive provisions on the German model.

There is little uniformity in the level of British union subscriptions which vary a great deal between one organization and another. In many cases unions dues are collected by shop stewards or other union representatives at the place of work. Until recently, in the engineering section of the AUEW, a provision in the rules, more honoured in the breach than in the observance, called for union dues to be paid by a personal visit during the branch meeting. In about one case in five dues are deducted by the employer from the pay packet, by means of the check-off and paid direct to the union. The TGWU, currently charge two main rates of subscription, one at 12p per week, the other at 20p. The difference is largely accounted for by varying rates of subscription to union social assurance schemes which continue to be an essential part of the service offered by almost all British unions to their members. The subscriptions of most members to their unions probably fall within the range of 10 to 20p per week. Unions pay an affiliation fee of 8p per member per year to the TUC. In one typical year, 1971, TUC income from affiliation fees amounted to some £640,000. British unions thus pay around 1 per cent of their income to the TUC. This must be measured against 12 per cent paid by German unions to the DGB and a comparable proportion paid by the Belgian socialist unions to the FGTB.

The aggregate funds of the British unions are very large, some £134 million overall. Yet these funds are by no means as large as they at first

1. Clegg, pp. 316–22.
2. Clegg, p. 314; Hansard, 26 May, 5 June 1972.

appear. The funds of the AUEW total some £14 million.[1] This calculates out at only £11 per head, sufficient to finance a national stoppage by the whole membership for only a matter of days. British union dues have not risen, over the years, in line with workers' wages. If, as seems likely, the new Industrial Relations Acts leads to longer and more frequent official disputes, union dues will need to rise.[2] Strike benefits remain low. Thus, those of the mighty TGWU, at £5 per week, are hardly sufficient to maintain a long dispute. This is not the whole story. In 1971 the Post Office Workers stood out for six weeks, in 1972 the miners for seven weeks, in each case without strike pay. Discretionary strike benefits were paid only to members hard pressed through special personal circumstances. One reason for this staying power is an unusually high sense of union solidarity. Another is the fact that the striker's family, although not the striker himself, is entitled to social security benefits provided by the state.

INCOMES POLICY

Over the twenty-five years since 1945, union strength has been higher than ever before. Throughout these years, the economy has run at around the level of full employment. These constraints have turned the attention of successive Labour and Conservative governments towards the elaboration of an incomes policy. The term itself is something of a misnomer. Thus a foremost authority defines 'an incomes policy . . . as an attempt to alter the level of wages or salaries, or to alter the pace of their change'. Although in exceptional circumstances such policies have sought to raise wages, 'such policies are far less common than attempts to hold back the rate of increase in incomes at times of rising or full employment'.[3] In British experience, incomes policy traditionally has been directed at holding back the rate of increase of wage and salary income rather than that derived from property and investment.

The Labour government of 1945–51 enforced a policy of wage restraint with some success between 1948 and 1950. In the end the dam broke. Wages moved forward. The Labour government lost the general election of 1951. The Conservative government announced its own short-lived pay pause in 1961, set up a National Incomes Commission, a National Economic Development Council and proposed a norm of 2–2½ per cent for future increases. The Labour government of 1964–70 made a fresh and more enthusiastic endeavour. A 'Declaration of Intent'

1. *Report of the Registrar of Friendly Societies*, Part 4, Trade Unions, 1970, p. 6; AUEW, *Annual Report*, pp. 60–61, 71.
2. On this 'Paying our dues', *Voice of the Unions*, Oct. 1972, p. 3.
3. Clegg, p. 413.

signed on behalf of the government, the TUC and the employers was inaugurated with a flourish of publicity in December 1964. The Declaration of Intent promised 'to maintain a stable price level' and 'to keep increases in total money incomes in line with increases in national output'. A National Board for Prices and Incomes was set up with a mandate to inquire into particular cases referred to it by the government. The Declaration of Intent, more ambitious than its predecessors, was no more successful. Prices rose. Voluntary wage and salary restraint, accepted by the unions, held the lines for a while only to be followed by an upsurge of wage claims. The government, against its will, was forced to devalue in November 1967. In part at least in response to foreign pressure the government introduced in 1969 proposals for legislation to limit the right to strike and to impose legal penalties on those who came into conflict with its terms. These proposals, introduced by a Labour government, created an uproar in the labour movement. In the end they had to be withdrawn. The government went out of office in 1970 in pronounced disfavour with its own supporters for which the incomes policy bore a heavy responsibility.

The Conservative government, elected in 1970, has made reform of industrial relations a keystone of its policy. An Industrial Relations Act on similar lines to that of the Labour government, but more stringent and extensive in its provisions, was passed into law in August 1971. This Act for the first time introduces the law into British industrial relations on a large scale. It sets out to make written agreements entered into or renewed since the passage of the Act legally binding, unless their terms expressly state the contrary; to make unions liable for damages in court of law in respect of the actions of their members; to limit the right to strike, backing this limitation with legal sanctions; to interfere in unions' internal procedures by withdrawing from unions which fail to 'register' important privileges, hitherto in their possession. The TUC refused co-operation. Most major unions refused to register. In response to union pressure the Labour Party gave specific undertakings to repeal the Act when next in office. The more important employers proved hesitant to take advantage of the provisions of the Act for fear that the damage such action might do to their relations with the unions would outweigh any benefits.[1] The Labour government returned in 1974 duly removed the Industrial Relations Act from the Statute Book. A large part of the provisions of the Act had remained ineffective even while legally it remained in force.

FUTURE TRENDS

The future trend of events in the British labour movement is far from

1. Actions under the Act were brought only by small employers.

clear. In part this is because in Britain, as in most other states of Western Europe, the post war patterns of labour movement behaviour are beginning to break up and it is too early yet to say definitely what will take their place. The Labour government of 1945–51, which national-ized coal, electricity, gas, steel, railways and parts of road transport, established the national health service and virtually created Britain's modern welfare state, seems in retrospect to have temporarily exhausted the reform capacity of the Labour Party. The Conservative Party now accepts Labour's reforms as part of the foundation of the modern state. The Conservatives, equally, if less explicitly, have adopted the Keynesian approach to government management of the economy. No Labour government, neither the 'minority' governments of 1924 and 1929–31, nor the 'majority' governments of 1945–51 and 1964–70, have yet elaborated adequate measures of strategic defence against crises of con-fidence resulting from 'runs' on the pound sterling, which orginate abroad. Over the last decade and a half the British economy has shown a lower rate of growth than that of most countries in Western Europe. If the economy has run to capacity the balance of payments deficit has risen alarmingly. When government intervention has lowered capacity utilization and improved the balance of payments, the rate of growth has fallen as a result. Thus, in 1971, government deflationary policies brought the level of unemployment to around 1 million, the highest figure since 1940. Government-induced deflation, by limiting growth and reducing investment, has undermined Britain's competitive position, thus reinforcing the 'stop–go' cycle already under way. Since Britain is deeply and inextricably involved in world economy the problem is a very real one.

What post war experience has demonstrated most of all is the increase in power of the unions. Union activity, undertaken by a kind of constitu-tionally unrecognized 'fourth estate', exercises influence of a major importance on economic behaviour throughout the economy. The dis-cussions about incomes policy, wage restraint, and related matters, are all a reflection of this fact. Whether such problems can be resolved without endowing organized labour with a far greater control of the enterprise remains to be seen.

The leadership of the trade union movement has shifted in the last years from right to left of centre. This has reflected the change in the power balance inside the unions where bargaining is now controlled much more directly by rank and file members. Union full-time officers now advise much more than direct. In time it seems probable that this shift will find reflections in the policies of the Labour Party both in Parliament and in the country. The legislation introduced by both Conservative and Labour governments, the incomes policy and wage restraint advocated and enforced by both, have tended to strengthen this drift to the left, which looks like becoming an institutionalized factor over the next decade. Britain's entry into the Common Market is likely to accentuate the process of change at work within the labour movement. British trade unionists are about to establish contact with new ideas, new situations and new problems, and are perhaps also about to be thrust into a position of leadership they were not hitherto aware it was their duty to fill. The same holds true of the Labour Party, which commands a position of authority within Europe only approached by the SPD in the Federal German Republic. British entry into Europe represents a major breach with the imperial–global role which has dominated British social life over some centuries past. It would be surprising if this breach were not to have as profound effect on the institutions and activity of the Labour movement as on the rest of British society.

8. Belgium

Brussels is nearer to London than either Newcastle upon Tyne or Plymouth. The whole tightly packed Belgian population, amongst the most densely congregated in the world, occupies only about 50 per cent more land space than the province of Wales in the United Kingdom. The population of Wales, which with its declining coal-mining industry shares problems in common with that of Belgium, stands at 2·7 million. Belgium reaches a total of some 9·5 million.

The geographical situation of the Belgian people has determined a great deal of their destiny. Belgium's coastline is strategically placed, separated by only a short sea route from southern England and the Thames estuary which commands the Port of London. Located between France and the territory of modern Germany, Belgium lies on crossroads at which the conflicting interests of greater European powers have frequently clashed in the past. On a direct line of lowland access from Germany to France, Belgium became a battleground in the First World War. Fought over in 1940, Belgium became a battlefield once again as the Allied armies swept forward towards the Rhine in 1944–5.

Belgium's history has been, in earlier years, inextricably linked with that of the Netherlands. The Low Countries (comprising present day Belgium and the Netherlands) shared a common heritage until the Reformation. Only during the sixteenth and seventeenth centuries when the Protestants of the United Provinces of the north asserted their independence through force of arms from Catholic Spain did experiences begin to diverge. In the territory of what is now Belgium and Northern France the Spanish repression was a great deal more successful than in the United Provinces. The supporters of Calvinism were killed, terrorized into submission or driven out. Protestantism was extirpated. The territory of present day Belgium became exclusively Catholic. The modern Belgian labour movement owes many of its characteristics to this fact.

At Ghent, Bruges, Ypres and elsewhere major commercial and manufacturing cities emerged in the early Middle Ages. The Low Countries stood close to London and the English Channel ports, at a northern extremity of the land route to Italy, with easy access by land and water to Germany and by sea to the Baltic. The economic importance of these cities enabled them to gain a large measure of autonomy and independence from the rule of the local feudal overlords. Within their walls grew up a ruling patrician bourgeoisie of great wealth whose public monuments can still impress us today.

English wool in these years was the basic raw material for the looms of Flanders. The population of Bruges and Ghent exceeded 20,000 already in the fourteenth century and in the next hundred years rose to 50,000 and above. By 1566 the population of Antwerp had reached 100,000. In these medieval townships there already existed strikes and elements of class conflict. Weavers and fullers attempted a rising against the oligarchy which ruled the town of Ghent as early as 1274 and other risings followed in the next hundred years.

The upsurge of the English woollen industry in the sixteenth century, the silting up of the approaches to the Flanders ports, the opening up of the New World, are among the factors which produced a catastrophic decline in the textile industry and with it the fortunes of the population. Nevertheless, when a large-scale capitalist textile industry appeared once more in the nineteenth century, it did so in some of those same Flemish towns where the textile industry had flourished centuries earlier. In the folk memory of the labour force recollections of that earlier era still lingered.

The Counts of Flanders, originally under the sovereignty of the French kings, educated their children in France, and contracted marital ties with the French aristocracy. The Flemish nobility in time did the same. Thus over centuries, French, which like Latin had claim to be the common European language of the cultivated elite, came to be the language of the present Belgian ruling class.

Education, compulsory and universal, is a phenomenon of twentieth-century Belgium. Until its advent, the working population, illiterate in the main, spoke a series of local dialects, rather than the cultivated French of the ruling class. Belgium divides on lines of differing linguistic heritage. In the southern Walloon provinces, Hainaut, Liège and Namur, approximately half the country, the prevailing language, historically, has borne a close affinity to French. In Flanders the prevailing language has been far closer to Dutch. Thus, especially after the advent of universal compulsory education, there have arisen complex regional, linguistic and class divisions within the Belgian state.

The Belgian ruling political and business elite spoke French, at least for all official, legal and political purposes. French became the legal language of the country. The working population in Flanders continued to speak its Dutch-based dialects. The Flemish working population was thus at a pronounced disadvantage within its own territory where the ruling elite spoke French, and the law courts and legal affairs were conducted in the French language. In Flanders the linguistic question was thus, in part at least, a class question as well.

The advent of universal literacy in the twentieth century created conditions which caused the language issue to become of greater importance than hitherto.[1] Flemish nationalism has become strong enough to provoke major strains within the Belgian state. Tuition in Flemish language became obligatory at the University of Ghent (in Flanders) in 1932. Tuition at primary schools in Flanders is now conducted in Flemish as a legal requirement. An acute and exaggerated sense of separate identity on the part of Flemings and Walloons has become a major force in Belgian social, political and trade union life. One contributory cause is the predominantly Catholic character of the Flemish provinces which tends to give the language issue both a linguistic and a confessional tone.[2]

In 1789 the territory of modern Belgium was under Austrian rule. The French Revolution sparked off a rising against Austria: the establishment of a shortlived Belgian Republic, later suppressed by Austrian arms. The revolutionary armies of France drove out the Austrians. Belgium was incorporated in the French Republic. Legal and administrative reforms were enforced which constitute the bedrock of the modern Belgian state. Napoleon's military defeat was followed by the Treaty of Vienna (1815) which detached Belgium once more from France. In the peace settlement the northern and southern (Protestant and Catholic) provinces of the Low Countries, without consultation with their inhabitants, were arbitrarily united into a single Netherlands state under a Protestant king. Conceived as a barrier to French expansion, the enforced fusion failed to last. A popular revolution in 1830, in which Catholic conservatives hostile to Protestantism combined with a liberal middle class influenced by the ideas of the French Revolution,[3] led to secession of the Catholic southern provinces, their incorporation into a new, independent Belgian state.

In 1831 the major powers recognized Belgium and guaranteed its existence as an independent, 'perpetually neutral' state.[4] Two buffer

1. Before the rise of the Flemish nationalist movement 'most Flemings spoke one of a number of often mutually incomprehensible local dialects. Only a tiny minority spoke a correct Flemish': Lorwin, in Dahl, ed., Political Oppositions in Western Democracies, p. 159. The linguistic issue in its present form is thus a product of nationalist agitation in the nineteenth and twentieth centuries as much as the modern form of an age-old cultural issue.

2. 'Flemish in the kitchen, French in the parlour', it was said of the Flanders new rich in the past. Now among wide strata of the Flemish population the situation has been reversed.

3. Verkade, Democratic Parties in the Low Countries and Germany, p. 28.

4. The resulting Treaty guaranteed Belgian neutrality and inviolability. It was this obligation of 1831 which provided Lord Grey's pretext for Britain's entry into World War One.

states, Belgium and the Netherlands emerged in place of one. Occupying the land mass between France and the borders of modern Germany in the north they divided the strategically important coastline facing Britain between them.

Modern Belgium was founded as a result of a diplomatic deal amongst great powers concerned to maintain the balance of power in Europe. The popular masses, whether Flemish or Walloon, were not consulted in any way. Real power in the new state was vested in an oligarchy, quite unrepresentative of the people as a whole. Many of the present problems of the Belgian state spring from this lack of any popular base at the time of its foundation.

The Belgian Revolution of 1830 established a system of parliamentary government with guarantees of the liberty of the press and free elections, under a constitutional monarch endowed with extensive powers. In 1847 the electorate mustered only 46,000 citizens out of a population of some 4·5 million. Belgium, in the most literal sense of the words, was a 'bourgeois democracy'. The mass of the population was denied the vote. Political sovereignty was vested in a propertied, privileged and self-authenticated elite. 'The Revolution of 1830', it has been said, 'made by the people was confiscated by the bourgeoisie.'[1]

The 1830 Revolution had been accomplished by two wings with a long term conflict of interests. On one side stood a liberal middle class which sought a measure of political power that the existing Netherlands regime was unwilling to concede, on the other a Catholic hierarchy opposed to the maintenance of a union with the Protestant Netherlands consummated under a Protestant king. Hostility between anti-clerical liberalism and a politically presumptuous Catholic hierarchy took particularly sharp form over popular education. To 'the Catholics, the neutrality of the state on religious questions was equivalent to the state's hostility'.[2] The issue of whether Church or state should control the schools, whether education should be secular or subordinated to the religious dogmatism of a politically motivated Church, became the axis around which revolved a large part of political debate and controversy from mid century onwards.

Close to Britain, possessed of important and accessible reserves of coal, with a textile industry, if outdated, still in being, Belgium led the continent of Europe in the industrial revolution. Coal mines in the province of Hainaut, close to the present French border, had been worked on a considerable scale since the sixteenth century.[3] Coal output, 4,800,000 tons already in 1841–50, rose to 11,780,000 tons in 1861–70.

1. Chlepner, *Cent ans d'histoire sociale en Belgique*, p. 19.
2. Pirenne, *Histoire de Belgique*, vol. vii, p. 99–114, 191.
3. One hundred and twenty workings with an average forty-five employed in each, according to one source: Delsinne, *Le Mouvement syndical en Belgique*, p. 8.

By 1870, after Britain, USA, France and Germany, Belgium was the world's fifth-largest steel-producer. The rate of growth of railway mileage in Belgium was by far the most intense in Europe.

The Belgian industrial upsurge drew on the labour of a disenfranchized population, predominantly rural in origin, whose conditions were deplorable even by comparison with those of other countries in the throes of industrialization. Despite the formal equality of individuals before the law, Article 415 of the penal code declared trade union action punishable by from two to ten years in jail. Until 1883 every worker was required by law to possess a workbook (*livret*). The workbook was held by the employer and might be annotated by him. Fresh employment could not be obtained without producing the workbook, a device which frequently produced a status more akin to sefdom than to free labour.

In the case of dispute between 'master' and 'man' the employer was accepted at his word, whereas under Article 1781 of the Code Civil (repealed in 1883) the employee was beholden to produce evidence in support of his testimony. The lack of proper school facilities, the customary use of child labour, the absence of compulsory education, which was not introduced in Belgium until 1914, led to widespread illiteracy. In one suburb of Charleroi in 1843 only one worker in forty could read and write. In a factory at the capital city of Brussels that same year only eight of 318 employees could read. Out of 14,312 workers examined in 306 plants through the country as a whole, only one in ten could read, write and calculate. Ground down by poverty, squalor and legal discrimination, deprived of the essentials of literacy indispensable for the creation of any lasting organization, it was not surprising that the creation of an effective Belgian labour movement did not get under way until the nineteenth century neared its end.

RISE OF THE LABOUR MOVEMENT

Belgium owes its existence as a state to the events which followed the French Revolution of 1789, and its political history was conditioned no less by the subsequent French revolutions of 1831, 1848 and the Paris Commune in 1871. Belgium was close enough to France, sufficiently similar in language and culture, to feel the transmitted shocks of these revolutions almost directly. Yet Belgium was at the same time sufficiently independent, sufficiently distant, to provide a haven for political refugees in the aftermath of these events. Socialist ideas first began to take hold in Belgium, primarily among bourgeois intellectuals, after the revolution of 1848.

Intellectuals influenced by French socialism found common ground with radical workers in the free thought movement provoked by the obscurantist outlook and reactionary social attitude of the Church.[1] The rising pace of industrial change precipitated resistance among artisans in Brussels. Unions of textile workers in the important Flemish city of Ghent appeared towards the end of the 1850s. Belgian socialists were prominently involved in the First International. By 1867 branches were established in Brussels, Ghent, the coalfields of Hainaut, the growing industrial city of Liège and the important textile town of Verviers nearby.[2] The collapse of the International which followed the fall of the Paris Commune in 1871 failed to halt the growth of the working-class movement. A *Chambre de Travail* (literally 'Chamber of Labour', i.e. Trades Council) uniting a number of working-class organizations was set up in Brussels in 1875. Organization was also consolidated in Ghent where the cooperative movement became firmly established with the foundation of the famous *Vooruit* cooperative society.

Separate Flemish and Brabant socialist parties founded in 1877[3] were fused into a united Belgian Workers' Party (*Parti Ouvrier Belge*: POB) in 1885. The choice of title was significant. Belgian socialists from the beginning were less interested in dialectical polemics than in achieving pragmatic compromise, a synthesis which might provide an effective basis for practical action.[4]

Belgian socialism, at the confluence of three great civilizations, possesses some of the characteristics of each. From the English the Belgians have learnt 'self-help', the idea of free association, principally under the form of co-operative organization; from the Germans the political tactics, and the fundamental doctrines, which were elaborated for the first time in the Communist Manifesto; from the French finally, their idealistic tendencies, their overall view of socialism as a prolongation of the revolutionary philosophy, as a new religion, continuing and carrying out all the aims of Christianity, but bringing it down to earth all illuminated with the light and clarity of the heavens.[5]

The Workers' Party was scarcely established before a wild and tumultuous 'rolling strike', characterized by mass picketing and demonstrations, swept through Liège, along the line of the mining and industrial district of the Borinage, up the valley of the Meuse and Sambre towards Mons and Charleroi. Factories went up in flames. A burst of spontaneous semi-insurrectionary violence drew tens and even hundreds of

1. Collard *et al.* in *Les Fastes du Parti*, pp. 20–21. Catholic opinion had gone so far as to show hostility to the legal regulation of child labour: Chlepner, p. 41.
2. Collard *et al.*, pp. 25–7. An English-language account will be found in Landauer, *European Socialism*, pp. 450–81.
3. *Parti Socialiste Flamand* and *Parti Socialiste Brabançon*. Brabant is the region around Brussels.
4. Destrée and Vandervelde, *Le Socialisme en Belgique*, pp. 17–18, Pierson, *Histoire du socialisme en Belgique*, p. 121.
5. Destrée and Vandervelde, p. 18.

thousands into action in its train. A number of strikers were shot dead by the soldiery. Others received jail sentences of ten to twelve years or even of life imprisonment. 'The terrible year' of 1886 established the social question on the agenda of Belgian bourgeois democracy for the first time. Alfred Defuisseaux's socialist pamphlet, *The Catechism of the People*, sold over 260,000 copies that year (200,000 in French, 60,000 in Flemish), an astonishing sale in a small nation with over one-third of the population illiterate.[1]

The Belgian Workers' Party (POB) was an alliance of separate and substantially autonomous working class and socialist organizations which largely anticipated the model established by the British Labour Party, some twenty years later. Co-operative organizations, which became very strong in Belgium; workers' friendly benefit societies; local, regional and national trade unions; socialist organizations: these comprised the bulk of the membership. Specifically socialist institutions in these early years were always a clear minority.

Belgium's first trade unions were thus organically associated with the POB. The unions saw their duty as 'above all of bringing to the party the support of workers not yet prepared to declare formal support for socialism'. Trade union business continued to be a normal part of Workers' Party activity for a number of years. Then, in 1898, steps were taken to ensure closer coordination of union activity by the constitution of a Trade Union Commission of the General Council of the Workers' Party (*Commission Syndicale Section du Conseil Général du Parti Ouvrier*). This Commission comprised nine members nominated by the party leadership and nine more nominated by the national trade union federations.

In these years, the POB's main activity was directed towards the achievement of universal suffrage. A setback to the suffrage agitation in 1902 made it clear that in the immediate future the unions could no longer look forward to major social advances springing from an increased socialist representation in parliament. Impressed by successes obtained by their counterparts in Britain and Germany, Belgian unionists began to put their movement on a sounder financial and organizational base than hitherto.[2]

Integral association with the POB constituted a barrier to the affiliation of a number of independent unions to the Commission Syndicale. After some debate the unions reconstituted themselves as the *Commission Syndicale du Parti Ouvrier Belge et des Syndicats Indépendants*. The leadership of the reconstituted *Commission Syndicale* was now elected

1. Destrée and Vandervelde, pp. 23–52.
2. Collard *et al.*, pp. 267–71. For the German influence, see Delsinne, *Le Mouvement syndicale*, pp. 221, and Delsinne, 'The trade union movement in Belgium', *International Labour Review*, 1950, p. 494.

solely from its own ranks. In 1907, following this constitutional change, a number of formerly independent unions joined the *Commission Syndicale*.[1]

In these years the tradition became 'firmly established that each time a social or political question of importance for the unions is on the order of the day it is discussed by the leadership of the two organizations (*Commision Syndicale* and POB) united in a single assembly'.[2] From 13,000 in 1898, 31,000 in 1900, the unions associated with the POB rose in numbers to 77,000 by 1911.[3] In 1913 the *Commission Syndicale* was able to claim 129,000 members.[4]

Until almost the end of the nineteenth century, in the eyes of those few Catholics who considered the question at all, the terms 'the workers' and 'the poor' were indistinguishable. Both categories were proper subjects for charity but not for organization. The growth of socialist influence among the working class brought a major change in this attitude.

At Ghent, in Flanders, an anti socialist Catholic workers' union had been set up as early as 1886. The Encyclical *Rerum Novarum* gave the first expressly Papal sanction to the legitimacy of Catholic trade union organization in 1891. In subsequent years a whole range of Catholic workers organizations, all operating under the patronage of the Church, came into being.

Mainly based in Flanders these organizations were relatively weak in the Walloon, Liège–Mons–Charleroi heavy industrial belt. Christian union membership has been put at 15,000 in 1904. A *Confédération Générale des Syndicales Chrétiens et Libres de Belgique* claimed 100,000 members in 1913.[5] Although this last figure seems grossly exaggerated, there can be no doubt that by this time a firm base had been created for Catholic unionism, especially amongst Catholics working for Catholic employers in Flanders. Originally for the most part 'yellow' organizations, the Catholic unions were now beginning to acquire cautious, conservative trade union attitudes of their own.

In this situation state-subsidized workers' travel was used to buttress

---

1. Spitaels, *Le Mouvement syndical en Belgique*, p. 14. On the leading committee of the *Commission Syndicale* two places were reserved for representatives of the POB. The Commission Syndicale received two seats on the POB leadership board in exchange.
2. Delsinne, pp. *326–7*. This happened in the case of the suffrage struggle of 1913.
3. Delsinne, p. 253. A figure of 130,000 in 1911 is quoted in *Les Fastes du Parti*, but this appears exaggerated.
4. The figure was probably inflated by the preparations for the suffrage general strike that were under way that year.
5. Chlepner, p. 118. Fogarty, *Christian Democracy in Western Europe, 1820–1953*, p. 220.

worker conservatism. Large numbers of workers were encouraged to maintain rural residence and commute daily to urban industrial employ-ment. Safe in the pastoral care of the village priest they were insulated from the drift to secularization and socialism considered inherent in city living. Over 1·5 million of such cheap season tickets were in circulation during 1900.[1]

The pastoral role allocated to the Catholic unions by the hierarchy led to forms of organization markedly more authoritarian than those of their socialist counterparts. 'Christian trade unionism is too important not to be placed under wise and prudent leadership,' declared one of the move-ment's founders. 'Without a central leadership established over the national federations, how can one be sure that its work is effectively carried out? What authority would be able to prevent it setting out on some dangerous road?'[2]

THE SUFFRAGE STRUGGLE

The deplorable social conditions of working people in the French and Belgian coal mines at the time of the industrial revolution have been vividly portrayed in Emile Zola's classic novel *Germinal*. The mass of the population remained totally excluded from participation in the government of civil society. A large proportion of the workforce was concentrated in the mines where both safety and other related factors made legal enactment vital. Excessive hours of work, not least in textiles, child labour, the employment of women for excessive hours on exhausting tasks, also brought the need for legal regulations to the fore.

The steadily emerging co-operative and workers' friendly benefit socie-ties, the more slowly growing unions, all required changes in legal statute to remove obstacles to their growth. These were amongst the factors inducing the Belgian working class movement to pay primary attention to the achievement of universal suffrage in its early years.[3] Disenfranchisement itself probably served to encourage a simplistic overestimation of the benefits which the right to vote might bring in its train.

Important also must have been the extreme partiality of the Belgian legal system, the persistent, outrageous and quite unnecessarily lethal violence used against strikers and demonstrators by the military.

1. Ministry of Foreign Affairs and External Trade, *Belgian News*, April 1968, Brussels p. 3.
2. J. Van Dyck, 25 Oct. 1908, quoted in Neuville, *Une Génération syndicale*, p. 103.
3. In Belgium, as in some other European countries, women did not receive the vote until after the Second World War; in this case in 1948: Chlepner, p. 18.

Sentences of life imprisonment and terms of up to twenty years solitary confinement were imposed in respect of the events of 1886. Seven persons were killed and seventeen injured in one incident in 1893, twelve killed in another incident the same year. Six were killed at Louvain as late as 1902.[1] In the short term there can be little doubt that concentration on the suffrage issue slowed down the rate of union growth. Whether in the long term this concentration proved justified is likely to remain an open question for years to come.

The social impact of the wild runaway strikes in the 'terrible year' of 1886 impressed Belgian socialist leaders. The government continued to withhold the right to vote from the majority of the population. Might not the working class then legitimately claim the right 'to refuse all labour for a society which treated it as a pariah and proclaim the general strike'?[2]

The general strike for the suffrage, as conceived by the POB, was no insurrectionary measure on the anarcho-syndicalist model. Rather it was a disciplined and carefully controlled manoeuvre designed to exercise pressure which would force established authority to concede reforms. The increasingly industrial character of the Belgian economy made it particularly vulnerable to an assault of this order. An important working-class population was quartered in the capital of Brussels. The textile industry of Ghent and Flanders, the mines of the Borinage in the Meuse-Sambre valley, the industrial population of Liège, circled the capital on three sides, no more than seventy miles distant.

The general strike nevertheless was a double-edged weapon. In the event of firm government resistance the leaders had either to back down defeated or to allow themselves to be carried forward into a revolutionary venture by militancy they had themselves unloosed. Yet for this, neither by temperament, nor by training, were they in any way prepared. It is in this context that the repeated hesitations of POB leadership at crucial moments in the suffrage struggle are best to be explained.

The political general strike may well be claimed as a specifically Belgian contribution to the history of labour. In the face of the refusal of the ruling oligarchy to concede universal suffrage, the Belgian labour movement, between 1888 and 1913, launched no less than five major political strikes designed to enforce reform.[3]

The first attempt, in 1887, prepared by a would-be revolutionary minority, thoroughly infiltrated by police provocateurs, proved a total failure. Four years later, on 1 May 1891, over 100,000 miners struck work

1. Collard et al., pp. 55, 63, 67; Pierson, pp. 89–90, 123, Braunthal, *History of the International*, pp. 209–10; Chlepner, pp. 53–4.
2. Manifesto of the POB to the Belgian People in 1886, quoted Bertrand, *Histoire de la démocratie et du socialisme en Belgique*, vol. ii, p. 401.
3. 1891, 1892, 1893, 1902 and 1913.

to demand the suffrage. The following year the POB decided to call a general strike. A stoppage led by the miners, which lasted from 1 to 11 May, drew from the government some promise of revision. When legislative progress reached a dead stop in April 1893, a fresh general strike call was issued. After ten days of turmoil accompanied by frequent violence, a revision of the law was voted.[1]

The 1893 suffrage reform, subject to certain residence qualifications, gave the vote to all adult males over the age of twenty-five. The electorate jumped from 137,000 to 1,350,000 at one bound. The reactionary majority in parliament, having reluctantly extended the right to vote to the working population, now conferred on the middle and upper classes the privilege of multiple voting, to redress the balance. After the suffrage reform 850,000 citizens were entitled to a single vote, a further 520,000 to multiple voting privileges. The minority of multiple voters, with a poll potential of some 1·25 million, were able to outvote the larger number of unitary voters by a margin of some one and a half to one.[2]

The suffrage reform of 1893 enabled the POB, with twenty eight deputies, to enter the parliamentary arena as a force of substance for the first time. Nevertheless the general aims of the suffrage reform were far from being realized. A fresh attempt at a breakthrough by means of a political general strike in 1902 lasted from 14 to 20 April. On this occasion the support of over 300,000 strikers was met by the mobilization of 60,000 men into the army. After a number of strikers had been shot dead by the military the stoppage was abandoned without achieving any practical result.[3] When in 1912, after over twenty years of struggle and agitation, both inside and outside parliament, universal and equal suffrage was still denied, the POB decided to resort to the political general strike again. Prolonged preparations were made. Funds collected at home and abroad were reckoned sufficient to maintain strikers and their families through a stoppage of some six to eight weeks' duration. The order for the strike was given on 14 April 1913. The larger part of Belgian industry stopped work. On 22 April the parliament voted a motion held by some to open the way to a revision of the electoral law. The POB leadership, without demanding more specific undertakings, called off the strike.[4] In the event, universal and equal suffrage was still not on the Statute Book when war broke out in August 1914. The suffrage reform was not conceded until a coalition government, including the socialists, had been formed in April 1919 in the revolutionary wave which followed the holocaust of 1914–18.

1. Pierson, pp. 104–7; Collard et al., pp. 60–62.
2. Pirenne, vol. vii, p. 320. Dahl, pp. 411–12.
3. Pirenne, vol. vii, p. 331; Pierson, pp. 122–3; Collard et al., pp. 66–8.
4. Pirenne, vol. vii, pp. 380–83; Pierson, pp. 224–6; Collard et al., pp. 75–6.

WAR AND INTER WAR YEARS

Emile Vandervelde, leader of the POB, with party endorsement, served in the oddly named government of 'sacred union', during the war years. The question of whether or not to serve in bourgeois Cabinets had caused serious disagreement in the POB as early as 1909–11.[1] In the first post war election of 1919 the POB, with seventy deputies, emerged as a major party for the first time.[2] The homogeneous Catholic majority which had ruled Belgium for the previous thirty years was replaced by a new and more changeable alliance of forces. A three party Catholic, socialist liberal system emerged, in which no single contender was able to muster an electoral majority on its own account. The socialist vote, 37 per cent in 1919, never varied as much as four points above or below this figure in the inter war decades. The Catholic vote meantime stabilized at between 40 per cent and 45 per cent.[3]

The Catholic Party,[4] confessionally based, was a multi class organization with both labour and business wings. The Liberals were the predominant party of Belgian business, the POB the party of labour. Liberals and socialists, springing from the common heritage of the French Revolution, were united in their opposition to clerical rule. The POB was most strongly based in Brussels and the Walloon provinces, but with additional points of strength in the larger Flemish cities.[5] Catholic support was predominant in Flanders and the rural regions of the country as a whole. Belgian politics thus came to take a particularly complex form. A straightforward confrontation between 'Labour and Conservative' on the British pattern was prevented by the divided nature of the contenders. Politics revolved around three issues: the conflicting interests of business and labour; the political clash between confessional and non-confessional forces; the growing rift between the French-speaking Walloon and the Dutch-speaking Flemish provinces of the nation. Since a Socialist–Liberal partnership was unthinkable, the alternatives were Catholic–Liberal (right of centre); Catholic–Socialist (left of centre); or tripartite governments, such as those of 1918–21, 1925–7, 1935–8 and 1939–44. Faced with such obstacles, the POB, although achieving reforms of significance, proved unable to effect any major

1. Pierson, p. 127; Collard et al., p. 89.
2. The socialists gained 70 seats, the Catholics 73, out of a total of 186. Dahl, p. 413.
3. Verkade, pp. 90–93. Flemish, Nationalist and Rexist votes have been counted as 'Catholic'. Communist votes have been combined with those of the socialists.
4. The Catholic Party became the Christian Social Party (*Parti Sociale Chrétien* – PSC) in 1945.
5. For a brief English-language account of Belgian labour in the inter war years, see Landauer, pp. 1560–70.

social transformation of Belgian society. Shut outside the true centres of power in the years before 1918, the party was to some degree tamed and domesticated in the years that followed.

The coalition government of 1918–21 lifted the remaining obstacles to trade union organization. The war, the disruption and hardship of the German occupation, the revolutionary wave which followed the Russian Revolution and the end of hostilities, generated a tidal wave of recruitment into the unions. Membership of the *Commission Syndicale* alone rose to 600,000 in 1919 and 700,000 in 1920.

At the beginning of 1919, as a result of disruption caused by the war there were 700,000 out of work in Belgium, an enormous number for a country of this size. Legislation enacted on the initiative of POB ministers brought state subsidies to union unemployment funds, guaranteeing them against bankruptcy when otherwise they might have been exhausted. These subsidies, maintained and to some extent amplified in the inter war years, played a very important part in enabling unions to recruit and retain members.[1] Largely one suspects due to this measure, 'in 1933, the worst year of the economic depression, the membership was higher than at any time since 1921'.[2] Government subsidies, which bound the unions closer to the state, gave them a vested interest in moderation and served to enhance social stability.

The main lines of the present Belgian labour movement were already laid down in the inter war years. In 1937 the *Commission Syndicale* formally asserted its independence of the POB, adopting new statutes and the fresh title, Belgian General Confederation of Labour (*Confédération Générale du Travail de Belgique*: CGTB). The Christian unions grew considerably, claiming 350,000 members against the 550,000 of the CGTB in 1939.

The Second World War shattered the existing framework. New organizations, born in the underground, threatened to replace the old, only to fall away in the post war years. In the 1950s and 1960s, as Walloon heavy industry declined, so new industry was installed in predominantly Flemish areas. The Catholic unions first caught up, then surpassed by a significant margin, the membership of their socialist rivals.

SECOND WORLD WAR

The German army's onslaught through the Low Countries in May 1940 forced the surrender of the Belgian army after an eighteen-day

1. Collard *et al.*, pp. 276–7. Union members may still draw their unemployment benefit through the union office. Seyfarth *et al.*, *Labor Relations and the Law in Belgium and the United States*, p. 314.
2. *ILO Review*, Geneva, 1950, pp. 502–3.

campaign. The tripartite Belgian Cabinet, comprising Catholic, Liberal and Socialist representatives, took refuge as a government in exile in Britain. The King, Leopold II, chose to remain behind in Belgium. Leopold's behaviour during the German occupation did much to bring the monarchy into disrepute. By the end of hostilities the King's continued tenure of the throne had become unacceptable to a large proportion of the Belgian people.

The Belgian Workers' Party (POB), in a country hit by heavy unemployment, constrained by the seeming impossibility of obtaining a single-party majority, had become strongly attracted to a programme of Keynesian planned economy during the inter war years. The architect of this new outlook was Henri de Man, the POB leader, whose ideas were also influential in the Netherlands and to a lesser extent in France as well. In midsummer 1940, following the collapse of France, there was some good ground for believing that the Germans had definitely won the war. That July, Henri de Man declared his faith in a Nazi victory and called on POB members to accept it as 'a starting-point towards a new social progress'.[1]

Towards the end of 1940 the occupation authorities decided to dissolve the FGTB. De Man, aided by renegade socialists and separatist minded Catholic unionists from Flanders, now launched a new *Union des Travailleurs Manuels et Intellectuels* (UTMI).[2] The UTMI was a collaborationist venture based on the German Labour Front, intended to encompass all Belgian workers, socialist and Catholic alike. Closely associated with the occupying authority, the UTMI, despite initial successes, subsequently failed to retain the allegiance of any significant part of the labour force. The bulk of the Flemish unionists withdrew their support in August 1941 following the German invasion of Russia.[3] In November of that same year employers formally recorded that it was impossible to collaborate with the UTMI.[4] Thus although de Man's defection did much to discredit the socialists, the labour movement as a whole refused to collaborate. The Belgian employers also failed to show any marked sympathy with the occupying power. Discussions between representatives of labour and employers which took place in the underground proved the preliminary to a government of national unity established in the post war years.[5]

Underground resistance to the Nazis demanded personal characteristics rather different from those developed by the legal, parliamentary and

1. 'Belgium in transition', *Annals of the American Academy of Political and Social Science* (hereafter cited as *Annals*), Sept. 1946, pp. 1–2, 69–70.
2. Collard *et al.* pp. 148–9, 282–4; Verkade, pp. 188–9; Spitaels, pp. 21–2.
3. Ebertzheim, *Les Syndicats ouvriers en Belgique*, p. 11.
4. Doucy, *Economie Sociale*, p. 232, quoted Spitaels, p. 22; Collard, *et al.* p. 284.
5. On this for example, Seyfarth *et al.*, *Labor Relations and the Law in Belgium and the United States*, p. 19.

trade union struggles of the inter war years. When old-line Catholic and socialist leaders proved unequal to the task, new men out of the rank and file came forward to fill the gap. Two main tendencies emerged in the underground.

One, the United Metal-workers' Movement (*Mouvement Métallurgiste Unifié*: MMU), was centred on the industrial region around Liège. The leaders of the MMU, some of whom, like André Renard, became prominent figures after the war, considered that the socialist movement had followed an excessively parliamentary and reformist course in the pre war years.[1] The MMU looked forward to a reconstitution of the labour movement after the war. It hoped to become the bedrock of a new union organization, uniting both Catholic and socialist workers around a radical if not a revolutionary programme.

The Belgian communists, never a powerful force in the inter war years, did not participate in the Resistance until after Hitler's attack on Russia in June 1941. Thereafter the communists played a most important role. At the end of the war Communist Party membership rose briefly to 100,000. The party itself joined the Liberal–Socialist–Catholic coalition established in 1944.[2] Inside the underground labour movement communist activity was concentrated not on the MMU but on the Trade Union Struggle Committees (*Comités de Lutte Syndicale*: CLS), most of which, although widely based in membership, functioned under party control.

BELGIAN LABOUR AFTER 1945

In Belgium, as in the Netherlands but unlike France, the business class as a whole did not willingly collaborate with the Nazi occupation. A question of some importance, this combined with socialist and communist participation in the government to ensure a peaceful transition at the end of hostilities. Partisan activity made possible the capture, intact, of the port of Antwerp. Several large communities were liberated by the underground before the arrival of the Allied forces. If the armed partisans had been unwilling to surrender their *de facto* sovereignty to that somewhat tenuously claimed by the 'government in exile', serious conflicts might have ensued.

The end of the war saw a most confused situation in the union ranks. The socialist CGTB seemed to have lost the bulk of its Walloon membership to rival organizations. The United Metal-workers' Movement (MMU) transformed itself into the United Trade Union Movement

1. For further details regarding the MMU see Ebertzheim, pp. 15–19; *Annals*, pp. 52–4.
2. In the 1946 general election the Communist Party polled 300,000 votes, electing twenty three deputies and seventeen senators: *Annals*, p. 19.

(*Mouvement Syndicale Unifié*: MSU). The Comités de Lutte Syndicale, not to be outdone, reconstituted themselves as a new *Confédération Belge des Syndicats Unifiés* (CBSU). Disarray amongst the radical wing of the trade union movement aided the revival of confessional unionism which once again began to appear as a force of significance in its own right.

In an endeavour to recover lost ground, in the hope of effecting a fusion with the Christians, the CGTB announced its willingness to fuse with other organizations. The confessional unions declined. The MSU and CBSU, after some hesitation, accepted the offer. The fusion into a newly titled General Federation of Belgian Labour (*Fédération Générale du Travail de Belgique*: FGTB) was completed in April 1945. Out of the seven full-time national secretaries who constituted the executive board, only three were former functionaries of the CGTB. On the National Committee, responsible for determining FGTB policy, former officials of the CGTB, although constituting the largest single group, remained a minority, filling only seven of the fifteen places available.

Tensions within the FGTB ran high for several years after the end of the war. The apparently strong position of the 'new guard' was undermined by the difficulties which adherents of the former MMU found in achieving a common front with members of the Belgian Communist Party (*Parti Communiste Belge*: PCB). Not the least reason was the policy of cautious moderation pursued by the communists throughout the whole period of their participation in the coalition governments of 1944–7.[1] The PCB was eased out of the Belgian coalition in March 1947 as one of the preliminaries to the launching of the Marshall Plan. At the congress following the Communist *coup* in Czechoslovakia in 1948, the communist national secretaries of the FGTB lost their posts. Thereafter PCB influence in the unions suffered a sharp decline.

The high hopes for the rebirth of the labour movement generated by the Resistance thus went unrealized. Once the smoke of battle cleared away the labour movement that emerged from the war looked remarkably similar to that which had existed before. The new FGTB represented the old CGTB, restaffed, with important shifts of internal structure and political outlook, a greater independence of the POB, but in essence the old CGTB, just the same. Alongside it stood a powerful Christian trade union confederation, *Confédération des Syndicats Chrétiens* (CSC) just as before.

1. The communists joined the coalition government on 26 September 1944 and finally departed on 20 March 1947. In the intervening years the PCB was out of office for the periods 26 September 1944 to 12 February 1945, and 13 to 31 March 1946: Senelle, *The Political and Economic Structure of Belgium*.

INDUSTRIAL RELATIONS

The Belgian economy, that of a small nation, is heavily involved in international trade. Balance of payment problems have been seen as a permanent constraint on collective bargaining in the post war years. The Belgian economy itself has been undergoing a process of profound structural change. Coal-mining has experienced a tremendous rundown following Belgium's entry into the European Coal and Steel Community: 115 pits were operating in the southern Walloon coalfields in 1956; only thirty nine remained in 1966. Employment in the Walloon coalfields, 115,000 in 1890, stood at 75,000 in 1956. Ten years later the figure had fallen to 36,000. A newer coalfield in the Flemish-speaking area adjacent to the Netherlands border, employs a further 26,000 workers. The centre of gravity of industrial activity, formerly in Wallonia and East Flanders, has shifted towards the regions around Brussels and Antwerp. Today, it is the Flemish provinces of Flanders, Antwerp and Limburg which employ the bulk of industrial workers and not the Walloon provinces of Hainaut, Liège and Namur as hitherto.[1]

The population of Walloon and Flemish provinces was originally approximately equal (2·5 million as against 2·8 million in 1890). During the present century, the Flemish population (borders remaining unchanged) has increased by some 2 million while the Walloon population has risen by barely 600,000. This population shift underlies much of present social tension in Belgium. Clearly it is also a factor behind the great increase in Christian union membership which has taken place in the post war years.

Some eighty legally constituted *commissions paritaires*, negotiating bodies covering different industrial sectors, roughly equivalent to Britain's Joint Industrial Councils but with greater power, constitute the main channel for Belgian collective bargaining. The *commissions paritaires* operate within the framework provided by a National Council of Labour and a Central Economic Council which provide means of labour–management–government consultation on questions of social and economic policy.

Belgian employers are represented by the national *Fédération d'Industrie Belge* (FIB). Where necessary, for example, over shop steward recognition, the FIB negotiates nationally, on an inter industrial basis, outside the *commissions paritaires*.

Much of Belgian industry is highly concentrated. As early as 1900 'the twelve largest joint stock companies provided work for half the

1. *Belgian News*, April 1968, Brussels: pp. 11–13: *Belgium at Work*, Belgian Information and Documentation Institute, Brussels, 1964, p. 26; European Community Statistical Office, *Year Book*, Brussels, 1966, p. 75.

Belgian workers employed in industry'.[1] Much the most important single company in Belgium is the massive conglomerate *Société Générale*. The biggest single force in Belgian banking, Société Générale also controls 60 per cent of insurance companies, 40 per cent of iron and steel, 30 per cent of coal production and 25 per cent of electrical energy. Awareness of this massive concentration stands at the background of all informal discussions of social and economic policy in Belgium.[2]

The life of the Belgian labour movement takes place against the back-cloth of a political system dominated by coalition politics. In this system, on past experience, one party, the confessional *Parti Sociale Chrétien* (PSC), can expect to be almost permanently in office. The PSC has been in the government for sixteen of the twenty-two years 1944–66. Of all the major parties[3] only the PSC has been able to muster the strength to govern alone, a feat accomplished during the four years 1950–54.[4] The central position occupied by the PSC strengthens the position of the Catholic *Confédération des Syndicats Chrétiens* (CSC), against its rival the FGTB. The CSC, through the labour wing of the PSC, is able to exercise influence upon a party almost permanently in office. CSC influence is likely to be much greater when there is a PSC–Socialist coalition than at any other time. The Parti Socialiste Belge (PSB) by contrast cannot expect to achieve office, except in coalition with the PSC.[5] Coalition politics, intermittent ministries, have not been without influence in eroding the socialist mystique of the PSB.[6] Under-standably, co-operation between the Catholic CSC and socialist FGTB is a great deal easier when Catholic PSC and socialist PSB are in coalition than when they are not.

THE BELGIAN GENERAL CONFEDERATION OF LABOUR – FGTB

The FGTB, with a membership of 800,000 in 1970, is a confederation of fourteen national unions.[7] The three largest national unions or *centrales* as they are known in Belgium, are the Metal-workers (200,000 members), the General Workers (180,000), and the Public Service Workers (170,000). These three together comprise some two thirds of

1. *Belgian News*, April 1968, p. 11.
2. For some details, Levinson, *International Trades Unionism*, pp. 385–7.
3. *Parti Sociale Chrétien* (PSC), *Parti Socialiste Belge* (PSB), *Parti Libéral Belge* (now *Parti pour la Liberté et le Progres*).
4. The PSC was out of office from August 1945 to March, 1947 and March 1954 to June 1958.
5. The *Parti Ouvrier Belge* (POB) became the *Parti Socialiste Belge* (PSB) in 1945.
6. The POB–PSB participated in ten governments out of eighteen between 1944 and 1966.
7. For a list see Ebertzheim, p. 50.

FGTB membership. No other *centrale* exceeds 100,000 members. The only two other unions to exceed 50,000 are the employees and the textile workers.

The structure of the *centrales* comprising the FGTB conforms to a generally similar pattern. The basic units of the *centrales* are the regional or provincial organizations. The line of responsibility of enterprise and local union branches runs upwards to the region rather than to the national union direct. The regional committee is elected by representatives of the local branches and appoints its own officers.

Control of union policy is vested in a congress meeting every two years. Delegates are chosen by regional organizations and not local union branches. Regions are represented at the congress in proportion to membership. Belgian unions are characterized by a firm determination to keep union leadership in touch with rank and file. Thus the constitution of the metal-workers' union lays it down that wherever the region is entitled to more than three congress delegates at least 50 per cent must be members still working at their trade.

The regional organizations, given the linguistic–regional conflicts which divide modern Belgium, are most important bodies. Above the regional organization stands the National Committee. Meeting as a rule three to four times a year the National Committee is a large assembly, a kind of congress in miniature. In the case of the metal-workers at least 60 per cent must be *délégués d'usine*, members still working at their trade.

Above the National Committee, smaller, meeting more frequently, is the Bureau, comprising representatives nominated by the most important regional organizations. In the case of the metal-workers, these are Antwerp, Brabant, the Centre, Charleroi, Flanders and Liège.

Control of union policy, between congresses, is vested in the National Committee and the Bureau. In the smaller *centrales* these two bodies may be fused into one.

The secretariat, comprising President (the chief officer), General Secretary, and a number of secretaries, each with specific responsibilities, carries out the day-to-day work of the national union. The secretariat meets, as a rule weekly, at the union head office.

In most countries, a certain tension exists between national union autonomy and the demands of confederal central authority. In the Netherlands and Italy the confederation is as a rule the stronger body. In Germany the situation is the other way about. In this comparison the FGTB stands somewhere between the two poles of centralism and autonomy. The pronounced regionalism of Belgian society means that in the FGTB, as also in the CSC, the regional organizations exercise rather more power than in most unions elsewhere. Belgian unionism is characterized not only by the customary tensions between national unions and the centre, but also by contradictory claims to sovereignty of the regional and the national organizations. The FGTB is not merely a federation of national unions, it is also an alliance of regional trade union organizations, each in itself a miniature FGTB. The FGTB Congress is held every two or three years. The congress decides policy and elects the full-time Bureau which undertakes the day-to-day execution of policy. Voting is by show of hands and not by card vote on the British model.

At the FGTB Congress both national unions and regional union organizations are represented. The congress musters some 500 delegates. Two thirds are elected by the fourteen affiliated *centrales*. One third are chosen by the twenty-six regional divisions of the FGTB.[1] Representation for regional organization guarantees a voice both for rank-and-file activists and for regional–linguistic attitudes which might otherwise fail to gain a proper hearing. FGTB regional organizations, which naturally vary from one to another in respect to the relative weight of their affiliations from the various *centrales*, are a most important part of the structure of the FGTB.

Between congresses control of FGTB policy is vested in an elected National Committee – *Comité National*, which numbers around 150 members. Delegates are elected for a two year term. *Centrales* and FGTB regional organizations divide representation in the ratio of two to one, as in the case of the congress. A relatively compact body, the National Committee can be summoned at two to three days' notice. In exceptional times it has been known to meet as often as four to five times in three months. More normally, the National Committee will meet three to four times a year. The National Committee decides FGTB policy between Congresses. Between meetings the day-to-day conduct of FGTB business is entrusted to a Secretariat of full-time officials. General supervision of the work of the Secretariat is entrusted to the Bureau.

The Secretariat, elected by the congress, comprises six full-time officials; General Secretary, Assistant General Secretary, two national secretaries and one assistant national secretary. Each is responsible for a specific field of activity, on which he must submit a report to congress. Endorsement of the report involves automatic renewal of the official's mandate for a further two years. Each national official, being separately elected, is a responsible functionary in his own right. As such he is not necessarily bound by the principle of collegial responsibility. In the event of serious differences within the Secretariat, an elected official retains the right to argue his case before the National Committee and indeed the Congress, until such time as the issue is formally decided by the FGTB. By virtue of their office all six members of the Secretariat are full-time members of both Bureau and National Committee.

1. Spitaels, p. 31; Ebertzheim, pp. 49, 60–63.

The twenty-one-man Bureau, which meets weekly, supervises the Secretariat's administration of FGTB affairs. Fifteen places on the Bureau are filled by key figures from the *centrales* and FGTB regional organizations. These representatives are elected by the congress, on the same year proportional basis as in the case of the National Committee, and sit for a two-year term. The remaining six seats are allocated to the full-time members of the Secretariat who sit by virtue of their function. The head office staff at the disposal of Bureau and Secretariat number around one hundred.

The linguistic–regional divisions which in recent years have begun to threaten the unity of the Belgian state have also forced changes of procedure inside the unions. In the Secretariat of the FGTB French and Flemish now rate as co-equal official languages. If the General Secretary speaks French then the Assistant General Secretary must be Flemish and vice versa. In the distribution of the remaining posts in the Secretariat, parity of representation between members of the two regional–linguistic groups is also obligatory. The same principles also hold for the Bureau. At Congresses of the FGTB and also at meetings of the National Committee, a motion must muster two thirds of the votes overall or 50 per cent of the votes cast by each of the two language groups before it can be considered as binding.

The FGTB has links with the other three arms of the socialist labour movement: the PSB, the Co-operatives and the Workers' Friendly Benefit Societies (*Mutualités*) through a common coordinating body, *L'Action Commune*. In this, as in the more rarely convened National Council of Labour in Britain, all four bodies meet as equals to discuss common action.

In the past it has been quite customary for members of the Secretariat to divide their time between the conduct of union business and membership of the Belgian parliament. In Belgium, as in Italy, where the issue of *incompatibilita* has become an issue during the last few years, critics of the leadership have demanded that such functionaries should choose one career or the other and not seek to combine both. In the FGTB the outcome has been a decision, taken in 1964, to declare the holding of a parliamentary mandate incompatible with a post in the Secretariat. Those members of the Secretariat who were already deputies at the time of this decision have been allowed to retain their seats for the time being.[1] The same privilege will not be accorded to their successors.

At an Extraordinary Congress to discuss future policy, held in January 1971, the FGTB adopted a number of important policy resolutions concerning workers' control. The essence of these proposals is a

1. The CSC took a similar decision in 1945, reaffirmed and amplified in 1953. See European Economic Community, *Monographies Syndicales – Belgique*, p. 17 (hereafter cited as EEC, *Monographies*).

strategy of moving the frontier of FGTB activity forward from the wages
front into fields formerly reserved for managerial prerogative. These
measures are considered an 'essential short term step towards the full
taking over of industry by the workers'. FGTB proposals include the
strengthening of existing 'in-plant' organs; the shop stewards (*délégation
syndicale*), the works council (*conseil d'entreprise*), and the Health and
Safety Committee. The FGTB want to give these bodies greater powers
of decision, greater access to information, and to obtain for their members more time off with pay in order that they may perform their duties
more effectively.[1]

THE CONFEDERATION OF CHRISTIAN UNIONS – CSC

The *Confédération des Syndicats Chrétiens* (CSC), with an enrolment of
900,000 in 1970, outnumbers its socialist rival by a clear 100,000 members. FGTB spokesmen claim with some justification that the influence
of the socialist centre amongst the working class exceeds that of the
CSC. Just the same the success of the CSC in first meeting and then
surpassing FGTB membership in the post war years is undeniable. In
Belgium as elsewhere in Europe the socialists have been inclined to see
themselves as the naturally ordained representatives of the proletariat.
The distinctive achievement of the CSC has been to show that, in terms
of union membership at least, socialist predominance can no longer be
taken for granted.

The CSC is a confederation of seventeen national unions (*centrales*).
Membership of the CSC is more evenly distributed amongst its affiliated
than that of the FGTB. Nevertheless, even in the case of the CSC,
the three largest *centrales*, the Construction-workers (160,000), the
Metal-workers (132,000), the Textile-workers (120,000) together comprise almost one half of the total membership. Three further unions,
the Employees, the Food-workers and the Public Service Workers, each
muster over 50,000 members. The Railway-workers and the Chemical-
workers follow not far behind.[2]

The CSC is defined by statute as an organization seeking to achieve a
society based on Christian principles.[3] Affiliates are required to accept
this aim and to conform to the governing disciplines of the central

1. On this see *Free Labour World*, March 1971 Brussels, pp. 20–23. For an
interesting background to these events, Desolre, *50 Ans de débats sur le contrôle
ouvrier, 1920–1970*.
2. Spitaels, pp. 50–51.
3. *Statuts de la CSC*, CSC, Brussels, 1966, p. 3. 'We do not require from our
members either proof of baptism or a certificate to show that they go to con-
fession. . . We remain convinced that their professional interests can only be
defended on the basis of Christian morality and social doctrine': A. Kool,
President of the CSC, November 1964, quoted in Spitaels, p. 46.

organization. In general the CSC statutes set up a model more centralized than that of the FGTB.[1] At the head of the CSC stands the President (since 1968 Henri Pauwels) elected for life and invested with greater powers than any comparable official in the FGTB. A Moral Counsellor appointed by the Catholic hierarchy participates as of right in the governing organ of the confederation.[2]

The constitution provides four main organs of self-government for the CSC; the General Congress, the *Comité Confédéral* (the *Comité*), the *Bureau* and the *Bureau Journalier*. All work under the supervision of the President as top official in the CSC.[3]

The General Congress plays a rather different role to that of the FGTB, devoting its attention to matters of general principle rather than to the enunciation of policy. Representation comes from both affiliated *centrales* and regional organizations of the CSC. *Centrales* and regional organizations are represented in accordance with their membership but in differing proportions. *Centrales* are entitled to a delegation based on two thirds of their membership, regional organizations to a delegation based on one third only.[4] The General Congress is required by statute to meet not less than once every four years. In fact, as a rule, it meets rather more frequently.[5]

The *Comité Confédéral* rather than the General Congress is the effective policy-making body of the CSC.[6] The *Comité* comprises delegates from each of the seventeen affiliated *centrales* plus delegates from each of the thirty-three regional federations. Representation is in accordance with membership on a weighted scale which gives a two-to-one advantage in favour of the *centrales*. The 'Moral Counsellor' appointed by the hierarchy sits on the *Comité* as a matter of right. Also present are the members of the Bureau Journalier, which is roughly the CSC equivalent to the Secretariat of the FGTB. The *Comité* meets not less than once in every two months and more often if required.[7]

Execution of policy decisions taken by the *Comité* is entrusted to two subsidiary organs, the *Bureau* and the *Bureau Journalier*.

1. For an interesting insight into the selection process of CSC union leaders, see Seyfarth *et al.*, p. 175.
2. Article 15 of the statutes. The status of the Moral Counsellor is analogous to that of the representatives of the Executive Committee of the Communist International (the C.I. Reps.) who were delegated to the executives of communist parties all over the world in the 1920s and 1930s.
3. *Statuts*, Articles 14, 15, 24, 32. Ebertzheim, p. 67.
4. *Statuts*, Article 19, also Spitaels, p. 45.
5. In the years after the Second World War General Congresses have been held in 1947, 1949, 1951, 1955, 1960, 1962, 1964. EEC, *Monographies*, p. 15.
6. *Statuts*, Article 21.
7. *Statuts*, Article 22. Spitaels, p. 45; Ebertzheim, pp. 88–9.

The *Bureau Journalier* comprises five members, the President, the General Secretary, the Moral Counsellor appointed by the Catholic hierarchy, plus two other chosen by the *Comité*. The President of the CSC like the other members is elected by the Comité Conféderal. The President's appointment is for life. As chief officer, somewhat in the manner of the President of a United States union, he is responsible for the conduct of the CSC and its business. As its title indicates the *Bureau Journalier* handles the day-to-day business of the CSC in line with policy decisions taken by the *Comité* and refined in their application by the *Bureau*. The constitution requires that three of the five members of the Bureau should be Flemings and two Walloons.[1]

General supervision of the work of the *Bureau Journalier* is in the hands of the *Bureau*. The *Bureau* comprises twenty-four members; twelve from the *centrales*, seven from the provincial federations, the President, the General Secretary, the Moral Counsellor appointed by the Catholic hierarchy, plus the two remaining members of the *Bureau Journalier*.

Out of the twelve places allocated to the *centrales* two are reserved for the *Centrale du Secteur Publique*, one for a representative of white-collar workers. Four of the seven seats allocated the provincial federation and seven places in the *Bureau* overall are reserved by statute for French-speaking Walloons. *Bureau* members, elected by a secret ballot of the *Comité*, serve a two-year term. The statutes require that one half of the membership of the *Bureau* be renewed by election every year.[2]

LEGAL STATUS

Laws of 31 March 1898 and 24 May 1921, allow unions to acquire the substantial benefits conferred by legal personality in exchange for accepting certain collateral social obligations laid down in the text of the laws. Belgian unions have considered that the consequences of 'registration' under the laws of 1898 and 1921 would involve a severe derogation from their rights as self-governing organizations. The requirement of publishing a full list of members, for example, has been held to lay trade unionists open to victimization by employers. As a result, over seventy years after the passage of the original legislation, neither the CSC nor FGTB have availed themselves of the advantages conferred by registration, nor are they likely to do so in the future. Lack of legal personality has not prevented the unions acquiring a large measure of

1. *Statuts*, Articles 24, 30–32; Spitaels, pp. 45–6. It is interesting to note that the equivalent body in the Netherlands Catholic union confederation NKV has a similar title, literally the 'committee which meets daily'.
2. *Statuts*, Article 27. On the constitution of the CSC, see Spitaels, pp. 45–6.

recognition and widespread representation on both state and para state boards. In practice *de facto* strength has necessarily brought *de facto* recognition of that strength in its train. The once important issues raised by the laws of 1898 and 1921 now belong to the past rather than to the present.

CONFEDERAL RELATIONS

In the past CSC and FGTB have at times been involved in sharp and bitter conflicts. The great increase in CSC membership has brought with it new parity in strength and has played some part in bringing the two organizations closer together. Certainly, when new industry has entered a Catholic area, the priest, the hierarchy and local Catholic politicians have been able to exercise powerful influence on the employer to accept the CSC as the union in the plant.[1] On the other hand, once established, the CSC has been increasingly constrained to act as a straightforward labour union rather than as an arm of the Church. The CSC, too, has moved to the left, in line with the shifts in the attitudes of the hierarchy, over the last two decades. Thus although each organization, CSC and FGTB, retains its distinctive principles, open hostility is now a thing of the past. CSC and FGTB normally present a common front in negotiations with the Belgian employers. Every major official stoppage in the last decade has been supported equally by CSC and FGTB.[2] Unity of action seems more likely to increase than decrease. Nevertheless, failing strong external pressure, steps towards organic unity do not seem likely in the immediate future.

UNION MEMBERSHIP

The shift of industry away from Wallonia towards Flanders and Brussels has markedly affected the fortunes of both FGTB and CSC. In 1967 the combined membership of CSC and FGTB amounted to approximately 1·5 million. Out of this total 62 per cent (911,000) were in Flemish regions, 29 per cent (416,000) in Walloon regions, and 9 per cent (132,000) in the linguistically divided but predominantly French-speaking region of Brussels. Wallonia's former predominance is clearly a thing of the past.

The extent to which the numerical predominance of the CSC is based on a shift of industry to Flanders is clearly shown by a regional breakdown of membership figures. Three quarters of CSC membership (570,000) is in Flanders, 17 per cent (130,000) in Walloon regions, only a bare 7·5 per cent (57,000) in Brussels and vicinity.

1. As in the case of the new Ford plant at Genk, for example: see Seyfarth *et al., Labor Relations in Belgium and the United States,* pp. 48–50.
2. Spitaels, pp. 83–5.

Flemish membership of the FGTB now also outranks that of Wallonia, although to a lesser degree: 49 per cent (341,000) of FGTB members are in Flemish-speaking areas as against 41 per cent (286,000) in Walloon regions; 10 per cent (75,000) of FGTB membership is found in Brussels region.

In Flemish regions the CSC outnumbers the FGTB by almost two to one (570,000–340,000). In Walloon regions FGTB membership exceeds that of the CSC by over 100 per cent (286,000–130,000). In the Brussels region, a far smaller catchment area, the two confederations are more evenly matched, but here too FGTB membership exceeds that of the CSC by a substantial margin (75,000–57,000).[1] In terms of sector membership the FGTB is ahead in steel, engineering and glass, all predominantly Walloon based. The CSC leads in chemicals, the food industry, and textiles, all rooted in Flanders. The FGTB remains ahead in its traditional strongholds of paper, printing, gas, electricity and city tramways. The CSC leads amongst bank and insurance employees. Overall the FGTB's main strength lies amongst industrial workers, skilled and unskilled alike. The CSC is strongest amongst the white collar employees and according to some evidence amongst young workers as well.

The level of unionization in Belgium is amongst the highest in the world. In some key sectors of industry organization amongst blue collar workers approaches 100 per cent. Approximately 70 per cent of blue-collar workers, 64 per cent of public service employees, 30 per cent of white collar workers were organized in either the CSC or FGTB in 1965. The level of unionization in Belgium is a great deal higher than most of the countries in the Economic Community, at the very least comparable with that of Great Britain and much greater than that of the United States. This achievement is remarkable by any standard. Given the confessional, non-confessional divisions of Belgian unionism and the regional–linguistic splits which divide the country as a whole, it is more than ever worthy of note.[2]

UNION DUES

Belgian union dues are relatively high. There is no check-off, but dues are nevertheless consistently well paid. One result is that membership figures quoted by unions are true and reliable, the two confederations going so far as to cross-audit one another's books to guarantee veracity. FGTB dues, fixed by the *centrales*, average around 1 per cent of salary.

1. On this, Ebertzheim, pp. 150–51; Spitaels, pp. 32–6, 47–50; Seyfarth *et al.*, *Labor Relations and the Law in Belgium and the United States*, p. 6.
2. On this, Ebertzheim, *Les Syndicals ouvriers en Belgique*, pp. 141–69; Spitaels, *B.* pp. 32–5, 47–52; EEC, *Monographies:* p. 7; Spitaels, ed., *L'Année Sociale 1968*, pp. 155–75; *Le Syndicalisme Belge*.

CSC dues, more standardized, are generally comparable. Both CSC and FGTB dues carry with them the right to a range of ancillary benefits. CSC dues for an adult male are in the region of 100 francs per month, 70 francs for an adult woman.[1] Ancillary benefits encourage membership stability and reduce membership turnover. Well-stocked strike funds greatly enhance the bargaining credibility of both CSC an FGTB.

In the middle 1950s FGTB unions negotiated a series of agreements providing premium payments to union members. The first, in the cement industry, was signed in 1953. At that time union membership had plunged to a low of 45 per cent. When the premium rose to double the level of union dues, membership swept up to above 85 per cent. Premium plans, which now cover some one third of the organized workforce, extend to engineering, chemicals, gas, electricity, textiles and clothing industries. Premium payments to union members provide cut-price or free unionism at the employers' expense.[2] Under the terms of certain agreements unofficial strikers are liable to forfeit their premium payments. The scheme is thus to be seen, at least in part, as a joint union–employer measure, designed to improve labour discipline.[3]

Differential payments to union members have undoubtedly helped to reduce the number of unorganized workers and to swell the ranks of both CSC and FGTB. Some observers suggest that those who decide to join a union only when 'free loading' becomes impossible have shown a preference for the CSC. If this is true, the initiative may have served to enhance the numerical superiority of the CSC.

The Belgian metal-workers' union has not only negotiated premium payments for union members, it has also enforced direct employer subsidies to union funds. Engineering employers are required to pay 0·5 per cent of the plant payroll expenditure, a kind of *per capita* fee, into a special fund. Proceeds are then paid out to union treasuries in proportion to membership in the enterprise. This measure, whilst enhancing union effectiveness, may also be construed as enhancing union–employer solidarity in the face of manifestations of rank-and-file rebellion in the workforce. The employers' association, *Fabrimetal*, has the right to discontinue the payment and impose what amounts to a *per capita* fine in the event of a stoppage.

1. EEC, *Monographies*, pp. 45, 77; Seyfarth *et al.*, *Labor Relations and the Law in Belgium and the United States*, p. 168.
2. Engineering, textiles, tobacco and food are amongst the industries covered by such agreements, Seyfarth *et al.*, *Labor Relations and the Law in Belgium and the United States*, pp. 45–9.
3. On this Blanpain, 'Labor relations in Belgium', in Kamin, ed., *Western European Labor and the American Corporation*, p. 224.

COLLECTIVE BARGAINING

The *commissions paritaires*, joint union–employer bodies, which constitute the main channel for collective bargaining in Belgium, were first
set up by a coalition government with socialist participation, in the
revolutionary wave which followed the end of the First World War. By
1921 there were some twenty *commissions paritaires* in being covering
some 600,000 workers.

Belgium's eighty or so *commissions paritaires* are governed by laws
of 9 June 1945, 4 and 11 March 1954 and 5 December 1968. Fifty deal
solely with blue collar negotiations, sixteen with white collar, while
fourteen cover workers in both categories within a particular industrial
sector. The *commissions* comprise equal numbers of union and employer
representatives with a President and Vice-President nominated by the
minister. Union representatives must be from recognized unions.[1]
Commission paritaire decisions require an unanimous vote. Thus each
party has a veto on the proposals of the other. No business can be conducted without a quorum. Since a quorum requires a minimum of one
half of the representatives of both employers and unions to be present,
either side has the opportunity to delay proceedings at will, should it so
desire.

The tasks of the *commissions paritaires*, as laid down by Article 39
of the 1968 statute, include the responsibility of concluding collective
agreements and preventing or conciliating disputes between employers
and workers. They also have the right to advise government on projected legislation and other matters.

The government *may*, at the request of a commission or one of its
member organizations, extend an agreement to all workers and employers within the commission's jurisdiction. In that case the terms of the
agreement become legally obligatory norms. Commission agreements
must be in both French and Flemish, except in cases where they apply to
only one linguistic region. In that case the local language alone rules.
The wages and conditions of the large majority of the Belgian workforce
are settled, either directly or indirectly, through *commission paritaire*
negotiations. One achievement of which Belgian labour is legitimately
proud is the legal entitlement to three weeks' annual holiday established
by law in 1966. Union bargaining has ensured that members will not be

---

1. Seyfarth *et al.*, *Labor Relations and the Law in Belgium and the United
States*, pp. 59–66; Belgian Institute for Information and Documentation, *Collective Bargaining in Belgian Labour*, (cited hereafter as *Collective Bargaining*)
pp. 6–8. A recognized union must have at least 50,000 members and be a
national organization represented on the National Labour Council and the
General Economic Council. In effect this limits access to C S C, F G T B and the
small predominantly white-collar C G S L B.

short of cash during their vacation by negotiating six weeks' pay for the three weeks' annual holiday.[1]

The *commissions paritaires* function with the framework provided by a Central Economic Council and a National Council of Labour. Each plays an advisory role in the formation of government policy.

The Central Economic Council (*Conseil Economique Central*: CEC) established in 1948, provides a forum for discussion and agreement regarding issues of national economic policy. The CEC comprises twenty members nominated by the unions, twenty-two members nominated by the employers, six 'independent' members, and a President appointed by the state. Matters may be referred to the CEC for consideration either by ministers or by one of the two houses of the legislature. CEC reports need not be unanimous but may reflect differences of opinion within the ranks of members.

The National Council of Labour, a consultative body the origins of which date back to 1944, exists to advise government and the legislature on social questions arising from collective bargaining, working conditions and hours of labour. This body decides jurisdictional disputes between *commissions paritaires* and also acts as a watchdog over the administration of legislation concerning hours of labour, works councils, etc. The National Council comprises twenty-three members, eleven nominated by unions, eleven nominated by employers, with an independent President nominated by the state.[2]

DÉLÉGATION SYNDICALE

The procedure regulating union representative rights in Belgian enterprises dates from a national agreement signed between the unions and the Federation of Belgian Employers in June 1947. This agreement makes provision for the recognition of a *délégation syndicale* (union committee – roughly shop stewards' committee) in all plants employing more than fifty workers. Members of the *délégation syndicale* must be over twenty-five years of age and have a minimum of one year's service in the industry. The *délégation syndicale* is normally appointed by the unions and ranges in size from one member in a plant of fifty workers to ten in a plant of between 1500 and 2000. In cases where inter union agreement is lacking the *commission paritaire* may hold an election. In such a case representation on the *délégation syndicale* is allocated in accordance with votes polled by the competing union *centrales*. A union must poll a minimum of 10 per cent of the vote to be entitled to a place in the *délégation*. Belgian stewards have some real protection against victimization.

1. *Collective Bargaining*, pp. 6–12; Seyfarth *et al.*, *Labor Relations and the Law in Belgium and the United States*, pp. 61–3, 279–83.
2. *Collective Bargaining*, p. 8.

In part this springs from the level of union strength, in part from provisions which lay down that the dismissed steward shall *retain* his post during the term of an appeal to the *commission paritaire*. Blue and white collar workers are normally represented separately on the *délégation syndicale*. Members are entitled to time off without loss of pay for the conduct of union business.[1]

The agreement which regulates the activity of the *délégation syndicale* provides the specific right to appear before the employer in respect of the application of collective agreements, statutory wage regulation within the plant, individual or collective grievances and the implementation of social legislation applicable to the enterprise. The *délégation* is entitled to meet the plant manager within three days of making the request.[2]

Belgian 'in-plant' industrial relations are characterized not only by the *délégation syndicale* but also by the work of two other organs, the *conseil d'entreprise* (works council) and the health and safety committee. The *délégation syndicale* springs from the FGTB's recognition of the clash of interests between employer and employed. The works council and the committee for health and safety by contrast reflect the emphasis placed by the CSC and the hierarchy on employer–employee cooperation.

CONSEIL D'ENTREPRISE (WORKS COUNCIL)

Comprised of equal numbers of persons elected by the workforce and appointed by management, the *conseil d'entreprise* is legally obligatory in all Belgian enterprises employing over 150 workers.

In *conseil d'entreprise* elections, all employees, not merely union members, are entitled to vote. The *conseil* is a fairly small body, the workers' side numbering six for an enterprise employing 150 and only ten for a plant employing 2000.[3] Elections for the workers' side take place every four years. Seats are reserved for workers, employees and young persons under twenty-one. Only union members are eligible for nomination. *In the event that there is no union then no works council may be formed.* The right to submit lists of candidates for the workers' side election is restricted by law to the three recognized unions. Candidates, whether successful, or unsuccessful, enjoy protection from dismissal except in cases of serious misconduct.

The works council meets not less than once a month under the

1. *Collective Bargaining*, p. 4. Seyfarth *et al.*, *Labor Relations and the Law in Belgium and the United States*, pp. 3, 22–6.
2. *Collective Bargaining*, p. 4. ICFTU *Labour Management Relations in Western Europe*, pp. 31–2. Seyfarth *et al.*, *Labor Relations and the Law in Belgium and the United States*, p. 75.
3. Six members for 100–500 workers, up to sixteen for 4000–6000 workers, and eighteen thereafter. Seyfarth *et al.*, *Labor Relations and the Law in Belgium and the United States*, p. 27.

presidency of the plant manager. It is entitled to certain limited information regarding the conduct of the firm's affairs, and is expected to work to enhance employer–employee cooperation. The works council may make recommendations regarding aspects of plant management and suggest criteria to govern hiring and firing procedure. It is also entitled to oversee the implementation of social and industrial legislation affecting the workplace. Perhaps most important of all, it manages company welfare schemes, canteens, sports clubs, etc. The works council also has powers of determination over the timing of plant holidays and the wording of plant regulations.[1]

By and large, the works council as at present constituted does not seem to have effected any major erosion of employer prerogatives. Reporting back to the workforce is severely hindered by the exaggerated business secrecy provisions which shroud works councillors' activity.

HEALTH AND SAFETY COMMITTEES

A law of 10 June 1952 makes health and safety committees (*Comités de Securité et d'Hygiène et d'Embellissement des Lieux de Travail*) obligatory in all Belgian plants employing more than fifty workers. The committee is comprised of equal numbers elected by workers and nominated by management under the chairmanship of the enterprise manager. Election of the workers' side is governed by the same general provisions as in the case of the works council. Here again the right to present candidates is reserved for the recognized unions. The committee watches over the enforcement of government safety regulations, encourages plant safety, generally oversees the health of workers and employees and does its best to ensure a satisfactory working environment.[2]

STRIKES

Although Belgium is a country in which the political general strike has been widely used, the general level of resort to industrial action remains low. Belgian strike figures have more in common with those of Germany and the Netherlands than of either Britain, France or Italy. In fact the disciplined character of the labour movement, which has enabled the limited general strike to be used with success, may well be one explanation. Moreover Belgium has strong unions and a relatively sophisticated

1. On all this, ICFTU, *Labour Management Relations*, pp. 32–3; Seyfarth et al., *Labor Relations and the Law in Belgium and the United States*, pp. 26–9. *Collective Bargaining*, pp. 4–5.
2. ICFTU Seyfarth et al., *Labor Relations and the Law in Belgium and the United States*, pp. 80, 82, 345. *Labour Management Relations*, p. 33, *Collective Bargaining*, pp. 5–6; Seyfarth et al., *Labor Relations and the Law in Belgium and the United States*, pp. 24–30, 401.

system of industrial relations. The need for stoppages in order to open channels of communication and achieve union aims may thus be less than in countries with less developed bargaining systems.

The political strike, too, is in part a reflection of the tripartite deadlock in the Belgium parliamentary system. On occasions this has left the P S B and F G T B with no alternative but resort to extra-parliamentary action to achieve essentially limited aims. Thus a socialist led general strike in July 1950, after much turmoil and some bloodshed, prevented the return to the throne of King Leopold, whose behaviour during the German occupation had deprived him of the confidence of a large part of the people. A largely Walloon based general strike lasting from December 1960 to January 1961, forced limitations on unpopular government economy measures. One price was severe strains between Walloon and Flemish members of the F G T B, increased stresses between the F G T B as a whole and the C S C.[1]

The rules governing the calling of official strikes are stringent and precise. Strike votes are conducted by ballot: 80 per cent of those likely to be involved must vote for a strike decision to be binding; a majority of 65 per cent in favour is required before a stoppage can be called official.[2] If the numbers involved are large the stoppage may require authorization from *centrale* or confederation leadership. In the C S C it is the confederation rather than the individual *centrales* which holds the strike fund. The confederation leadership may thus wield considerable influence over the conduct of negotiation. Given the strength and solidarity of Belgian unions, their well-established strike funds, a stoppage once begun in Belgium may last some considerable time.

There are some signs that the relative industrial peace of the post war decades may be ending. Early in 1970, 20,000 Catholic miners in Limburg came out on a five-week unofficial stoppage. The Ford plant nearby at Genk came out unofficially at the same time, whereupon the union leaders backed the movement to keep it under control. In February 1970 foreign workers, the bulk of the workforce at Michelin came out on strike against union advice in a tearaway stoppage which culminated in a sit-down in the plant. These stoppages, while not in themselves conclusive, do suggest that in Belgium, as elsewhere in Western Europe, the pattern of labour relations established in the post war years is undergoing severe strain.

FUTURE TRENDS

The characteristics of the Belgian labour movement, it has been sug-

1. Collard *et al.*, pp. 203–7, Verkade, pp. 211–16, 200–204. Spitaels, pp. 23–6, Ebertzheim, pp. 19–25.
2. Seyfarth *et al.*, *Labor Relations and the Law in Belgium and the United States*, pp. 176–7.

gested, spring from the size and nature of the economy, the regional–linguistic–confessional–industrial and occupational differences which exist among the labour force. In post war years the regional–linguistic conflicts have grown a great deal sharper. The labour movement is going to find it hard to resist their divisive effects.

The Catholic CSC, which in 1945 lagged 200,000 members behind the socialist FGTB, is now by a margin of a clear 100,000 members the largest trade union confederation in Belgium. There does seem to be evidence to suggest that the larger a Catholic trade union confederation grows, the more it tends to become a lay rather than a confessional organization. Beset by problems on all sides the Catholic Church appears to be making real endeavours to come to terms with the twentieth century. Not least the hierarchy seems to seek doctrinal innovation which will accommodate state-owned industry, in both East and West, within the framework of Catholic social thought. In the event that these doctrinal shifts, either voluntarily or involuntarily, are carried into the trade union movement, then part of the ideological rationale of divided unionism in Belgium may be called into question. In that case the tripartite system of Belgian politics, which depends on the incorporation of the Catholic working-class vote into that of the multiclass *Parti Social Chrétien*, might in time be challenged as well.

Rumblings from below, now to be heard, suggest that the satisfied and somewhat bureaucratized union hierarchies, with their close and intimate links with parties, employers and governments, are getting out of touch with their rank and file. If this be true it will not be at all a bad thing. The real centres of wealth and social power have not changed that much in Belgian society over the last hundred years. There remains plenty of work for new radicals to do.

9. The Netherlands

ECONOMIC AND SOCIAL BACKGROUND

The distance from Groningen in the far north of the Kingdom of the Netherlands to Eindhoven in the far south is scarcely 220 miles. The land area of the Netherlands is less than that of the single state of Maryland in the USA. Yet as late as the eighteenth century the population of the United Provinces of the Netherlands exceeded that of the whole of North America. In those years the great trading city of Amsterdam, its concentric rings of canals lined with trees and graceful merchants' houses, conducted a trade which reached to the uttermost ends of the globe. Amsterdam, like London and New York in later ages, stood at the centre of the commerce of the world.

The strategic position of the Low Countries (the territory comprised by the contemporary states of the Netherlands and Belgium), located at the mouth of the Rhine and the junction of several smaller rivers leading into the interior of Western Europe, opposite the southern and most highly developed part of Great Britain, led them to become a major centre of commerce at a very early date. In the Middle Ages the towns of Flanders, whose bygone magnificence still survives in the burgher architecture of Bruges and Ghent, developed a measure of commercial importance and political independence which can only be compared with the free cities of northern Italy. The wool trade with England, buying raw wool, weaving it in the Low Countries and shipping it back to England, made the territory outward-looking which to some extent it remains to this day.[1] In the wars against France in the fourteenth century, the three provinces of Holland, Brabant and Flanders (the neighbouring regions of modern Belgium and the Netherlands combined), provided England with a firm base of operations. The interest of England's ruling elite that the Low Countries should be independent of great powers to the east (Germany) and to the south (France) has been a permanent factor in the history of the region. In

1. The Belgian Congo and the Netherlands East Indies, both lost after the Second World War, made Belgium and the Netherlands colonial powers of importance. The Netherlands, with a population of some 8 million, was at one time governing the East Indies with a population of 100 million.

1914, following Germany's invasion of Belgium, it led Britain directly into the First World War.

In the sixteenth century, by one of those convoluted concatenations of legitimate and illegitimate succession in which monarchic history abounds, the Netherlands was in the possession of the King of Spain. Philip's centralizing absolutism disturbed the Netherlands' nobility. The rigours of the Inquisition alienated still wider sections of the population. The urban centres of the Netherlands as trading cities were unusually open to influence from outside.[1]

The entrepreneurial activity and ambitions of the trading bourgeoisie generated an ideology at odds with the formal doctrine of the Catholic Church. In the 1560s a great Calvinist upsurge swept from France northwards through what is now Belgium, Holland and Luxembourg, setting off reciprocating waves of angry revolt and brutal repression which historians have termed the Eighty Years' War. The Spanish campaign of reconquest, like Montgomery's Arnhem assault in 1944, came to a halt against the river barriers of the Rhine and the Scheldt. In the area of the present-day Netherlands the forces of militant Calvinism triumphed over a recalcitrant Catholic minority. In the southern Walloon provinces, Calvinism was literally extirpated by fire and sword.[2] The Catholicism of Belgium, the Protestantism of the Netherlands, with all that this involves for the modern labour movement, is a direct outcome of this bloodshed and slaughter which swept the Low Countries between three and four centuries ago.

The northern Low Countries benefited from an emigration from the south. Their strategic control of the Scheldt virtually put Antwerp out of business as a rival port. A naturally favourable position for world trade was now enhanced by the opening up of the Indies and the New World.

The United Provinces[3] which emerged from the Eighty Years' War constituted a loose federation in which sovereignty resided not with the (Federal) States General but with the Estates of the Seven Provinces.[4] The successful revolt 'did for the Dutch bourgeoisie more than the civil

1.   'Hence Amsterdam, Turk, Christian, Pagan, Jew,
                  Staple of sects and mint of schisme grew;
                  That bank of conscience, where not one so strange
                  Opinion but finds credit and exchange.'
                  Andrew Marvell, 'The Character of Holland'.
   2. Thus 'the Books of deceased persons could not be taken over by their legatees before they had been approved by the censor': Renier, *The Dutch Nation*, p. 15; Geyl, *Holland and Belgium*, p. 19.
   3. Holland, Zeeland, Utrecht, Gelderland, Friesland, Overijssel and Gröningen.
   4. As late as the end of the eighteenth century the state of Holland still addressed the state of Zeeland as: 'Honourably High Mighty Gentlemen, Favoured Friends, Neighbours and Allies'; Daalder in Dahl, *Political Opposi- tions in Western Democracies*, p. 188.

war was able to do for the English upper middle class in the seventeenth century; it accomplished what 1789 and 1815 did for the French'.[1] The bourgeoisie became, both in fact and in name, the ruling class. Although each province cast one equal vote in the States General, Holland, which as the largest trading centre provided over half the federal treasury,[2] emerged as the major force. The dominant position in civil life was occupied by the regents, a class of urban merchants and traders, who gradually assumed unto themselves the powers and functions of city government.

A haughty patrician class, consisting in each town of a very limited number of families, closely interrelated, little by little had possessed itself, as a matter of hereditary right, of all the offices and dignities of the town, of the province and of the state; their fellow citizens . . . were regarded as belonging to an inferior caste.[3]

The particular form taken by political and social development was crucial for the subsequent history of the Netherlands State. The continuous threat of flooding from the North Sea imposed permanently predetermined limits on the intensity of internal conflict if a large part of the Netherlands was not to disappear beneath the ocean for ever. Once the United Provinces were established, the long maritime seaboard, 'the rivers and canals of the Netherlands made [them] . . . to a large extent immune against invasion on land. Consequently there was no urgent need for them to develop large standing armies.'[4] The Crown, given the pre-eminence gained by the burgher middle class and the social structure of the country, lacked the capacity to impose its will. The naval rather than military role of the kingdom not only weakened the King, it also positively strengthened the merchants whose aid was essential for the furnishing of warships and crews. The religious content of the political revolt, the theocratic ambitions of Calvinist clergy, clothed the discussion of political issues in religious terminology. The presence of an important Catholic minority constituted a permanent spur to Protestant vigilance. The need to stand solid against powerful external enemies, the latitudinarian outlook engendered by a mercantile society, the co-existence of multiple centres of power within a single state, all counselled a certain tolerant moderation in internal political affairs.[5]

1. Renier, p. 23.
2. 'In the province of Holland this dictatorship of the urban oligarchy was a tangible reality': Renier, p. 20.
3. Landheer, p. 178.
4. Lapalombara and Weiner, eds., *Political Parties and Political Development*, p. 47.
5. Thus 'it was not so much in their religion as in their approach to religion that the Netherlanders suffered from their ruler. They had the tolerance of merchants who are in the habit of rubbing shoulders with men from many

The Netherlands bourgeoisie became accustomed to rule in the seventeenth century. The bourgeoisie as a class thus acquired self-confidence, self-possession and political expertise through over two centuries of dominance *before* the modern labour movement appeared on the scene. Government in the United Provinces was the prerogative of a series of localized, mainly urban, oligarchies. Influenced by the need to maintain a united front against threats from without, these oligarchies developed manifold and sophisticated modes of adjusting their conflicting interests. Open splits or appeals to the masses were not accepted as part of the rules of the game. Modes of political behaviour were established in which real decisions were evolved by process of wheeling and dealing amongst initiated leaders of authoritative groups, each with a constituency to serve. None was responsible directly to popular opinion, which was at a discount. In their dealings with religion the *regents*, as men of power, were not inclined to put too fine an emphasis on points of doctrine. Such a course of action would have involved ceding part of their own authority to the Church. The ministers nevertheless were able to maintain a firm hold on their well indoctrinated flock. Aristocracy, *regents*, *predikants* and people became the axes around which Netherlands politics revolved.

At a time in which primitive communication and imperfect knowledge made widespread bilateral trade impossible:

Amsterdam became the *entrepôt* where the merchandise of the world was brought, unloaded, warehoused and eventually distributed. Dutch carriers were indispensable while the rest of the world was still in the early stages of commercial development ... Amsterdam ... in 1700 was the staple market about which international trade and finance revolved.[1]

Later development undermined the *entrepôt* role of Amsterdam. Divisions amongst the commercial class hindered a valid adaptation. The eighteenth and nineteenth centuries became for the Netherlands a time of stagnation and decline. The industrial revolution in the Netherlands took place in a country where the bourgeoisie had been enthroned for centuries, where the self-confidence and self-reliance of the workforce had been ground down, if not broken, by well over a hundred years of stagnation and decline.

RISE OF LABOUR MOVEMENT

The federal United Provinces lasted until replaced by a centralized state

1. Wilson, *Anglo-Dutch Commerce and Finance in the Eighteenth Century*, pp. 3–4.

climes, varying in creed and outlook ... The Netherlanders did not learn tolerance from Erasmus: the great humanist was the product of Netherlands tolerance': Renier, p. 13.

borne on the bayonets of Revolutionary France in 1795. The peace treaty concluded at the Congress of Vienna established an enlarged Kingdom of the Netherlands which included all of present day Belgium. The object was to create a powerful buffer state against France. The political, religious, linguistic and national strains which resulted proved too strong. A popular national revolt centred on Brussels broke out in 1830. The outcome was the formation of an independent Belgian state. At the Congress of London in 1831 the major powers, although not without some misgivings, allowed the new state to remain. Discontent with the handling of the Belgian revolt by the Netherlands' King William I led to his abdication in 1840. In 1848, under the impact of revolution elsewhere in Europe, his successor accepted major parliamentary reforms.

The Catholic episcopal hierarchy was re-established following the enactment of the 1848 constitution. Hereafter much of Netherlands political life hinged around conflicts between Liberals, Calvinists and Catholics especially over the control of public education.[1] Voting blocs of Catholic, Liberal and Calvinist derivation were formed.[2] The Calvinists split in two on the basis of doctrinal division and, to some extent, class composition. Abraham Kuyper, a political pastor, pioneered the Calvinist cause. Learning from the Anti Corn Law League in Britain, Kuyper brilliantly applied modern techniques of mass agitation in the Netherlands a generation before their time. In the Anti-Revolutionary Party Kuyper created the first mass-based party in Netherland history.[3]

Like the conduct of affairs by the regents, the esoteric manoeuvres of Dutch parliamentary life remained the concern of an arbitrarily selected few. The electorate in 1853 was confined to some 80,000 persons in a population of around 3 million. Thirty years later the percentage of the adult population entitled to vote still remained around 6 per cent.[4] Women did not obtain the right to vote in the Netherlands before 1920. The social conditions of the disenfranchised masses were, on the kindest portrayal, deplorable.

1. The episcopacy was re-established in 1853. The schools issue arose over the Education Act of 1878.

2. At present the Catholic People's Party and a liberal People's Party for Freedom and Democracy. The Calvinists comprise an Anti-Revolutionary Party and the Christian Historical Union. The Catholics command 30 per cent of the vote, the Liberals and each of the Calvinist parties about 10 per cent each. The Christian Historicals are somewhat more 'higher class' than the 'little people' of the Anti-Revolutionary Party. The split arose over a proposed extension of suffrage in 1894.

3. Kuyper was able to obtain 300,000 signatures for a petition over the 1878 Education Act. At this time the electorate numbered barely 120,000.

4. The right to vote was restricted to males over twenty-three years of age. Of these only 11 per cent were entitled to vote in 1854, only 12 per cent in 1880, only 49 per cent in 1900. When the suffrage was enlarged in 1900 the qualifying age was raised to twenty-five years of age at the same time.

The shift to an industrial economy in the Netherlands did not get properly under way until the last two decades of the nineteenth century, later than in either Belgium or Germany. Part at least of the motor force seems to have come from the German expansion which followed the Franco-Prussian War of 1870–71.[1] Further factors were the flight from the land provoked by the opening up of the prairies in the USA, the global revolution in the cheap transport of food caused by steamship transportation.

In areas such as Gröningen, Friesland and Noord Holland, the instability precipitated by rapid social change among an agricultural workforce with long experience of depressed social conditions created a working class movement with a tendency towards radicalism. In Amsterdam the workforce of the diamond industry, organized in a craft-dominated luxury trade with a uniquely high skilled content and bargaining capacity to match, was more inclined towards moderation. The sharp discipline enforced by a rapidly advancing railway system on a new railway proletariat combined with the prevailing social context to press in the direction of moderation.

In the initial years of the Dutch labour movement the radicals, under the leadership of a former Lutheran pastor, Domela Nieuwenhuis, who resigned his Friesland living in order better to serve his cruelly deprived flock, were in the ascendant. After the turn of the century, the radicals found themselves increasingly isolated and finally lost control altogether.

The response of the Netherlands' working population to the industrial revolution was less volatile than in France and Italy, less powerfully organized than in either Germany or Britain. The commercial–mercantile–maritime–imperial–parasitic nature of much of the economy was probably one cause, the firm hold of the bourgeoisie as a long-standing ruling class another.[2] Social conditions too seem to have been exceptionally bad, and this is likely to have been an influential factor.[3] The absence of a large labour force in engineering, heavy industry and mining was probably a further contributory cause. The deferential qualities imbued by a deeply entrenched Calvinist piety cannot have

1. Thus Verkade, *Democratic Parties in the Low Countries and Germany*, p. 43; Windmuller, *Labor Relations in the Netherlands*, p. 3. Windmuller's book is essential reading for anyone in the English-speaking world who wishes to understand the Netherlands labour movement. My own work owes much to Windmuller's text and I gladly acknowledge the debt. However, the reader should be warned, the conclusions we draw from the evidence, the value-judgements we place upon events, often differ profoundly.

2. A most valuable insight into Netherland society around this time will be obtained from Max Havelaar's remarkable novel *Multatuli*.

3. The worker's average life-expectation has been put at thirty-two years: quoted in Verkade, p. 43.

248 THE LABOUR MOVEMENT IN EUROPE

been without effect either. In her classic *Capital and Labour in the Netherlands*, Henriette Roland Holst wrote:

The Dutch proletarian felt not indispensable but instead superfluous. Far from claiming his 'right to work' he begged for it as he would for charity. The rich were not his enemies living off his sweat and blood but good people, bene-factors, on whose generosity he depended. The mood of the Dutch people was not one of fundamental resistance but of resigned suffering.[1]

Ingrained localism, an historically determined, religiously prescribed, divinely ordained spirit of submission and, one suspects, a marked lack of alternative sources of employment, were all factors tending to produce this situation.

The first socialist organization in the Netherlands, the Social Democratic League (*Sociaal Democratische Bond*: SDB), was founded in 1881. In 1887, the SDB leader Domela Nieuwenhuis went so far as to suggest in the socialist journal *Justice for All* that the great public welcome given to King William III in Amsterdam that year was scarcely appropriate for 'a man who made so little of his job'. Nieuwenhuis was rewarded with a sentence of two years in jail (reduced on appeal to one year). A national outcry followed. Released after serving only eight months, Nieuwenhuis was elected to parliament from a Friesian constituency in 1888. Experience of parliament, scepticism regarding the possibilities of parlia-mentary action,[2] dissatisfaction with the slow pace of reform in the Netherlands, drove Nieuwenhuis farther to the left, in the direction of syndicalism and the general strike.

In 1893, under the influence of Nieuwenhuis, the Social Democratic League adopted a specifically anti-parliamentarian programme. A split followed. A new organization, the Social Democratic Workers' Party (*Sociaal Democratische Arbeiders Partij*: SDAP) was set up in 1894. The SDB disintegrated in 1897. A number of its members subsequently joined the SDAP. The SDAP, aided by suffrage reforms in 1900 and 1910, made rapid progress, returning two deputies in 1897; fifteen by the time of the outbreak of war in 1914.[3] Both the original SDB and its successor the SDAP were heavily indebted to the Marxist ideology of German Social Democracy for their ideas. Germany's SPD also seems to have provided material aid from time to time. In 1913 the SDAP had made sufficient ground for three of its leaders to be offered posts in the

1. *Kapitaal en Arbeid en Nederland*, vol. i, p.132, quoted in Windmuller, p. 5.
2. In 1890 the electorate was still restricted to 296,000, 27 per cent of the *male* population over twenty-three years of age. Daalder in Dahl, p. 417.
3. Constitutional amendments raised the electorate to 570,000 in 1900 and 855,000 in 1910. Verkade, p. 22.

government. The proposal was rejected by the party congress by a vote of 375 to 320.[1]

The conversion of Domela Nieuwenhuis to anarchism did not leave an entirely clear field to the leaders of the SDAP. In 1906, a left wing, prominent amongst whom were David Wjnkoop, Herman Gorter and Henriette Roland Holst, formed around the journal *Tribune*. Ordered to close their press by the party in 1908 the 'Tribunists' refused and were expelled. The 'Tribunists' now set up their own left wing Social Democratic Party (*Sociaal Democratische Partij*: SDP), which continued to maintain an independent existence until it affiliated to the Communist International in 1919.

NETHERLANDS TRADES UNIONISM

The unions in the Netherlands, in their early days, were no more free of internal conflicts and dissensions than were the socialist parties. A Netherlands section of the First International perished in the dispute between Marx and Bakunin. Print-workers and diamond-cutters formed their first organizations in the 1860s. Carpenters, cabinet makers, cigar makers, painters and masons (all skilled trades), railwaymen and others followed suit. In 1893, following a decision of the Socialist International, the Netherlands socialist and union organizations established a joint National Labour Secretariat (*Nationaal Arbeids Secretariaat*: NAS). Inside the NAS, an exclusively union body after 1896, two clearly defined tendencies were at work. One, syndicalist, voluntarist in conception, militant in outlook, wedded to a low-dues fighting policy, with a view of the strike as a means of social and economic emancipation. The other, typified by the diamond-workers' leader, Henry Polak, in favour of high dues, social benefits, strike funds, professional leadership, discipline, and an essentially parliamentary socialist orientation. Each wing, one suspects, was rationalizing ideology out of its own conditions of employment and job opportunities.[2]

Up to 1903 the syndicalists were probably the dominant element. In that year employer counter measures against attempts to organize the Amsterdam port labour force led to a general stoppage. Railway wages and conditions were deplorable. A call, issued by the dockers, for the railwaymen to refuse to handle 'black goods' led to a total rail stoppage in defiance of union instructions. The railway companies, taken

1. Verkade, p. 43. Daalder in Dahl, p. 209–20; Windmuller, pp. 15, 33–4.
2. Both elements had a British connection. The British trade unionist, Tom Mann, had set up a branch of the Dock, Wharf, Riverside and General Labourers' Union at Rotterdam during an international organizing tour in 1896. Mann, *Tom Mann's Memoirs*, p. 136; Windmuller, p. 13. Henry Polak had worked in England and taken his organizational ideas in large measure from the British craft unions.

aback, capitulated, granting a whole series of major concessions, including union recognition. The government now took alarm and introduced legislation banning strikes on railways and in public services, providing penalties of up to six years' imprisonment. Socialists and unionists, some with mixed feelings, replied with the threat of a general strike. In the event the rail union leaders proved to have no heart in the venture. Newly formed Protestant scab unions kept trains running. Although the port of Amsterdam was closed and important successes were obtained elsewhere, the strike committee called off the stoppage on the third day, a total defeat.[1]

The 1903 rail dispute widened the breach between socialists and syndicalists in the labour movement and shifted the balance heavily in the socialist favour. In 1905–6 some fifteen national unions, under socialist influence, set up a strongly centralized confederation on the model of the German ADGB. Henry Polak was elected first President of this newly founded confederation, the *Nederlands Verbond van Vakverenigingen* (NVV). Jan Oudegeest, a railway unionist, became general secretary. The pre war decade was tumultuous. Lock outs accounted for over half the number of days lost through strikes.[2] In 1910 lock outs exceeded strikes as much as three to one. The NVV proved able to stand the strain. In 1910 membership stood at 41,000. By 1914 NVV membership doubled to 80,000.[3] A united campaign for universal suffrage waged by the SDAP and NVV proved an important solidifying factor. In 1900 most workers had no vote.[4] In 1917, following the reform of that year, male suffrage was universal.[5]

By 1914 therefore, the Netherlands possessed a coherent and firmly established trade union and socialist movement. Each co-operated closely with the other. Each had a financial and membership base, a cadre of voluntary officials and full time functionaries at its command. Each, and this is crucial, had in its own way waged a battle with a left wing within its own ranks. Each in turn had emerged victorious, in command of a largely homogeneous organization from which the left had, substantially, been excluded.

The strong hold of the Calvinist Church over the Protestant laity, the

1. There is a parallel with the British rail strike of 1911, and the conduct of the TUC in 1926. Strikes in Netherlands public services were still illegal in the 1960s. In the Netherlands the rail unions had sought to negotiate a return to work before the first day of the strike was over.

2. Lijphart, p. 109.

3. At that time NAS membership stood at 10,000. Windmuller, p. 39.

4. Up to at least 1908 two thirds of SDAP votes came from rural areas. It is interesting to speculate on the impact this had on the party's policy and character.

5. A further reform in 1920 extended the suffrage to women. The voting age was then twenty-five, it is now twenty-three. Dahl, p. 417.

grip exercised by the Catholic hierarchy over its own faithful, were not basically undermined by the rise of either Netherlands socialism or the NVV. Nor did the socialist challenge cause Catholics and Protestants to sink their differences and form a common front. An early attempt, begun in 1895, to set up a joint Catholic–Protestant textile union foundered on a 1906 directive that Catholics might join only organizations of their own denomination. The outcome was the birth of separate Catholic and Protestant organizations, each anti-socialist, each dedicated to the rejection of the class struggle. By 1914 the membership of confessional union organizations stood at around 40,000 (29,000 Catholic, 11,000 Protestant), one half the membership of the NVV. The confessional organizations, however, remained more a dependency of the employers, more an arm of the hierarchy among the working class, than trade unions in the normally accepted sense of that term.

The Netherlands labour movement assumed the essential outlines of its modern form in the years between 1880 and 1918. A competently organized, moderate socialist party, a like minded trade union confederation constituted one element. A would-be revolutionary fringe on the left of both constituted another. Rival Catholic and Protestant union organizations stood on the right of the socialist unions. Each was tied to its respective hierarchy, each linked to one or other of the Protestant and Catholic parties in the Netherlands parliament. This remarkably stable constellation of forces was briefly threatened by a radicalization which undermined the hold of the established organizations in 1945–7. Changes in industrial structure after the Second World War have helped produce a shift towards confessional unionism. There has been a general lessening of tension between the three union confederations. Otherwise the situation remains substantially the same today.

THE INTER WAR YEARS

The Netherlands did not join the holocaust of 1914–18. The war brought to certain sectors of the economy a major boom, to others an unprecedented slump. To help reduce the impact of unemployment the government decided first to subsidize union benefit funds, later to match, florin for florin, the contributions of union members. Government subsidies to union unemployment benefit funds continued until administration was passed over to the state following the Second World War. The 1920s and particularly the 1930s were years of specially high unemployment. Government aid not only guaranteed union funds against bankruptcy, it also enabled union treasuries to pay union members, through union offices, benefits which exceeded those available to non-members outside union ranks. This system clearly provided marked incentives for individuals to swell the union ranks. At the same time, the possibility that the subsidy might be withdrawn, should union–employer–government conflicts grow too sharp, acted as a moderating factor on union behaviour. Limited union dependence on government aid thus constitute done important stage in the integration of the unions into the social system.

By 1920 membership of the NVV had boomed to around 250,000. Membership in confessional and independent organizations brought the total enrolment up to almost double this figure. The number of workers covered by collective agreements mushroomed from the meagre 23,000 of 1910 (10,000 of whom were Amsterdam diamond-workers) to 275,000. The Russian Revolution, the hardships of the war years, heightened social tensions. The German revolution of 1918 began at Bremen and Kiel, just across the northern border. Encouraged by mass discontent and news of outbreaks of indiscipline in the Netherlands army, Pieter Jelles Troelstra, the socialist party leader, announced that the revolution would not stop at the border.[1] The government mobilized its reserves. Troelstra now found himself without the support of the party leadership. The SDAP beat a rapid retreat. The administration rushed through a bumper package of long-overdue reforms including female suffrage. Moderation, at least on the part of the leaders of the labour movement, became once more the order of the day.

In the depression which followed 1920 union membership fell rapidly. As employers sought to cut wages and increase hours, strikes brought man days lost to an average of 1,700,000 a year between 1919 and 1924. A limited economic recovery was followed by a cataclysmic decline in 1932. Unemployment reached a peak of 33 per cent in 1936 and did not fall below 25 per cent in the remaining pre war years. Overall unemployment amongst NVV members rose as high as 36 per cent. In painting and plastering as many as two thirds of union members were out of work. Government action quite failed to cope with the crisis. The government aided employers in their efforts to reduce wages, sought to cut state expenditure and reduce the costs of its own public works. Only the continuing state guarantee saved union benefit funds from disaster. The subsidies which safeguarded the viability of union insurance funds also provided a powerful lever with which to ensure the loyalty of the union apparatus to the status quo.[2]

The course of events after 1920 was very different from that in the years before. The slump and the employers' offensive forced the labour movement to fight hard simply to maintain gains already made. Hitler's conquest of power on the Netherlands eastern border, the rise of fascism

1. 'The revolution would not stop at the eastern frontier station of Zevenaar': Verkade, *Democratic Parties in the Low Countries and Germany*, pp. 109–10.
2. R. Stenhuis, NVV President, was forced to resign when he pressed for a more vigorous socialist policy in 1928. See Verkade p. 120; Windmuller, p. 62.

both at home and abroad, seemed to put the continued existence of the Netherlands state in danger. The socialist vote, which hitherto had grown steadily, now stabilized itself at around one quarter of the total poll and seemed unable to grow further. Attempts to head the SDAP and NVV in a more radical direction in the late 1920s and early 1930s came to nothing. A group of left-wingers were expelled from the Socialist Party in 1932. The SDAP now moved towards the Keynesian 'Plan Socialism' of the Belgian Henry de Man, which it adopted in 1935. In the Netherlands both communists and Nazis made gains, but never sufficiently serious to threaten the balance of power. The SDAP, in the fashion of pre war German Social Democracy, refused to participate in any coalition government through all the years up to 1939. Republican up to 1937, the party refused for a considerable time to attend the royal opening of parliament, to cheer the Queen, or to vote for the defence budget. In August 1939, however, under the threat of imminent hostilities, J. W. Albarda, the SDAP leader, and Van den Tempel, another SDAP deputy, with the approval of the party Congress, crossed the line and entered the Cabinet.[1]

In the new coalition cabinet, Albarda was awarded the portfolio of Minister of Waterways, while Van den Tempel became Minister of Social Affairs.[2] The socialist ministers had held these scarcely distinguished offices for less than a year when in May 1940 the German army occupied the Netherlands. After remaining outside the government for more than fifty years the representatives of Netherlands socialism now spent five of their first six years of office as part of a 'government' in exile.

THE SECOND WORLD WAR

Inside the occupied Netherlands life at first went on very much as before. A civil government under Seyss-Inquart was appointed. Every effort was made to employ the existing organs of administration for German purposes, an endeavour which very largely succeeded.[3] Only in later years, when it became clear that Germany was losing the war, when serious social hardship and mass deportation of Jews began,[4] when above all the Germans attempted large scale conscription of Netherlands workers for forced labour in Germany, did resistance on a large scale get under way.

1. Daalder in Dahl, pp. 211–12; Verkade, pp. 116–20.
2. Laurens in Landheer pp. 201–2.
3. For example the Dutch parliament, provincial and other bodies were suspended rather than disbanded, thus leaving the members free to draw their salaries. Warmbrunn, *The Dutch under German Occupation*, p. 37.
4. Especially important, since the largest concentration of Jewish citizens was in Amsterdam, the *de facto* capital, and traditionally a centre of radical thought and feeling. For one account see Jacob Presser, *The Destruction of the Dutch Jews*.

The record of the NVV was not a particularly happy one. In July 1940 the Germans dismissed the President and Vice-President of the NVV and appointed a Dutch Nazi, J. H. Woudenberg, Commissioner in charge of the NVV in their place. Shortly afterwards German observers were appointed to all NVV union headquarters. Several union leaders were removed from office, the NVV executive itself dissolved. 'A few high officials threatened to withdraw, but the threat of reprisals sufficed to make them change their minds.' The whole team of leading function-aries remained at their posts under Woudenberg[1] until the NVV was dissolved into a specifically Nazi Netherlands Labour Front in the spring of 1942.[2] This was despite the fact that the employers themselves refused to recognize the NVV as representative after July 1941.

The confessional unions behaved somewhat better than the NVV. Yet they too, once assured that their independence would be main-tained, adopted a stance of loyal cooperation with the occupation regime.[3] However, when, in July 1941, the Nazis decided to place both Catholic and Protestant federations under Woudenberg's administra-tion, the officers of most confessional unions resigned on the spot and called on the members to follow them out of the organizations.[4]

In July 1940 the Dutch Nazi, Rost van Tonningen, was appointed Commissioner in charge of the SDAP. The SDAP leadership refused to co-operate. The party nevertheless remained in being until dissolved by the Nazis in 1941. The railway unions, whose bureaucracy, in the words of one observer, 'was closer in mentality to the management than to its own constituency', went along without dissent with management's policy of loyal collaboration with the Germans.[5] When in 1944 the railwaymen undertook a prolonged strike in aid of the Allies, they did so on the understanding, which was honoured, that full wages including overtime and Christmas bonuses would be paid.[6]

The groups which sprang up to conduct the Resistance were largely divorced from the old-line organizations. Foremost, *after* Hitler's on-

1. An account of this affair will be found in 'The Netherlands during the German occupation', ed. Postumus, in *Annals of the American Academy of Political and Social Science*, May 1946, pp. 2–64, 66. More accessible is Windmuller, pp. 92–8, 100.
2. To their great credit a few staff members resigned in 1940; 95 per cent of the officers and two thirds of members withdrew in 1942 to avoid enrolment in the Labour Front. NVV members showed more spirit than their leaders: see Warmbrunn, pp. 137–8, 269.
3. Thus in November 1940 a delegation of leaders from all three confedera-tions toured Nazi Germany under the auspices of the Labour Front: Wind-muller, p. 95.
4. Warmbrunn, pp. 137–8; Windmuller, pp. 98–9.
5. Management's aim was allegedly to prevent infiltration by Nazis on the one hand and left-wing radicals on the other. Warmbrunn, p. 139.
6. Warmbrunn, pp. 143–5.

slaught on Russia in June 1941, was the Netherlands Communist Party, hitherto an insignificant force on the political scene.[1] On the other hand an important part of the activity initiated by the government in exile seems to have been designed to ensure the post war preservation of the *status quo*.

The development of thought and activity in the labour movement under the occupation proceeded on two very different lines. Resistance to the occupation (in which members of the confessional organizations participated), the collaboration of leading NVV officials up to 1942, the general suffering and hardship of the wartime years, all served to force a radicalization of labour's ranks. Many activists were disgusted with the role played by the NVV. Many also believed that the time had come to end the division of the organized labour movement into socialist, protestant and catholic wings. Many sought a radical restructuring of Netherlands society in line with the sufferings and hardship imposed by the occupation and the Resistance. Such forces joined with the Netherlands Communist Party, which was pursuing objectives of its own, to set up a radically motivated movement for trade union unity. By 1945, this Unity Trade Union Centre (*Eenheids Vakcentraal*: EVC) with 176,000 members, including important support among Catholic miners in Limburg, bid fair to outrank the NVV and the confessional organizations as well.[2]

Meantime the formation of a Nazi-led Netherlands Labour Front on 1 May 1942, the rising tide of the Resistance in the years that followed, had caused former officials of all three federations to move closer together. NVV spokesmen proposed the establishment of a single united trade union confederation after the war. The confessional union leaders had not been impressed by the NVV's role in the early years of the occupation and were unwilling to consider organic unity except on a specifically confessional base.[3] The Catholics seem to have been influenced in this by the hierarchy and the Dutch employers.[4] The most that could be agreed was to undertake the establishment of a Council of Trade Union Confederations (*Raad van Vaakcentralen*), to make provision for joint co-operation at all levels of union organization. Given the deep historic splits in the Netherlands labour movement this represented a most important advance.

1. Warmbrunn, pp. 132–3, 233–5, 196–8; Frits Kool, 'Communism in Holland', in *Problems of Communism*, Sept–Oct. 1960.
2. Verkade, pp. 234–5. Kool, *Communism in Holland*, quoted above. Windmuller, pp. 109–10.
3. The NVV's acceptance of the Nazi Commissioner Woudenberg was one reason. The willingness of some of its officials to take over the assets of confessional organizations and incorporate them in the NVV under Nazi command was another. See Windmuller, pp. 99–100, 105.
4. See statement of Dirk Stikker, quoted in Windmuller, p. 105.

Radical and conservative wings of the labour movement were not alone in making plans for the Netherlands on the conclusion of hostilities. Dirk U. Stikker, a leading representative of the Netherlands employers, in consultation with Professor Molenaar of Leiden University, conceived the idea of a Foundation of Labour in which employers, unions and government would combine to deal with problems of social and economic policy and industrial relations. Representatives of employer organizations, former functionaries of the now dissolved union confederations and higher civil servants met to discuss this proposition. Well before the Liberation, aided by concessions made by union representatives, the main outline of the proposal had been agreed.

A common desire to preserve social stability after liberation undoubtedly helped to achieve the agreement to set up a Foundation of Labour.[1] The legitimacy of the 'government' in exile in Britain was in certain eyes somewhat tenuous. The possibility of a conflict with the claims of the Resistance in the Netherlands was exercising Cabinet members as early as 1943. One main concern of the government in exile was to 'maintain peace and order and to prevent a "hatchet day" during the transition period after the German surrender'.[2] The advance of the Allied armies was halted at Arnhem in the southern Netherlands in September 1944. The rest of the country remained under German control until the success of the final Allied offensive in April–May 1945. In terms of membership the left wing Trade Union Unity Centre at this time was pressing the still somewhat discredited NVV very hard. The Communist Party, which was to poll 10 per cent of the vote, win a third of the poll in Amsterdam, and return ten MPs the following year, was stronger and more popular than ever before.[3] With the front line running across the country, large-scale flooding, enormous damage caused by land and air bombardment, a yawning deficit in essential food supplies, the last winter of the war proved by far the worst for the Netherlands population. Who could claim the most right to rule? The government in exile, now returned to one part of the country? Or the Resistance, already present on the ground both there and in the territory still under German occupation? The issue could not fail to be to some extent in question.

In these and later years both government and established labour organizations were striving to establish their legitimacy against a challenge from grass-roots. It is against this background that the subsequent course of Netherlands labour politics and labour relations must be

1. See the delicate phrasing used by Windmuller (p. 106) for example.
2. Warmbrunn, pp. 219, 186–7. The government in exile went so far as to prepare to endow the extreme right wing 'Order Service' with police authority in the interim, a quite startling proposal.
3. Kool, in *Problems of Communism*, p. 19; Lazitch, *Les Partis communistes d' Europe*, p. 218.

examined if it is to be properly understood. The Netherlands economy, heavily dependent on world trade, was badly damaged by the war; recovery was handicapped by the loss of unearned income from the Netherlands East Indies, now independent and under nationalist control. In such serious circumstances, appeals to class unity and individual self-sacrifice in the interests of national recovery were likely to carry much more weight than might otherwise have been the case.

NETHERLANDS LABOUR AFTER 1945

Socialist participation in the Netherlands government had begun in 1939. Socialist ministers continued to serve in the 'government in exile' through the war, also during the interregnum between the partial liberation of the Netherlands in 1944 and the first post war general election in 1946. In that election the old SDAP, now merged with other organizations and launched as a broader Labour Party (*Partij van den Arbeid*: PvdA), won 28 per cent of the poll. In the ten difficult years that followed the Labour Party leader, W. Drees, presided over a coalition Cabinet.[1] The coalition, whilst enacting important social reforms, also involved the Labour Party in supporting ill-conceived and costly endeavours to regain the Indonesian Empire lost to the Japanese during the war and now in the hands of nationalist forces. If the Netherlands communists had not been so discredited by their servile pro-Russian stance the PvdA might have lost much of its support at this time. Willem Drees, as Minister of Social Affairs, introduced in 1945 an Extraordinary Decree on Labour Relations. This soon became a basic regulator of post war industrial relations. The decree established a four man Board of Government Conciliators endowed with massive powers over wages and conditions. (Employees drawing *over* a specified income were exempt from these provisions.) This Board found its origins partly in a law of 1923, partly in a similar board set up in May 1940, which established a number of important precedents before being dissolved by the Germans in October 1942.[2] The Decree fixed a compulsory forty eight hour week. In the event of a dispute between the parties, it fixed the employee to his place of employment, prohibiting either firing or resignation without Board sanction. Normal collective bargaining prerogatives were transferred to the Board, which received powers to fix wages and conditions of employment. Employers were prohibited from altering wages rates or conditions of work without prior Board approval. The same sanctions applied to collective agreements.[3]

1. The Netherlands government was headed by a socialist prime minister until 1959.
2. Edelman and Fleming, p. 226; Windmuller, pp. 90–2, 269–72.
3. Edelman and Fleming, pp. 225–6. Windmuller, pp. 268–72.

In practice it became customary for government to issue general directives to the Board. The Board in its turn, following a somewhat amplified interpretation of its original constitution, would then refer every agreement which came before it to the Foundation of Labour, established in 1945 for examination and advice. The Foundation, comprised of representatives of employers' organizations and the three 'orthodox' union federations (but not the EVC, which was excluded), would then refer the agreement to its wage committee for closer examination and, if thought appropriate, revision. The final package then went back to the Board, where approval was normally in the nature of a formality.[1]

This convoluted procedure, whereby guidelines were established in a ministry composed of a coalition of conflicting interests, and their interpretation passed to a neo-corporative institution of employers and 'recognized' organizations of the employed, constituted the keystone of Netherlands labour relations policy in the decade and a half after 1945.[2] One effect, as will readily be appreciated, was to eliminate the EVC entirely from the bargaining table. Yet at the end of the war the EVC was larger than the Protestant CNV, only slightly smaller than the Catholic NKV and at least comparable in size to the NVV. Representation on the Foundation of Labour was exclusively from the central labour confederations, NVV, NKV, CNV and not from their individual affiliated unions. The powers of the central confederation machinery, as against that of the affiliated unions, were thus greatly strengthened, a tendency already apparent before 1940 and further accelerated during the war years.

The EVC itself was severely hampered by the offensive countermeasures undertaken by government, business and the established organizations of labour. It was also badly hit by internal divisions of its own. Once the first flush of enthusiasm was over it became clear that the communists were a most powerful influence within the EVC. The Netherlands Communist Party sought with some success to subordinate EVC activity to the rapidly changing power imperatives of Russian state policy during the Cold War. Internal conflicts weakened EVC, outside influence eroded its power still further. By the middle 1950s, the EVC challenge to the entrenched orthodoxies of Netherlands labour was clearly overcome. A communist decision to disband the remnants of EVC with a view to re-entering the NVV led to a split in both EVC and the Communist Party during 1958.[3] A syndicalist offshoot of the

1. Windmuller, p. 272; Edelman and Fleming, pp. 224–6.
2. For a valuable insight into its effect on union behaviour, see Flanders, 'Manpower utilization and the American investor', in Kamin, ed., *Western European Labor and the American Corporation*, p. 424.
3. Kool, in *Problems of Communism*, p. 21.

EVC continues in existence as an independent organization up to the present day.

The Netherlands Communist Party in 1955 stood at around 16,000 members.[1] The party vote, 10 per cent of the electorate in 1945, had fallen to 2·4 per cent by 1959. In the election of 1967 the Communist Party could elect only five deputies, as against the thirty-seven of the Labour Party and four from its rival on the left, the Pacifist Socialist Party. A loosely applied ban on membership by NVV has not prevented the emergence of isolated pockets of party strength in certain shipyards and in sections of the construction industry. Nevertheless the Communist Party, thoroughly stalinist, is hardly a major force in Netherlands political life today.

The effects of the Second World War on the Netherlands labour movement were manifold and important. Under the stress of impending hostilities the Socialist Party (SDAP) broke with its original abstentionist tradition and joined a coalition government in 1939. Thereafter the SDAP (from 1946 the Labour Party – PvdA) continued to participate in a series of coalition governments, which collectively lasted the nineteen years 1939–58. The war and the occupation thus changed the socialists from a party of opposition to a party of government. The war marks a watershed in party history, as a result of which the socialists entered the administration and remained within its ranks for almost two decades.

In the case of the unions the leadership decision to continue to serve under the Nazi Commissioner Woudenberg did a great deal to discredit the NVV. This loss of credibility was reflected in an initial failure to regain pre war membership levels at the conclusion of hostilities. The NVV lost power and influence relative to its confessional rivals. A serious challenger emerged on the left. Enormous destruction and extreme hardship characterized much of the fabric of life in the Netherlands at the end of the war. The fear of radical social change, shared by coalition government, employers, socialist and confessional unions, resulted in the establishment of an unique, neo-corporative 'incomes policy'. This policy was designed not only to ensure post war stability and economic recovery, but also to eliminate the threat to the existing power structure represented by the EVC. The oligarchic modes of mutual interaction and accommodation thus established show astonishing resemblance to those devised by the regents of the United Provinces some centuries earlier.[2]

1. The party does not at present publish or reveal membership figures.
2. Thus the Secretary of the Economic and Social Council of the Netherlands writes of inter-union co-operation: 'The objectives of the Central organizations . . . their administration, how their decisions are made and carried out, and their financial conduct are matters for free disposition by the organizations themselves; *in the last resort* it is the individual membership which determines them': Pels, *International Labour Review*, Sept., 1966, p. 275. The Michels-like

THREE PILLAR SOCIETY

The Netherlands labour movement, in the second half of the twentieth century, operates in a specific social context which conditions its outlook and behaviour. Netherlands society, with its firmly rooted localized traditions, comprises three specific subcultures, the three pillars (*zuilen*) of the Netherlands' confessionally exclusive society. A Calvinist pillar comprises between one fifth and one quarter of the population; a Catholic pillar encompasses something over one third. Rather less than one half of the population stands outside the expressly confessional blocs. Here are found an important part of business, the largest single trade union organization, an important part of the conservative, or in the Netherlands' terms 'liberal' vote, plus the adherents of the Labour Party (PvdA). Also properly to be included in the non-confessional bloc are those religious persons not primarily motivated by their confessional affiliation.[1]

Political allegiance, which in the Netherlands is closely linked to confessional affiliation, is stabilized by a situation in which over three quarters of children attend denominational schools.[2] Over half of Netherlands Catholics are concentrated in the two southernmost provinces of Limburg and Brabant. Here, comprising some 90 per cent of the population, the Catholics are a factor of predominant political importance.

The division of the electorate into three competing blocs, none able to win an absolute majority on its own account, each divided from the other on what it considers grounds of fundamental principle, is the decisive characteristic of Netherlands political life. Catholics marginally outnumber Protestants, who are themselves divided into competing, doctrinally divided, Calvinist groups. Labour and 'liberal' parties stand apart from the confessional blocs altogether. Proportional representation ensures a close match between votes polled and seats obtained in the national parliament. One result is that the Catholic 'Centre', which stands between a Protestant bloc divided between Calvinist sects on the one hand, and a non-confessional bloc divided between capital and

1. The 1960 census shows 40 per cent Catholic, 37 per cent Calvinist (divided between two groups), 18 per cent unattached. Since religious opinion does not in every case determine political behaviour, even in the Netherlands, these figures should be regarded as indicative rather than absolute.

2. In 1900 however, two out of every three attended *public* schools. This regression was the fruit of the School Pacts of 1916–17 to which the socialists assented as part of the deal for universal suffrage and other reforms. Daalder, pp. 205–14; Verkade, pp. 54–5.

differentiation between the organization and its members is revealing. Pels's comment on the media and the press (p. 278) is also illuminating. The emphasis in the quotation is my own.

labour on the other, has been represented 'in all regular Cabinets' since 1918.[1] The consequent mechanics of Netherlands coalition politics has placed disproportionate power in the hands of party political, parliamentary and clerical elites. The socialists, with a peak vote of 33 per cent in 1956,[2] have never been able to form a government on their own account. Since 1939 the SDAP and its successor the PvdA have been numbered amongst eligible partners for the coalition tango.[3]

NETHERLANDS EMPLOYERS

Netherlands employers are divided on confessional–non-confessional lines in much the same way as the rest of this pillar society. Even milk-traders have the choice of Catholic, Protestant and non-denominational employer associations. A non-denominational Central Social Federation of Employers (*Centraal Sociaal Werkgevers Verbond*: CSWV)[4] represents some 12,000 companies. A smaller Netherlands Catholic Employers Federation (*Nederlands Katholiek Werkgevers Verbond*: NKWV) comprises some 4000 firms, mostly in the Catholic south. A still smaller Federation of Protestant Employers (*Verbond van Protestants – Christelijke Werkgevers in Nederland*: VPCW) claims some 660 affiliated enterprises. According to the OECD, 80 per cent of employers in industry belong to CSWV, 15 per cent to NKWV and 5 per cent to the VPCW.[5] A desire to avoid the bewilderingly complex pattern of industrial negotiations likely to arise from the existence of three employers' organizations and three union confederations, each side divided amongst itself on comparable political–confessional lines, was probably a part at least of the rationale of centralized bargaining policy in post war years.

In 1967 the two confessional organizations established a Federation of Catholic and Protestant Employers' Associations (*Federatie van de Katholieke en Protestants–Christelijke Werkgeversbonden*: FCWV) with a view to a subsequent full unification. Confessional and non-confessional employers' associations are linked in a central co-ordinating body, the Council of Netherlands Employers' Associations (*Raad van Nederlandse Werkgeversbonden*). Links between employers' associations, political parties and government are close. One past secretary of a Catholic employers' association, M. G. M. Marijnen, served as prime minister between 1963 and 1965.[6]

As might be expected, the three 'Giants of the Netherlands', Philips,

1. Daalder, in Dahl, pp. 221–4.
2. Daalder in Dahl, p. 213.
3. The PvdA in 1969 enrolled 117,000 members.
4. The term for employer, *Werkgever*, literally 'work-giver', speaks a whole volume about Netherlands social attitudes.
5. OECD, *Growth and Economic Policy*, p. 174.
6. Windmuller, p. 256.

Royal Dutch Shell and Unilever, play a disproportionate role in determining employer attitudes and policy. Philips, a multi-national giant
specializing in consumer electrics, represents the prime source of income
and employment for the city of Eindhoven, with a population of close on
300,000 people. Critics speak of Eindhoven as a company town and
have been known to hint darkly of company pressures on the whole
fabric of civic life and action.[1] The turnover of these three companies,
Royal Dutch Shell (9·7 million dollars), Unilever (6 million dollars)
and Philips (3·6 million dollars), amounted to 69 per cent of the gross
national product of the whole Netherlands in the year 1969.[2] Whilst all
three are multi-national, rather than solely national companies, their
significance for the Netherlands economy is self-evident. The extent to
which the Netherlands' unique post war incomes policy finds some
special explanation in the preponderant influence of these three giants in
the Netherlands economy certainly merits further investigation.

The three giants which overshadow the Netherlands are unrepresentative of the economy as a whole. In 1964, one half of the 1·2 million
workers in manufacturing industry were employed in undertakings with
500 workers or less. Almost all these are likely to have been businesses
under family ownership and management.[3] In these undertakings a
spirit of paternalism more appropriate to a century or more ago is frequently the rule.[4] Upward mobility into management is at a pronounced
discount. Government and legislation combine to maintain in existence
an employer class which can claim continuity from the seventeenth
century and often continues to manifest the same arrogant and self-
opinionated 'regent's mentality' which characterized the oligarchs of
that earlier era. The entrepreneur's view of the productive enterprise
as inviolable personal property produces inbred hostility to any suggestion of a union presence in the plant. This again is one reason for the
pattern of national bargaining preferred by both employers and the three
big union organizations in the last decades.

NETHERLANDS UNIONS

Labour organizations in the Netherlands possess all the inherent advantages of an industrial union structure. All three federations, NVV,
NKV and CNV, were reorganized on a mutually agreed industrial

1. For example, the allegations of police provocation reported in *Agenor*,
Brussels, Nov.–Dec. 1971.
2. Levinson, *Capital, Inflation and the Multinationals*, p. 105.
3. Small employers are defined as employing between ten and forty nine
workers; medium employers as employing fifty to four hundred and ninety nine,
see Windmuller, p. 237.
4. One authority has referred to the 'enlightened despotism' which ruled in
textiles: see Windmuller, p. 236.

union basis in 1946. In 1968 there were only twenty unions in the NVV, twenty one in the Catholic NKV and twenty four in the Protestant CNV. However, the advantages of rational union organization are somewhat reduced by the presence of three competing industrial unions in every jurisdiction. The triplication of industrial union structure keeps individual unions small. Only five Netherlands unions enrol more than 50,000 members, only fifteen more than 25,000, a further factor enhancing the power of the federation centre against the base.[1] The size of the average union is only some 17,000 members.

Again, the endeavour to translate plan rationality into organizational form has not entirely succeeded. To define the boundaries of an industrial union in a homogeneous industry like rail transport or coalmining is not too difficult. In other cases jurisdictional boundaries are not so easily defined. In the Netherlands, as in other countries where organization is conducted on industrial union lines, the metal-working, public service and general unions, by virtue of their 'catch-all' jurisdiction, have grown unusually large and tend to overshadow their rivals. The somewhat arbitrary definition of union boundaries, while aiding central control and discounting jurisdictional disputes, also seems to have contributed to a lessening of interest and participation at the base.

The structure of national unions in the NVV, NKV and CNV is essentially similar. A Congress, normally held at three year intervals, decides fundamental policy issues and elects the top union officials. Supervision of union policy between infrequent congresses is assigned to a union General Council which meets, as a rule, quarterly. The General Council, which is comprised in the main of members elected from union locals and districts, acts as a kind of congress in miniature and is a body of major importance. Policy laid down by the Congress and interpreted by the General Council is carried out by a board of full-time functionaries. The top official is the union President. The full board may number as many as ten. An inner cabinet, composed normally of President, Vice-President, General Secretary and Treasurer, the *dagelijks bestuur* or 'board which meets daily', controls the day to day conduct of union business.

The Netherlands is a small country so that the ties between the national union centre and its regional and local organizations are much closer than might otherwise be the case. The NVV metal-workers' union, ANMB, the largest in the federation, is organized into thirteen districts in each of which there are between three and five full-time officials. The functional division of other unions is less, although since most are a great deal smaller, the staffing is at a markedly lower level. The union divisional officers are responsible upwards to the national

1. The NVV enrols 560,000 members in twenty unions; NKV – 420,000 members in twenty one unions; CNV – 240,000 members in twenty four unions.

office, rather than downwards to the locals in their areas. The constitution of Netherlands national unions does not make provision for the election of a district committee to supervise or control either district officers or district activity.

The power of Netherlands union branches (*afdelingen*) is by Anglo-American standards severely limited. Membership meetings, as a rule, are held only three to four times a year. The full time secretaries and dues-collection officers found in the larger locals are employees of the national union, not of the union local itself. These branch officials are thus responsible upwards to the national union, rather than downwards to their own members. Union branches themselves have only limited powers. In the absence of effective shop floor organization, issues in dispute are passed to the district office for action rather than dealt with on the initiative of the members. Union dues are normally paid to a house-to-house collector, rather than collected in the plant or at branch meetings. This factor too detracts from union activity at the base and contributes to apathy among members. The level of union dues in the Netherlands is high. Moreover, in comparison with either France or Italy, where dues are far lower, they are consistently well paid. Union contributions average 1·5–2 per cent of wages. As a result both national unions and national federations are well staffed and able to maintain a high level of union activity and organization. By mutual agreement, the industrial unions with comparable jurisdictions in each of the three main confederations hold dues and benefits at similar levels, thus eliminating the use of the dues structure as a means of competitive bidding for membership.

THE THREE CONFEDERATIONS

The three main union centres (NVV 620,000 members), (NKV 400,000), (CNV 240,000), together comprise some 1,260,000 members, or 80 per cent of the organized labour force. A further 300,000 workers are organized in independent, mostly white-collar, unions, and the small syndicalist centre. Unlike unions in France and Italy, Netherlands labour organizations have grown rapidly in line with the boom economy of post war years. Membership of the Big Three (NVV, NKV, CNV) 640,000 in 1947 had passed 1,260,000 by 1972.

Each national centre maintains close ties with one or other of the main contenders for office in the Netherlands political system. The NVV is linked informally with the PvdA, the NKV with the Catholic People's Party, the CNV through different elements of its Calvinist membership with both the Anti-Revolutionary Party and the Christian Historical Union. Out of the three confederations, the CNV, deeply influenced by Calvinist theology, stands farthest to the right. Nevertheless, despite political and confessional differences, the three union centres have achieved a surprising amount of agreement on common action and policy in the post war years.

The structure of the three federations, NVV, NKV, and CNV, is essentially similar. The Congress of NVV, the largest of the confederations, is held not less than once in every three years. Representation is confined to full-time officials and members of the executive board of the affiliated unions. Constitutionally, the prime task of the NVV Congress is to elect the President, Vice-President, General Secretary and Treasurer of the confederations. The NVV President is the chief official and public spokesman of the confederation. In general it is left to the NVV leaders themselves to decide the subjects for report and discussion at the three-yearly Congress. Thus, in 1962 the twenty third Congress of the NVV discussed a report of federation activity over the last three years, documents on 'European Integration' and a paper on 'The Position of the Trade Union Movement in Modern Society'. All these items were introduced by the platform. The NVV constitution makes no provision for the submission of resolutions from affiliated organizations.[1] In the nature of things the official leadership exercises largely unchallenged control of the proceedings. As will be observed there is no provision for representatives of the base to attend the Congress. The most important policy-making body in the NVV is the Executive Board, comprising the President and the eight full-time national officers, plus members of the executive boards of each of the affiliated organizations. In the Executive Board of the NVV, which meets quarterly, is vested much of the power normally apertaining to a Congress in other countries.

Co-equal in authority with the NVV Congress and a great deal more important in practice is the General Assembly. The General Assembly decides the general policy of the NVV and appoints the five co-equal secretaries who, with the other four officers elected at the Congress, handle the day-to-day business of the NVV. The General Assembly comprises the members of the executives of the affiliated unions, plus the President, Vice-President, General Secretary, Treasurer and five secretaries of the NVV. Since there are twenty unions affiliated to the NVV it will be appreciated that the General Assembly is a somewhat unwieldy body.

Between 1962 and 1966 the NVV General Assembly was convened on eight occasions, twice in 1962, 1963 and 1966, once in each of the intervening years. Among other matters the 1964 and 1965 assemblies filled vacancies that had arisen on the NVV Executive Board. A major function of these gatherings seems to have been to discuss and decide wages

1. Offermans, *Details on the Netherlands Federation of Trade Unions*, pp. 1–3; *The Dutch Trade Union Movement – Historical Data*, NVV, Amsterdam, p. 24; Windmuller, pp. 144–5.

policy in the light of the prevailing economic situation. The Executive Committee of the NVV, which meets once or twice every month, supervises the day-to-day management of confederation affairs. The Executive Committee comprises the President of the NVV, the eight other members of the NVV full-time Executive Board, plus the presidents of each of the NVV's twenty affiliated unions.

Day-to-day management of NVV affairs is in the hands of the Executive Board. The Executive Board convenes every Monday with the President in the Chair. The nine members, President, Vice-President, General Secretary, Treasurer and five secretaries, each have special responsibility for some aspect of NVV affairs. The NVV President, who was, until recently, Andree Kloos (now chairman of the Labour Party television network), far outranks all other Executive Board members in terms of standing and prestige. The presence of the National President and eight other NVV full-time officials on the twenty nine man Executive Board gives the NVV apparatus exceptional weight in confederation deliberations. An affiliate like the metal-workers, with 100,000 members and more in its strike fund than the NVV, can afford to be independent. Smaller organizations have less scope to exercise their autonomy. Yet the votes of large and small unions in the councils of the NVV Executive are the same. Centralized wage bargaining may well have served the smaller unions in the past as a means of counterbalancing the otherwise predominant influence of the larger unions in this field.

NVV organization extends from national to regional level. Regional offices staffed by NVV employees watch over NVV interests in their localities. In major urban areas there also exist union city councils. Composed of delegates from affiliated unions these councils watch over the collective interests of their members and the NVV within their districts.

The Executive Board of the Catholic NKV is smaller than that of the NVV, consisting of the federation's full-time officers, plus the presidents of only seven of the twenty-four affiliated unions. The Protestant CNV is a more unitary organization than either NVV or NKV. The CNV Executive Board comprises only the four chief officers of the federation.

NVV affiliates pay approximately 10 per cent of their dues income in fees to the confederation. In the case of the Catholic NKV this rises as high as 20 per cent. NVV dues are slightly lower than those paid by unions affiliated to the German DGB but a great deal higher than those charged by the British TUC. Part of this income goes to meet the cost of various social service benefits provided by the NVV, another part for the NVV's strike fund which stood at around 10 million florins in 1966. The strike fund of the NVV metal-workers' union, ANMB, stood at 150 million florins at this time.

Confessional unionism is firmly rooted in the culture of Netherlands society. The Catholic trade union centre mustered 150,000 members as early as 1923 and claimed over 300,000 before the outbreak of war in 1939. During the depression years of the 1930s the three union centres began to move closer together. After the Liberation, the NVV, NKV and CNV collaborated in the *Raad van Vaakcentralen*. At this time the Netherlands hierarchy viewed the prospect of a leftward move by Catholic workers with much concern. In 1954 a pastoral letter declared the NVV forbidden ground for the faithful. Catholics who remained in membership after the publication of the pastoral letter were declared ineligible to receive the Holy Sacraments and denied the right to a church burial. This edict led to the break-up of the Council of Central Trade Union organizations. In the end, however, the underlying forces working for greater unity proved too strong for the bishops. Informal collaboration continued between the top leaders of the three federations. A co-ordinating body (*Overlegorgan*) established in 1958 replaced the former tripartite council and remains in being up to the present day. The coordinating body, which comprises the President, General Secretary and one Executive Board member from each confederation, meets at regular intervals in Utrecht. Inside the co-ordinating body, despite confessional ties that might lead the outside observer to think otherwise, NVV and NKV find it easier to establish common ground than the Catholic NKV and Protestant CNV. In 1965 the hierarchy's ban on Catholic membership of the NVV was withdrawn. Two years later, all three organizations were able to agree on a common *Programme of Action*.

The relations between all three confederations, above all between NKV–CNV and NKV, have been greatly affected by changes which have taken place in the hierarchy of the Vatican and the Netherlands since 1945. The conservative hierarchy which imposed the ban on the NVV in 1954 has now become one of the more radical sections of the Catholic Church on a world scale. One consequence was the revocation of the ban on the NVV. Another has been the hierarchy's assent to important changes in the structure of Catholic unionism itself.

In the Catholic attitude to labour organization, as in that of the communists, there has always been an implicit dualism. To some, Catholic unions have always appeared as an extended arm of the Church, 'front organizations' for Catholic aims and principles amongst the working class, organizations in which confessional, rather than secular aims were paramount. To others such organizations have appeared primarily as workers' organizations, but with a Catholic ethical and religious bias.

These two views assumed discrete organizational forms. Leagues of Catholic Workers and Catholic unions were both set up. In each of the five diocese, the Leagues of Catholic Workers worked alongside the twenty five or so unions organizing workers of Catholic faith, in a common-roof organization.

Arising in part from the experience of common resistance to Nazi occupation, Netherlands Catholicism in recent years has benefited from a greater acceptance by the public at large. One result has been the decline of a 'fortress mentality' amongst Catholics themselves. As in post war years the Catholic unions have grown in numbers and organization, so they have sought to achieve great independence from hierarchic control. In 1964 the Catholic unions were able to assert their independent identity, establishing the NKV in the form which it possesses today, with as its aim 'the protection, both direct and indirect, of the interests of the workers and their families in general and of the affiliated organizations and their members in particular'. The NKV constitution (Article 2) lays down that 'the activities of the federation are based on Christian principles', a phraseology which leaves a great deal of scope for interpretation Of recent years the role of the clerical 'counsellors' appointed to the executives of NKV unions has greatly declined. Outside evidence does seem to show that once a Catholic union moves out of organizing only Catholic workers employed by Catholic entrepreneurs into the wider world of labour it is constrained to adopt new rules and procedures if it is to succeed. There is no reason to expect the NKV will prove an exception to this rule.

UNION MEMBERSHIP

Union membership (including independents) in the Netherlands rose from 790,000 in 1947 to 1·5 million in 1968, a quite phenomenal increase. The NVV, 300,000 in 1947, rose to 620,000 in 1972. The NKV, 220,000 in 1947, rose to 400,000 in 1972 the CNV from 120,000 to 240,000 in the same period. Taking account of the increase in the labour force, the global strength of trade unions within the economy (i.e. including approximately 300,000 independents) rose from 30 per cent to 40 per cent.[1] Most surprisingly, despite an overall increase of almost 100 per cent in union membership, the relationship of forces between the three main federations remained substantially unchanged. One explanation may be that the confessional character of NKV and CNV makes their constituencies mutually exclusive. Only the non-confessional NVV might reasonably hope to make significant gains at the expense of its confessional rivals. In the past the NVV has sought repeatedly to over-

1. Since the official figures for 1947 exclude EVC the growth shown is somewhat exaggerated.

come hierarchical decrees which have operated against the recruitment of Protestant and Catholic workers into its ranks.

The strength of the three confederations is far from uniform over the Netherlands as a whole. The Catholic unions are especially strong in Limburg and Brabant in the south. The Catholic miners' union has been hit by the rundown of the industry. The Catholic textile union remains an important force. The NVV is ahead in engineering, printing, chemicals and food-processing, most of these concentrated in the urban–industrial Randstadt complex of Rotterdam–Amsterdam–The Hague. In agriculture, where a switch from casual labour to machinery has aided unionization, the Protestant agricultural workers' union is the strongest in the field.

The level of unionization in the Netherlands, at 40 per cent is unusually high. Blue collar organization in private industry probably stands at nearer 50 per cent. The general level is brought down by the lower level of organization of white collar workers, which barely exceeds one fifth of the potential.

UNION BEHAVIOUR

The moderation of the Netherlands labour movement, to an extent explicable in terms of historical conditioning, is somewhat remarkable in the light of the population boom which the Netherlands has undergone during the twentieth century. One might have expected an increase of specific weight of young people within the population to produce pressure in a radical direction. The population, 5 million in 1900, more than doubled to 13 million in 1970. In the Amsterdam–The Hague–Rotterdam industrial triangle population density rises to as high as 800 to 1000 per square mile, making the Netherlands one of the most highly populated areas in the world.[1] Yet neither this high degree of urbanization, a high level of union organization, nor the close proximity of industrial areas to the national capital seems to have produced any perceptible political effect.

The explanation would seem to lie, at least in part, in the general characteristics of Netherlands society. The organizational forms adopted by the unions in particular seem to have both expressed and perpetuated aspects of the prevailing cultural norms within the organization of the labour movement.

The Netherlands labour movement, at its origins, stood markedly to the left of centre. The present attitudes of both the NVV and PvdA can be traced back to the victory of right over left in the movement's

1. Pels, 'Organized industry and planning in the Netherlands', *International Labour Review*, September 1966, p. 274. The Netherlands population density of 356 per square kilometre is 12 per cent higher than Belgium, 50 per cent higher than Britain.

early struggles. The SDAP took its original ideology from German Social Democracy. Both socialism and unionism in the Netherlands seem to have been markedly influenced by models of German origin. Lenin, in his *What is to be Done?*, which constitutes the organizational basis of Russian communism, repeatedly draws attention to German Social Democracy, as a model to be followed. The Netherlands labour movement seems to have done no less. In its own explanatory literature, the NVV lists the union hierarchy as Executive Board, Executive Committee, Meeting of the Executive Board with the Executives of the affiliated organizations and Congress last of all. The order of priority is less a slip of the pen, than a true indication of the extent to which power in labour organizations lies at the summit rather than at the base.[1]

Underlying the structure of Netherlands unionism there seems to be an organic view which sees the confederation as a unitary whole with specific subdivisions, rather than as an aggregation of independent units, each voluntarily ceding part of its sovereignty to a higher authority. In line with this view the constitutions of NVV, NKV and CNV claim the right to review and approve rules and constitutions of affiliated bodies.[2] The confederation thus appears as an entity in its own right, rather than as an emanation of the basic national union organizations.

Centralization of authority in the confederation at the expense of the national unions was already a significant factor before the Second World War, and was accentuated by developments during the first years of the German occupation. The highly centralized bargaining policy pursued during the post war years further strengthened the position of the confederation as against its affiliates. In this system, the NVV, NKV and CNV rather than the individual national unions became the effective bargaining agent on behalf of union members.[3] Union policy originating with the national unions was not articulated through a central confederation. Instead decisions originating with the confederation became obligatory for the individual affiliates. The national unions thus became executors rather than originators of union policy.

The question remains: how were the three Netherlands federations able to carry out an integrated policy of long term wage restraint without a massive revolt from the ranks of the members? The dire economic straits of the Netherlands after 1945 is certainly one reason. In part at least, as has already been indicated, the answer also may lie in the nature of the working class.[4] Again, it is clear that in some cases at least, the

1. *Details on the Netherlands Federation of Trades Unions*, pp. 3–4.
2. Windmuller, pp. 165–6.
3. It is interesting to note that in Italy after the war the communist-led CGIL bargained on behalf of its 'affiliates' in exactly the same way.
4. One probable cause of Netherlands conservatism is the market localism of the population and the exceptionally tight family structure. On this see Warmbrunn, pp. 99–100.

courts have sought to protect the 'Big Three' from incursions by possible rivals.[1] More important would seem to be the prevailing organizational norms of Netherlands unionism. These norms to an important extent express a view of the union as a democracy of functionaries rather than a democracy of participating union members. The resulting attitudes are more akin to those of a socially minded business union than to those which spring from the more participatory models of union organization prevalent elsewhere. Certainly, without the concentration of power which exists at the summit of trade union organization in the Netherlands, it is difficult to believe that a policy of long-term wage restraint could ever have been carried out. Yet when all is said and done one ought not to give this aspect of the matter too much emphasis. The whole NVV confederation still remains less than half the size of one British union, the TGWU, around one quarter the size of Germany's IG Metall. Britain's three largest unions, the TGWU, AUEW and GMWU, are all larger than the whole union confederation NVV. Centralization is not an independent factor; its consequences cannot be considered without some thoughtful attention to the size of the organization involved.

Examination of union rules and statutes suggests that a further explanation of the character of Netherlands unions lies in the method of recruitment to positions of professional leadership and authority. In this self-reproducing system leaders choose their subordinates, and by implication their successors, without the possibility of any intervention from the rank and file. Excluding technical staff, Netherlands unions employ altogether some 800 full-time officials. The mode of recruitment of these officials and the nature of their career structure give them every incentive to unite in the face of any demands for greater participation from below. One leading NVV official has written:

The average member is as a rule not able to appreciate the job qualifications which leaders in important positions must meet. A judgement on the question of who among available candidates should be considered for an important leadership position can be made in the trade union movement only by a small group of knowledgeable persons, for they alone are conversant with all the factors necessary to reach a decision.[2]

Essentially the same view, that 'the choice of officers is too important

1. The NVV seafarers' union argued in a court test case that 'because the federations are bound by the "rules of the game" set by the government and the independent unions do not abide by them, the position of the federations is not an equal one, and they therefore have the *right* to be protected in their position against the independent unions' (italics added). On this, Windmuller, p. 176.

2. Quoted in Windmuller, p. 212. This same view is shared by communists and business management. The author once heard a leading functionary of the British Communist Party justify the non-election of top officials in exactly this fashion.

to be left to a more or less arbitrary election', has been expressed by a former president of the Protestant CNV.

Entry to a professional union career usually begins via appointment as a union district officer. Such posts are publicly advertised. Applicants are interviewed and provisionally selected by a sub-committee of the union executive board. The trainee official then serves one year's trial in office. At the end of that period, if considered satisfactory, the Executive Board will recommend permanent appointment to the legislative assembly. The recommendation is customarily endorsed as a matter of course.[1] Once appointed, the official may look to a line of promotion leading to the union full time executive board and perhaps eventually to the hierarchy of the NVV. Positions in the savings banks, insurance companies and other enterprises controlled by the unions represent a further possibility.[2] Given the close link between unions and government, transfer to state or para-state employment provides additional opportunities. Union officials, traditionally, have also played an important role as officials of international union organizations. Two General Secretaries of the ICFTU, Harm Buiter and Jacob Oldenbroek, began their careers as members of the NVV.

There can be little doubt [writes one by no means unsympathetic observer] that the procedure for selecting and promoting union officers has made a decisive contribution to the ability of union leaders to exercise wage restraint and to collaborate closely with employers and government in administering the economy ... Union leaders have the same tendency to deal with their members in a spirit of benevolent authoritarianism, or high-handed paternalism, which they want employers to abandon.[3]

STRIKES

Both relatively and absolutely, the number of man-days lost through strikes and lock-outs in the Netherlands is amongst the lowest in the world. The organized labour force is around 1·5 million, the total workforce amounts to some 4·6 million. Yet between 1950 and 1967, mandays lost through stoppages have exceeded 100,000 in only three years, 1955, 1956 and 1960. In most years the loss through strikes and lockouts has been economically and statistically negligible.

The causes of this phenomenon would seem to lie in large part in

1. A similar procedure is followed by one of Britain's more bureaucratic unions, the GMWU.
2. The NKV owns a daily paper, *De Volksrant*, a savings bank, CVB, a life insurance company, Concordia, and other institutions: *This is the NKV*, Amsterdam (undated). Netherlands union leaders are well, although not excessively well, paid. The CNV fixes its top officers' salaries at a level comparable to that of a high-level civil servant, a not insignificant choice of method: Windmuller, pp. 221, 224.
3. Windmuller, pp. 221–3.

factors already outlined. Yet further examination reveals a note of deep unexplained mystery about the whole proceedings. In the years before the Second World War the unions were numerically weaker than they are now. During the inter war years the fighting power of the unions was gravely impaired by mass unemployment. The labour force itself was far smaller. Yet both before and after the First World War the level of strikes in the Netherlands was a great deal higher than at the present time. Man-days lost between 1919 and 1924 never fell below 1 million, exceeded 2 million in 1920 and 3 million in 1924. More man-days were lost in the single year 1924 than in the whole two post war decades 1947–67.

A phenomenon of similar order can be observed in Germany. Yet for the relative quiescence of post war Germany one can adduce as explanation a whole series of special features not to be found in the Netherlands: total devastation, mass starvation, foreign occupation, a great influx of population from the East, the division of the national territory, the threat of a Russian army and a communist regime on the eastern border.

Nor can we look to legislation as an explanation. Strikes were illegal until 1872. Strikers have remained liable to action at civil law in all the years that followed. The judiciary has been consistently hostile to the right to strike.[1] Following the rail stoppage of 1903, legislation, still in force on the statute book, was introduced, banning strikes by both railway and government employees.[2] Yet, as will readily be appreciated, none of these factors seem to have been especially effective before 1939.

It is true that in more recent years a Netherlands High Court decision of 1960, by somewhat devious judicial logic, seems virtually to have abolished the right to strike. Whether this verdict will, in the medium term, be maintained, remains to be seen.[3] Nevertheless no legal decision in 1960 can be invoked to explain the absence of serious stoppages before this date. Nor does the strike record *after* 1960, look significantly different from that of the years before.

There are a number of possible explanations that suggest themselves. In the years before the Second World War the number of workers covered by collective agreements remained low, reaching no more than 293,000 in 1938. In the post war years the unions were involved with

1. In 1966, one prominent jurist, Professor N. E. H. van Esveld of Leiden University, considered that to legalize the right to strike would be to put the clock back by a quarter of a century.

2. This law was applied against a strike of Amsterdam municipal employees in 1955: Windmuller, pp. 319–20; for more recent cases see *IMF News*, Geneva, no. 5, 1971, no. 22, 1972.

3. In 1966 it was proposed to exempt strikes called by the 'Big Three' from penal sanctions while leaving unofficial stoppages exposed to the full rigour of the law.

employers and government, at national level, via the Foundation of Labour and other institutions, in discussions affecting the conditions of the whole workforce, organized and unorganized alike. In line with this development the number of workers covered by collective agreements rose to 1 million by 1952 and 2 million by 1962. This suggests that the war and immediate post war years constitute the decisive watershed for the achievement of union recognition in the Netherlands. The consequent close association of unions with government involved a move upwards of authority from base to vertex. Union leaders, perhaps, were now more involved in holding their members to the terms of agreements already reached at national level than in calling strikes to enforce union demands that employers refused to concede. Employers too saw no need to lock out their employees to enforce wage reductions, when the unions themselves now constituted the major bulwark against 'excessive' wage demands. In the most difficult transition period, 1945–7, the task of union leaders was aided by the Netherlands Communist Party which as a party of government with two ministers in the coalition acted as a brake on industrial and social militancy. Whether now, after a quarter of a century in which union recognition has become not the exception but the rule, this post war quiescence will continue indefinitely remains open to doubt.

WORKS COUNCILS

In the wave of radicalization which followed the Second World War, the Netherlands parliament, like its counterparts in France, Belgium and the Federal Republic, enacted legislation designed to give elected representatives of the workforce a limited voice in the conduct of certain aspects of plant affairs. Inspiration for this legislation would seem to owe a great deal to the Works Council Law first enacted in Germany under the Weimar Republic.

The original Netherlands Works Council Act (*Wet op de Onder-negingsgraden*) of 1950 requires the establishment of works councils in all enterprises with twenty five or more employees. The prime task of the works council as laid down by the statute is 'to contribute to its utmost to the best possible functioning of the enterprise'. At a more mundane level the works council is entrusted with the handling of individual grievances, and is allocated certain rights concerning the planning of holidays, hours, shift work, and the enforcement of national legislation regarding obligatory safety procedures. Perhaps more important, the works council is entrusted with the policing, at plant level, of national agreements concluded between unions and employers' associations. As will be seen, the works council is intended to facilitate employer–employee cooperation and not to represent the interests of one group as against the other. As an insurance against any too wide-ranging ambition the legislation places the employer in the chair at all works council meetings. Finance of works council activities is a plant, not a personnel, responsibility.

The 1960 Works Council Law provided no sanctions against employers who failed to comply with its provisions. Most small employers, a proportion of both medium and large employers also, took advantage of the absence of compulsion to ignore the responsibilities placed upon them by law. Amongst firms with less than fifty employees, the rate of non-compliance rose as high as 80 per cent. Over one quarter of companies with between 100 and 500 employees similarly failed to honour the terms of the Act. In 1966 it was claimed that as many as four out of every five workers were covered by existing works councils. Nevertheless less than half the eligible enterprises (2278 of 4800) had honoured the obligation set upon them by the law.[1] Amended legislation passed under union pressure in September 1970 has made obligatory the establishment of works councils in enterprises employing over 100 workers. It is too early yet to comment on the effectiveness of this legislation in bringing the 20 per cent out of compliance in line with the provisions of the original Act of 1950.

Election of works councillors takes place by means of a ballot on predetermined lists. The first prerogative for proposing election slates is vested in affiliates of the Big Three, NVV, NKV, CNV. Unitary slates are not permitted. Each list must comprise a coalition of members of all three federations. Councillors serve for a two year term and are eligible for re-election. The law does not provide works council members with protection against victimization or arbitrary dismissal. Constitutional provisions safeguard the representations of white collar interests. In Amsterdam and neighbouring shipyards enough opposition feeling exists for an opposition 'Free List' sometimes to succeed in making much of the running.

Councillors are bound by long-outdated conceptions of business secrecy. Information made available to third parties by councillors, either by intent or by accident, can lay them open to a prison term. Union advisers are denied access to works council meetings. As a result both consultation with union officers and report-back meetings with the plant workforce are severely circumscribed. The function of the works council, as expressed in law and to a large degree embodied in practice, is firmly in line with the paternalistic spirit which characterizes a great deal of Netherlands life and industry. The absence of union 'in-plant' representation, the lack of preparation of works council members, the failure to provide proper links between works council and the shop floor, the

1. Windmuller, pp. 414–16. *Bulletin of the International Union of Food and allied Workers' Associations*, Geneva, 1971, no. 3, p. 6.

presence of the employer as chairman of works council meeting, the attitude of the employers, the defects of the legislation itself, have combined
to prevent the Works Council Law of Act of 1950 making radical changes
in shop floor life.

The joint *Programme of Action*, published by the 'Big Three' in 1967,
made several demands for the revision of the works council legislation.
One calls expressly for the protection of works council members against
employer victimization. Others propose closer ties between works councillors and their union, with provision for expert advice (presumably
from the unions) for council members in their work. The Verdam Commission, appointed to go into the whole issue, has made a series of
recommendations for improving the operation of the works council law.
The eventual outcome of these developments is still not clear. To date at
any rate, the works councils in the Netherlands appear a great deal less
important than either their counterparts in Germany or the *commissione
interne* in Italy.

PLANT NEGOTIATIONS

The top heavy structure of union bargaining, the tough resistance of
employers to 'in-plant' bargaining, the establishment of the works
council as an enterprise, rather than a union work-force representative
body, means that until now a union presence at the point of production
has not existed in the Netherlands.

In 1965 the metal-workers' union – the ANMB – set out to remedy
this situation. It proposed to appoint a plant representative (*bedriffscon-
tactman*) chosen from the existing workforce, in all organized shops.
Where the size of the plant made this advisable, this representative was
to be backed up by a plant committee (*bedriffscontactcomissie*). The plant
representative was to act as liaison between union and plant, receiving
complaints, transmitting workforce problems to the union district office
for processing and action. The employers' association after initial hesitation returned a favourable response. Company hostility has since made
it impossible so far to operate the proposals in more than a small number
of enterprises.

In the 1967 *Programme of Action* the combined unions call for the
right to meet management at plant level and the right also to a say in
handling grievances. Until now this last prerogative has been reserved
for the works council alone.

FUTURE TRENDS

The tight control of wage policy by joint government–employer–union
decision, which characterized labour relations in the 1940s and 1950s,
went far towards breakdown in the 1960s. In this the Netherlands, like

other countries, seems to be moving rapidly away from the pattern of labour relations established in the immediate post war years towards one based on changed economic, social and political circumstances.

By the early 1960s signs of strain were already becoming clearly apparent. The gap between wages in the Netherlands and elsewhere in the Community was clearly felt by the workforce. The number of Netherlands workers employed in Germany was rising. Employers, competing with one another in a tight labour market, were paying 'black market' wages in order to recruit and retain their labour force. The widespread presence of 'labour-only contractors' (in Britain 'the lump', in the Netherlands, *Koppelbazen*) led to a situation in which workers in the same plant, on the same job, worked alongside one another with a 30 per cent wage differential between them. In 1964 the dam broke. Wage increases of 10 per cent and over were recorded all along the line.

Economic discontent accompanied widespread movements in society at large. In 1966 the PvdA lost its place in the government, which then became a Catholic–Liberal (i.e. Conservative) coalition. That year anarchist smoke bombs disrupted the wedding celebrations of Princess Beatrice and her German fiancé Claus von Amsberg. Attempts to impose a wage agreement giving preferential treatment to members of the Big Three unions in the building industry at the expense of the 'independents' led to a strike in Amsterdam followed by riots in which one person was killed.[1] Subsequently both the mayor and the police chief in the city resigned. More significantly for the future, the discriminatory clause in the agreement was subsequently ruled out of order by the courts. In 1969 Netherlands students occupied university buildings in Amsterdam and Utrecht. The Catholic hierarchy, hitherto a stronghold of conservatism, faced with a fall in recruitment and losses from the priesthood, called, in 1970, for an end to compulsory celibacy for priests, a shift in attitude of hitherto inconceivable magnitude.

In 1969 the imposition of value-added tax (VAT), in line with EEC budgetary requirements, led to a direct 7 per cent increase in the cost of living and brought tensions to a still higher level. A strike at a low wage fibreboard plant in the depressed northern province of Gröningen mushroomed into a general stoppage through all plants in the industry. In defiance of union back-to-work calls the strikers achieved massive wage gains. Elsewhere fears of redundancies arising from mergers and modernization led to further unofficial stoppages.[2]

1. In the building industry the Big Three together organize only one-third of the labour force, the remainder being either members of the 'independents' or outside union ranks altogether.
2. In April 1970 angry members of the Food and Agricultural Workers Union (AGV) occupied the offices of the NVV and NKV as protest against the policies followed by union leaders. *International Union of Food and Drink Workers, Bulletin*, 1970, no. 4, p. 7.

In autumn 1970 an isolated stoppage over low wages, the high cost of living and the inequities of the 'labour-only' contracting system in the Raandstadt spread until it shut down the ports of Rotterdam and Amsterdam. The stoppage then rolled around the whole country with such intensity that the unions were forced to back it under fear of losing control of their members altogether. The outcome here again was a major wages advance.[1]

The Catholic–Liberal government, seeking anxiously to bring wage movements under control, introduced legislation enabling it to impose a wage pause and delay the effective date of wage settlements. The outcome was that all three union federations, NVV, Catholic and Protestant, called a one hour general strike for the day the bill was to be discussed in parliament. The co-ordinated official political stoppage which took place on 1 December 1970 was a landmark in the history of Netherlands labour. When the bill passed into law both NVV and NKV (but not the Protestant CNV) withdrew from all discussions on wage questions in both the Foundation of Labour and the Social and Economic Council, thus depriving government policy of much of its credibility.[2] As if to emphasize the changing situation, the PvdA shed its right wing around the same time and emerged in control of a left-of-centre leadership in 1970.

It is too soon to point to the ultimate outcome of these novel developments, but it is clear that the Netherlands labour movement, and with it industrial relations, are entering a new era,[3] the characteristics of which will be radically different from those of 1945–60.

1. For a revealing account of some past and present events, Albeda, 'Recent trends in collective bargaining in the Netherlands', *International Labour Review*, March 1971, pp. 247–68.

2. Tensions continue. In February 1972 some 30,000 metal-workers came out on unofficial strike following judicial intervention in a wage dispute: *IMF News*, Feb. 1972, no. 5, p. 7.

3. On this see, J. Raven, 'Industrial relations; crisis in the Netherlands', *Free Labour World*, March 1970, pp. 13–15; also Albeda, 'Les Pays Bas, les relations de travail', in Spitaels, ed., *La Crise des relations industrielles en Europe*, pp. 139–60.

10. Europe International

There are some 26 million trade unionists in the nine countries of the enlarged European Economic Community.[1] These 26 million give their allegiance to three rival international organizations of trade union national centres. Two at least of these internationals have global affiliations. The International Confederation of Free Trade Unions (ICFTU), with headquarters in Brussels, is by far the largest, with affiliates in eight of the nine nations totalling in all some 21 million members.[2] The Russian-dominated World Federation of Trade Unions (WFTU), with headquarters in Prague and most of its members in Eastern Europe, has affiliates in only two countries of the Nine, France and Italy. WFTU membership in the Nine would seem to be around 3 million, though the membership *claims* of its affiliates are considerably greater.[3] The World Confederation of Labour (WCL; formerly the International Federation of Christian Trade Unions, IFCTU), with affiliates in France, Belgium and the Netherlands, musters an affiliation of some 2·3 million.[4] On Europe-wide issues ICFTU and WCL unions have shown in recent years what comes remarkably close to a common front. The rift between the ICFTU and the Russian-dominated WFTU remains very wide.

International cooperation between unions in similar trades can be traced back at least one hundred years, but international organizations uniting the different national movements did not appear before the first decade of the twentieth century. The split between Christian and non-Christian trade unions finds its origins at the very beginnings of the

1. Belgium 1·7m, France 2·6m, Germany 6·5m, Italy 3·2m, Britain 10m, Luxembourg 40,000, Netherlands 1·2m, Denmark 910,000, Ireland 390,000. There are additionally some 3·75m in the four Scandinavian countries, 1·3m in Austria and a further 440,000 in Switzerland. These figures exclude independent white-collar organizations.
2. Belgium: FGTB, 800,000; France: FO, 600,000; Germany: DGB, 6·5m; Italy: Britain: TUC, 10m; CISL, 1·2m and UIL, 300,000; Netherlands: NVV, 600,000: Denmark 910,000.
3. Italy, CGIL, 1·7m; France: CGT, 1·2m.
4. Belgium: CSC, 900,000; Netherlands: NKV, 400,000 and CNV, 240,000; France: CFDT, 800,000.

European labour movement. The separate organization of Communist-dominated labour, by contrast, is a direct consequence of the endeavours of the Russian Bolsheviks to extend their influence and ideology in the aftermath of the Revolution of October 1917.[1]

The idea of the international association of radical working men can be traced at least as far back as the British Chartists. The first lasting and important organization was the International Working Men's Association (IWMA), better known as the First International, founded in London during 1864, originally with its main base amongst British trade unionists. The International, which as a force in being lasted some eight years, exercised an influence out of all proportion to its size. Links were established between groups of skilled workers, trade unions and a limited number of intellectuals (of whom Marx was one) in countries as far apart as France, Belgium, Switzerland, Germany, Austria, Hungary, Italy, Spain, Denmark, the Netherlands and the United States. The International is best remembered as a progenitor of Marxist socialism. Marx himself drafted its statutes and Inaugural Address. But the International was far more than that. The IWMA did not restrict itself to propagating ideas of independent working class organization. The International took positive action to limit the transfer of scabs from one country to break strikes in another. The IWMA also organized international aid funds to help affiliates out on strike. As such it deserves to be remembered as the direct antecedent of the international trade union organizations of the present day.

The First International broke up following the defeat of the Paris Commune of 1871. During the celebrations of the hundredth anniversary of the French Revolution in 1889, the socialist parties of all the major European countries came together in Paris to form a successor, under the title of the Second International. One of the first acts of this 1889 congress was to organize worldwide support for the demonstrations called by the American Federation of Labor (AFL) in support of the claim for the eight hour day, on 1 May 1890. In this was the origin of the modern labour tradition of 'May Day'.[2]

The British trade unions were the strongest in Europe. Yet in the nature of things the interests of British trade unionists were directed more towards the English-speaking world of the Empire and the United States than to continental Europe. In certain fields, notably coal-mining, textiles, shipping and port labour, British unions played a decisive role in the establishment of international union collaboration. In other areas the main initiative lay elsewhere.

1. On this for example; Walter Kendall, 'Folk myths of the western world', in *Bulletin of the Society for the Study of Labour History*, spring 1972, pp. 78–82.
2. For an outline of these events see Lorwin, *The International Labor Movement*, pp. 7–20.

Coal, textiles and maritime transport, (at this time inextricably connected with the problem of the organization of port labour), were basic British industries, heavily involved in the growing world market. The pressure of foreign competition gave British unionists a vital interest in ensuring that conditions overseas were not allowed to undermine those won with great effort at home. International ties between mining unions were set up in Manchester in 1890, between textile unions in the same town four years later, between shipping and port workers in London in 1896. These ties were maintained in the years that followed.

Such endeavours were not, however, either the first or the most typical of the early attempts of unionized workers to organize international collaboration. The first steps seem to have been taken rather by trades which employed predominantly skilled labour. It may well have been that the old craft custom of the *wanderjahr*, in which the apprentice 'out of his time' set out on a working tour in search of trade experience and knowledge, made such links an occupational necessity. Problems of organizing high craft content luxury trades may also have made close union ties across national borders desirable, especially where employers sought to break strikes in one country by bringing in blackleg labour from another. Skilled workers, whose craft training ensured higher pay, enjoyed more independence from their employers than the unskilled, whose bargaining power was in the nature of things a great deal less.

Such factors, the existence in certain cases of linguistic or cultural links, made the growth of international organization easier in some trades than others. Germany's central position, her rapidly growing economy, which attracted large numbers of workers from abroad, also gave the German unions a special reason for taking a lead in these affairs.[1]

Although formal international organization was not established until 1889, eleven years later, discussions between unions of hatters in Germany, Italy and Denmark took place as early as the Paris Exhibition of 1878; shoe-makers and cigar-makers established international ties that same year. Printers and glass-workers followed in 1892, tailors and metal-workers in 1893. Furriers, lithographers and brewery workers all established union internationals in the years before 1900. That some at least of these ventures were a 'spin-off' from the activities of the Second International seems probable. By 1914 some twenty eight international union associations, known as International Trade Secretariats (ITS) were in existence. Collectively these covered most of the main spheres of union operation.

The unions of Denmark, Norway and Sweden, with their respective socialist parties, had participated in periodic Scandinavian labour

1. On this for example, ibid., p. 35. One needs also to remember that frontier changes may have separated groups of workers previously united. This possibility merits further study.

conferences ever since 1886. On the initiative of J. Jensen, President of the Danish trade union confederation, a conference of representatives of European trade union centres was held in Copenhagen in 1901, at the same time as that year's meeting of the Scandinavian Labour Conference. The outcome was a decision to set up an International Secretariat of the National Trade Union Federations, with headquarters in Germany under the presidency of Karl Legien, President of the German ADGB. A series of international conferences followed. These were held in Stuttgart in 1902, Dublin in 1903, Amsterdam in 1905. Oslo in 1907, Paris in 1909, Budapest in 1911 and Zürich in 1913. At these conferences practical collaboration and exchange of views was further developed. The unions continued to acknowledge the supremacy of the Socialist International on matters of general strategy. Yet at the same time they were greatly strengthening their autonomy in affairs more specifically their own concern.

The International Secretariat operated out of Berlin, thus emphasizing the pre-eminent role played by the German unions in international union co-operation at that time. The American Federation of Labor (AFL), the first non European organization, was persuaded to affiliate in 1911. AFL representatives attended that year's conference in Budapest. At the Zürich conference in 1913, on the proposal of the AFL, the title of the International Secretariat was changed to that of the International Federation of Trade Unions (IFTU). The Zürich conference was attended in a fraternal capacity by representatives of the ITS, who also held the first international conference of their own at that time. On the eve of the First World War the IFTU mustered nineteen affiliates and a total membership of some 7·7 million. Of these almost half came from Germany and Austria–Hungary; the next largest contingent came from the USA. The ITS conference of 1913 reported twenty-five affiliates with a combined membership of some 5·6 million. The three largest ITS, Metal, Mine-workers and Transport, represented rather more than half the total.[1]

The First World War broke up the IFTU. The affiliates, in the main, supported the war effort undertaken by their respective governments. Legien and the German unions refused to allow the IFTU headquarters to be removed from Germany to neutral territory. Once the war was over national antagonism, notably between the unions of Belgium and Germany, threatened to make a re-establishment of the IFTU impos-

1. Austria 424,000, Germany 2·5m, USA 2m, Belgium 127,000, Bosnia 5,000, Croatia 7,000, Denmark 114,000, Finland 28,000, France 600,000, Great Britain 970,000, Hungary 107,000, Italy 327,000, Netherlands 86,000, Norway 64,000, Romania 10,000, Serbia 10,000, Spain 128,000, Sweden 97,000. The smallness of the British figure is due to the failure of the majority of British unions to affiliate until a later date. Schevenels, *Forty five years of the IFTU*, pp. 23, 64.

sible. In the end, with difficulties and continuing strains, the task was accomplished; the headquarters of the IFTU were moved to Amsterdam where they remained until 1928.[1] In general, British unionists tended to take over the leading posts hitherto occupied by the Germans.

Membership of the IFTU rose to 23 million by 1919, and this despite the fact that the AFL had allowed its affiliation to lapse. Although numbers subsequently fell by more than half, membership of the IFTU continued at around double the 1914 figure throughout the inter war years. The inability of the revived Second International to re-assert anything approaching its old doctrinal authority and the crucial role now played by mass trade unions as axes of social and governmental power combined to make the IFTU a considerably more important force than hitherto.

The IFTU thus found itself pitchforked into intense political conflicts. In Moscow during 1921 the Russian Bolsheviks had set up a Red International of Labour Unions (RILU), the main membership base of which was the Russian unions under tight communist control. The RILU was specifically created to smash the IFTU. Those unions which could not be captured from within were to be split, or, if this was impossible, destroyed.[2] A period of violent internecine civil war ensued in the European labour movement. In France the CGT split. As a rival to the CGT proper, a hostile communist controlled CGTU emerged. In Germany the social democratic union leaders found themselves involved in a life or death struggle with a RILU based communist opposition. In the years 1925–7 British and Russian unions were linked through an Anglo-Russian Joint Trade Union Committee. No ties between the IFTU and the Russian unions existed at that time. Serious strains developed between the British unions and the rest of the IFTU membership, particularly the hard pressed Germans, over the attitude to be taken towards the Russian unions, whose approach to the IFTU vacillated between courtship and downright disruption and abuse. In the end the RILU failed to establish itself as in any sense an organizational rival to the IFTU. Yet its foundation had served to open up an almost unbridgeable chasm between the Russians, the communists and the major trade union organizations. The hostility caused by these events lasted up to and even beyond the Second World War. The AFL had stood aside from IFTU after the First World War. Under pressure from a left wing CIO, the AFL decided in 1937 to rejoin.

1. The IFTU with Walter Schevenels as General Secretary was moved to Berlin in 1928, then to Paris in 1933 on eve of the Nazis' final conquest of power.
2. On this for example, Carr, *The Bolshevik Revolution, 1917–1923*, vol. iii, pp. 395–8, 454–6; Martin, *Communism and the British Trade Unions*, pp. 11–15, 124–33; Murphy, *The Reds in Congress*, London, 1925, pp. 4–5, 16–18, 29; 'The Red Labour Union International', *Bulletin of the Executive Bureau*, no. 3, 17, Sept. 1921, pp. 3–5.

Christian unionism arose as a religious response to the socialist organization of the labour force, especially after Pope Leo XIII's Encyclical
Rerum Novarum in 1891. At first the Christian unions constituted only
an unimportant fragment of the organized labour force, restricted in the
main to predominantly Catholic areas and in particular to enterprises
owned by Catholic employers. In 1908 the Christian unions too established their own international organization. A conference held in Zürich
led to the establishment of an international secretariat which by 1914
claimed a membership of some 540,000. Germany, with over 200,000
members, represented by far the largest component of the Christian
international. In 1920 at a Congress in The Hague, the Christians established an International Federation of Christian Trade Unions (IFCTU),
which claimed some 3·4 million adherents, with affiliates, in Germany,
Austria, Belgium, Spain, France, Hungary, Italy, the Netherlands,
Switzerland and Czechoslovakia.

The limited membership base of the Christian unions meant that they
did not benefit to anything like the same extent as the socialists from
the war and post war membership boom. Germany, Italy and Austria,
three major areas of recruitment, went down before Nazi and fascist
coups in the inter war years. On the other hand, in France, Belgium and
the Netherlands the confessional unions markedly consolidated their
base. In France and Belgium in particular the Young Christian Workers'
Movement created a new and important tradition of working class leadership. In France, too, the mass move into the unions following the sit-
downs of 1936 enabled the Christian unions to extend their base for the
first time outside the specifically Catholic workforce, a factor of great
significance for the future.[1]

The Second World War transformed the international trade union
movement. The seemingly irresistible onrush of the Nazis quickly swept
the IFTU apparatus out of its headquarters in Paris into exile in
Britain. Yet this was not the end. By now the IFTU was no longer a
purely European phenomenon. Nine of its twenty seven affiliates were
outside Europe.[2] The leaders of the IFTU quickly rallied to the Allied
cause. Russian communists and German Nazis, however, joined hands
to occupy Poland in 1939. When the German armies invaded Norway,
Denmark, Belgium, the Netherlands and France, the Communist–Nazi
Pact was still in force. All this served to widen still further the breach
between the IFTU and its communist critics. Not until Hitler invaded
Russia in June 1941 did the Pact end and an almost total reversal of
front on the part of the world communist movement ensue.

1. For a brief history: WCL, *Fifty Years: the WCL from 1920 to 1970* and
The WCL: Unity in Diversity.
2. USA, Canada, Mexico, Argentine, Palestine, India, China, Dutch East
Indies and New Zealand.

The Russians had allowed the organization of the RILU to lapse in 1935. The issue of Russian union affiliation to the IFTU had become the subject of prolonged and unproductive negotiation during the years 1937–8. The unwilling entry of the Russians into the war on the side of the Allies now brought the issue of cooperation to the fore again. In September 1941 the British TUC, on a motion which had originated with the General Council, took steps which led to the formation of a new Anglo-Soviet Trade Union Committee the following month.[1] Endeavours intended, it has plausibly been suggested, to extend this committee across the Atlantic to include both AFL and CIO (thus outflanking the IFTU altogether), came to nothing. However, a separate TUC–AFL Anglo-American Trade Union Committee (again outside the IFTU) was set up in July 1942. There now ensued a series of complex and confusing manoeuvres which have not been completely unravelled up to the present day. Nevertheless the essential lines of motion seem clear. The Russian government, as a major strategic aim, sought to integrate the state-controlled Russian unions into a new, unified, world wide union international. The officers of the IFTU had acquired, on the basis of experience, a well justified hostility to the Russian unions and the communists. Russian policy therefore necessarily discounted the legitimate claims of the IFTU to be considered the basis for a re-formed post war trade union international.

In this endeavour the Russian government could count on important forces in their favour. First, a deep seated and widely held spirit of solidarity with the Russian people for their part in the battle against Hitler; second, the reflection of this sentiment in mass union organizations in Britain and the USA, where on this issue the communists acquired influence out of all proportion to their actual following; third, the influence gained by the communists in the CIO, their ability to manipulate that organization's legitimate wish for greater influence in the wider world trade union movement for purposes of their own.

In November 1943, when the turning-point in the war was already passed, the TUC sent out invitations to seventy one union organizations in thirty one countries to attend a conference in London in June 1944 to consider problems of post war reconstruction. In the event the Allied invasion of Europe that month forced a cancellation. In October 1944 the TUC issued fresh invitations. A conference was called for early in 1945. In deference to objections from the CIO and the Russians a preliminary conference with the TUC was held in December 1944 to finalize plans for the conference itself. It was clear by now that the intention was the formation of a united world trade union movement extending from the Russian communists, via the AFL, to the Catholic unions in France and the Netherlands.

1. TUC, *Congress Report*, 1941, pp. 243–57.

The conference that met in London on 6 February 1945 brought together 204 delegates from some sixty three labour organizations claiming around 60 million members. It soon became plain that there existed a tacit alliance between the French CGT,[1] the CIO[2] and the Russians, to put on one side plans prepared to make the reorganized IFTU the basis of a new organization and start entirely afresh. One outcome was that the conference decided to establish a committee with instructions to prepare draft statutes for a new organization to be presented to a fresh conference to be held at a later date. This conference mustered in Paris on 25 September 1945. Out of it was born the short-lived World Federation of Trade Unions (WFTU).[3]

The WFTU was the labour movement counterpart of the wartime Grand Alliance of the 'democratic powers' against fascism.[4] The official sanction given to the WFTU inaugural conferences in London and Paris, the facilities accorded its activities at that time, are ample evidence of the favour with which it was then regarded by the Allied governments.[5] The officially expressed aims of the WFTU were blandly non-socialist and quite uncontroversial. This indeed was essential if they were to be acceptable to the US unions and some others. That these aims were wholeheartedly endorsed both by the Russian unions and the communist-dominated organizations under their influence is further evidence of the extent to which the WFTU was seen by the Russians as part of a global diplomatic manoeuvre.

The problems that arose as a result were manifold. Neither side was being honest with the other. Each had consented to compromises in which they had no real confidence. The communists could not have believed a word of the honeyed sentiments they voiced towards some of their new found allies. The Western unions in their turn had consented to admit the Russian unions as equal partners, though they knew quite

1. In the course of 1945 the CGT had established both a Franco-British Trade Union Committee and a Franco-Soviet Trade Union Committee. In January 1945, according to Lorwin, 'they made an agreement with the leaders of the Soviet unions for common action in favour of a new world labor organisation' (pp. 206–7).

2. The AFL had refused to attend the proposed conference, raising objections to both its competence and its composition. Lorwin, pp. 204–5 ; Schevenels, pp. 329–31.

3. The WFTU, founded in 1945, lasted only until 1949. The Russian-dominated rump which continues to use that title has claim to continuity in neither membership, organization or principle. It is in fact an entirely different organization which has usurped the original name.

4. But not of course *Spanish* fascism, the survival of which has been heavily dependent on aid from one at least of the 'democratic' powers.

5. As shown by the visas, permits, travel documents and travel facilities, all in the shortest supply, which were made available to delegates from all over the world.

well that they were no more than extended arms of the Russian state and party machine. The manifest unreality of the compromises reached made it highly unlikely that they could last. Unification was the product of a post war diplomatic honeymoon; once this was over internal tensions tore the whole fragile structure apart.

WFTU headquarters were established in Paris under the secretaryship of Louis Saillant. Expensive offices and a large staff were made possible by affiliation income derived in the main from British, United States and Russian unions. It fairly soon became clear that the Executive Board had a concealed bias towards the Russian cause. Saillant increasingly revealed himself as an explicit fellow traveller; V. V. Kuznetzov of Russia and Di Vittorio of Italy were both Communist Party members; Vicente Toledano of Mexico and H. F. Chiu of China sided fairly consistently with the Russians. Léon Jouhaux of France[1] and Frank Rosenblum,[2] the representative of the CIO, took something of a middle position. Walter Citrine, later replaced by Arthur Deakin (both of the TUC), and Evert Kupers of the Netherlands represented the bedrock of the opposite point of view. Such differences would have been difficult to reconcile even if all parties had been willing to place purely political matters on one side and concentrate on trade union issues. This was not the case. Saillant and the communists were intent on using the WFTU to support Russian foreign policy objectives. The non-communist majority was bound to resist. Subjected to internal strains of a high order, the WFTU survived as an united organization for less than four years, from October 1945 until January 1949.

Saillant's endeavour to use the WFTU as an agency for the pursuit of Russian state interests within the international labour movement was one primary cause of the eventual split. In line with this objective, the communists in the WFTU sought from the very beginning to reduce the International Trade Secretariats (ITS), which functioned as independent associates, to the status of mere departments of the centrally administered WFTU organization.[3] In the event no such forced fusion was ever consummated. A running battle between communists and non-communists over the status of the independent ITS characterized the whole of the short history of the 'united' WFTU.

The WFTU was also involved, whatever its wish, in the great power conflict over the future of Germany, in these years still divided into four separately administered occupation zones.[4] In the Eastern zone, the

1. Jouhaux withdrew following the CGT–FO split of December 1947.
2. Later for practical purposes substituted by James B. Carey, Secretary of the CIO.
3. There are no international trade secretariats in the present 'WFTU', only trade departments of the central organization with headquarters in Prague.
4. For the communist view of these events see Behrendt, *The WFTU and the German Trade Unions*.

least industrial part of surviving German territory, with a population of 19 million, the Russians rapidly dragooned into existence a communist-controlled 'trade union movement' which claimed 5 million members. By contrast, the three Western zones, which included the Ruhr and the bulk of German industry, with a population of 48 million, claimed only 4·5 million union members. After the currency reform and Berlin Blockade which began in July 1948, Germany split into hostile Eastern and Western blocs. The German labour movement, against its will, became a cockpit, in which were fought battles crucial to the outcome of the Cold War.[1] Saillant sought to exercise the WFTU influence in Germany in Russia's favour,[2] not least by seeking to produce a 'unification' which would have placed the whole German trade union movement under communist control. The reconciliation between Russia's 'unions' and those of Britain and the USA was a direct consequence of Hitler's attack on Russia, which brought Britain, Russia and the USA into a common military alliance. The progressive break-up of this alliance between 1946 and 1949 brought the dissolution of the WFTU in its train.

Between March and May 1947 the communist parties one by one lost their places in the governments of Belgium, France and Italy. The Marshall Plan, announced in June, was denounced by the Russian Foreign Minister, Molotov, at the Paris Big Four talks in July. The Cominform, uniting the communist parties of Eastern and Western Europe, much on the lines of the Communist International disbanded in 1943, was founded the following September as a Russian counter-measure. In February 1948 the communist *coup d'état* in Czechoslovakia took place. The communists in the 'West' now switched from a policy of exaggerated class collaboration to one of equally exaggerated industrial militancy. A wave of communist inspired strikes swept France and Italy in particular during the winter of 1947–8. The CGT split in two in April 1948. The formerly united Italian trade union movement began to split asunder not long after.

The inaugural meeting of the Communist Information Bureau (Cominform), held in September 1947, had formally denounced the Marshall Plan, thus signalling all-out communist opposition, not least in the Councils of the WFTU. Blocked by the communists from obtaining serious discussion of the Plan proposals inside the councils of the WFTU the TUC, in March 1948, convened its own conference to discuss the European Recovery Programme (ERP) which had emerged

1. The Russian side is imperfectly documented; for the performance of the remarkable Irving Brown of the 'Western' team, see Lorwin, *International Labor Movement*, pp. 236–7; for other aspects, Braden, 'I'm glad the CIA is immoral', *Saturday Evening Post*, 20 May 1967.
2. Lorwin, *International Labor Movement*, pp. 248–52; Schevenels, pp. 358–9.

from the Marshall Plan. Delegates from all non-communist unions in Europe attended, together with representatives of both A F L and C I O. Belated attempts to prevent what was now an incipient split, undertaken at the Rome W F T U Executive meeting in May 1948, came to nothing. In October 1948 the T U C proposed that the W F T U suspend all activity for a twelve-month 'breathing-space'. In November the C I O convention rejected a proposition to endorse the W F T U.[1] At the January 1949 W F T U Executive meeting, Deakin presented the T U C motion for a suspension, citing the breakdown of negotiations between the W F T U and the Trade Secretariats as a major cause. Carey of the C I O spoke on similar lines, asserting that the communists had acquired a virtual veto over the operation of the W F T U and that there was nothing left but to bury it. On their inability to muster a majority Deakin of the T U C, Carey of the C I O and Kupers of the Netherlands N V V walked out. The life of the W F T U, as conceived in 1944–5, was virtually at an end.

The secessions which followed the January 1949 walkout left the W F T U as a shell of its former self, a rump organization, dominated by the state-controlled unions of Russia and Eastern Europe. The only European affiliates of importance which remained were the CGIL in Italy and the CGT in France. The T U C in Britain, the AFL and the CIO in the United States, now combined with representatives of European, Latin American, Asian and Australian unions to call a fresh world conference at London in November–December 1949. At this gathering the present International Confederation of Free Trade Unions (I C F T U) was founded. The conference was attended by 251 delegates from eighty seven union organizations in fifty two different countries. The I C F T U claimed some 48 million adherents, 21 million of these in Europe, 15 million more in the U S A (A F L and C I O combined). The statutes sought to provide a balance between British, North American, continental European and other regions on the executive. Efforts were made to avoid the over centralization of authority which had been a prime cause of the disintegration of the old W F T U. To this end the General Secretary was, by common consent, nominated from a minor rather than a major union centre. The central headquarters, for the same reason, were sited in Brussels, outside the direct ambit of any one of the major powers. The I T S retained full organizational autonomy, with the right to exchange representatives with the I C F T U at congresses and important executive meetings. At the same time the I T S recognized that they were part of the same international trade union movement, thus tacitly accepting a moral obligation to be bound by the general policy decisions of the I C F T U. The structure of the I C F T U remains sub-stantially as at the time of its original establishment. There has been only

1. Lorwin, *International Labor Movement*, pp. 258–9.

one major change in composition. Following disputes between the United States unions and the I C F T U the A F I–C I O withdrew from the I C F T U altogether in 1969.[1] Whether this breach will become permanent remains to be seen.

Employers apart, the main beneficiaries of these post war dissensions proved to be the European Christian organizations, which for the first time emerged as strong, powerful, fully legitimate trade union organizations in their own right. The Christian organizations had attended W F T U preliminaries but refused to join when the draft statutes denied them 'dual union' status in their respective countries. In Belgium the Christian C S C displaced the socialist F G T B as that country's major union confederation. In the Netherlands the combined membership of Catholic and Protestant organizations came to exceed that of the socialist confederation N V V by a considerable margin. In France, by the early 1960s, the Christian C F T C, now reorganized as the C F D T, displaced the Force Ouvrière as the main rival to the communist-controlled C G T. On the issue of the Marshall Plan the Christian unions organized in the *Confédération Internationale des Syndicats Chrétiens* (C I S C) and stood shoulder to shoulder with the I C F T U. On most matters arising in regard to the European Economic Community the C I S C and the I C F T U found themselves occupying common ground. In 1968 the reorganization of the C S C under non-confessional statutes with the new title of World Confederation of Labour (W C L) gave some hopes, so far unfulfilled, that old and bitter differences might at last be coming to an end.

The rump of the W F T U has suffered further severe setbacks since the secessions of 1949. The disputes between the Russian and Chinese governments provoked severe internal strains within the W F T U. The All China Federation of Trade Unions (A C F T U) was virtually dissolved in December 1966, during the 'cultural revolution'. The Chinese failed to attend the seventh W F T U Congress held in Budapest in October 1969 and there are at present no Chinese representatives on the W F T U General Council. The W F T U 'trade departments', intended as rivals to the independent I T S, have never seriously got off the ground. The W F T U's campaigns against the Common Market have ended in defeat. At the present time both C G T and C G I L send their delegates to meetings of the Economic and Social Committee of the EEC in Brussels. Each organization is seeking closer links with the Community in line with those long ago achieved by affiliates of the I C F T U and W C L. In Italy the socialist minority within the C G I L has declared for the disaffiliation of the C G I L from the W F T U, which now appears thoroughly discredited on every side.

Relations amongst I C F T U unions in Community Europe have been

1. AFL and CIO merged into the AFL–CIO in December 1955.

coloured in the past by the disproportionate size and influence of some organizations as against the others. Whereas Belgium's FGTB (800,000), the Netherlands' NVV (600,000), France's Force Ouvrière (600,000), Luxembourg's CGTL (30,000) and Italy's CISL (1·2 million) together muster some 3·2 million members, Germany's DGB alone enrols 6·9 million. The DGB nevertheless has sought meticulously not to assert its predominance, a fact to which the important posts occupied by representatives of the less powerful union confederations in Community-wide union offices bears witness.[1] The entry of Britain's 10 million strong TUC into the Community has already profoundly changed this balance, constituting something of a watershed in the history of trade unionism in continental Europe.

Britain, Denmark and the Republic of Ireland together add a further 11·3 million members to the forces of organized labour within the EEC.[2] The entry of Britain and Denmark doubles the membership of ICFTU affiliates in the Community, lifting it almost overnight from the former level of 10 million, to a figure in excess of 21 million.[3] The unions in these countries have been accustomed to exercise serious influence on national government policy. Assuredly they will wish to exercise at least comparable influence on the organs of the enlarged Community.

British entry raises one further question. Although hitherto the ICFTU affiliates at 10 million have outnumbered those of the WCL (2·3 million) and the WFTU (2·9 million) by a wide margin, their superiority in numbers was not so large as to be overwhelming. The entry of Britain changes this situation altogether. The ICFTU membership of some 21 million in the EEC, now outnumbers that of each of the two rival confederations by over seven to one. In such circumstances there will certainly be a rising pressure, especially from the British, for a merger of the competing forces. Some indications of this are already visible.[4] There are signs that the Christian unions would be prepared to accept a merger on suitable terms. Whether the communists would be prepared to place sectional prejudice on one side and sacrifice their ties with the Russian based WFTU for the sake of working class unity in Europe seems more doubtful.

ICFTU unions in the Community established, in 1958, a European

1. The election, in 1972, of Otto Kersten from the DGB as General Secretary of the ICFTU, as successor to Harm Buiter, may suggest a change in this attitude is getting under way.

2. Denmark 910,000, Republic of Ireland 390,000.

3. The Irish unions are affiliated to neither ICFTU, WCL not WFTU.

4. See for example the article *World Union Crisis* proposing that the WCL and WFTU affiliates should consider breaking their present ties and joining the ICFTU, in the widely read and influential *Voice of the Unions*, London, September 1972.

Secretariat with headquarters in Brussels, designed to organize collaboration and communication on matters of joint concern. The first secretary, Harm Buiter, a Netherlands metal workers' union representative, later became General Secretary of the ICFTU. Community-wide collaboration was carried a stage further at Rome in April 1971, when a conference of delegates from unions in the Six decided to refashion the European Secretariat into a new European Confederation of Trade Unions (ECTU) within the ICFTU.

The main task of the European Confederation will be to co-ordinate union action and policy in the territory of the EEC, but it also has wider aims. To date the unions have been consistently disappointed at their inability to exercise adequate influence on economic and social policy. As a result they now seek a thoroughgoing democratization of Community institutions. Thus the founding conference of the European Confederation called for a European parliament elected by universal suffrage to which the present Community institutions would be responsible. The conference also sought the setting up within the framework of the EEC of joint bodies of employers and workers for each branch of industry within the Community. The Confederation seeks to ensure that the projected European Company Law will include *Mitbestimmung* provisions of the type already in force in the coal, iron and steel industries of the Federal German Republic. Already an important body, the European Confederation carries still more weight now that the entry of Britain, and with it the TUC, is finally accomplished.[1] The extension of the European Confederation to cover Swiss, Scandinavians and Austrians (with only Community countries voting on 'Community' issues) has strengthened its authority still further. There are indeed signs, already plainly manifest at the ICFTU world congress held in London in July 1972, that the ECTU is bidding to become a serious rival for the authority of both the ICFTU and the ITS. Such proposals gather support from the most disparate and divergent interests. The Russians, the communists, their friends and others in the international trade union movement wish to devalue the ICFTU as against the WFTU and clear the way for the communist-led CGT in France and the communist-controlled CGIL in Italy to gain closer association with the European Confederation without paying the price of disaffiliation from the WFTU that ought properly to be demanded. The AFL–CIO and the US State Department, whose ventures in influencing international labour, notably in Africa, Asia and Latin America, at present involve jurisdictional conflicts with the ICFTU, also wish to devalue that organization. Certain sections of British labour seem to believe that by

1. For the European Confederation see *European Community*, London May 1970, pp. 17–18, also Eli Marx, 'Trade union activities in the European communities', in Marx and Kendall, *Unions in Europe*.

virtue of its longstanding 'special relationship' the TUC might act as intermediary between America's AFL–CIO and the ECTU, whilst at the same time retaining considerable freedom to act on its own account. A stratum of 'super-centralizers' in the top leadership of the European national confederations see in the EEC-wide organization the means to enhance their own power and prestige, in regard both to the EEC and to their own members, whilst at the same time laying claim to a new jurisdiction in the international bargaining field from which hitherto they have been excluded.

To the outside observer this procedure smacks of the primacy of bureaucratic self-interest over principles of organizational rationality. The TUC excluded the locally based trades councils from its Congress deliberations over seventy years ago. Since then it has based its organization largely on the national federations. The logical structure for the ECTU would seem to be one of direct affiliation from national union *federations*. This would place the emphasis of discussion and action on matters of specifically labour interest rather than those matters in which national union *confederations* tend to identify their interests with that of the national bourgeoisie. Clearly it would not be wise to exclude the national confederations entirely from the ECTU; nor would it be wise to exclude the ITS, or to set up the European Confederation as a rival to the ICFTU. Yet the proposal to base representation on national *confederations* does bring a note of unreality into the whole proceedings. Germany's IG Metall, Britain's TGWU, Germany's OTV, Britain's AUEW, each represent more workers than any of the three national confederations of the Netherlands, NVV, CNV, NKV, more than two of the national confederations of France, FO and CFDT, more than either of the national confederations of Belgium, CSC and FGTB. Each union is also far larger than Italy's national confederation, UIL.[1] Decisions arising from democratic debate can only be acceptable if the basis of representation in the policy-making body has some real relation to underlying strength. The proposals to make the ECTU a confederation of confederations is not only top heavy and unwieldy, it is also unjust. If proceeded with it is likely to generate severe strains in the future. All this suggests that the European Confederation will become a great deal more important in the future than in the past, its future activity is likely to have great significance both for the ICFTU and for the future of international trade unionism as a whole.

1. The membership of IG Metall is 2·3 million, that of OTV 1m, TGWU membership stands at 1·5m, that of the AUEW 1·3m. By contrast, in the Netherlands, NVV 560,000, NKV 430,000, CNV 240,000; in France, CFDT 800,000, FO 600,000, in Belgium, CSC 900,000, FGTB 800,000, in Italy CISL 1·2m UIL 300,000.

11. The European Motor Industry

The international company[1] poses in a particularly sharp form problems with which the trade union and labour movement has been faced almost from its foundation.[2] Although at least one farsighted trade union leader paid very serious attention to the issues involved as early as the 1920s[3] it is only in the last two decades that union reactions have begun to assume specific and concrete forms. Chemicals (including oil-refining), electronics and automobiles are the sectors in which the process of internationalization is most advanced at the present time. In each of these sectors the United States commands the larger producers. In each, equally, giants of US origin are subject to competition by rivals from continental Europe. Of the three sectors, the motor industry is the major employer of manpower. The motor industry also, because of its manifold and perhaps unequalled backward and forward linkages,[4] has now become a crucial, if not decisive element in the economic mechanism of the Western advanced industrial society. At the same time it is an industry which has seen the major US producers allocating a growing share of overall output to plants outside the boundaries of the USA. The socio-economic political motives for this development ought not to detain us here. The major union in the US auto industry is the United Automobile, Aerospace and Agricultural Implement Workers of America (UAW). The UAW is a key participant in the Automotive Department of the International Metal-workers' Federation (IMF). The displacement of production outward from the home base has

1. For two views see Kindleberger, ed., *The International Corporation*, and Levinson, *Capital, Inflation and the Multinationals*.
2. The establishment of the ITF for example was directly due to the need of British unionists in ports and shipping to protect their flanks from lower wage competition; on this Mann, *Tom Mann's Memoirs*, pp. 135–45.
3. Fimmen, *Labour's Alternative: United States of Europe or Europe Limited*, 1924. Formerly Secretary of the IFTU, Fimmen was at this time secretary of International Transport Workers' Federation (ITF).
4. The motor industry generates much secondary employment, 'backward' via component manufacturers, the oil and rubber industry, etc., 'forward' via garages, petrol stations, enforced destruction of city property, rebuilding, motorways, etc.

encouraged the U A W to play a most active part inside and alongside the I M F in developing modes of international union organization properly suited to meet and combat on equal ground, the vastly expanded scale of company international operation which typifies all the major producers in this second half of the twentieth century. In scale of production the European motor industry now equals or exceeds that of the U S A. As a result it shows a mirror to the probable future of other industries which stand to gain from the economies of scale offered by the E E C.

In Europe the motor, pre-eminently a product of twentieth century mass production, has in the years since the Second World War seen a boom on the scale of that of the United States in the first half of the century. 'In 1968 world output of motor vehicles of all kinds reached the record figure of 28 million whereas at the beginning of the 1950s it had been about 8 million.'[1] The largest single national producer remains the U S A with an output (in 1968) of 10·8 million vehicles, equivalent to 39 per cent of world production. Taken as a whole the European nations that year ran the U S A very close with a combined total of some 10 million vehicles.[2] The comparison is of course not precise. Japan, in 1968, was the world's second largest national producer with an output of 4·1 million against the 3·3 million of the next runner, the Federal Republic of Germany. The more highly diversified European industry cannot avail itself of either the same long runs, or the generally similar social conditions, which help to explain the giant size of the motor industry in the U S A. Nevertheless the significance of the industry in Europe is already immense.

It has been estimated that in the motor industry in Europe 'nine boards of directors make decisions affecting the security of income and the standard of living of one million *families* of workers employed in the European automobile industry properly speaking, or two million *families* when the labour force in ancillary industries is taken into account'.[3] The international integration of the industry is so great that it is by no means certain that a compilation of national employment statistics is the best manner to elucidate its significance. Through its backward and forward linkages the motor industry generates a great deal more employment than that registered in the figures of the workforce employed by the production plants.

1. 'The European Automobile Industry: problems and prospects in the world context', Report to the European I M F Automotive Conference, Paris, 3–5 December 1969.
2. But with some twenty motor companies as compared to only four in the U S A, ibid., p. 5. In 1970, European production taken as a whole outranked that of the U S A.
3. 'Priority demands and means of action of European auto workers', report of Daniel Benedict, Assistant General Secretary I M F, European I M F Automotive Conference, Paris, 3–5 December 1969.

Yet on this basis alone, in 1967, the three major French producers, Renault (66,000 workers), Citroën (62,000) and Peugeot (35,000), together employed over 160,000 men and women. Simca, a Chrysler subsidiary, employed a further 20,000 workers. In Germany Volkswagen employs 104,000 workers, Mercedes 80,000 and BMW 12,000, a total of 196,000. The two major subsidiaries of foreign-owned companies, Opel (General Motors – 57,000 workers) and Ford (33,000), brought the total work force of the five main producers to a total of 286,000. In Italy FIAT alone employs 142,000 workers, its two small competitors Alfa Romeo (12,000) and Lancia (9000) a further 21,000, a total of 163,000. Most of the major producers also have a toehold in assembly in Belgium. The two major producers here, Ford and General Motors, each employ around 6500 persons. Volkswagen, Citroën and Renault also operate in Belgium; between them they employ a further 6000 workers. There is one small native producer in the Netherlands, DAF, with a workforce of some 9000. In Spain there are two large manufacturing plants, one, SEAT owned by FIAT, the other owned by Chrysler. Spain also has a number of small assembly or partial manufacturing plants. In the main these are offshoots of the other major producers.

An indication of the overall allocation of the labour force employed in the European auto industry in 1967 will be found in the following table.[1] It will be observed that Britain, France, Germany and Italy emerged unchallengeably as the major producers:

Country		Workforce (1967)
Belgium		30,000
France		200,000
Germany		450,000
Italy		175,000
Netherlands		16,000
	Total	871,000
Great Britain		450,000
	Total	1,321,000
Scandinavia (of which Volvo and Saab = 20,000)		34,000
Spain		60,000
Switzerland		10,000
	Total	104,000
	Gross	1,425,000

1. Adapted from 'The state of the West European motor industry', document submitted to the Sixth World Auto Conference of the IMF in May 1968.

National statistics, however, provide a very inadequate picture of international production. On a global scale General Motors (GM), Ford and Chrysler in Detroit, Volkswagen in Wolfsburg, FIAT in Turin, directly decide the economic future and employment prospects of some 1,750,000 workers. The payroll of General Motors alone reaches 750,000.[1] The three US giants, General Motors, Ford and Chrysler, together produce some 60 per cent of world auto output, employing almost 1 million workers in the United States and a further 300,000 overseas.[2] In 1967 the two largest European producers, FIAT and Volkswagen, reached an output of 1,310,000 and 1,200,000 vehicles respectively.[3] Ford output in Belgium and Germany (550,000) plus that of Britain (488,000) exceeded 1 million vehicles in 1966. The two European subsidiaries of GM, Vauxhall in Britain (283,000) and Opel in Germany (662,000), produced an output in excess of 900,000 that same year. The three Chrysler subsidiaries in Europe, Rootes in Britain (213,000), Simca in France (280,000), Barreiros in Spain (50,000), topped the half million mark.[4] In Britain the subsidiaries of the US Big Three (GM, Ford and Chrysler) took 54 per cent of the market share in 1968. That same year Ford and Opel (GM) combined claimed 31 per cent of the German market.[5]

A moment's consideration will show that international operations on this scale pose to the trade unions and the labour movement problems of a very special order. It is not merely that the shift of production by US companies overseas gives US unions a greater practical interest than ever before in the level of organization and bargaining power achieved by unions in the subsidiaries of US companies abroad. Nor is it merely that the workers employed by US companies operating in Europe may find their bargaining power eroded or destroyed by the transfer of production to plants owned by the same company elsewhere. The European companies themselves are now beginning to diversify into assembly plants abroad, to develop the global scale of their operations in precisely the American manner. Thus FIAT is establishing a plant for the Russians at Togliattigrad in the Soviet Union. Volkswagen exports one quarter of its output to the USA. Plants in Brazil, Mexico and

1. Daniel Benedict, Report on 'International Problems of the Automobile Industry', presented to UILM Conference on the European motor industry, Turin, June 1967.
2. Benedict, quoted above, p. 7.
3. *State of the European Motor Industry*, London, May 1968. British Leyland output that year was 671,000 vehicles.
4. Report to the Sixth World Automotive Conference, May 1968. See also table, ILO Metal Trades Committee Report, 1970, p. 166.
5. 'United States companies' interests in the European automotive industry' Burton B. Bendiner, IMF Conference, Dec. 1969, p. 3.

elsewhere give Volkswagen 30 per cent of the output of motor vehicles in South and Central America.[1]

Under the pressure of competition from the US giants the twenty European producers are already beginning to undergo a further process of concentration. Volkswagen has swallowed NSU. Auto Union is linked to Porsche. Daimler Benz has interests in BMW. Rumours suggest that Volkswagen plans a merger with BMW through purchase of the 50 per cent shareholding currently in the hands of the Quandt family. In Italy the field is practically down to FIAT and the state-owned Alfa Romeo. In France, Renault, a nationalized concern, closely associated with Peugeot, is developing links with Alfa Romeo. Citroën, nominally an independent, is closely involved with FIAT. One can already see the prospect of a cross-frontier FIAT–Citroën merger, the possible eventual growth of a Volkswagen–FIAT–Citroën European giant, which could apply economies of scale in a truly American manner.[2] It is clear that the existing level and scope of union and labour organization is inadequate to meet a challenge on this scale.

The problems raised for the unions by the multi-national corporation are manifold. In the first place the union can no longer be certain that the management with whom it deals in the course of local or national negotiations is competent to take decisions on its own account. The true locus of sovereignty may lie at some higher level of the company's international management executive team. Equally, the international 'spread' of the company's operation may enable it to 'ride out' a strike on one national front of its productive activities simply by switching output to another. The corporation's ability to juggle international book keeping through transfer pricing, makes it possible to switch profits from one arena of operation to another at will. In such circumstances the claim of 'inability to pay' loses whatever small measure of credibility it ever possessed for union bargainers (or public opinion) in the first place. The company is able to meet hard union bargaining or plans to enforce sophisticated social security provisions for its workforce with the threat to switch output to nations with lower wages and less stringent social security provisions. The corporation may go even farther and threaten to relocate projected new investment, or to shut down its plants in one single nation altogether. The multi-national character of enterprise operation enables the company to evade the fiscal provisions and planning measures elaborated by the government of any single national state

1. 'Economic and social development in the European motor industry', Report by Gunter Kopke, Secretary of the European Committee of Metalworkers' Unions, Brussels, December 1969. Production at Volkswagen's giant plant at São Bernardo, outside São Paulo in Brazil already exceeds 200,000 a year. São Bernardo employs some 20,000 workers.

2. Kopke, quoted above.

should it so desire. In this way the multi-national corporation may become almost a law unto itself, slipping off whatever shackles of social responsibility labour has been able to fasten on its activity by means of parliamentary political action in the past.

The corporation may, for reasons of its own, allocate specific sectors of the world market to particular plants, shutting out others as an act of policy, whatever the innate merits of the case. 'General Motors reportedly imports Opel cars into the United States and Vauxhall cars into Canada and at one time decided not to export Holden (Australia) cars to Japan but to keep this market for the General Motors plants in California.'[1] 'Ford imports the Ford Cortinas made in the United Kingdom into the United States but excludes the cars produced by its subsidiary in the Federal Republic of Germany.'[2] Plants required to supply industry in one country may, as an act of policy, be planned for establishment in another.[3] Production of particular models may be concentrated in the plants of one nation rather than another. Specific aspects of research, development and other functions may be located in one country at the expense of others.[4] The individual national companies may even be subsumed into an international 'Big Brother'. Thus Ford of Europe Incorporated has been established in the UK specifically to supervise the European automotive activities of the Ford Motor Company of the USA.[5] Design and production planning for the eminently successful Ford Capri was shared between Britain and Germany. Capri production is now under way at both Dagenham and Cologne. The Escort saloon originally designed and built in Britain is now also assembled at the Ford plant at Genk in Belgium.[6]

Ford of Europe Incorporated is in an excellent position to elaborate a unified Europe-wide policy for its dealings with the unions in auto. The unions, by contrast, are badly divided amongst themselves, both within and between the nations comprising the European auto-productive market.

In Britain Ford deals with a whole constellation of rival unions, the bulk of the membership being divided between one craft union (AUEW) and one general union (TGWU). In Belgium the Ford plant at Genk in Catholic Limburg is organized by a Catholic union affiliated to the CSC, which is outside the IMF. At Genk the socialist FGTB possesses only a minority status. At the Ford tractor plant in Antwerp CSC and FGTB divide the membership equally. At Cologne the metal-workers'

1. Layton, *Trans-Atlantic Investments*, p. 86.
2. *Financial Times*, 8 April 1969, p. 19.
3. *Financial Times*, 30 Dec. 1966.
4. Quoted International Labour Office, Metal Trades Committee Report, 1970, pp. 167–8.
5. *International Herald Tribune*, Paris, 16 June 1967.
6. Metal Trades Committee Report, p. 168.

union, I G Metall, embraces the whole organized workforce. Up to this time meetings between these unions to discuss matters of common concern have been sparse indeed. The first meeting of British and German Ford workers did not take place until 27 March 1971, during the British Ford strike.[1] This meeting followed the discussions which had taken place at I M F World Auto Council meetings during the preceding days.

The isolation of workers in the Ford plants of different nations is no exception. The degree of liaison between workers employed by General Motors, Britain (Vauxhall), and General Motors, Germany (Opel), is just as limited as in the case of Ford. Where Chrysler is concerned the situation for the unions is even less satisfactory. Chrysler, Britain (Rootes), is well organized. Chrysler, France (Simca), maintains a hostile anti-union shop and has kept the level of unionization very low indeed. In Chrysler, Spain, all unions are outlawed by the fascist government. Nevertheless in the Spanish plants there do exist clandestine union organizations, notably the U S O, led in the main by left socialists of Christian origin. There are also underground groups led by communists and others.

The union situation in the major European producers can be summarized fairly briefly.[2] In Britain, despite jurisdictional rivalry amongst several different unions, almost the whole of the workforce is organized. The level of organization in Germany is lower, but in this case all workers are in the same union, IG Metall. In Belgium workers are divided between the Christian CSC and the socialist FGTB. The CSC has majority status at Ford, Genk. At Ford, Antwerp, socialists and Christians divide the organized workforce in almost equal proportions. In the Netherlands the Catholic NKV organizes the majority of the works in the DAF plant, the socialist NVV a minority. In France the level of union organization in the motor industry, as elsewhere, is low. At Renault, Boulogne-Billancourt, Paris, the largest plant, the level of unionization has been put at 20 per cent overall. The union allegiance of this small minority is divided three ways between CGT, CFDT and FO, with the CGT some distance ahead of the others. Citroën and Simca have been charged with encouraging anti-union strong-arm tactics more typical of the United States of the 1920s and 1930s than of Europe at the present time. Chrysler (Simca) and Citroën have also supported a 'yellow' company union the CFT (*Confederation Française du Travail* in the endeavour to forestall genuine union organization in their plants. In Italy the three confederations, CISL, CGIL, and UIL,

1. For text of resolution passed at IMF World Auto Company Council Conference, London, 23–5 May 1971, see *Bulletin of the International Metalworkers' Federation*, Geneva, no. 37, May 1971, p. 6.
2. For the sake of clarity I have excluded any mention of white-collar workers from this account.

are all in the field. Organization overall is not particularly strong. At Turin FIAT has been accustomed to shift its favours from one confederation to another as it thought fit. Union membership has fluctuated widely as a result. SIDA, originally a company union, has also been a powerful factor in the Turin plant. All four unions together organize at the outside perhaps 40 per cent of the workforce at the present day. Management at the new Alfa Romeo plant in Naples is expected to favour CISL as against its rivals, but it is too early yet to foretell the final outcome.

Looking at the situation overall, about one half of the labour force in the major European auto-producers are at present trade union members. The bulk of this membership is organized, through its national unions, into the International Metal-workers' Federation (IMF). The IMF is an organization in its own right, quite separate from the ICFTU, financing its own activities from its own affiliation fees, deciding its own policies, as it sees fit, from time to time. On a global scale only one half of IMF members are linked with the ICFTU. In Europe however, with four exceptions, the most important being the CFDT in France, most IMF members are also ICFTU affiliates.

In France, Italy, Belgium and the Netherlands there exist important groups of workers organized in national unions of either communist or Catholic orientation which for one reason or another stand outside the IMF. These groups are linked respectively via the Russian and ex-Catholic-led confederations of national union centres, the World Federation of Trade Unions (WFTU) and the World Confederation of Labour (WCL). The highly centralized constitution of the WFTU makes no provision for independent action by workers in specific industries. All such action is tightly controlled by the so-called 'Trade Departments' which are an integral part of the WFTU headquarters apparatus in Prague. The same holds true, although in somewhat lesser degree, as far as the WCL is concerned. The WCL has membership in the motor industry in Belgium and the Netherlands, the WFTU in France and Italy.

The November 1964 IMF World Automotive Conference, held at Frankfurt, devoted an important part of its time to discussing how to bargain more effectively with the multinational corporation. One outcome was the establishment, at a global conference held at the UAW Detroit headquarters in June 1966, of a series of World Motor Councils covering employees of Ford, General Motors and the Chrysler–FIAT–Simca–Rootes complex. A further World Council covering Volkswagen–Mercedes Benz was set up in Wolfsburg in November of that same year.[1] At each of these conferences, union representatives from the global

1. On this, in particular, IMF, *World Company Councils, Auto Workers' Answer to World Company Power*, Geneva, 1967.

locations of company activity were brought together for discussions on policy and an exchange of experience. In the case of Ford, GM and Volkswagen–Mercedes, but not of Chrysler, joint exchanges with top management also took place.

The unions have now decided to work towards a system of bargaining co-ordinated round a limited series of internationally agreed priority demands. Since the four Europe owned giants, FIAT, Volkswagen, British Leyland and Renault, together with the subsidiaries of the US Big Three, between them control 90 per cent of European motor vehicle production, this is a course which offers real possibilities. Strategy was elaborated in some detail at the First European Automotive Conference, held in Paris during December 1969. The outcome was a twelve-point list of 'priority collective bargaining goals':

First: The 40-hour week
                  Security of employment
                  Equal rights for women workers
                  Trade union rights in the shop
Other demands: Guaranteed annual wage
                  Humanization of rest and relief time
                  Trade union control on work speeds
                  Improved holidays and holiday pay
                  Adequate retirement pensions
                  Improved vocational training
                  Paid educational and cultural leave
                  Protection of older workers

It is intended that each union will press for those priority items still to be achieved. The outcome should be a levelling out of the differences in conditions and wages which divide producers and national workforces one from another. Closer contact, meetings, seminars and exchanges between workers in the different national plants of the same international combine are now firmly under way. The achievement of these co-ordinated demands should clear the ground for the negotiation of Europe-wide collective agreements at a later date. Such agreements, are likely to be based on the major corporations, as is already the case in the USA.

The European Automotive Conference also called for the elaboration of special codes governing investment and mergers, so as to protect both workers and consumers in the face of the international auto corporation, not least those giants in which fundamental policy decisions may be taken outside Europe altogether. The Conference proposed a number of measures designed to enhance the degree of social responsibility shown by the companies. Proposals intended to ease the achievement of full trade union recognition in the industry were also agreed.

One event to which the European Automotive Conference devoted particular attention was the hard-fought strike at the Ford plant at Genk in Belgium during 1968. Particularly significant was the support rendered by the IMF despite the fact that the union primarily involved was part of the Belgian Christian confederation CSC, and not an affiliate of the IMF at all.

Ford, Genk, employs some 10,000 workers. Situated in Limburg, a predominantly Catholic rural area, hitherto characterized by low wages and high unemployment, the plant went into operation in 1961 and produced its 500,000th vehicle in May 1967. Genk is approximately sixty miles due west of the older-established and much larger Ford plant at Cologne which employs some 25,000 workers. Some fifty miles to the north-east Ford also operate a longstanding tractor plant in the major city and port of Antwerp. The wage scale at Ford, Genk, was some 30 per cent below that at Antwerp. Genk craftsmen in particular objected that their work week was considerably longer than the forty hours negotiated in the agreement covering Ford, Cologne.[1]

The original Genk agreement expired during 1968. The union now called for parity in wages and conditions with Ford, Antwerp. Negotiations proved abortive. An official strike was declared on 21 October.[2] The strike did not end until 22 November. During the stoppage approaches were made by the unions not only to workers at Ford, Antwerp, but also to workers at Ford, Cologne in Germany, Ford, Dagenham and Ford, Halewood in Britain. I G Metall, the union at Ford, Cologne, gave undertakings not to accept work transferred from Genk. Cologne workers also undertook not to step up output to replace production lost at Genk. German workers employed on special tasks at Genk were called out in sympathy by their unions. When the Belgian unions organized a solidarity demonstration on 2 November, a delegation from Ford, Cologne, marched alongside the Belgian workers as an indication of support. The visit of a Belgian delegation to Britain gained further promises of solidarity. Assurances were given that the British workers would not permit an increase in production of the Ford Escort at Halewood so as to fill gaps left by the stoppage of the Escort line at Genk. The strikers remained solid throughout the whole month-long stoppage. This in itself was something of an achievement for a work force in an hitherto non-industrial area. The strike ended with major gains for the union. The Antwerp differential, although not abolished, was reduced by half.

1. Kopke, Report to the IMF European Automotive Conference, Paris, 3–5 Dec. 1969, p. 7.
2. For a detailed account of the Genk strike, see Spitaels, *L'Année sociale, 1968*, pp. 130–51; also Blanpain, 'American involvement in Belgium', in Kamin, ed., *Western European Labor and the American Corporation*, pp. 460–61.

304 THE LABOUR MOVEMENT IN EUROPE

The Genk conflict has to be seen in the context of the claim by Ford Dagenham for parity with the industrial Midlands which in 1971 led to a five-week official stoppage involving some 50,000 workers. A precedent of importance for both disputes existed in the UAW's 1967 contract negotiations in the USA. Here the outcome of an official strike was the ending of the differential between contracts governing Canada and the United States. The world auto market is now continental or even global in nature. The auto *labour* market is still astonishingly local. The Belgian Genk–Antwerp, the British, Dagenham–Midlands parity disputes illustrate this very well. If their negotiations with the companies are to be fully effective the unions must work towards a unified labour market, with comparable wages and conditions operating right across the board of the particular combines[1] in both national and continental operations. In the medium-long term a bid to equalize wages *up* towards the United States level would seem to be necessary if only to safeguard and maintain the rate of progress of auto workers in the USA. In this connection the levelling *up* of the wages of Canadian workers to the US level may be seen as a portent of future relations between Europe and the USA in this field.

In the past, trade union affiliation in European countries has been largely determined by local political or confessional allegiance. The nature of the bargaining situation with which unions have been confronted has meant that the choice of affiliation has only rarely possessed important international connotations. The Ford, Genk, stoppage provides one indication of the way in which tradition is likely to change in the future. In the case of Ford, Genk, the metal-workers' union of the Christian confederation CSC, basing itself on the predominantly Catholic composition of rural Limburg, had originally demanded sole negotiation rights in the Ford plant. This was despite the presence of the socialist FGTB, which represented about one quarter of the labour force. Nevertheless, when once the stoppage began the Christian union found it necessary to appeal for solidarity to nonconfessional organizations in Germany and the United Kingdom. These in their turn, putting aside sectional differences, and with the full approval of the Belgian FGTB, found it proper to give support. The casual reader of most accounts of these events, indeed, would not become aware of the rift in international allegiance were he not already informed of the fact. In auto at least, the pressures of international bargaining are likely to do a great deal to erode existing political and confessional union divisions.

The difficulties of organizing effective international inter-union solidarity would appear to lie much more in the mind of unionists than in external objective economic and social conditions. Over centuries, Euro-

1. Thus in 1970 Ford, Dagenham, stewards hired a bus and visited their counterparts in Genk, Antwerp and Cologne.

peans, in certain aspects of their activity, have been so accustomed to think on a petty local scale, that the breakout to new dimensions involves something of a revolution. A United States company like Du Pont customarily organizes its marketing operation on the West Coast, 3000 miles from its East Coast Delaware headquarters, without any obvious difficulty. A similar facility on an international scale is already becoming the hallmark of the global corporation. The Ford Genk–Antwerp–Cologne complex lies within a radius of less than eighty miles from Genk. The whole 'Ford of Europe' operation, including outposts in Liverpool and Southampton, lies within a 200-mile radius from London. Chrysler's Franco–British operations are more extensive, but not vastly so. Chrysler–Simca's plants in Paris, Sully and La Rochelle[1] and Chrysler–Rootes's factories at Coventry, Luton, Dunstable in England and Paisley in Scotland are all comfortably within a 400-mile radius from London. General Motors runs plants at Luton, Dunstable and Ellesmere Port (near Liverpool). General Motors also owns the large Opel operation at Russelsheim in Germany. None of these is more than 300 miles from Rotterdam.

Although travel expenses and language difficulties remain problems to be overcome, these are clearly not on such a scale in themselves as to inhibit close union and workforce ties. Rather it is the deeply ingrained localist thinking of the members of the workforce and the unions themselves. The individuals who comprise the workers and union officials in each plant, brought up behind curtains of national sovereignty, have been walled off from one another by traditions with their origins in centuries of war and national prejudice. As far as day-to-day experience is concerned, the workforce of plants in other countries frequently seem as far away as Australia, or almost, the moon.

Nevertheless, pressures are at work which seem to place international bargaining on the order of the day for the late 1970s and early 1980s.[2] The precondition for the successful establishment of such a revitalized system of bargaining seems to lie in a clear breach with existing craft, local, national and political sectarian prejudices. These prejudices spring from the closed nature of the national, regional and local labour and product markets, in which union organization has operated up to now. Locals organizing auto plants have traditionally been part of the metal-working unions in their respective countries. As such they have been involved in all the political sectarian quarrels which have characterized the relations between organized workers in the national economy. These

1. Even La Rochelle, on the coast, farthest away, is only some 350 miles south-west of Paris.
2. On this, Nunn, 'World councils of employees; a challenge to the supranational corporation?', in Kamin, ed., *Western European Labour and the American Corporation*, p. 18.

306 THE LABOUR MOVEMENT IN EUROPE

quarrels may in the past have been inevitable. Now it is unmistakably clear that at a moment in which multi-national, industrial, combine-wide bargaining is the order of the day, such union divisions are out-dated and almost totally disfunctional. The need is for a large degree of sectoral autonomy for auto-workers within the metal-workers' unions of each national economy. The assumed framework of *national* economic bargaining is called into question. If the companies' mode of behaviour is multi-national it is difficult to see how union organization can fail to follow the employer onto the multi-national arena. The alternative is for the unions to be outflanked and outgeneralled at every point as a result of their own insularity. The fact that its statutes make the IMF independent of any of the competing international confederations of national union centres is one factor here likely to prove of positive significance for the future.[1]

Longer-term needs would seem to require decentralization of union bargaining power from national to plant and combine level. Above this would arise a new hierarchy of negotiation, essentially concerned with multi-national bargaining at the level of the individual corporation. The national organization of the national union would remain primary in all those industries largely devoted to the national market. The national union would also remain supreme in the pursuance of socio-political objectives at the level of the national economy and for the achievement of those policy goals which require intervention by the national government. Other functions would either be devolved downwards or become more and more the preserve of international industrial bargaining on a corporation basis. The long-term outcome might be the emergence of 'International Industrial Unions', each with internal trade departments, operating on a Europe-wide basis. Regional organization of such 'International Industrial Unions' might or might not correspond to national boundaries, depending on the nature of the problems involved. Effective international industrial action would certainly require a recognition that international mobility of labour had now become a necessary counterpart to the international mobility of capital. In the short term labour mobility between major national producers might raise real difficulties. In the medium term such difficulties are likely to be more than outweighed by the consolidation and enhanced solidarity of the abour force which would result.

The problem of how to bring the multi-national automotive concern

1. At least one other ITS has drawn this moral. At its Fourteenth Congress in October 1969, the International Chemical Workers' Federation removed the constitutional provision that all affiliates must also be affiliates of the ICFTU and substituted in its place a requirement that 'the organization subscribe to democratic principles in their internal and external relations', *IUF Bulletin*, vol. 40, no. 10, 1970.

under effective social control seems likely to occupy the labour movement for some time to come. State ownership of the individual national units of multi-national companies would in itself seem to be no solution, not least because the national enterprise in isolation cannot take proper advantage of the international division of labour. Proposals have been made for control of merger, employment and industrial investment-plant-location policy. Such proposals possess some merit. Yet, given the multi-national corporation's ability to evade or override restrictions imposed by national sovereignty should it so desire, can such restrictions ever be fully enforced? The problems of legislation and enforcement on a European-wide or international scale are, if anything, more difficult still. The First European Automotive Conference in 1969 made proposals for union representation on the management boards of multi-national companies on the lines of the German *Mitbestimmung* and European Confederation proposals. This may be one possibility. In the long term the only sure way in which to enforce social responsibility would seem to be to vest the whole corporation in the work force, at the multi-national level. In the meantime, the IMF's work to build up co-ordinating committees between plant and union representatives in the various multi-national combines, to establish a comprehensive data bank on global wages, working conditions and other aspects of company operations, seem to be indispensable.

Across the board, Europe-wide collective bargaining agreements are not yet in view. On the other hand, Europe-wide, combine frame agreements, on specific aspects of working conditions, such as hours, relief times, holidays, and similar matters, seem quite possible within the next decade. Europe-wide demonstrations and limited industrial stoppages in support of such demands are well within the bounds of probability.

The activity of unions in Europe, from their origins in the second half of the nineteenth century up to the present time, have been dominated by the endeavour to gain full recognition on a nation-wide basis. The struggle to extend those bargaining rights into the transnational sphere is likely to dominate the next hundred years as surely as strictly national struggles have dominated the last.

12. Conclusion

No individual or social group makes history out of the whole cloth. The actions of every performer in the social drama are conditioned by circumstances. Man may define absolute minima of human needs. The possibilities of meeting them remain manifold, even numberless. The drives which motivate the social action of working people customarily find their origins in the deprivations, relative or absolute, to which they are subject. Yet the needs *felt* by individuals and social groups are conditioned by the nature of the social environment. Subjectively this limits the capacity to envisage possible solutions; objectively it imposes arbitrary limits to the modes in which it is reasonable to seek to fulfil these needs.

The 'laws' of economics no less than the 'laws' of society are in the last analysis statements about the required behaviour of persons. As such, both their effects and their enforcement vary according to the human context in which they operate. It is possible to lay down a series of criteria to define the term 'labour movement'. Barring a grey area of give and take at the margin, such criteria would assuredly achieve a very wide measure of acceptance by all involved in the field. One might in the same sense lay down criteria to define the product mix for an omelette. Yet not all omelettes are the same. Ingredients differ both in quality and in substance. The ingredients in the mixture themselves vary in proportion. The frying pan is too hot, or too cold. The butter varies in quality. Not all cooks exercise the same skills or concern for their craft. The finished product may be served hot from the kitchen, it may have grown stale on a cold plate before reaching the table. In much the same way the modern mass labour movement stands at a nodal point where some of the most complex and varied forces of industrial society interact. The economic, social, cultural and historical experience which condition its organization, attitudes and behaviour are infinitely varied.[1]

1. On this, for example, Lapalombara and Weiner, eds., *Political Parties and Political Development*, pp. 45–7, 54–5, 62–6; Moore, *Soviet Politics: the Dilemma of Power*, pp. 412–15; Hobsbawm, *Labouring Men*, pp. 371–3; Mitchell and Stearns *Workers and Protest*, pp. 3–4, 17–20, 65–70, ff; and Thompson, *The Making of the English Working Class*, p. 1.

That in different nations the labour movement should present itself under a wide range of organizational forms and adopt many different modes of behaviour is therefore no cause for surprise.

The Italian worker of the older generation experienced three decades of fascism, war, defeat, reconstruction. He lives in a pronouncedly disaggregated society, with marked regional differences, unified and freed from foreign occupation barely a hundred years ago. His country is the administrative centre of a cult of global dimensions. The attitudes of upward deference, the bureaucratic and hierarchic modes of behaviour engendered by this cult, seem to have become an integral part of the political life of the nation.

The German worker lives in the industrial heartland of Europe. His nation has a powerful military tradition and strong ties of internal cohesion. His working-class movement set the pace of world socialism over decades. He is conscious that Germany is one of the axes around which the future of European society revolves. German society, too, has experienced a decade of one of the most ruthless dictatorships in history, a dictatorship imposed with aid and sustenance from German business. German cities were ruined and millions of Germans died in the Second World War. Currency reforms in 1923 and 1948 wiped out the savings of two successive generations. At the end of the war life in West Germany was further disrupted by the influx of millions of refugees forcibly expelled from the East. To the present day its existence is conditioned by the presence of a hostile and alien regime on part of the soil of what was formerly a unified German state.

The Netherlands and Belgium, by contrast, are both small nations, buffer states occupying a no man's land between three great powers. Confessional issues play a major role in the social and political life of each. In Belgium in particular, where linguistic, regional and confessional issues to a marked extent coincide, these fix to a great degree the framework within which other social forces must operate. Belgium and the Netherlands are highly dependent on foreign trade. The social balance of forces in both countries varies markedly from that of their neighbours.

In France the whole of socio-political life has taken place in the shadow of the Revolution of 1789. Revolution in France has a national patriotic note unknown elsewhere. Pyrrhic victory in 1914–18, outright defeat in 1940, the loss of overseas possessions after 1945, late and limited industrialization, a highly centralized state, the narrow horizons of the entrepreneurial bourgeoisie, have all in their own way conditioned the outlook, beliefs and behaviour of the French workforce, which in the nature of things comprises the majority of the nation.

Our own thinking on these matters is bedevilled by a species of Anglo-American exceptionalism. Britain was the initiator of the industrial revolution, the classic country of entrepreneurial capitalism, showing in a pure form its nature and mode of operation. The United States, a great continental republic, was even more free of the trammels of a pre-capitalist past. No other nations fitted the same mould. The superiority of British goods and the supremacy of the British navy in the nineteenth century justified and made effective the British belief in free trade. The continental scope of the United States market acted in much the same way. In Britain the power of the Church as an independent social force had been broken in the sixteenth century. The USA was a lay state from the moment of its foundation. In Britain the dominant power of the monarchy had been ended already in the seventeenth century. The United States was a parliamentary republic from the very beginning.

Compare this with the situation in continental Europe. The continuity of the English state goes back in an unbroken line to the eleventh century, that of the USA to 1789. The bourgeois revolution in Britain and the USA is complete at an early date. Each is a lay state in a predominantly lay society. In each parliamentary institutions are dominant. In each the prevailing modes of human economic behaviour are characterized by rules of abstract economic rationality.

Many nations of continental Europe do not fit this model at all. The modern Belgian state dates from 1830. The present Italian state was established only in 1861. The unification of Germany was not accomplished until 1867–71. Relations between Church and state have been an issue of major controversy in these countries at intervals all through the nineteenth century and to some degree in the twentieth century as well. The standards of behaviour of the entrepreneurial bourgeoisie, which in some respects owe more to the past than to the present, have not been fully determined by considerations of abstract economic rationality. The end of absolutism in France is the product of the Revolution of 1789. The power of the monarchy in Germany was not broken before 1919. In Italy one may almost say that the establishment of parliamentary democracy is a product of the second rather than the first half of the twentieth century.

The close ties between state and industry through tariffs, military requirements, or as in the case of the railways, subsidies, state participation or outright state ownership, have meant that in continental Europe the boundary line between politics and economics has not been drawn with anything like the same precision as in Britain or the USA. The labour movement and the labour unions arise as a response to specific social conditions, in a specific historical context, at a series of specific moments in time. As the challenge varies, so must the response. Let us examine a few examples.

The rise of the German labour movement, the unitary character of the dominant SPD, can surely not be separated from the incomplete character of the German bourgeois revolution, the fact that German industry developed very rapidly, on a large scale, and with close links with the banks. In France, where the bourgeois revolution was far more complete, but the urbanization–industrialization process more retarded, there emerged multiple divisions within the ranks of French socialism, a clear breach between the SFIO and CGT. The character of both French entrepreneurial activity and the political system were different from the pattern in Germany. These factors encouraged the growth of a labour force and a labour movement of a very different type.

The industrial revolution in Italy did not, until the last decades, extend far beyond the 'iron triangle' of Genoa–Milan–Turin. Italy itself was divided into metropolitan and near-colonial regions above and below a line drawn across the peninsula near Rome. In the country as a whole there survived a species of dual economy in which advanced modern industry co-existed alongside sectors of archaic peasant and artisan economy. Italian entrepeneurs, in their dealings with employees, have customarily assumed attitudes more appropriate to relations between the country squire and his dependent tenantry. The existence of large scale agricultural unionism, until recently based largely on share cropping tenancies, has helped to contribute a flavour of near anarchic violence to sections of the labour movement. If one is to accept the claim of the CGIL, 151 Italian workers have been killed in demonstrations by police and soldiers in the years since 1945. This claim may well be exaggerated. Yet, even after making all due allowances, the figure which remains is one which scarcely belongs to our conception of civilized government in twentieth-century Europe at all.[1]

If the entrepreneurial class fails to perceive its interests entirely in terms of abstract economic rationality, this holds too, in some measure, for the labour force as well. The significance of Christian unionism in Belgium and the Netherlands, its integral role in the development and evolution of the CFDT in France, the overriding importance of the confessional spirit embodied in the Catholic workers' organization ACLI, in the appearance and consolidation of CISL in Italy, all demonstrate this fact beyond any possibility of contradiction. Such features of the European labour movement seem to drive a coach and horses through any such simplistic typologies as that epitomized by Selig Perlman's *Theory of the Labour Movement* with its 'three factors . . . as basic in any modern labour situation' hingeing on the 'resistance power of capitalism', 'the dominance over the labour movement by the

1. According to the Polish Communist Party leader, Edward Gierek, forty five people were killed and 1165 injured in riots which followed the Polish government decision to reduce wages and increase prices in the weeks before Christmas 1970. But this, one supposes, is not quite the same thing? See *Guardian*, London, 8 Feb. 1971.

intellectual's "mentality"', and 'the degree of maturity of a trade union "mentality"'.[1] The 'three pillar society' of the Netherlands and the 'two-pillar' union structure in Belgium are factors which cannot adequately be explained by reference to the economic behaviour of modern capitalism, but only by reference to factors outside this frame of reference altogether. If we find ourselves in one society in which employers and employees speak of themselves as *datori del lavoro* and *prestati d'opera*, and another in which they refer to themselves as *arbeitgeber* and *arbeitnehmer*, ('givers of work' and 'receivers of work'), then we are justified in asserting that in such social contexts, both the fashion in which the participants view the relationship and the relationship itself are very different from the simple abstractions of 'employer' and 'employee'.

In fact the significance of the term 'wage worker' cannot properly be understood outside of the specific social context in which the wage worker himself exists. In Britain this largely urban phenomenon developed over several centuries. In the United States, the immigrant, cut off from his country of origin, lived in a society which had been dominated from the beginning by an ethic derived from a system of commodity circulation. This society too had been established on what was practically virgin soil.[2] The capitalist commodity ethic had no antecedent tradition with which to compete for the minds of the population. In Europe, wage workers frequently had close ties with a rural peasant economy. Physical factors such as population distribution, urban and architectural environment, more intangible factors such as religious belief, social custom, modes of thought and social reference, the very political institutions themselves, were all inherited from the past and weighed heavily on the future in formation. Thus the fact that a man performed the 'role' of a wage worker in no way necessitated that he should entirely act and think like one, or more precisely in the manner in which thinking derived from the premises of classical economics (and this includes Marx) predicated that he *ought* to act. The 'pure' wage worker in the past, and up to the present time, is the exception rather than the rule. The 'average' worker manifests strong objection to the labour mobility essential to the workings of a free market economy, he continues to resist social pressures which seek to utilize his labour power and his person as no more than commodities to be bought and sold in the market place. The European worker, firmly rooted in a local environment, has proved singularly reluctant to move in response to the imperative signals of market forces. A great deal of his social, economic and

1. Perlman, *A Theory of the Labor Movement*, p. x.
2. This is not to deny the significance of pre-existing Indian and Spanish cultures but merely to point out that their influence, for our purposes, was minimal.

political activity derives from *resistance* to these very forces. Employers too, for paternalistic and other reasons of their own, have acted in a precisely similar way, seeking to tie labour to the plant, to domesticate it, thus narrowing the social horizons of the working man, establishing a closed sector of the labour market appropriated to themselves, relatively immune to external market forces.

In those countries in which an important part of the organized labour force either resides in, or resides and works in rural areas, similar phenomena may recur with added force. Thus, within the close confines of the tiny Belgian state, heavily subsidized workmen's fares helped to ensure that Catholic factory-workers continued to reside in rural areas, in an ambience dominated by the village priest. By this means they were removed from the de-confessionalizing pressures of a largely impersonal urban environment. On the other hand, in Italy the agricultural unionists of Tuscany, Emilia and the Po Valley, placed in a position in which mass action rather than normal trade union activity was required to bring results, imparted a revolutionary and insurrectionist note to much of labour union activity in the country as a whole.

The sense of homogeneity of the national labour force, too, cannot but be influenced by the degree of internal labour migration, and more important, the sense of common identity in the nation as a whole. If, as in Belgium, the citizen thinks of himself at least as much as a Fleming or a Walloon as a Belgian; if, as in Italy, citizens associate themselves as much or more with their own town and its community, or with their province, then with the state; then the problems of national union organization are likely to be materially affected as a result.

The balance of industrial sectors in the economy, too, the progress of their rise or decline, cannot be without importance for the character and behaviour of both bourgeoisie and proletariat. Coal-miners, concentrated in relatively large units of employment and bound together by a common sense of danger, frequently in isolated single-industry communities, men faced with common problems many of which are capable of solution or amelioration by legislative means, are likely to be to the fore in both union and political action. Railwaymen, united by a single nation-wide employer, usually linked with the state, are in some ways in a similar situation. The behaviour of white collar workers and of workers in industries based predominantly on female labour such as textiles, are likely to conform to a markedly different model.

One suspects, although much detailed study would be required to produce adequate proof, that a great many of the differences between national labour movements are due to factor composition shifts of this kind. That the fortunes of an industry will directly condition the behaviour of both the workforce and employers in that sector is self-evident. Industrial relations in Turin cannot be separated from the fortunes of FIAT, nor over half a century could the fortunes of the Borinage in Belgium be separated from the price of coal.

Sectoral shifts in the economy may contribute to major social convulsions, as in the link between the rundown of the coal mines of the Borinage and the prolonged Belgian general strike of December 1960 to January 1961; or between the crisis in the British coal industry and the general strike of 1926, or more recently the great British coal strike of 1972. Sectoral shifts may also lead to important changes in the allegiance of the organized workforce, as illustrated by the rise of the Catholic CSC to majority status over the socialist FGTB, alongside the growth of new industry in Flanders, in the years after the Second World War.

The internal class–economic relationships, which led to the formation of the modern working class, seem also to have been affected in an important way by outside factors. The arrival of the railway on the prairies of the United States and a fall in ocean freight rates combined to expose large areas of European agriculture to a terrifying blast of competition.[1] The shift from the land and the social dislocation that resulted from urbanization made a major contribution to the rise of the modern labour movement. Some 'displaced persons' went to swell the European proletariat, others crossed the Atlantic as part of the greatest wave of inter-continental migration the world has ever known.

Another, too infrequently considered, aspect of the growth of the modern labour movement, is the extent to which the labour movement itself has been conditioned by the environment into which it has grown. It seems generally agreed that the Anti-Socialist Laws did a great deal to strengthen the revolutionary stance of German Social Democracy. The allegiance of the bourgeoisie to the cause of the Prussian state after 1848 similarly strengthened the position of the SPD as unchallenged advocate of the pre-requisites of a modern parliamentary democracy. The gains made by the Italian Socialist Party in the years before the First World War were to an important extent the consequence of the extreme weakness of a parliamentary regime based on *trasformismo* and a *clientela* relationship between the state and its patrons. The early years of the Belgian socialist movement were dominated by the struggle for the right to vote to an extent which would have been inconceivable had the suffrage been distributed as widely as in France or even Great Britain. French memories of 1789, 1830, 1848 and the Commune of 1871 served to legitimize revolutionary attitudes and the use of revolutionary phrase-

1. On this Landauer, *European Socialism*, p. 375, Landes, *The Unbound Prometheus*, p. 342. For Britain see Court. *A Concise Economic History of Britain*, pp. 200–7. Both Landes and Court point also to the significance of south Russian production in this regard. Two remarkable novels by Frank Norris, *The Octopus* (1901) and *The Pit* (1903), deal with the North American end of this phenomenon.

ology among the working class. The nature of the French political system favoured existing tendencies towards a lack of discipline among socialist deputies and acted as a force limiting the homogeneity of the political wing of the socialist movement. To the extent that laissez faire ideas had never taken root in continental Europe to the same extent as in Britain and the USA, so the advance of socialist thought was aided, since in some aspects this represented a re-alignment of earlier patterns of social thought, rather than a later innovation.

The rise of the modern labour movement during the last quarter of the nineteenth century, represented the emergence of an entirely new phenomenon, radically and permanently altering the balance of power between the social classes. In each country a socialist party was formed. In each the socialist party soon polled votes in millions. Sometimes, as in Germany and also in Italy, the socialist party emerged as the largest single force on the parliamentary scene. The trade unions, which outside Britain scarcely existed in 1880, rose to 5 million strong by 1914 and reached some 15 million in 1919 in the aftermath of the First World War.[1] If socialist and trade union development had continued the upward march manifested between 1880 and 1910 then the advent of the socialist millennium might reasonably have been predicted for the 1930s and the 1940s. Instead the advance, speeded up by the First World War, subsequently halted and went into retreat during the inter war years. A number of key factors seem to have been responsible. The urbanization process slowed down. The rate of augmentation of the proletarian labour force declined or went down to zero. The labour movement met a solid confessional bloc against which it proved impossible to make further electoral progress. The divisions in the labour movement engendered by the foundation of the communist parties in the aftermath of the Russian Revolution also hindered its growth. Fear of the export of the Russian Revolution to Western Europe set off anti-democratic countermeasures. In the form of fascism and Nazism these triumphed in Italy and Germany. At times they also constituted a significant threat elsewhere.

The slowdown in the motor force of social progress was not without its effect on social democracy. Just as the emergence of a mass labour movement represented a real shift in the balance of social forces, so its institutionalization over time gave it vested interests to protect, both in the field of organization and political achievement, and in the job fiefs and expectations which went along with these things. In Germany in

1. Trade union membership, in 1914: Belgium, 200,000; France, 1m; Germany, 2m; Italy, 950,000; Netherlands, 225,000. By 1919 these figures had risen to Belgium, 750,000; France, 2·5m; Germany, 9m, Italy, 1·8m, Netherlands, 625,000: International Labour Office, Geneva, *Studies and Reports*, Series A, no. 17, 16 Feb. 1921, p. 2.

particular, and in varying degrees in other countries, the 'apparatus' developed a life of its own, with interests which by no means ran alongside those of the class it was supposed to defend and represent.[1] This was also true of the unions, the cooperatives and other working class organizations. All these were hard hit by the depression in the inter war years.

The dilemma of the socialist parties was particularly acute. They had created an organization, mustered a considerable vote, elected an important parliamentary delegation. They possessed real power. Whether they chose to lead, participate in, or oppose particular governments, their action, or inaction, could not be without effect on the social situation, the welfare of their supporters, and by implication the party's future hopes. The forces on which social democracy had relied to carry it over the top into a new society seemed to have halted their operation or even gone into reverse. In the event, social democracy, lacking an alternative strategy, or any adequate will to power, found itself increasingly assimilated into the existing socio-political system.

The whole situation was complicated by the appearance of communist parties, each an integral part of the Communist International, as major forces in France, Germany and Italy. The socialist parties and the unions in their original form represented an endeavour to express, articulate and enforce the short and long term interests of the working class. No doubt these interests were imperfectly perceived. No doubt the organizations themselves became to some extent corroded by the self interest of the bureaucratic apparatus they produced to serve their ends. The basic link between interest and organization was no less real for that. The communist parties introduced a factor of a rather different order. Allegedly the outcome of the 'betrayal' of the socialist parties in the First World War, they were, in fact, something a great deal more. Improvised in great haste, under the direction of the Russian Communist Party in Moscow, almost totally dependent on it for ideology and practical inspiration, they were also in most cases heavily dependent on it for finances with which to maintain their grossly inflated scale of operations. The communist parties thus became, without the intent of their founders either at home or in Moscow, a kind of arm of Russian state policy within the working class and socialist movement. In this they had much in common with the Christian trade union organizations which themselves represented an extended arm of the Vatican and the Church.

1. On this in particular, Landauer, *European Socialism*, pp. 482–6, also the illuminating remark of the German Socialist Ignaz Auer on the Bernstein controversy, quoted Walter Kendall, *The Revolutionary Movement in Britain, 1900–1921*, p. 10. The classic statement is Michels, *Democracy and Political Parties*.

The Christian organizations however did not set out to capture the *whole* labour movement and run it on Vatican instructions. As a rule they were content to accept a 'dual union' status. The communist parties claimed to possess a 'higher truth' of universal validity, embodied in the theory and practice of the Russian state. Policies derived from the paramount interests of this state they sought to impose on the labour movement in every country where they were to be found. The communist parties were thus strangely independent of their own social base and social environment: *in* particular countries but not, properly speaking, *of* them. Their behaviour could not be predicted on the basis of local causation but only by reference to the presumed interests of the ruling group in the Russian state. The policy of 'social fascism', which led the communists almost to welcome Hitler's assumption of power, is one example of a whole series that can only adequately be explained on this basis. That this development has done enormous harm to the development of the European labour movement there can be no doubt.

The other great factor of which socialist theory took no adequate account was that of war, for there can be no doubt that the great turning-points in the history of the European labour movement have been the two world wars. The effect of each war was vastly to increase the size and influence of mass trade union and socialist organizations. War brought down the Hohenzollern regime and installed the Weimar Republic in its place. War shattered the Austro-Hungarian Empire, redrew the map of Europe and in the process generated catastrophic social consequences over much of the continent. The First World War installed social democracy as the first or second party in most countries in Europe. In France and Italy at least the Second World War demoted the socialist parties to a secondary role and installed the communist parties as a dominant force in their place. German labour was split into two halves, one in the Federal Republic, the other under the Ulbricht regime. In the Federal Republic the pre-existing union divisions were overcome. A single union confederation, the DGB, emerged in their place. The influx of refugees from the East, the conduct of the East German regime, combined to eliminate the once powerful German Communist Party from the Federal Republic almost entirely.

Two world wars have shown conclusively that cataclysm alone is not sufficient to produce a social revolution. In the Europe of 1945 the consequence of catastrophe was prostration, not revolution, above all in Germany. Nor was there revolution in France and Italy, the two other countries in which the old ruling elite was most badly compromised by its dealings with fascism. Here the communists replaced the social democrats as the essential anchor of social stability. Only by means of their aid did the established order accomplish the difficult transition to a new normality and re-establish the old organs of state power, military and judiciary, substantially unchanged from an earlier age.[1] This was not a development which anyone could have prophesied in advance. More than any other single event it revealed the extent to which the communist party had emerged as a bureaucratic organism serving interests of its own, quite separate from those of its popular base.

In the post war years, after 1947 in particular, the European labour movement became a cockpit of the Cold War. Western Europe became a prize which could tip the scales either way in the global struggle between the USA and the USSR. In Germany the survival of the newly formed Federal Republic as a separate state was at issue. In France and Italy there was real concern that these countries might be assimilated to the Eastern bloc on the model of the Czech *coup* of 1948. The forcible imposition of Stalinist rule in Czechoslavakia, Poland, Eastern Germany and throughout Eastern Europe; the subsequent repression of socialist and all other parties, the suppression of free trade unions in the 'East'; the total subordination of the Western communist parties to the day-to-day interests of Russian policy all combined to give the struggle a particularly frenetic quality. The post war course of the labour movement could no longer be derived from analysis of the class forces at work in any given country. As the communist parties lined up alongside the Russian government, so, as a reaction, the socialist parties began to line up alongside the Americans. The communist parties now, as for twenty years past, were backed by a whole series of international front organizations, lavishly financed from the East.[2] Now the same phenomena began to appear on the other side. Where the Russian government and the MVD participated in the struggle on the communist side, the American state and the CIA participated on the other.[3] Mass labour organizations became a war-torn territory fought over by the intelligence organizations of either side. The resulting internecine warfare of the 1940s and 1950s is something from which the European labour movement has still to recover.

The Cold War, with its forced alliances on either side, stepped up the instrumentalization of trade union action in regard to the presumed interests of third parties in a most unfortunate fashion. Communist unions called strikes on any issue, irrespective of its merits, without consideration of their effects on the working class movement, provided only that their leaders considered that such strikes would serve the higher strategic interest of the Russian ruling elite. That being so, other

1. For one view on this see Kendall, 'McInnes and social democracy', *Survey*, summer 1969, pp. 86–90.

2. For a critique of the WFTU as a Russian agency, see Donahue, *Focus on a Communist Front*.

3. For the most exhaustive, easily accessible account of the 'Western' end of this affair, 'Is your union affiliated to the CIA?', *Voice of the Unions*, London, May 1967, pp. 4–5.

organizations were under the strongest pressure to refuse support for all communist-led stoppages, for exactly the same reason. The communist misuse of the unions as a 'transmission belt to the masses' tended to produce a similar phenomenon on the part of their opponents.

Instrumentalization of the unions was not a totally new phenomenon. In those countries where the foundation of the socialist party had preceded that of the unions, these had in the early days usually been regarded, in part at least, as recruiting agents for the party, a means by which the party might extend its influence over the less conscious sections of the working class. In Russia during the 1920s the unions had little by little been stripped of every vestige of independence and reduced to appendages of the state and party machine. In Italy under Mussolini, in Germany under Hitler, the trade unions had been dissolved and replaced by 'Labour Front' style organizations which were no more than state agencies for the management and control of the labour force. Membership of the 'Labour Front' became the precondition for a whole series of direct and indirect benefits. That this experience in both cases contributed to internal union passivity and strengthened pre-existing tendencies of upward deference towards official union leaders seems very likely.

The unions in any case, especially in Germany, had established considerable assets in their own right, a fact which gave them a sound reason for hesitating over courses of action which might put these assets in jeopardy. In Belgium and the Netherlands another factor tended towards the domestication of union leadership. Parliamentary pressure had acquired for the unions special status as agencies for the payment of unemployment benefit. The state undertook to subsidize union unemployment funds in case of need. To the unions, therefore, rising unemployment meant not a fall in membership but an increase, not the threat of bankruptcy but on the contrary a guarantee of financial stability. Yet what the state might confer, government might also take away. The general conduct of union affairs could not fail to be influenced by an awareness of this fact.[1] In a similar fashion, but on a far less important scale, all unions in France, the CGT included, accept state aid for their educational programme.[2] The same holds true for the DGB in Germany and the TUC in Britain.[3] In the Netherlands after the war part at least of the attraction of super-centralized bargaining conducted between

1. On this, for example, Trotsky's criticism of the Netherlands revolutionary trade union leader Henriek Sneevliet, in Trotsky, *The Writings of Leon Trotsky*, p. 133.

2. On this see, Marcel David, 'Universities and workers' education in France', *International Labour Review*, Feb. 1970, pp. 109–32.

3. On this, in part, see Deutsche Gewerkschaftsbund, *The Educational Activities within the German Federation of Trade Unions*, pp. 30–32. In the same way the German political parties, including the SPD, receive a state subsidy in

a government with socialist participation and the Catholic, socialist and Protestant union confederations was that it enabled all parties concerned to combine against the threat of the new union confederation EVC, which each, for its own reasons, wished to shut out from the game. Similarly, just as in Eastern Europe only communist-controlled 'unions' are permitted, so, in France and Italy in particular, governments have favoured unions belonging to FO, CISL, and UIL, as against those apertaining to the communist controlled CGT and CGIL.

If government has shown a bias against communist-led unions there can be no doubt that the communists themselves have a vested interest in keeping unions weak, holding union autonomy within limits pre-determined by the exigencies of external communist party control. Strong communist parties and weak unions go together. Weak unions, unable to finance their activity by dues income alone, become in the nature of things a dependency of the party apparatus. The fact that neither the CGT nor the CGIL, each of which goes to great length to acquire the reputation of a militant union, possesses strike funds, is but one manifes-tation of this situation. The formal argument that large strike funds lead to conservatism can hardly be taken seriously, not least when the United Auto Workers have recently conducted a ten-week stoppage against General Motors, in which over 390,000 workers participated.[1] The truth is that the longer a strike continues the more it tends to generate forces of its own, the more difficult it becomes to use for purely instrumental party aims. The party is interested in short, sharp stoppages, for political objectives. Long-drawn-out slogging matches which win big economic gains *raise* the status of union leaders and *devalue* that of communist party functionaries. The absence of strike funds makes the conduct of union stoppages dependent on propaganda campaigns for financial aid mounted and controlled by the party apparatus. This in turn serves to limit union autonomy and enhance the power of party bureaucrats over the administration of union affairs. Autonomous and financially inde-pendent unions challenge the view that the workers and their organiza-tions, afflicted with 'false consciousness', are unfit to manage their own affairs, that only a party politbureau, endowed with some power of mystic infallibility, is fit to decide the 'true interest' of the working class. Weak unions are eminently suited for instrumental use, strong unions are not. No proper understanding of the union situation in France and Italy can be achieved without a recognition of this fact.

Other factors remain to be stressed. The separation of the state and the economy in Europe has never been as wide as in Britain and the

1. From 7 Sept. to 12 Nov. 1971.

proportion to the vote they poll in general elections. In Britain the aid is indirect via the use of facilities made available by the WEA, University Extra-Mural Departments and other institutions.

USA.[1] Nor has the relation between unions and the socialist movement been the same. In the early years of the labour movement union bargaining power in continental Europe was weaker than in Britain. The degree of socialist representation in parliament was a great deal stronger. Up to the present time, unions, unable to win demands on their own account, have often achieved them through mass pressure and legislative action.[2] The large public demonstrations which accompany major trade union claims in Italy should not be seen as particularly radical gestures, as some observers seem to believe. On the contrary they are a means of influencing public opinion, of exercising political pressure to persuade employers to settle claims which the unions themselves are unable to enforce by industrial action. As a result the interpenetration of political and union activity is usually a great deal higher in continental Europe than in Britain or the USA.[3]

The assumption, implicit in most Anglo-American discussions of industrial relations, that the union is to be understood as solely or primarily a wage bargaining institution is a questionable one. Even in Britain and the USA, countries in which the unions' wage bargaining role has been primary, the very presence of the unions has introduced new elements into the political game. The scope for freedom of operation open to governments of whatever political persuasion has been limited as a result. The briefest consideration of relations between government and unions during the First and Second World Wars should make this plain. In the United States the organization of mass production industry, the establishment of the CIO, was certainly not without significance for the fortunes of the Democratic Party. The CIO provided a countervailing force to the hitherto unchallenged power of the corporate giants in auto and steel. This in itself was an economic fact of real political significance. Strong unions possess great economic bargaining power. The exercise of this power, irrespective of the subjective wishes or intentions of union leaders, cannot fail to exercise important influence over a whole range of political decisions.

In a state such as Italy, where the collective bargaining system is weak, intervention by means of political strikes and demonstrations may be one of the few functional modes of operation open to working people. Conversely, given the highly disfunctional nature of Italian political institutions, extra-parliamentary pressure may be one of the few ways in which the ordinary population can force the lumbering legislative

1. Thus Britain was the only country in Europe to build its railways solely by means of private capitalist endeavour.
2. For example the Matignon Agreement, the legal enactment of the forty-hour week, which followed the 1936 sit-downs in France, the changes which have followed the French events of May 1968, the *Statuto dei Lavoratori* which followed the Italy's 'hot autumn' of 1969.
3. Germany is a probable exception.

machine into action. Belgium is a nation divided between geographically separate populations of Flemings and Walloons. If the assumption of office by the king of such a state is unacceptable to almost half the nation, then a political general strike may become a highly functional measure, without which the disintegration of a whole society may result. In France, where employers deny union recognition and refuse to concede justified demands which unions lack the strength to enforce, spontaneous uprisings like those of 1936 and 1968 may prove the only way in which rank and file pressure can override union rivalry and incompetence, break employer resistance and achieve improved wages and conditions of labour. The shift from a high strike record under Weimar to a low one under the Federal Republic is in part to be explained by the level of pauperization of a ruined post war Germany. Yet one must take account too of Germany's position as a front line nation in the Cold War, the ever present 'menace' of East Germany beyond the wall, which sets predetermined limits to the level of acceptable social conflict within the borders of the Federal Republic. Such external factors, automatically excluded from a narrow collective bargaining approach, are crucial to the understanding of the behaviour of labour in continental Europe.

The limits of effective bargaining are set, too, not only by union strength and capability, but also by employer attitudes and willingness to 'bargain in good faith'. Experience in Britain and the USA shows that a great deal of violence and suffering may be required before employers can be 'broken in' to accept union intrusion into hitherto unchallenged areas of entrepreneurial autonomy. In France and Italy at any rate, this breakthrough does not seem yet to have been made. Employers' associations, especially in France, Germany and Italy, and to a lesser extent perhaps in the other countries, are not ideologically neutral, exclusively wage bargaining bodies. Their attitude to union bargaining is conditioned by their political outlook. Their views of desirable economic policy are influenced by ideology. Frequently they possess quite open and specific ties with newspapers, political parties and other organizations designed to influence or determine public opinion. If employers' associations are dominated by a multiplicity of small businesses, they may seek to safeguard the marginal employer by linking bargaining to *rates* rather than *earnings*. Larger corporations are then left free to bid superior quality labour into the market by unilaterally offering wages above the negotiated rates. Such tactics undermine union credibility and limit the extent of union organization within their plants. Factors of this kind seem to be at work in both France and Italy.

The Netherlands, a society with a long standing oligarchic tradition, a small state within which giant corporations such as Philips, Shell, Hoogovens and Unilever can exercise disproportionate influence, stands at the other end of the scale. Here one has seen over a number of years the persistence of a highly centralized national wage policy, one which would have proved quite impossible in other countries where the unique features of the Netherlands social matrix do not appear. However caution is needed here. Centralized wage decision in a small nation with a workforce of 4·5 million is not at all the same thing as a centralized wage bargain in a state with a workforce of 27 million like the German Federal Republic or 81 million as in the USA. There must be a number of industry wide bargains in both Britain and the USA which cover almost as many workers as the central bargain at the level of the Netherlands national economy.

At first sight the organization of most confederations in Europe, based as they are on industrial union lines, seems more precise and logical than that of their counterparts in either Britain's TUC or America's AFL. The advantages of more coherent organization are, however, largely dissipated by confessional and political divisions. In every country except the Federal Republic there are two, three or more industrial unions competing for membership in the same jurisdiction. The hostility provoked by these divisions has on occasion made an old-line AFL craft dispute seem like a summer holiday outing. Duplication of union organization leads to bloated staffing, and increased organizational costs, weakens bargaining potential and strengthens the position of bureaucracy as against the rank and file. Yet even these ideological and confessional divisions ought not to be taken entirely at their face value. Subsumed behind some of them, one suspects, are craft, industrial, white collar preferences of exactly the same order as in Britain and the USA.

Experience has shown that industrial union territories are easier to envisage in theory than to lay down in practice. The boundaries of rail transport and coal mining are fairly easy to define. In other cases the problem is not so simple. As a result unions like the metal-workers and the public service employees which have something of a 'catch all' jurisdiction have grown much larger than others in which the sector boundaries can be more closely defined. The consequent predominance of two or three major unions in each confederation has not been entirely without merit, since it acts as a break on the centralizing ambitions of confederation leadership. One needs to remember too that the nature of union democracy cannot always be fully comprehended by reference to the statutes alone. The rules of CGT and CGIL make no provision for leadership and control by members of the communist parties of France and Italy. Yet it is in the decisions of the PCF and PCI, rather than in the respective union congresses, that the key to union behaviour is to be found.

Collective bargaining in continental Europe has a greater legal content than in Britain or even the USA. In part this is derived from a cultural tradition in which the state has been accustomed to regulate aspects of the job relation by reference to a long standing concern for the welfare of the citizen which antedates his status as a wage worker or an employee.[1] In part, too, this attitude springs from the use of legislation to resolve issues which the unions felt unable to settle by collective action on their own account. Perhaps the most important example is the works council legislation, which in one form or another exists in all the continental European states.

Works councils, as a rule obligatory by law, exist in each country of the original Six: *comités d'entreprises* in France, *conseils d'entreprises* in Belgium, *ondernemingsraads* in the Netherlands, *commissione interne* in Italy, *delegations d'employés* in Luxembourg and *betriebsrat* in Germany.[2] In France, Belgium and the Netherlands the employer sits in the chair, a provision which markedly undermines works council independence and authority. The constitution of the German *betriebsrat* prescribes 'co-operation in a spirit of mutual trust having regard to the common good'. The constitutions of the works councils in other countries contain generally similar clauses. In general works councils possess limited powers of consultation, sometimes amounting to a temporary veto on layoffs and dismissals, some say in hiring, a say in the formulation of works rules, the authority to supervise the application of legally obligatory safety regulations, plus those aspects of the union agreement which have validity at plant level. In France the *comités d'entreprises* often administer large and important social funds in respect of canteens and recreation facilities. In terms of power and influence, the German *betriebsrat* are the most important. In nearly every case (except the German) the constitution ascribes to the works council some consultative functions in regard to the management of the enterprise. These provisions have remained a dead letter. Experience suggests that without independent union organization the works councils are unable to carry out effectively even the limited tasks allotted to them by the law.

More important for the operation of the enterprise than the works council legislation, either in Germany or elsewhere, are the *Mitbestimmung*, co-determination provisions, which apply to the coal, iron and steel industries in the Federal Republic. The *Mitbestimmung* law gives 50 per cent representation on the supervisory board and one executive director out of three to nominees of German workers and their unions. The extension of these provisions to all large enterprises in the Federal Repub-

1. On this see Benenstein and Levenbach in Kahn-Freund *et al.*, *Labour Law in Europe*, pp. 17–23, 31.
2. For an easily accessible reference see ICFTU, *How Your Union Works*, pp. 117–23, also ILO, *Participation of Workers in Decisions Within Undertakings*, Geneva, 1969. The *commissione interne* arise from a confederal agreement.

lic is a major aim of the German union confederation DGB. The German unions also wish to see similar *Mitbestimmung* provisions included in any European company law that may eventually be approved by the Community.

The Community itself, now in its second decade and enlarged by the adhesion of Britain, Denmark and Ireland, is already making its impact felt on the scale and nature of union operation in Europe. The Community sprang from fears that the European mainland, in a state of economic and social prostration at the end of the war, but still the greatest centre of industrial production outside the USA and the USSR, might fall, through internal divisions, into the Russian orbit. Once it had been decided to re-activate the German economy and to include contingents from a new German army into the NATO forces, a number of consequential measures followed, designed to limit the capacity of a revived Germany once again to dominate continental Europe. German heavy industry was integrated with that of the rest of the Six by the establishment of the European Coal and Steel Community (ECSC) in 1952. A course was set towards full economic, and possible eventual political, unification, by the Treaty of Rome which came into effect in 1958.

Progress towards unification posed real problems for the labour movements of the Six.[1] The breakdown of barriers between national product markets made likely serious shifts in sector labour demand, perhaps also the shift of whole branches of industry from one country to another. Free movement of labour posed problems of a similar order. The bureaucratic character of the Community, its lack of responsibility to any representative federal institutions, also caused the unions much concern. In the union view this left the Commission far too open to business influence, without any adequate countervailing force either from labour or from the population at large. As a result the unions have constantly pressed for greater representation in Community affairs and also for the establishment of federal institutions better able to supervise the activities of the Commission.[2] The unions, too, have sought to influence the proposed statute for a European company, a device which, it is feared, with some justification, could enable German employers in heavy industry to circumvent *Mitbestimmung* provisions by switching their statutes to those of the European company, when once it is inaugurated.[3] Finally, the ECTU has been set up to co-ordinate action not only within the Community but also in its new extended form between all unionists in

1. For one view on this, Kendall, *Mercato Comune e Movimento Operaio in Europa*.
2. ECTU unions are seriously considering deploying 'all available resources in order to hinder the further development of the Economic and Monetary Union if trade union conditions in this regard are not fulfilled'.
3. For the ECTU proposals, Braun, 'The European Company', *Free Labour World*, Brussels, June 1970, pp. 15–17.

Europe, including the Scandinavians, the Swiss and the Austrians. The ITS, similarly, are beginning a move to establish special European sections within the framework of their more global operations.

The labour movement from its very beginnings had placed great stress on internationalism. Moral fervour was great, organizational support enormously weaker. Socialist and trade union organizations in the first decade of the present century were far less powerful than at the present time. The resources of the Bureau of the Socialist International were more appropriate to a postal clearing house than to an international organization seriously able to influence the course of events. The war of 1914–18 swept the Socialist International aside. In retrospect one is less surprised at the collapse than at the fact that so many otherwise perceptive historians appear to believe that it could have been otherwise. The Socialist International never recovered from its failure to fulfil exaggerated hopes in 1914. The Communist International substituted for the international solidarity of workers in all lands one with another the overriding duty of workers everywhere, always and in all circumstances, unhesitatingly to support the Russian state.[1] Internationalism was redefined as Great Russian chauvinism. The truth would seem to be that it was difficult for the *ideal* of international brotherhood to have much effective significance as long as most of the immediate and medium term economic *interests* of the workers were intractably bound up with those of the nation state. The growing unification of the European economy, the increasing significance of the multi-national company, have now begun to bring principle and ideal more closely into line.

In such circumstances the existing pattern of union organization, already absurdly divided before corporate economic interest on the national plane, becomes quite obsolete. The multi-national company may plan investment, fix prices, allocate markets to plants, co-ordinate collective bargaining policy, all on the same European scale. The unions need to co-ordinate the views of never less than five or six national union federations or confederations, perhaps as many as ten or twelve, before they can present a common front. The justification for union organization at national level has been the decisive significance of the nation state as an arena within which industrial and political decisions affecting the workforce take place. As economic barriers within the Community come down, especially if, as projected, a unified currency is introduced in the 1980s, so the predominant role of national union centres will be undermined. In the end perhaps the national union centres will be more involved with political–industrial issues settled at the level of the national economy than with industrial bargaining itself.

One might legitimately anticipate two main lines of union develop-

1. On this in particular, the excellent statement of the communist view by Joseph R. Starobin in Calmann, ed., *Western Europe*, p. 300.

CONCLUSION 327

ment. First, an increasing integration of national unions into something approaching an 'International Industrial Union' on the lines of the ITS. These 'International Industrial Unions' would be empowered to levy limited funds on their own account. They would conduct negotiations around specifically defined matters of a general nature at global and European level, dealing both with the Commission and with companies in the EEC. In the case of Europe-wide companies this would raise the unions to the same level of organizational integration as their adversaries. In the case of smaller companies operating in only one or two of the Community nations, it might confer on the unions significant advantages. An 'International Industrial Union', able to gross up Europe-wide re-sources against an employer operating only in a single territory, would deploy bargaining power which the employers' associations of some whole nations would find it difficult to resist. The Teamsters Union in the United States achieved remarkable successes with the 'over the road' contract, originated in Minneapolis, in precisely this fashion.[1] There are large-scale gains awaiting collection by the unions just as soon as they can learn to overcome outdated divisions and organize at the level which the working of the economy itself demands.

Alongside this development of Europe-wide framework bargaining would go a decentralization to new areas, no longer exclusively demarcated by national boundaries. Contiguous regions of Belgium and France or Luxembourg, France and Germany, maybe larger areas, might be brought into a natural bargaining net defined by economic circumstance. Plant and enterprise bargaining, too, would assume far greater importance than now in the general scheme of things. More bargaining would take place both *above* and *below* national level. National unions and national confederations would become more concerned with those aspects of social security, safety, taxation, employment policy, etc., which remained the preserve of national government, where the workforce would continue to need powerful and effective representation.

The meetings which have already taken place between the European Metal Workers Federation of the IMF and Philips top management at Eindhoven; the decision of the International Union of Food and Allied Workers Associations to set up a World Council of Nestlé Workers' Unions are some examples of the course events are likely to follow.[2] As long ago as 1969 ICF affiliated unions in ten countries prepared a common front of workers employed by the giant French glass conglomerate San Gobain. Unions in France, Germany, Italy and the USA agreed to provide mutual financial support, guaranteed solidarity action in case of need and set up a joint co-ordinating committee in

1. On this James and James, *Hoffa and the Teamsters*, pp. 89–101, 122–4.
2. *Report of World Conference of Nestlé Workers*, IUF, Geneva, May 1972. 'EMF meets Philips', *IMF News*, Geneva, June 1972, p. 3.

constant session via phone and cable. It was agreed that no final settlement in negotiations in any one country would be made without prior
consultations and agreement by the joint committee. Co-ordinated
international bargaining brought marked successes, the US company
finally settling on the basis of the profitable world accounts other than on
its own far less profitable balance sheet.[1] Since then ICF multi-national
councils have extended greatly, the meeting of the ICF's Dunlop–
Pirelli World Council in June 1972 in particular commanding widespread attention. Multi-national plant and company councils have
already become part of the common currency of trades unionism in
Europe. The level of internationally co-ordinated common action is
likely to rise still further in the future.

The need to raise unionism to the level of the Common Market and
the existing capitalist institutions questions the legitimacy of the confessional and political divisions which continue to divide organized
workers within Europe one from another. These divisions now rest
more on artificial than on natural grounds. The confessional issue, in
union terms, remains important only in Belgium and the Netherlands.
The nuances which continue to separate the ECTU and the WCL at
European level are, to most observers, scarcely visible. The Italian communist-led CGIL and the French communist-led CGT have both
abandoned their original all out opposition to the Community.[2] There
are already signs that the Russian state is softening its previous hostility
to the EEC.[3] In that case, we shall see the communist parties abandon their criticism too, well before the 1970s are over. In the event
that a communist party gained admission to the cabinet of either France
or Italy, a prompt about-turn could be expected almost as a matter of
course.

The Ford Antwerp–Genk parity dispute of winter 1969 illustrated
quite well the obsolescence of instrumental union divisions in the era of
the multi-national company. The Christian union which enjoyed majority
status at Genk nevertheless needed to call up assurances of support
from Ford workers in Britain and Germany who stood outside the ranks
of the WCL. The same problem will arise for CGIL members in
FIAT and for CGT (and CFDT) members in Renault when once
these companies broaden, as they must, their interests in the EEC.

1. On this *inter alia see* Charles Levinson, *International Trade Unionism*,
London, 1972, pp. 8–21.
2. Since 1967 the Italian CGIL and the French CGT have maintained a
joint Standing Committee for Liaison and Initiative in Brussels so as to keep in
contact with the organs of the Community. For an account see *Bulletin of the
CGT–CGIL Standing Committee*, no. 1, Brussels, May 1967. See also *Agenor*
Brussels, Nov.–Dec. 1971, pp. 7–8.
3. On this 'Moscow less hostile to the Community?', *European Community*,
London, May 1972, pp. 12–13.

The ties which bind some Belgian and Netherlands trade unions to the ex-Christian WCL and some French and Italian unions to the WFTU are similar, and all of an instrumental order. The affiliation of CGT and CGIL to the Russian-dominated WFTU brings their members no tangible benefit. The WFTU has no other affiliate in Europe and scarcely any other of importance in the capitalist world. This same affiliation, isolates the CGT and CGIL from other unions and positively disrupts prospects of Europern union unity. Nevertheless the Russian 'unions' which dominate the WFTU, the native communist parties which stand behind both CGT and CGIL, oppose disaffiliation. A WFTU without the CGT and CGIL would leave the Russians without any union propaganda base in Western Europe. In the case of the Christian unions and the WCL, the Church and the Vatican stand in place of the communists and the Russian state. Without Belgian and Netherlands affiliates, the credibility of the WCL would vanish. It is forces outside the labour movement, rather than those intrinsic to its operation, which in this case, as in the other, are responsible for the continuing divisions amongst European labour.

Instrumental use of unions by political parties rests on the premiss, sometimes open, sometimes concealed, that workers do not have either the education or the good sense to run their own organizations for themselves. As a result intellectuals, Christian or communists, are to decide by institutionalized means what is best for the workers to whom they presume to stand in loco parentis.[1] The essential arrogance of this view is well expressed in Lenin's almost octogenarian chestnut, What is to be Done? 'Social-Democratic consciousness among the workers . . . could only be brought to them from without.' 'The history of all countries shows that the working class, exclusively by its own effort, is able to develop only trade union consciousness.'[2] Lenin's implicit assumption that the working class is a tabula rasa in the field of ideas, without either sense of class consciousness or traditions of struggle derived from human experience in an earlier age, a class homogeneous and not varied in composition, without specific national or regional characteristics, is too self-evidently erroneous to require refutation here. This piece of middle class condescension may have possessed relevance for a half formed proletariat in Russia scarcely one generation removed from serfdom. It certainly has very little relevance for the working class with close on a century's tradition of self-organization and activity, as it exists in Western Europe today. In any case, ideas once received are self-acting in the popular mind. They assume a development of their own in the light

1. For the communist version see Stalin, Problems of Leninism, pp. 77–8, 131–2; Otto Kuusinen, 'International Press Correspondence', vol. vi, no. 28, April 1926.
2. Lenin, What is to be Done?, pp. 32–3.

of social experience. There is no intrinsic reason why socialist (or Christian) ideas, once accepted by the working class movement, should not thereafter be self-generating. In the light of this any intellectually credible justification for either communist or Christian paternalism flies out of the window.

The fundamental factor, largely unperceived, which underlies the halt in the strategic advance of working class and socialist influence in Europe has been the failure of social forces to move the real power index forward in favour of the working class in the years after 1920, as they had done before. This in turn seems to have been rooted in peasant immobility, the conservative attitudes, and sometimes the confessionalism, with which it is closely linked. Three quarters of farmers in the original Six still vegetate on unprofitable holdings,[1] whilst producing unmarketable surpluses which cost as much a year as the Americans spent to reach the moon. It has been estimated that if the 1970 rate of increase were to continue the surplus budget would soon suffice to put a man on Mars.[2] Yet the advent of the Common Market has not been without effect. The agricultural population of the original Six has shrunk by ten million in the last twenty years and is planned to diminish a further five million by 1980. A revised common agricultural policy, with proper human safeguards, ought to prove capable of liquidating this legacy of the past. British entry is likely to prove an important incentive. Over the medium term, a run down of the peasantry is likely to produce a shift in the internal balance of power and remove much of the socio-economic underpinning of the '33⅓ per cent barrier'. A shift in the social balance of power could give further impetus to the renewal of existing organizations of the labour movement which is in some cases already under way. Among the younger generation the myth of the Russian Revolution, and with it the mystique of the orthodox communist parties, has already lost much of its fascination. The communist parties themselves are becoming so discredited that it is difficult to see anything but an era of gradual decline ahead. Even now it is the incompetence of their rivals rather than any innate merit of their own that enables them still to wield the influence that they do.

Yet in retrospect it would be folly not to recognize that an important part of the doctrine of 'scientific socialism' has ended as utopia. The so-called 'socialist' regimes are no more than crude dictatorships which for

1. The average size of farms in the nations of the Nine is: United Kingdom 85 acres, Denmark 48 acres, France 47 acres, Luxembourg 43 acres, Ireland 41 acres, Netherlands 27 acres, Federal Republic 26 acres, Belgium 26 acres, Italy 18 acres, *Farming Facts, the EEC and the Four*, Barclays Bank, London, Booklet no. 2, Dec. 1971, p. 9.

2. Sicco Mansholt, at this time Vice-President of the Commission of the EEC, 'Farm reform', *European Community*, Nov. 1970, p. 9.

a generation have used police measures to hold down public consumption for the benefit of state accumulation. The identification of these regimes with the cause of socialism has done the whole labour movement enormous harm. Failing a clear and bold critique, this damage is likely to prove irreparable. A socialist critique of the activities of the entrepreneurial bourgeoisie in a relatively free society, however valid in itself, lacks credibility when the onlooker, with some justification, perceives the proferred alternative as rule by a materialist theocracy backed by a ruthless and all-powerful secret police.

The truth seems to be that the early socialists, Marx and Engels in particular, were motivated by a somewhat simplified view of the fashion in which power could meaningfully be transferred from an entrepreneurial bourgeoisie to the working class. The bourgeosie attained its dominance in a process extended over centuries. Marx anticipated already in 1848 that the death knell of capitalism was about to sound. Yet such a fore-shortened time scale could scarcely be justified, least of all by reference to his own precedents. The lesson of nationalization in the West and total state ownership in the East seems to be that working class rule does not arrive simply by the expropriation of part or the whole of the bourgeoisie. In each case the wage labour, employee–employer relation remains substantially unchanged. Ownership, to be meaningful, cannot be separated from control.

In the West, hopes that parliamentary gradualism would over time *fundamentally* transform society have so far proved unfulfilled. There is little reason to suppose that parliamentary gradualism alone will succeed in the future where it failed in the past. In the East the Leninist–Stalinist model, despite all its boastful claims abroad, lacks the confidence even to put them to the test of a single free election at home. The failures of Social Democracy are used to justify the crimes of Stalinism. The crimes of Stalinism are used to justify the failure of Social Democracy fundamentally to transform the *status quo*. Clearly something new, different from both, is urgently required. The use of aggressive unionism steadily to encroach on entrepreneurial authority, prerogative and control, may here serve to provide the so far missing link between reform and revolution.[1] Already it seems reasonable to suggest that the emergence of powerful unions as centres of independent economic power, *within* the bourgeois state, has forced the ruling class to make a surrender, so far unlegitimized, of an important part of its power. Aggressive bargaining and encroaching control, backed and supported by legislative measures, may indeed, in the next decades, begin radically to transform our society. To the extent that the workforce challenges entrepreneurial decision, beginning a shift from autocracy to democracy in the plant, so

1. For one (Swedish) view on this, see Geijer, 'Industrial democracy in the seventies', *Free Labour World*, April 1971, pp. 15–18.

it prepares the workers themselves to assume the responsibility for entrepreneurial decisions.

In the scale of history the advance in socio-economic power achieved by the organized labour movement in this century has been nothing less than stupendous. Given the use of intelligence and foresight, the transformation in the course of the next half century is likely to be no less.

Statistical Appendix

LIVING CONDITIONS INDICATORS

TRADE UNION MEMBERSHIP

UNEMPLOYMENT

INDUSTRIAL DISPUTES

SOCIALIST PARTY MEMBERSHIP

COMMUNIST PARTY MEMBERSHIP

SOCIALIST AND COMMUNIST ELECTION RESULTS

IMMIGRANTS AND FOREIGN WORKERS

The choice of the Europe-wide indices was made by Walter Kendall, who also undertook the initial research. A large part of the data was assembled by Bob Holton, originally of the University of Sussex, and latterly of the University of Glasgow. Further material was collected, the difficult and time consuming task of filling gaps in the data, undertaken by Tony Carew of the University of Sussex. Tony Carew was also responsible for the collation of the data into Europe wide tables.

Attention is drawn to the fact that the reliability of these statistics is uneven and that some sets of statistics are incomplete. The figures shown in the overall compilations in particular should be regarded as illustrative rather than precise. Thus in regard to Italy and France, the figures of trade union membership shown are usually those claimed by unions. These often overstate the true figures by a very wide margin. National unemployment statistics do not conform to standard criteria. All are likely to exclude 'uninsured' unemployed, thus on occasion materially understating the true total. In short, although the author and his aides have gone to very great pains to assemble the most comprehensive possible set of data they recognize that the final result is necessarily imperfect. Further refinement would have been utterly beyond the very limited economic resources at their disposal. In the event that funds are forthcoming the author would hope to elaborate the data further. In the meantime the reader should bear these factors in mind when forming value judgements based on the data provided.

Living Conditions Indicators

HOURS OF WORK (APRIL 1971)
Basic weekly working hours as laid down by law and by collective agreement in major manufacturing sectors, and average hours actually worked

	Basic working week[1]		Average hours worked[2]
	by legislation	by collective agreement	
Belgium	45	42–44	42·2
France	40[3]	40–41¼	44·6
Germany	48	40–41	42·9
Italy	48	40–43	42·2
Luxemburg	44½	41–44	42·4
Netherlands	48	40–43¾	43·8
UK	—	39½–40½	44·9[4]

[1] Adult workers.
[2] All workers.
[3] Nominal total only, providing basis for overtime payments.
[4] October 1970, men over 21 only.
SOURCES: EEC and Department of Employment; quoted in EEC Information Office, 'The Common Market and the Common Man', p. 16.

PAID HOLIDAYS
Situation in April 1971 for adult workers in industry

	Legal minimum (working weeks)[1]	Minimum under collective agreements (working weeks)[1] [2]	Supplementary holidays (days)[3]	Public holidays (days)
Belgium	3	rare	rare	10
France	4	4	6	8–10
Germany	2½–3	3–4	6	10–13
Italy	2½	2½–3	6	17
Luxemburg	3–4	—	rare	10
Netherlands	3	3–3½	6	7
UK	—	sometimes 2 generally 3	n.a.	6

[1] Working week may be of 5 or 6 days.
[2] Varies according to industry
[3] Maximum additional days granted under collective agreements in some industries according to age and length of employment.
SOURCES: EEC and Department of Employment; quoted in EEC Information Office, 'The Common Market and the Common Man', p. 17.

UNIONS IN EUROPE – STATISTICAL SUMMARY 1900–1968

Years	France[10] CGT	CFTC/CFDT	CGT–FO	Germany Socialist	Christian	Italy[12] CGIL	CISL	UIL
1904	150,000			1,052,000	—	—		
1910	357,000			2,017,000	316,000	302,000		
1914	400,000[3]			2,075,000	218,000	320,000		
1918-21[5]	2,000,000	140,000		7,570,000	1,000,000	2,200,000		
1931[6]	736,000	70,000[4]		4,418,000	678,000			
1937	4,743,000	500,000	—	—	—			
1946	5,579,000	365,000		—		4,680,000		
1950	3,993,000	330,000	400,000[6]	5,449,000		4,782,000	1,489,000	40(
1959	1,000,000	650,000	400,000	6,273,000		3,600,000	2,357,000	50(
1966	1,200,000	500,000	400,000	6,537,000		3,347,000	2,000,000[4]	1,50(
1968	1,300,000[4]	700,000[4]	500,000[4]	6,375,000		1,700,000[4]	1,200,000[4]	30(

NOTES
[1] 1900 figure.
[2] 1909 figure.
[3] 1912 figure.
[4] Estimate. In the case of France and Italy, estimates rather than claims are included for the year 1968, in the hope that this will aid the reader to obtain a better overall appreciation.
[5] The peak post war year has been taken: France 1920: Germany – socialist and Husch-Duncker 1921, Christian 1919; Italy 1920; Britain 1919; Belgium FGTB 1920; Netherlands (NVV) 1920; Denmark 1920; In the case of Belgium, CSC (1923), Netherlands NKV and NV C(1921), the only years for which details were available.
[6] The figures for France and for the Netherlands NVV are for 1930.
[7] 1947 figures.
[8] The total is an underestimate since although no figures were available for inclusion in

in	Belgium		Netherlands[9]			Denmark	Total
	CSC	FGTB	NVV	NKV	CNV	LO	
,000	14,000	31,000[1]	—	—	—	65,000	2,853,000
,000	49,000[2]	68,000	41,000	12,000	7,000	102,000	5,055,000
,000	123,000	129,000	80,000	29,000	11,000	121,000	6,266,000
,000	150,000[1]	688,000	247,000	146,000	73,000	279,000	21,223,000
,000	239,000	522,000	251,000	190,000[4]	100,000[4]	270,000	11,268,000
,000	305,000	546,000	283,000	190,000[4]	118,000[4]	452,000	11,597,000
,000	402,000	612,000	242,000	224,000[7]	119,000[7]	605,000	20,368,000[8]
,000	567,000	631,000	381,000	296,000	155,000	656,000	27,356,000
,000	737,000	723,000	476,000	395,000	218,000	740,000	25,997,000
,000	872,000	770,000[11]	535,000	419,000	234,000	835,000	27,944,000
,000	920,000	800,000	559,000	423,000	241,000	865,000	24,767,000

the table the trade unions were already established in each of the four occupational zones of Germany.

[9] The Netherlands figures take no account of the union confederation EVC which claimed 176,000 members in 1945. The figures for the immediate post war years are thus something of an understatement.

[10] This table takes no account of CGTU membership of which details have proved difficult or impossible to obtain. The figures for the years 1920–1934 are thus something of an understatement.

[11] 1967 figure.

[12] The Italian figures for the years up to 1921 take no account of the Christian union CIL for which figures have not been forthcoming. Italian union membership for these years is thus somewhat understated.

The national tables, equally the Europe wide table, exclude specifically white collar unions, independent of the various national confederations.

Trade Union Membership

FRANCE *General – 1894–1910*

Year	Total workers organized	CGT membership
1894	404,440	—
1896	422,777	—
1898	437,793	—
1900	491,647	—
1902	614,173	—
1904	715,576	150,000
1906	836,134	203,273
1908	957,102	294,398
1910	977,350	357,814

SOURCE: *Annuaire des syndicats professionels*, 1911. Quoted in J. A. Estey, *Revolutionary Syndicalism*, London, 1913, pp. 33, 48.

Years	CGT	CFTC/CFDT	CGT-FO
1904	150,000		
1906	203,273		
1908	294,398		
1910	357,814		
1912	400,000		
1918	2,000,000		
1919	2,000,000	140,000	
1920	2,000,000		
1921	1,000,000		
1930	736,800		
1934	600,000	100,000	
1936	1,043,000	150,000	
1937	4,743,000	500,000	
1939	2,000,000	303,000	
1940	800,000		
1945	4,500,000	300,000	
1946	5,579,000	365,000	
1947	5,480,257	380,000	
1948	4,079,943	385,000	2,000,000
1949	3,887,412	320,000	
1950	3,993,800	330,000	
1951	3,076,211	335,000	
1952	2,505,357	350,000	
1953	1,500,000	340,000	
1959	1,000,000	650,000	400,000
1961	1,722,000	471,000	
1963	1,773,000	562,000	
1964		549,000	
1965	1,939,000	519,000	
1966	1,200,000	500,000	400,000
1967	1,942,000	545,000	
1968	2,000,000	623,000	5–600,000
1969	2,301,000	675,000	
1970		678,000	
1972	2,333,000	800,000	663,158

SOURCES: *Annuaire des syndicats professionels*, 1911. Quoted in J. A. Estey, *Revolutionary Syndicalism*, London, 1913, pp. 38, 46. International Institute of Social History, *Mouvements ouvriers et dépression économique de 1929–39*, Asser, 1966, p. 170. Val R. Lorwin *The French Labour Movement*, pp. 74–6, 176–189, 324–5. J. Capdevielle and R. Mouriaux, *Les syndicats ouvriers en France*, Paris, 1970, p. 74. Syndicalisme, *Hebdomadaire de CFDT*, 6 January 1972. G. Lefranc, *Le Mouvement syndical de la Libératión aux évenèments de mai–juin 1968*, pp. 79, 97, 205. G. Lefranc, *Les Espériences syndicales en France de 1939 à 1950*, p. 367. G. Lefranc, *Le Mouvement syndicale sous la Troisième République*, pp. 315, 409–11. CGT official figures.

GERMANY *Socialist unions*

Year	Membership	Year	Membership
1891	277,659	1925	4,156,000
1892	237,094	1927	4,150,000
1893	223,530	1929	4,906,000
1894	246,494	1931	4,418,000
1895	259,175		
1896	329,230	1949	480,000
1897	412,359	1950	5,449,990[1]
1898	493,742	1951	5,980,298
1899	580,473	1952	6,047,387
1900	680,427	1953	6,051,221
1901	677,510	1954	6,103,343
1902	733,206	1955	6,104,872
1903	887,698	1956	6,124,547
1904	1,052,108	1957	6,244,386
1905	1,344,803	1958	6,331,735
1906	1,689,709	1959	6,273,741
1907	1,865,506	1960	6,378,820
1908	1,831,731	1961	6,382,896
1909	1,832,667	1962	6,430,428
1910	2,017,298	1963	6,430,978
1911	2,339,785	1964	6,485,471
1912	2,553,162	1965	6,574,491
1913	2,573,718	1966	6,537,160
1914	2,075,759	1967	6,407,733
		1968	6,375,972
1919	5,419,000	1969	6,500,000
1921	7,568,000	1970	6,700,000
1923	7,138,000	1971	6,800,000

SOURCES: K. Zwing, *Geschichte der deutscher Freier Gewerkschafter*, Jena 1969, p. 82. Quoted in W. Galenson, *Comparative Labour Movements*, p. 261. *Encyclopedia of Social Sciences*, vol. 15, p. 14, New York, 1935. DGB official statistics.

NOTES

[1] Figures from 1949 onwards are for the DGB.

Christian unions

Year	Membership	Year	Membership
1910	316,115	1918	538,559
1911	350,574	1919	1,00,770
1912	350,930	1921	986,000
1913	341,735	1923	938,000
1914	218,197	1925	588,000
1915	162,425	1927	606,000
1916	178,970	1929	673,000
1917	293,187	1931	678,000

SOURCE: *Encyclopedia of Social Sciences*, New York, 1935, vol. 15, p. 14.

Hirsch Duncker unions

Year	Membership	Year	Membership
1910	122,571	1918	113,792
1911	107,743	1919	189,831
1912	109,225	1921	225,000
1913	106,618	1923	185,000
1914	77,749	1925	158,000
1915	61,086	1927	168,000
1916	57,666	1929	169,000
1917	79,113	1931	181,000

SOURCE: *Encyclopedia of Social Sciences*, New York, 1935, vol. 15, p. 14.

ITALY   *Confederazione Generale del Lavoro* (CGL)

Year	Membership	Year	Membership
1907	190,422	1916	201,291
1908	258,515	1917	237,560
1909	292,905	1918	249,039
1910	302,400	1919	1,150,062
1911	383,770	1920	2,200,100
1912	309,671	1921	1,128,915
1913	327,312	1922	401,054
1914	320,858	1923	211,016
1915	233,863	1924	201,049

	CGIL	CISL	UIL
1946	4,680,987		
1947	5,958,722		
1948	5,588,370		
1949	5,037,089	1,221,523	
1950	4,782,090	1,489,682	400,000
1951	—	1,812,501	
1952	4,938,000	1,800,000	
1953	—	2,000,000	
1954	4,625,000	2,045,542	500,000
1955	4,622,343	—	—
1956	—	2,138,300	—
1957	4,078,000		—
1958	3,678,000	2,316,896	552,000
1959	3,600,000	—	—
1960	3,745,000	2,357,000	—
1961	3,673,430	2,425,262	1,547,491
1962	3,495,971	—	1,507,059
1963	3,509,882	—	—
1964	—		1,511,425
1965	3,316,729	—	—
1966	3,347,941	—	1,508,170
1967	3,352,251	—	1,503,428
1968	3,352,251	2,000,000	1,510,772
1969	—	—	—
1970	—		—
1971	—	1,700,000	552,000

SOURCES: W. Galenson (ed.), *Comparative Labor Movements*, p. 427. *Almanacco Socialista, 1931*, edito del Partito Socialista Italiano Sezione della Internazionale operaia socialista, Paris, p. 138. A. Manoukian (ed.), *La presenza sociale del PCIe della DC*, Instituto di Studi e Ricerche 'Carlo Cattaneo', Bologna, 1968. pp. 41, 109. *Annuario politico Italiano* (Milan) 1963, 1964, 1966, 1967, 1968 and 1969. ICFRU official affiliation figures.

ITALY   *Italian Confederation of Workers Unions – CISL*
MEMBERSHIP CLAIMED 1968, 1972

According to official claims membership of the Italian Confederation of Workers Unions increased markedly between 1968 and 1972. The table which follows shows the allocation of claimed membership amongst the national unions.

National Union	1968	1972	% Increase
Food Workers	30,390	45,280	49
Chemical Workers	66,460	118,970	79
Construction Workers	74,310	115,180	55
Electricians	41,970	47,430	13
Miners	7,060	8120	15
Gas and Oil Refineries	11,580	17,250	49
Metal Workers	169,960	278,730	64
Printers	25,210	36,560	45
Textiles and clothing	127,524	182,360	43
Agricultural Workers	193,920	213,310	11
Peasants	77,610	83,040	7
Local Government	84,130	106,850	27
Hospitals	60,940	106,030	74
Civil Service	54,850	68,020	24
State employees	59,180	75,160	27
Elementary School Teachers	88,650	97,510	10
Secondary School teachers	790	30,630	3894
University Lecturers	—	1070	—
Scientists	—	1570	—
Railwaymen	26,050	38,810	49
Post and Telegraphs	73,580	81,770	22
Telephones (State)	6470	6660	3
State Monopolies	5500	5660	3
Commerce	46,150	74,300	61
News Vendors	7480	7780	4
Bank Employees	18,960	32,230	72
Insurance Workers	4840	5030	4
Telephones (IRI)	14,130	16,390	16
Tramwaymen	29,970	35,960	20
Seamen	10,200	12,240	20
Traffic wardens	28,810	38,320	33
Air line	2650	4030	52
Self employed fishermen	9200	12,610	37
Port Workers	3910	5940	52
Theatre and Cinema	6330	7780	23
Pensioners	142,890	158,610	11
Others	4540	6910	52

SOURCE: *Conquiste del lavoro*, Rome, July 1973, p. 24. The 1968 membership figures have been calculated from the percentage gain claimed in the original text.

BRITAIN *TUC Affiliated membership*[1]

Year	Membership	Year	Membership	Year	Membership
1893	1,100,000	1920	6,417,910	1947	7,791,470
1894	1,000,000	1921	5,128,648	1948	7,937,091
1895	1,076,000	1922	4,369,268	1949	7,883,355
1896	1,093,191	1923	4,328,325	1950	7,827,945
1897	1,184,241	1924	4,350,982	1951	8,020,079
1898	1,200,000	1925	4,365,619	1952	8,088,450
1899	1,250,000	1926	4,163,994	1953	8,093,837
1900	1,200,000	1927	3,874,842	1954	8,106,958
1901	1,400,000	1928	3,673,144	1955	8,263,741
1902	1,500,000	1929	3,744,320	1956	8,304,709
1903	1,422,518	1930	3,719,401	1957	8,337,325
1904	1,541,000	1931	3,613,273	1958	8,176,252
1905	1,555,000	1932	3,367,911	1959	8,128,251
1906	1,700,000	1933	3,294,581	1960	8,299,393
1907	1,777,000	1934	3,388,810	1961	8,312,875
1908	1,705,000	1935	3,614,551	1962	8,315,332
1909	1,647,715	1936	4,008,647	1963	8,325,790
1910	1,662,133	1937	4,460,617	1964	8,771,012
1911	2,001,633	1938	4,669,186	1965	8,867,522
1912	2,232,446	1939	4,866,711	1966	8,787,282
1913	—	1940	5,079,094	1967	8,725,604
1914	2,682,357	1941	5,432,644	1968	8,875,381
1915	2,850,547	1942	6,024,411	1969	9,402,170
1916	3,082,352	1943	6,642,317	1970	10,002,204
1917	4,532,085	1944	6,575,654	1971	9,894,881
1918	5,283,676	1945	6,671,120		
1919	6,505,482	1946	7,540,397		

SOURCE: *TUC Annual Report, 1972*, p. 642.

[1] TUC membership figures understate the total number of trade unionists since not all trade unions are affiliated to the TUC. This discrepancy was far more important before the First World War than at the present time.

BELGIUM

Year	Potential trade unionists not including domestic workers	Combined membership of CSC and FGTB	percentage organized
1910	1,725,783	118,848	6·88
1930	1,914,596	671,091	35·05
1947	2,456,489	1,004,623	40·89
1948	2,294,492	1,086,692	47·36
1949	2,308,987	1,142,310	49·47
1950	2,282,920	1,173,362	51·40
1951	2,342,603	1,219,851	52·07
1952	2,457,669	1,272,240	51·76
1953	2,354,045	1,284,580	54·57
1954	2,344,532	1,274,888	54·37
1955	2,349,950	1,290,029	54·90
1956	2,376,125	1,310,122	55·13
1957	2,416,898	1,342,185	55·53
1958	2,471,087	1,401,256	56·70
1959	2,437,208	1,446,988	59·37
1960	2,457,156	1,467,792	59·73
1961	2,475,578	1,462,570	59·07
1962	2,540,502	1,444,916	56·87
1963	2,575,830	1,510,978	58·65

NOTE: These figures exclude both white collar unions and the Liberal CGSLB organization.
SOURCE: Memo from Belgium Feb./April 1966. *The Political and Economic Structure of Belgium*, R. Senelle. Ministry of Foreign Affairs and External Trade.

BELGIUM *CSC (Christian)*

Year	Membership	Year	Membership
1901	11,000	1949	547,129
1904	14,759	1950	567,587
1909	49,478	1951	607,363
1913	100,000	1952	625,011
1914	123,000	1953	642,303
		1954	645,192
1923	149,481	1955	653,636
1925	133,156	1956	669,284
1929	181,407	1957	684,526
1930	209,311	1958	715,563
1931	238,799	1959	737,286
1932	300,713	1960	761,705
1933	304,010	1961	771,576
1934	296,684	1962	772,208
1935	297,296	1963	812,257
1936	280,796	1964	834,196
1937	304,999	1965	844,420
1938	325,711	1966	872,245
1939	350,000	1967	904,672
		1968	920,000
1945	294,207	1969	950,233
1946	402,536	1970	965,208
1947	437,129	1971	995,520
1948	503,384	1972	1,023,000

SOURCES: Official CSC statistics. *Movements ouvriers et dépression économique de 1929 à 1939*, International Institute of Social History, Asser, 1966, pp. 81–2.

FGTB *(Socialist)*

Year	Membership	Year	Membership
1900	31,311	1939	546,224
1910	68,844		
1911	77,000	1945	511,851
1914	129,177	1946	612,003
1919	576,890	1950	631,075
1920	687,610	1955	679,116
1925	525,039	1957	698,825
1929	504,605	1958	714,382
1930	502,708	1959	723,242
1931	522,476	1960	715,628
1932	572,171	1963	712,646
1933	591,976	1964	724,102
1934	580,074	1965	750,318
1935	545,119	1967	770,816
1936	573,839	1968	800,851
1937	546,469	1969	823,379
1938	581,951		

SOURCES: Official FGTB statistics. *Mouvements ouvriers et dépression economique de 1929–1939*, International Institution of Social History, Asser, 1966, pp. 81–2.

CGSLB

Year	Members
1920	12,000
1930	30,000
1940	100,000
1960	111,407
1961	111,765
1962	119,012
1963	120,886

SOURCE: *Monographies syndicales.*

DENMARK LO

Year	Membership	Year	Membership	Year	Membership
1899	75,000	1924	237,000	1949	636,000
1900	77,000	1925	240,000	1950	656,000
1901	73,000	1926	156,000	1951	662,000
1902	64,000	1927	156,000	1952	671,000
1903	63,000	1928	156,000	1953	687,000
1904	65,000	1929	250,000	1954	686,000
1905	69,000	1930	259,000	1955	687,000
1906	78,000	1931	270,000	1956	705,000
1907	91,000	1932	300,000	1957	714,000
1908	97,000	1933	302,000	1958	719,000
1909	99,000	1934	355,000	1959	739,500
1910	102,000	1935	381,000	1960	776,400
1911	105,000	1936	407,000	1961	789,600
1912	107,000	1937	452,000	1962	802,600
1913	115,000	1938	470,000	1963	818,000
1914	121,000	1939	500,000	1964	833,900
1915	132,000	1940	516,000	1965	840,700
1916	151,000	1941	527,000	1966	835,000
1917	179,000	1942	545,000	1967	844,300
1918	255,000	1943	564,000	1968	865,300
1919	277,000	1944	579,000	1969	894,300
1920	279,000	1945	604,000	1970	895,900
1921	244,000	1946	605,000	1971	909,400
1922	233,000	1947	614,000		
1923	233,000	1948	623,000		

SOURCE: Official statistics of Danish trade union confederation LO.

LUXEMBOURG

Confédération Générale du Travail – CGT
Members 1965 29,000

Of which
Fédération nationale des ouvriers luxembourgeois (FNOL) 20,150
Fédération national des cheminots, travailleurs, du transport,
functionnaires et employés du Luxembourg (FNCTTFEL) 7800

Confédération luxembourgeoise des syndicats chrétiens – LCGB
Members 1965 18,000

Fédération des employés privés du grand-duché de Luxembourg [1918] – FEP
Members 1965 10,000

NETHERLANDS *NVV (Socialist)*

Year	Membership	Year	Membership
1906	19,000	1953	435,683
1910	40,660	1954	453,949
1914	80,000	1955	463,121
		1956	468,047
1920	247,000	1957	500,332
1921	216,600	1958	486,249
1923	196,800	1959	476,894
1924	180,340	1960	486,743
1930	251,500	1961	506,964
1933	336,158	1962	507,666
1937	283,400	1963	512,751
1940	319,099	1964	529,173
		1965	526,433
1946	242,645	1966	535,746
1947	300,341	1967	556,143
1948	330,889	1968	559,259
1949	365,391	1969	554,895
1950	381,554	1970	562,548
1951	405,570	1971	611,401
1952	420,776	1972	623,810

SOURCES: ICFTU, 'The European Trade Union Movement Within the ICFTU', *Know Your Facts No. 4*, 1964. S. H. Scholl (ed.), *150 ans de mouvement ouvrier Chrétien en Europe de l'ouest*, Louvain, 1966, p. 394. Central Bureau of Statistics, The Hague. NVV official statistics.

THE NETHERLANDS *NKV (Catholic)*

Year	Membership	Year	Membership
1910	11,650	1956	381,733
1914	29,000	1957	411,991
		1958	395,047
1921	146,030	1959	395,869
1926	90,475	1960	400,396
1933	192,655	1961	411,785
1940	186,943	1962	417,780
		1963	418,018
1947	224,885	1964	420,849
1948	251,510	1965	415,384
1949	268,896	1966	419,755
1950	296,410	1967	428,661
1951	311,427	1968	432,502
1952	321,478	1969	412,560
1953	334,714	1970	400,032
1954	347,268	1971	401,802
1955	360,986	1972	399,732

SOURCES: S. H. Scholl (ed.) *150 ans de mouvement ouvrier chrétien en Europe de l'ouest*, Louvain, 1966, pp. 394–5. Central Bureau of Statistics, The Hague. NKV official statistics.

CNV (Protestant)

Year	Membership	Year	Membership
1910	6,587	1956	206,283
1914	11,000	1957	215,956
		1958	218,683
1921	73,819	1959	218,449
1926	48,327	1960	219,019
1934	115,606	1961	223,789
1940	121,179	1962	224,865
		1963	226,808
1947	119,051	1964	229,068
1948	131,560	1965	228,900
1949	147,477	1966	234,200
1950	155,627	1967	238,500
1951	166,487	1968	241,000
1952	174,750	1969	240,500
1953	182,293	1970	238,500
1954	191,138	1971	237,800
1955	199,693	1972	239,100

SOURCES: S. H. Scholl (ed.) *150 ans de mouvement ouvrier Chrétien en Europe de l'ouest*, 1966, pp. 394–5. Central Bureau of Statistics, The Hague.

Unemployment

UNEMPLOYMENT (Five-year Averages)

Years	France	Germany	Italy	Britain	Belgium	Netherlands	Ireland	Denmark
1922–25	1900	—	221,800	1,264,400	10,300	32,400	—	38,800
1926–30	8200	1,696,000	291,100	1,433,800	17,200	27,600	25,600	53,900
1931–35	275,500	3,953,800	930,800	2,440,900	195,300	289,900	72,300	75,500
1936–40	379,900	978,000	796,600	1,606,900	162,200	319,400	86,800	94,000
1941–45	—	—	—	—	—	—	67,200	—
1946–50	96,800	997,000	1,662,000	473,700	163,800	39,800	58,100	53,700
1951–55	155,100	1,243,800	1,741,000	274,000	208,400	71,300	59,800	65,100
1956–60	111,300	564,800	1,360,000	344,900	107,700	46,300	62,200	58,000
1961–65	126,000	154,800	619,000	390,700	65,000	23,700	48,300	24,100
1966–70	216,500	245,900	686,000	504,400	81,200	57,400	56,600	26,700

NOTES

Belgium   average for 1936–40 based on 1936–9 only
     average for 1946–50 based on 1947–50 only

France   average for 1936–40 based on 1936–9 only
     average for 1946–50 based on 1947–50 only

Italy   average for 1931–5 based on 1931–4 only
     average for 1936–40 based on 1937–9 only
     average for 1946–50 based on 1947–50 only

Germany   average for 1936–40 based on 1936–38 only
     average for 1946–50 based on 1947–50 only

Netherlands   average for 1936–40 based on 1936–39 only
     average for 1946–50 based on 1947–50 only

Ireland   average for 1926–30 based on 1926–29 only
     average for 1931–35 based on 1931, 1933 and 1935 only
     average for 1936–40 based on 1937–40 only

Denmark   average for 1926–30 based on 1926–29 only
     average for 1931–35 based on 1931–33 and 1935 only

Britain   average for 1922–25 based on 1923–25 only
     average for 1936–40 based on 1936–39 only

GENERAL *Number of trade unionists unemployed 1913–20*

Year	Germany	Belgium	Netherlands	Denmark
1913	1,973,000	77,000	65,000	117,000
1914	1,635,000	77,000	76,000	128,000
1915	1,019,000	—	106,000	134,000
1916	818,000	—	132,000	145,000
1917	939,000	—	148,000	160,000
1918	1,248,000	—	190,000	218,000
1919	3,686,000	—	300,000	296,000
1920	5,260,000	—	400,000	306,000

SOURCE: *International Labour Review*, vol. i, Jan. 1921, p. 116; vol. iii July–Sept. 1921, pp. 138, 339.

GENERAL *Percentage of trade unionists unemployed 1920–21*

Year	France	Germany	Britain	Belgium	Netherlands	Denmark
1910	5·9	2·0	4·7	1·7	—	8·1
1911	6·0	1·8	3·0	1·9	1·9	9·4
1912	5·7	1·8	3·2	1·7	3·6	7·7
1913	5·3	2·6	2·1	2·1	5·0	7·1
1914	4·1	6·3	2·3	3·3	13·1	9·6
1915	—	3·9	1·1	—	18·2	8·7
1916	—	2·3	0·4	—	6·5	6·2
1917	—	0·9	0·7	—	8·9	6·9
1918	—	0·8	0·8	—	9·2	17·9
1919	—	3·4	2·4	—	10·5	13·0
1920	—	3·2	2·4	—	6·6	7·0
1921	—	2·4	14·8	10·2	9·8	18·5

SOURCES: ILO, *Statistics of Unemployment in Various Countries, 1910–22. Studies and Reports, 1922*, no. 1, Unemployment Series, Geneva. *British Labour Statistics, Historical Abstract 1886–1968*, Department of Employment, 1971, Table 159.

FRANCE *Unemployed on relief (1912–41) and registered unemployed (1947–71)*

Year	No.	Year	No.
1922	4708	1950	132,891
1923	1615		
1924	631	1951	120,129
1925	726	1952	131,799
		1953	179,967
1926	4636	1954	183,933
1927	29,646	1955	159,981
1928	3397		
1929	928	1956	112,286
1930	2514	1957	80,731
		1958	93,083
1931	56,112	1959	139,724
1932	273,412	1960	131,115
1933	276,033		
1934	345,033	1961	111,000
1935	426,931	1962	122,600
		1963	140,300
1936	431,897	1964	114,100
1937	350,333	1965	142,100
1938	375,742		
1939	361,930	1966	147,700
1940	—	1967	196,100
		1968	253,800
1941	337,000	1969	223,000
		1970	262,100
1947	45,777		
1948	77,803	1971	288,900
1949	131,062		

SOURCES: *International Labour Review*, 1922–29, Statistics on Unemployment. *ILO Yearbooks*, 1942, 1954, 1968, 1971.

GERMANY   *Wholly unemployed trade unionists*

Year	No.	%
1922	85,000	1·3
1923	595,000	11·9
1924	415,000	11.4
1925	229,000	8·2
1926	610,000	17·7
1927	339,000	8·8
1928	423,000	9·6

SOURCE: *International Labour Review*, vols. 1–9, 1921–9, Statistics of Unemployment.

Unemployed

Year	No.	%	Year	No.	%
1926	1,706,000[1]	—	1953	1,258,597	7·5
1927	801,000[1]	—	1954	1,220,607	7·0
1928	1,002,000[1]	—	1955	928,308	5·1
1929	1,898,604	9·3			
1930	3,075,580	15·3	1956	761,412	4·0
			1957	662,334	3·4
1931	4,519,704	23·3	1958	683,117	3·5
1932	5,575,492	30·1	1959	479,924	2·4
1933	4,804,428	26·3	1960	237,427	1·2
1934	2,718,309	14·9			
1935	2,151,039	11·6	1961	161,075	0·8
			1962	142,400	0·7
1936	1,592,655	8·3	1963	174,200	0·8
1937	912,312	4·6	1964	157,400	0·7
1938	429,461	2·1	1965	139,200	0·6
1947	588,050	—	1966	154,300	0·7
1948	591,532	4·2	1967	444,600	2·1
1949	1,229,711	8·3	1968	313,600	1·5
1950	1,579,766	10·2	1969	173,200	0·8
			1970	143,800	0·7
1951	1,432,323	9·0			
1952	1,379,203	8·4	1971	129,200	0·6

[1] The figures for these years relate to numbers unemployed in receipt of benefit. From 1929 onwards the figures relate to registered unemployed. The post 1938 figures are for the Federal Republic alone.

SOURCES: *International Labour Review*, 1927–9, Statistics of Unemployment. *ILO Yearbooks*, 1942, 1954, 1962, 1968 and 1971.

ITALY *Registered wholly unemployed*

Year	No.	%	Year	No.	%
1922	391,322	—	1951	1,721,088	8·8
1923	234,050	—	1952	1,849,680	9·5
1924	153,893	—	1953	1,946,533	10·0
1925	108,262	—	1954	1,699,000	8·8
			1955	1,491,000	7·6
1926	115,915	—			
1927	290,690	—	1956	1,867,000	9·4
1928	322,810	—	1957	1,662,000	8·2
1929	300,786	—	1958	1,322,000	6·6
1930	425,437	—	1959	1,117,000	5·6
			1960	836,000	4·2
1931	734,454	—			
1932	1,006,442	—	1961	710,000	3·5
1933	1,018,955	—	1962	611,000	3·0
1934	963,677	—	1963	504,000	2·5
			1964	549,000	2·7
1937	874,000	4·6	1965	721,000	3·6
1938	810,000	4·3			
1939	705,866	3·8	1966	769,000	3·9
			1967	689,000	3·5
1947	1,620,000	8·3	1968	694,000	3·5
1948	1,742,000	8·9	1969	663,000	3·4
1949	1,673,000	8·6	1970	615,000	3·1
1950	1,614,940	8·3			
			1971	566,000	2·9

SOURCES: *International Labour Review*, 1922–9, Statistics on Unemployment. *ILO Yearbooks*, 1942, 1954, 1962, 1968 and 1971.

BRITAIN *Percentage of trade unionists unemployed*

Year	%	Year	%
1888	4·9	1906	3·6
1889	2·1	1907	3·7
1890	2·1	1908	7·8
1891	3·5	1909	7·7
1892	6·3	1910	4·7
1893	7·5	1911	3·0
1894	6·9	1912	3·2
1895	5·8	1913	2·1
1896	3·3	1914	2·3
1897	3·3	1915	1·1
1898	2·8	1916	0·4
1899	2·0	1917	0·7
1900	2·5	1918	0·8
1901	3·3	1919	2·4
1902	4·0	1920	2·4
1903	4·7	1921	14·8
1904	6·0	1922	15·2
1905	5·0		

SOURCE: *British Labour Statistics, Historical Abstract 1886–1968*, Department of Employment 1971, Table 159.

Percentage of insured workers unemployed 1913–22

Year	%	Year	%
1913	3·6	1918	0·8
1914	4·2	1919	—
1915	1·2	1920	3·9
1916	0·6	1921	16·9
1917	0·7	1922	14·3

SOURCE: *British Labour Statistics, Historical Abstract 1886–1968*, Department of Employment, 1971, Table 160.

Numbers of insured persons unemployed 1923-47 and wholly unemployed 1948-70

Year	No.	Year	No.
1923	1,297,700	1950	305,600
1924	1,087,200		
1925	1,408,500	1951	237,000
		1952	328,700
1926	1,751,100	1953	319,900
1927	1,069,400	1954	271,600
1928	1,273,400	1955	213,200
1929	1,163,700		
1930	1,911,700	1956	229,600
		1957	294,500
1931	2,706,800	1958	410,100
1932	2,842,800	1959	444,500
1933	2,498,100	1960	345,800
1934	2,124,400		
1935	2,032,600	1961	312,100
		1962	431,900
1936	1,729,000	1963	520,600
1937	1,399,300	1964	372,200
1938	1,885,400	1965	317,000
1939	1,414,200		
		1966	330,900
1945	144,900	1967	521,000
		1968	549,400
1946	1,042,200	1969	541,100
1947	418,500	1970	579,700
1948	302,500		
1949	300,100	1971	799,100

SOURCE: *British Labour Statistics, Historical Abstract 1886-1968*, Department of Employment, 1971, Table 163, p. 165. *British Labour Statistics, Year-book*, 1970.

BELGIUM *Insured unemployed*

Year	No.	%	Year	No.	%
1922	19,564	2·7	1950	223,537	10·9
1923	6104	0·6			
1924	6165	0·9	1951	206,520	9·8
1925	9388	1·5	1952	246,538	11·8
			1953	245,807	11·8
1926	9059	1·5	1954	224,752	10·9
1927	23,918	3·8	1955	118,400	5·8
1928	4155	0·6			
1929	13,000	1·9	1956	94,500	4·6
1930	36,000	5·4	1957	81,400	3·9
			1958	116,400	5·5
1931	110,000	14·5	1959	132,300	6·3
1932	211,000	23·5	1960	114,300	5·4
1933	210,000	20·5			
1934	235,000	23·4	1961	89,100	4·2
1935	210,927	21·7	1962	70,900	3·3
			1963	59,400	2·7
1936	154,038	16·2	1964	50,400	2·2
1937	125,929	13·1	1965	55,400	2·4
1938	173,913	17·6			
1939	195,211	18·8	1966	61,500	2·7
			1967	85,300	3·7
1941	123,192	—	1968	102,700	4·5
			1969	85,300	3·6
1947	67,560	3·4	1970	71,300	3·0
1948	129,203	6·4			
1949	234,906	11·6	1971	62,800	2·0

SOURCES: *International Labour Review*, 1922–9, Statistics of Unemployment. *ILO Yearbooks*, 1942, 1954, 1962, 1971.

NETHERLANDS   *Insured unemployed (1922–30); wholly unemployed (1931–36); registered unemployed (1937–71)*

Year	No.	%	Year	No.	%
1922	40,900	11·9	1951	67,750	—
1923	36,600	12·6	1952	104,256	—
1924	25,000	9·3	1953	83,338	—
1925	27,400	9·9	1954	60,214	1·9
			1955	41,407	1·3
1926	24,100	8·4			
1927	30,900	10·2	1956	30,326	0·9
1928	21,100	6·5	1957	41,359	1·2
1929	24,300	7·1	1958	81,472	2·3
1930	37,800	9·7	1959	48,500	1·5
			1960	30,100	0·9
1931	138,231	—			
1932	271,092	—	1961	22,400	0·7
1933	322,951	—	1962	22,700	0·7
1934	332,772	—	1963	25,000	0·7
1935	384,691	—	1964	22,100	0·6
			1965	26,700	0·7
1936	414,512	—			
1937	324,044	—	1966	37,300	1·0
1938	303,421	—	1967	78,500	2·0
1939	235,642	—	1968	71,900	1·9
			1969	52,900	1·4
1947	30,701	—	1970	46,400	1·1
1948	29,033	—			
1949	42,125	—	1971	45,100	1·1
1950	57,681	—			

SOURCES: *International Labour Review*, 1922–9, Statistics of Unemployment. *ILO Yearbooks*, 1942, 1954, 1962, 1968, and 1971.

IRELAND   *Insured unemployed (1925-8); registered applicants for work (1929-71)*

Year	No.	Year	No.
1925	42,400	1949	60,606
		1950	53,415
1926	29,400		
1927	25,100	1951	50,453
1928	27,200	1952	60,688
1929	20,702	1953	70,562
1930	—	1954	62,436
		1955	55,200
1931	25,230		
1932	—	1956	61,400
1933	72,472	1957	69,700
1934	—	1958	65,300
1935	119,498	1959	61,700
		1960	52,900
1936	—		
1937	81,760	1961	46,600
1938	88,714	1962	46,600
1939	93,074	1963	50,000
1940	84,054	1964	48,900
		1965	49,400
1941	74,656		
1942	76,887	1966	47,700
1943	66,884	1967	55,000
1944	59,047	1968	58,000
1945	58,999	1969	57,300
		1970	64,900
1946	59,726		
1947	55,623	1971	54,900
1948	61,203		

SOURCES: *International Labour Review*, 1925–9, Statistics of Unemployment. *ILO Yearbooks*, 1942–71.

DENMARK *Unemployed trade unionists*

Year	No.	%	Year	No.	%
1922	49,900	18·0	1951	63,024	9·7
1923	32,700	12·7	1952	81,645	12·5
1924	29,100	11·1	1953	61,018	9·2
1925	43,700	16·4	1954	54,143	8·0
			1955	65,939	9·7
1926	60,000	22·1			
1927	62,800	22·6	1956	75,492	11·1
1928	50,000	18·0	1957	70,900	10·2
1929	42,817	15·5	1958	68,400	9·6
1930	—	—	1959	44,100	6·1
			1960	31,400	4·3
1931	53,019	17·9			
1932	—	—	1961	28,900	3·9
1933	97,478	28·8	1962	25,000	3·3
1934	—	—	1963	32,000	4·2
1935	76,195	19·7	1964	18,500	2·4
			1965	16,100	2·0
1936	—	—			
1937	95,630	21·7	1966	18,300	2·3
1938	97,707	21·3	1967	21,800	2·7
1939	88,924	18·4	1968	38,700	5·0
			1969	31,200	3·9
1946	51,636	8·9	1970	23,900	2·9
1947	51,998	8·9			
1948	51,644	8·6	1971	30,000	3·7
1949	59,041	9·6			
1950	54,829	8·7			

SOURCES: *International Labour Review*, 1922–9. *ILO Yearbooks*, 1942–71.

LUXEMBOURG *Registered unemployed*

Year	No.	Year	No.
1955	200	1964	50
1956	110	1965	50
1957	120	1966	20
1958	150	1967	170
1959	140	1968	90
1960	120	1969	40
1961	120	1970	40
1962	80	1971	20
1963	220		

SOURCE: *ILO Yearbook*, 1971.

Industrial Disputes

NUMBER OF DISPUTES (Five-year Averages)

Years	France	Germany	Italy	Britain	Belgium	Netherlands	Ireland	Denmark
1896–1900	568	774	282	758	122	—	—	69
1901–5	691	1363	970	427	94	—	—	91
1906–10	1236	2712	1566	479	155	⎱ 241	—	55
1911–15	886	2101	953	961	201	⎰	—	250
1916–20	1073	1380	1060	1077	444	435	—	63
1921–5	844	2997	567	656	179	282	68	24
1926–30	1035	549	—	357	157	218	83	22
1931–5	350	567	—	438	90	183	115	16
1936–40	6914	—	—	936	369	105	78	17
1941–5	—	—	—	1765	—	—	—	29
1946–50	1930	—	1204	1690	212	185	150	12
1951–55	2035	—	1577	1917	130	67	94	46
1956–60	1804	—	1993	2612	84	71	54	31
1961–65	2036	—	3666	2416	42	56	80	31
1966–70	2444	—	3274	2690	88	33	117	37

NOTES

France   1936–40 figures based on 1936–38 only
1946–50 figures based on 1947–50 only
1966–70 figures exclude 1968

The absence of data for 1945, 1946 years in which the incidence of strikes was low makes the five-year average unduly high

Germany   1911–15 figures excludes 1914
1916–20 figures based on 1916, 1917 and 1920 only
1931–35 figures based on 1931 and 1932 only
post-1945 figures for Federal Republic only

Italy   1921–25 figures based on 1921–24 only
1946–50 figures based on 1949–50 only

Belgium   1911–15 figures based on 1911–14 only
1916–20 figures based on 1919–20 only
1936–40 figures based on 1936–39 only
1946–50 figures based on 1947–50 only

Netherlands   1936–40 figures based on 1936–39 only

Ireland   1926–30 figures based on 1929–30 only

WORKING DAYS LOST (Five-year Averages)

Years	France	Germany	Italy	Britain	Belgium	Netherlands	Ireland	Denmark
1896–1900	1,990,600	—	—	6,948,000	800,700	—	—	—
1901–5	3,132,200	2,852,700	—	2,744,000	2,450,500	—	—	155,400
1906–10	4,628,600	4,954,100	—	5,701,000	1,605,800	{ 494,000	—	105,400
1911–15	2,176,000	4,325,300	—	14,736,000	1,286,300		—	233,600
1916–20	8,257,600	5,648,300	—	15,101,000	2,501,700	988,600	—	574,600
1921–25	4,208,600	23,843,500	—	26,554,000	2,595,400	1,532,900	—	1,583,600
1926–30	4,293,800	7,408,000	—	35,496,000	1,331,600	482,600	89,300	63,500
1931–35	1,593,600	1,515,700	—	3,491,000	941,500	711,800	204,000	102,200
1936–40	—	—	—	1,774,000	2,008,700	87,400	481,500	615,600
1941–45	—	—	—	2,192,000	—	—	107,200	39,800
1946–50	13,665,700	325,400	—	1,946,000	1,917,000	293,600	269,400	375,400
1951–55	3,893,400	1,193,400	5,499,000	2,381,000	662,700	63,600	291,800	8,400
1956–60	1,937,400	706,700	5,580,200	4,450,000	1,269,600	147,700	94,100	236,400
1961–65	2,793,400	485,200	12,816,000	3,160,000	224,800	339,400	362,400	521,200
1966–70	32,128,000	156,800	17,676,000	5,540,000	534,800	63,300	663,000	431,800

NOTES

France 1936–40 figures based on 1936–38 only
1946–50 figures based on 1947–50 only
1966–70 figures exclude 1961

The absence of data for 1945, 1946 years in which the incidence of strikes was low makes the five year average unduly high.

Germany 1911–15 figures exclude 1914
1916–20 figures exclude 1918–19
1931–35 figures based on 1931–32 only
1946–50 figures based on 1949–50 only
post-1945 figures for Federal Republic only

Italy 1951–55 figures based on 1954–55 only

Belgium 1911–15 figures based on 1911–14 only
1916–20 figures based on 1919–20 only
1936–40 figures based on 1936–39 only
1946–50 figures based on 1947–50 only

Netherlands 1936–40 figures based on 1936–39 only

Ireland 1926–30 figures based on 1929–30 only

FRANCE

Year	No. of strikes	No. of strikers	Days lost
1890	313	118,900	1,340,000
1891	267	108,900	1,717,000
1892	261	48,500	918,000
1893	634	70,100	3,175,000
1894	391	54,600	1,062,000
1895	405	45,800	617,000
1896	476	49,900	644,000
1897	356	68,900	781,000
1898	368	82,100	1,216,000
1899	739	176,800	3,551,000
1900	902	222,700	3,761,000
1901	523	111,400	1,862,000
1902	512	212,700	4,675,000
1903	567	123,200	2,442,000
1904	1026	271,100	3,935,000
1905	830	177,700	2,747,000
1906	1309	438,500	9,439,000
1907	1275	198,000	3,562,000
1908	1073	99,000	1,752,000
1909	1025	167,500	3,560,000
1910	1502	281,400	4,830,000
1911	1471	230,600	4,096,000
1912	1116	267,600	2,318,000
1913	1073	220,400	2,224,000
1914	672	160,600	2,187,000
1915	98	9400	55,000
1916	314	41,400	236,000
1917	696	293,800	1,482,000
1918	499	176,200	980,000
1919	2026	1,151,000	15,478,000
1920	1832	1,317,000	23,112,000
1921	475	402,400	7,027,000
1922	665	290,300	3,935,000
1923	1068	331,000	4,172,000
1924	1083	274,900	3,863,000
1925	931	249,200	2,046,000
1926	1660	349,300	4,072,000
1927	396	110,500	1,046,000
1928	816	204,100	6,377,000

Year	No. of strikes	No. of strikers	Days lost
1929	1213	239,900	2,765,000
1930	1093	581,900	7,209,000
1931	286	48,300	950,000
1932	362	71,600	2,244,000
1933	343	87,100	1,199,000
1934	385	100,600	2,393,000
1935	376	108,900	1,182,000
1936	16,907	2,423,000	—
1937	2616	323,800	—
1938	1220	1,333,000	—
1946	—	—	312,000
1947	2285	2,997,500	22,673,000
1948	1425	6,561,100	13,133,000
1949	1426	4,329,900	7,129,000
1950	2586	1,527,200	11,728,000
1951	2514	1,754,400	3,495,000
1952	1749	1,155,200	1,732,000
1953	1761	1,783,600	9,722,000
1954	1479	1,318,900	1,440,000
1955	2672	1,060,600	3,078,000
1956	2440	981,600	1,422,000
1957	2623	2,963,837	4,121,000
1958	954	1,112,459	1,137,000
1959	1512	939,798	1,938,000
1960	1494	1,071,513	1,069,000
1961	1963	2,551,800	2,600,000
1962	1884	1,472,400	1,901,000
1963	2382	2,646,000	5,991,000
1964	2281	2,603,000	2,496,000
1965	1674	1,237,000	979,000
1966	1711	3,341,000	2,523,000
1967	1675	2,823,600	4,203,000
1968	—	—	150,000,000[1]
1969	2480	1,536,000	2,172,000
1970	3912	1,159,200	1,742,000
1971	4332	4,387,800	4,387,000

[1] Estimate provided by French Embassy.

SOURCES: *ILO Yearbooks*. French Embassy. *Revue Française de Travail.*

GERMANY

Year	No. of strikes	No. of strikers	Days lost
1890–1	226	38,536	—
1892	73	3022	—
1893	116	9356	—
1894	131	7328	—
1895	204	14,032	—
1896	483	128,808	—
1897	578	63,119	—
1898	985	60,162	—
1899	976	100,779	—
1900	852	115,761	1,234,025
1901	727	48,522	1,194,553
1902	861	55,715	964,317
1903	1282	121,593	2,622,232
1904	1625	135,957	2,120,154
1905	2323	507,964	7,362,802
1906	3480	316,042	6,317,675
1907	2792	281,030	5,122,467
1908	2052	126,885	2,045,585
1909	2045	131,244	2,247,512
1910	3194	369,011	9,037,575
1911	2914	325,253	6,846,240
1912	2825	479,589	4,776,818
1913	2600	248,986	5,672,034
1915	66	2221	6511
1916	142	14,639	36,555
1917	193	66,634	152,802
1920	3807	1,429,116	16,755,614
1921	4455	1,489,454	25,874,432
1922	4785	1,823,921	27,732,832
1923	2046	1,606,501	12,477,712
1924	1973	1,618,011	36,197,888
1925	1730	753,647	16,934,820
1926	358	92,436	1,251,366
1927	853	485,658	7,148,250
1928	743	719,850	20,355,365
1929	435	179,667	4,254,877
1930	356	213,201	4,030,717

Year	No. of strikes	No. of strikers	Days lost
1931	478	167,572	1,893,723
1932	657	127,720	1,137,890
1949	—	58,133	270,716
1950	—	79,270	380,121
1951	—	174,325	1,592,892
1952	—	84,097	442,877
1953	—	50,625	1,488,218
1954	—	115,899	1,586,523
1955	—	600,410	856,752
1956	—	52,467	1,580,247
1957	—	45,321	1,071,846
1958	—	202,614	782,254
1959	—	21,648	61,825
1960	—	17,065	37,723
1961	—	21,052	64,350
1962	—	79,177	450,948
1963	—	316,397	1,846,025
1964	—	5629	16,711
1965	—	6250	48,520
1966	—	196,013	27,086
1967	—	59,604	389,581
1968	—	25,167	25,249
1969	—	89,571	249,184
1970	—	184,269	93,203
1971	—	536,300	4,483,700

NOTE: post-1945 figures for Federal Republic only.

SOURCES: S. Nestriepke, *Die Gewerkschaftsbeweging*, Stuttgart, 1921–3, vol. i, p. 395 and vol. ii, p. 38. Quoted in W. Galenson, *Comparative Labor Movements*, pp. 270, 274. Nathan Reich, *Labour Relations in Republican Germany*, pp. 63–5. *ILO Yearbooks*, 1954, 1962, 1968, 1971.

ITALY

Year	No. of strikes	No. of strikers	Days lost
1881	45	8372	—
1882	49	8054	—
1883	76	13,162	—
1884	91	24,212	—
1885	151	43,017	—
1886	113	20,797	—
1887	78	27,302	—
1888	106	30,340	—
1889	130	24,409	—
1890	147	40,352	—
1891	156	42,528	—
1892	129	34,304	—
1893	149	44,499	—
1894	117	32,343	—
1895	133	21,072	—
1896	211	96,151	—
1897	229	100,705	—
1898	292	44,200	—
1899	268	45,089	—
1900	410	93,375	—
1901	1671	419,525	—
1902	1031	344,106	—
1903	596	131,834	—
1904	839	219,590	—
1905	715	154,527	—
1906	1649	381,624	—
1907	2258	575,630	—
1908	1745	371,383	—
1909	1062	187,021	—
1910	1118	198,774	—
1911	1255	385,591	—
1912	1090	239,965	—
1913	907	464,567	—
1914	905	216,922	—
1915	608	179,644	—
1916	577	138,508	—
1917	470	174,817	—
1918	313	158,711	—
1919	1871	1,554,566	—
1920	2070	2,313,685	—

Year	No. of strikes	No. of strikers	Days lost
1921	1734	723,862	—
1922	575	447,919	—
1923	201	66,213	—
1924	361	165,216	—
1949	1159	2,894,000	—
1950	1250	3,537,000	—
1951	1178	2,134,000	—
1952	1338	1,471,000	—
1953	1401	4,675,000	—
1954	1990	2,045,000	5,376,000
1955	1981	1,403,000	5,622,000
1956	1904	1,677,000	4,136,000
1957	1731	1,226,000	4,618,000
1958	1937	1,283,000	4,171,000
1959	1925	1,900,000	9,190,000
1960	2471	2,337,000	5,786,000
1961	3502	2,697,000	9,890,000
1962	3652	2,909,000	22,716,000
1963	4145	3,693,000	11,394,000
1964	3841	3,245,000	13,088,000
1965	3191	2,309,000	6,992,000
1966	2387	1,887,000	14,473,000
1967	2658	2,244,000	8,568,000
1968	3377	4,862,000	9,239,000
1969	3788	7,506,000	37,824,000
1970	4162	3,721,000	18,276,000
1971	5598	3,891,000	12,948,000

SOURCE: M. F. Neufeld, *Italy, School for Developing Countries*, quoting from *Annuario statistico Italiano*, 1919–21. *ILO Yearbooks*, 1954, 1962, 1968, 1971.

BRITAIN

Year	No. of strikes	No. of strikers	Days lost
1893	599	597,000	30,439,000
1894	903	254,000	9,506,000
1895	728	205,000	5,701,000
1896	906	142,000	3,565,000
1897	848	166,000	10,327,000
1898	695	199,000	15,257,000
1899	710	137,000	2,503,000
1900	633	132,000	3,088,000
1901	631	111,000	4,130,000
1902	432	115,000	3,438,000
1903	380	93,000	2,320,000
1904	346	56,000	1,464,000
1905	349	67,000	2,368,000
1906	479	158,000	3,019,000
1907	585	100,000	2,148,000
1908	389	221,000	10,785,000
1909	422	168,000	2,687,000
1910	521	384,000	9,867,000
1911	872	824,000	10,155,000
1912	834	1,232,000	40,890,000
1913	1459	497,000	9,804,000
1914	972	326,000	9,878,000
1915	672	401,000	2,953,000
1916	532	235,000	2,446,000
1917	730	575,000	5,647,000
1918	1165	923,000	5,875,000
1919	1352	2,401,000	34,969,000
1920	1607	1,779,000	26,568,000
1921	763	1,770,000	85,872,000
1922	576	512,000	19,850,000
1923	628	343,000	10,672,000
1924	710	558,000	8,424,000
1925	603	401,000	7,952,000
1926	323	2,724,000	162,233,000
1927	308	90,000	1,174,000
1928	302	80,000	1,388,000
1929	431	493,000	8,287,000
1930	422	286,000	4,399,000

Year	No. of strikes	No. of strikers	Days lost
1931	420	424,000	6,983,000
1932	389	337,000	6,488,000
1933	357	114,000	1,072,000
1934	471	109,000	959,000
1935	553	230,000	1,955,000
1936	818	241,000	1,829,000
1937	1129	388,000	3,413,000
1938	875	211,000	1,334,000
1939	940	246,000	1,356,000
1940	922	225,000	940,000
1941	1251	297,000	1,079,000
1942	1303	349,000	1,527,000
1943	1785	454,000	1,808,000
1944	2194	716,000	3,714,000
1945	2293	447,000	2,835,000
1946	2205	405,000	2,158,000
1947	1721	489,000	2,433,000
1948	1759	324,000	1,944,000
1949	1426	313,000	1,807,000
1950	1339	269,000	1,389,000
1951	1719	336,000	1,694,000
1952	1714	303,000	1,792,000
1953	1746	1,329,000	2,184,000
1954	1989	402,000	2,457,000
1955	2419	599,000	3,781,000
1956	2648	464,000	2,083,000
1957	2859	1,275,000	8,412,000
1958	2629	456,000	3,462,000
1959	2093	522,000	5,270,000
1960	2832	698,000	3,024,000
1961	2686	675,000	3,046,000
1962	2449	4,297,000	5,798,000
1963	2068	455,000	1,755,000
1964	2524	700,000	2,277,000
1965	2354	673,000	2,925,000
1966	1937	414,000	2,398,000
1967	2116	551,000	2,787,000
1968	2378	2,073,000	4,690,000
1969	3116	1,426,000	6,846,000
1970	3906	1,460,000	10,980,000
1971	2,228	1,178,000	13,551,000

SOURCE: *British Labour Statistics, Historical Abstract 1886–1968*, Department of Employment, 1971, Table 197. *British Labour Statistics Yearbook* 1970.

BELGIUM

Year	No. of strikes	No. of strikers	Days lost
1896	139	23,204	438,639
1897	130	35,958	755,475
1898	91	13,101	116,313
1899	104	57,931	2,270,649
1900	146	32,443	422,910
1901	117	43,814	2,951,104
1902	73	10,477	176,880
1903	70	7649	172,334
1904	81	12,375	577,251
1905	133	75,672	8,375,259
1906	212	48,513	1,436,487
1907	224	51,454	4,088,004
1908	108	17,085	594,727
1909	123	15,469	423,638
1910	110	27,257	1,486,573
1911	310	54,947	1,836,235
1912	220	61,654	2,138,065
1913	167	15,930	835,692
1914[1]	109	24,431	335,590
1919	372	164,030	2,545,535
1920	517	296,192	2,457,949
1921	258	127,293	2,339,454
1922	172	85,605	1,591,490
1923	168	104,980	2,067,965
1924	188	84,447	2,252,622
1925	112	81,988	4,726,081
1926	140	77,362	1,881,453
1927	186	39,873	941,875
1928	201	74,707	2,254,424
1929	168	49,236	799,177
1930	93	54,149	781,646
1931	74	20,648	399,037
1932	63	161,422	580,670
1933	87	35,664	664,044
1934	79	33,628	2,441,335
1935	150	98,543	623,002

[1] Jan.–May 1914, only

Year	No. of strikes	No. of strikers	Days lost
1936	999	774,266	6,939,353
1937	209	81,844	647,647
1938	144	34,467	290,937
1939	126	32,338	157,242
1947	473	353,732	2,211,786
1948	155	341,422	1,858,190
1949	99	50,134	829,850
1950	122	149,936	2,768,535
1951	163	121,240	593,164
1952	122	278,064	863,377
1953	115	116,724	411,903
1954	107	60,168	443,706
1955	143	118,578	1,001,769
1956	148	176,140	948,170
1957	115	339,055	3,788,738
1958	43	62,803	293,767
1959	57	123,473	983,147
1960	61	19,140	334,446
1961	38	12,622	92,092
1962	40	21,995	270,975
1963	48	17,722	247,381
1964	41	40,682	443,835
1965	43	18,774	70,131
1966	74	41,629	533,239
1967	58	37,621	181,713
1968	71	29,338	364,363
1969	88	24,691	162,898
1970	151	107,670	1,432,274
1971	184	86,900	1,240,400

SOURCES: *Belgian Ministry of Labour. ILO Yearbooks.*

NETHERLANDS

Year	No. of strikes	No. of strikers	Days lost
1906–13 (average)	184	—	911,500
1914	271	15,700	393,100
1915	269	15,200	177,600
1916	377	18,100	260,700
1917	344	31,300	554,500
1918	325	39,700	716,100
1919	649	61,700	1,056,800
1920	481	66,400	2,354,900
1921	299	47,700	1,281,800
1922	325	44,000	1,223,900
1923	289	56,400	1,216,400
1924	239	27,700	3,156,000
1925	262	33,600	786,600
1926	212	9,900	281,300
1927	239	13,500	220,500
1928	205	16,900	647,700
1929	226	21,300	990,800
1930	212	11,000	273,000
1931	215	28,200	856,100
1932	216	32,000	1,772,600
1933	184	14,800	553,800
1934	152	6,200	114,200
1935	152	12,900	262,400
1936	96	10,400	94,800
1937	95	4,600	38,800
1938	141	6,400	124,800
1939	90	5,300	91,400
1945 (July–Dec.)		36,500	
1946	270	72,100	681,600
1947	272	59,920	203,400
1948	183	17,740	131,400
1949	116	14,340	289,400
1950	79	17,640	162,200
1951	85	14,230	66,700
1952	40	3790	31,200
1953	58	10,800	28,300
1954	91	18,744	59,200
1955	63	21,190	132,900

Year	No. of strikes	No. of strikers	Days lost
1956	80	37,026	212,800
1957	37	1435	7200
1958	73	5123	37,300
1959	48	7635	13,900
1960	121	75,500	467,300
1961	43	8578	24,600
1962	24	2156	9085
1963	104	26,055	37,757
1964	53	8498	43,862
1965	60	23,213	54,607
1966	20	11,188	12,647
1967	8	4,371	6165
1968	11	4599	13,698
1969	28	12,403	21,687
1970	99	52,333	262,810

SOURCES: *ILO Yearbooks*, 1954, 1962, 1968 and 1971. Netherlands Central Bureau of Statistics.

IRELAND

Year	No. of strikes	No. of strikers	Days lost
1929	53	4533	101,397
1930	83	3410	77,417
1931	60	5431	310,199
1932	70	4222	42,152
1933	88	9039	200,126
1934	99	9288	180,080
1935	99	9513	288,077
1936	107	9443	185,623
1937	145	26,734	1,754,949
1938	137	13,736	208,784
1939	99	6667	106,476
1940	89	7715	152,076
1941	71	4895	77,133
1942	69	5132	115,039
1943	81	5921	61,809
1944	84	4387	38,308
1945	87	8785	243,932

Year	No. of strikes	No. of strikers	Days lost
1946	105	10,896	150,108
1947	194	22,253	449,438
1948	147	16,567	258,166
1949	153	9837	273,151
1950	154	18,559	216,505
1951	138	24,777	545,133
1952	82	14,851	529,089
1953	75	7144	82,046
1954	81	8294	66,734
1955	96	11,841	236,324
1956	67	4420	48,069
1957	45	4059	92,040
1958	51	12,043	126,143
1959	58	9305	124,479
1960	49	5865	80,349
1961	96	27,437	377,264
1962	60	9197	104,024
1963	70	16,067	233,617
1964	87	25,245	545,384
1965	88	38,917	552,351
1966	112	52,238	783,635
1967	79	20,925	182,645
1968	126	38,880	405,686
1969	134	61,760	935,900
1970	134	28,752	1,007,714
1971	133	43,700	273,700

SOURCE: *ILO Yearbooks*, 1954, 1962, 1968, 1971.

DENMARK

Year	No. of strikes	No. of strikers	Days lost
1900	82	7,600	236,000
1901	56	4,100	57,000
1902	68	2,400	133,000
1903	61	1,100	19,000
1904	86	2,600	69,000
1905	75	5,700	499,000

Year	No. of strikes	No. of strikers	Days lost
1906	90	3,900	68,000
1907	105	8,100	255,000
1908	122	7,600	85,000
1909	65	2,400	58,000
1910	71	2,500	61,000
1911	51	28,800	648,000
1912	60	4,100	50,000
1913	76	9,700	382,000
1914	44	3,400	56,000
1915	43	1,900	32,000
1916	66	14,300	241,000
1917	215	10,100	214,000
1918	253	9,800	194,000
1919	472	35,600	916,000
1920	243	22,000	1,306,000
1921	110	48,100	1,321,000
1922	31	48,900	2,272,000
1923	58	1,900	20,000
1924	71	9,800	175,000
1925	48	102,300	4,130,000
1926	32	1,000	23,000
1927	17	2,900	119,000
1928	11	500	11,000
1929	22	1040	41,283
1930	37	5349	144,000
1931	16	3692	246,000
1932	17	5760	87,000
1933	26	492	18,000
1934	38	11,546	146,000
1935	14	827	14,000
1936	12	98,862	2,946,000
1937	22	1372	21,000
1938	21	3650	90,000
1939	19	523	16,000
1940	9	257	5000
1941	2	65	3000
1942	7	3155	11,000
1943	8	14,627	31,000
1944	34	7690	88,000

Year	No. of disputes	No. of strikers	Days lost
1945	35	8526	66,000
1946	59	54,241	1,389,000
1947	29	7542	467,000
1948	24	2722	8200
1949	17	2654	10,400
1950	18	2849	3700
1951	12	1701	3700
1952	9	2397	3600
1953	8	403	2300
1954	20	7673	22,700
1955	13	6257	9900
1956	98	66,306	1,086,600
1957	14	2540	7210
1958	15	9474	9400
1959	23	5859	18,100
1960	82	19,787	60,900
1961	34	153,304	2,308,200
1962	26	9518	14,600
1963	19	6527	23,600
1964	40	7530	17,500
1965	37	14,194	242,100
1966	22	10,369	15,400
1967	22	10,442	9900
1968	17	28,772	33,600
1969	48	35,856	56,200
1970	76	55,515	100,800

SOURCES: *ILO Yearbooks*, 1954, 1962, 1968, 1971. Danish Statistical Department.

Socialist Party Membership

Year	France	Germany	Italy	Britain[4]	Belgium	Netherlands	Total
1906	43,000	384,000	43,000	998,000	—	7000	1,475,000
1910	53,000	720,000	31,000	1,430,000	—	10,000	2,244,000
1914	90,000	1,085,000	45,000	1,612,000	—	25,000	2,857,000
1919	133,000	1,012,000	81,000	3,511,000	—	37,000	4,774,000
1925	111,000	844,000	—	3,373,000	—	37,000	4,365,000
1931	130,000	1,008,000	—	2,358,000	—	69,000	3,565,000
1946	354,000	701,000	860,000	3,322,000	—	77,000	5,314,000
1951	116,000[1]	649,000	720,000	5,849,000	126,000	112,000	7,572,000
1957	107,000[2]	626,000	477,000	6,582,000	140,000	140,000	8,072,000
1963	102,000	650,000	491,000	6,358,000	196,000	145,000	7,942,000
1969	90,000	739,000	500,000[3]	6,163,000	194,000	116,000	7,793,000

NOTES
[1] 1952 figure.
[2] 1950 figure.
[3] 1968 figure (estimate).
[4] Labour Party: affiliated and individual membership combined.

FRANCE

Year	No.	Year	No.
1905	40,000	1929	119,519
1906	43,462	1930	125,563
1907	48,237	1931	130,864
1908	49,348	1932	137,684
1909	51,692	1933	131,044
1910	53,928	1934	110,000
1911	63,358	1935	120,083
1912	63,657	1936	202,000
1913	68,800	1937	286,604
1914	90,700	1938	275,377
1915	25,393		
1916	25,879	1945	335,705
1917	28,000	1946	354,858
1918	35,793	1947	323,368
1919	133,327	1948	238,762
1920	180,000	1949	156,828
1921	50,000	1952	116,327
1922	49,174	1953	113,455
1923	50,496	1954	115,494
1924	72,659	1959	107,600
1925	111,276	1961	102,284
1926	111,368	1963	102,284
1927	98,034	1966	102,284
1928	109,892	1969	90,000

SOURCES: J. Braunthal, *Yearbook of the International Socialist Labour Movement*. Socialist International.

GERMANY

Year	No.	Year	No.
1906	384,327	1928	937,381
1907	530,466	1929	1,021,777
1908	587,336	1930	1,037,384
1909	683,309	1931	1,008,953
1910	720,038		
1911	836,562	1946	701,448
1912	970,112	1947	875,479
1913	982,850	1948	844,653
1914	1,085,905	1949	736,218
1915	585,898	1950	684,698
1916	432,618	1951	649,529
1917	243,061	1952	627,827
1918	249,411	1953	607,456
1919	1,012,299	1954	585,479
1920	1,180,208	1955	589,051
1921	1,028,574	1956	601,196
1922	1,464,868	1957	626,189
1923	1,261,072	1958	623,816
1924	940,078	1959	623,817
1925	844,495	1961	650,000
1926	823,526	1963	650,000
1927	867,671	1966	704,152
		1969	730,000

SOURCES: J. Braunthal, *Yearbook of the International Socialist Labour Movement*. Socialist International.

ITALY

Year	No.	Year	No.
1896	19,121	1946	860,300
1897	27,281	1947	822,000
1900	19,194	1948	531,031
1901	47,098	1949	430,258
1902	37,778	1950	700,000
1903	42,451	1951	720,000
1904	45,800	1952	750,000
1905	43,905	1953	780,000
1906	43,654	1954	754,000
1907	43,953	1955	770,000
1908	43,788	1956	710,000
1909	28,835	1957	477,000
1910	31,960	1958	486,000
1911	30,220	1959	484,652
1912	30,233	1960	489,337
1913	37,151	1961	465,259
1914	45,102	1962	491,216
		1963	491,676
1918	25,030	1964	446,250
1919	81,463	1965	437,458
1921	216,327	1966	697,588
1922	106,841	1967	633,573
		1968	500,000[1]
1945	700,000	1972	400,000[1]

[1] estimates

SOURCES: Spartaco Cannarsa, *Il Socialismo e i XXV Congressi Nazionali de Partito Socialista Italiano*, Società Editrice 'Avanti!', Florence 1950. F. Cazzola, *Il Partito come organizzazione; Studio di un caso – il PSI*, Edizioni del Tritone, Rome, 1970.

BRITAIN *Labour Party*

Year	No.	Year	No.	Year	No.
1900	375,900	1924	3,194,300	1948	5,422,400
1901	469,300	1925	3,373,800	1949	5,716,900
1902	861,100	1926	3,388,200	1950	5,920,100
1903	969,800	1927	3,293,600	1951	5,849,000
1904	900,000	1928	3,292,100	1952	6,107,600
1905	921,200	1929	2,330,800	1953	6,096,000
1906	998,300	1930	2,346,900	1954	6,498,000
1907	1,072,400	1931	2,358,000	1955	6,483,900
1908	1,158,500	1932	2,371,700	1956	6,537,200
1909	1,486,300	1933	2,305,000	1957	6,582,500
1910	1,430,500	1934	2,278,400	1958	6,542,100
1911	1,539,000	1935	2,377,500	1959	6,436,900
1912	1,895,400	1936	2,444,300	1960	6,328,300
1913	—	1937	2,527,600	1961	6,325,600
1914	1,612,100	1938	2,630,200	1962	6,295,700
1915	2,093,300	1939	2,663,000	1963	6,358,436
1916	2,219,700	1940	2,571,100	1964	6,353,317
1917	2,465,100	1941	2,485,400	1965	6,439,893
1918	3,013,100	1942	2,453,900	1966	6,335,612
1919	3,511,200	1943	2,503,200	1967	6,294,614
1920	4,359,800	1944	2,672,800	1968	6,086,625
1921	4,010,300	1945	3,038,600	1969	6,163,882
1922	3,311,000	1946	3,322,300	1970	6,222,580
1923	3,155,900	1947	5,040,200		

SOURCE: *Labour Party Annual Report*, 1971, pp. 397–8.

NOTES
The Labour Party membership comprises both affiliated and individual members. The party's ranks were opened to individual members only in 1918. In 1970 there were 5,542,389 affiliated and 680,191 individual members.

BELGIUM

Year	No.	Year	No.
1951	126,000	1963	196,700
1952	126,000	1966	196,500
1953	126,000	1969	194,253
1955	140,000	1970	216,500
1957	140,000	1971	216,500
1959	182,542	1972	216,500
1961	196,700		

SOURCE: Socialist International. Emile Vandervelde Institute, Brussels.

NETHERLANDS

Year	No.	Year	No.	Year	No.
1895	700	1917	24,893	1939	82,145
1896	1000	1918	27,093		
1897	1500	1919	37,628	1945	56,000
1898	2100	1920	47,870	1946	77,000
1899	2500	1921	37,412	1947	115,000
1900	3200	1922	41,472	1948	108,000
1901	4000	1923	42,047	1949	117,000
1902	6500	1924	41,230	1950	110,000
1903	5600	1925	37,894	1951	112,000
1904	6000	1926	41,221	1952	110,000
1905	6816	1927	43,196	1953	111,000
1906	7471	1928	46,169	1954	112,000
1907	8423	1929	53,395	1955	125,000
1908	8748	1930	61,162	1956	143,000
1909	9504	1931	69,263	1957	140,000
1910	9980	1932	78,920	1958	136,000
1911	12,582	1933	81,914	1959	153,000
1912	15,667	1934	87,212	1961	145,000
1913	25,708	1935	84,269	1963	145,000
1914	25,609	1936	87,826	1966	140,000
1915	25,642	1937	87,312	1969	116,922
1916	24,018	1938	88,897		

SOURCE: J. Braunthal, *Yearbook of the International Socialist Labour Movement*. Socialist International.

Communist Party Membership

Year	France	Germany	Italy	Britain	Belgium	Netherlands	Total
1922	78,000	226,000	24,000	5000	517	2500	336,017
1925	83,000	122,000	12,000	5000	590	1700	224,290
1929	46,000	106,000	—	3500	1000	1100	157,600
1936	150,000[1]	—	—	11,500	8000	6000	175,500
1946	804,000	300,000	2,068,000	42,000	100,000	53,000	3,367,000
1949	786,000	215,000	2,242,000	40,000	35,000	33,000	3,351,000
1954	506,000	65,000[2]	2,145,000	34,000	14,000	16,000	2,780,000
1964	252,000[3]	13,000	1,641,000	34,000	14,000	15,000	1,969,000

[1] June 1936. Membership increased from 80,000 in January 1936 to 280,000 in January 1937 following the Popular Front election victory in May and the sit down strikes of June–July 1936.
[2] 1956 figure.
[3] June 1965.

FRANCE

Year	No.	Year	No.
1921	131,000	1937 (Jan.)	280,000
1922	78,828	1937 (Dec.)	328,296
1924	68,187		
1925	83,326	1944	309,681
1926	75,000	1945 (June)	544,989
1927	52,376	1945 (Dec.)	775,342
1928	52,372	1946	804,229
1929	46,000	1947 (Jan.)	809,030
1930	38,248	1947 (June)	895,130
1931	30,743	1947 (Dec.)	907,785
1932	34,580	1948	798,459
1933	28,000	1949	786,855
1934	40,000	1954	506,250
1935	60,000	1959	225,000
1936 (Jan.)	80,000	1965	252,000
1936 (June)	150,000		

SOURCES: B. Lazitch, *Les Partis communistes d'Europe, 1919–55*, pp. 192/3. W. S. Sworatowski: ed., *World Communism: a handbook*, Hoover Institution Press, 1973, pp. 142, 146.

GERMANY *(Weimar and Federal Republic)*

Year	No.	Year	No.
1919	106,656	1931	206,000
1920	45,000	1932	360,000
1921	360,000		
1922	226,000	1945 (June)	300,000
1924	121,394	1947	325,000
1925	122,755	1949	215,000
1926	134,248	1951	178,000
1927	124,729	1956	65,000
1929	106,000	1964	13,000
1930	240,000		

SOURCE: B. Lazitch, *Les Partis communistes d'Europe*, p. 163. W. S. Sworatowski, ed., *World Communism: a handbook*, p. 158.

EAST GERMANY (later DDR)

Year	No.	Year	No.
1946	1,298,415	1951	1,298,000
1947	1,793,951	1953	1,230,000
1948	2,000,000	1954	1,300,000
1949	1,770,000	1963	1,650,000
1950	1,550,000		

SOURCE: J. M. Vincent, in *Socialist Register*, 1964, p. 70. W. S. Sworatowski, ed., *World Communism: a handbook*, p. 161.

ITALY

Year	No.	Year	No.
1921	70,000	1957	1,825,342
1922	24,638	1958	1,818,606
1924	12,000	1959	1,789,269
		1960	1,792,974
1943 (Jan.)	5,000	1961	1,728,620
1943 (Dec.)	110,000	1962	1,630,550
1944	401,960	1963	1,615,112
1945	1,718,000	1964	1,641,214
1946	2,068,282	1965	1,615,296
1949	2,242,719	1966	1,575,935
1950	2,112,593	1967	1,534,705
1951	2,117,000	1968	1,502,889
1953	2,134,285	1969	1,503,816
1955	2,145,317	1970	1,507,047
1956	2,035,353	1971	1,521,642

SOURCES: B. Lazitch, *Les Partis communistes d'Europe 1919–55*, p. 225. Italian Communist Party – official figures.

BRITAIN

Year	No.	Year	No.
1920	3000–5000	1946	42,000
1922	5116	1947	39,000
1924	3000	1948	44,000
1925	5000	1949	40,000
1926	6000 (April)	1950	39,000
1926	10,730 (Oct.)	1951	35,000
1927	7377	1952	36,000
1929	3500	1953	35,000
		1954	34,000
1930	2555	1955	33,000
1931	2756 (June)	1956	33,000
1931	6263 (Sept.)	1957	27,000
1932	9000 (Jan.)	1958	25,000
1932	5600 (Nov.)	1959	26,000
1933	—	1960	27,000
1934	5800	1961	29,000
1935	7700	1962	30,000
1936	11,500	1963	33,000
1937	12,250	1964	34,000
1938	15,750	1965	34,000
1939	17,756	1966	33,000
		1967	33,000
1941	22,738	1968	30,000
1942	56,000	1969	31,000
1943	55,138	1970	29,000
1944	47,513	1971	29,000
1945	45,435		

SOURCES: Communist Party: Congress Reports and official figures. Henry Pelling, *The British Communist Party*, London, 1958, pp. 192/193. Walter Kendall, *The Revolutionary Movement in Britain 1900–1921*, London 1969, pp. 303/5.

BELGIUM

Year	No.	Year	No.
1922	517	1939	9000
1924	590		
1927	1500	1945	100,000
1928	500	1949	35,000
1929	less than 1000	1954	14,000
1935	2500	1959	11,345
1936	8000	1962	14,353
1938	7000		

SOURCES: B. Lazitch, *Les Partis communistes d'Europe 1919–55*, p. 174.
W. S. Sworatowski, ed., *World Communism : a handbook*, pp. 31,33, 35.

NETHERLANDS

Year	No.	Year	No.
1919	500	1935	6000
1920	2431	1938	10,000
1922	2500		
1924	1700	1946	53,000
1927	1400	1950	33,000
		1952	25,000
1929	1100	1955	16,000
1931	1600	1960	15,000
1932	3700		

SOURCES: B. Lazitch, *Les Partis communistes d'Europe 1919–55*, p. 217.
W. S. Sworatowski, ed., *World Communism : a handbook*, pp. 333/4, 336.

LUXEMBOURG

Year	No.	Year	No.
1921	500	1948	3000
1925	210	1950	1500
1945	5000	1954	800

SOURCES: B. Lazitch, *Les Partis communistes d'Europe 1919–55*, p. 235.
W. S. Sworatowski, *World Communism : a handbook*, p. 312.

Socialist and Communist Election Results

GENERAL   *Votes*

Year	France		Germany		Italy		Britain	
	Socialist	*Communists*	*Socialist*	*Communist*	*Socialist*	*Communist*	*Socialist*	*Commu*
1900–5	878,000		3,010,000		325,000		63,000	
1909–12	1,106,000		4,250,000		341,000		506,000	
1918–20	1,729,000		6,104,000	589,000	1,834,000		2,245,000	
1924–25	1,687,000	875,000	7,880,000	2,709,000	783,000	268,000	5,488,000	55,000
1932–33	1,975,000	796,000	7,250,000	5,980,000	—		6,363,000[1]	51,000
1946–49	3,432,000	5,489,000	6,935,000	1,360,000	4,758,000	4,356,000	11,992,000[2]	92,000
1954–58	3,180,000	5,514,000	9,496,000		4,198,000	6,704,000	12,405,000	32,000
1960–63	2,300,000	4,010,000	11,427,000		4,255,000	7,767,000	12,205,000[3]	46,000
1967–70	4,224,000	5,029,000	14,074,000		4,604,000	8,557,000	12,142,000	50,000

[1] 1931
[2] 1945
[3] 1964
[4] Estimate

gium alist	Communist	Netherlands Socialist	Communist	Denmark Socialist	Communist	Total Electoral Support Socialists	Communists
6,000		65,000				4,807,000	
4,000		82,000				6,529,000	
7,000		294,000	31,000			12,853,000	620,000
0,000	29,000	706,000	36,000			17,364,000	3,972,000
6,000	65,000	789,000	118,000			17,243,000	7,010,000
0,000[4]	300,000	1,347,000	502,000	834,000	141,000	30,098,000	12,240,000
7,000	184,000	1,871,000	272,000	910,000	73,000	33,987,000	12,779,000
3,000	162,000	1,750,000	173,000	1,024,000	27,000	34,894,000	12,185,000
9,000	170,000	1,619,000	248,000	968,000	29,000	39,080,000	14,083,000

FRANCE

Year	Socialist Votes	Seats	%	Communist Votes	Seats	%
1905	878,000	52	—			
1910	1,106,000	76	—			
1914	1,397,373	103	—			
1919	1,729,307	—	—			
1924	1,687,668	105	17·2	875,000	26	9·7
1928	1,719,115	100	17·4	1,063,000	14	11·6
1932	1,975,593		20·0	796,000	12	9·6
1936	1,922,493	146	19·2	1,502,000	72	18·3
1945	4,561,000	150	18·5	5,004,121	161	26·4
1946 (June)	4,188,000	129	17·0	5,199,111	153	26·2
1946 (Nov.)	3,432,000	105	13·7	5,489,288	183	28·6
1951	2,744,842	107	14·3	5,041,593	103	25·6
1956	3,180,000	99	15·0	5,514,945	146	25·6
1958	3,193,000	47	15·5	3,882,204	10	18·9
1962	2,300,000	66	12·7	4,010,809	41	21·8
1967	4,224,000		18·9	5,029,808	73	22·4
1968	3,654,000		16·5	4,435,357	33	20·0

SOURCES: J. Braunthal, *Yearbook of the International Socialist Labour Movement*. B. Lazitch, *Les Partis communistes d'Europe*, p. 193. C. Willard, *Socialisme et Communisme Français*, Paris, p. 155. Institut Maurice Thorez, Williams, *Politics in Post-War France*, pp. 440, 441. Williams, *The French Parliament*, 1956–67, p. 29.

GERMANY

Year	Socialist Votes	Seats	%	Communist Votes	Seats	%
1871	123,975	2	—			
1874	351,952	9	—			
1877	493,288	12	—			
1878	437,158	9	—			
1881	311,961	12	—			
1884	549,990	24	—			
1887	763,128	11	—			
1890	1,427,298	35	—			
1893	1,786,738	44	—			
1898	2,107,076	56	—			
1903	3,010,771	81	—			
1907	3,259,029	43	—			
1912	4,250,401	110	—			
1919	13,826,400	187[1]	—			
1920	11,151,211	194[2]	45·5%	589,500	4	2·1
1924 (May)	6,014,000	100	21·0	3,693,300	62	12·6
1924 (Dec.)	7,880,963	131	26·0	2,709,100	45	9·0
1928	9,146,165	152	29·6	3,264,800	54	10·6
1930	8,575,240	143	24·4	4,592,100	77	13·1
1932 (July)	7,959,700	133	21·6	5,282,000	89	14·6
1932 (Nov.)	7,248,000	121	20·4	5,980,200	100	16·9
1933	7,181,600	120	18·3	4,848,100	81	12·3
1949*	6,935,000	—	29·2	1,360,443	15	5·7
1953	7,940,000	151	28·8	607,413	—	2·2
1957	9,496,000	169	31·8			
1961	11,427,000	190	36·2			
1965	12,813,186	202	39·3			
1969	14,074,455	224	42·7			

NOTES
[1] SPD 11,509,100 – 165 seats.
  USPD 2,317,300 – 22 seats.
[2] SPD 6,104,398 – 113 seats.
  USPD 5,046,813 – 81 seats.
[3] Federal Republic only 1949 onwards.
SOURCES: K. S. Pinson, *Modern Germany*, pp. 572–5. B. Lazitch, *Les Partis communistes d'Europe*, p. 164. SPD official figures.

ITALY

Year	Socialist Votes	Seats	%	Communist Votes	Seats	%
1892	26,000	6	—			
1895	76,000	12	—			
1897	135,000	15	—			
1900	175,000	33	13			
1904	325,960	30	—			
1909	341,387	41	—			
1913	961,703	53	—			
1919	1,834,792	156	—			
1921	1,628,753	123	24·7	304,719	15	4·6
1924	{ 360,694[1]	22	5·0	268,191	19	3·7
	422,957[2]	24	5·9			
1946	4,758,129	—	21·0	4,356,686	104	19·0
1948	1,838,116	52	—	8,136,637[7]	131	31·0
1953	{ 3,441,014[3]	75	12·7	6,120,709	143	22·7
	1,222,957[4]	19	4·5			
1958	4,198,522	84	14·2	6,704,706	140	22·7
1963	4,255,836	87	13·8	7,767,601	166	25·3
1968	4,604,329[5]	91	14·5	8,557,404	177	26·9
1972	3,224,778[6]	61	10·7	9,097,847	179	27·2

[1] Serrati group.
[2] Turati group.
[3] Nenni Socialists – PSI.
[4] Saragat Socialists – PSDI.
[5] Nenni Socialists (PSI) plus Saragat Socialists (PSDI).
[6] Nenni Socialists (PSI) alone.
[7] The socialist figure is for the Saragat group. The socialists and communists fought on a common slate. The Nenni Socialist-Communist vote is shown under the communist heading.

SOURCES: B. Lazitch, *Les Partis communistes d'Europe*, pp. 225–6. Italian Communist Party figures.

Spartaco Cannarsa, *Il Socialismo e i XXV Congress Nazionali del Partito Socialista Italiano*, Società Editrici Avanti!, Florence, 1950.

BRITAIN

Year	Labour Party Vote	Seats	%	Communist Party Vote	Seats	%
1900	62,600	2	1·8			
1906	323,100	29	5·9			
1910 (Jan.)	505,600	40	7·6			
1910 (Dec.)	370,800	42	7·1			
1918	2,244,900	57	22·2	—	—	—
1922	4,236,700	142	29·5	52,639	2	
1923	4,348,300	191	30·5	76,741	—	
1924	5,487,600	151	33·0	55,355	1	
1929	8,364,800	287	37·1	50,164	—	
1931	6,362,500	46	30·6	74,824	—	
1935	8,325,200	154	37·9	27,117	1	
1945	11,992,200	393	47·8	102,780	2	
1950	13,295,700	315	46·1	91,746	—	
1951	13,948,300	295	48·8	21,640	—	
1955	12,405,200	277	46·4	33,144		
1959	12,216,100	258	43·8	30,897	—	
1964	12,205,200	317	44·1	45,932	—	
1966	13,064,951	363	47·9	62,112	—	
1970	12,141,676	287		38,431	—	

SOURCES: David Butler and Jennie Freeman, *British Political Facts, 1900–1968*, London, 1969, pp. 141/4. Henry Pelling, *A Short History of the Labour Party*, p. 136. Keesings Contemporary Archives.

BELGIUM

Year	Socialist Votes	Seats	%	Communist Votes	Seats	%
1894	308,932	28	16·15			
1900	466,898	32	30·0			
1912	{ 244,773[1]	39	9·35			
	{ 782,332	—	—			
1919	647,000	69	37·0			
1921	672,474	68	35·8	3164	—	—
1925	820,650	78	39·4	29,422	2	0·3
1929	803,347	70	36·0	43,237	1	1·9
1932	866,361	73	37·1	65,905	3	2·8
1936	757,537	70	32·0	143,223	9	6·0
1939	704,582	64	30·2	125,428	9	5·3
1946	—	69	31·5	300,099	23	12·6
1949	1,496,890	66	28·7	376,765	12	7·4
1950	1,755,216	77	35·6	234,541	7	4·7
1954	1,927,015	86	37·3	184,000	4	3·5
1958	1,897,646	84	35·7	100,113	2	1·8
1961	1,933,424	84	36·7	162,238	4	3·0
1965	1,464,635	64	28·2	236,702	5	4·5
1968	1,449,172	59	27·99	170,625	5	3·3
1971	1,438,626	61	27·2	163,785	5	3·2

[1] In 1912 there were two lists: socialists (*top*) and socialist-liberal. The number of seats is the total for the two groups.

SOURCE: B. Lazitch, *Les Partis communistes d'Europe*, p. 173. Emile Vandervelde Institute. Belgian Communist Party.

NETHERLANDS

Year	Socialist Votes	Seats	%	Communist Votes	Seats	%
1897	12,451	2	2·0			
1901	38,279	2	5·0			
1905	65,561	6	6·0			
1909	82,855	7	7·0			
1913	144,249	15	16·0			
1918	294,495	22	22·0	31,010	2	2·3
1922	567,769	20	20·0	53,664	2	1·8
1925	706,704	24	23·0	36,786	1	1·2
1929	804,714	24	24·0	37,622	2	2·0
1933	798,632	22	22·0	118,354	4	3·2
1937	890,661	23	22·0	115,845	3	3·3
1946	1,347,940	29	28·0	502,963	10	10·6
1948	1,263,366	27	26·0	382,001	8	7·7
1952	1,545,867	30	29·0	328,571	6	6·2
1956	1,871,990	50	33·0	272,167	4	4·8
1959	1,821,677	48	30·0	144,371	3	2·4
1963	1,750,808	43	28·0	173,457	4	2·8
1967	1,619,694	37	23·5	248,008	5	3·6
1971	1,552,276	39	24·6	246,299	6	3·9
1972	2,021,473	43	24·7	329,973	7	4·5

SOURCES: J. Braunthal, *Yearbook of the International Socialist Labour Movement.* B. Lazitch, *Les Partis communistes d'Europe*, p. 218. Netherlands Embassy. Keesings Contemporary Archives. Dehl (Ed.), *Political Oppositions in Western Democracies*, pp. 418–22.

DENMARK

Year	Socialist Votes	Seats	%	Communist Votes	Seats	%
1935	759,069	68	—	27,140	2	—
1945	610,966	48	—	218,054	18	—
1947	834,089	57	—	141,094	9	—
1950	813,590	59	—	94,495	7	—
1953	894,913	74	—	93,824	8	—
1957	910,862	70	—	73,310	6	—
1960	1,024,039	76	—	27,345	—	—
1964	1,103,667	76	41·9	32,390	—	1·2
1966	1,070,043	69	38·3	21,536	—	0·7
1968	968,706	62	34·2	29,738	—	1·1
1971	1,074,777	70	37·3	39,564	—	1·4

SOURCE: Keesings Contemporary Archives.

LUXEMBOURG

Year	Socialist Vote	Seats	%	Communist Votes	Seats	%
1922	17,379	—	15·0	965	—	0·8
1925	—	—	—	—	—	3·1
1931	32,000	13	—	—	—	5·6
1934	400,000	10	42·0	70,000	1	7·4
1945	—	—	—	295,701	7	13·4
1948	372,177	19	16·0	228,982	4	10·0
1954	831,836	17	29·0	211,121	3	5·4
1959	848,523	17	30·0	220,425	3	4·8
1964	999,843	21	33·4	330,909	5	7·8

SOURCES: B. Lazitch, *Les Partis communistes d'Europe*, p. 235. Keesings Contemporary Archives.

Immigrants and Foreign Workers

Statistics regarding immigrants and foreign workers raise many difficulties. Not all immigrants need be foreign workers, they may also be self-employed persons, professional people or even political refugees. Statistics for active (employed) workers understate the true immigrant population by a wide margin since they make no allowance either for the numbers of dependents, or for elder persons outside the active labour force. All figures will exclude 'illegal' immigrants, who as in France in recent years, may be very numerous. On the other hand they may *include* foreign born groups such as the Poles in Britain and France, now more properly understood as permanently domiciled in their country of residence, who may indeed have acquired nationality. Further, statistics from different sources, which ought to be comparable, frequently show wide disparities for which no reason is obviously apparent. The reader would do well to bear these factors in mind.

Ireland and Italy, countries in which the numbers of immigrants and foreign workers do not reach significant proportions have been excluded from the tables. Figures for Denmark were still awaited when the volume closed for the press.

FRANCE

Algeria	700,000
Germany	50,000
Italy	590,000
Morocco	170,000
Poland	110,000
Portugal	610,000
Spain	620,000
Tunisia	100,000
Yugoslavia	60,000
	3,010,000

NOTE
Algeria, Morocco, Poland, Portugal, and Tunisia 1970; other countries 1968.

GERMANY

Austria	143,000
France	47,000
Greece	343,000
Italy	574,000
Netherlands	104,000
Portugal	54,000
Spain	246,000
Turkey	469,000
Yugoslavia	515,000
Other	482,000
	2,977,000

BRITAIN

Austria	30,000
British West Indies (including Jamaica)	270,000
Cyprus	60,000
France	34,000
Germany	140,000
Greece	9000
India	240,000
Irish Republic	740,000
Italy	100,000
Netherlands	17,000
Pakistan	75,000
Poland	120,000
Portugal	6000
Spain	35,000
Turkey	4000
Yugoslavia	13,000
Others	710,000
	2,603,000

Figures for persons from outside the United Kingdom.

BELGIUM

Total_____ 172,000
of which   70,000 Italy

The figures are for the year 1968. Castles and Kosack, (p. 4), however, put the number of foreign *immigrants* in Belgium at 679,000.

NETHERLANDS

Total_____ 100,000
of which   9500 Italy
                            20,000 crossfrontier
workers from Belgium and Netherlands

SOURCES: OECD *Social Statistiques*, Supplement A, Paris, 1969. S. Castles and G. Kosack, *Immigrant Workers and Class Structure in Western Europe*, Oxford 1973, pp. 4–5. Nicolas Deakin (ed.). *Immigrants in Europe*, Fabian Text No. 300, London 1973, p. 10.

Maps and Diagrams

2. BELGIUM: LINGUISTIC REGIONS

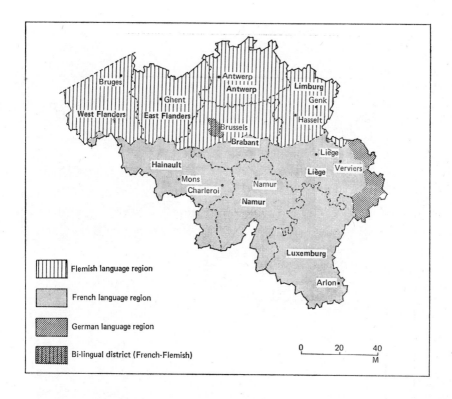

Bruges

Antwerp
Antwerp

Limburg
Genk

Ghent

East Flanders

Hasselt

West Flanders

Brussels

Brabant

Liège

Hainault

Liège
Verviers

Mons

Charleroi

Namur

Namur

Luxemburg

Arlon

Flemish language region

French language region

German language region

Bi-lingual district (French-Flemish)

0   20   40
                M

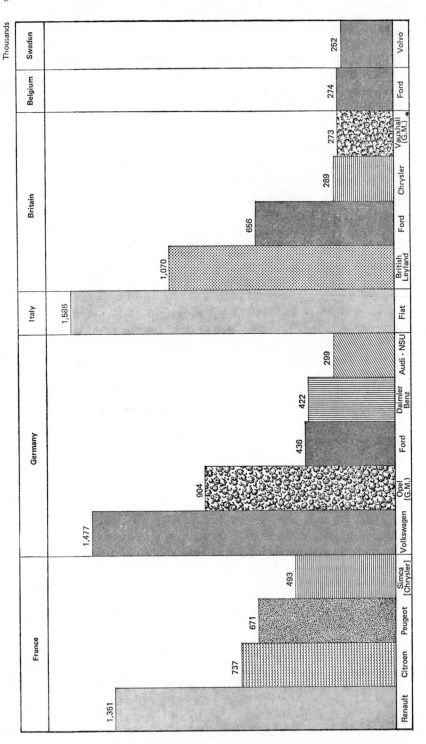

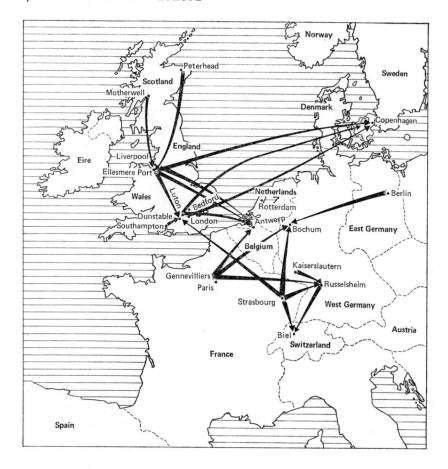

GENERAL MOTORS — EUROPE

Production flow

General Motors operates as Vauxhall in Great Britain, as Opel in Germany, under its own name in Belgium and France. The chart which follows shows the extent of Europe wide integration. Given the variable fortunes of the automotive industry the data given should be regarded as subject to change.

Subsidiary	Product	Plant	Specific Operations
BELGIUM			
GM Continental	**Cars:** Opel Kadett, Rekord, Olympia **Trucks:** Vauxhall, Bedford Automotive parts	*Antwerp*	**Final assembly** of cars and trucks, radiator production, warehouse, administration centre

Subsidiary	Product	Plant	Specific Operations
BRITAIN **Vauxhall**	**Cars:** Viva, Victor, Ventora, Cresta, Viscount	*Ellesmere Port*	Transmissions, axles, power train components, stampings, body build-up, paint and trim, **final assembly**
	Trucks and vans: Bedford	*Dunstable*	Power train and engines, axles, truck frames, **final assembly** (trucks)
		Bedford	Die construction
		Luton	Stampings, engines, body build-up, paint and trim, **final assembly**
		Toddington	Parts depot
		Lidlington	Proving grounds
FRANCE **GM Strasbourg**	Automotive parts	*Strasbourg*	3-speed automatic transmission production
GERMANY **Opel**	**Cars:** Kadett, Olympia, Rekord, Kapitan, Admiral, Diplomat	*Rüsselsheim*	Transmissions, axles, power train components, stampings, body build-up, paint and trim, **final assembly** (cars and trucks), product engineering
	Trucks and vans: Opel	*Bochum*	Engines, mechanical components, stampings, body build-up, **final assembly**
		Kaiserslautern	Chassis components
		Berlin	Bearing shells
		Dudenhofen	Proving grounds

Source: I.M.F. Situation as at January, 1972.

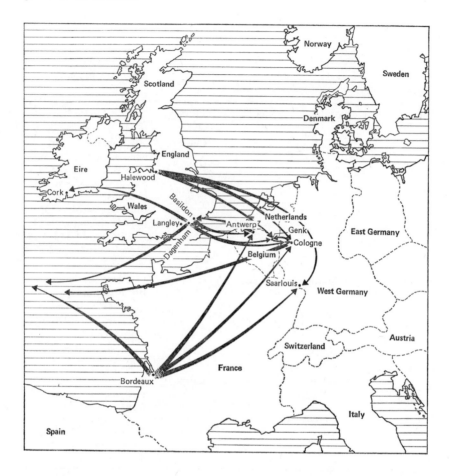

FORD OF EUROPE

Production flow
The major vehicle producers are now organized on a continental and international scale. This chart shows the basic inter-state production flow of Ford of Europe. Given the changeable fortunes of the automotive industry the details should be treated as approximate. Only major operations are shown.

Country	Plant Location	Number of Employees	Vehicle	Specific Operations
Belgium	Antwerp	2,000	Tractors	Tractor operations, rear axles and transmissions. Supplies parts for Basildon

Country	Plant Location	Number of Employees	Vehicle	Specific Operations
	Genk	10,000	Escort	Wheels, stampings, **final assembly.** Supplies wheels, body stampings to Cologne
Britain	Basildon	2,000	Tractors	Supplies parts for Antwerp
	Dagenham	25,000	Cars	Stampings, foundry, wheels, body build-up, chassis, paint and trim, transmissions, engines, tractor components, **final assembly.** Supplies body stampings to Cologne and Genk, CKD Cortinas to Amsterdam
	Halewood	11,000	Cars	Gearboxes, stampings, **final assembly.** Supplies body stampings to Cologne and Genk
	Langley	5,000	Trucks	**Final assembly** for other units
	Leamington and Swansea	—	Parts	Foundry, castings, power train, transmission parts
France	Bordeaux	1,600		Produces automatic transmission, supplies all 5 car plants
Germany	Cologne	25,000	Cars	Stampings, foundry, engines, body build-up, **final assembly.** Supplies engines and transmissions to Genk
	Saarlouis	5,000	Cars	Stampings, sub-assembly, **final assembly**
Ireland	Cork	800	Cortina, Escort	Assembly plant
Netherlands	Amsterdam	1,400	Cortina, trucks	Assembly plant

Source: I.M.F. Situation as at January 1972.

6. MOTOR INDUSTRY EUROPE

The diagram shows the distance of the main motor plants from London.
Each circle equals fifty miles

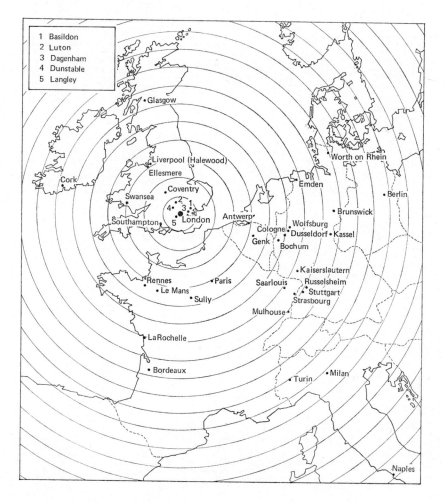

A. INTERNATIONAL CONFEDERATION OF FREE TRADE UNIONS — ICFTU

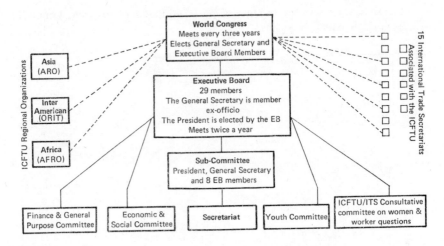

Note

A representative of the ICFTU/ITS Advisory Committee on Women Worker questions is entitled to take part in Executive Board meetings on a consultative basis. Four representatives from ITS are entitled to attend Executive Board meetings on a consultative basis.

Source: ICFTU

B. GENERAL CONFEDERATION OF LABOUR-WORKER'S FORCE – CGT-FO

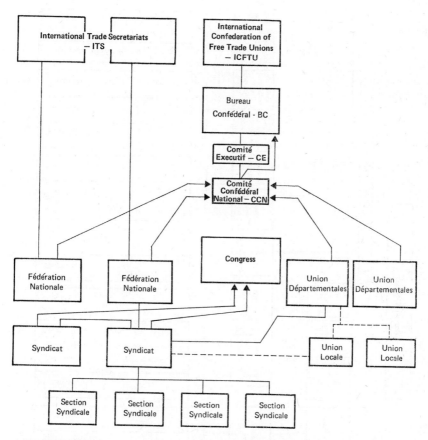

Notes

In addition to the elements shown above, the CGT-FO also embraces young workers (*Fédération Nationale des Jeunes Syndicalistes*) and old age pensioners (*Fédération Nationale des Vieux Travailleurs*). In each case the organization exists at local, *département* and national level. *Département* should be understood in the sense of the administrative divisions of the French state to which the CGT-FO '*Union Départementales*' correspond. An elaboration of the working of the structure will be found in the text.

It will be noted that in the CGT-FO, as in the CGT, the Congress which decides policy does not elect the CCN and higher organs to which the execution of policy is entrusted.

Source: CGT-FO

C. **FRENCH DEMOCRATIC CONFEDERATION OF LABOUR – CFDT** head
office chart

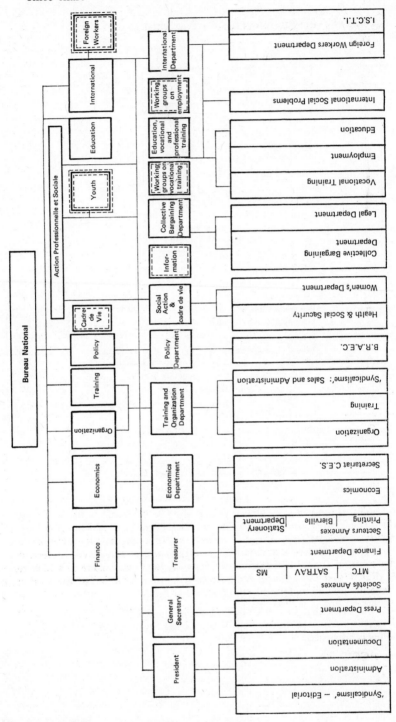

Source: CFDT

D. GENERAL CONFEDERATION OF LABOUR – CGT

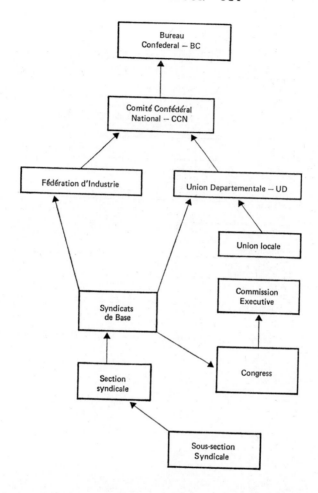

Notes

Féderation d'Industrie represents the equivalent of the British trade union. The Union Départementale represents the regional organization at the level of the départements, the administrative divisions of the French state to which the union structure, here, corresponds. It will be observed that in the CGT, as in the CGT-FO, the Congress which decides policy does not elect the CCN and higher organs to which the execution of policy is entrusted.

E. ITALIAN CONFEDERATION OF WORKERS UNIONS — CISL

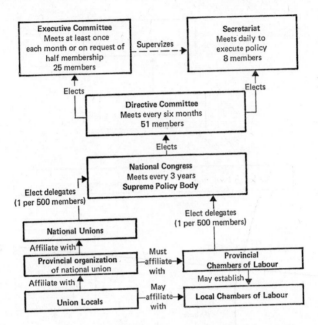

Adapted from Joseph La Palombara, *The Italian Labour Movement*, Ithaca, 1957, p. 51

F. ITALIAN UNION OF LABOUR – UIL

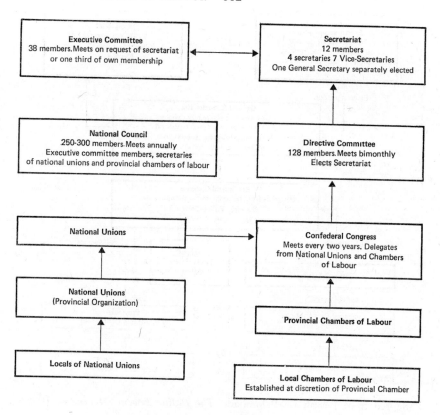

Source: Adapted from Joseph La Palombara, *The Italian Labour Movement*, Ithaca, 1957, p. 53

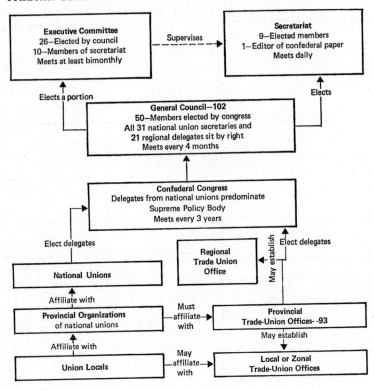

Adapted from Joseph La Palombara, *The Italian Labour Movement*, Ithaca, 1957, p. 52

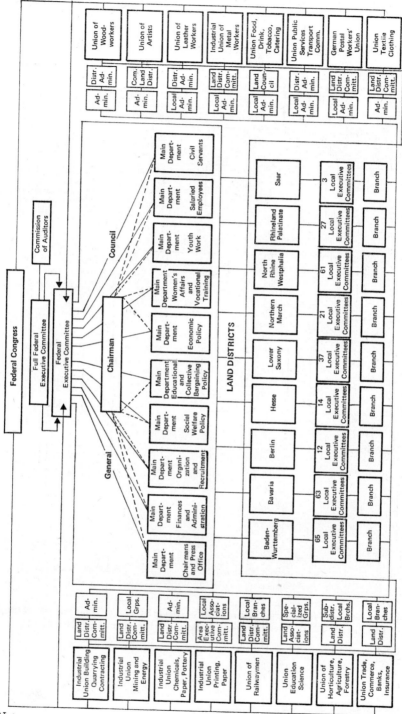

Note

The Land Districts of the DGB correspond to the states (Lander) of the German Federal Republic.

I. BELGIAN GENERAL FEDERATION OF LABOUR – FGTB

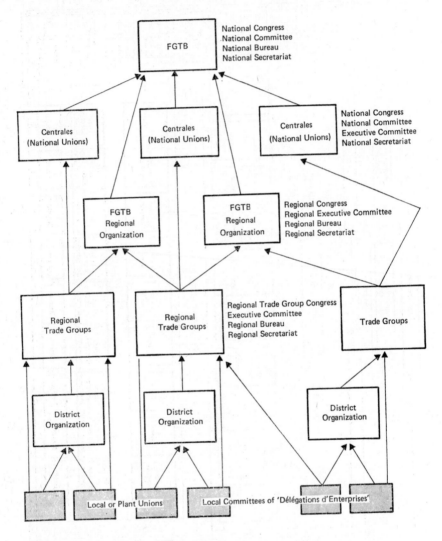

Note

I have rendered the Belgian *Section Professionelle* as *Trade Group*, the term used in the British TGWU which would seem to be the nearest equivalent.

Source: FGTB

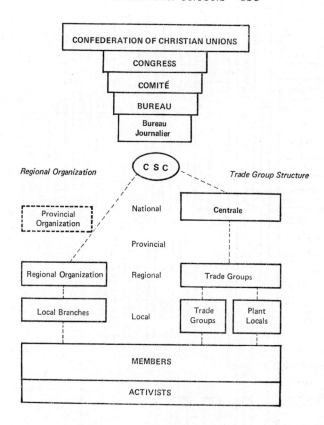

Note

I have translated the Belgian *Secteur Professionelle* as *Trade Group*, the term used in the British TGWU which would seem to be the nearest equivalent: the Belgian *Secteur Interprofessionel* as *Regional Organization*: the term *militants* which has no true equivalent in English as *activists*: the term *Centrale*, roughly the equivalent of national union I have left in the original so as to convey more precisely the Belgian connotation.

Source: 'Catechisme Syndicale', CSC, Brussells, 1972

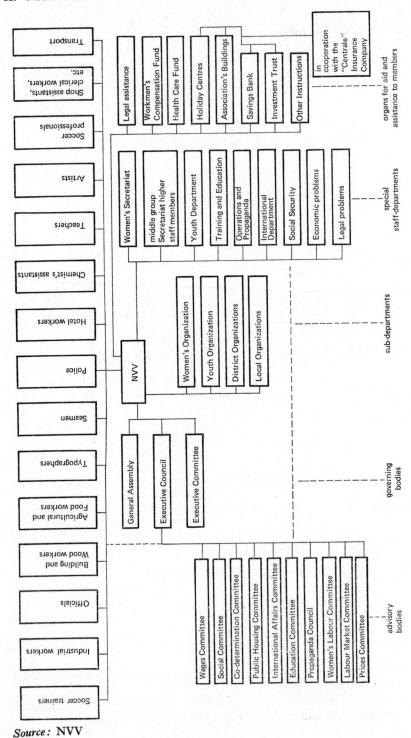

Source: NVV

Bibliography

GENERAL

Books

AARON, B., *Labor Courts and Grievance Settlement in Western Europe*, University of California Press, 1971.

BROAD, ROGER and JARRETT, R. J., *Community Europe Today*, rev. edn, Wolff, 1972.

CALMANN, JOHN, ed., *Western Europe: a handbook*, Blond, 1967.

CARSTEN, F. L., *Revolution in Central Europe, 1918-1919*, Temple Smith, 1972.

CROZIER, MICHEL, *The Bureaucratic Phenomenon*, Tavistock, 1964.

DAHL, ROBERT A., *Political Oppositions in Western Democracies*, Yale University Press, 1968.

DALLIN, DAVID J., *Soviet Espionage*, Yale University Press, 1955.

DESPICHT, NIGEL, *Policies for Transport in the Common Market*, London, Lambarde Press, 1964.

EDELMAN, M. and FLEMING, R. W., *The Politics of Wage-Price Decisions*, University of Illinois Press, 1965.

EEC INFORMATION OFFICE, *The Common Market and the Common Man*, London, 1969.

EINAUDI, L. and GOGUEL, F., *Christian Democracy in France and Italy*, Notre Dame, 1952.

GERSCHENKRON, A., *Economic Backwardness in Historical Perspective*, Harvard University Press, 1962.

HENDERSON, W. O., *The Industrial Revolution on the Continent*, Cass, 1961.

HOBSBAWM, ERIC, *The Age of Revolution*, Weidenfeld & Nicolson, 1962.

HOBSBAWM, ERIC, *Labouring Men*, Weidenfeld & Nicolson, 1964.

JAMES, RALPH and JAMES, ESTELLE, *Hoffa and the Teamsters*, New York, Van Nostrand, 1965.

KAHN-FREUND, OTTO, et al., *Labour Law in Europe with special reference to the Common Market*, Stevens, 1962.

KAHN-FREUND, OTTO, et al., *Labour Relations and the Law: a comparative study*, Stevens, 1965.

KENDALL, WALTER, *Mercato Comune e movimento operaio in Europa*, Milan, Azione Comune, 1965.

KINDLEBERGER, CHARLES P., ed., *The International Corporation: symposium proceedings*, Massachusetts Institute of Technology Press, 1970.

422 THE LABOUR MOVEMENT IN EUROPE

LANDES, DAVID S., *The Unbound Prometheus*, Cambridge University Press, 1969.
LAPALOMBARA, J. and WEINER, M., eds., *Political Parties and Political Development*, Princeton University Press, 1966.
LAYTON, C., *Trans-Atlantic Investments*, Boulogne-sur-Seine, 1968.
LEVARD, G., *Chances et périls du syndicalisme chrétien*, Paris, 1955.
LEVINSON, CHARLES, *Capital, Inflation and the Multinationals*, Allen & Unwin, 1971.
LIPSET, S. M., and ROKKAN, S., *Political Party Systems and Voter Alignments*, New York, Free Press, 1967.
MICHELS, ROBERT, *Democracy and Political Parties*, Jarrold 1915.
MITCHELL, H. and STEARNS, P. V., *Workers and Protest*, Cornell University Press, 1971.
MOODY, JOSEPH N., ed., *Church and Society*, New York, Arts, 1963.
MOORE, BARRINGTON, *Soviet Politics: the dilemma of power*, New York, Harper, 1965.
NORRIS, FRANK, *The Octopus*, Nelson, 1901.
NORRIS, FRANK, *The Pit*, London, Grant Richards, 1903.
OECD, *Growth and Economic Policy*, Paris, 1964.
PERLMAN, SELIG, *A Theory of the Labor Movement*, New York, 1928.
POSTAN, M. M., *An Economic History of Western Europe, 1945–1964*, Methuen, 1967.
SHONFIELD, ANDREW, *Modern Capitalism*, Oxford University Press, 1969.
SPITAELS, G., *L'Année sociale 1968*, Brussels, 1969.
SPITAELS, G., ed., *La Crise des relations industrielles en Europe*, Bruges, 1972.
STALIN, JOSEPH, *Problems of Leninism*, Moscow, 1940.
STURMTHAL, ADOLF, *Contemporary Collective Bargaining in Seven Countries*, University of Illinois Press, 1957.
THOMPSON, E. P., *The Making of the English Working Class*, Penguin, 1968.
TRIFFIN, ROBERT, *Europe and the Money Muddle*, Yale University Press, 1957.
TROTSKY, LEON, *The Writings of Leon Trotsky*, New York, Pathfinder Press, 1969.
VIGNAUX, PAUL, *Traditionalisme et syndicalisme*, New York, 1943.
Yearbook of the International Free Trade Union Movement, 1957–58, London.

Articles

BRAUN, WALTER, 'The European company', *Free Labour World*, Brussels, June 1970.
DESPICHT, NIGEL, 'Esquisse historique de la politique britannique des transports intérieures, *Transports*, Paris, Nov. 1967.
KENDALL, WALTER, 'Folk myths of the western world', *Bulletin of the Society for the Study of Labour History*, London, spring 1972.

INTERNATIONAL LABOUR MOVEMENT
Books
BARKIN, S., DYMOND and KASSALOW, E. M., eds., *International Labor*, New York, Harper & Row, 1961.

BECU, OMAR, *The International Trade Secretariats*, Brussels, ICFTU, 1952.
BECU, OMAR, *The International Transport Workers' Federation*, ITWF, 1952.
BEEVER, R. COLIN, *European Unity and the Trade Union Movement*, Leiden, 1960.
BEHRENDT, ALBERT, *The WFTU and the German Trade Unions*, Berlin, 1965.
BORKENAU, F., *The Communist International*, Faber & Faber, 1938.
BORKENAU, F., *World Communism*, University of Michigan Press, 1962.
BRAUNTHAL, JULIUS, *The International Federation of Trades Unions of the Textile and Clothing Workers*, Ghent, 1928.
BRAUNTHAL, JULIUS, *In Search of the Millennium*, Gollancz, 1945.
BRAUNTHAL, JULIUS, *The History of the International 1914-43*, 2 vols., Nelson, 1966, 1967.
BRAUNTHAL, JULIUS, ed., *Yearbook of the International Socialist Labour Movement*, Nelson, 1960.
CALMANN, JOHN, ed., *Western Europe: a handbook*, Blond, 1967.
CARR, E. H., *The Bolshevik Revolution 1917-1923*, 3 vols., new edn, Penguin, 1966.
CAUTE, D., *The Left in Europe since 1789*, Weidenfeld & Nicolson, 1966.
CONNOLLY, JAMES, *The Workers' Republic*, Dublin, Three Candles, 1951.
DOLLEANS, E., *Histoire du mouvement ouvrier 1830-1936*, Paris, 1953.
DOLLEANS, E. and CROZIER, M., *Mouvement ouvrier et socialiste: chronologie et bibliographie*, Paris, 1950.
DONAHUE, GEORGE R., *Focus on a Communist Front*, Phoenix House, 1958.
FIMMEN, EDO, *The International Federation of Trade Unions*, Amsterdam, 1922.
FIMMEN, EDO, *Labour's Alternative: United States of Europe or Europe Limited*, Labour Publishing Co., 1924.
FORTMAN, W. F., and DE GAAY, *Aims and Purposes of Christian Trade Unionism*, Utrecht, 1958.
GALENSON, WALTER, *Comparative Labor Movements*, New York, Russell, 1952.
GALENSON, WALTER, *Trade Union Democracy in Western Europe*, University of California Press, 1961.
GOMPERS, SAMUEL, *Labour in Europe and America*, London, Harper, 1910.
GORZ, ANDRÉ, *Strategy for Labor*, Boston, Beacon Press, 1967.
GRIFFITH, W. E., ed., *Communism in Europe*, 2 vols., Massachusetts Institute of Technology Press, 1964; Pergamon, 1967.
ICFTU, *How Your Union Works*, Brussels, 1964.
ICFTU, *Labour Management Relations in Western Europe*, Brussels, 1966.
ICFTU, *Twenty Years ICFTU, 1949-1969*, Brussels, 1969.
ILO, *Participation of Workers in Decisions within Undertakings*, Geneva, 1969.
ILO, *The Protection of Trade Union Funds and Property*, Geneva, 1970.
JOLL, JAMES, *The Second International 1889-1915*, Weidenfeld & Nicolson, 1955.
KAMIN, ALFRED, ed., *Western European Labor and the American Corporation*, Washington DC, Bureau of National Affairs, 1970.

424 THE LABOUR MOVEMENT IN EUROPE

KASSALOW, EVERETT M., *National Labor Movements in the Post-War World*, Northwestern University Press, 1963.

KASSALOW, EVERETT M., *Trade Unions and Industrial Relations: an international comparison*, New York, Random House, 1969.

LANDAUER, CARL A. *European Socialism*, 2 vols., University of California Press, 1959.

LAZITCH, B., *Les Partis communistes d'Europe*, Paris, 1956.

LENIN, V. I., *Imperialism, the Highest Stage of Capitalism*, London, Martin Lawrence, 1948.

LEVINSON, CHARLES, *International Trades Unionism*, Allen & Unwin, 1972.

LORWIN, LEWIS L., *The International Labor Movement*, New York, Harper, 1953.

LOUIS, PAUL, *Syndicalisme européenne*, Paris, 1914.

MACDONALD, DWIGHT, *Memoirs of a Revolutionist*, New York, Farrar Straus, 1957.

MARQUAND, H. A., *Organized Labour in Four Continents*, Longmans, 1939.

MARX, ELI and KENDALL, WALTER, *Unions in Europe*, University of Sussex, 1971.

MEYERS, FREDERICK, *European Coal Mining Unions*, University of California Press, 1961.

MEYNAUD, J., *L'action syndicale et la Communauté Européenne*, Lausanne, 1962.

MOODY, JOSEPH N., 'Christian trade unions since World War II', in Moody, ed., *Church and Society*, New York, 1953.

NEUMANN, FRANZ, *European Trade Unionism and Politics*, New York, League for Industrial Democracy, 1936.

PERLMAN, S., *A Theory of the Labor Movement*, New York, Kelley, 1949.

PRAEM, O., *150 Ans de mouvement ouvrier chrétien européen de l'ouest, 1789–1939*, Louvain, 1966.

PRICE, JOHN, *The International Labour Movement*, Oxford University Press, 1945.

REYNAUD, J., *The Future of Industrial Relations in Europe*, Geneva, International Institute of Labour Studies, 1968.

ROSENBERG, ARTHUR, *A History of Bolshevism*, Oxford University Press, 1954.

SASSENBACH, J., *Twenty-five Years of International Trade Unionism*, Amsterdam, 1926.

SCHEVENELS, WALTER, *Forty-five Years of the IFTU*, Brussels, 1956.

SCHOLL, S. H., ed., *150 Ans de mouvement chrétien en Europe de l'ouest*, Louvain, 1966.

SOBOLEV, A. I. et al., *Outline History of the Communist International*, Moscow, 1971.

STURMTHAL, ADOLF, *Contemporary Collective Bargaining in Seven Countries*, University of Illinois Press, 1957.

STURMTHAL, ADOLF, *The Tragedy of European Labor*, Columbia University Press, 1943.

STURMTHAL, ADOLF, *Unity and Diversity in European Labor*, New York, Free Press, 1953.

STURMTHAL, ADOLF, *White-Collar Trade Unions*, University of Illinois Press, 1967.
SWORATOWSKI, W. S., ed., *World Communism, a handbook*, Hoover Institution Press, 1973.
TACK, B., *Labour Management Relations in Western Europe*, Brussels, 1966.
WINDMULLER, JOHN P., *American Labor and the International Labor Movement, 1940-1953*, Cornell University Press, 1953.
WCL, *The WCL; Unity in Diversity*, Brussels, 1970.
WCL, *Fifty Years: the WCL from 1920 to 1970*, Brussels, 1970.
ZIRNHELD, J., *Cinquante années de syndicalisme chrétien*, Paris, 1937.

Articles
'Anglo-American negotiations and the Soviet trade unions', *International Labour Review*, Geneva, Sept. 1942.
BRADEN, T. W., 'I'm glad the CIA is immoral', *Saturday Evening Post*, 20 May 1967.
DAVIES, E., 'Anglo-American trades union co-operation', *Political Quarterly*, London, 1943.
DRAPER, THEODORE, 'The ghost of social fascism', *Commentary*, New York, Feb. 1969.
'The facts about unofficial strikes', *Free Labour World*, Brussels, April 1970.
GEIJER, ARNE, 'Industrial democracy in the seventies', *Free Labour World*, Brussels, April 1971.
'The international trades union movement in the postwar period', *International Labour Review*, Geneva, Sept. 1941.
'Is your union affiliated to the CIA?', *Voice of the Unions*, London, May 1967.
LAPALOMBARA, J, 'The political role of organized labour in Western Europe', *Journal of Politics*, Feb. 1955.
'The Red Labour Union International', *Bulletin of the Executive Bureau*, Moscow, no. 317, Sept. 1921, pp. 3-5.

FRANCE
Books
ADAM, GÉRARD, *Atlas des élections sociales en France*, Paris, 1964.
ADAM, GÉRARD, *La CFTC 1940-1958*, Paris, 1964.
ADAM, GÉRARD, *La CGT - FO*, Paris, 1965.
ADAM, GÉRARD, et al., *L'Ouvrier français en 1970*, Paris 1970.
ADAM, GÉRARD, et al., *Le Négociation collective en France*, Paris, 1972.
BARJONET, ANDRÉ, *La CGT*, Paris, 1960.
BARJONET, ANDRÉ, 'CGT 1968: subjectivism to the rescue of the status quo', in Charles Posner, ed., *Reflections on the Revolution in France 1968*, Penguin, 1970.
BAUM, WARREN C., *The French Economy and the State*, Princeton University Press, 1958.
BELLEVILLE, PIERRE, *Une Nouvelle classe ouvrière*, Paris, 1963.

BORKENAU, F., *The Communist International*, Faber & Faber, 1938.
BOSWORTH, WILLIAM, 'Catholicism and crisis', in E. M. Earle, ed., *Modern France*, Princeton University Press, 1951.
LE BOURRE, RAYMOND, *Le Syndicalisme français sous la Cinquième République*, Paris, 1959.
BOWDITCH, JOHN, 'The concept of élan vital, a rationalization of weakness' in E. M. Earle, ed., *Modern France*, Princeton University Press, 1951.
BRAYANCE, ALAIN, *Anatomie du parti communiste français*, Paris, 1952.
BREÇY, ROBERT, *La Grève générale en France*, Paris, 1961.
BREÇY, ROBERT, *Le Mouvement syndical en France, 1871–1921*, Paris, 1963.
BROWER, DANIEL R., *The New Jacobins: the French Communist Party and the Popular Front*, Cornell University Press, 1968.
BRUHAT, JEAN, *Histoire du mouvement ouvrier français*, Paris, 1952.
BRUHAT, J. and PIOLOT, M., *Esquisse d'une histoire de la CGT*, Paris, 1966.
CAUTE, D., *Communism and the French Intellectuals, 1914–1960*, Deutsch, 1964.
CFDT, *Histoire du mouvement ouvrier et des Centrales Syndicales en France*, Paris, 1966.
CHEVALIER, LOUIS, *Classes laborieuses et classes dangereuses en France*, Paris, 1958.
CLAPHAM, J. H., *The Economic Development of France and Germany, 1815–1914*, Cambridge University Press, 1923.
CLARKE, MARJORIE R., *A History of the French Labor Movement, 1910–1928*, University of California Press, 1930.
COLLINET, MICHEL, *Esprit de syndicalisme*, Paris, 1952.
COLLINET, MICHEL, *Essai sur la condition ouvrière*, Paris, 1951.
COLLINET, MICHEL, *L'Ouvrier français*, Paris, 1951.
COLLINET, MICHEL, *La Tragédie du marxisme*, Paris, 1951.
CUTHBERT, NORMAN, 'Fayol and the principles of organization', in A. Tillett, T. Kempner and G. Wills, eds., *Management Thinkers*, Penguin, 1970.
DALE, LEON, *Marxism and French Labor*, New York, Vantage, 1956.
DESCHAMPS, EUGÈNE, *Militer en toute liberté*, Paris, 1971.
DESCHAMPS, EUGÈNE, 'La France, pratique syndicale, action directe et mouvements spontanés', in G. Spitaels, ed., *La Crise des relations industrielles en Europe*, Brussels, 1971.
DOLLEANS, E., *Histoire du mouvement ouvrier, 1830–1936*, Paris, 1953.
EARLE, E. M., ed., *Modern France*, Princeton University Press, 1951.
EHRMANN, H. W., 'The decline of the French Socialist Party' in E. M. Earle, ed., *Modern France*, Princeton University Press, 1951.
EHRMANN, H. W., *French Labor from Popular Front to Liberation*, Cornell University Press, 1947.
EHRMANN, H. W., *Organized Business in France*, Princeton University Press, 1957.
FAUVET, JACQUES, *Histoire de parti communiste français*, Paris, 1964, 1965.
FROSSARD, L. A., *De Jaurès à Lénine*, Paris, 1930.
FURNISS, E. S., *France – Troubled Ally*, Oxford University Press, 1960.
GALENSON, W., *Comparative Labor Movements*, New York, Russell, 1952.

GALENSON, W., *Trade Union Democracy in Western Europe*, University of California Press, 1961.

GEORGES, D., TINTANT, D. and RENAULD, M. A., *Léon Jouhaux, cinquante ans de syndicalisme*, Paris, 1962.

GODFREY, E. D., jr., *The Fate of the French Non-Communist Left*, New York, Random House, 1955.

GOGUEL, F. and GROSSER, A., *La Politique en France*, Paris, 1964.

GRAHAM, B. D., *The French Socialists and Tripartisme, 1944–1947*, Weidenfeld & Nicolson, 1965.

GREENE, NATHANIEL, *Crisis and Decline : the French Socialist Party in the Popular Front Era*, Cornell University Press, 1969.

GUÉRIN, D., *Front Populaire*, Paris, 1962.

HAMILTON, RICHARD, *Affluence and the French Worker in the Fourth Republic*, Princeton University Press, 1967.

HUMBERT-DROZ, J., *L'Oeil de Moscou à Paris*, Paris, 1964.

HUMBERT-DROZ, J., *Origines et débuts des partis communistes des pays latins, 1919–1923*, Amsterdam, 1970.

JACKSON, J. H., *Jean Jaurès : his life and work*, Allen & Unwin, 1943.

KASSALOW, EVERETT M., *Trade Unions and Industrial Relations : an international comparison*, New York, Random House, 1969.

KEMP, T., *The French Economy*, Longman, 1972.

KOESTLER, A., *The Age of Longing*, Collins, 1951.

KRIEGEL, ANNIE, *Aux Origines du communisme français, 1914–1920*, 2 vols., Paris, 1964.

KRIEGEL, ANNIE and BECKER, JEAN J., *1914 : La Guerre et le mouvement ouvrier français*, Paris, 1964.

LANDAUER, CARL, *European Socialism*, 2 vols., University of California Press, 1959.

LANDES, DAVID S., 'French business and the businessman', in E. M. Earle, ed., *Modern France*, Princeton University Press, 1951.

LAROQUE, PIERRE, *Les Relations entre patrons et ouvriers*, Paris, 1938.

LEBRUN, PIERRE, *Questions actuelles du syndicalisme*, Paris, 1965.

LEFRANC, G., *Les Éxpériences syndicales en France de 1939 à 1950*, Paris, 1950.

LEFRANC, G., *Le Front Populaire*, Paris, 1965.

LEFRANC, G., *Histoire du Front Populaire*, Paris, 1965.

LEFRANC, G., *Juin 1936*, Paris, 1966.

LEFRANC, G., *Le Mouvement socialiste sous la Troisième République, 1875–1940*, Paris, 1963.

LEFRANC, G., *Le Mouvement syndical de la Libération aux événements de mai-juin 1968*, Paris, 1969.

LEFRANC, G., *Le Mouvement syndical en France*, Paris, 1967.

LEFRANC, G., *Le Mouvement syndical sous la Troisième République, 1871–1940*, Paris, 1967.

LEFRANC, G., *Le Syndicalisme en France*, Paris, 1964.

LESIRE-OGREL, H., *Le Syndicat dans l'entreprise*, Paris, 1967.

LEVINE, LOUIS, *The Labor Movement in France*, New York, 1912.

LEVINE, LOUIS, *Syndicalisme en France*, New York, 1914.

LICHTHEIM, G., *Marxism in Modern France*, Columbia University Press, 1966.

LIGOU, D., *Histoire du socialisme en France, 1871–1961*, Paris, 1962.

LORWIN, LEWIS, *The International Labor Movement*, New York, Harper, 1953.

LORWIN, VAL R., *The French Labor Movement*, Harvard University Press, 1954.

MCPHERSON, W. H. and MEYERS, F., *French Labor Courts : judgement by peers*, University of Illinois Press, 1966.

MALLET, SERGE, *La Nouvelle classe ouvrière*, Paris 1963.

MARCUS, J. T., *French Socialism in the Crisis Years, 1933–1936*, New York, 1963.

MARQUAND, H. A., *Organized Labour in Four Continents*, Longmans, 1939.

MEYERS, F., *European Coal Mining Unions*, University of California Press, 1961.

MICAUD, CHARLES, *Communism and the French Left*, Weidenfeld & Nicolson, 1963.

MONATTE, PIERRE, *Left Wing Trade Unionism in France*, Workers' Library, 1922.

MONATTE, PIERRE, *Trois scissions syndicales*, Paris, 1958.

MONTLUCARD, M., *La Dynamique des comités d'entreprises*, Paris, 1963.

MONTREUIL, JEAN, *Histoire du mouvement ouvrier en france*, Paris, 1974.

MOTHÉ, DANIEL, *Journal d'un ouvrier, 1956–1958*, Paris, 1959.

MOTHÉ, DANIEL, *Militant chez Renault*, Paris, 1965.

NOGUÈRES, HENRI, *Histoire de la Résistance en France*, Paris, 1967.

NOLAND, A., *The Founding of the French Socialist Party 1893–1905*, Harvard University Press, 1956.

PARAF, PIÈNE, *Le Syndicalisme pendant et après la guerre*, Paris, 1923.

PEDRONCINI, GUY, *Les Mutineries de l'armée français*, Paris, 1963.

PICKLES, D. M., *The Fifth French Republic*, Methuen, 1962.

POSNER, CHARLES, ed., *Reflections on the Revolution in France, May 1968*, Penguin, 1970.

PROST, ANTOINE, *La CGT à l'époque du Front Populaire, 1934–1939*, Paris, 1964.

REYNAUD, J. D., *Les Syndicats en France*, Paris, 1963.

RIDLEY, F. F., *Revolutionary Syndicalism in France*, Cambridge University Press, 1970.

RIEBER, ALFRED J., *Stalin and the French Communist Party, 1940–1947*, Columbia University Press, 1962.

RIOUX, L., *Le Syndicalisme*, Paris, 1960.

ROSMER, ALFRED, *Le Mouvement ouvrier pendant la guerre*, Paris, 1936.

ROSSI, A., *A Communist Party in Action*, Yale University Press, 1949.

ROSSI, A., *Les Communistes français pendant la drôle de guerre*, Paris, 1951.

ROSSI, A., *La Guerre des papillons*, Paris, 1954.

ROSSI, A. *Physiologie du parti communiste français*, Paris, 1948.

SAPOSS, DAVID J., *The Labor Movement in Post-war France*, Columbia University Press, 1931.

SEALE, P. and MCCONVILLE, M., *French Revolution 1968*, Heinemann, 1968.

SHAW, LEE C., 'The French general strike of 1968', in Alfred Kamin, ed.,

Western European Labor and the American Corporation, Washington DC, Bureau of National Affairs, 1970.

STURMTHAL, ADOLF, *The Tragedy of European Labour, 1918–1939*, Gollancz, 1944.

STURMTHAL, ADOLF, *Unity and Diversity in European Labor*, New York, Free Press 1953.

STURMTHAL, ADOLF, *Workers' Councils*, Harvard University Press, 1964.

THOREL, G., *Chronologie du mouvement syndicale d'ouvriers en France, 1791–1946*, Paris, 1947.

TIANO, A. H., LESIRE-OGREL, H. and ROCHARD, M., *Expérience française d'action ouvrière*, Paris, 1956.

TOURAINE, ALAIN, *L'Evolution du travail ouvrier aux usines Renault*, Paris, 1955.

TOURAINE, ALAIN, *Ouvriers d'origine agricole*, Paris, 1961.

TROTSKY, LEON, *Whither France?*, New York, Pioneer Publications, 1936.

VERDIER, R., *La Vie clandestine du parti socialiste*, Paris, 1944.

VIDALENC, G., *Aspects du mouvement ouvrier français*, Brussels, IFCTU.

WILLIAMS, PHILIP M., *Crisis and Compromise*, Longmans, 1964.

WOHL, ROBERT, *French Communism in the Making, 1919–1924*, Stanford University Press, 1966.

ZIRNHELD, J., *Cinquante années de syndicalisme chrétien*, Paris, 1937.

Articles

ADAM, G., 'CGT 1963', *Revue Française de Science Politique*, 1963, pp. 965–76.

ADAM, G., 'Situation de Force Guvrière', ibid, 1964, pp. 95–108.

ADAM, G., 'De la CFTC à la CFTD', ibid., 1965, pp. 87–103.

ADAM, G., 'CGT et CFDT 1967', ibid., 1967, pp. 576–90.

BARNES, W. F., 'The politics of French Christian labor', *Journal of Politics*, Feb. 1959.

COLLINET, M., 'Communism and French labour: the post-war struggle for leadership', *Problems of Communism*, May–June 1951.

DELAMOTTE, YVES, 'Recent collective bargaining trends in France', *International Labour Review*, Geneva, April 1971.

DRAPER, THEODORE, 'The ghost of social fascism', *Commentary*, New York, Feb. 1969.

EHRMANN, H. W., 'The French peasant and communism', *American Political Science Review*, vol. 26, no. 1, March 1952, pp. 19–43.

EHRMANN, H. W., 'The trade union movement in the framework of the French war economy, 1939–1940', *Journal of Politics*, Aug. 1944.

GOLDEY, DAVID, 'The events of May and the French general election of June 1968', *Political Affairs*, 1969.

LORWIN, VAL R., 'Collective bargaining in post-war France', *Assembly of the Associated Academy of Politics and Social Science*, March 1957.

LOVET, R., 'Financial participation: change or illusion for the ordinary man?', *Free Labour World*, Brussels, June 1971.

MARCEL, DAVID, 'Universities and workers' education in France', *International Labour Review*, Geneva, Feb. 1970.

MEYERS, F., 'The role of collective bargaining in France', *British Journal of Industrial Relations*, Nov. 1965.

MONTLUCARD, M., 'La participation ouvrière dans l'institution française des comités d'entreprises', Paper presented at International Seminar on Workers' Participation in Management, Experiences Institutions and Perspectives, University of Bologna, Dec. 1969.

SCHWARZ, SOLOMON, 'Les occupations d'usines en France de mai et juin 1936', *International Review for Social History*, Amsterdam, 1937.

'Works agreements of the "Renault Type"', *International Labour Review*, Geneva, March 1960.

GERMANY
Books

ABENDROTH, W., *Wirtschaft, Gesellschaft und Demokratie in der Bundesrepublik*, Frankfurt am Main, 1959.

ANDERSON, EVELYN, *Hammer or Anvil*, Gollancz, 1945.

BAADE, FRITZ, ed., WOYTINSKY, E. S., *So much Alive*, New York, Vanguard, 1962.

BALFOUR, MICHAEL, *Survey of International Affairs*, vol. 8, *Four-Power Control in Germany and Austria, 1945-1946*, Oxford University Press, 1956.

BALFOUR, MICHAEL, *The Kaiser and his Times*, London, Cresset, 1964.

BELOFF, MAX, *The United States and the Unity of Europe*, Faber & Faber, 1963.

BERLAU, A. J., *The German Social Democratic Party, 1914-1921*, Columbia University Press, 1949.

BERNSTEIN, E., *Evolutionary Socialism*, London, 1909.

BLUMENTHAL, W. M., *Co-determination in the German Steel Industry*, Princeton University Press, 1956.

BOHNING, WOLF R., *Foreign Workers in Post-War Germany*, University of Kent, 1971.

BRADY, ROBERT A., *The Rationalization Movement in German Industry*, University of California Press, 1933.

BRADY, ROBERT A., *The Spirit and Structure of German Fascism*, Gollancz, 1937.

BRANDT, WILLY, *In Exile*, London, Wolff, 1971.

BRAUNTHAL, GERARD, *The Federation of German Industry in Politics*, Cornell University Press, 1965.

BRETT-SMITH, RICHARD, *Berlin '45. The Grey City*, Macmillan, 1966.

BROCKWAY, FENNER, *German Diary*, Gollancz, 1946.

CARSTEN, F. L., *Revolution in Central Europe, 1918-1919*, Temple Smith, 1972.

CHALMERS, DOUGLAS A., *The Social Democratic Party of Germany*, Yale University Press, 1964.

CLAPHAM, J. H., *The Economic Development of France and Germany, 1815-1914*, Cambridge University Press, 1923.

CRAWFORD, R., ed., *The Cultural Migration*, Pennsylvania, University Press, 1953.

DAHRENDORF, ROLF, *Society and Democracy in Germany*, New York, Double-day, 1969.

DAWSON, W. H., *The Evolution of Modern Germany*, London, 1908.

Deutsche Gewerkschaftsbund, *Co-determination: a contemporary demand*, Düsseldorf, DGB, 1970.

Deutsche Gewerkschaftsbund, *The Basic Programme of the German Trade Unions' Federation*, Düsseldorf, DGB, 1964

Deutsche Gewerkschaftsbund, *The Educational Activities within the German Federation of Trade Unions*, Düsseldorf, DGB, 1965.

DIETZ, J. H. *et al.*, *Le Syndicalisme allemand contemporain*, Paris, 1968.

EDELMAN, M. and FLEMING, R. W., *The Politics of Wage-Price Decisions*, University of Illinois, 1965.

EDINGER, LEWIS J., *German Exile Politics: The Social Democratic Executive Committee in the Nazi Era*, Stanford University Press, 1966.

EDINGER, LEWIS J., *Kurt Schumacher*, Stanford University Press, 1965.

FRIEDMANN, W., *The Allied Military Government of Germany*, Stevens & Sons, 1947.

GALENSON, WALTER, *Comparative Labor Movements*, New York, Russell, 1952.

GERSCHENKRON, ALEXANDER, *Bread and Democracy in Germany*, New York, Fertig, 1966.

GOTTFURCHT, H., *Trade Unions in Germany*, London, 1944.

GREBING, HELGA, *History of the German Labour Movement*, Wolff, 1969.

GROSSER, A., *The Federal Republic of Germany*, Pall Mall Press, 1964.

GROSSER, A., *Western Germany*, Allen & Unwin, 1955.

GUILLEBAULD, C. W., *The Works Council*, Cambridge University Press, 1928.

HARTMANN, H., *Authority and Organization in German Management*, Princeton University Press, 1959.

HESSELBACH, WALTER, *Co-operative Enterprises in West Germany*, Frankfurt am Main, 1967.

HILL, RUSSELL, *The Struggle for Germany*, Gollancz, 1947.

HUNT, RICHARD, N., *German Social Democracy 1918–1933*, Yale University Press, 1964.

KITZINGER, U., *German Electoral Politics*, Oxford University Press, 1960.

KNIGHT, M., *The German Executive*, Stanford University Press, 1952.

LANDAUER, CARL A., *European Socialism*, University of California Press, 1959.

LEPINSKI, FRANZ, *The German Trade Union Movement*, Düsseldorf, 1959.

LIDTKE, V. L., *The Outlawed Party: Social Democracy in Germany, 1878–1890*, Princeton University Press, 1966.

MCKITTERICK, TOM and ROBERTS, R. D. V., *Workers and Management: The German Co-determination Experiment*, Gollancz, 1953.

MARKMANN, H., 'Les grèves spontanées de l'automne 1969', in G. Spitaels, ed., *La Crise des relations industrielles en Europe*, Brussels, 1972.

MARX, KARL and ENGELS, FREDERICK, *Communist Manifesto*, centenary edn, Lawrence & Wishart, 1948.

MEHRING, FRANZ, *Karl Marx*, Lane, 1936.

MERKL, PETER H., *Origins of the West German Republic*, Oxford University Press, 1963.

MEYERS, FREDERICK, *European Coal Mining Unions*, University of California Press, 1961.

MICHELS, ROBERT, *Democracy and Political Parties*, Jarrold, 1915.

MORGENTHAU, HANS J., *Germany and the Future of Europe*, University of Chicago Press, 1951.

NATHAN, OTTO, *The Nazi Economic System*, Durham, 1944.

NEUMANN, FRANZ, *Behemoth : the practice and structure of National Socialism, 1933–44*, Gollancz, 1942.

NEUMANN, FRANZ, 'The Labor Movement in Germany', in H. J. Morgenthau, *Germany and the Future of Europe*, University of Chicago Press, 1951.

OLIVEIRA, A. RAMOS, *A People's History of Germany*, Gollancz, 1942.

PETROFF, PETER and PETROFF, IRMA, *The Secret of Hitler's Victory*, Hogarth, 1934.

PINSON, K. S., *Modern Germany*, New York, Macmillan, 1954.

PRITTIE, TERENCE, *Konrad Adenauer 1876–1967*, Stacey, 1972.

PROUDFOOT, MALCOLM J., *European Refugees*, Faber & Faber, 1952.

REICH, NATHAN, *Industrial Relations in the Weimar Republic*, Oxford University Press, 1938.

REICH, NATHAN, *Labor Relations in Republican Germany*, New York, Oxford University Press, 1938.

ROSENBERG, ARTHUR, *The Birth of the German Republic*, Oxford University Press, 1931.

ROSENBERG, ARTHUR, *A History of the German Republic*, Methuen, 1936.

ROSENBERG, LUDWIG, *The German Experiences with Inflation*, Düsseldorf, 1958.

ROTH, GÜNTHER, *Social Democrats in Imperial Germany*, New Jersey, Bedminster Press, 1963.

RUSSELL, BERTRAND, *German Social Democracy*, London School of Economics, 1896.

RYDER, A. J., *The German Revolution of 1918*, Cambridge University Press, 1967.

SCHECHTMANN, J. B., *Postwar Population Transfers in Europe, 1944–1955*, Oxford University Press, 1962.

SCHLESINGER, RUDOLF, *Central European Democracy and its Background*, Routledge, 1953.

SCHORSKE, CARL E., *German Social Democracy 1905–1917*, Harvard University Press, 1955.

SCHORSKE, C. and PRICE, H., *The Problem of Germany*, New York, Council on Foreign Relations, 1947.

SEIDEL, RICHARD, *The Trade Union Movement of Germany*, Amsterdam, 1928.

SEYFARTH, SHAW, FAIRWEATHER and GERALDSON, *Labor Relations and the Law in West Germany and the United States*, University of Michigan Bureau of Business Research, 1969.

SHUCHMAN, A., *Co-determination – Labor's Middle Way*, Washington DC, Public Affairs Press, 1957.

SPIRO, HERBERT J., *The Politics of German Co-determination*, Harvard University Press, 1958.

STUMPF, RICHARD, *War, Mutiny and Revolution in the German Navy*, Rutgers University Press, 1967.

STURMTHAL, ADOLF, *Workers' Councils*, Harvard University Press, 1964.

Trades Union Congress, *Trades Unionism in Central Europe*, TUC, 1946.

VERKADE, WILLEM, *Democratic Parties in the Low Countries and Germany*, Leiden, 1965.

WOYTINSKY, E. S., ed., *So Much Alive*, New York, Vanguard, 1962.

WOYTINSKY, W., *The Social Consequences of the Economic Depression*, Geneva, 1936.

WOYTINSKY, W., *Stormy Passage*, New York, Vanguard, 1961.

Articles

BARNES, S. H. *et al.*, 'The German party system and the 1961 Federal election', *American Political Science Review*, Sept. 1962.

HAMBURGER, ERNST, 'The German labor front – DAF', *Monthly Labor Review*, Washington DC, Nov. 1944.

KELLEY, MATTHEW A., 'Communists in German labor organizations', *Journal of Political Economy*, June 1949.

KELLEY, MATTHEW A., 'The re-constitution of the German trade union movement', *Political Science Quarterly*, March 1949.

KERR, CLARK, 'The trade union movement and the re-distribution of power in post-war Germany', *Quarterly Journal of Economics*, 1954.

LEPINSKI, FRANZ, 'The German trade union movement', *International Labour Review*, Geneva, vol. 79, Jan. 1959.

MARKMANN, HEINZ, 'Incomes policy in Germany: a trade union view', *British Journal of Industrial Relations*, Nov. 1964.

MASON, TIMOTHY W., 'Labour in the Third Reich 1933–1939', *Past and Present*, April 1966.

REICHEL, HANS, 'Recent trends in collective bargaining in the Federal Republic', *International Labour Review*, Geneva, Dec. 1971.

VINCENT, J. MARIE, 'West Germany: the reactionary democracy', *Socialist Register*, London 1964.

Thesis

MASON, TIMOTHY W., 'National Socialist policies towards the German working class, 1925–1939', unpublished D.Phil. thesis, Oxford, 1971.

Other sources

Articles in *British Zone Review*, Düsseldorf, 1946.

'The Federal Republic at a Glance', Press and Information Department of the Federal Republic, Bonn, 1971.

ITALY
Books

ADAMS, J. and BARILE, PAOLO, *The Government of Republican Italy*, Boston, Houghton Mifflin, 1961.

ARFÉ, G., *Storia del socialismo italiano*, Turin, 1965.

BARNES, S. H., *Party Democracy: politics in an Italian Socialist Federation*, Yale University Press, 1967.

BARZINI, LUIGI, *The Italians*, Hamish Hamilton, 1964.

BINCHY, D. A., *Church and State in Fascist Italy*, Oxford University Press, 1941.

BLACKMER, D. L. M., *Unity in Diversity: Italian communism and the communist world*, Massachusetts Institute of Technology Press, 1966.

BOCA, ANGELO DEL, *Giornali in crisi*, Turin, 1968.

BORGHI, ARMANDO, *La revoluzione mancata*, Milan, 1964.

CARLYLE, MARGARET, *Modern Italy*, Hutchinson, 1957.

DOGAN, MATTEI, 'Political cleavage and social stratification in France and Italy', in S. M. Lipset and S. Rokkan, eds., *Political Party Systems and Voter Alignments*, New York, Free Press, 1967.

EDELMAN, MURRAY and FLEMING, R. W., *The Politics of Wage-Price Decisions*, University of Illinois Press, 1965.

EINAUDI, M. et al., *Nationalization in France and Italy*, Cornell University Press, 1956.

EINAUDI, M. and GOGUEL, F., *Christian Democracy in Italy and France*, Notre Dame, 1952.

FORCELLA, E. and MONTICONE, A., *Platone di Esecuzione. I processi della Prima Guerra Mondiale*, Bari, 1968.

GALENSON, WALTER, ed., *Comparative Labor Movements*, New York, Russell, 1952.

GALENSON, WALTER, *Trade Union Democracy in Western Europe*, University of California Press, 1961.

GALLI, GIORGIO, *Il bipartismo difetto*, Bologna, 1967.

GALLI, GIORGIO, 'Italian Communism', in W. E. Griffith, ed., *Communism in Europe*, vol. 1, Massachusetts Institute of Technology Press, 1964.

GALLI, GIORGIO, *La Sinistra italiana nel Dopoguerra*, Bologna, 1958.

GIUGNI, G., 'Articulated bargaining in Italy', in Allen Flanders, ed., *Collective Bargaining*, Penguin, 1969.

GRINDROD, MURIEL, *The New Italy*, Oxford University Press, 1947.

GUÉRIN, DANIEL, *Fascism and Big Business*, New York, Pioneer Publications, 1939.

HOLLAND, STUART, ed., *The State as Entrepreneur*, Weidenfeld & Nicolson, 1972.

HOROWITZ, DANIEL L., *The Italian Labor Movement*, Harvard University Press, 1963.

Istituto Nazionale di Economia Agraria, *Annuario dell' agricoltura nazionale*, vol. 23, Rome, 1969.

KENDALL, WALTER, 'Labour Relations in IRI', in Stuart Holland, ed., *The State as Entrepreneur*, Weidenfeld & Nicolson, 1972.

LANZARDO, LILIANO, *Classe operaia e Partito Comunista alla FIAT. La strategia della collaborazione*, Turin, 1971.

LAPALOMBARA, J., *Interest Groups in Italian Politics*, Princeton University Press, 1964.

LAPALOMBARA, J., *The Italian Labor Movement*, Cornell University Press, 1958.

LAPALOMBARA, J. and WEINER, M. eds., *Political Parties and Political Development*, Princeton University Press, 1966.

LIPSET, S. M. and ROKKAN, S., eds., *Political Party Systems and Voter Alignments*, New York, Free Press, 1967.

LUTZ, VERA, *Italy – a study in economic development*, Oxford University Press, 1962.

MACK-SMITH, DENIS, *Italy*, Ann Arbor, 1959.

NEUFELD, MAURICE F., *Italy, School for Developing Countries*, Cornell University Press, 1961.

NEUFELD, MAURICE F., *Labor Unions and National Politics in Italian Industrial Plants*, Cornell University Press, 1954.

POSNER, M. V. and WOOLF, S. J., *Italian Public Enterprise*, Duckworth, 1967.

PRYCE, ROY, *The Italian Local Elections 1956*, Chatto, 1956.

RAFFAELE, JOSEPH A., *Labor Leadership in Italy and Denmark*, University of Wisconsin Press, 1962.

ROSSI, A., *Rise of Italian Fascism 1918–1922*, Methuen, 1938.

SARTI, ROLAND, *Fascism and the Industrial Leadership in Italy 1919–1940*, University of California Press, 1971.

SARTORI, GIOVANNI, in Lapalombara, J., and Weiner, M., ed. *Political Parties and Political Development*. Princeton University Press, 1966.

The School of Barbiana, *Letter to a Teacher*, Penguin, 1972.

SEYFARTH, SHAW, FAIRWEATHER and GERALDSON, *Labor Relations and the Law in Italy and the United States*, University of Michigan Bureau of Business Research, 1970.

SPRIANO, PAOLO, *L'occupazione delle fabbriche nel Settembre 1920*, Turin, 1964.

SPRIANO, PAOLO, *Storia del Partito Comunista Italiana*, vols. i and ii, Turin, 1967, 1969.

SPRIGGE, C. J. S., *The Development of Modern Italy*, Duckworth, 1943.

VALIANI, LEO, *L'avento di De Gasperi*, Turin, 1949.

WEBSTER, RICHARD A., *Christian Democracy in Italy 1860–1960*, Hollis & Carter, 1961.

WISKEMANN, ELIZABETH, *Italy*, Oxford University Press, 1947.

WISKEMANN, ELIZABETH, *Italy since 1945*, Macmillan, 1971.

ZACCARIA, GUELFO, *200 Communisti Italiani tra le vittime dello Stalinismo*, Milan, 1964.

Articles and pamphlets

AGOSTINONE, VALERIO, 'L'unità sindicale e la incompatibilità', *Critica Sociale*, Milan, 20 Feb. 1972.

BAGLIONI, G., 'L'istituto della Commissione Interne e la questione della rappresentanza dei lavoratori nei luoghi di lavoro', *Studi di Sociologia*, Milan, June 1970.

BIANCO, GINO, 'To use the Communist Party – or be used', *Socialist Affairs*, London, March 1972.

CASTELLINA, LUCIANA, 'Rapporto sulla FIAT', *Il Manifesto*, July–Aug. 1970, pp. 12–24.

FIOM/FIM/UILM, *Contratto Nazionale del Lavoro*, Rome, 1967.

FIOM/FIM/UILM, *Unity and Victory*, Rome, 1969.

FIM, *Sull' Organizzazione*, no. 3, Rome, 1971.

GARAVINI, SERGIO, 'Gli anni cinquanta alla FIAT: un esperienza storica', *Politica ed Economia*, Rome, Sept.–Oct. 1970.

GIUGNI, GINO, 'Articulated bargaining in Italy' in Allen Flanders, ed., *Collective Bargaining*, London, 1969.

GIUGNI, GINO, 'Recent developments in collective bargaining in Italy', *International Labour Review*, Geneva, April 1965.

JACOBSON, JULIUS, ed., 'Currents in Italian Socialist Thought', symposium in *New Politics*, New York, vol. i, no. 4, 1962.

SPRIANO, PAOLO, 'I Comunisti nella Resistenza', *Rinascita*, Rome, 30 July 1971.

MONTANA, VANNI B., 'The plight of Italian democracy', *Free Trade Union News*, Washington DC, AFL–CIO, March 1972.

MONTANA, VANNI B., 'Projected merger of Italian unions follows communist blueprint', *Free Trade Union News*, Washington DC, AFL–CIO, March 1972.

BRITAIN

Books

BAIN, G. S., *Trade Union Growth and Recognition*, research paper no. 6 for the Royal Commission on Trade Unions, HMSO, 1967.

CARROTHERS, W. A., *Emigration from the British Isles*, London, P. S. King, 1929.

CLAPHAM, J. H., *An Economic History of Modern Britain*, Cambridge University Press, vol. ii, 1932, vol. iii, 1938.

CLEGG, H. A., *The System of Industrial Relations in Britain*, Oxford, Blackwell, 1970.

CLEGG, H. A., KILLICK, A. J. and ADAMS, REX, *Trade Union Officers*, Oxford, Blackwell, 1961.

COLE, G. D. H. and POSTGATE, R., *The Common People*, Methuen, 1947.

COURT, W. H. B., *A Concise Economic History of Britain*, Cambridge University Press, 1954.

EDELMAN, MURRAY and FLEMING, R. W., *The Politics of Wage-Price Decisions*, University of Illinois Press, 1965.

FLANDERS, A. and CLEGG, H. A., *The System of Industrial Relations in Great Britain*, Oxford, Blackwell, 1954.

FROW, R. E., FROW, E. and KATANKA, MICHAEL, *Strikes: a documentary history*, C. Knight, 1971.

HOWELL, GEORGE, *Labour Legislation, Labour Movements and Labour Leaders*, London, T. Fisher Unwin, 1905.

HUGHES, JOHN, *Trade Union Structure and Government*, research paper no. 5 for the Royal Commission on Trade Unions, HMSO, 1968.

JEFFERYS, JAMES B., *The Story of the Engineers, 1800–1945*, Lawrence & Wishart, 1946.

KENDALL, WALTER, *The Revolutionary Movement in Britain, 1900–1921*, Weidenfeld & Nicolson, 1969.

LILJEGREN, S. B., *Fall of the Monasteries and Social Changes in England leading up to the Great Revolution*, Lund, 1924.

MCCARTHY, W. E. J., *The Closed Shop in Britain*, Oxford, Blackwell, 1964.

MCCARTHY, W. E. J., *The Role of Shop Stewards in British Industrial Relations*, research paper no. 1 for the Royal Commission on Trade Unions, HMSO, 1966.

MCCARTHY, W. E. J. and PARKER, S. R., *Shop Stewards and Workshop Relations* research paper no. 10 for the Royal Commission on Trade Unions, HMSO, 1968.

MANN, TOM, *Tom Mann's Memoirs*, Labour Publishing Co., 1923.

MARTIN, RODERICK, *Communism and the British Trade Unions, 1924–1933*, Oxford University Press, 1969.

MARSH, A., *Industrial Relations in the Engineering Industry*, Oxford, Pergamon, 1965.

MORRIS, WILLIAM, *News from Nowhere*, Nelson, 1891.

MURPHY, J. T., *The Workers' Committee*, Sheffield, 1917.

PELLING, HENRY, *A History of British Trade Unionism*, Macmillan, 1969.

PELLING, HENRY, *A Short History of the Labour Party*, Macmillan, 1968.

PRIBICEVIC, BRANCO, *The Shop Stewards' Movement and Workers' Control, 1910–22*, Oxford, Blackwell, 1956.

TAYLOR, A. J. P., *English History, 1914–1945*, Oxford University Press, 1965.

TRADES UNION CONGRESS, *Trade Unionism*, TUC, 1966.

WEBB, SIDNEY and WEBB, BEATRICE, *History of Trade Unionism*, Longmans, 1917.

BELGIUM
Books

BAUDHUIN, F., *Belgique, 1900–1960*, Louvain, 1961.

Belgian Institute for Information and Documentation, *Collective Bargaining in Belgian Labour*, Brussels, 1969.

BERTRAND, L., *Histoire de la démocratie et du socialisme en Belgique, depuis 1830*, 2 vols., Brussels, 1906, 1907.

BLANPAIN, ROGER, 'American involvement in Belgium', in Alfred Kamin, ed., *Western European Labor and the American Corporation*, Washington DC, Bureau of National Affairs, 1970.

BLANPAIN, ROGER, 'Labor relations in Belgium', ibid.

BONDAS, JOSEPH, *Un Demi-siècle d'action syndicale 1898–1948*, Brussels, 1953.

BRAUNTHAL, JULIUS, *The History of the International*, 2 vols., Nelson, 1966, 1967.

CHLEPNER, B. S., *Cent ans d'histoire sociale en Belgique*, Brussels, 1956.

CLARKE, M. V., *The Medieval City State*, London, 1926.

COLE, G. D. H., *The Second International 1889–1914*, Macmillan, 1956.

COLLARD, LEO, et al., *Les Fastes du Parti 1885–1914*, Brussels, 1960.

DAHL, ROBERT, ed., *Political Oppositions in Western Democracies*, Yale University Press, 1968.

DEBUNNE, G., 'La crise des relations industrielles', in G. Spitaels, ed., *La Crise des relations industrielles en Europe*, Brussels, 1972.

DELSINNE, LÉON, *Le Mouvement syndical en Belgique*, Brussels, 1936.
DELSINNE, LÉON, *Le Parti Ouvrier Belge des origines à 1894*, Brussels, 1955.
DESOLRE, GUY, *50 Ans de débats sur le contrôle ouvrier 1920–1970*, Brussels, 1970.
DESTRÉE, J. and VANDERVELDE, E., *Le Socialisme en Belgique*, Paris, 1898.
DOLLEANS, E., *Histoire du mouvement ouvrier*, vol. ii, Paris, 1953.
DOUCY, A., *Economie sociale*, Brussels, 1966.
EBERTZHEIM, RENÉ, *Les Syndicats ouvriers en Belgique*, Liège, 1959.
EEC, *Monographies Syndicales – Belgique*, Brussels, 1966.
FOGARTY, MICHAEL P., *Christian Democracy in Western Europe 1820–1953*, Routledge, 1957.
GALENSON, WALTER, *Comparative Labor Movements*, New York, Russell, 1952.
HUGGETT, F. E., *Modern Belgium*, Pall Mall Press, 1969.
LANDAUER, CARL, *European Socialism*, University of California Press, 1959.
LIJPHART, AREND, *The Politics of Accommodation : Pluralism and democracy in the Netherlands*, University of California Press, 1968.
LORWIN, VAL R., 'Labor organizations and politics in Belgium and France', in E. M. Kassalow, ed., *National Labor Movements in the Post-War World*, Northwestern University Press, 1963.
LORWIN, VAL R., 'Religion, class and language in national politics', in Robert A. Dahl, ed., *Political Oppositions in Western Democracies*, Yale University Press, 1968.
MAN, HENRI DE, *Après Coup* (memoirs), Paris, 1941.
MAN, HENRI DE, *The Psychology of Socialism*, Allen & Unwin, 1928.
MEYERS, FREDERICK, *European Coal Mining Unions*, University of California Press, 1961.
MEYNAUD, J., *L'Action syndicale et la Communauté Economique Européenne*, Lausanne, 1962.
MEYNAUD, J., *La Décision politique en Belgique*, Paris, 1965.
NEUVILLE, J., *Une Génération syndicale*, Brussels, 1959.
NEUVILLE, J., *Le Taux de syndicalisation en Belgique en 1967*, Brussels, CRISP, 1969.
PIERSON, MARC A., *Histoire du socialisme en Belgique*, Brussels, 1953.
PIRENNE, H., *Belgian Democracy : its early history*, Manchester University Press, 1915.
PIRENNE, H., *Histoire de Belgique*, vol. vii, Brussels, 1932.
POSTAN, M. and RICH, E. E., eds., *Trade and Industry in the Middle Ages*, Cambridge University Press, 1952.
SENELLE, ROBERT, *The Political and Economic Structure of Belgium*, Brussels, Ministry of Foreign Affairs and External Trade, 1966.
SEYFARTH, SHAW, FAIRWEATHER and GERALDSON, *Labor Relations and the Law in Belgium and the United States*, University of Michigan Bureau of Business Research, 1969.
SPITAELS, G., *Le Mouvement syndicale en Belgique*, Bruges, 1967.
SPITAELS, G., ed., *L'Année sociale 1968*, Brussels, 1969.
Le syndicalisme belge – documentation européenne, EEC, Brussels, 1968.
VANDERVELDE, E., *Le Parti Ouvrier Belge 1885–1925*, Brussels, 1925.
VANDERVELDE, E., *Souvenirs d'un militant socialiste*, Paris, 1939.

VERKADE, WILLEM, *Democratic Parties in the Low Countries and Germany*, Leiden, 1965.
WEIL, GORDON L., *The Benelux Nations*, New York, Holt, Rinehart & Winston, 1970.

Articles
'Belgium in transition', *Annals of the American Academy of Political and Social Science*, Philadelphia, Sept. 1946.
DELSINNE, LÉON, 'The trade union movement in Europe', *International Labour Review*, Geneva, May 1950.

THE NETHERLANDS
Books
ALBEDA, W. R., 'Les Pays Bas, les relations de travail', in G. Spitaels, ed., *La Crise des relations industrielles en Europe*, Brussels, 1972.
BARKER, J. E., *The Rise and Decline of the Netherlands*, London, 1906.
BARNOUW, A. J., *The Making of Modern Holland*, Allen & Unwin, 1948.
BARNOUW, A. J., *The Pageant of Netherlands History*, Longmans, 1952.
BLOK, P. J., *The History of the People of the Netherlands*, London, Putnam, 1912.
BORKENAU, FRANZ, *World Communism*, University of Michigan Press, 1962.
DAALDER, HANS, 'The Netherlands: opposition in a segmented society', in Robert A. Dahl, ed., *Political Oppositions in Western Democracies*, Yale University Press, 1968.
DAHL, ROBERT A., ed., *Political Oppositions in Western Democracies*, Yale University Press, 1968.
EDELMAN, M. and FLEMING, R. W., *The Politics of Wage-Price Decisions*, University of Illinois Press, 1965.
FLANDERS, ALLEN, 'Manpower utilization and the American investor', in Alfred A. Kamin, ed., *Western European Labor and the American Corporation*, Washington DC, Bureau of National Affairs, 1970.
GEYL, PIETER A., *History of the Low Countries*, Macmillan, 1964.
GEYL, PIETER A., *Holland and Belgium*, Leiden, 1921.
GOUDSBLOM, JOHAN, *Dutch Society*, New York, Random House, 1967.
HAVELAAR, MAX (Edward Dowes Dekker), *Multatuli*, Amsterdam, 1967.
HOLST, HENRIETTE ROLAND, *Kapitaal en Arbeid en Nederland*, 2 vols., Rotterdam, 1932.
LANDHEER, B., ed., *The Netherlands*, University of California Press, 1943.
LAZITCH, B., *Les Partis communistes d'Europe*, Paris, 1956.
LENIN, V. I., *What is to be done?*, London, Martin Lawrence, 1947.
LIJPHART, A. J., *The Politics of Accommodation*, University of California Press, 1968.
LAPALOMBARA, J. and WEINER, M., eds., *Political Parties and Political Development*, Princeton University Press, 1966.
MANN, TOM, *Tom Mann's Memoirs*, Labour Publishing Co., 1923.
Netherlands Zone Handbook, HMSO for Foreign Office, 1944.
OFFERMANS, TH., *The Three Dutch Trade Unions and their Affiliated Unions*, Amsterdam, NVV, 1968.

PRESSER, JACOB, *The Destruction of the Dutch Jews*, New York, 1969.
RENIER, G. J., *The Dutch Nation*, Allen & Unwin, 1944.
RIEMANS, HENDRIK, 'The growth of Netherlands economy', in B. Landheer, ed., *The Netherlands*, University of California Press, 1943.
SHOTWELL, J. T., ed., *Governments of Continental Europe*, New York, Macmillan, 1940.
TAWNEY, R. H., *Religion and the Rise of Capitalism*, Murray, 1926.
VERKADE, WILLEM, *Democratic Parties in the Low Countries and Germany*, Leiden, 1965.
VLEKKE, BERNARD, 'The Dutch before 1581', in B. Landheer, ed., *The Netherlands*, University of California Press, 1943.
WARMBRUNN, W., *The Dutch under German Occupation*, Stanford University Press, 1963.
WILSON, CHARLES, *Anglo-Dutch Commerce and Finance in the Eighteenth Century*, Cambridge University Press, 1941.
WINDMULLER, JOHN P., *Labor Relations in the Netherlands*, Cornell University Press, 1969.

Articles
ALBEDA, W., 'Recent trends in collective bargaining in the Netherlands', *International Labour Review*, Geneva, March 1971.
KOOL, FRITZ, 'Communism in Holland', *Problems of Communism*, Washington D.C., Sept.–Oct. 1960.
PELS, P. S., 'Organized industry and planning in the Netherlands', *International Labour Review*, Geneva, Sept. 1966.
POSTUMUS, N. W., ed., 'The Netherlands during the German Occupation', *Annals of the American Academy of Political and Social Science*, Philadelphia, 1946.
WILSON, CHARLES H., 'The economic decline of the Netherlands', *Economic History Review*, May 1939.

Other Sources
Details on the Netherlands Federation of Trade Unions, Amsterdam, NVV, 1968.
Programme of Action, Amsterdam, NVV/NKV/CNV, 1967.
'The trade union movement in the Netherlands', *Trade Union News from the European Community*, London, summer 1970.

ADDITIONAL SOURCES
Publications of the CFTC, CFDT, CGT, CGT–FO, in France; CISL, CGIL, UIL, FIM, FIOM and UILM in Italy; DGB in Germany; NVV, CNV, NKV in the Netherlands; CSC and FGTB in Belgium; TUC in Britain.
Also publications of the International Confederation of Free Trade Unions – ICFTU; the International Metalworkers' Federation – IMF; the International Federation of Chemical and General Workers' Unions – ICF; the International Union of Food and Allied Workers' Association – IUF; the United Automobile, Aerospace and Agricultural Implement Workers of

America – UAW; the World Confederation of Labour – WCL; the World Federation of Trade Unions – WFTU; the International Labour Office – ILO; the Organization for Economic Cooperation and Development – OECD; and the European Economic Community – EEC.

Also *The British Zone Review*, Düsseldorf, 1946, and *Netherlands Zone Handbook*, Foreign Office, 1944.

Periodicals
American Political Science Review.
Annals of the American Academy of Political and Social Science.
British Journal of Industrial Relations.
Bulletin of the International Metalworkers' Federation.
Bulletin of the International Union of Food and Allied Workers' Associations.
Bulletin of the Society for the Study of Labour History.
Commentary, New York.
Critica Sociale, Milan.
Economia e Lavoro, Rome.
European Community, London.
France Nouvelle, Paris.
Free Labour World, Brussels.
Free Trade Union News, AFL–CIO, Washington DC.
Guardian, London.
International Herald Tribune, Paris.
International Labour Review, Geneva.
International Review of Social History, Amsterdam.
Journal of Political Economy.
Journal of Politics.
New Politics, New York.
Le Nouvel Observateur, Paris.
Observer, London.
Past and Present.
Political Affairs.
Problems of Communism.
Quarterly Journal of Economics.
Revue Française de Science Politique.
Rinascità, Rome.
Saturday Evening Post, New York.
Soccorso Rosso, Turin.
Socialist Affairs, London.
Socialist Register.
Studi di Sociologia.
Sunday Times, London.
Survey, London.
The Times, London.
Transports, Paris.
UNIAPAC International, Brussels.
Voice of the Unions, London.
World Trade Union Movement, Prague.

Index

United Metal-workers' Movement
(MMU) (Belgium), 223
United Provinces, 243 and n3, 244,
245
United Socialist Party (PSU) (Italy),
147
United States (US), 1, 4, 87, 130
and n, 247, 314
anti-communism, 56
armed forces, 7
capitalist-industrialism, 5, 7
Constitution, 14
Ford plant 'militia', 83
immigration, 181, 312
Marshall Plan, 33, 56, 57, 75, 108,
153, 224, 288, 289
motor industry, 83, 294, 295 and
n2, 296, 297
occupation of Germany, 108, 288
Second World War, 49
social organization, 4, 35, 310
Teamsters Union, 327
trade unionism, 2, 7, 64, 97, 195,
232
international, 282, 289, 292, 297
membership, 234
wage agreements, 77n1, 172, 321
and USSR, 318
United Trade Union Movement
(MSU) (Belgium), 223-4
Unity of Action Pact, socialist-
communist, 42 and n3

Vaillant, Allemane, 38, 39n2
Van den Tempel, J. 253
Van Tonningen, Rost, 254

Vandervelde, Emile, 220
Victor Emmanuel III, King, 150, 151

Wages Councils (UK), 201-2, 203
Webb, Sidney and Beatrice, 184
Weber, Max, 5
Whitley Report, 201
Wilson, Havelock, 19
Wjnkoop, David, 249
Workers' Friendly Benefit Societies
(Mutualités) (Belgium), 229
Workers' and Soldiers' Councils
(Germany), 100
World Conference of Labour (WCL),
155n2, 279, 290, 301, 328, 329
affiliations, 279 and n4, 290, 291
World Federation of Trade Unions
(WFTU), 52n4, 301
affiliates, 291
and ERP, 288-9
German future, 287-8
membership in the Nine, 279 and
n3
Russian dominated, 155, 279, 286
and n3, 287, 289, 292, 329
short-lived, 286 and nn3 and 5,
287-8, 289
trade departments, 287n3, 290
USSR-China disputes, 290
World Motor Councils, 301-2
Woudenberg, J. H., 254, 255n3, 259

Young Christian Workers' Movement
(Belgium), 284
Yugoslavia, 120

Zola, Émile, 186, 217

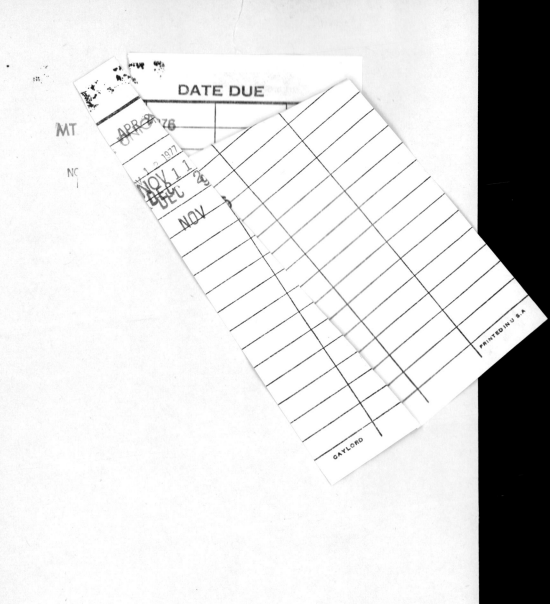